W9-BJD-447

READINGS IN MEDIEVAL HISTORY

READINGS IN MEDIEVAL HISTORY

Volume I: The Early Middle Ages

FIFTH EDITION

EDITED BY PATRICK J. GEARY

UNIVERSITY OF TORONTO PRESS

Copyright © University of Toronto Press 2016

Higher Education Division

www.utppublishing.com

All rights reserved. The use of any part of this publication reproduced, transmitted in any form or by any means, electronic, mechanical, photocopying, recording, or otherwise, or stored in a retrieval system, without prior written consent of the publisher—or in the case of photocopying, a licence from Access Copyright (Canadian Copyright Licensing Agency), One Yonge Street, Suite 1900, Toronto, Ontario M5E 1E5—is an infringement of the copyright law.

LIBRARY AND ARCHIVES CANADA CATALOGUING IN PUBLICATION

Readings in medieval history / edited by Patrick J. Geary.—Fifth edition.
Includes bibliographical references.
Contents: Volume 1. The early Middle Ages—Volume 2. The later Middle Ages.
Issued in print and electronic formats.

ISBN 978-1-4426-3433-6 (volume 1: paperback).—ISBN 978-1-4426-3436-7 (volume 2: paperback).—ISBN 978-1-4426-3434-3 (volume 1: html).—ISBN 978-1-4426-3435-0 (volume 1: pdf).—ISBN 978-1-4426-3437-4 (volume 2: html).—ISBN 978-1-4426-3438-1 (volume 2: pdf).

1. Middle Ages—Sources.   I. Geary, Patrick J., 1948–, editor

D113.R42 2015b   940.1   c2015-906782-0
                                   c2015-906783-9

We welcome comments and suggestions regarding any aspect of our publications—please feel free to contact us at news@utphighereducation.com or visit our Internet site at www.utppublishing.com.

North America
5201 Dufferin Street
North York, Ontario, Canada, M3H 5T8

2250 Military Road
Tonawanda, New York, USA, 14150

ORDERS PHONE: 1-800-565-9523
ORDERS FAX: 1-800-221-9985
ORDERS E-MAIL: utpbooks@utpress.utoronto.ca

UK, Ireland, and continental Europe
NBN International
Estover Road, Plymouth, PL6 7PY, UK
ORDERS PHONE: 44 (0) 1752 202301
ORDERS FAX: 44 (0) 1752 202333
ORDERS E-MAIL: enquiries@nbninternational.com

Every effort has been made to contact copyright holders; in the event of an error or omission, please notify the publisher.

The University of Toronto Press acknowledges the financial support for its publishing activities of the Government of Canada through the Canada Book Fund.

Printed in Canada.

For my students and especially in memory of BRIDGET BERNADETTE PHILLIPS *1966–1989 whose tragic death cut short a career of great promise*

Contents

Color Plates

Preface

Any historian will tell you that the real fun in history comes from reading and analyzing primary sources: those documents, monuments, tools, and buildings actually created by the people we study. Regardless of how well researched or written, no secondary history book can provide the same thrill as reading the actual words of a twelfth-century abbot or following the testimony of a woman hauled before a court of inquisition. History, after all, is the active and creative process of interpreting the distant echoes of the past; it is not the passive memorization of facts, dates, and other people's theories. Canned history is no more appealing than canned food: fresh is always better, and growing your own is the best. Even the best textbook or scholarly synthesis is only the opinion of some historian about the significance of the material that he or she has read. In a sense, the author has already had all the fun: reading, interpreting, synthesizing, and making sense of these voices of the past. Unless we know the sources that the author has used, we can have only a distant sense of whether to accept, reject, or modify his or her conclusions. Only by reading these primary sources for ourselves can we develop our own critical, independent evaluation of the people who produced them and thus become historians, ready to participate in a dialogue with others who have read these texts before and offered their interpretations.

Because this active involvement with primary sources is at the heart of studying history, this volume places at the disposal of students beginning their exploration of medieval Europe some of these documents so that they can actually participate in the historical enterprise. Obviously this book cannot reproduce the feeling of anticipation as one sits in a great European library and opens a massive parchment manuscript, or the excitement of untying a bundle of charters written by monastic scribes over a thousand years ago. Nor can translations convey the complexities and problems of the original languages: every translation, it has been said, is a "polite lie." Still, I hope that these documents will bring students more than merely a deeper knowledge of the received tradition of medieval history. The recognition of the fragmentary and ambiguous nature of the documentation with which historians have reconstructed the past should inspire in students a healthy skepticism toward these syntheses. Moreover, it should engender in them an impatience to acquire the necessary linguistic and technical skills to do their own medieval history and to do it better than their predecessors and teachers.

Accordingly this book is designed to provide primary material with which students can participate in the historical process, not to argue for any particular interpretations or to serve merely as an illustration of currently fashionable historical theses. Four principles have guided the selection of the documents it contains.

First, entire documents or long excerpts have been included whenever possible. Truncated and severely abridged "snippets" do not allow students to understand enough of the form and context of these sources to attempt their own analyses. The result is a volume containing fewer texts than might be desired, but because of their length students and instructors should be able to do more with those that are included. I particularly regret that, with the exception of the Old High German *Song of Hildebrand*, I was forced to exclude literary sources. However, excellent and inexpensive translations of the classics of medieval literature are generally available for students and can supplement the harder-to-find historical sources in this volume. Likewise, I regret that except to a very limited extent, the Orthodox and Islamic worlds of the Middle Ages are not represented in this reader. To do these complex civilizations justice would have fundamentally changed the nature of this volume: they deserve primary source readers of their own.

Second, rather than selecting widely different texts to illustrate particular issues, I have grouped some texts to form a dossier in which the individual documents relate to each other. This is of course what the practicing historian attempts to compile and examine. Examples such as the series of documents concerning land holding from Cluny, two accounts of the meeting between Otto III and the Polish prince Bolesław Chrobry in 1000, a group of Florentine catasto filings from a single family, or two Spanish law codes dealing with Jews, Muslims, and heretics, provide students with the opportunity to pose historical questions from a variety of differing perspectives. Likewise, it should be possible for students to make valid connections among documents across units. Thus, for example, the selection from the *Theodosian Code* can be related to texts from the Salic law, Anglo-Saxon law, twelfth-century Italian legal contracts, the *Saxon Mirror*, and Spanish urban law. Guibert of Nogent's autobiography can be compared with that of Emperor Charles IV and *The Book of Margery Kempe*. Anselm of Canterbury's argument for the existence of God can be compared with that of Thomas Aquinas. The selection from the eleventh-century *Domesday Book* concerning Huntingdonshire lends itself to comparison with the Huntingdonshire Eyre of 1286.

Third, whenever possible the documents presented here have been selected because they have been the objects of significant scholarship available in English. Nothing is more frustrating for a student beginning to develop an interest in medieval history than to find the issues he or she raises in relationship to a particular text have been discussed only in continental languages. Thus, for example, one reason for the selection of the book of the *Miracles of St. Foy* rather than other hagiographic texts is that it has been the subject of a number of recent studies in English from a variety of perspectives. The example of an inquisitorial dossier comes from Montaillou, brilliantly if controversially studied by Emmanuel Le Roy Ladurie. Similarly, the growing interest in the multi-ethnic and multi-cultural world of the Iberian peninsula explains the inclusion of Spanish material.

Finally, although I have my own prejudices and preferences in terms of how one does history, I have made a sincere effort to provide the raw material for many types of historical investigations. There is no one exercise that can be done with each document, no single way that an instructor can make use of them. Nor is there one point of view toward which the selection of documents tacitly point.

Of course, the perspective and competence of the investigator limit every historical enterprise, and this volume is no exception. One could easily compile an equally valuable alternative list of readings to this one, and one could validly object to the geographical limitations from which the sources are taken. I have tried to take into account the range of documents my colleagues are currently using by surveying and examining medievalist syllabuses and other source books. I have selected accurate translations or made new ones, attempting whenever possible to select translations whose publishers charge reasonable fees to reproduce in order to keep the price of the book as low as possible. Finally, I have included a number of hitherto untranslated texts in order to provide the sorts of documents representative of the types of sources to which medievalists are turning in contemporary research.

Don LePan of Broadview Press, who first suggested that a new medieval reader was needed and encouraged me to undertake it, deserves much of the credit for this book. I would also like to thank Barbara Rosenwein, Susanna Foster Baxandall, George Beech, and Jonathan M. Elukin for their contributions. I owe a lasting debt of gratitude to John William Rooney, Jr., who first introduced me to the joy of reading the sources of medieval history. Wolter Braamhorst, Anne Picard, and Julian Hendrix spent many hours assisting me in finding and revising appropriate translations and editions. Edward Schoolman worked with me on the glossary. J. Patout Burns, Richard Kay, and Ronald Finucane provided many useful corrections and suggestions for revisions. Also critical to the success of this *Reader* has been the feedback I have received from the users of the first four editions. Clearly the book has proven useful to many teachers and students, and many have shared with the editors, first at Broadview and more recently at the University of Toronto Press, as well as with me their suggestions for how to make the book still better. I would particularly like to thank Terrie Bramley, Brett Savage, and Julia Bernheim for their assistance in preparing this latest edition.

In this new, fifth edition, we have taken advantage of the many written comments that we have received through the years. In addition to keeping innovations from the fourth edition such as a glossary of technical vocabulary, recommended readings that can provide students with more information on the text, and more women's voices, we have added a new section on the Black Death, as well as a section that deals with Europe's encounter with the Mongol Empire, and provided questions for study at the end of each section. This edition also contains for the first time a number of color images since objects, like written texts, are also the raw stuff of history. We hope that this new edition, like the four that preceded it, will continue to open a world of excitement and wonder to students of the Middle Ages by allowing them to participate in the joys of the historian's craft.

Patrick J. Geary

Late Antiquity

1. THEODOSIAN CODE

The *Theodosian Code* was the first official collection of imperial general constitutions (composed between 313 and 438) dealing with a large number of public, private, and church issues. Its compilation was ordered by Emperor Theodosius II (401–450) as part of his concern with legal education. It was completed in 438 and adopted in both the eastern and western portions of the Roman Empire.

The work is arranged in 16 books, each composed of a number of titles. In the east it was superseded by the codification of Justinian but continued to be the authoritative collection of Roman law in the barbarian kingdoms of western Europe. As such, it had an enormous influence on the formation of western barbarian and medieval law.

The following selection is Book III, which treats contracts, betrothal, marriage, dowries, divorce, and care of minors.

Source: The Theodosian Code and Novels and the Sirmondian Constitutions, trans. Clyde Pharr with Theresa Sherrer Davidson and Mary Brown Pharr (Princeton, NJ: Princeton University Press, 1952), 63–81.

Further Reading: John F. Matthews, *Laying Down the Law: A Study of the Theodosian Code* (New Haven, CT: Yale University Press, 2000).

Title I: Contracts of Purchase (*De Contrahenda Emptione*)

1. Emperor Constantine Augustus to Profuturus, Prefect of the Annona.

It is not at all fitting that the good faith of sale and purchase should be broken, when no duress was exerted through fraud. For a contract that has been executed without any flaw must not be disturbed by a litigious controversy because of the sole complaint that the price was too cheap.

Posted on the ides of August in the fifth consulship of Constantine Augustus and the consulship of Licinius Caesar.—August 13, 319.

Interpretation: When a thing has been purchased for a definite price that is agreed upon between the buyer and seller, although it is worth more than it is sold for at the present, this only must be investigated, whether the person who is proved to have purchased it has committed no fraud or violence. If the seller should wish to revoke the sale, by no means shall he be permitted to do so.

2. The Same Augustus to Gregorius.

The purchaser shall assume the tax assessment[1] of property that is purchased, and no person shall be permitted either to buy or sell property without its tax assessment.

1. Moreover, in accordance with this law, there must henceforth be a public or fiscal inspection, so that if any property should be sold without its tax assessment and this fact should be reported by another, the seller, indeed, shall lose the landholding, and the purchaser for his part shall lose the price that he has paid, since the fisc shall vindicate both.

1a. It is also Our pleasure that no person shall engage in the sale of anything whatsoever unless at the time when the contract between the seller and the buyer is formally executed, a certain and true ownership is proved by the neighbors. To such an extent shall the precaution prescribed by this law be observed that even if "benches," or strips of land, as they are commonly called, are sold, the proof of showing ownership shall be fulfilled.

2. Nor shall the formalities between the buyer and the seller be solemnized in hidden corners, but fraudulent sales shall be completely buried and shall perish.

Given on the day before the nones of February at Constantinople in the year of the consulship of Felicianus and Titianus.—February 4, 337.

Interpretation: If any person should purchase a villa, he shall know that he has purchased the obligation of the tribute of the thing itself as well as the right to the landholding, because no person is permitted either to buy or sell a farm without the tribute or fiscal payment. But if any person should dare to sell or presume to purchase anything when the fiscal payment had been concealed, those between whom such a contract has been made by a secret transaction should know that both the purchaser shall lose the price and the seller shall lose the landholding, because it is ordered that the neighbors of the property which is sold must be witnesses and present, to the extent that even in the case of things of slight value, if anything is sold for use, it is Our pleasure that it shall be shown to the neighbors and thus purchased, in order that the property of others may not be sold.

3. Emperor Julian Augustus to Julianus, Count of the Orient.

We order that the constitution of My paternal uncle, Constantine, shall be repealed, in which he commanded that minor women who were united with husbands in marriage should be able to negotiate sales without the interposition of a decree, if their husbands should suppose that they ought to give their consent as well as provide their subscription to the documents. For it is absurd that husbands who are at times needy men should be obligated for their wives, because when the right itself of the sale is not valid, these women are able to recover their own property from those persons who have participated in the illicit contracts. 1. Therefore We revive the old law, that on no account shall any sale whatsoever be valid when it has been contracted by a minor, whether a man or a woman, without the interposition of a decree.

Given on the eighth day before the ides of December at Antioch in the year of the consulship of the Most Noble Mamertinus and Nevitta.—December 6, 362.

Interpretation: It had been ordained by a law of the Emperor Constantine that minor women who had husbands could sell anything from their own resources with the consent of their husbands. But this ordinance is abrogated by the present law, and the following rule must be observed, namely, that if under the compulsion of necessity men or women who are minors should wish to sell anything, whoever should wish to buy it shall be protected by the authorization of the judge or by the consent of the municipal council; for otherwise a sale made by minors will not be valid.

4. Emperors Gratian, Valentinian, and Theodosius Augustuses to Hypatius, Praetorian Prefect.

If a person in his majority and approved as capable of administering his own patrimony should sell a landed estate, even though it is situated at a distance and even though, perchance, in some cases the entire estate has not been sold, he shall not thereafter obtain the right of recovery on the ground that the price was too cheap.

1. He shall not be allowed to contrive delays by means of unfounded objections, namely, that he should allege that the value of the property was unknown to him, since he ought to know the value, that is, the worth and income of his own family property.

Given on the sixth day before the nones of May at Milan in the year of the second consulship of Merobaudes and the consulship of Saturninus.—May 2, 383.

Interpretation: If any person, already of full legal age and able to manage his own household, should sell his villa, house, or anything else at a definite price and if, perchance, later he should wish to claim in opposition that he received a smaller price than the property was worth, because he says, perhaps, that he was ignorant of the value of the land which he sold, since it was located at

---

[1] That is, payments of the taxes assessed on the property.

a distance, the sale cannot be revoked for that reason. For a person of full age could have known what sort of thing he sold or at what price the thing to be sold could be valued.

5. *The Same Augustuses to Cynegius, Praetorian Prefect.*

No Jew whatever shall purchase a Christian slave or contaminate an ex-Christian with Jewish religious rites. But if a public investigation should disclose that this has been done, the slave shall be forcibly taken away, and such masters shall undergo a punishment suitable and appropriate for the crime. It is further added that if there should be found among the Jews any slaves who are either still Christians or ex-Christian Jews, they shall be redeemed from this unworthy servitude by the Christians upon payment of a suitable price.

Received on the tenth day before the kalends of October at Rhegium in the year of the consulship of Richomer and Clearchus.—September 22, 384.

Interpretation: It must be observed above all things else that no Jew shall be permitted to have a Christian slave; indeed, if a Jew should have a Christian slave, he shall under no circumstances dare to presume to transfer him to his own religious faith. If he should do this, he shall know that his slaves will be forcibly taken from him, and he shall undergo a punishment suited to so great a crime. For before this law was issued, it had been decreed that if a Christian slave had been contaminated by Jewish pollution, his master should know that the price which he had paid for the slave would be refunded to him by the Christians in order that the slave might remain in the Christian faith.

6. *The Same Augustuses to Flavianus, Praetorian Prefect of Illyricum and Italy.*

Formerly the right had been granted to near kinsmen and to co-owners to exclude extraneous persons from a purchase,[2] and men could not, in accordance with their own decision, sell any property which they had for sale. But because this appears to be a grave injustice, which is veiled by the empty pretext of honor, that men should be compelled to do anything about their own property against their will, this former law is hereby annulled, and each person shall be able to seek and approve a purchaser according to his own decision.

Given on the sixth day before the kalends of June at Vincentia in the year of the consulship of Titianus and Symmachus.—May 27, 391.

Interpretation: A former ordinance of the law had provided that if one co-owner, because of some necessity, should wish to sell a thing, an extraneous person should not have the opportunity to buy it. But this imperial indulgence is approved as better, namely, that any person shall have the right to use his unconstrained decision concerning his own property. He may pass over his co-owners and near kinsmen and have the unrestricted privilege of selling to whomever he wishes.

7. *The Same Augustuses to Remigius, Augustal Prefect.*

If persons of full legal capacity should once enter into a contract of purchase and sale, it cannot be invalidated on the ground that too small a price has been paid.

Given on the third day before the kalends of April at Constantinople in the year of the fourth consulship of Arcadius Augustus and the third consulship of Honorius Augustus.—March 30, 396.

Interpretation: When an agreement has been made between any two persons concerning the price of anything, although the thing has been bought for a less price than it was worth, the sale shall by no means be revoked.

8. *The Same Augustuses to Messala, Praetorian Prefect.*

(After other matters.) If any persons by flight should desert the compulsory public services, either municipal or provincial, that have been enjoined upon them and should suppose that they may enter into clandestine contracts, they shall understand that these artifices will profit them nothing, and the purchaser shall be fined the price that he has paid. (Etc.)

Given on the twelfth day before the kalends of September in the year of the consulship of the Most Noble Theodorus.—August 21, 399.

Interpretation: If any persons should attempt to escape the compulsory public services which are due to the municipal council or their own municipality and should wish to sell their property secretly, they shall know that what they have done cannot be valid, and that they themselves will be recalled to the services due. Those persons also who bought the property shall lose the price.

9. *Emperors Honorius and Theodosius Augustuses to the People.*

We command that the sales, gifts, and compromises which have been extorted through the exercise of power[3] shall be invalidated.

---

[2] Of property held in common.

[3] The merciless exploitation of the poor and weak by the rich and powerful was extremely common. It was often forbidden by the emperors, but the various laws against it were apparently ineffectual.

Given on the thirteenth day before the kalends of March at Constantinople in the year of the tenth consulship of Honorius Augustus and the sixth consulship of Theodosius Augustus.—February 17, 415.

Interpretation: All men shall know that whatever they have given or sold under the compulsion of very powerful persons can be recovered.

10. *Honorius and Theodosius Augustuses to Palladius, Praetorian Prefect.*

There is said to exist a superfluous belief of some persons that the right to purchase has been denied to persons placed in administrative offices and in the imperial service, although a law of the sainted Honorius, issued to Palladius, Praetorian Prefect, and included in the Theodosian corpus, is read as having given this right to such persons.

Title 2: The Annulment of Provisions for Forfeiture (De Commissoria Rescindenda)

1. *Emperor Constantine Augustus to the People.*

Since among other captious practices, the harshness of the provision for forfeiture is especially increasing, it is Our pleasure that such provision shall be invalidated and that hereafter all memory of it shall be abolished. If any person, therefore, is suffering under such a contract, he shall be relieved by this sanction which cancels all such past and present arguments and prohibits them for the future. For We order that creditors shall surrender the property[4] and recover that which they have given.[5]

Given on the day before the kalends of February at Sofia (Serdica) in the year of the seventh consulship of Constantine Augustus and the consulship of Constantius Caesar.—January 31, 326; [320].[6]

Interpretation: Those written acknowledgements of debt are called agreements for forfeiture in which a debtor through necessity promises in a written acknowledgement of debt to sell to his own creditor a thing which he had pledged for a time to the creditor. This law cancels any such agreement for forfeiture which has been made and absolutely prohibits one to be made. Thus if any

creditor should appear to have bought property of his debtor under such a pretext, he shall not delude himself with written documents, but as soon as the debtor wishes, who sold when oppressed by debt, the creditor shall recover his money, and the debtor shall receive back his property.

Title 3: Fathers Who Have Sold Their Children (De Patribus Qui Filios Distraxerunt)

1. *Emperors Valentinian, Theodosius, and Arcadius Augustuses to Tatianus, Praetorian Prefect.*

All those persons whom the piteous fortune of their parents has consigned to slavery while their parents thereby were seeking sustenance shall be restored to their original status of free birth. Certainly no person shall demand repayment of the purchase price, if he has been compensated by the slavery of a free-born person for a space of time that is not too short.

Given on the fifth day before the ides of March at Milan in the year of the consulship of Tatianus and Symmachus.—March 11, 391.

Interpretation: If a father, forced by need, should sell any free-born child whatsoever, the child cannot remain in perpetual slavery, but if he has made compensation by his slavery, he shall be restored to his free-born status without even the repayment of the purchase price.

Title 4: Aedilician Actions (De Aedilicis Actionibus)

1. *Emperors Valentinian, Theodosius, and Arcadius Augustuses to Nebridius, Prefect of the City.*

Once a contract of good faith has been completed and a slave has been received and the price paid, the right to recover the purchase price shall be granted to the purchaser of the slave only if he can produce the slave who he claims is a fugitive. This rule, indeed, is prescribed by law not only in the case of barbarian slaves, but also in the case of provincial slaves.

Given on the third day before the kalends of July at Constantinople in the year of the consulship of Emperor Designate Honorious and the Most Noble Evodius.—June 29, 386.

Interpretation: When the price of a slave has been agreed upon between the buyer and seller and a deed of sale has been written, such sale can by no means be revoked, unless by chance the buyer should prove that the

---

[4] Which they have accepted as a pledge.

[5] As a loan.

[6] Some of the dates provided in the text are incorrect; suggested corrections appear after these.

slave is a fugitive, and then he shall have permission to recover the price if he should restore the slave to the seller.

Title 5: Betrothal and Prenuptial Gifts (*De Sponsalibus et Ante Nuptias Donationibus*)

1. Emperor Constantine Augustus to Rufinus, Praetorian Prefect.

It was the will of Our father that no act of generosity should be valid unless it was entered in the public records. We decree also that, after the time of promulgation of this law, gifts between betrothed persons, as well as those between all other persons, shall be valid only if they are accompanied by the attestation of the public records.

Given on the fourth day before the ides of May at Sirmium in the year of the fifth consulship of Constantine Augustus and the consulship of Licinius Caesar.—May 12, 319 or 352.

Interpretation: Before the time of the above law, gifts were valid even without the attestation of the public records. But now, after the above law, no nuptial or any other gift of anything whatsoever, between any persons whatsoever, can be valid if it has not been formally registered in the public records.

2. The Same Augustus to Maximus, Prefect of the City.

Since We are displeased with the opinion of the ancients which decreed that gifts to a betrothed woman were valid even though the marriage did not follow, We order that those negotiations between betrothed persons which are conducted with due legal formality with the intention of making gifts shall be made subject to the following conditions: whether it appears that persons live under paternal power or that they are in any manner legally independent, if, either of their own volition or with the mutual consent of their parents, they should make presents to each other as though with a view to future matrimony, and if indeed the man of his own accord should be unwilling to take the woman as his wife, he shall not recover that which has been given and delivered by him; if any part of the promised gift remains in the possession of the donor, it shall be transferred to the betrothed woman without any evasion. 1. But if the responsibility for failure to contract the marriage is revealed to have been that of the betrothed woman or of the person under whose power she lives, then all gifts shall be returned to the betrothed man or his heirs without any diminution.

2. These provisions shall similarly be observed also if a gift has been made to a betrothed man on the part of the woman betrothed to him. There shall be no further inquiry into reasons for failure to contract the marriage. Thus, for example, the morals or the low birth, perhaps, of either party may not be alleged, and no other obstacle may be adduced which anyone might consider unsuitable, since long before the betrothal was contracted, all these things should have been foreseen. Therefore, only the intention shall be investigated, and a change of intention shall suffice for either restitution or recovery of the gifts that have been made, since, after the elimination of all pretexts, it shall be necessary for nothing further to be established, except the evidence as to which party said that the marriage which was to be contracted was not acceptable.

3. Since it is possible that before the marriage is contracted, one of the two may die while his intention to marry is still unchanged, We consider it suitable that when the one to whom a gift has been made completes his days before the marriage, whatever has been given under the title of a betrothal gift or donated in any other way shall be restored to the person who made the gift. Also, if the person who presented a gift should die before the wedding, the gift shall be immediately invalidated and that property which was presented shall be restored to the heirs of the donor without any hindrance.

4. We decree that this benefit shall extend even to the person of the father and mother and of children also, if there were any from a former marriage; if in any manner any of these persons should succeed to the inheritance of the deceased. But if none of these persons should be an heir of the deceased, but some one from the remaining[7] degrees should succeed to the inheritance, the gifts shall become valid even though because of death the marriage was not confirmed, since We believe that suitable provisions should be made only for those persons.[8]

Given on the seventeenth day before the kalends of November: October 16. Posted on the sixth day before the aforesaid kalends at Rome in the year of the fifth consulship of Constantine Augustus and the consulship of Licinius Caesar.—October 27, 319.

Interpretation: Whenever betrothed persons have made a specific agreement concerning their future

---

[7] The more remote degrees of kinship than those mentioned above.

[8] The ones specified above.

marriage, and the man, either with the consent of his parents or of his own free will if he is legally independent, has written a deed of gift of his betrothal bounty to his betrothed and has confirmed this deed of gift with all the formality of written documents, provided also that it shall be proved that public records were made in conformity with the law and that formal induction into the land and delivery of movables followed, then if anything should pass into the right and ownership of the betrothed woman by such a formal gift and if later, after the aforesaid formal documents have been executed, the man should voluntarily refuse to accept as his wife the woman whom he betrothed, he shall not demand back anything that has been delivered. If he is proved to have in his possession any of the property thus formally specified and delivered, it shall be transferred without any delay to the ownership of the betrothed woman whom he was unwilling to accept.

It is unnecessary to explain the remainder of the above law because it is annulled by the subsequent laws.

3. The Same Augustus to Valerianus, Acting Vicar of the Prefect.

Although in matters of gain it is not customary to assist women who are ignorant of the law, the statutes of former emperors declare that this rule does not apply as against one who is still under age. 1. Lest, therefore, when marital affection has vanished, some cruel decision should be made, We decree that if property has been given and delivered to a prospective wife who is under age at the time of marriage, this property cannot be recovered on the grounds that the former husband refused to register the gift in the public records.

Given on the fourth day before the kalends of May in the year of the consulship of Gallicanus and Symmachus.—April 28, 330.

Interpretation: Although even in the case of women, who can at times be excused because of their frailty, the law is unwilling to assist them in some cases if they have been negligent, nevertheless, in the above law it was the emperor's will that especial provision should be made for them, so that if any girl should be united to a husband in her pupillary years and her husband should through negligence fail to register his betrothal bounty in the public records, she shall know that by the benefit of this law, even if public records are lacking, the gift will remain in her ownership with indefeasible title.

4. The Same Augustus to Pacatianus, Praetorian Prefect.

If any man should contract for the marriage of a girl to himself and should fail to effect such marriage within two years, and if after this time has elapsed the girl should proceed to marry another, no fraud shall be imputed to her for hastening her marriage and not allowing her marriage vows to be mocked any longer.

Given on the day before the ides of April at Marcianopolis in the year of the consulship of Pacatianus and Hilarianus.—April 12, 332.

5. The Same Augustus to Pacatianus, Praetorian Prefect.

The father of a girl or her tutor, curator, or any kinsman, shall not be permitted to give her in marriage to another after having previously betrothed her to a soldier. If the girl should be given in marriage to another within two years, the person guilty of such perfidy shall be exiled by relegation to an island. But if after an interval of two years has elapsed since the marriage was agreed upon, the person who betrothed the girl[9] should marry her to another, it shall be attributed to the fault of the betrothed man[10] rather than to that of the girl, and the person who gave the girl in marriage to another husband after two years shall suffer no injury.

Given on the day before the ides of April at Marcianopolis in the year of the consulship of Pacatianus and Hilarianus.—April 12, 332.

Interpretation: If any person, either a private citizen or a soldier, after his betrothal to a girl, should make a definite agreement concerning the marriage with her father, tutor, curator, or near kinsman, he must effect the marriage within two years after this definite agreement. But if on account of the procrastination or negligence of the betrothed man, a period of two years should elapse and the girl should marry another man, both she herself and the kinsman who delivered her in marriage shall be free from calumny. For the fault is that of the man who, by delaying his own marriage, gave to another man the opportunity to marry the girl. If she should be given in marriage to another man within two years, the rules to be observed will be understood more clearly from the subsequent law.

6. The Same Augustus to Tiberianus, Vicar of Spain.

If a man should make gifts to his betrothed when a kiss has been exchanged as a pledge and if it should happen that either the man or the woman should die before the marriage, We order that one half of the things given shall belong to the survivor; the other half shall belong

---

[9] To a soldier.

[10] The soldier who had thus delayed the marriage of the girl to himself.

to the heirs of the deceased man or woman, of whatever degree such heirs may be and by whatever right they may succeed to the inheritance, so that it appears that one half the gift shall remain valid and one half shall be annulled. But when no kiss has been exchanged as a pledge, if either of the betrothed persons should die, the whole gift shall be invalidated and shall be restored to the betrothed donor or to his heirs.

1. If a woman should give anything to her betrothed under the title of betrothal gifts, a thing which rarely occurs, and if it happens that either the man or the woman dies before the marriage, whether or not a kiss has been exchanged as a pledge, the whole gift shall be invalidated, and the ownership of the things shall be transferred to the betrothed woman who gave it or to her heirs.

Given on the ides of July at Constantinople: July 15, 335. Received on the fourteenth day before the kalends of May at Hispalis in the year of the consulship of Nepotianus and Facundus.—April 18, 336.

Interpretation: If when a betrothal has been solemnized and a kiss has been exchanged as a pledge, the betrothed man should make some gift to the betrothed woman, and if perchance he should die before the marriage, then the girl, in case she survives, shall be able to vindicate one half of the things which had been formally given to her, and the heirs of the deceased shall acquire one half, in whatsoever order, according to the degree of succession, they may come. But if a kiss should not be exchanged as a pledge, and the betrothed man should die, the girl shall not be able to vindicate any of the things given or delivered to her. But if anything should be given by the girl to the betrothed man and she should die, whether or not a kiss has been exchanged as a pledge, the parents or near kinsmen of the girl shall recover all that which the girl gave.

7. . . . [11]

. . . provided that . . . has been preserved, the gift shall have complete validity, although he did not arrange for the certification of public records in testimony thereof. Certainly, a group of people assembled as witnesses of these vows is sufficiently competent. But in the case of all other gifts, the execution of public records shall be required in accordance with the constitutions of Our sainted father.[12]

Given on the fifth day before the ides of Ju . . . [13] *at Köln in the year of the consulship of Amantius and Albinus.—June 9 (July 11), 345.*

8. *Emperor Julian Augustus to Hypatius, Vicar of the City of Rome.*[14]

Whenever any gifts consisting of landed estates that are subject to either Italian, stipendiary, or tributary rights are given and pledged by a stipulation to a betrothed woman in her minority, with a view to future marriage, such bounty shall be supported by perpetual validity, even though it should appear that the formality of delivery was lacking; provided, however, that even in the case of those gifts which are bestowed upon minors, the execution of public records shall be demanded in all cases.

Given on the ninth day before the kalends of M(arch) at Antioch in the year of the fourth consulship of Julian Augustus and the consulship of Sallustius.—February 21, 363.

9. *Emperors Valentinian, Valens, and Gratian Augustuses to Probus, Praetorian Prefect.*

Before marriage many things are delivered with all due formality under the title of betrothal gifts, and these gifts must not by any means contribute to loss on the part of the donor. But if the girl should die during the marriage, they shall revert to the advantage of the said donor in disregard, of course, of the old law. Therefore, the claim of the father and other near kinsmen shall be annulled, and such gifts shall be returned without delay to those persons who appear to have presented them before the marriage was contracted.

Given on the third day before the ides of July at Trier in the year of the consulship of Valentinian and Valens Augustuses.—July 13, 368 (or 367 or 373).

10. *Emperors Gratian, Valentinian, and Theodosius Augustuses to Eutropius, Praetorian Prefect.*

If, after anything has been given as earnest under the title of betrothal gifts, either of the betrothed persons should die, We order that whatever has been given shall be restored, unless the deceased person had previously given cause for the non-performance of the marriage rites.

---

[11] The first part of the constitution has been lost.

[12] Constantine the Great.

[13] Since the MS. is defective, the month is uncertain.

[14] Estates subject to Italian rights had certain privileges that were not held by stipendiary or tributary estates, since Italian estates were originally those of the Roman conquerors, while stipendiary and tributary estates were originally those of conquered peoples. These distinctions were gradually abolished in the time of the Empire.

Given on the fifteenth day before the kalends of July at Thessalonica in the year of the fifth consulship of Gratian Augustus and the first consulship of Theodosius Augustus.—June 17, 380.

11. The Same Augustuses to Eutropius, Praetorian Prefect.

When betrothal gifts have been made to a girl before her tenth year, We remit the fourfold penalty for the father, mother, tutor, or any person, even though the marriage should not follow; and if the girl should die in the meantime, We order that the betrothal gifts shall be restored to her betrothed.

1. But if the father or any other person who has charge of the girl's affairs should suppose that he should retain the pledges which he has received in the girl's tenth year or later, and before her twelfth year, that is, until the end of her eleventh year, then if, when the time for the marriage arrives, he should be false to his trust, he shall become obligated to the fourfold penalty.

2. But for a widow, since she is not assisted by the privilege of age, there is a different rule, namely, that if she does not effect her marriage, she shall be liable to the fourfold penalty according to the ancient constitution.

3. Moreover, when any person makes an agreement concerning the marriage of a girl after the completion of her twelfth year, if indeed the person making the agreement is the girl's father, he shall obligate himself, but if her mother or a curator or other near kinsman, the girl shall become obligated.

4. But there shall be reserved to the girl against her mother, tutor, curator, or such near kinsman, an unimpaired action, on the basis of what is fair and just with regard to those pledges which she restored from her own resources according to the penalty of the law, provided that she can prove that she had been compelled by the aforesaid persons to consent to receive what was given as earnest.

Given on the fifteenth day before the kalends of July at Thessalonica in the year of the fifth consulship of Gratian Augustus and the first consulship of Theodosius Augustus.—June 17, 380.

Interpretation: If, before a girl has reached her tenth year, her father or mother or, if the father should be lacking, her tutor, curator, or any near kinsman, should make an agreement concerning her marriage and should accept betrothal gifts, and if afterwards he should change his mind and wish to reject the person whom he had formerly accepted, he shall not be condemned to the fourfold penalty, but shall restore only what he had received. Certainly, also if the girl should die, only that shall be

returned which had been received. But if, when the girl is in her tenth year and until the completion of her eleventh year, she herself, or her parents, tutors, and curators should retain the earnest which had been received, the following rule must be observed, namely, that if the person who made the agreement concerning the marriage of the girl should wish to prove false to the agreement and should reject the man whose betrothal gifts had been received, he shall be liable to the fourfold penalty, without doubt. But if he should return the pledges received before the girl's eleventh year is completed, he shall fear no malicious charges concerning the earnest which had been accepted. On the other hand, if the girl should be a widow, she shall not be able to defend herself on the ground of her age,[15] if she should turn her affections elsewhere and should wish to reject her former betrothed. Then whatever she has accepted under the title of betrothal gifts she shall return fourfold. But if after the girl's twelfth year, her father should wish to do otherwise than he promised concerning her marriage, her father himself shall be held liable to the fourfold penalty. If the father is dead and the mother, tutor, curator, or any near kinsman should make a definite agreement concerning the marriage of the girl and the girl should prefer to wed another, she herself out of her own resources shall make reparation to her former betrothed in the amount of four times the value of what she received. This condition, however, shall be observed, that she can bring suit afterwards against the aforesaid persons, if under their compulsion she unwillingly accepted the pledges of the man whom she later refused.

12. Emperors Honorius and Theodosius Augustuses to Marinianus, Praetorian Prefect.

(After other matters.) If a father should enter into a pact concerning the marriage of his daughter and he should not be able to reach the time of the marriage because he perished by human lot, the decision which is proved to have been made by the father shall remain valid and binding between the betrothed, and a compromise shall not be permitted to have any weight if it is proved to have been made by the guardian to whose administration the interests of the minor pertain. 1. For it is thoroughly unjust that the decision of a tutor or curator, who has perhaps been bribed, should be admitted as against the father's wish, since frequently even the determination

---

[15] That is, she may not claim the privileges granted to women who were minors.

of a woman herself is found to work against her own interests. (Etc.)

Given on the third day before the nones of November at Ravenna in the year of the thirteenth consulship of Our Lord Honorius Augustus and the tenth consulship of Our Lord Theodosius Augustus.—November 3, 422.

Interpretation: When a definite agreement concerning the marriage of a girl has been made by the decision of her father, if by human lot the father should die before the girl is married, the agreement cannot be changed in any way, and the girl shall not have the liberty to do anything else even if her mother or tutor or curator or near kinsmen should perhaps wish that she accept another rather than the man her father chose. But the promise of her father with reference to the man whom he himself accepted as her betrothed shall remain valid, and in no way shall the girl be permitted in accordance with her own plan to desire anything contrary to the wishes of her father.

13. *Emperors Theodosius and Valentinian Augustuses to Hierius, Praetorian Prefect.*

(After other matters.) If a deed or gift has been validated before marriage by the formality of registration in the public records, there shall be no inquiry as to whether delivery of the gift either preceded or followed the marriage or was altogether omitted. In the case of a gift which is less than two hundred solidi in its total value, the execution of public records shall not be required. 1. We do not permit these advantages to be denied to a wife or to those persons who succeed to her rights, who may be deceived through the fraud of her husband or the dishonesty of his heirs or through legal technicalities, even though either through ignorance or cunning the deed of gift should make mention of things to be given as dowry, but such gifts shall be extracted from the husband or his heirs and shall be restored. That law also shall remain in force which makes just provision for women of minor age, even when the attestation of the public records has been omitted, if they have been deprived of their father's aid. (Etc.)

Given on the tenth day before the kalends of March at Constantinople in the year of the consulship of Taurus and Felix.—February 21, 428.

Interpretation: If a betrothal gift should be entered in the public records before marriage, it cannot be invalidated even though the thing given is not delivered. But in the case of a gift, the total value of which is found to be less than two hundred solidi, even when a public record of it is lacking, no chicanery can be employed against women under cover of any cunning device or objection, but any writing whatever which indicates the day and the time shall suffice. Therefore, whether a gift is one which is made by entry in the public records without delivery, or whether it is one which is less than two hundred solidi in value, it shall not be invalidated by any arguments resting upon chicanery in any respect, but the things shall be exacted from the husband or his heirs who shall be ordered to restore them to the woman. Nevertheless, the benefit of the law shall remain valid concerning those women who are married during their minority after their father's death, so that a deed of gift of any amount whatever, when made in writing, shall stand with complete validity, even though it has not been registered in the public records.

14. ...[16]

... the betrothed man or the betrothed woman may violate this regulation without any hazard. But the fifteenth constitution of the fifteenth title of the third book of the Theodosian Code confirms the threatened penalty to the extent of double indemnity in cases of agreements for marriage.

Title 6: If the Governor of a Province or Persons Connected with Him Should Give Betrothal Gifts (*Si Provinciae Rector Vel Ad Eum Pertinentes Sponsalia Dederint*)

1. *Emperors Gratian, Valentinian, and Theodosius Augustuses to Eutropius, Praetorian Prefect.*

(After other matters.) If betrothal gifts should be given by persons who hold positions of public power and honor in the administration of provinces and who, therefore, can intimidate parents, tutors, curators, or the women themselves who are about to contract the marriage, We order that if either the parents or the women themselves should change their minds thereafter, they shall not only be released from the toils of the law and free from the fourfold penalty which it has established, but in addition they shall keep as gain the things given as pledges if they should suppose that they ought not to be returned. 1. So widely do We intend this provision to extend that We decree that it shall apply not only to such administrators, but also to sons, grandsons, near kinsmen, associates and confidential advisers of

---

[16] The text has been lost at this point.

administrations, provided, however, that the administrators had given them assistance. 2. However, We do not forbid that marriage to be effected thereafter which was obligated by means of an earnest at the time of such administration, on account of those persons about whom We have spoken, if the consent of the betrothed woman should accede thereto.

Given on the fifteenth day before the kalends of July at Thessalonica in the year of the fifth consulship of Our Lord Gratian Augustus and the first consulship of Our Lord Theodosius Augustus.—June 17, 380.

Interpretation: If any judges[17] of provinces or any persons in administrative offices, while holding the aforesaid positions of honor, should have with them their adult sons or near kinsmen or any persons who appear to be associated with them in their administration, if they should use their power to threaten the parents or perchance to intimidate tutors or curators or the girls themselves, if they should give anything in the name of betrothal gifts or as earnest for the purpose of obligating the household of any person, and if the parents or the girls themselves should wish to resist this desire,[18] they shall have the unrestricted right to refuse that which they appear to have thus accepted. They shall know that the fourfold penalty shall not be exacted of them, but also those gifts which it appears that they accepted through terror they shall retain to their own profit, if they so wish, and they cannot be constrained to return them unless perchance they should wish to do so of their own free will. For if, after the end of such administration, the desire of the parents or the girls should remain unchanged with regard to marriage with those persons who had given betrothal gifts, the marriage thus chosen may follow.

Title 7: Marriage (*De Nuptiis*)

1. Emperors Valentinian, Valens, and Gratian Augustuses to the Senate.

A widow less than twenty-five years of age, even though she enjoys the freedom derived from emancipation, shall not enter into a subsequent marriage without the consent of her father or in opposition to his will. Therefore, the intermediaries and marriage brokers, the corrupt bearers of secret messages back and forth, shall cease. No person shall purchase a noble marriage,[19] no person shall solicit one; but the kinsmen shall be consulted publicly, and a number of nobles shall be admitted. 1. But if in the choice of a marriage the woman's desire should conflict with the decision of her near kinsmen, it is Our pleasure that, as has been sanctioned in the case of marriages of girls who are pupils, the authority of a judicial trial shall be added to the investigation that must be held, so that if the suitors are equal in birth and character, the person whom the woman herself approves, consulting her own interests, shall be adjudged preferable. 2. But lest perchance even honorable marriages should be impeded by those persons who, as kinsmen in the nearest degree, would be called to the inheritances of such widows, if a suspicion of this kind should arise, it is Our will that the authority and judgment of those persons shall prevail who, even though death should intervene, could not receive the benefit of the inheritance.

Given on the seventeenth day before the kalends of August in the year of the second consulship of Gratian Augustus and the consulship of Probus.—July 16, 371.

Interpretation: If a widow who has not yet arrived at her twenty-fifth year during her father's lifetime should wish to enter into a subsequent marriage, she shall know that, even though she has acquired her freedom by emancipation, her marriage is subject to the control of her father and does not rest upon her own desire, and her consent must conform to the choice of her father and not that of any friends or comrades whatever. But if indeed the father of such a widow is dead, even so she shall not have the right to marry according to her own individual choice, but in the interests of an honorable condition of marriage, the judgment of the near kinsmen must be followed. But if there should be two suitors, the near kinsmen must certainly be consulted, and the judge also must not be ignored, who shall take into consideration the desire of the woman only in the interest of the more honorable man. He shall not give assent to the wishes of those near kinsmen only who labor under the suspicion of desiring the inheritance and who, perhaps, while they delay the wedding, appear to be awaiting the death of the woman with a view to their succession to the inheritance. But if such a condition should arise, the choice of those persons rather must be followed who can acquire nothing from the inheritance of the aforesaid woman.

---

[17] Governors, the judges ordinary.

[18] Of the administrators. Or: if the parents or the girls themselves should wish to oppose their previous agreement.

[19] Marriage with a person of noble rank.

2. Emperors Valentinian, Theodosius, and Arcadius Augustuses to Cynegius, Praetorian Prefect.

No Jew shall receive a Christian woman in marriage, nor shall a Christian man contract a marriage with a Jewish woman. For if any person should commit an act of this kind, the crime of this misdeed shall be considered as the equivalent of adultery, and freedom to bring accusation shall be granted also to the voices of the public.

Given on the day before the ides of March at Thessalonica in the year of the second consulship of Theodosius Augustus and the consulship of the Most Noble Cynegius.—March 14, 388.

Interpretation: By the severity of this law it is prohibited that a Jew should enjoy marriage with a Christian woman or that a Christian man should receive a Jewish woman as his wife. But if any persons should involve themselves in such a union, contrary to Our prohibition, they shall know that they will be prosecuted and subjected to the same punishment as that which is inflicted upon adulterers, and that the right to bring accusation of this crime and the prosecution of it shall be allowed not only to near kinsmen but also to everyone.

3. Emperors Theodosius and Valentinian Augustuses to Hierius, Praetorian Prefect.

If instruments[20] of prenuptial gifts or dowries should be lacking and if the solemn procession and other wedding ceremonies should be omitted, no person shall suppose that on this account a marriage otherwise legally entered into shall lack validity or that the rights of legitimacy can be taken from children born of such a marriage, when the marriage is contracted of persons of equally honorable status, when it is preceded by no law, and when it is confirmed by the consent of the parties and the reliable testimony of friends. (Etc.)

Given on the tenth day before the kalends of March at Constantinople in the year of the consulship of Felix and Taurus.—February 21, 428.

Interpretation: If any such exigency should arise that a marriage should lack the due formalities, or even that betrothal gifts cannot be made or the bestowal of a dowry executed, yet if the parties should unite in marriage by mutual consent, when they are persons of equal status, a suitable choice and the agreement of the parties shall suffice, provided, however, that the knowledge of friends shall act as surety of the marriage; then if such a situation should occur, the marriage shall be approved as valid and the children as legitimate.

---

[20] Documentary evidence, such as deeds of gift and dowry agreements.

Title 8: Subsequent Marriages
(*De Secundis Nuptiis*)

1. Emperors Gratian, Valentinian, and Theodosius Augustuses to Eutropius, Praetorian Prefect.

If any woman who has lost her husband should hasten to marry another man within the period of a year (for We add a small amount of time to be observed after the ten months period, although We consider even that to be very little) she shall be branded with the marks of disgrace and deprived of both the dignity and rights of a person of honorable and noble status. She shall also forfeit all the property which she has obtained from the estate of her former husband, either by the right of betrothal gifts or by the will of her deceased husband. She shall know also that she shall expect no help from Us through either a special grant of imperial favor or an annotation.

Given on the third day before the kalends of June at Constantinople in the year of the consulship of Eucherius and Syagrius.—May 30, 381.

Interpretation: If within a year after the death of her husband a woman should marry another man, she shall know that she will subject herself to infamy and be rendered infamous to such a degree that she shall forfeit any betrothal gifts that she has received by the bounty of her former husband or anything that he has given to her by his testament, and all this property shall go to his children. If there should be no children, the said property shall profit those persons who are akin to the former husband in the nearest degree, and they shall be able to vindicate this property for themselves through the right of inheritance.

2. The Same Augustuses to Florus, Praetorian Prefect.

When a woman passes to a subsequent marriage, if she has children born from a prior marriage, anything that she has received from the property of her former husband by right of betrothal gifts, or anything that she has also received upon celebration of the marriage, or anything that she has acquired from the property of her former husband by gifts made in expectation of death or by testament, either by direct right or under the title of a trust or legacy or as a reward through any other form of munificent liberality, all this she shall have the right to transmit undiminished, just as she received it, to the children which she has from her prior marriage, or to any one of these children upon whom the mother believes she ought to bestow the judgment of her liberality in view of the merits of such child, provided that this child should be one of those whom We consider most worthy of such a succession. Such a woman shall not presume or have the power to alienate any part of such property to any extraneous person whatsoever or to successors born from the union of the second marriage. She shall have the right of possession only to the last day of her life, and she shall not be allowed the power of alienation also. For if any of the aforesaid property, through a fraud of evil intent, should be transferred by the mother who possesses it to any other person whatsoever, it must be restored by compensation out of her own resources, whereby the property shall go undiminished and unimpaired to those persons whom We have designated as heirs.

1. We also add to the law the following provision, namely, that if any son from the aforesaid children who are proved to have been born from the former marriage should perhaps die, leaving one or more sisters but no brother, and thus, by benefit of the decree of the Senate, he should appear to provide for the mother a place as heir along with the sisters; or if a daughter should die leaving no brother alive, but only her mother and sisters as survivors and should thus preserve for the mother an opportunity to enter upon the inheritance for a half portion, whatever the mother shall appear to have obtained by the benefit of succession,[21] she shall be granted only the possession thereof to the last day of her life in accordance with her due portion. She shall leave everything to the surviving children who were born of her prior marriage, and she shall not have the power to will such property to any extraneous person or to alienate any of it.

2. But if she should have no children as her successors from the prior marriage, or if such child or children should have died, she shall hold in fully legal ownership all property which she has received in any manner, and she shall have the unlimited power to acquire ownership from these children and to give it by testament to whomever she wishes.

3. It is Our will that husbands also shall be admonished by a similar example of both piety and law. Although We do not constrain them by the bond, so to speak, of a sanction very severely imposed upon them, nevertheless We restrain them by the law of religion, that they may know that which is enjoined upon mothers by the necessity of the law, as here set forth, is more readily expected of them in consideration of justice, in order that, if necessity should so persuade, in the case of men, too, there should not have to be exacted from them by the aid of a sanction that which meanwhile may properly be desired and expected.

Given on the sixteenth day before the kalends of January at Constantinople in the year of the consulship of Antonius and Syagrius.—December 17, 382.

---

[21] As an heir.

Interpretation: If a woman should lose her husband and afterward should enter into another marriage at the statutory time, that is, when a year has elapsed, and if she should have children by her former husband, she shall preserve for such children all the property which she has received through any betrothal bounty or gift made at the time of the wedding, and she shall know that this property must not be transferred to other or extraneous persons. But whatever the former husband has given to his wife by a testament or trust fund or under the title of legacy or in expectation of death, this property that the wife has received by such a gift, she shall have the unlimited power to bestow, either upon all the children or upon one for the merit of such child's service, if she should so wish; but she shall not be permitted to alienate any of the property of her former husband away from his children. But if she should presume to do this, she must know that compensation must be made out of her own resources.

The emperor supposed that the following provision especially should be included in this law, namely, that if a woman should proceed to another marriage, and if, of the children which she had born from her prior marriage, a son should die, in case that he leaves surviving a mother and sisters, or at least a sister and does not leave a brother, who would be able to exclude the mother, then by the benefit of the law the mother and the daughters or daughter shall succeed to equal shares. But if a daughter should die and should leave only a mother and sisters, the mother shall acquire half the inheritance of the deceased daughter, and half shall accrue to the sisters, whether there be one or many, under the condition, however, that while the mother lives, she shall possess only in usufruct the half which she has acquired from such inheritance of a son or daughter. After her death she shall leave this property to the remaining children, if any have survived from her former marriage, and she shall not have the liberty to transfer it to other persons either by testament or by gift. But if no children by her former husband should survive, then any property whatever that she has received on this account she shall vindicate for herself as though it were her own property, and she shall lawfully transmit it to whomever she may wish. In this law also it was the emperor's will that a similar condition should be observed if a father whose wife had died should proceed to a subsequent marriage, so that, if there should be sons or daughters by his former wife, of whom some should die and make a place for the father in the succession to their own portion, after the father's death, this portion which was left to him should accrue to the brothers and sisters who survive from his prior marriage, and it could not pass to other persons through paternal power.

3. Emperors Honorius and Theodosius Augustuses to Johannes, Praetorian Prefect.

No person shall have any doubt that a woman shall have a usufruct to the last day of her life in the property which she received at the time of her marriage, even though she should perchance proceed to a subsequent marriage after the statutory time has elapsed and even though there should be children of the prior marriage. The ownership of such property shall be preserved for those persons to whom the most sacred imperial laws have reserved the entire right after the death of the woman, which right it is manifestly established is transmitted to the children of the prior marriage.

Given on the tenth day before the kalends of July at Ravenna in the year of the ninth consulship of Our Lord Honorius Augustus and the fifth consulship of Our Lord Theodosius Augustus.—June 22, 412.

Interpretation: It is very well known that a woman vindicates to her ownership such property as she receives from her husband at the time of her wedding. If her husband should chance to die, leaving children, however, and the woman should lawfully proceed to another marriage after the period of mourning has elapsed, to the last day of her life she shall hold a usufruct of the property thus given to her. But after the death of the woman, all such property shall revert to the children of the former husband, and the mother is not permitted to transfer any of it to the ownership of others while the children are living.

Title 9: If a Woman to Whom Her Husband Left a Usufruct Should Subsequently Marry (*Si Secundo Nupserit Mulier Cui Maritus Usumfructum Reliquerit*)

1. Emperors Arcadius and Honorius Augustuses to Asterius, Count of the Orient.

By a clear decision We indicate that the regulations which have been established by Our Clemency concerning prenuptial gifts are far different from those which have been established concerning property from a man's own patrimony, the usufruct of which he has left to his wife by his own will. For in the case of such usufruct of a portion of his own property which a man by executing his last will leaves to his wife, it is Our will that the woman shall be threatened with the loss of this usufruct immediately after her subsequent marriage, in accordance with

that law which has indubitably been issued concerning this special point. But as to the usufruct of property given before marriage, those rules shall be observed which an earlier, most salutary law has decreed with a full regulation.

Given on the sixteenth day before the kalends of March at Constantinople in the year of the fourth consulship of Honorius Augustus and the consulship of Eutychianus.—February 14, 398.

Interpretation: With a clear interpretation the emperor has explained these two legal provisions, namely, that if the husband at his death should leave to his wife, in addition to the betrothal gift, a usufruct on property of his own patrimony, she shall possess that which has been left to her according to his will, on condition that if afterwards the woman should marry another man, she shall immediately restore the usufruct acquired under the will to the children of the man from whom she had obtained the usufruct. But she shall rightfully retain the usufruct of the betrothal gift until her death, just as another law previously indicated. Whence the ownership of this property shall revert after the mother's death to the children of the husband who gave it.

Title 10: If Marriage Should Be Petitioned for in Accordance with a Rescript (*Si Nuptiae Ex Rescripto Petantur*)

1. Emperors Honorius and Theodosius Augustuses to Theodorus, Praetorian Prefect.

Some men, in disregard of the provision of the ancient law, suppose that they may request from Us by surreptitious supplication permission for a marriage to which they know they are not entitled, and they pretend that they have the girl's consent. Therefore We prohibit betrothals of such a kind by the ordinance of the present law. 1. If any person, therefore, in violation of this ordinance, should obtain such permission to marry by a surreptitious supplication, he shall not doubt that he will suffer the forfeiture of his goods and the punishment of deportation. He shall also know that he forfeits the right of marriage which he obtained by such a forbidden usurpation; that he cannot have legally born children in this manner; and that he has never obtained an effective permission by the grant of the requested indulgence or the imperial annotation. Excepted herefrom are those persons whom the law of Our father of triumphal memory[22] did not forbid to supplicate, after the pattern of the imperial indulgences, for the marriage of cousins, that is, of persons related in the fourth degree. Those persons also shall be excepted who desire that the solemn engagement of parents as to the marriage of their daughters shall be fulfilled or who request the return of betrothal gifts, that is, of gifts given in the name of earnest, together with the fourfold penalty, under the provisions of the laws. 2. For We forbid that We be requested by supplication to grant permission for a marriage which should properly be impetrated[23] in accordance with the wish of the parents or of the adult girls or the women themselves. But if a marriage is refused which has previously been promised and some lawsuit arises under the provision of these statutes, We do not forbid that We be consulted about the law.

Given on the tenth day before the kalends of February at Ravenna in the year of the eighth consulship of Our Lord Honorius Augustus and the third consulship of Our Lord Theodosius Augustus.—January 23, 409.

Interpretation: Occasionally it happens that some man, forgetful of the severity of the law, dares to employ surreptitious methods in dealing with the imperial majesty, that he seeks for himself permission granted by an imperial order for a marriage which he is not entitled to obtain, and that he lies about the consent of the parents or of the girl; wherefore, the emperor prohibits such audacity. If any man, therefore, should suppose that he should obtain the right to marry through such surreptitious methods, he shall know that he will be punished by the forfeiture of his property and exile by relegation; that he shall not have the marriage which he sought in such a manner; that the children born of a union contracted through such an arrangement and by such corrupt solicitation shall not be called legitimate, and that not even through a supplication to the emperor shall he obtain pardon for such presumption. But in the case of persons connected by kinship in the fourth degree who have entered into a presumptuous union, although such a union is infamous, nevertheless, if the parties should supplicate the emperor, he will grant a pardon. Those persons shall not be prohibited from seeking an ordinance of His Majesty, since they are united in marriage pursuant to an agreement of the parents. But if any man to whom a girl was betrothed while her parents were

living is scorned by the girl after the death of her parents, according to the tenor of the law he shall recover fourfold those things which he has given or presented in the name of earnest. But if arrangements have not previously been made, the emperor, with all severity, prohibits the request by supplication of permission to marry. But if any man should make a marriage agreement with the parents of a girl or with the girl herself, and one of the contracting parties should wish to abandon the agreement, We do not forbid the person who is scorned to consult Us. (The remainder of this law has already been expounded elsewhere.)

Title 11: If a Person Endowed with Any Administrative Power Should Seek to Marry a Woman Against Her Will (*Si Quacumque Praeditus Potestate Nuptias Petat Invitae*)

1. Emperors Gratian, Valentinian, and Theodosius Augustuses to Neoterius, Praetorian Prefect.

If a person endowed with ordinary authority[24] or with any administrative authority whatever, should use the advantage of his power in connection with contracting a marriage to which the woman herself or her parents are averse, whether the girl is a pupil, a maiden or widow living with her father, a widow of independent status, or in short, a woman of any condition whatever, and if such administrator should be found to show or to have shown his menacing favor toward unwilling persons whose interests are here considered, We decree that he shall be liable to a fine of ten pounds of gold, and We forbid him, when he has retired from his high office, to usurp the high rank thus acquired. If he should refuse to obey the sanction of Our statute with respect to the vindication of the honor which he has wrongfully used, the following penalty is provided, namely, that in every case for a continuous period of two years he shall not be allowed to live in the province in which he committed such usurpation.

1. Because, however, We realize that certain households and certain parents must be further protected against hidden malice, We order that if any parent or

---

[22] Theodosius I. The law is not extant.

[23] Obtained by request or entreaty.

[24] Administrative authority, as of the governors, the judges ordinary.

any woman whatsoever should be assailed by hidden promises or threats through the judge with regard to that marriage to which the woman has disdained to give her consent, such persons may immediately file an attestation. Whereupon they, together with their household and that of their family, shall cease to belong to his jurisdiction; the defenders of each municipality and the apparitors of the aforesaid judge shall attend to this matter. 2. If such depravity should be that of the judge ordinary, all jurisdiction over the aforesaid household in all matters, civil and criminal, shall belong to the vicar as long as the aforesaid judge ordinary is in authority. However, if the vicar or a person of similar authority should undertake to exercise coercion in contracting such a marriage, the judge ordinary in turn shall become the intercessor. But if the judge and vicar should both be suspected, the protection of such households particularly shall devolve upon the illustrious prefect as long as the aforesaid judge or vicar is in office.

Given on the fifteenth day before the kalends of July at Thessalonica in the year of the fifth consulship of Gratian Augustus and the first consulship of Theodosius Augustus.—June 17, 380.

Interpretation: If any judge who administers a province, or even if any person to whom is entrusted the administration of municipalities or districts, through his authority should assign to himself for marriage a maiden, against the will of her parents, or even a widow who is either of independent status or a pupil, and if, contrary to the interests of this woman, by means of terror and collusion of any persons whatever, such woman should be assigned against her will to be married to those persons concerning whom the emperor speaks—if anyone should presume to do this, he shall know that he will be condemned to the payment of ten pounds of gold, stripped of his high rank, and prohibited for a period of two years from entering the province in which he had been judge. But this law provides a special grant of imperial favor, as a protection against such men, to parents and to women themselves when they are of independent status, and to those persons who exercise guardianship over minors, namely, that they shall have the right to file their attestations before other judges or in the nearest municipalities and to be defended by their protection. Thus if there should be another high official in the same province, as, for example, if there should be two judges, one administering private rights and the other imperial rights, and if, in this situation, any person is oppressed by one of these judges, he shall be defended by the protection of the

other, or at least he shall have recourse to the magnificent authority,[25] who can bring this information to the ears of the emperor.

Title 12: Incestuous Marriages (*De Incestis Nuptiis*)

1. Emperors Constantius and Constans Augustuses to the Provincials of Phoenicia.

If any man should be so abominable as to presume that a daughter of a brother or of a sister should be made his wife, and if he should fly to her embrace, not as her paternal or maternal uncle, he shall be held subject to a sentence of capital punishment.

Given on the day before the kalends of April at Antioch in the year of the third consulship of Constantius Augustus and the second consulship of Constans Augustus.—March 31, 342.

Interpretation: If any man should presume to enter into an incestuous union with the daughter of his brother or of his sister, he shall know that he will undergo the peril of capital punishment.

2. Emperors Constantius and Constans Augustuses and Julian Caesar to Volusianus, Praetorian Prefect.

Although the ancients believed it lawful for a man to marry his brother's wife after the marriage of his brother had been dissolved, and lawful also for a man, after the death or divorce of his wife, to contract a marriage with a sister of the said wife, all men shall abstain from such marriages, and they shall not suppose that legitimate children may be begotten from such a union. For it is established that children so born are spurious.

Given on the day before the kalends of May at Rome in the year of the consulship of Arbitio and Lollianus.—April 30, 355.

Interpretation: Licence is absolutely denied a man to marry a woman who has been his brother's wife or for the same man to have two sisters to wife, for the children born of such a union are not considered legitimate.

3. Emperors Arcadius and Honorius Augustuses to Eutychianus, Praetorian Prefect.

The decrees shall remain undisturbed with regard to those persons who have been either absolved or punished in any manner under the law formerly issued. But hereafter, if any person should defile himself by an incestuous

---

[25] The praetorian prefect.

marriage with his own first cousin, the daughter of his sister or brother, or finally with any man's wife whose marriage to him has been forbidden and condemned, he shall indeed be exempt from the punishment designated by the law, that is, the punishment of fire and proscription, and he shall have the right to hold his own property as long as he lives. But he shall not be considered as having a wife or as having children born from her. 1. Absolutely nothing shall be given by him during his lifetime or left by him at his death to the aforesaid wife, even through an interposed person. 2. If perchance any dowry has been formally given, specified, or promised, it shall accrue to the resources of Our fisc in accordance with the ancient law. 3. He shall leave nothing by his testament to extraneous persons, but whether he dies testate or intestate, he shall be succeeded, according to the statutes and the law, by those persons, if there be any, who are born of statutory and legal marriage; that is, in the case of descendants, by a son, daughter, grandson, granddaughter, great grandson, great granddaughter; in the case of ascendants, by a father, mother, grandfather, grandmother; in the case of collaterals, by a brother, sister, paternal uncle, or paternal aunt.

4. Indeed, he shall have the power to make a testament only to the extent that he may leave what he wishes, subject to the provisions of the law and statutes, to those persons alone whom We order to succeed by the terms of the imperial statute; provided, however, that if any of those persons whom We have mentioned should be proved to have participated in contracting the incestuous marriage and to have entered into the plan, he shall be absolutely barred from the inheritance of the deceased, and into his place shall succeed that person who is found to rank next after him in the order of kinship. 5. Certainly these provisions which We have made concerning men shall be observed also by women who pollute themselves by marriage with the aforesaid persons. 6. But if none of the aforementioned persons should survive, a place shall be open to the fisc.[26] 7. We order to be subject to the restraints and conditions of this law any person who perchance previously, that is, before the promulgation of this law, has been contaminated by the illicit crimes of the aforesaid marriages and has been able in any manner to avoid detection.

Given on the seventh day before the ides of December at Constantinople in the year of the fourth consulship of

Arcadius Augustus, and the third consulship of Honorius Augustus.—December 7 (6), 396.[27]

Interpretation: After the provisions of the former law which was issued about such persons, the emperor commands that the following rules shall be observed, namely, that if any person should unite to himself in a criminal marriage a sister's or a brother's daughter, a cousin of the third degree,[28] or even a cousin of more remote degree, or the wife[29] of his brother, such person shall be exempt from the penalty of the law, that is, severe punishment and proscription, but he shall be subjected to the punishment that he shall be separated from such a union and that if there are any children, they shall not be considered his heirs. But both parties[30] shall be branded with infamy, with the provision that, by special grant of imperial favor, they shall appear only to have possession of their own property; but they shall presume to enter into no contract. They shall be deprived of the right to make gifts and to execute testaments. But such a husband shall bestow nothing upon the woman herself whom he has thus married, and if the husband and wife have exchanged gifts at the time of the marriage, such gifts shall be confiscated to the fisc. Even if they should have children, none of their property shall pass to such children through a supposititious[31] person or any other person or by fictitious gift, but at their death their property shall pass by intestate succession to those lawful heirs who are admitted to the inheritance according to their rank in the line of succession, up to a certain degree of kinship. They are permitted the right to make a testament for the benefit of those persons only for whom they are allowed by law to make testaments, so that from these persons they may designate as heirs those persons whom they choose; provided, however, that if any of these persons are shown to have given their approval to such a union, they shall be excluded from the inheritance, and they shall make place for others who come in the next degree. Indeed, if there should be a lack of such near kinsmen that the law calls to the succession, then the fisc shall take possession of their property.

4. Emperors Honorius and Theodosius Augustuses to Aurelianus, Praetorian Prefect for the second time.

---

[26] That is, the right to receive the inheritance shall be available to the fisc, if the properly qualified heirs are lacking.

[27] The date is doubtful, since Caesarius was prefect until July 13, 397, and was succeeded by Eutychianus on September 4, 397.

[28] A first cousin.

[29] The former wife.

[30] Both parties to the union.

[31] Fraudulently substituted or pretended.

A man shall be considered as though he had committed incest, if after the death of a former wife he should presume to select her sister for marriage. A woman, also, shall be held to an equal and similar accountability if after the death of her husband she should presume to aspire to a marriage with his own brother. It will undoubtedly follow that the children of such a cohabitation will not be considered legitimate, they shall not be in the power of their father, and they shall not receive the paternal inheritance as family heirs.

Given on the seventeenth day before the kalends of January at Constantinople in the year of the tenth consulship of Our Lord Honorius Augustus and the sixth consulship of Our Lord Theodosius Augustus.—December (May) 16, 415.

Interpretation: If any woman should marry the husband[32] of her sister after the death of the latter, or if any man should be united by a subsequent marriage to his deceased wife's sister, such persons shall know that they are infamous as a result of such a union. The children born of this union are excluded from the succession and shall not be reckoned as children.

Title 13: Dowries (*De Dotíbus*)

1. Emperors Constantius and Constans Augustuses to Philippus, Praetorian Prefect.

An action on morals cannot be extended beyond the person accused, and it shall not be granted against an heir nor assigned to an heir.

Given on the twelfth day before the kalends of October in the year of the consulship of Limenius and Catullinus.—September 20, 349.

Interpretation: If a husband should accuse his wife with respect to her morals, that is, of sorcery, adultery, or other similar crimes, and if his wife should then die, her heirs cannot be accused because a crime dies with its author. Also if a husband who has accused his wife should die, the wife cannot be accused by the heir of the husband.

2. Emperor Julian Augustus to Mamertinus, Praetorian Prefect.

In the restoration of dowries, it is Our pleasure that rights of retention created by law and by pacts shown to be consistent with the law shall also be preserved unbroken and inviolate by the authority of this sanction.

Given on the fourth day before the kalends of March in the year of the fourth consulship of Julian Augustus and the consulship of Sallustius.—February 26, 363.

Interpretation: This law prescribes that pacts made between a husband and wife, which were made relative to a dowry and which are consistent with the law, shall be valid, just as all other pacts. But since this statute evidently does not set forth the provisions concerning retentions from a dowry, such provisions must be sought in the body of the law, that is, in the Sentences of Paulus under the title, Dowries, or at any rate in the Responses of Paulus under the title, A Wife's Property.

3. Emperors Honorius and Theodosius Augustuses to Marinianus, Praetorian Prefect.

(After other matters.) If while a marriage subsists it should chance that the husband should be destroyed by the lot of fate, the dowry which is said to have been given or promised out of his wife's property shall revert to the woman, and the heir of the deceased shall not dare to vindicate for himself any of the property which has reverted to the woman as the result of her husband's death.

1. If perchance, while the marriage subsists, the dowry has been returned to a wife by her husband, a transaction which cannot stand according to the laws, because it is understood to be analogous to a gift,[33] and if the wife should die, the dowry, together with the fruits thereof from the day that the dowry was returned to her, shall be restored to the husband by her heirs; but the ownership of the same cannot be alienated by the husband away from the children born of the aforesaid woman. (Etc.)

Given on the third day before the nones of November at Ravenna in the year of the thirteenth consulship of Honorius Augustus and the tenth consulship of Theodosius Augustus.—November 3, 422.

Interpretation: If perchance a husband should die and his wife should survive him, the woman shall recover for her own ownership any property which had been given to her husband as a dowry, and the heirs of the deceased husband shall not presume to vindicate it. Indeed, if the husband, while he was living, had perhaps returned that property which he had received from his wife as dowry, since such a return is like a gift, this act shall have no validity. If the woman should die, such property cannot be vindicated by her heirs, but it is ordered that, together with its fruits, it shall be restored to her husband; provided, however, that if there should be children, they shall not vindicate this property for themselves as though a part of their mother's estate during the lifetime of their father, and the father shall have nothing therefrom except the usufruct, nor shall he have the unrestricted right to

---

[32] The former husband.

[33] Gifts between husbands and wives were forbidden.

transfer such property to another person; but after his death all of it shall revert to their common children.

4. Emperors Theodosius and Valentinian Augustuses to Hierius, Praetorian Prefect.

(After other matters.) We decree that any sort of words whatever shall suffice for the exaction of a dowry, if its delivery has once been agreed upon, even though a formal statement or stipulation with reference to the promise of the property of the dowry did not follow. (Etc.)

Given on the tenth day before the kalends of March at Constantinople in the year of the consulship of Felix and Taurus.—February 21, 428.

Interpretation: A dowry, that is, whatever is given by[34] a woman to her husband at the time of marriage, is ordered to be valid with respect to its fulfillment or its exaction, even though a stipulation of the promiser and the legally prescribed words should be lacking.

Title 14: Marriages with Foreigners (De Nuptiis Gentilium)

1. Emperors Valentinian and Valens Augustuses to Theodosius, Master of the Horse.

No provincial, of whatever rank or class he may be, shall marry a barbarian wife, nor shall a provincial woman be united with any foreigner. But if there should be any alliances between provincials and foreigners through such marriages and if anything should be disclosed as suspect or criminal among them, it shall be expiated by capital punishment.

Given on the fifth day before the kalends of January in the year of the consulship of Valentinian and Valens Augustuses.—December 28, 370 or 373; May 28, 368.

Interpretation: No Roman shall presume to have a barbarian wife of any nation whatever, nor shall any Roman woman be united in marriage with a barbarian. But if they should do this, they shall know that they are subject to capital punishment.

Title 15: Sureties of Dowries (De Fidejussoribus Dotium)

1. Emperors Valentinian, Theodosius, and Arcadius Augustuses to Martinianus, Count of the Orient.

Henceforth We absolve all sponsors or sureties from their promises in guaranteeing any solemn agreement for a dowry.

Given on the third day before the ides of November at Constantinople in the year of the second consulship of Arcadius Augustus, and the consulship of Rufinus.—November 11 [10], 392.

Interpretation: If any person should become surety of a woman for the payment of a dowry, he shall not be held liable for such guaranty.

Title 16: Notices of Divorce (De Repudiis)

1. Emperor Constantine Augustus to Ablavius, Praetorian Prefect.

It is Our pleasure that no woman, on account of her own depraved desires, shall be permitted to send a notice of divorce to her husband on trumped up grounds, as, for instance, that he is a drunkard or a gambler or a philanderer, nor indeed shall a husband be permitted to divorce his wife on every sort of pretext. But when a woman sends a notice of divorce, the following criminal charges only shall be investigated, that is, if she should prove that her husband is a homicide, a sorcerer, or a destroyer of tombs, so that the wife may thus earn commendation and at length recover her entire dowry. For if she should send a notice of divorce to her husband on grounds other than these three criminal charges, she must leave everything, even her last hairpin, in her husband's home, and as punishment for her supreme self-confidence, she shall be deported to an island. In the case of a man also, if he should send a notice of divorce, inquiry shall be made as to the following three criminal charges, namely, if he wishes to divorce her as an adultress, a sorceress, or a procuress. For if he should cast off a wife who is innocent of these crimes, he must restore her entire dowry, and he shall not marry another woman. But if he should do this, his former wife shall be given the right to enter and seize his home by force and to transfer to herself the entire dowry of his later wife in recompense for the outrage inflicted upon her.

Given . . . in the year of the consulship of Bassus and Ablavius.—331

Interpretation: The right to send a notice of divorce is extended to a wife or husband for certain approved reasons and causes; for they are forbidden to dissolve a marriage for a trivial charge. If perchance a woman should say that her husband is either a drunkard or given to licentiousness, she shall not send him notice of divorce on that account. But if perchance she should prove that he is either a homicide, a sorcerer, or a violator of tombs,

---

[34] On behalf of.

the husband who is convicted of these crimes appears to be justly divorced, without any fault of the woman; and she may recover her dowry and depart. If the woman should not be able to prove such crimes, she shall be subjected to the following punishment: namely, that she shall forfeit both the dowry which she had given or which had been given on her behalf and the gift[35] which she received, and she shall also be liable to exile by relegation. But if a man should cast off his wife, he also is not permitted to divorce her for a trivial quarrel, as often happens, unless perhaps he should be able to prove that she is an adultress, a sorceress, or a procuress. But if he cannot prove this, he shall restore her dowry to the woman, and he shall not presume to take another wife. But if perchance he should attempt to do so, the woman who was cast off, though innocent, shall have the right to vindicate for herself her husband's home and all his substance. It is recognized that this is ordained in order that if a woman should be unjustly divorced, she is ordered to acquire the dowry of the second wife also.

2. *Emperors Honorius, Theodosius, and Constantius Augustuses to Palladius, Praetorian Prefect.*

If a woman should serve notice of divorce upon her husband and separate from him and if she should prove no grounds for divorce, the gifts shall be annulled which she had received when betrothed. She shall also be deprived of her dowry, and she shall be sentenced to the punishment of deportation. We deny her not only the right to a union with a subsequent husband, but even the right of postliminium.[36] But if a woman who has revolted against her marriage should prove merely flaws of character and ordinary faults, she shall lose her dowry and restore to her husband all gifts, and never at all shall she be associated in marriage with any man. In order that she may not defile her widowhood with wanton debauchery, we grant to the repudiated husband the right to bring an accusation.

1. It remains to say that if a woman who withdraws should prove serious grounds and a conscience involved in great crimes, she shall obtain possession of her dowry and shall also retain the betrothal bounty, and she shall regain the right to marry after a period of five years from the day of the divorce. For then it will appear that she has

done this from loathing of her own husband rather than from a desire for another husband.

2 (1). Certainly if the husband should be the first to give notice of divorce and if he should charge his wife with a grave crime, he shall prosecute the accused woman in accordance with the law, and when he has obtained his revenge, he shall both get possession of her dowry and recover his bounty to her, and he shall acquire the unrestricted right to marry another woman immediately. 3. If it is a fault of character and not of criminality, the husband shall recover his gifts but relinquish the dowry, and he shall have the right to marry another woman after a period of two years. 4. But if the husband should wish to dissolve the marriage because of a mere disagreement and should charge the repudiated woman with no vices or sins, he shall lose both his gifts and the dowry and be compelled to live in perpetual celibacy; he shall suffer punishment for his insolent divorce in the sadness of solitude; and the woman shall be granted the right to marry after the termination of a year. Moreover, We order to be preserved the guarantees of the ancient law in regard to the retentions of dowries, on account of children.

Given on the sixth day before the ides of March at Ravenna in the year of the consulship of Eustathius and Agricola.—March 10, 421.

Interpretation: If a woman should be the first to serve a notice of divorce upon her husband and should not prove the statutory grounds for divorce, she shall forfeit the betrothal bounty, and she shall not recover that which she gave her husband as dowry. In addition, she shall also be sent into exile by relegation, and she shall not have the right to marry another man. If, however, after divorcing her husband, she should become involved in adultery, her husband shall have the right to prosecute her even after the divorce. But if a woman who has separated from her husband should prove that he is guilty of grave and definite crimes, she shall both recover her dowry and vindicate that which her husband bestowed upon her as a betrothal bounty, and she shall have the unrestricted right of marriage after five years.

Indeed, if the husband should be the first to serve notice of divorce, he shall secure his revenge on grounds approved by law, he shall vindicate his dowry of his repudiated wife, shall recover his betrothal gifts, and shall have the right to marry another woman immediately if he wishes. If indeed there were no definite crimes, but, as often happens, the husband is displeased with the frivolity of his wife's character, he shall recover his gifts and shall restore to her immediately anything which he has received from her, after a period of two years he shall

---

[35] The betrothal and prenuptial gifts.

[36] Under Roman law, those who return from banishment or exile after a proscribed period of time are entitled to regain former privileges and rights under the right of postliminium.

have the right to marry another wife. But if no defect of character should be proved but merely mental discord, the innocent woman who is rejected by her husband shall both vindicate the gifts made to her by the man and shall recover her dowry. But he shall remain alone forever and shall not presume to associate himself in marriage with another woman. The woman, however, is permitted to proceed to another marriage after a year if she should so wish. But for the sake of their common children, if there should be any, the emperor orders those rules to be observed which have been established in the law concerning retentions according to the number of children, which law Paulus sets forth in his Book of Responses under the title A Wife's Property.

Title 17: The Creation of Tutors and Curators (*De Tutoribus et Curatoribus Creandis*)

1. Emperor Constantine Augustus and the Caesar to Bassus, Prefect of the City.

It is Our pleasure that in all litigation, no person who has attained the age of puberty[37] shall have legal capacity unless by the interposition of a decree a curator has been appointed for him,[38] either for the purpose of administering his patrimony or for the purpose of the lawsuit, so that, in accordance with the preceding statutes of Our Providence, when a suit has been legally instituted, the controversy may be tried in the courts and settled.

Given on the fourth day before the ides of October at Aquileia in the year of the fifth consulship of Constantine Augustus and the consulship of Licinius Caesar.—October 12, 319 or 318.

Interpretation: If an action is brought as though against a pupil,[39] although he should appear to be an adult,[40] such person cannot take part in the lawsuit unless perchance his age should be confirmed by attestation of the municipal council, or at any rate a curator should be provided who may defend the patrimony or lawsuit of the ward.

---

[37] *Puber*, an adult, a male over 14 or a female over 12 and under 25 years of age.

[38] The guardianship of minors was a compulsory public service, without remuneration. It could not be evaded except by some legally recognized excuse.

[39] Under the age of puberty.

[40] Under 25 years of age, but over the age of puberty.

2. The Same Augustus and Caesar to the People.

A consanguineous paternal uncle shall not refuse the statutory guardianship over a woman.

Given on the day before the kalends of January in the year of the seventh consulship of the Augustus Himself and the consulship of the Caesar.—December 31, 326.

3. Emperors Valentinian, Theodosius, and Arcadius Augustuses to Proculus, Prefect of the City.

The Illustrious prefect of the City, with the assistance of ten men selected from the membership of the Most August Senate, together with the Most Noble praetor who presides over suits involving guardianship, shall provide that suitable persons, of any rank whatever, shall be obligated to act as tutors and curators.

1. Certainly, those who judge this matter shall decide with free judgment and without liability. If one nominee should not be adequate for administering the pupil's property, it shall be proper, according to the ancient law, that several shall be called to this duty and that the person whom the aforesaid group adjudges the most competent for administering the pupil's affairs shall obtain such administration by the decision of the prefect alone.

2. Hence in this manner, those present at the council shall remain free of fear, and from this deliberation of prudent men, legalized protection shall be provided for both young children and adults.

3 (1). However, it is evident that We have decreed the preceding regulation concerning those persons for whom there are available neither testamentary nor statutory guardians of a suitable mode of life, age, and property. For when, perchance, such men are offered, We rightly prescribe that they can be held obligated if they should acquire no grounds of defense through their privileges. 4 (2). Moreover, We decree that all other provisions that have been prescribed by the ancient laws concerning the case of minors shall remain inviolate.

Given on the sixth day before the kalends of January at Milan in the year of the consulship of Timasius and Promotus.—December 27, 389.

Interpretation: As often as the problem arises concerning the guardianship of pupils, the chief decurions of the municipality, along with the judge, must select either a tutor or a curator, according to the age of the minor, so that a person who undertakes a tutelage as the result of such a selection can be secure. However, this manner of selection shall be observed in connection with those persons whose appointment has not been directed by testament and who have not been assigned to this office through close kinship. Concerning the other interests of minors, indeed, the emperor commands that the provisions of former laws shall be observed.

4. The Same Augustuses to Tatianus, Praetorian Prefect.

If mothers who have lost their husbands should demand tutelage over their children to administer their affairs, before confirmation of such an office can legally come to them, they shall state in the public records that they will not proceed to another marriage.

1. Certainly, no woman is forced to make such a choice, but she shall comply of her own free will with the conditions which We have prescribed. For if she prefers to choose another marriage, she must not administer the guardianship of her children.

2. In order that such a woman may not easily be taken by storm after she has lawfully undertaken the guardianship, We order that, first of all, the property of any man who eagerly seeks the marriage of a woman who is administering the guardianship shall be obligated and held liable for the accounts of the children, so that nothing may be lost to them through negligence or through fraud.

3. To the aforesaid provisions We add the following: that a woman who has attained her majority shall have the right to petition for a guardianship when a statutory tutor is lacking or when such a person is excused from serving as tutor by reason of his privilege, or when he is excluded as being of the class of suspect, or when he is found to be incapable of managing even his own property because of mental or physical infirmity. 4. But if women should avoid the guardianship and should prefer marriage, and no statutory tutor can be called to such cases, then only the Illustrious prefect of the City, with the assistance of the praetor who presides over the appointment of tutors or the judges who administer the law in the provinces, shall, after investigation, order guardians of another order to be appointed for minors.

Given on the twelfth day before the kalends of February at Milan in the year of the fourth consulship of Valentinian Augustus and the consulship of Neoterius.—January 21, 390.

Interpretation: If women whose husbands are dead should themselves wish to undertake the guardianship of their children, before they may assume this responsibility, they shall formally declare in the public records that they will not marry. However, this declaration must not be extorted from them, but if they prefer, they shall so state of their own free will. For if they desire to proceed to subsequent marriages, they cannot administer the guardianship of their children. When men request the mothers of young children to marry them, they too shall know that if a woman has begun to administer the tutelage of her children, and later marries, the man whom she takes as her consort in marriage shall know that his property will be obligated, and he himself will be responsible for rendering an account to the minors.

There is the further provision that a woman is forbidden to undertake a guardianship unless she has attained her majority. As to those persons, indeed, who come to a guardianship by statute, if any one of them should appear either to be mistaken as to his resources or to be worthless in character, he cannot be admitted to the guardianship, lest the property of the minors should be lost. But those persons shall undertake the guardianship who are characterized by integrity of mind and who are definitely connected by a near degree of kinship. For if the aforesaid persons should be lacking and the mother should be unwilling to undertake the guardianship, then, as has been previously provided, tutors shall be assigned to minors by the selection of the judges or the provincials.[41]

Title 18: Those Persons Who Shall Petition (*Qui Petant*)

1. Emperors Constantius Augustus and Julian Caesar to Our Very Dear Orfitus, Greetings.

Grandfathers also and grandmothers shall be held obligated to the necessity of requesting the appointment of tutors if both testamentary and statutory guardianship should be lacking for their grandchildren of pupillary age. For if perchance a tutor should not be requested, in accordance with the provisions of the ancient laws, those persons to whom the inheritance could have come shall forfeit the benefit of the succession.

Given on the ides of July in the year of the ninth consulship of Constantius Augustus and the second consulship of Julian Caesar.—July 15, 357.

Interpretation: If there should be no paternal grandfather, the emperor orders that even the maternal grandfather and the paternal and maternal grandmothers shall be bound by the command of the law to request tutors for young children, provided that testamentary or statutory tutors are proved to be lacking. But if they should scorn to provide tutors for their young grandchildren, the emperor orders that they shall be subjected to the following penalty, namely, that if perchance the "mournful"

---

[41] The municipal councils.

inheritance should accrue from the estates of minors for whom they have either not sought or not wished to provide tutors, they shall be considered as extraneous persons.

2. . . . [42]

Title 30: The Administration and Liability of Tutors and Curators (De Administratione et Periculo Tutorum et Curatorum)

1. Emperor Constantine Augustus.

Minors shall not be prohibited from vindicating for themselves the property of their tutors or curators, as though it were obligated under title of a pledge, if such tutors or curators should become indebted to them on account of the duties of their administration.

Given on the seventh day before the kalends of April in the year of the consulship of Volusianus and Annianus.—March 26, 314.

Interpretation: If any tutor or curator should be proved to be a debtor to minors through negligence of his administration, he shall know that his own property is so obligated that if he should not render satisfaction, after his account has been deducted,[43] his goods shall be held as a pledge by the minors.

2. The Same Augustus to Maximus, Prefect of the City.

(After other measures.) The guardians of minors shall make good the value of the property lost,[44] if through them the conditions attached to the gifts should be neglected. (Etc.)

Given on the third day before the nones of February at Rome in the year of the consulship of Sabinus and Rufinus Augustus.—(January 30) February 3, 316 (or 323 or 320).

Interpretation: If in the case of gifts which can be made to minors, the formality or condition of a gift should not be fulfilled through the tutor's negligence or collusion, he shall be compelled to pay out of his own property that which the minor has lost.

3. The Same Augustus to the People.

. . . or curator shall be solicitous to make repeated inspections in order to see that the aforesaid articles are unharmed. As to superfluous animals of minors also, We do not forbid that they be sold.

Given on the ides of March at Sirmium in the year of the seventh consulship of Constantine Augustus and the consulship of Constantius Caesar.—March 15, 326 or 329.

4. The Same Augustus to all Provincials.

(After other matters.) If guardians of minors, that is, tutors or curators, as co-owners of property that is being sued for in litigation should decline to declare, as the law requires, but contrary to the prohibition, they should name the aforesaid minors, the guardians shall pay to the fisc out of their own resources as much money as is computed to be a third of the estimated value of the property involved in the litigation, since minors, whether pupils or adults, must lose nothing, no matter what the outcome of the suit. However, if the guardians should be paupers, they shall suffer diminution of status and shall cease to be Roman citizens, but in such a way that the rights of the minors themselves shall be preserved unimpaired. (Etc.)

Given on the kalends of August 12 in the year of the consulship of Bassus and Ablavius.—August 1, 331.

5. The Same Augustus to Felix.

Since landholdings held by emphyteutic tenure[45] are being torn from the possessions of minors as a result of default involving forfeiture which occurred through neglect or betrayal by tutors or curators, it is Our pleasure that if during the administration of a tutor or curator, the landed estates of a minor should lose the prerogative of emphyteutic tenure through an offense involving forfeiture, they shall restore to the minor from their own resources, under the threat of a severe sentence, as much as it shall be determined that the property forfeited was worth.

Given on the fourteenth day before the kalends of May at Constantinople in the year of the consulship of Dalmatius and Zenophilus.—April 18, 333.

Interpretation: If perchance it should occur that, subject to any kind of payment whatever, minors should hold by emphyteutic tenure a landed estate, that is, property of the fisc which their parents had obtained the right to hold, and if this estate should be diminished or certainly if it should be taken away from them through the negligence or betrayal of the tutor, whatever may be lost shall be restored by the tutor or curator.

---

[42] A constitution has been lost.

[43] An account of his own expenses incurred for the benefit of the minor during the course of his guardianship.

[44] To the minors by reason of the negligence of the guardians.

[45] A form of lease requiring the lessee to make improvements to the property during the term of the lease.

6. Emperors Arcadius and Honorius Augustuses to Euty-chianus, Praetorian Prefect.

The very moment that they are instituted, tutors shall immediately appear before the judges, so that, in the presence of the chief decurions, the defender, and public office staffs,[46] an inventory shall be made with due formality, and all the gold and silver found in the pupil's substance, as well as anything else that does not suffer change with the lapse of time, shall be marked with the seals of the judges, senators and public office staffs, and placed in safest custody by the authorization of a public order. There shall be no expectation of interest, nor shall any change be made in any event whatever, until the ward, having become an adult, attains legal age, when he does not so much begin to have time for lawsuits as to rejoice that he has been restored so soon to his whole patrimony.

1. Since a moderate fortune, too, must be considered, if perchance movables alone, and no immovables, are left to a person as an inheritance, and no income from landed estates can be reckoned upon, out of which the pupil's household or the pupil himself can be supported, either suitable estates shall be purchased with the aforesaid movables, or if perchance, as usually happens, suitable estates cannot be found, in accordance with the general rule of the ancient law, an income shall accrue from interest. Thus in this case also, in which there is no hope for income from landed estates, the needs of the minor shall be provided from the income of his movable property; and in the former case[47] interest shall by no means be sought without the risk of the tutor.

Given on the sixth day before the kalends of March at Constantinople in the year of the fourth consulship of Arcadius Augustus, and the third consulship of Honorius Augustus.—February 25, 396(?).

Interpretation: As soon as any person enters upon a guardianship, he shall immediately summon the chief decurions of the municipality and the defender, together with his office staff, while he takes an inventory and makes a written record of the property of the pupil which he has received. If there should be any money or silver or things which cannot perish with age, he shall deposit them after they have been marked with the seals of the aforesaid officials, and in no event shall such property be diminished. The aforesaid persons

shall know that while the pupil is in his minority, this property shall not be entrusted to him for the purpose of lawsuits or for any other reasons, but it shall be preserved in all its entirety until his mature age. In all other matters there shall be profitable diligence. If the resources of a minor are of less value, so that he has no patrimony, and his substance is found to consist of movables only, the tutors shall know that they will be permitted to undertake to sell the movables and to purchase fields, so that they may provide for the minors in this respect. But if there is no substance of such value that a land estate can be purchased with it, the tutors are ordered to use diligence in collecting the money and to acquire profit for the pupil from the earnings of interest or from any other sources. If perchance the substance of the minor should be very small, then the property shall be kept intact, and means of subsistence shall be furnished to the pupil. If this is done, the pupil shall not seek interest from the tutor.

Title 31: Exemption from Tutelage (*De Excusatione Tutelae*)

1. Emperors Arcadius and Honorius Augustuses to Flavianus, Prefect of the City.

(After other matters.) We grant to the shipmasters themselves exemption from tutelage or curatorship to this extent, namely, that they shall be obligated to perform such duties for minors of their own guild only.

Given on the third day before the nones of March at Milan in the year of the consulship of Stilicho and Aurelianus.—March 5, 400.

Title 32: The Landed Estates of Minors Shall Not Be Alienated without a Decree (*De Praendiis Minorum Sine Decreto Non Alienandis*)

1. Emperor Constantine Augustus to Severus.

A minor who is less than twenty-five years of age shall be able to vindicate a landed estate or a rustic slave which was alienated without the issuance of a decree, even though he has not applied for restoration to his original condition; provided that if, following upon the publication of this law, so little time before the end of the twenty-fifth year should remain that a lawsuit already begun cannot be terminated within the limits of the

---

[46] The office staffs of the public officials of the district.

[47] If suitable estates can be purchased for the minor.

aforesaid year, the lawsuit that is begun can be continued. 1. Those persons also whom this same law has found past their twenty-fifth and within their twenty-sixth year shall not delay to commence their petitions, since the time limits for a lawsuit thus begun shall be concluded at the twenty-sixth year.

2. But if any persons should attempt to sue after this time, they shall be rejected, so that the possessor shall now be certain and secure.[48]

Given on the fifteenth day before the kalends of January at Sofia (Serdica) in the year of the consulship of Probianus and Julianus.—December 18, 322 or 325.

2. *Emperors . . .*

Even if any minor should be found obligated, either in the name of his father or in his own name, on account of urgent fiscal debts only or as a consequence of private contracts, the interposition of a decree shall be granted by the Constantinian Praetor after the reasons have been exactly proved, so that after the reliability of the facts has been revealed, a sale may remain valid.[49] Since these things are so, tutors also who are suspect must be sued in the court of the said praetor; an action also must be granted, provided, of course, that the laws shall be observed and that recourse may be had finally to Your Experience, if, while the trial is being conducted before either of the two praetors, the aid of an appeal should be interposed by one of the parties, so that you as the sublime judge may weigh the merits of the appeal.

Given . . .—December 31, 326(?).

2. AUGUSTINE OF HIPPO

Augustine of Hippo (354–430) had the most profound influence in medieval culture of any ancient writer. Born in North Africa to Roman non-Christian parents, his transformation to being the most important Christian thinker of his time was a long process, which included a pagan education followed by work as a teacher of rhetoric, as well as periods when he followed Manichaeism (as outlined in his autobiographical *Confessions*). After Augustine's conversion in 386, his writings demonstrate his strong opposition to both Manichaeism and Christian heresies; however, his most influential works were his treatise *On Christian Doctrine* and his great *City of God*.

In the first, finished in 426, Augustine outlined what became the universal means of interpreting sacred Scripture and other texts through to the twelfth century. The particular passages below discuss his fundamental distinction between the use and enjoyment of creation, and his theory of signs.

Augustine wrote the *City of God* over a long period, completing it only in 426. The work began as a defense against the charge that Christianity had led to the misfortunes of the Roman Empire culminating in the sacking of Rome by the Visigoths in 410. It became a broad-ranging meditation on the nature of good and evil, human society, and government and formed the foundation of all medieval political theory.

Source: Philip Schaff (ed.), *A Select Library of the Nicene and Post-Nicene Fathers of the Christian Church*, vol. II, trans. Marcus Dods (Buffalo, NY: Christian Literature Co., 1987). *Further Reading:* G. O'Daly, *Augustine's* City of God: *A Reader's Guide* (Oxford: Clarendon Press, 1999).

---

[48] In his possession.

[49] Minors were not permitted to sell property without a decree, which could be granted for various reasons, such as urgent debts.

ON CHRISTIAN DOCTRINE

Preface: Showing that to teach rules for the interpretation of scripture is not a superfluous task.

1. There are certain rules for the interpretation of Scripture which I think might with great advantage be taught to earnest students of the word, that they might profit not only from reading the works of others who have laid open the secrets of sacred writings, but also from themselves opening such secrets to others. These rules I propose to teach to those who are able and willing to learn, if God our Lord do not withhold from me, while I write, the thoughts He is wont to vouchsafe to me in my meditations on this subject. But before I enter upon this undertaking, I think it well to meet the objections of those who are likely to take exception to the work, or who would do so, did I not conciliate them beforehand. And if, after all, men should still be found to make objections, yet at least they will not prevail with others over whom they might have influence, did they not find them forearmed against their assaults, to turn them back from a useful study to the dull sloth of ignorance.

2. There are some, then, likely to object to this work of mine, because they have failed to understand the rules here laid down. Others, again, will think that I have spent my labour to no purpose, because, though they understand the rules, yet in their attempts to apply them and to interpret Scripture by them, they have failed to clear up the point they wish cleared up; and these, because they have received no assistance from this work themselves, they will give it as their opinion that it can be of no use to anybody. There is a third class of objectors who either really do understand Scripture well, or think they do, and who, because they know (or imagine) that they have attained a certain power of interpreting the sacred books without reading any directions of the kind that I propose to lay down here, will cry out that such rules are not necessary for any one, but that everything rightly done towards clearing up the obscurities of Scripture could be better done by the unassisted grace of God.

3. To reply briefly to all these: To those who do not understand what is here set down, my answer is, that I am not to be blamed for their want of understanding. It is just as if they were anxious to see the new or the old moon, or some very obscure star, and I should point it out with my finger; if they had not sight enough to see even my finger, they would surely have no right to fly into a passion with me on that account. As for those who, even though they know and understand my directions, fail to penetrate the meaning of obscure passages in Scripture, they may stand for those who, in the case I have imagined, are just able to see my finger, but cannot see the stars at which it is pointed. And so both these classes had better give up blaming me, and pray instead that God would grant them the sight of their eyes. For though I can move my finger to point out an object, it is out of my power to open men's eyes that they may see either the fact that I am pointing, or the object at which I point.

4. But now as to those who talk vauntingly of Divine Grace, and boast that they understand and can explain Scripture without the aid of such directions as those I now propose to lay down, and who think, therefore, that what I have undertaken to write is entirely superfluous. I would such persons could calm themselves so far as to remember that, however justly they may rejoice in God's great gift, yet it was from human teachers that they themselves learned to read. Now, they would hardly think it right that they should be held in contempt by the Egyptian monk Antony, a just and holy man, who, not being able to read himself, is said to have committed the Scriptures to memory through hearing them read by others, and by dint of wise meditations to have arrived at a thorough understanding of them; or by that barbarian slave Christianus, of whom I have lately heard from very respectable and trustworthy witnesses, who, without any teaching from man, attained a full knowledge of the art of reading simply through prayer that it might be revealed to him; after three days' supplication obtaining his request that he might read through a book presented to him on the spot by the astonished bystanders.

5. But if any one thinks that these stories are false, I do not strongly insist on them. For, as I am dealing with Christians who profess to understand the Scriptures without any directions from man (and if the fact be so, they boast of a real advantage, and one of no ordinary kind), they must surely grant that every one of us learnt his own language by hearing it constantly from childhood, and that any other language we have learnt,—Greek, or Hebrew, or any of the rest,—we have learnt either in the same way, by hearing it spoken, or from a human teacher. Now, then, suppose we advise all our brethren not to teach their children any of these things, because on the outpouring of the Holy Spirit the apostles immediately began to speak the language of every race; and warn every one who has not had a like

experience that he need not consider himself a Christian, or may at least doubt whether he has yet received the Holy Spirit? No, no; rather let us put away false pride and learn whatever can be learnt from man; and let him who teaches another communicate what he has himself received without arrogance and without jealousy. And do not let us tempt Him in whom we have believed, lest, being ensnared by such wiles of the enemy and by our own perversity, we may even refuse to go to the churches to hear the Gospel itself, or to read a book, or to listen to another reading or preaching, in the hope that we shall be carried up to the third heaven, "whether in the body or out of the body," as the apostle says, and there hear unspeakable words, such as it is not lawful for man to utter, or see the Lord Jesus Christ and hear the Gospel from his own lips rather than from those of men.

6. Let us beware of such dangerous temptations of pride, and let us rather consider the facts that the Apostle Paul himself, although stricken down and admonished by the voice of God from heaven, yet was sent to a man to receive the sacraments and be admitted into the Church; and that Cornelius the centurion, although an angel announced to him that his prayers were heard and his alms had in remembrance, yet was handed over to Peter for instruction, and not only received the sacraments from the apostle's hands, but was also instructed by him as to the proper objects of faith, hope, and love. And without doubt it was *possible* to have done everything through the instrumentality of angels, but the condition of our race would have been more degraded if God had not chosen to make use of men as the ministers of His word to their fellow-men. For how could that be true which is written, "The temple of God is holy, which temple ye are," if God gave forth no oracles from His human temple, but communicated everything that He wished to be taught to men by voices from heaven, or through the ministration of angels? Moreover, love itself, which binds men together in the bond of unity, would have no means of pouring soul into soul, and, as it were, mingling them one with another, if men never learnt anything from their fellow-men.

7. And we know that the eunuch who was reading Isaiah the prophet, and did not understand what he read, was not sent by the apostle to an angel, nor was it an angel who explained to him what he did not understand, nor was he inwardly illuminated by the grace of God without the interposition of man; on the contrary, at the suggestion of God, Philip, who *did* understand the prophet, came to him, and sat with him, and in human words, and with a human tongue, opened to him the Scriptures. Did

not God talk with Moses, and yet he, with great wisdom and entire absence of jealous pride, accepted the plan of his father-in-law, a man of an alien race, for ruling and administering the affairs of the great nation entrusted to him? For Moses knew that a wise plan, in whatever mind it might originate, was to be ascribed not to the man who devised it, but to Him who is the Truth, the unchangeable God.

8. In the last place, every one who boasts that he, through divine illumination, understands the obscurities of Scripture, though not instructed in any rules of interpretation, at the same time believes, and rightly believes, that this power is not his own, in the sense of originating with himself, but is the gift of God. For so he seeks God's glory, not his own. But reading and understanding, as he does, without the aid of any human interpreter, why does he himself undertake to interpret for others? Why does he not rather send them direct to God, that they too may learn by the inward teaching of the Spirit without the help of man? The truth is, he fears to incur the reproach: "Thou wicked and slothful servant, thou oughtest to have put my money to the exchangers." Seeing, then, that these men teach others, either through speech or writing, what they understand, surely they cannot blame me if I likewise teach not only what they understand, but also the rules of interpretation they follow. For no one ought to consider anything as his own, except perhaps what is false. All truth is of Him who says, "I am the truth." For what have we that we did not receive? and if we have received it, why do we glory, as if we had not received it?

9. He who reads to an audience pronounces aloud the words he sees before him: he who teaches reading, does it that others may be able to read for themselves. Each, however, communicates to others what he has learnt himself. Just so, the man who explains to an audience the passages of Scripture he understands is like one who reads aloud the words before him. On the other hand, the man who lays down rules for interpretation is like one who teaches reading, that is, shows others how to read for themselves. So that, just as he who knows how to read is not dependent on some one else, when he finds a book, to tell him what is written in it, so the man who is in possession of the rules which I here attempt to lay down, if he meet with an obscure passage in the books which he reads, will not need an interpreter to lay open the secret to him, but, holding fast by certain rules, and following up certain indications, will arrive at the hidden sense without any error, or at least without falling into any gross absurdity. And so although it will sufficiently appear in the course of the work itself that no one can justly object to this

undertaking of mine, which has no other object than to be of service, yet as it seemed convenient to reply at the outset to any who might make preliminary objections, such is the start I have thought good to make on the road I am about to traverse in this book.

BOOK I. Containing a general view of the subjects treated in Holy Scripture.

Chapter 1.—The interpretation of Scripture depends on the discovery and enunciation of the meaning, and is to be undertaken in dependence on God's aid.

1. There are two things on which all interpretation of Scripture depends: the mode of ascertaining the proper meaning, and the mode of making known the meaning when it is ascertained. We shall treat first of the mode of ascertaining, next of the mode of making known, the meaning;—a great and arduous undertaking, and one that, if difficult to carry out, it is, I fear, presumptuous to enter upon. And presumptuous it would undoubtedly be, if I were counting on my own strength; but since my hope of accomplishing the work rests on Him who has already supplied me with many thoughts on this subject, I do not fear but that He will go on to supply what is yet wanting when once I have begun to use what He has already given. For a possession which is not diminished by being shared with others, if it is possessed and not shared, is not yet possessed as it ought to be possessed. The Lord saith, "Whosoever hath, to him shall be given," He will give, then, to those who have; that is to say, if they use freely and cheerfully what they have received, He will add to and perfect His gifts. The loaves in the miracle were only five and seven in number before the disciples began to divide them among the hungry people. But when once they began to distribute them, though the wants of so many thousands were satisfied, they filled baskets with the fragments that were left. Now, just as that bread increased in the very act of breaking it, so those thoughts which the Lord has already vouchsafed to me with a view to undertaking this work will, as soon as I begin to impart them to others, be multiplied by His grace, so that, in this very work of distribution in which I have engaged, so far from incurring loss and poverty, I shall be made to rejoice in a marvellous increase of wealth.

Chapter 2.—What a thing is, and what a sign.

2. All instruction is either about things or about signs; but things are learnt by means of signs. I now use the word "thing" in a strict sense, to signify that which is never employed as a sign of anything else: for example, wood, stone, cattle, and other things of that kind. Not, however, the wood which we read Moses cast into the bitter waters to make them sweet, nor the stone which Jacob used as a pillow, nor the ram which Abraham offered up instead of his son; for these, though they are things, are also signs of other things. They are signs of another kind, those which are never employed except as signs: for example, words. No one uses words except as signs of something else; and hence may be understood what I call signs: these things, to wit, which are used to indicate something else. Accordingly, every sign is also a thing; for what is not a thing is nothing at all. Every thing, however, is not also a sign. And so, in regard to this distinction between things and signs, I shall, when I speak of things, speak in such a way that even if some of them may be used as signs also, that will not interfere with the division of the subject according to which I am to discuss things first and signs afterwards. But we must carefully remember that what we have now to consider about things is what they are in themselves, not what other things they are signs of.

Chapter 3.—Some things are for use, some for enjoyment.

3. There are some things, then, which are to be enjoyed, others which are to be used, others still which enjoy and use. Those things which are objects of enjoyment make us happy. Those things which are objects of use assist, and (so to speak) support us in our efforts after happiness, so that we can attain the things that make us happy and rest in them. We ourselves, again, who enjoy and use these things, being placed among both kinds of objects, if we set ourselves to enjoy those which we ought to use, are hindered in our course, and sometimes even led away from it; so that, getting entangled in the love of lower gratifications, we lag behind in, or even altogether turn back from, the pursuit of the real and proper objects of enjoyment.

Chapter 4.—Difference of use and enjoyment.

4. For to enjoy a thing is to rest with satisfaction in it for its own sake. To use, on the other hand, is to employ whatever means are at one's disposal to obtain what one

desires, if it is a proper object of desire; for an unlawful use ought rather to be called an abuse. Suppose, then, we were wanderers in a strange country, and could not live happily away from our fatherland, and that we felt wretched in our wandering, and wishing to put an end to our misery, determined to return home. We find, however, that we must make use of some mode of conveyance, either by land or water, in order to reach that fatherland where our enjoyment is to commence. But the beauty of the country through which we pass, and the very pleasure of the motion, charm our hearts, and turning these things which we ought to use into objects of enjoyment, we become unwilling to hasten the end of our journey; and becoming engrossed in a factitious delight, our thoughts are diverted from that home whose delights would make us truly happy. Such is a picture of our condition in this life of mortality. We have wandered far from God; and if we wish to return to our Father's home, this world must be used, not enjoyed, that so the invisible things of God may be clearly seen, being understood by the things that are made,—that is, that by means of what is material and temporary we may lay hold upon that which is spiritual and eternal.

BOOK II.

Chapter 1.—Signs, their nature and variety.

1. As when I was writing about things, I introduced the subject with a warning against attending to anything but what they are in themselves, even though they are signs of something else, so now, when I come in its turn to discuss the subject of signs, I lay down this direction, not to attend to what they are in themselves, but to the fact that they are signs, that is, to what they signify. For a sign is a thing which, over and above the impression it makes on the senses, causes something else to come into the mind as a consequence of itself: as when we see a footprint, we conclude that an animal whose footprint this is has passed by; and when we see smoke, we know that there is fire beneath; and when we hear the voice of a living man, we think of the feeling in his mind; and when the trumpet sounds, soldiers know that they are to advance or retreat, or do whatever else the state of battle requires.

2. Now some signs are natural, others conventional. Natural signs are those which, apart from any intention or desire of using them as signs, do yet lead to the knowledge of something else, as, for example, smoke when it indicates fire. For it is not from any intention of making it a sign that it is so, but through attention to experience we come to know that fire is beneath, even when nothing but smoke can be seen. And the footprint of an animal passing by belongs to this class of signs. And the countenance of an angry or sorrowful man indicates the feeling in his mind, independently of his will: and in the same way every other emotion of the mind is betrayed by the tell-tale countenance, even though we do nothing with the intention of making it known. This class of signs, however, it is no part of my design to discuss at present. But as it comes under this division of the subject, I could not altogether pass it over. It will be enough to have noticed it thus far.

Chapter 2.—Of the kind of signs we are now concerned with.

3. Conventional signs, on the other hand, are those which living beings mutually exchange for the purpose of showing, as well as they can, the feelings of their minds, or their perceptions, or their thoughts. Nor is there any reason for giving a sign except the desire of drawing forth and conveying into another's mind what the giver of the sign has in his own mind. We wish, then, to consider and discuss this class of signs so far as men are concerned with it, because even the signs which have been given us of God, and which are contained in the Holy Scriptures, were made known to us through men—those, namely, who wrote the Scriptures. The beasts, too, have certain signs among themselves by which they make known the desires in their mind. For when the poultry-cock has discovered food, he signals with his voice for the hen to run to him, and the dove by cooing calls his mate, or is called by her in turn; and many signs of the same kind are matters of common observation. Now whether these signs, like the expression or the cry of a man in grief, follow the movement of the mind instinctively and apart from any purpose, or whether they are really used with the purpose of signification, is another question, and does not pertain to the matter in hand. And this part of the subject I exclude from the scope of this work as not necessary to my present object.

Chapter 3.—Among signs, words hold the chief place.

4. Of the signs, then, by which men communicate their thoughts to one another, some relate to the sense of

sight, some to that of hearing, a very few to the other senses. For, when we nod, we give no sign except to the eyes of the man to whom we wish by this sign to impart our desire. And some convey a great deal by the motion of the hands: and actors by movements of all their limbs give certain signs to the initiated, and, so to speak, address their conversation to the eyes: and the military standards and flags convey through the eyes the will of the commanders. And all these signs are as it were a kind of visible words. The signs that address themselves to the ear are, as I have said, more numerous, and for the most part consist of words. For though the bugle and the flute and the lyre frequently give not only a sweet but a significant sound, yet all these signs are very few in number compared with words. For among men words have obtained far and away the chief place as a means of indicating the thoughts of the mind. Our Lord, it is true, gave a sign through the odour of the ointment which was poured out upon his feet; and in the sacrament of His body and blood He signified His will through the sense of taste; and when by touching the hem of His garment the woman was made whole, the act was not wanting in significance. But the countless multitude of the signs through which men express their thoughts consist of words. For I have been able to put into words all those signs, the various classes of which I have briefly touched upon, but I could by no effort express words in terms of those signs. . . .

Chapter 17.—Origin of the legend of the nine Muses.

27. For we must not listen to the falsities of heathen superstition, which represent the nine Muses[50] as daughters of Jupiter and Mercury. Varro refutes these, and I doubt whether any one can be found among them more curious or more learned in such matters. He says that a certain state (I don't recollect the name) ordered from each of three artists a set of statues of the Muses, to be placed as an offering in the temple of Apollo, intending that whichever of the artists produced the most beautiful statues, they should select and purchase from him. It so happened that these artists executed their works with equal beauty, that all nine pleased the state, and that all were bought to be dedicated in the temple of Apollo; and he says that afterwards Hesiod the poet gave names

to them all. It was not Jupiter, therefore, that begat the nine Muses, but three artists created three each. And the state had originally given the order for three, not because it had seen them in visions, nor because they had presented themselves in that number to the eyes of any of the citizens, but because it was obvious to remark that all sound, which is the material of song, is by nature of three kinds. For it is either produced by the voice, as in the case of those who sing with the mouth without an instrument; or by blowing, as in the case of trumpets and flutes; or by striking, as in the case of harps and drums, and all other instruments that give their sound when struck.

Chapter 18.—No help is to be despised, even though it come from a profane source.

28. But whether the fact is as Varro has related, or is not so, still we ought not to give up music because of the superstition of the heathen, if we can derive anything from it that is not of use for the understanding of Holy Scripture; nor does it follow that we must busy ourselves with their theatrical trumpery because we enter upon an investigation about harps and other instruments, that may help us to lay hold upon spiritual things. For we ought not to refuse to learn letters because they say that Mercury discovered them; nor because they have dedicated temples to Justice and Virtue, and prefer to worship in the form of stones things that ought to have their place in the heart, ought we on that account to forsake justice and virtue. Nay, but let every good and true Christian understand that wherever truth may be found, it belongs to his Master; and while he recognizes and acknowledges the truth, even in their religious literature, let him reject the figments of superstition, and let him grieve over and avoid men who, "when they knew God, glorified him not as God, neither were thankful; but became vain in their imaginations, and their foolish heart was darkened. Professing themselves to be wise, they became fools, and changed the glory of the uncorruptible God into an image made like to corruptible man, and to birds, and four-footed beasts, and creeping things."[51]

Chapter 19.—Two kinds of heathen knowledge.

29. But to explain more fully this whole topic (for it is one that cannot be omitted), there are two kinds of

---

[50] In Greek and Roman mythology, the divinities of the inspiration of literature, science, and the arts.

[51] Romans 1:20.

knowledge which are in vogue among the heathen. One is the knowledge of things instituted by men, the other of things which they have noted, either as transacted in the past or as instituted by God. The former kind, that which deals with human institutions, is partly superstitious, partly not.

Chapter 20.—The superstitious nature of human institutions.

30. All the arrangements made by men for the making and worshipping of idols are superstitious, pertaining as they do either to the worship of what is created or of some part of it as God, or to consultations and arrangements about signs and leagues with devils, such, for example, as are employed in the magical arts, and which the poets are accustomed not so much to teach as to celebrate. And to this class belong, but with a bolder reach of deception, the books of the haruspices and augurs.[52] In this class we must place also all amulets and cures which the medical art condemns, whether these consist in incantations, or in marks which they call *characters*, or in hanging or tying on or even dancing in a fashion certain articles, not with reference to the condition of the body, but to certain signs hidden or manifest; and these remedies they call by the less offensive name of *physica*, so as to appear not to be engaged in superstitious observances, but to be taking advantage of the forces of nature. Examples of these are the ear-rings on the top of each ear, or the rings of ostrich bone on the fingers, or telling you when you hiccup to hold your left thumb in your right hand.

31. To these we may add thousands of the most frivolous practices, that are to be observed if any part of the body should jump, or if, when friends are walking arm-in-arm, a stone, or a dog, or a boy, should come between them. And the kicking of a stone, as if it were a divider of friends, does less harm than to cuff an innocent boy if he happens to run between men who are walking side by side. But it is delightful that the boys are sometimes avenged by the dogs; for frequently men are so superstitious as to venture upon striking a dog who has run between them,—not with impunity however, for instead of a superstitious remedy, the dog sometimes makes his assailant run in hot haste for a real surgeon. To this class,

too, belong the following rules: To tread upon the threshold when you go back to bed if any one should sneeze when you are putting on your slippers; to return home if you stumble when going to a place; when your clothes are eaten by mice, or to be more frightened at the prospect of coming misfortune than grieved by your present loss. Whence that witty saying of Cato, who, when consulted by a man who told him that mice had eaten his boots, replied, "That is not strange, but it would have been very strange indeed if the boots had eaten the mice."

Chapter 21.—Superstition of astrologers.

32. Nor can we exclude from this kind of superstition those who were called *genethliaci*, on account of their attention to birthdays, but are now commonly called *mathematici*. For these, too, although they may seek with pains for the true position of the stars at the time of our birth, and may sometimes even find it out, yet in so far as they attempt thence to predict our actions, grievously err, and sell inexperienced men into a miserable bondage. For when any freeman goes to an astrologer of this kind, he gives money that he may come away the slave either of Mars or of Venus, or rather, perhaps, of all the stars to which those who first fell into this error, and handed it on to posterity, have given the names either of beasts, or of men with a view to confer honor on those men. And this is not to be wondered at, when we consider that even in times more recent and nearer our own, the Romans made an attempt to dedicate the star which we call Lucifer to the name and honor of Caesar. And this would, perhaps, have been done, and the name handed down to distant ages, only that his ancestress Venus had given her name to this star before him, and could not by any law transfer to her heirs what she had never possessed, nor sought to possess, in life. For where a place was vacant, or not held in honor of any of the dead of former times, the usual proceeding in such cases was carried out. For example, we have changed the names of the months Quintilis and Sextilis to July and August, naming them in honor of the men Julius Caesar and Augustus Caesar; and from this instance any one who cares can easily see that the stars spoken of above formerly wandered in the heavens without the names they now bear. But as the men were dead whose memory people were either compelled by royal power or impelled by human folly to honor, they seemed to think that in putting their names upon the stars they were raising the dead men themselves to heaven. But whatever they may be called by men, still there are stars

---

[52] Roman religious officials sought to predict future events using these methods, the haruspex through the examination of entrails, the augur through the flight of birds.

which God has made and set in order after His own pleasure, and they have a fixed movement, by which the seasons are distinguished and varied. And when any one is born, it is easy to observe the point at which this movement has arrived, by use of the rules discovered and laid down by those who are rebuked by Holy Writ in these terms: "For if they were able to know so much that they could weigh the world, how did they not more easily find out the Lord thereof?"

Chapter 22.—The folly of observing the stars in order to predict the events of a life.

33. But to desire to predict the characters, the acts, and the face of those who are born from such an observation, is a great delusion and great madness. And among those at least who have any sort of acquaintance with matters of this kind (which, indeed, are only fit to be unlearnt again), this superstition is refuted beyond the reach of doubt. For the observation is of the position of the stars, which they call constellations, at the time when the person was born about whom these wretched men are consulted by their still more wretched dupes. Now it may happen that, in the case of twins, one follows the other out of the womb so closely that there is no interval of time between them that can be apprehended and marked in the position of the constellations. Whence it necessarily follows that twins are in many cases born under the same stars, while they do not meet with equal fortune either in what they do or what they suffer, but often meet with fates so different that one of them has a most fortunate life, the other a most unfortunate. As, for example, we are told that Esau and Jacob were born twins, and in such close succession, that Jacob, who was born last, was found to have laid hold with his hand upon the heel of his brother, who preceded him. Now, assuredly, the day and the hour of the birth of these two could not be marked in any way that would not give both the same constellation. But what a difference there was between the characters, the actions, the labors, and the fortunes of these two, the Scriptures bear witness, which are now so widely spread as to be in the mouth of all nations.

34. Nor is it to the point to say that the very smallest and briefest moment that separates the birth of twins, produces great effects in nature, and in the extremely rapid motion of the heavenly bodies. For, although I may grant that it does produce the greatest effects, yet the astrologer cannot discover this in the constellations, and it is by looking into these that he professes to read the fates. If, then, he does not discover the difference when he examines the constellations, which must, of course, be the same whether he is consulted about Jacob or his brother, what does it profit him that there is a difference in the heavens, which he rashly and carelessly brings into disrepute, when there is no difference in his chart, which he looks into anxiously but in vain? And so these notions also, which have their origin in certain signs of things being arbitrarily fixed upon by the presumption of men, are to be referred to the same class as if they were leagues and covenants with devils.

Chapter 23.—Why we repudiate arts of divination.

35. For in this way it comes to pass that men who lust after evil things are, by a secret judgment of God, delivered over to be mocked and deceived, as the just reward of their evil desires. For they are deluded and imposed on by the false angels, to whom the lowest part of the world has been put in subjection by the law of God's providence, and in accordance with His most admirable arrangement of things. And the result of these delusions and deceptions is, that through these superstitions and baneful modes of divination, many things in the past and future are made known, and turn out just as they are foretold; and in the case of those who practice superstitious observances, many things turn out agreeably to their observances, and ensnared by these successes, they become more eagerly inquisitive, and involve themselves further and further in a labyrinth of most pernicious error. And to our advantage, the Word of God is not silent about this species of fornication of the soul; and it does not warn the soul against following such practices on the ground that those who profess them speak lies, but it says, "Even if what they tell you should come to pass, hearken not unto them." For though the ghost of the dead Samuel foretold the truth to King Saul, that does not make such sacrilegious observances as those by which his ghost was brought up the less detestable; and though the ventriloquist woman in the Acts of the Apostles bore true testimony to the apostles of the Lord, the Apostle Paul did not spare the evil spirit on that account, but rebuked and cast it out, and so made the woman clean.

36. All arts of this sort, therefore, are either nullities, or are part of a guilty superstition, springing out of a baleful fellowship between men and devils, and are to be utterly repudiated and avoided by the Christian as the covenants of a false and treacherous friendship. "Not as

if the idol were anything," says the apostle; "but because the things which they sacrifice they sacrifice to devils and not to God; and I would not that ye should have fellowship with devils."[53] Now, what the apostle has said about idols and the sacrifices offered in their honor, that we ought to feel in regard to all fancied signs which lead either to the worship of idols, or to worshipping creation or its parts instead of God, or which are connected with attention to medicinal charms and other observances; for these are not appointed by God as the public means of promoting love towards God and our neighbor, but they waste the hearts of wretched men in private and selfish striving after temporal things. Accordingly, in regard to all these branches of knowledge, we must fear and shun the Devil their prince, strive only to shut and bar the door against our return. As, then, from the stars which God created and ordained, men have drawn lying omens of their own fancy, so also from things that are born, or in any other way come into existence under the government of God's providence, if there chance only to be something unusual in the occurrence,—as when a mule brings forth young, or an object is struck by lightning,—men have frequently drawn omens by conjectures of their own, and have committed them to writing, as if they had drawn them by rule.

Chapter 24.—The intercourse and agreement with demons which superstitious observances maintain.

37. And all these omens are of force just so far as has been arranged with the devils by that previous understanding in the mind which is, as it were, the common language, but they are all full of hurtful curiosity, torturing anxiety, and deadly slavery. For it was not because they had meaning that they were attended to, but it was by attending to and marking them that they came to have meaning. And so they are made different for different people, according to their several notions and prejudices. For those spirits which are bent upon deceiving, take care to provide for each person the same sort of omens as they see his own conjectures and preconceptions have already been entangled in. For, to take an illustration, the same figure of the letter X, which is made in the shape of a cross, means one thing among the Greeks and another among the Latins, not by nature, but by agreement and pre-arrangement as to its signification; and

so, any one who knows both languages uses this letter in a different sense when writing to a Greek from that in which he uses it when writing to a Latin. And the same sound, *beta*, which is the name of a letter among the Greeks, is the name of a vegetable among the Latins; and when I say, *lege*, these two syllables mean one thing to a Greek and another to a Latin. Now, just as all these signs affect the mind according to the arrangements of the community in which each man lives, and affect different men's minds differently, because these arrangements are different; and as, further, men did not agree upon them as signs because they were already significant, but on the contrary they are now significant because they have agreed upon them; in the same way also, those signs by which the ruinous intercourse with devils is maintained have meaning just in proportion to each man's observations. And this appears quite plainly in the rites of the augurs; for they, both before they observe the omens and after they have completed their observations, take pains not to see the flight or hear the cry of the birds, because these signs are of no significance apart from the previous arrangement in the mind of the observer.

Chapter 25.—In human institutions which are not superstitious, there are some things superfluous and some convenient and necessary.

38. But when all these have been cut away and rooted out of the mind of the Christian, we must then look at human institutions which are not superstitious, that is, such as are not set up in association with devils, but by men in association with one another. For all arrangements that are in force among men, because they have agreed among themselves that they should be in force, are human institutions; and of these, some are matters of superfluity and luxury, some of convenience and necessity. For if those signs which the actors make in dancing were of force by nature, and not by the arrangement and agreement of men, the public crier would not in former times have announced to the people of Carthage, while the pantomime was dancing, what it meant to express,—a thing still remembered by many old men from whom we have frequently heard it. And we may well believe this, because even now, if any one who is unaccustomed to such follies goes into the theater, unless some one tells him what these movements mean, he will give his whole attention to them in vain. Yet all men aim at a certain degree of likeness in their choice of signs, that the signs may as far as possible be like the

---

[53] 1 Corinthians 10:20.

things they signify. But because one thing may resemble another in many ways, such signs are not always of the same significance among men, except when they have mutually agreed upon them.

39. But in regard to pictures and statues, and other works of this kind, which are intended as representations of things, nobody makes a mistake, especially if they are executed by skilled artists, but every one, as soon as he sees the likenesses, recognizes the things they are likenesses of. And this whole class are to be reckoned among the superfluous devices of men, unless when it is a matter of importance to inquire in regard to any of them, for what reason, where, when, and by whose authority it was made. Finally, the thousands of fables and fictions, in whose lies men take delight, are human devices, and nothing is to be considered more peculiarly man's own and derived from himself than anything that is false and lying. Among the convenient and necessary arrangements of men with men are to be reckoned whatever differences they choose to make in bodily dress and ornament for the purpose of distinguishing sex or rank; and the countless varieties of signs without which human intercourse either could not be carried on at all, or would be carried on at great inconvenience; and the arrangements as to weights and measures, and the stamping and weighing of coins, which are peculiar to each state and people, and other things of the same kind. Now these, if they were not devices of men, would not be different in different nations, and could not be changed among particular nations at the discretion of their respective sovereigns.

40. This whole class of human arrangements, which are of convenience for the necessary intercourse of life, the Christian is not by any means to neglect, but on the contrary should pay a sufficient degree of attention to them, and keep them in memory.

Chapter 26.—What human contrivances we are to adopt, and what we are to avoid.

For certain institutions of men are in a sort of way representations and likenesses of natural objects. And of these, such as have relation to fellowship with devils must, as has been said, be utterly rejected and held in detestation; those, on the other hand, which relate to the mutual intercourse of men, are, so far as they are not matters of luxury and superfluity, to be adopted, especially the forms of letters which are necessary for reading, and the various languages as far as is required—a matter I have spoken of above. To this class also belong shorthand characters, those who are acquainted with

which are called shorthand writers. All these are useful, and there is nothing unlawful in learning them, nor do they involve us in superstition, or enervate us by luxury, if they only occupy our minds so far as not to stand in the way of more important objects to which they ought to be subservient.

Chapter 27.—Some departments of knowledge, not of mere human invention, aid us in interpreting Scripture.

41. But, coming to the next point, we are not to reckon among human institutions those things which men have handed down to us, not as arrangements of their own, but as the result of investigation into the occurrences of the past, and into the arrangements of God's providence. And of course, some pertain to the bodily senses, some to the intellect. Those which are reached by the bodily senses we either believe on testimony, or perceive when they are pointed out to us, or infer from experience.

Chapter 28.—To what extent history is an aid.

42. Anything, then, that we learn from history about the chronology of past times assists us very much in understanding the Scriptures, even if it be learnt without the pale of the Church as a matter of childish instruction. For we frequently seek information about a variety of matters by use of the Olympiads, and the names of the consuls; and ignorance of the consulship in which our Lord was born, and that in which He suffered, has led some into the error of supposing that He was forty-six years of age when He suffered, that being the number of years He was told by the Jews the temple (which He took as a symbol of His body) was in building. Now we know on the authority of the evangelist that He was baptized; but the number of years He lived afterwards, although by putting His actions together we can make it out, yet that no shadow of doubt might arise from another source, can be ascertained more clearly and more certainly from a comparison of profane history with the Gospel. It will still be evident, however, that it was not without a purpose it was said that the temple was forty and six years in building; so that, as this cannot be referred to our Lord's age, it may be referred to the more secret formation of the body which, for our sakes, the only-begotten Son of God, by whom all things were made, condescended to put on.

43. As to the utility of history, moreover, passing over the Greeks, what a great question our own Ambrose[54] has set at rest! For, when the readers and admirers of Plato dared calumniously to assert that our Lord Jesus Christ learnt all those sayings of His, which they are compelled to admire and praise, from the books of Plato—because (they urged) it cannot be denied that Plato lived long before the coming of our Lord!—did not the illustrious bishop, when by his investigations into profane history he had discovered that Plato was through Jeremiah's means initiated into our literature, so as to be able to teach and write those views of his which are so justly praised? For not even Pythagoras himself, from whose successors these men assert Plato learnt theology, lived at a date prior to the books of that Hebrew race, among whom the worship of one God sprang up, and of whom as concerning the flesh our Lord came. And thus, when we reflect upon the dates, it becomes much more probable that those philosophers learnt whatever they said that was good and true from our literature, than that the Lord Jesus Christ learnt from the writings of Plato,—a thing which it is the height of folly to believe.

44. And even when in the course of an historical narrative former institutions of men are described, the history itself is not to be reckoned among human institutions; because things that are past and gone and cannot be undone are to be reckoned as belonging to the course of time, of which God is the author and governor. For it is one thing to tell what has been done, another to show what ought to be done. History narrates what has been done, faithfully and with advantage; but the books of the haruspices, and all writings of the same kind, aim at teaching what ought to be done or observed, using the boldness of an adviser, not the fidelity of a narrator.

Chapter 29.—To what extent natural science is an exegetical aid.

45. There is also a species of narrative resembling description, in which not a past but an existing state of things is made known to those who are ignorant of it. To this species belongs all that has been written about the situation of places, and the nature of animals, trees, herbs, stones, and other bodies. And of this species I have treated above, and have shown that this kind of knowledge is serviceable in solving the difficulties of Scripture, not that these objects are to be used

conformably to certain signs as nostrums or the instruments of superstition; for that kind of knowledge I have already set aside as distinct from the lawful and free kind now spoken of. For it is one thing to say: If you bruise down this herb and drink it, it will remove the pain from your stomach; and another to say: If you hang this herb round your neck, it will remove the pain from your stomach. In the former case the wholesome mixture is approved of, in the latter the superstitious charm is condemned; although indeed, where incantations and invocations and marks are not used, it is frequently doubtful whether the thing that is tied or fixed in any way to the body to cure it, acts by a natural virtue, in which case it may be freely used; or acts by a sort of charm, in which case it becomes the Christian to avoid it the more carefully, the more efficacious it may seem to be. But when the reason why a thing is of virtue does not appear, the intention with which it is used is of great importance, at least in healing or in tempering bodies, whether in medicine or in agriculture.

46. The knowledge of the stars, again, is not a matter of narration, but of description. Very few of these, however, are mentioned in Scripture. And as the course of the moon, which is regularly employed in reference to celebrating the anniversary of our Lord's passion, is known to most people; so the rising and setting and other movements of the rest of the heavenly bodies are thoroughly known to very few. And this knowledge, although in itself it involves no superstition, renders very little, indeed almost no assistance, in the interpretation of Holy Scripture, and by engaging the attention unprofitably is a hindrance rather; and as it is closely related to the very pernicious error of the diviners of the fates, it is more convenient and becoming to neglect it. It involves, moreover, in addition to a description of the present state of things, something like a narrative of the past also; because one may go back from the present position and motion of the stars, and trace by rule their past movements. It involves also regular anticipations of the future, not in the way of forebodings and omens, but by way of sure calculation; not with the design of drawing any information from them as to our own acts and fates, in the absurd fashion of the *genethliaci*, but only as to the motions of the heavenly bodies themselves. For, as the man who computes the moon's age can tell, when he has found out her age to-day, what her age was any number of years ago, or what will be her age any number of years hence, in just the same way men who are skilled in such computations are accustomed to answer like questions about every one of the heavenly

[54] Bishop of Milan, ca. 340–397.

bodies. And I have stated what my views are about all this knowledge, so far as regards its utility.

Chapter 30.—What the mechanical arts contribute to exegetics.

47. Further, as to the remaining arts, whether those by which something is made which, when the effort of the workman is over, remains as a result of his work, as, for example, a house, a bench, a dish, and other things of that kind; or those which, so to speak, assist God in His operations, as medicine, and agriculture, and navigation; or those whose sole result is an action, as dancing, and racing, and wrestling;—in all these arts experience teaches us to infer the future from the past. For no man who is skilled in any of these arts moves his limbs in any operation without connecting the memory of the past with the expectation of the future. Now of these arts a very superficial and cursory knowledge is to be acquired, not with a view to practicing them (unless some duty compel us, a matter on which I do not touch at present), but with a view to forming a judgment about them, that we may not be wholly ignorant of what Scripture means to convey when it employs figures of speech derived from these arts.

Chapter 31.—Use of dialectics. Of fallacies.

48. There remain those branches of knowledge which pertain not to the bodily senses, but to the intellect, among which the science of reasoning and that of number are the chief. The science of reasoning is of very great service in searching into and unraveling all sorts of questions that come up in Scripture, only in the use of it we must guard against the love of wrangling, and the childish vanity of entrapping an adversary. For there are many of what are called *sophisms*, inferences in reasoning that are false, and yet so close an imitation of the true, as to deceive not only dull people, but clever men too, when they are not on their guard. For example, one man lays before another with whom he is talking, the proposition, "What I am, you are not." The other assents, for the proposition is in part true, the one man being cunning and the other simple. Then the first speaker adds: "I am a man"; and when the other has given his assent to this also, the first draws his conclusion: "Then you are not a man." Now of this sort of ensnaring arguments, Scripture, as I judge, expresses detestation in that place where it is said, "There is one that showeth wisdom in words, and is hated"; although indeed, a style of speech which is not intended to entrap, but only aims at verbal

ornamentation more than is consistent with seriousness of purpose, is also called sophistical.

49. There are also valid processes of reasoning which lead to false conclusions, by following out to its logical consequences the error of the man with whom one is arguing; and these conclusions are sometimes drawn by a good and learned man, with the object of making the person from whose error these consequences result, feel ashamed of them, and of thus leading him to give up his error, when he finds that if he wishes to retain his old opinion, he must of necessity also hold other opinions which he condemns. For example, the apostle did not draw true conclusions when he said, "Then is Christ not risen," and again, "Then is our preaching vain, and your faith is also vain";[55] and further on drew other inferences which are all utterly false; for Christ has risen, the preaching of those who declared this fact was not in vain, nor was their faith in vain who had believed it. But all these false inferences followed legitimately from the opinion of those who said that there is no resurrection of the dead. These inferences, then, being repudiated as false, it follows that since they would be true if the dead rise not, there will be a resurrection of the dead. As, then, valid conclusions may be drawn not only from true but from false propositions, the laws of valid reasoning may easily be learnt in the schools, outside the pale of the Church. But the truth of propositions must be inquired into in the sacred books of the Church.

Chapter 32.—Valid logical sequence is not devised but only observed by man.

50. And yet the validity of logical sequences is not a thing devised by men, but is observed and noted by them that they may be able to learn and teach it; for it exists eternally in the reason of things, and has its origin with God. For as the man who narrates the order of events does not himself create that order; and as he who describes the situations of places, or the natures of animals, or roots, or minerals, does not describe arrangements of man; and as he who points out the stars and their movements does not point out anything that he himself or any other man has ordained;—in the same way, he who says, "When the consequent is false, the antecedent must also be false," says what is most true; but he does not himself make it so, he only points out that it is so. And it is upon this rule that the reasoning I have

---

[55] 1 Corinthians 15:14.

quoted from the Apostle Paul proceeds. For the antecedent is, "There is no resurrection of the dead,"—the position taken up by those whose error the apostle wished to overthrow. Next, from this antecedent, the assertion, viz., that there is no resurrection of the dead, the necessary consequence is, "Then Christ is not risen." But this consequence is false, for Christ has risen; therefore the antecedent is also false. But the antecedent is, that there is no resurrection of the dead. Now all this is briefly expressed thus: If there is no resurrection of the dead, then is Christ not risen; but Christ is risen, therefore there is a resurrection of the dead. This rule, then, that when the consequent is removed, the antecedent must also be removed, is not made by man, but only pointed out by him. And this rule has reference to the validity of the reasoning, not to the truth of the statements.

Chapter 33.—False inferences may be drawn from valid reasonings, and vice versa.

51. In this passage, however, where the argument is about the resurrection, both the law of the inference is valid, and the conclusion arrived at is true. But in the case of false conclusions, too, there is a validity of inference in some such way as the following. Let us suppose some man to have admitted: If a snail is an animal, it has a voice. This being admitted, then, when it has been proved that the snail has no voice, it follows (since when the consequent is proved false, the antecedent is also false) that the snail is not an animal. Now this conclusion is false, but it is a true and valid inference from the false admission. Thus, the truth of a statement stands on its own merits; the validity of an inference depends on the statement or the admission of the man with whom one is arguing. And thus, as I said above, a false inference may be drawn by a valid process of reasoning, in order that he whose error we wish to correct may be sorry that he has admitted the antecedent, when he sees that its logical consequences are utterly untenable. And hence it is easy to understand that as the inferences may be unsound where the opinions are false, so the inferences may be unsound where the opinions are true. For example, suppose that a man propounds the statement, "If this man is just, he is good," and we admit its truth. Then he adds, "But he is not just;" and when we admit this too, he draws the conclusion, "Therefore he is not good." Now although every one of these statements may be true, still the principle of the inference is unsound. For it is not true that, as when the consequent is proved false the antecedent is also false, so when

the antecedent is proved false the consequent is false. For the statement is true, "If he is an orator, he is a man." But if we add, "He is not an orator," the consequence does not follow, "He is not a man."

Chapter 34.—It is one thing to know the laws of inference, another to know the truth of opinions.

52. Therefore it is one thing to know the laws of inference, and another to know the truth of opinions. In the former case we learn what is consequent, what is inconsequent, and what is incompatible. An example of a consequent is, "If he is an orator, he is a man"; of an inconsequent, "If he is a man, he is an orator"; of an incompatible, "If he is a man, he is a quadruped." In these instances we judge of the connection. In regard to the truth of opinions, however, we must consider propositions as they stand by themselves, and not in their connection with one another; but when propositions that we are sure about are joined by a valid inference to propositions that are true and certain, they themselves, too, necessarily become certain. Now some, when they have ascertained the validity of the inference, plume themselves as if this involved also the truth of the propositions. Many, again, who hold the true opinions have an unfounded contempt for themselves, because they are ignorant of the laws of inference; whereas the man who knows that there is a resurrection of the dead is assuredly better than the man who only knows that it follows that if there is no resurrection of the dead, then is Christ not risen.

Chapter 35.—The science of definition is not false, though it may be applied to falsities.

53. Again, the science of definition, of division, and of partition, although it is frequently applied to falsities, is not itself false, nor framed by man's device, but is evolved from the reason of things. For although poets have applied it to their fictions, and false philosophers, or even heretics—that is, false Christians—to their erroneous doctrines, that is no reason why it should be false, for example, that neither in definition, nor in division, nor in partition, is anything to be included that does not pertain to the matter in hand, nor anything to be omitted that does. This is true, even though the things to be defined or divided are not true. For even falsehood itself is defined when we say that falsehood is the declaration of a state of things which is not as we declare it to be; and this definition is true, although falsehood itself cannot be true. We can also divide it, saying that there are two

kinds of falsehood, one in regard to things that cannot be true at all, the other in regard to things that are not, though it is possible that they might be, true. For example, the man who says that seven and three are eleven, says what cannot be true under any circumstances; but he who says that it rained on the kalends of January, although perhaps the fact is not so, says what possibly might have been. The definition and division, therefore, of what is false may be perfectly true, although what is false cannot, of course, itself be true.

Chapter 36.—*The rules of eloquence are true, though sometimes used to persuade men of what is false.*

54. There are also certain rules for a more copious kind of argument, which is called eloquence, and these rules are not the less true that they can be used for persuading men of what is false; but as they can be used to enforce the truth as well, it is not the faculty itself that is to be blamed, but the perversity of those who put it to a bad use. Nor is it owing to an arrangement among men that the expression of affection conciliates the hearer, or that a narrative, when it is short and clear, is effective, and that variety arrests men's attention without wearying them. And it is the same with other directions of the same kind, which, whether the cause in which they are used be true or false, are themselves true just in so far as they are effective in producing knowledge or belief, or in moving men's minds to desire and aversion. And men rather found out that these things are so, than arranged that they should be so.

Chapter 37.—*Use of rhetoric and dialectic.*

55. This art, however, when it is learnt, is not to be used so much for ascertaining the meaning as for setting forth the meaning when it is ascertained. But the art previously spoken of, which deals with inferences, and definitions, and divisions, is of the greatest assistance in the discovery of the meaning, provided only that men do not fall into the error of supposing that when they have learnt these things they have learnt the true secret of a happy life. Still, it sometimes happens that men find less difficulty in attaining the object for the sake of which these sciences are learnt, than in going through the very intricate and thorny discipline of such rules. It is just as if a man wishing to give rules for walking should warn you not to lift the hinder foot before you set down the front one, and then should describe minutely the way you ought to move the hinges of the joints and knees.

For what he says is true, and one cannot walk in any other way; but men find it easier to walk by executing these movements than to attend to them while they are going through them, or to understand when they are told about them. Those, on the other hand, who cannot walk, care still less about such directions, as they cannot prove them by making trial of them. And in the same way a clever man often sees that an inference is unsound more quickly than he apprehends the rules for it. A dull man, on the other hand, does not see the unsoundness, but much less does he grasp the rules. And in regard to all these laws, we derive more pleasure from them as exhibitions of truth, than assistance in arguing or forming opinions, except perhaps that they put the intellect in better training. We must take care, however, that they do not at the same time make it more inclined to mischief or vanity,—that is to say, that they do not give those who have learnt them an inclination to lead people astray by plausible speech and catching questions, or make them think that they have attained some great thing that gives them an advantage over the good and innocent.

Chapter 38.—*The science of numbers not created, but only discovered, by man.*

56. Coming now to the science of numbers, it is clear to the dullest apprehension that this was not created by man, but was discovered by investigation. For, though Virgil could at his own pleasure make the first syllable of *Italia* long, while the ancients pronounced it short, it is not in any man's power to determine at his pleasure that three times three are not nine, or not make a square, or are not the triple of three, nor one and a half times the number six, or that it is not true that they are not the double of any number because odd numbers have no half. Whether, then, numbers are considered in themselves, or as applied to the laws of figures, or of sounds, or of other motions, they have fixed laws which were not made by man, but which the acuteness of ingenious men brought to light.

57. The man, however, who puts so high a value on these things as to be inclined to boast himself one of the learned, and who does not rather inquire after the source from which those things which he perceives to be true derive their truth, and from which those others which he perceives to be unchangeable also derive their truth and unchangeableness, and who, mounting up from bodily appearances to the mind of man, and finding that it too is changeable (for it is sometimes instructed, at other times uninstructed), although it holds a middle

place between the unchangeable truth above it and the changeable things beneath it, does not strive to make all things redound to the praise and love of the one God from whom he knows that all things have their being;—the man, I say, who acts in this way may seem to be learned, but wise he cannot in any sense be deemed.

Chapter 39.—To which of the above-mentioned studies attention should be given, and in what spirit.

58. Accordingly, I think that it is well to warn serious and able young men, who fear God and are seeking for happiness of life, not to venture heedlessly upon the pursuit of the branches of learning that are in vogue beyond the pale of the Church of Christ, as if these could secure for them the happiness they seek; but soberly and carefully to discriminate among them. And if they find any of those which have been instituted by men varying by reason of the varying pleasure of their founders, and unknown by reason of erroneous conjectures, especially if they involve entering into fellowship with devils by means of leagues and covenants about signs, let these be utterly rejected and held in detestation. Let the young men also withdraw their attention from such institutions of men as are unnecessary and luxurious. But for the sake of the necessities of this life we must not neglect the arrangements of men that enable us to carry on intercourse with those around us. I think, however, there is nothing useful in the other branches of learning that are found among the heathen, except information about objects, either past or present, that relate to the bodily senses, in which are included also the experiments and conclusions of the useful mechanical arts, except also the sciences of reasoning and of number. And in regard to all these we must hold by the maxim, "Not too much of anything"; especially in the case of those which, pertaining as they do to the senses, are subject to the relations of space and time.

59. What, then, some men have done in regard to all words and names found in Scripture, in the Hebrew, and Syriac, and Egyptian, and other tongues, taking up and interpreting separately such as were left in Scripture without interpretation; and what Eusebius has done in regard to the history of the past with a view to the questions arising in Scripture that require a knowledge of history for their solution;—what, I say, these men have done in regard to matters of this kind, making it unnecessary for the Christian to spend his strength on many subjects for the sake of a few items of knowledge, the same, I think, might be done in regard to other matters, if any competent man were willing in a spirit of benevolence to undertake the labor for the advantage of his brethren. In this way he might arrange in their several classes, and give an account of the unknown places, and animals, and plants, and trees, and stones, and metals, and other species of things that are mentioned in Scripture, taking up these only, and committing his account to writing. This might also be done in relation to numbers, so that the theory of those numbers, and those only, which are mentioned in Holy Scripture, might be explained and written down. And it may happen that some or all of these things have been done already (as I have found that many things I had no notion of have been worked out and committed to writing by good and learned Christians), but are either lost amid the crowds of the careless, or are kept out of sight by the envious. And I am not sure whether the same thing can be done in regard to the theory of reasoning; but it seems to me it cannot, because this runs like a system of nerves through the whole structure of Scripture, and on that account is of more service to the reader in disentangling and explaining ambiguous passages, of which I shall speak hereafter, than in ascertaining the meaning of unknown signs, the topic I am now discussing.

Chapter 40.—Whatever has been rightly said by the heathen, we must appropriate to our use.

60. Moreover, if those who are called philosophers, and especially the Platonists, have said aught that is true and in harmony with our faith, we are not only not to shrink from it, but to claim it for our own use from those who have unlawful possession of it. For, as the Egyptians had not only the idols and heavy burdens which the people of Israel hated and fled from, but also the vessels and ornaments of gold and silver, which the same people when going out of Egypt appropriated to themselves, designing them for a better use, not doing this on their own authority, but by the command of God, the Egyptians themselves, in their ignorance, providing them with things which they themselves were not making a good use of; in the same way all branches of heathen learning have not only false and superstitious fancies and heavy burdens of unnecessary toil, which every one of us, when going out under the leadership of Christ from the fellowship of the heathen, ought to abhor and avoid; but they contain also liberal instruction which is better adapted to the use of the truth, and some most excellent precepts of morality; and some

truths in regard even to the worship of the One God are found among them. Now these are, so to speak, their gold and silver, which they did not create themselves, but dug out of the mines of God's providence which are everywhere scattered abroad, and are perversely and unlawfully prostituting to the worship of devils. These, therefore, the Christian, when he separates himself in spirit from the miserable fellowship of these men, ought to take away from them, and to devote to their proper use in preaching the Gospel. Their garments, also,—that is, human institutions such as are adapted to that intercourse with men which is indispensable in this life,—we must take and turn to a Christian use.

61. And what else have many good and faithful men among our brethren done? Do we not see with what a quantity of gold and silver and garments Cyprian, that most persuasive teacher and most blessed martyr, was loaded when he came out of Egypt? How much Lactantius brought with him? And Victorinus, and Optatus, and Hilary, not to speak of living men! How much Greeks out of number have borrowed! And prior to all these, that most faithful servant of God, Moses, had done the same thing; for of him it is written that he was learned in all the wisdom of the Egyptians. And to none of all these would heathen superstition (especially in those times when, kicking against the yoke of Christ, it was persecuting the Christians) have ever furnished branches of knowledge it held useful, if it had suspected they were about to turn them to the use of worshipping the One God, and thereby overturning the vain worship of idols. But they gave their gold and their silver and their garments to the people of God as they were going out of Egypt, not knowing how the things they gave would be turned to the service of Christ. For what was done at the time of the exodus was no doubt a type prefiguring what happens now. And this I say without prejudice to any other interpretation that may be as good, or better.

Chapter 41.—*What kind of spirit is required for the study of Holy Scripture.*

62. But when the student of the Holy Scriptures, prepared in the way I have indicated, shall enter upon his investigations, let him constantly meditate upon that saying of the apostle's, "Knowledge puffeth up, but charity edifieth."[56] For so he will feel that, whatever may be the riches he brings with him out of Egypt, yet unless he has kept the passover, he cannot be safe. Now Christ

is our passover sacrificed for [...] the sacrifice of Christ more cl[...] call which He himself addresse[...] toiling in Egypt under Pharoah[...] that labor and are heavy laden, [...] Take my yoke upon you, and lear[...] and lowly in heart; and ye shall fir[...] For my yoke is easy, and my burd[...] is it light but to the meek and lowly in heart, whom knowledge doth not puff up, but charity edifieth? Let them remember, then, that those who celebrated the passover at that time in type and shadow, when they were ordered to mark their door-posts with the blood of the lamb, used hyssop to mark them with. Now this is a meek and lowly herb, and yet nothing is stronger and more penetrating than its roots; that being rooted and grounded in love, we may be able to comprehend with all saints what is the breadth, and length, and depth, and height,—that is, to comprehend the cross of our Lord, the breadth of which is indicated by the transverse wood on which the hands are stretched, its length by the part from the ground up to the cross-bar on which the whole body from the head downwards is fixed, its height by the part which is hidden, being fixed in the earth. And by this sign of the cross all Christian action is symbolized, viz., to do good works in Christ, to cling with constancy to Him, to hope for heaven, and not to desecrate the sacraments. And purified by this Christian action, we shall be able to know even "the love of Christ which passeth knowledge," who is equal to the Father, by whom all things, were made, "that we may be filled with all the fullness of God." There is besides in hyssop a purgative virtue, that the breast may not be swollen with that knowledge which puffeth up, nor boast vainly of the riches brought out from Egypt. "Purge me with hyssop," the psalmist says, "and I shall be clean; wash me, and I shall be whiter than snow. Make me to hear joy and gladness." Then he immediately adds, to show that it is purifying from pride that is indicated by hyssop, "that the bones which Thou hast broken may rejoice."[58]

Chapter 42.—*Sacred Scripture compared with profane authors.*

63. But just as poor as the store of gold and silver and garments which the people of Israel brought with them out of Egypt was in comparison with the riches

---

[56] 1 Corinthians 8:1.

[57] Matthew 11:28.
[58] Psalm 51:8.

they afterwards attained at Jerusalem, and which reached their height in the reign of King Solomon, so poor is all the useful knowledge which is gathered from the books of the heathen when compared with the knowledge of Holy Scripture. For whatever man may have learnt from other sources, if it is hurtful, it is there condemned; if it is useful, it is therein contained. And while every man may find there all that he has learnt of useful elsewhere, he will find there in much greater abundance things that are to be found nowhere else, but can be learnt in the wonderful sublimity and wonderful simplicity of the Scriptures.

When, then, the reader is possessed of the instruction here pointed out, so that unknown signs have ceased to be a hindrance to him; when he is meek and lowly of heart, subject to the easy yoke of Christ, and loaded with His light burden, rooted and grounded and built up in faith, so that knowledge cannot puff him up, let him then approach the consideration and discussion of ambiguous signs in Scripture. And about these I shall now, in a third book, endeavor to say what the Lord shall be pleased to vouchsafe.

CITY OF GOD

BOOK I.

Preface, explaining his design in undertaking this work.

The glorious city of God is my theme in this work, which you, my dearest son Marcellinus,[59] suggested, and which is due to you by my promise. I have undertaken its defense against those who prefer their own gods to the Founder of this city,—a city surpassingly glorious, whether we view it as it still lives by faith in this fleeting course of time, and sojourns as a stranger in the midst of the ungodly, or as it shall dwell in the fixed stability of its eternal seat, which it now with patience waits

for, expecting until "righteousness shall return unto judgment,"[60] and it obtain, by virtue of its excellence, final victory and perfect peace. A great work this, and an arduous; but God is my helper. For I am aware what ability is requisite to persuade the proud how great is the virtue of humility, which raises us, not by a quite human arrogance, but by a divine grace, above all earthly dignities that totter on this shifting scene. For the King and Founder of this city of which we speak, has in Scripture uttered to His people a dictum of the divine law in these words: "God resisteth the proud, but giveth grace unto the humble."[61] But this, which is God's prerogative, the inflated ambition of a proud spirit also affects, and dearly loves that this be numbered among its attributes, to

Show pity to the humbled soul,
And crush the sons of pride.[62]

And therefore, as the plan of this work we have undertaken requires, and as occasion offers, we must speak also of this earthly city, which, though it be mistress of the nations, is itself ruled by its lust of rule.

Chapter 1.—Of the adversaries of the name of Christ, whom the barbarians for Christ's sake spared when they stormed the city.

For to this earthly city belong the enemies against whom I have to defend the city of God. Many of them, indeed, being reclaimed from their ungodly error, have become sufficiently creditable citizens of this city; but many are so inflamed with hatred against it, and are so ungrateful to its Redeemer for His signal benefits, as to forget that they would now be unable to utter a single word to its prejudice, had they not found in its sacred places, as they fled from the enemy's steel, that life in which they now boast themselves.[63] Are not those very Romans, who were spared by the barbarians through

---

[59] Marcellinus was a friend of Augustine who urged him to write this work. He was commissioned by the Emperor Honorius to convene a conference of Catholic and schismatic Donatist bishops in the summer of 411, and conceded the victory to the Catholics; but on account of his rigor in executing the laws against the Donatists, he fell victim to their revenge and was honored by a place among the martyrs.

[60] Psalm 94:15.

[61] James 4:6.

[62] Aeneid VI, 853.

[63] Augustine refers to the sacking of the city of Rome by the West Gothic King Alaric in 410. He was the most humane of the barbaric invaders and conquerors of Rome and had embraced Arian Christianity (probably from the teaching of Ulphilas, the Arian bishop and translator of the Bible). He spared the Catholic Christians.

their respect for Christ, become enemies to the name of Christ? The reliquaries of the martyrs and the churches of the apostles bear witness to this; for in the sack of the city they were open sanctuary for all who fled to them, whether Christian or pagan. To their very threshold the bloodthirsty enemy raged; there his murderous fury owned a limit. Thither did such of the enemy as had any pity convey those to whom they had given quarter, lest any less mercifully disposed might fall upon them. And, indeed, when even those murderers who everywhere else showed themselves pitiless came to those spots where that was forbidden which the license of war permitted in every other place, their furious rage for slaughter was bridled, and their eagerness to take prisoners was quenched. Thus escaped multitudes who now reproach the Christian religion, and impute to Christ the ills that have befallen their city; but the preservation of their own life—a boon which they owe to the respect entertained for Christ by the barbarians—they attribute not to our Christ, but to their own good luck. They ought rather, had they any right perceptions, to attribute the severities and hardships inflicted by their enemies, to that divine providence which is wont to reform the depraved manners of men by chastisement, and which exercises with similar afflictions the righteous and praiseworthy,—either translating them, when they have passed through the trial, to a better world, or detaining them still on earth for ulterior purposes. And they ought to attribute it to the spirit of these Christian times, that, contrary to the custom of war, these bloodthirsty barbarians spared them, and spared them for Christ's sake, whether this mercy was actually shown in promiscuous places, or in those places specially dedicated to Christ's name, and of which the very largest were selected as sanctuaries, that full scope might thus be given to the expansive compassion which desired that a large multitude might find shelter there. Therefore ought they to give God thanks, and with sincere confession flee for refuge to His name, that so they may escape the punishment of eternal fire—they who with lying lips took upon them this name, that they might escape the punishment of present destruction. For of those whom you see insolently and shamelessly insulting the servants of Christ, there are numbers who would not have escaped that destruction and slaughter had they not pretended that they themselves were Christ's servants. Yet now, in ungrateful pride and most impious madness, and at the risk of being punished in everlasting darkness, they perversely oppose that name under which they

fraudulently protected themselves for the sake of enjoying the fruits of this brief life. . . .

Chapter 8.—Of the advantages and disadvantages which often indiscriminately accrue to good and wicked men.

Will someone say, Why, then, was this divine compassion extended even to the ungodly and ungrateful? Why, but because it was the mercy of Him who daily "maketh His sun to rise on the evil and on the good, and sendeth rain on the just and on the unjust."[64] For though some of these men, taking thought of this, repent of their wickedness and reform, some, as the apostle says, "despising the riches of His goodness and long-suffering, after their hardness and impenitent heart, treasure up unto themselves wrath against the day of wrath and revelation of the righteous judgment of God, who will render to every man according to his deeds":[65] nevertheless does the patience of God still invite the wicked to repentance, even as the scourge of God educates the good to patience. And so, too, does the mercy of God embrace the good that it may cherish them, as the severity of God arrests the wicked to punish them. To the divine providence it has seemed good to prepare in the world to come for the righteous good things, which the unrighteous shall not enjoy; and for the wicked evil things, by which the good shall not be tormented. But as for the good things of this life, and its ills, God has willed that these should be common to both; that we might not too eagerly covet the things which wicked men are seen equally to enjoy, nor shrink with an unseemly fear from the ills which even good men must suffer.

There is, too, a very great difference in the purpose served both by those events which we call adverse and those called prosperous. For the good man is neither uplifted with the good things of time, nor broken by its ills; but the wicked man, because he is corrupted by this world's happiness, feels himself punished by its unhappiness. Yet often, even in the present distribution of temporal things, does God plainly evince His own interference. For if every sin were now visited with manifest punishment, nothing would seem to be reserved for the final judgment; on the other hand, if no sin received now a plainly divine punishment, it would be concluded that there is no divine providence at all. And so of the good

---

[64] Matthew 5:45.
[65] Romans 2:6.

things of this life: if God did not by a very visible liberality confer these on some of those persons who ask for them, we should say that these good things were not at His disposal; and if He gave them to all who sought them, we should suppose that such were the only rewards of His service; and such a service would make us not godly, but greedy rather, and covetous. Wherefore, though good and bad men suffer alike, we must not suppose that there is no difference between the men themselves, because there is no difference in what they both suffer. For even in the likeness of the sufferings, there remains an unlikeness in the sufferers; and though exposed to the same anguish, virtue and vice are not the same thing. For as the same fire causes gold to glow brightly, and chaff to smoke; and under the same flail the straw is beaten small, while the grain is cleansed; and as the lees are not mixed with the oil, though squeezed out of the vat by the same pressure, so the same violence of affliction proves, purges, clarifies the good, but damns, ruins, exterminates the wicked. And thus it is that in the same affliction the wicked detest God and blaspheme, while the good pray and praise. So material a difference does it make, not what ills are suffered, but what kind of man suffers them. For, stirred up with the same movement, mud exhales a horrible stench, and ointment emits a fragrant odor.

Chapter 9.—Of the reasons for administering correction to bad and good together.

What, then, have the Christians suffered in that calamitous period, which would not profit every one who duly and faithfully considered the following circumstances? First of all, they must humbly consider those very sins which have provoked God to fill the world with such terrible disasters; for although they be far from the excesses of wicked, immoral, and ungodly men, yet they do not judge themselves so clean removed from all faults as to be too good to suffer for these even temporal ills. For every man, however laudably he lives, yet yields in some points to the lust of the flesh. Though he do not fall into gross enormity of wickedness, and abandoned viciousness, and abominable profanity, yet he slips into some sins, either rarely or so much the more frequently as the sins seem of less account. But not to mention this, where can we readily find a man who holds in fit and just estimation those persons on account of whose revolting pride, luxury, and avarice, and cursed iniquities and impiety, God now smites the earth as His predictions threatened? Where is the man who lives with them in the style in which it becomes us to live with them?

For often we wickedly blind ourselves to the occasions of teaching and admonishing them, sometimes even of reprimanding and chiding them, either because we shrink from the labor or are ashamed to offend them, or because we fear to lose good friendships, lest this should stand in the way of our advancement, or injure us in some worldly matter, which either our covetous disposition desires to obtain, or our weakness shrinks from losing. So that, although the conduct of wicked men is distasteful to the good, and therefore they do not fall with them into that damnation which in the next life awaits such persons, yet, because they spare their damnable sins through fear, therefore, even though their own sins be slight and venial, they are justly scourged with the wicked in this world, though in eternity they quite escape punishment. Justly, when God afflicts them in common with the wicked, do they find this life bitter, through love of whose sweetness they declined to be bitter to these sinners.

If anyone forbears to reprove and find fault with those who are doing wrong, because he seeks a more seasonable opportunity, or because he fears they may be made worse by his rebuke, or that other weak persons may be disheartened from endeavoring to lead a good and pious life, and may be driven from the faith; this man's omission seems to be occasioned not by covetousness, but by a charitable consideration. But what is blameworthy is, that they who themselves revolt from the conduct of the wicked, and live in quite another fashion, yet spare those faults in other men which they ought to reprehend and wean them from; and spare them because they fear to give offense, lest they should injure their interests in those things which good men may innocently and legitimately use,—though they use them more greedily than becomes persons who are strangers in this world, and profess the hope of a heavenly country. For not only the weaker brethren who enjoy married life, and have children (or desire to have them), and own houses and establishments, whom the apostle addresses in the churches, warning and instructing them how they should live, both the wives with their husbands, and the husbands with their wives, the children with their parents, and parents with their children, and servants with their masters, and masters with their servants,—not only do these weaker brethren gladly obtain and grudgingly lose many earthly and temporal things on account of which they dare not offend men whose polluted and wicked life greatly displeases them; but those also who live at a higher level, who are not entangled in the meshes of married life, but use meager food and raiment, do not often take thought of their own safety and good name, and abstain from finding fault with the wicked, because they fear their wiles and violence. And although they do not fear them to such an extent as to be drawn to the commission of like iniquities, nay, not by any threats or violence soever; yet those very deeds which they refuse to share in the commission of, they often decline to find fault with, when possibly they might by finding fault prevent their commission. They abstain from interference, because they fear that, if it fail of good effect, their own safety or reputation may be damaged or destroyed; not because they see that their preservation and good name are needful, that they may be able to influence those who need their instruction, but rather because they weakly relish the flattery and respect of men, and fear the judgments of the people, and the pain or death of the body; that is to say, their non-intervention is the result of selfishness, and not of love.

Accordingly this seems to me to be one principal reason why the good are chastised along with the wicked, when God is pleased to visit with temporal punishments the profligate manners of a community. They are punished together, not because they have spent an equally corrupt life, but because the good as well as the wicked, though not equally with them, love this present life; while they ought to hold it cheap, that the wicked, being admonished and reformed by their example, might lay hold of life eternal. And if they will not be the companions of the good in seeking life everlasting, they should be loved as enemies, and be dealt with patiently. For so long as they live, it remains uncertain whether they may not come to a better mind. These selfish persons have more cause to fear than those to whom it was said through the prophet, "He is taken away in his iniquity, but his blood I will require at the watchman's hand."[66] For watchmen or overseers of the people are appointed in churches, that they may unsparingly rebuke sin. Nor is that man guiltless of the sin we speak of, who, though he be not a watchman, yet sees in the conduct of those with whom the relationships of this life bring him into contact, many things that should be blamed, and yet overlooks them, fearing to give offense, and lose such worldly blessings as may legitimately be desired, but which he too eagerly grasps. Then, lastly, there is another reason why the good are afflicted with temporal calamities—the reason which Job's case exemplifies: that the human spirit may be

proved, and that it may be manifested with what fortitude of pious trust, and with how unmercenary a love, it cleaves to God. . . .

BOOK XIX

Chapter 4.—What the Christians believe regarding the supreme good and evil, in opposition to the philosophers, who have maintained that the supreme good is in themselves.

If, then, we be asked what the city of God has to say upon these points, and, in the first place, what its opinion regarding the supreme good and evil is, it will reply that life eternal is the supreme good, death eternal the supreme evil, and that to obtain the one and to escape the other we must live rightly. And thus it is written, "The just lives by faith,"[67] for we do not as yet see our good, and must therefore live by faith; neither have we in ourselves power to live rightly, but can do so only if He who has given us faith to believe in His help do help us when we believe and pray. As for those who have supposed that the sovereign good and evil are to be found in this life, and have placed it either in the soul or the body, or, to speak more explicitly, either in pleasure or in virtue, or in both; in repose or in virtue, or in both; in pleasure and repose, or in virtue, or in all combined; in the primary objects of nature, or in virtue, or in both,—all these have, with a marvelous shallowness, sought to find their blessedness in this life and in themselves. Contempt has been poured upon such ideas by the Truth, saying by the prophet, "The Lord knoweth the thoughts of men" (or, as the Apostle Paul cites the passage, "The Lord knoweth the thoughts of the *wise*") "that they are vain."[68]

For what flood of eloquence can suffice to detail the miseries of this life? Cicero, in the *Consolation* on the death of his daughter, has spent all his ability in lamentation; but how inadequate was even his ability here? For when, where, how, in this life can these primary objects of nature be possessed so that they may not be assailed by unforeseen accidents? Is the body of the wise man exempt from any pain which may dispel pleasure, from any disquietude which may banish repose? The amputation

---

[66] Ezekiel 33:6.

[67] Habakkuk 2:4; Romans 1:17.
[68] 1 Corinthians 3:20.

or decay of the members of the body puts an end to its integrity, deformity blights its beauty, weakness its health, lassitude its vigor, sleepiness or sluggishness its activity,—and which of these is it that may not assail the flesh of the wise man? Comely and fitting attitudes and movements of the body are numbered among the prime natural blessings; but what if some sickness makes the members tremble? what if a man suffers from curvature of the spine to such an extent that his hands reach the ground, and he goes upon all-fours like a quadruped? Does not this destroy all beauty and grace in the body, whether at rest or in motion? What shall I say of the fundamental blessings of the soul, sense and intellect, of which the one is given for the perception, and the other for the comprehension of truth? But what kind of sense is it that remains when a man becomes deaf and blind? where are reason and intellect when disease makes a man delirious? We can scarcely, or not at all, refrain from tears, when we think of or see the actions and words of such frantic persons, and consider how different from and even opposed to their own sober judgment and ordinary conduct their present demeanor is. And what shall I say of those who suffer from demoniacal possession? Where is their own intelligence hidden and buried while the malignant spirit is using their body and soul according to his own will? And who is quite sure that no such thing can happen to the wise man in this life? Then, as to the perception of truth, what can we hope for even in this way while in the body, as we read in the true book of Wisdom, "The corruptible body weigheth down the soul, and the earthly tabernacle presseth down the mind that museth upon many things?"[69] And eagerness, or desire of action, if this is the right meaning to put on the Greek ὁρμήν, is also reckoned among the primary advantages of nature; and yet is it not this which produces those pitiable movements of the insane, and those actions which we shudder to see, when sense is deceived and reason deranged?

In fine, virtue itself, which is not among the primary objects of nature, but succeeds to them as the result of learning, though it holds the highest place among human good things, what is its occupation save to wage perpetual war with vices,—not those that are outside of us, but within; not other men's, but our own,—a war which is waged especially by that virtue which the Greeks call σωφροσύνη, and we temperance, and which bridles carnal lusts, and prevents them from winning the consent of the spirit to wicked deeds? For we must not fancy that there is no vice in us, when, as the apostle says, "The flesh lusteth against the spirit"; for to this vice there is a contrary virtue, when, as the same writer says, "The spirit lusteth against the flesh."[70] "For those two," he says, "are contrary one to the other, so that you cannot do the things which you would." But what is it we wish to do when we seek to attain the supreme good, unless that the flesh should cease to lust against the spirit, and that there be no vice in us against which the spirit may lust? And as we cannot attain to this in the present life, however ardently we desire it, let us by God's help accomplish at least this, to preserve the soul from succumbing and yielding to the flesh that lusts against it, and to refuse our consent to the perpetration of sin. Far be it from us, then, to fancy that while we are still engaged in this intestine war, we have already found the happiness which we seek to reach by victory. And who is there so wise that he has no conflict at all to maintain against his vices?

What shall I say of that virtue which is called prudence? Is not all its vigilance spent in the discernment of good from evil things, so that no mistake may be admitted about what we should desire and what avoid? And thus it is itself a proof that we are in the midst of evils, or that evils are in us; for it teaches us that it is an evil to consent to sin, and a good to refuse this consent. And yet this evil, to which prudence teaches and temperance enables us not to consent, is removed from this life neither by prudence nor by temperance. And justice, whose office it is to render to every man his due, whereby there is in man himself a certain just order of nature, so that the soul is subjected to God, and the flesh to the soul, and consequently both soul and flesh to God,—does not this virtue demonstrate that it is as yet rather laboring towards its end than resting in its finished work? For the soul is so much the less subjected to God as it is less occupied with the thought of God; and the flesh is so much the less subjected to the spirit as it lusts more vehemently against the spirit. So long, therefore, as we are beset by this weakness, this plague, this disease, how shall we dare to say that we are safe? and if not safe, then how can we be already enjoying our final beatitude? Then that virtue which goes by the name of fortitude is the plainest proof of the ills of life, for it is these ills which it is compelled to bear patiently. And this holds good, no matter though the ripest wisdom co-exists with it. And I am at a loss to understand how the Stoic philosophers can presume to

---

[69] Wisdom 9:15.

[70] Galatians 5:17.

say that these are no ills, though at the same time they allow the wise man to commit suicide and pass out of this life if they become so grievous that he cannot or ought not to endure them. But such is the stupid pride of these men who fancy that the supreme good can be found in this life, and that they can become happy by their own resources, that their wise man, or at least the man whom they fancifully depict as such, is always happy, even though he become blind, deaf, dumb, mutilated, racked with pains, or suffer any conceivable calamity such as may compel him to make away with himself; and they are not ashamed to call the life that is beset with these evils happy. O happy life, which seeks the aid of death to end it? If it is happy, let the wise man remain in it; but if these ills drive him out of it, in what sense is it happy? Or how can they say that these are not evils which conquer the virtue of fortitude, and force it not only to yield, but so to rave that it in one breath calls life happy and recommends it to be given up? For who is so blind as not to see that if it were happy it would not be fled from? And if they say we should flee from it on account of the infirmities that beset it, why then do they not lower their pride and acknowledge that it is miserable? Was it, I would ask, fortitude or weakness which prompted Cato to kill himself? for he would not have done so had he not been too weak to endure Caesar's victory. Where, then, is his fortitude? It has yielded, it has succumbed, it has been so thoroughly overcome as to abandon, forsake, flee this happy life. Or was it no longer happy? Then it was miserable. How, then, were these not evils which made life miserable, and a thing to be escaped from?

And therefore, those who admit that these are evils, as the Peripatetics [Aristotelians] do, and the Old Academy, the sect which Varro advocates, express a more intelligible doctrine; but theirs also is a surprising mistake, for they contend that this is a happy life which is beset by these evils, even though they be so great that he who endures them should commit suicide to escape them. "Pains and anguish of body," says Varro, "are evils, and so much the worse in proportion to their severity; and to escape them you must quit this life." What life, I pray? This life, he says, which is oppressed by such evils. Then it is happy in the midst of these very evils on account of which you say we must quit it? Or do you call it happy because you are at liberty to escape these evils by death? What, then, if by some secret judgment of God you were held fast and not permitted to die, nor suffered to live without these evils? In that case, at least, you would say that such a life was miserable. It is soon relinquished, no doubt, but this does not make it not miserable; for were

it eternal, you yourself would pronounce it miserable. Its brevity, therefore, does not clear it of misery; neither ought it to be called happiness because it is a brief misery. Certainly there is a mighty force in these evils which compel a man—according to them, even a wise man—to cease to be a man that he may escape them, though they say, and say truly, that it is as it were the first and strongest demand of nature that a man cherish himself, and naturally therefore avoid death, and should so stand his own friend as to wish and vehemently aim at continuing to exist as a living creature, and subsisting in this union of soul and body. There is a mighty force in these evils to overcome this natural instinct by which death is by every means and with all a man's efforts avoided, and to overcome it is desired, sought after, and if it cannot in any other way be obtained, is inflicted by the man on himself. There is a mighty force in these evils which make fortitude a homicide,—if, indeed, that is to be called fortitude which is so thoroughly overcome by these evils, that it not only cannot preserve by patience the man whom it undertook to govern and defend, but is itself obliged to kill him. The wise man, I admit, ought to bear death with patience, but when it is inflicted by another. If, then, as these men maintain, he is obliged to inflict it on himself, certainly it must be owned that the ills which compel him to this are not only evils, but intolerable evils. The life, then, which is either subject to accidents, or environed with evils so considerable and grievous, could never have been called happy, if the men who give it this name had condescended to yield to the truth, and to be conquered by valid arguments, when they inquired after the happy life, as they yield to unhappiness, and are overcome by overwhelming evils, when they put themselves to death, and if they had not fancied that the supreme good was to be found in this mortal life; for the very virtues of this life, which are certainly the best and most useful possessions, are all the more telling proofs of its miseries in proportion as they are helpful against the violence of its dangers, toils, and woes. For if these are true virtues,—and such cannot exist save in those who have true piety,—they do not profess to be able to deliver the men who possess them from all miseries; for true virtues tell no such lies, but they profess that by the hope of the future world this life, which is miserably involved in the many and great evils of this world, is happy as it is also safe. For if not yet safe, how could it be happy? And therefore the Apostle Paul, speaking not of men without prudence, temperance, fortitude, and justice, but of those whose lives were regulated by true piety, and whose virtues were therefore true, says, "For we are saved by hope: now hope which is not seen is not hope; for what a man seeth, why doth he yet hope for? But if we hope for that we see not, then do we with patience wait for it."[71] As, therefore, we are saved, so we are made happy by hope. And as we do not as yet possess a present, but look for a future salvation, so is it with our happiness, and this "with patience"; for we are encompassed with evils, which we ought patiently to endure, until we come to the ineffable enjoyment of unmixed good; for there shall be no longer anything to endure. Salvation, such as it shall be in the world to come, shall itself be our final happiness. And this happiness these philosophers refuse to believe in, because they do not see it, and attempt to fabricate for themselves a happiness in this life, based upon a virtue which is as deceitful as it is proud.

Chapter 5.—Of the social life, which, though most desirable, is frequently disturbed by many distresses.

We give a much more unlimited approval to their idea that the life of the wise man must be social. For how could the city of God (concerning which we are already writing no less than the nineteenth book of this work) either take a beginning or be developed, or attain its proper destiny, if the life of the saints were not a social life? But who can enumerate all the great grievances with which human society abounds in the misery of this mortal state? Who can weigh them? Hear how one of their comic writers makes one of his characters express the common feelings of all men in this matter: "I am married; this is one misery. Children are born to me; they are additional cares." What shall I say of the miseries of love which Terence also recounts—"slights, suspicions, quarrels, war to-day, peace tomorrow?" Is not human life full of such things? Do they not often occur even in honorable friendships? On all hands we experience these slights, suspicions, quarrels, war, all of which are undoubted evils; while, on the other hand, peace is a doubtful good, because we do not know the heart of our friend, and though we did know it to-day, we should be as ignorant of what it might be tomorrow. Who ought to be, or who are more friendly than those who live in the same family? And yet who can rely even upon this friendship, seeing that secret treachery has often broken it up, and produced enmity as bitter as the amity was sweet, or seemed sweet by the most perfect

dissimulation? It is on this account that the words of Cicero so move the heart of every one, and provoke a sigh: "There are no snares more dangerous than those which lurk under the guise of duty or the name of the relationship. For the man who is your declared foe you can easily baffle by precaution; but this hidden, intestine, and domestic danger not merely exists, but overwhelms you before you can foresee and examine it."[72] It is also to this that allusion is made by the divine saying, "A man's foes are those of his own household,"[73]—words which one cannot hear without pain; for though a man have sufficient fortitude to endure it with equanimity, and sufficient sagacity to baffle the malice of a pretended friend, yet if he himself is a good man, he cannot but be greatly pained at the discovery of the perfidy of wicked men whether they have always been wicked and merely feigned goodness, or have fallen from a better to a malicious disposition. If, then, home, the natural refuge from the ills of life, is itself not safe, what shall we say of the city, which, as it is larger, is so much the more filled with lawsuits civil and criminal, and is never free from the fear, if sometimes from the actual outbreak, of disturbing and bloody insurrections and civil wars? . . .

Chapter 9.—Of the friendship of the holy angels, which men cannot be sure of in this life, owing to the deceit of the demons who hold in bondage the worshippers of a plurality of gods.

The philosophers who wished us to have the gods for our friends rank the friendship of the holy angels in the fourth circle of society, advancing now from the three circles of society on earth to the universe, and embracing heaven itself. And in this friendship we have indeed no fear that the angels will grieve us by their death or deterioration. But as we cannot mingle with them as familiarly as with men (which itself is one of the grievances of this life), and as Satan, as we read, sometimes transforms himself into an angel of light, to tempt those whom it is necessary to discipline, or just to deceive, there is great need of God's mercy to preserve us from making friends of demons in disguise, while we fancy we have good angels for our friends; for the astuteness and deceitfulness of these wicked spirits is equaled by their hurtfulness. And is this not a great misery of human life, that we are involved in such ignorance as, but for God's mercy,

---

[71] Romans 8:25.

[72] *In Verrem*, ii. 1. 15.

[73] Matthew 10:36.

makes us a prey to these demons? And it is very certain that the philosophers of the godless city, who have maintained that the gods were their friends, had fallen a prey to the malignant demons who rule that city, and whose eternal punishment is to be shared by it. For the nature of these beings is sufficiently evinced by the sacred or rather sacrilegious observances which form their worship, and by the filthy games in which their crimes are celebrated, and which they themselves originated and exacted from their worshippers as a fit propitiation.

Chapter 10.—The reward prepared for the saints after they have departed the trial of this life.

But not even the saints and faithful worshippers of the one true and most high God are safe from the manifold temptations and deceits of the demons. For in this abode of weakness, and in these wicked days, this state of anxiety has also its use, stimulating us to seek with keener longing for that security where peace is complete and unassailable. There we shall enjoy the gifts of nature, that is to say, all that God the Creator of all natures has bestowed upon ours,—gifts not only good, but eternal,—not only of the spirit, healed now by wisdom, but also of the body renewed by the resurrection. There the virtues shall no longer be struggling against any vice or evil, but shall enjoy the reward of victory, the eternal peace which no adversary shall disturb. This is the final blessedness, this the ultimate consummation, the unending end. Here, indeed, we are said to be blessed when we have such peace as can be enjoyed in a good life; but such blessedness is mere misery compared to that final felicity. When we mortals possess such peace as this mortal life can afford, virtue, if we are living rightly, makes a right use of the advantages of this peaceful condition; and when we have it not, virtue makes a good use even of the evils a man suffers. But this is true virtue, when it refers all the advantages it makes a good use of, and all that it does in making good use of good and evil things, and itself also, to that end in which we shall enjoy the best and greatest peace possible.

Chapter 11.—Of the happiness of the eternal peace, which constitutes the end or true perfection of the saints.

And thus we may say of peace, as we have said of eternal life, that it is the end of our good; and the rather because the Psalmist says of the city of God, the subject of this laborious work, "Praise the Lord, O Jerusalem; praise thy God, O Zion: for He hath strengthened the bars of thy gates; He hath blessed thy children within thee; who hath made thy borders peace."[74] For when the bars of her gates shall be strengthened, none shall go in or come out from her; consequently we ought to understand the peace of her borders as that final peace we are wishing to declare. For even the mystical name of the city itself, that is, *Jerusalem*, means, as I have already said, "Vision of Peace." But as the word peace is employed in connection with things in this world in which certainly life eternal has no place, we have preferred to call the end or supreme good of this city life eternal rather than peace. Of this end the apostle says, "But now, being freed from sin, and become servants to God, ye have your fruit unto holiness, and the end life eternal."[75] But, on the other hand, as those who are not familiar with Scripture may suppose that the life of the wicked is eternal life, either because of the endless punishment of the wicked, which forms a part of our faith, and which seems impossible unless the wicked live forever, it may therefore be advisable, in order that every one may readily understand what we mean, to say that the end or supreme good of this city is either peace in eternal life, or eternal life in peace. For peace is a good so great, that even in this earthly and mortal life there is no word we hear with such pleasure, nothing we desire with such zest, or find to be more thoroughly gratifying. So that if we dwell for a little longer on this subject, we shall not, in my opinion, be wearisome to our readers, who will attend both for the sake of understanding what is the end of this city of which we speak, and for the sake of the sweetness of peace which is dear to us all. . . .

Chapter 21.—Whether there ever was a Roman Republic answering to the definitions of Scipio in Cicero's dialogue.

This, then, is the place where I should fulfill the promise I gave in the second book of this work, and explain, as briefly and clearly as possible, that if we are to accept the definitions laid down by Scipio in Cicero's *De Re publica*, there never was a Roman republic; for he briefly defines a republic as the commonweal of the people. And if this definition be true, there never was a Roman republic, for the commonweal was never attained among the

---

[74] Psalm 147:13.
[75] Romans 6:22.

Romans. For the people, according to his definition, is an assemblage associated by a common acknowledge-ment of right and by a community of interests. And what he means by a common acknowledgment of right he explains at large, showing that a republic cannot be administered without justice. Where, therefore, there is no true justice, there can be no right. For that which is done right is justly done, and what is unjustly done can-not be done by right. For the unjust inventions of men are neither to be considered nor spoken of as rights; for even they themselves say that right is that which flows from the fountain of justice, and deny the definition which is commonly given by those who misconceive the matter, that right is that which is useful to the stron-ger party. Thus, where there is not true justice there can be no assemblage of men associated by a common acknowledgment of right, and therefore there can be no people, as defined by Scipio or Cicero; and if no people, then no commonweal of the people, but only of some promiscuous multitude unworthy of the name of peo-ple. Consequently, if the republic is the commonweal of the people, and there is no people if it be not associated by a common acknowledgment of right, and if there is no right where there is no justice, then most certainly it follows that there is no republic where there is no jus-tice. Further, justice is that virtue which gives every one his due. Where, then, is the justice of man, when he des-erts the true God and yields himself to impure demons? Is this to give every one his due? Or is he who keeps back a piece of ground from the purchaser, and gives it to a man who has no right to it, unjust, while he who keeps back himself from the God who made him, and serves wicked spirits, is just?

This same book, *De Re publica*, advocates the cause of justice against injustice with great force and keenness. The pleading for injustice against justice was first heard, and it was asserted that without injustice a republic could neither increase nor even subsist, for it was laid down as an absolutely unassailable position that it is unjust for some men to rule and some to serve; and yet the imperial city to which the republic belongs cannot rule her provinces without having recourse to this injustice. It was replied in behalf of justice, that this ruling of the provinces is just, because servitude may be advanta-geous to the provincials, and is so when rightly admin-istered,—that is to say, when lawless men are prevented from doing harm. And further, as they became worse and worse so long as they were free, they will improve by subjection. To confirm this reasoning, there is added an eminent example drawn from nature: for "why," it is

asked, "does God rule man, the soul the body, the rea-son the passions and other vicious parts of the soul?" This example leaves no doubt that, to some, servitude is useful; and, indeed, to serve God is useful to all. And it is when the soul serves God that it exercises a right control over the body; and in the soul itself the reason must be subject to God if it is to govern as it ought the passions and other vices. Hence, when a man does not serve God, what justice can we ascribe to him, since in this case his soul cannot exercise a just control over the body, nor his reason over his vices? And if there is no justice in such an individual, certainly there can be none in a community composed of such persons. Here, therefore, there is not that common acknowledgment of right which makes an assemblage of men a people whose affairs we call a republic. And why need I speak of the advantageousness, the common participation in which, according to the definition, makes a people? For although, if you choose to regard the matter attentively, you will see that there is nothing advantageous to those who live godlessly, as every one lives who does not serve God but demons, whose wickedness you may measure by their desire to receive the worship of men though they are most impure spirits, yet what I have said of the common acknowledgment of right is enough to demonstrate that, according to the above definition, there can be no people, and therefore no republic, where there is no justice. For if they assert that in their republic the Romans did not serve unclean spirits, but good and holy gods, must we therefore again reply to this evasion, though already we have said enough, and more than enough, to expose it? He must be an uncommonly stupid, or a shamelessly contentious person, who has read through the foregoing books to this point, and can yet question whether the Romans served wicked and impure demons. But, not to speak of their character, it is written in the law of the true God, "He that sacrificeth unto any god save unto the Lord only, he shall be utterly destroyed."[76] He, therefore, who uttered so menacing a commandment decreed that no worship should be given either to good or bad gods. . . .

Chapter 24.—*The definition which must be given of a people and a republic, in order to vindicate the assumption of these titles by the Romans and by other kingdoms.*

But if we discard this definition of a people, and, assuming another, say that a people is an assemblage of

[76] Exodus 22:20.

reasonable beings bound together by a common agreement as to the objects of their love, then, in order to discover the character of any people, we have only to observe what they love. Yet whatever it loves, if only it is an assemblage of reasonable beings and not of beasts, and is bound together by an agreement as to the objects of love, it is reasonably called a people; and it will be a superior people in proportion as it is bound together by higher interests, inferior in proportion as it is bound together by lower. According to this definition of ours, the Roman people is a people, and its commonweal is without doubt a commonwealth or republic. But what its tastes were in its early and subsequent days, and how it declined into sanguinary seditions and then to social and civil wars, and so burst asunder or rotted off the bond of concord in which the health of a people consists, history shows, and in the preceding books I have related at large. And yet I would not on this account say either that it was not a people, or that its administration was not a republic, so long as there remains an assemblage of reasonable beings bound together by a common agreement as to the objects of love. But what I say of this people and of this republic I must be understood to think and say of the Athenians or any Greek state, of the Egyptians, of the early Assyrian Babylon, and of every other nation, great or small, which had a public government. For, in general, the city of the ungodly, which did not obey the command of God that it should offer no sacrifice save to Him alone, and which, therefore, could not give to the soul its proper command over the body, nor to the reason its just authority over the vices, is void of true justice.

Chapter 25.—That where there is no true religion there are no true virtues.

For though the soul may seem to rule the body admirably, and the reason the vices, if the soul and reason do not themselves obey God, as God has commanded them to serve Him, they have no proper authority over the body and the vices. For what kind of mistress of the body and the vices can that mind be which is ignorant of the true God, and which, instead of being subject to His authority, is prostituted to the corrupting influences of the most vicious demons? It is for this reason that the virtues which it seems to itself to possess, and by which it restrains the body and the vices that it may obtain and keep what it desires, are rather vices than virtues so long as there is no reference to God in the matter. For although some suppose that virtues which have a

reference only to themselves, and are desired only on their own account, are yet true and genuine virtues, the fact is that even then they are inflated with pride, and therefore to be reckoned vices rather than virtues. For as that which gives life to the flesh is not derived from the flesh, but is above it, so that which gives blessed life to man is not derived from man, but is something above him; and what I say of man is true of every celestial power and virtue whatsoever.

Chapter 26.—Of the peace which is enjoyed by the people that are alienated from God, and the use made of it by the people of God in the time of its pilgrimage.

Wherefore, as the life of the flesh is the soul, so the blessed life of man is God, of whom the sacred writings of the Hebrews say, "Blessed is the people whose God is the Lord."[77] Miserable, therefore, is the people which is alienated from God. Yet even this people has a peace of its own which is not to be lightly esteemed, though, indeed, it shall not in the end enjoy it, because it makes no good use of it before the end. But it is our interest that it enjoy this peace meanwhile in this life; for as long as the two cities are commingled, we also enjoy the peace of Babylon. For from Babylon the people of God is so freed that it meanwhile sojourns in its company. And therefore the apostle also admonished the Church to pray for kings and those in authority, assigning as the reason, "that we may live a quiet and tranquil life in all godliness and love."[78] And the prophet Jeremiah, when predicting the captivity that was to befall the ancient people of God, and giving them the divine command to go obediently to Babylonia, and thus serve their God, counselled them also to pray for Babylonia, saying, "In the peace thereof shall ye have peace,"[79]—the temporal peace which the good and the wicked together enjoy.

Chapter 27.—That the peace of those who serve God cannot in this mortal life be apprehended in its perfection.

But the peace which is peculiar to ourselves we enjoy now with God by faith, and shall hereafter enjoy eternally with Him by sight. But the peace which we enjoy

---

[77] Psalm 33:12.
[78] 1 Timothy 2:2.
[79] Jeremiah 29:7.

in this life, whether common to all or peculiar to ourselves, is rather the solace of our misery than the positive enjoyment of felicity. Our very righteousness, too, though true in so far as it has respect to the true good, is yet in this life of such a kind that it consists rather in the remission of sins than in the perfecting of virtues. Witness the prayer of the whole city of God in its pilgrim state, for it cries to God by the mouth of all its members, "Forgive us our debts as we forgive our debtors."[80] And this prayer is efficacious not for those whose faith is "without works and dead," but for those whose faith "worketh by love."[81] For as reason, though subjected to God, is yet "pressed down by the corruptible body,"[82] so long as it is in this mortal condition, it has not perfect authority over vice, and therefore this prayer is needed by the righteous. For though it exercises authority, the vices do not submit without a struggle. For however well one maintains the conflict, and however thoroughly he has subdued these enemies, there steals in some evil thing, which, if it do not find ready expression in act, slips out by the lips, or insinuates itself into the thought; and therefore his peace is not full so long as he is at war with his vices. For it is a doubtful conflict he wages with those that resist, and his victory over those that are defeated is not secure, but full of anxiety and effort. Amidst these temptations, therefore, of all which it has been summarily said in the divine oracles, "Is not human life upon earth a temptation?"[83] who but a proud man can presume that he so lives that he has no need to say to God, "Forgive us our debts?" And such a man is not great, but swollen and puffed up with vanity, and is justly resisted by Him who abundantly gives grace to the humble. In this, then, consists the righteousness of a man, that he submit himself to God, his body to his soul, and his vices, even when they rebel, to his reason, which either defeats or at least resists them; and also that he beg from God grace to do his duty, and the pardon of his sins, and that he render to God thanks for all the blessings he receives. But, in that final peace to which all our righteousness has reference, and for the sake of which it is maintained, as our nature shall enjoy a sound immortality and incorruption, and shall have

no more vices, and as we shall experience no resistance either from ourselves or from others, it will not be necessary that reason should rule vices which no longer exist, but God shall rule the man, and the soul shall rule the body, with a sweetness and facility suitable to the felicity of a life which is done with bondage. And this condition shall there be eternal, and we shall be assured of its eternity; and thus the peace of this blessedness and the blessedness of this peace shall be the supreme good.

Chapter 28.—The end of the wicked.

But, on the other hand, they who do not belong to this city of God shall inherit eternal misery, which is also called the second death, because the soul shall then be separated from God its life, and therefore cannot be said to live, and the body shall be subjected to eternal pains. And consequently this second death shall be the more severe, because no death shall terminate it. But war being contrary to peace, as misery to happiness, and life to death, it is not without reason asked what kind of war can be found in the end of the wicked answering to the peace which is declared to be the end of the righteous? The person who puts this question has only to observe what it is in war that is hurtful and destructive, and he shall see that it is nothing else than the mutual opposition and conflict of things. And can he conceive a more grievous and bitter war than that in which the will is so opposed to passion, and passion to the will, that their hostility can never be terminated by the victory of either, and in which the violence of pain so conflicts with the nature of the body, that neither yields to the other? For in this life, when this conflict has arisen, either pain conquers and death expels the feeling of it, or nature conquers and health expels the pain. But in the world to come the pain continues that it may torment, and the nature endures that it may be sensible of it; and neither ceases to exist, lest punishment also should cease. Now, as it is through the last judgment that men pass to these ends, the good to the supreme good, the evil to the supreme evil, I will treat of this judgment in the following book.

---

[80] Matthew 6:12.

[81] Galatians 5:6.

[82] Wisdom 9:15.

[83] Job 7:1.

3. ST. PERPETUA

THE PASSION OF SAINTS PERPETUA AND FELICITAS

Vibia Perpetua, a member of a high-ranking Roman family, was arrested along with four other Christians under a decree of Emperor Septimus Severus in 202 during a period of intense persecution. She was executed in the arena in Carthage on March 7, 203. Her *Passion*, or account of her martyrdom, was apparently written in large part by Perpetua herself, making it one of the few texts by a woman from this period. An unknown contemporary author wrote the beginning and end of the text, placing it in the tradition of Monatism, a Christian movement that emphasized female prophesy and strict asceticism, and encouraged Christians to seek martyrdom. *The Passion*, with its prophetic visions linked to scriptural imagery and its prominent female voice, had a great influence in later martyrologies not only in North Africa, but in the eastern Mediterranean as well.

Source: Acts of the Christian Martyrs, trans. H.R. Musurillo (Oxford: Clarendon Press, 1972), 106–31.

Further Reading: Brent D. Shaw, "The Passion of Perpetua," *Past & Present* 139 (1993): 3–45.

1. The deeds recounted about the faith in ancient times were a proof of God's favor and achieved the spiritual strengthening of men as well; and they were set forth in writing precisely that honor might be rendered to God and comfort to men by the recollection of the past through the written word. Should not then more recent examples be set down that contribute equally to both ends? For indeed these too will one day become ancient and needful for the ages to come, even though in our own day they may enjoy less prestige because of the prior claim of antiquity.

Let those then who would restrict the power of the one Spirit to times and seasons look to this: the more recent events should be considered the greater, being later than those of old, and this is a consequence of the extraordinary graces promised for the last stage of time. For *in the last days, God declares, I will pour out my Spirit upon all flesh and their sons and daughters shall prophesy and on my manservants and my maidservants I will pour my Spirit, and the young men shall see visions and the old men shall dream dreams.* So too we hold in honor and acknowledge not only new prophecies but new visions as well, according to the promise. And we consider all the other functions of the Holy Spirit as intended for the good of the Church; for the same Spirit has been sent to distribute all his gifts to all, as the Lord apportions to everyone. For this reason we deem it imperative to set

them forth and to make them known through the word for the glory of God. Thus no one of weak or despairing faith may think that supernatural grace was present only among men of ancient times, either in the grace of martyrdom or of visions, for God always achieves what he promises, as a witness to the non-believer and a blessing to the faithful.

And so, my brethren and little children, *that which we have heard and have touched with our hands we proclaim also to you, so that* those of you that were witnesses may recall the glory of the Lord and those that now learn of it through hearing *may have fellowship* with the holy martyrs and, through them, *with the Lord Christ Jesus*, to whom belong splendor and honor for all ages. Amen.

2. A number of young catechumens were arrested, Revocatus and his fellow slave Felicitas, Saturninus and Secundulus, and with them Vibia Perpetua, a newly married woman of good family and upbringing. Her mother and father were still alive and one of her two brothers was a catechumen like herself. She was about twenty-two years old and had an infant son at the breast. (Now from this point on the entire account of her ordeal is her own, according to her own ideas and in the way that she herself wrote it down.)

3. While we were still under arrest (she said) my father out of love for me was trying to persuade me and shake

my resolution. "Father," said I, "do you see this vase here, for example, or water pot or whatever?"

"Yes, I do," said he.

And I told him: "Could it be called by any other name than what it is?"

And he said: "No."

"Well, so too I cannot be called anything other than what I am, a Christian."

At this my father was so angered by the word "Christian" that he moved towards me as though he would pluck my eyes out. But he left it at that and departed, vanquished along with his diabolical arguments. For a few days afterwards I gave thanks to the Lord that I was separated from my father, and I was comforted by his absence. During these few days I was baptized, and I was inspired by the Spirit not to ask for any other favor after the water but simply the perseverance of the flesh. A few days later we were lodged in the prison; and I was terrified, as I had never before been in such a dark hole. What a difficult time it was! With the crowd the heat was stifling; then there was the extortion of the soldiers; and to crown all, I was tortured with worry for my baby there. Then Tertius and Pomponius, those blessed deacons who tried to take care of us, bribed the soldiers to allow us to go to a better part of the prison to refresh ourselves for a few hours. Everyone then left that dungeon and shifted for himself. I nursed my baby, who was faint from hunger. In my anxiety I spoke to my mother about the child, I tried to comfort my brother, and I gave the child in their charge. I was in pain because I saw them suffering out of pity for me. These were the trials I had to endure for many days. Then I got permission for my baby to stay with me in prison. At once I recovered my health, relieved as I was of my worry and anxiety over the child. My prison had suddenly become a palace, so that I wanted to be there rather than anywhere else.

4. Then my brother said to me: "Dear sister, you are greatly privileged; surely you might ask for a vision to discover whether you are to be condemned or freed." Faithfully I promised that I would, for I knew that I could speak with the Lord, whose great blessings I had come to experience. And so I said: "I shall tell you tomorrow." Then I made my request and this was the vision I had.

I saw a ladder of tremendous height made of bronze, reaching all the way to the heavens, but it was so narrow that only one person could climb up at a time. To the sides of the ladder were attached all sorts of metal weapons: there were swords, spears, hooks, daggers, and spikes; so that if anyone tried to climb up carelessly or without paying attention, he would be mangled and his flesh would adhere to the weapons.

At the foot of the ladder lay a dragon of enormous size, and it would attack those who tried to climb up and try to terrify them from doing so. And Saturus was the first to go up, he who was later to give himself up of his own accord. He had been the builder of our strength, although he was not present when we were arrested. And he arrived at the top of the staircase and he looked back and said to me:

"Perpetua, I am waiting for you. But take care; do not let the dragon bite you."

"He will not harm me," I said, "in the name of Christ Jesus."

Slowly, as though he were afraid of me, the dragon stuck his head out from underneath the ladder. Then, using it as my first step, I trod on his head and went up.

Then I saw an immense garden, and in it a gray-haired man sat in shepherd's garb; tall he was, and milking sheep. And standing around him were many thousands of people clad in white garments. He raised his head, looked at me, and said:

"I am glad you have come, my child."

He called me over to him and gave me, as it were, a mouthful of the milk he was drawing; and I took it into my cupped hands and consumed it. And all those who stood around said: "Amen!" At the sound of this word I came to, with the taste of something sweet still in my mouth. I at once told this to my brother, and we realized that we would have to suffer, and that from now on we would no longer have any hope in this life.

5. A few days later there was a rumor that we were going to be given a hearing. My father also arrived from the city, worn with worry, and he came to see me with the idea of persuading me.

"Daughter," he said, "have pity on my gray head—have pity on me your father, if I deserve to be called your father, if I have favored you above all your brothers, if I have raised you to reach this prime of your life. Do not abandon me to be the reproach of men. Think of your brothers, think of your mother and your aunt, think of your child, who will not be able to live once you are gone. Give up your pride! You will destroy all of us! None of us will ever be able to speak freely again if anything happens to you."

This was the way my father spoke out of love for me, kissing my hands and throwing himself down before me. With tears in his eyes he no longer addressed me as his daughter but as a woman. I was sorry for my father's sake, because he alone of all my kin would be unhappy to see me suffer.

I tried to comfort him saying: "It will all happen in the prisoner's dock as God wills; for you may be sure that we are not left to ourselves but are all in his power."

And he left me in great sorrow.

6. One day while we were eating breakfast we were suddenly hurried off for a hearing. We arrived at the forum, and straight away the story went about the neighborhood near the forum and a huge crowd gathered. We walked up to the prisoner's dock. All the others when questioned admitted their guilt. Then, when it came my turn, my father appeared with my son, dragged me from the step, and said "Perform the sacrifice—have pity on your baby!"

Hilarianus the governor, who had received his judicial powers as the successor of the late proconsul[84] Minucius Timinianus, said to me: "Have pity on your father's gray head; have pity on your infant son. Offer the sacrifice for the welfare of the emperors."

"I will not," I retorted.

"Are you a Christian?" said Hilarianus.

And I said: "Yes, I am."

When my father persisted in trying to dissuade me, Hilarianus ordered him to be thrown to the ground and beaten with a rod. I felt sorry for father, just as if I myself had been beaten. I felt sorry for his pathetic old age.

Then Hilarianus passed sentence on all of us: we were condemned to the beasts, and we returned to prison in high spirits. But my baby had got used to being nursed at the breast and to staying with me in prison. So I sent the deacon Pomponius straight away to my father to ask for the baby. But father refused to give him over. But as God willed, the baby had no further desire for the breast, nor did I suffer any inflammation; and so I was relieved of any anxiety for my child and of any discomfort in my breasts.

7. Some days later when we were all at prayer, suddenly while praying I spoke out and uttered the name Dinocrates. I was surprised; for the name had never entered my mind until that moment. And I was pained when I recalled what had happened to him. At once I realized that I was privileged to pray for him. I began to pray for him and to sigh deeply for him before the Lord. That very night I had the following vision. I saw Dinocrates coming out of a dark hole, where there were many others with him, very hot and thirsty, pale and dirty. On his face was the wound he had when he died.

Now Dinocrates had been my br[other in] the flesh; but he had died horribly of [a cancer] when he was seven years old, and his d[eath was a cause] of loathing to everyone. Thus it was for [him that I made] my prayer. There was a great abyss bet[ween us, so that neither] could approach the other. Where Dinoc[rates stood there] was a pool full of water; and its rim was [higher than] the child's height, so that Dinocrates had to stretch himself up to drink. I was sorry that, though the pool had water in it, Dinocrates could not drink because of the height of the rim. Then I woke up, realizing that my brother was suffering. But I was confident that I could help him in his trouble; and I prayed for him every day until we were transferred to the military prison. For we were supposed to fight with the beasts at the military games to be held on the occasion of the Emperor Geta's birthday. And I prayed for my brother day and night with tears and sighs that this favor might be granted me.

8. On the day we were kept in chains, I had this vision shown to me. I saw the same spot that I had seen before, but there was Dinocrates all clean, well dressed, and refreshed. I saw a scar where the wound had been; and the pool that I had seen before now had its rim lowered to the level of the child's waist. And Dinocrates kept drinking water from it, and there above the rim was a golden bowl full of water. And Dinocrates drew close and began to drink from it, and yet the bowl remained full. And when he had drunk enough of the water, he began to play as children do. Then I awoke, and I realized that he had been delivered from his suffering.

9. Some days later, an adjutant named Pudens, who was in charge of the prison, began to show us great honor, realizing that we possessed some great power within us. And he began to allow many visitors to see us for our mutual comfort.

Now the day of the contest was approaching, and my father came to see me overwhelmed with sorrow. He started tearing the hairs from his beard and threw them on the ground; he then threw himself on the ground and began to curse his old age and to say such words as would move all creation. I felt sorry for his unhappy old age.

10. The day before we were to fight with the beasts I saw the following vision. Pomponius the deacon came to the prison gates and began to knock violently. I went out and opened the gate for him. He was dressed in an unbelted white tunic, wearing elaborate sandals. And he said to me: "Perpetua, come; we are waiting for you."

Then he took my hand and we began to walk through rough and broken country. At last we came to

---

[84] Roman provincial governor.

the amphitheater out of breath, and he led me into the center of the arena.

Then he told me: "Do not be afraid. I am here, struggling with you." Then he left.

I looked at the enormous crowd who watched in astonishment. I was surprised that no beasts were let loose on me; for I knew that I was condemned to die by the beasts. Then out came an Egyptian against me, of vicious appearance, together with his seconds, to fight with me. There also came up to me some handsome young men to be my seconds and assistants. My clothes were stripped off, and suddenly I was a man. My seconds began to rub me down with oil (as they are wont to do before a contest). Then I saw the Egyptian on the other side rolling in the dust. Next there came forth a man of marvelous stature, such that he rose above the top of the amphitheater. He was clad in a beltless purple tunic with two stripes (one on either side) running down the middle of his chest. He wore sandals that were wondrously made of gold and silver, and he carried a wand like an athletic trainer and a green branch on which there were golden apples.

And he asked for silence and said: "If this Egyptian defeats her he will slay her with the sword. But if she defeats him, she will receive this branch." Then he withdrew.

We drew close to one another and began to let our fists fly. My opponent tried to get hold of my feet, but I kept striking him in the face with the heels of my feet. Then I was raised up into the air and I began to pummel him without as it were touching the ground. Then when I noticed there was a lull, I put my two hands together linking the fingers of one hand with those of the other and thus I got hold of his head. He fell flat on his face and I stepped on his head.

The crowd began to shout and my assistants started to sing psalms. Then I walked up to the trainer and took the branch. He kissed me and said to me: "Peace be with you, my daughter!" I began to walk in triumph towards the Gate of Life.[85] Then I awoke. I realized that it was not with wild animals that I would fight but with the Devil, but I knew that I would win the victory. So much for what I did up until the eve of the contest. About what happened at the contest itself, let him write of it who will.

11. But the blessed Saturus has also made known his own vision and he has written it out with his own hand. We had died, he said, and had put off the flesh, and we

began to be carried towards the east by four angels who did not touch us with their hands. But we moved along not on our backs facing upwards but as though we were climbing up a gentle hill. And when we were free of the world, we first saw an intense light. And I said to Perpetua (for she was at my side): "This is what the Lord promised us. We have received his promise."

While we were being carried by these four angels, a great open space appeared, which seemed to be a garden, with rose bushes and all manner of flowers. The trees were as tall as cypresses, and their leaves were constantly falling. In the garden there were four other angels more splendid than the others. When they saw us they paid us homage and said to the other angels in admiration: "Why, they are here! They are here!"

Then the four angels that were carrying us grew fearful and set us down. Then we walked across to an open area by way of a broad road, and there we met Jucundus, Saturninus, and Artaxius, who were burnt alive in the same persecution, together with Quintus who had actually died as a martyr in prison. We asked them where they had been. And the other angels said to us: "First come and enter and greet the Lord."

12. Then we came to a place whose walls seemed to be constructed of light. And in front of the gate stood four angels, who entered in and put on white robes. We also entered and we heard the sound of voices in unison chanting endlessly: "*Holy, holy, holy!*" In the same place we seemed to see an aged man with white hair and a youthful face, though we did not see his feet. On his right and left were four elders, and behind them stood other aged men. Surprised, we entered and stood before a throne: four angels lifted us up and we kissed the aged man and he touched our faces with his hand. And the elders said to us: "Let us rise." And we rose and gave the kiss of peace. Then the elders said to us: "Go and play."

To Perpetua I said: "Your wish is granted."

She said to me: "Thanks be to God that I am happier here now than I was in the flesh."

13. Then we went out and before the gates we saw the bishop Optatus on the right and Aspasius the presbyter and teacher on the left, each of them far apart and in sorrow. They threw themselves at our feet and said: "Make peace between us. For you have gone away and left us thus."

And we said to them: "Are you not our bishop, and are you not our presbyter? How can you fall at our feet?"

We were very moved and embraced them. Perpetua then began to speak with them in Greek, and we drew them apart into the garden under a rose arbor.

---

[85] The *Porta Sanavivaria* by which victorious gladiators or those spared by the people could leave.

While we were talking with them, the angels said to them: "Allow them to rest. Settle whatever quarrels you have among yourselves." And they were put to confusion. Then they said to Optatus: "You must scold your flock. They approach you as though they had come from the games, quarreling about the different teams."

And it seemed as though they wanted to close the gates. And there we began to recognize many of our brethren, martyrs among them. All of us were sustained by a most delicious odor that seemed to satisfy us. And then I woke up happy.

14. Such were the remarkable visions of these martyrs, Saturus and Perpetua, written by themselves. As for Secundulus, God called him from this world earlier than the others while he was still in prison, by a special grace that he might not have to face the animals. Yet his flesh, if not his spirit, knew the sword.

15. As for Felicitas, she too enjoyed the Lord's favor in this wise. She had been pregnant when she was arrested, and was now in her eighth month. As the day of the spectacle drew near she was very distressed that her martyrdom would be postponed because of her pregnancy; for it is against the law for women with child to be executed. Thus she might have to shed her holy, innocent blood afterwards along with others who were common criminals. Her comrades in martyrdom were also saddened; for they were afraid that they would have to leave behind so fine a companion to travel alone on the same road to hope. And so, two days before the contest, they poured forth a prayer to the Lord in one torrent of common grief. And immediately after their prayer the birth pains came upon her. She suffered a good deal in her labor because of the natural difficulty of an eight months' delivery.

Hence one of the assistants of the prison guards said to her: "You suffer so much now—what will you do when you are tossed to the beasts? Little did you think of them when you refused to sacrifice."

"What I am suffering now," she replied, "I suffer by myself. But then another will be inside me who will suffer for me, just as I shall be suffering for him."

And she gave birth to a girl; and one of the sisters brought her up as her own daughter.

16. Therefore, since the Holy Spirit has permitted the story of this contest to be written down and by so permitting has willed it, we shall carry out the command or, indeed, the commission of the most saintly Perpetua, however unworthy I might be to add any thing to this glorious story. At the same time I shall add one example of her perseverance and nobility of soul.

The military tribune had treated them with extraordinary severity because on the information of certain very foolish people he became afraid that they would be spirited out of the prison by magical spells.

Perpetua spoke to him directly. "Why can you not even allow us to refresh ourselves properly? For we are the most distinguished of the condemned prisoners, seeing that we belong to the emperor; we are to fight on his very birthday. Would it not be to your credit if we were brought forth on the day in a healthier condition?"

The officer became disturbed and grew red. So it was that he gave the order that they were to be more humanely treated; and he allowed her brothers and other persons to visit, so that the prisoners could dine in their company. By this time the adjutant who was head of the jail was himself a Christian.

17. On the day before, when they had their last meal, which is called the free banquet,[86] they celebrated not a banquet but rather a love feast. They spoke to the mob with the same steadfastness, warned them of God's judgment, stressing the joy they would have in their suffering, and ridiculing the curiosity of those that came to see them. Saturus said: "Will not tomorrow be enough for you? Why are you so eager to see something that you dislike? Our friends today will be our enemies on the morrow. But take careful note of what we look like so that you will recognize us on the day." Thus everyone would depart from the prison in amazement, and many of them began to believe.

18. The day of their victory dawned, and they marched from the prison to the amphitheater joyfully as though they were going to heaven, with calm faces, trembling, if at all, with joy rather than fear. Perpetua went along with shining countenance and calm step, as the beloved of God, as a wife of Christ, putting down everyone's stare by her own intense gaze. With them also was Felicitas, glad that she had safely given birth so that now she could fight the beasts, going from one blood bath to another, from the midwife to the gladiator, ready to wash after childbirth in a second baptism. They were then led up to the gates and the men were forced to put on the robes of priests of Saturn, the women the dress of the priestesses of Ceres. But the noble Perpetua strenuously resisted this to the end. "We came to this of our own free will that our freedom should not be violated. We agreed to pledge our lives provided that we would do no such thing. You agreed with us to do this." Even injustice recognized

---

[86] The public feast given to the condemned.

justice. The military tribune agreed. They were to be brought into the arena just as they were. Perpetua then began to sing a psalm: she was already treading on the head of the Egyptian. Revocatus, Saturninus, and Saturus began to warn the onlooking mob. Then when they came within sight of Hilarianus, they suggested by their motions and gestures: "You have condemned us, but God will condemn you" was what they were saying.

At this the crowds became enraged and demanded that they be scourged before a line of gladiators. And they rejoiced at this that they had obtained a share in the Lord's sufferings.

19. But he who said, "Ask and you shall receive," answered their prayer by giving each one the death he had asked for. For when ever they would discuss among themselves their desire for martyrdom, Saturninus indeed insisted that he wanted to be exposed to all the different beasts, that his crown might be all the more glorious. And so at the outset of the contest he and Revocatus were matched with a leopard, and then while in the stocks they were attacked by a bear. As for Saturus, he dreaded nothing more than a bear, and he counted on being killed by one bite of a leopard. Then he was matched with a wild boar; but the gladiator who had tied him to the animal was gored by the boar and died a few days after the contest, whereas Saturus was only dragged along. Then when he was bound in the stocks awaiting the bear, the animal refused to come out of the cages, so that Saturus was called back once more unhurt.

20. For the young women, however, the Devil had prepared a mad heifer. This was an unusual animal, but it was chosen that their sex might be matched with that of the beast. So they were stripped naked, placed in nets and thus brought out into the arena. Even the crowd was horrified when they saw that one was a delicate young girl and the other was a woman fresh from child birth with the milk still dripping from her breasts. And so they were brought back again and dressed in unbelted tunics.

First the heifer tossed Perpetua and she fell on her back. Then sitting up she pulled down the tunic that was ripped along the side so that it covered her thighs, thinking more of her modesty than of her pain. Next she asked for a pin to fasten her untidy hair: for it was not right that a martyr should die with her hair in disorder, lest she might seem to be mourning in her hour of triumph.

Then she got up. And seeing that Felicitas had been crushed to the ground, she went over to her, gave her hand, and lifted her up. Then the two stood side by side. But the cruelty of the mob was by now appeased, and so they were called back through the Gate of Life.

There Perpetua was held up by a man named Rusticus who was at the time a catechumen and kept close to her. She awoke from a kind of sleep (so absorbed had she been in ecstasy in the Spirit) and she began to look about her. Then to the amazement of all she said: "When are we going to be thrown to that heifer or whatever it is?"

When told that this had already happened, she refused to believe it until she noticed the marks of her rough experience on her person and her dress. Then she called for her brother and spoke to him together with the catechumens and said: "You must all *stand fast in the faith* and love one another, and do not be weakened by what we have gone through."

21. At another gate Saturus was earnestly addressing the soldier Pudens. "It is exactly," he said, "as I foretold and predicted. So far not one animal has touched me. So now you may believe me with all your heart: I am going in there and I shall be finished off with one bite of the leopard." And immediately as the contest was coming to a close a leopard was let loose, and after one bite Saturus was so drenched with blood that as he came away the mob roared in witness to his second baptism: "Well washed! Well washed!"[87] For well washed indeed was one who had been bathed in this manner.

Then he said to the soldier Pudens: "Goodbye. Remember me, and remember the faith. These things should not disturb you but rather strengthen you."

And with this he asked Pudens for a ring from his finger, and dipping it into his wound he gave it back to him again as a pledge and as a record of his bloodshed.

Shortly after he was thrown unconscious with the rest in the usual spot to have his throat cut. But the mob asked that their bodies be brought out into the open that their eyes might be the guilty witnesses of the sword that pierced their flesh. And so the martyrs got up and went to the spot of their own accord as the people wanted them to, and kissing one another they sealed their martyrdom with the ritual kiss of peace. The others took the sword in silence and without moving, especially Saturus, who being the first to climb the stairway was the first to die. For once again he was waiting for Perpetua. Perpetua, however, had yet to taste more pain. She screamed as she was struck on the bone; then she took the trembling hand of the young gladiator and guided it to her throat. It was as though so great a woman, feared as she was by the unclean spirit, could not be dispatched unless she herself were willing.

---

[87] An ironic use of the greeting to bathers in the public baths.

Ah, most valiant and blessed martyrs! Truly are you called and chosen for the glory of Christ Jesus our Lord! And any man who exalts, honors, and worships his glory should read for the consolation of the Church these new deeds of heroism which are no less significant than the tales of old. For these new manifestations of virtue will bear witness to one and the same Spirit who still operates, and to God the Father almighty, to his Son Jesus Christ our Lord, to whom is splendor and immeasurable power for all the ages. Amen.

Questions for Study

The rise of Christianity is one of the major phenomena of late antiquity and visible in all the texts in this section. In what ways do the texts illustrate the effect of Christianity's increasing prominence? How might one compare the legal status of women in the *Theodosian Code* with the behavior of Perpetua? How does Augustine contrast the history of Rome with Christian belief?

The Barbarian World

4. TACITUS Cornelius (c. 56–120)

GERMANIA

In 98 the Roman historian Cornelius Tacitus (ca. 56–ca. 120) wrote a brief description of the Germanic peoples living beyond the Rhine. The *Germania* was his second work, written after the *Life of Agricola* (a biography and tribute to his father-in-law and the elaboration of his life as a model for Roman senatorial behavior) but in the years before his two major historical works, the *Historiae* and *Annales*. His account is based on the secondary? writings of previous geographers and historians, especially Pliny the Elder's lost *German Wars*, as well as on interviews with people who had first-hand experience with the Germanic peoples. Although largely accurate in its details, the treatise organizes and filters Tacitus's data through the classical ethnological categories. Its purpose was less to inform Romans about the Germans than to criticize Roman customs and morals by contrasting them with those of the barbarians.

Source: Tacitus, *Dialogus, Agricola, Germania* (London: Heineman, 1914). *Germania* trans. Maurice Hutton, rev. D. LePan, 1989.
Further Reading: Ronald H. Martin, *Tacitus* (Berkeley: University of California Press, 1981).

1 Undivided Germany is separated from the Gauls, Rhaetians, and Pannonians by the rivers Rhine and Danube: from the Sarmatians and Dacians by mutual fear or mountains: the rest of it is surrounded by the ocean, which enfolds wide peninsulas and islands of vast expanse, some of whose people and kings have but recently become known to us: war has lifted the curtain.

The Rhine, rising from the inaccessible and precipitous crest of the Rhaetian Alps, after turning west for a reach of some length is lost in the North Sea. The Danube pours from the sloping and not very lofty ridge of Mount Abnoba, and visits several peoples on its course, until at length it emerges by six of its channels into the Pontic Sea: the seventh mouth is swallowed in marshes.

2 As for the Germans themselves, I should suppose them to be native to the area and only very slightly blended with new arrivals from other races or regions; for in ancient times people who sought to migrate reached their destination by sea and not by land; while, in the second place, the great ocean on the further side

of Germany—at the opposite end of the world, so to speak, from us—is rarely visited by ships from our world. Besides, even apart from the perils of an awful and unknown sea, who would have left Asia or Africa or Italy to look for Germany? With its wild scenery and harsh climate it is pleasant neither to live in nor look upon unless it be one's home.

Their ancient hymns—the only record of history which they possess—celebrate a god Tuisto, a scion of the soil, and his son Mannus as the founders of their race. To Mannus they ascribe three sons, from whose names the tribes of the seashore came to be known as Ingaevones, the central tribes as Herminones, and the rest as Istaevones. Some authorities, using the license which pertains to antiquity, claim more sons for the god and a larger number of race names: Marsi, Gambrivii, Suebi, Vandilii. These are, they say, real and ancient names, while the name of "Germany" is new. The first tribes in fact to cross the Rhine and expel the Gauls, though now called Tungri, were then styled Germans: so little by little the name—a tribal, not a national, name—prevailed, until the whole people were called by the artificial name of "Germans," first only by the victorious tribe in order to intimidate the Gauls, but afterwards among themselves also.

3 The authorities also record how Hercules appeared among the Germans, and on the eve of battle the natives chant "Hercules, the first of brave men." They use as well another chant—"barritus" is the name they use for it—to inspire courage; and they forecast the results of the coming battle from the sound of the cry. Intimidation or timidity depends on the concert of the warriors; the chant seems to them to mean not so much unison of voices as union of hearts; the object they specially seek is a certain volume of hoarseness, a crashing roar, their shields being brought up to their lips, that the voice may swell to a fuller and deeper note by means of the echo.

To return. Ulysses also—in the opinion of some authorities—was carried during his long and legendary wanderings into this ocean, and reached the lands of Germany. Asciburgium, which stands on the banks of the Rhine and has inhabitants today, was founded, they say, and named by him; further, they say that an altar dedicated by Ulysses, who added to his own inscription that of his father Laertes, was once found at the same place, and that certain monuments and barrows, marked with Greek letters, are still extant on the borderland between Germany and Rhaetia. I have no intention of furnishing evidence to establish or refute these assertions: every one according to his temperament may minimize or magnify their credibility.

4 Personally, I agree with those who hold that in the peoples of Germany there has been given to the world a nation untainted by intermarriage with other peoples, a peculiar people and pure, like no one but themselves; whence it comes that their physique, in spite of their vast numbers, is identical: fierce blue eyes, red hair, tall frames. They are powerful too, but only spasmodically; they have no fondness for feats of endurance or for hard work. Nor are they well able to bear thirst and heat; to cold and hunger, thanks to the climate and the soil, they are accustomed.

5 There are some varieties in the appearance of the country, but in general it is a land of bristling forests and unhealthy marshes; the rainfall is heavier on the side of Gaul; the winds are higher on the side of Noricum and Pannonia.

It is fertile in cereals, but unkind to fruit-bearing trees; it is rich in flocks and herds, but for the most part they are undersized. Even the cattle lack natural beauty and majestic brows. The pride of the people is rather in the number of their beasts, which constitute the only form of wealth they value.

The gods have denied them gold and silver, whether in mercy or in wrath I find it hard to say. Not that I would assert that Germany has no veins bearing gold or silver, for who has explored there? At any rate, they are not affected, like their neighbors, by the use and possession of such things. One may see among them silver vases, given as gifts to their commanders and chieftains, but treated as of no more value than earthenware. Although the border tribes for purposes of trade treat gold and silver as precious metals, and recognize and collect certain coins of our money, the tribes of the interior practice barter in the simpler and older fashion. The coinage which appeals to them is the old and long-familiar: the denarii with milled edges, showing the two-horsed chariot. They prefer silver to gold: not that they have any feeling in the matter, but because a number of silver pieces is easier to use for people whose purchases consist of cheap objects of general utility.

6 Even iron is not plentiful among them, as may be gathered from the style of their weapons. Few have swords or the longer kind of lance: they carry short spears, in their language "*frameae*," with a narrow and small iron head, so sharp and so handy in use that they fight with the same weapon, as circumstances demand, both at close quarters and at a distance. The mounted man is content with a shield and *framea*: the infantry launch showers of spears as well, each man a volley, and

are able to hurl these great distances, for they wear no outer clothing, or at most a light cloak.

Their garb is for the most part quite plain; only shields are decorated, each a few colors. Few have breast-plates: scarcely one or two at most have metal or hide helmets. The horses are conspicuous for neither beauty nor speed; but then neither are they trained like our horses to run in shifting circles: the Germans ride them forwards only or to the right, with but one turn from the straight, dressing the line so closely as they wheel that no one is left behind. In general there is more strength in their infantry, and accordingly cavalry and infantry fight in one body; the swift-footed infantryman, whom they pick out of the whole body of warriors and place in front of the line, are well-adapted to cavalry battles. The number of these men is fixed—one hundred from each canton, and among themselves "the Hundred" is the precise name they use. What was once a number only has become a title and a distinction. The battle-line itself is arranged in wedges. To retire, provided you press on again, they treat as a question of tactics, not of cowardice; they carry off their dead and wounded even in drawn battles. To have abandoned one's shield is the height of disgrace. The man so dishonored cannot be present at religious rites, nor attend a council; many survivors of war have ended their infamy with a noose.

7 They choose their kings on the grounds of birth, their generals on the basis of courage. The authority of their kings is not unlimited or arbitrary; their generals control them by example rather than command, the troops admiring their energy and the conspicuous place they take in front of the line. But anything beyond this—capital punishment, imprisonment, even a blow—is permitted only to the priests, and then not as a penalty or under the general's orders, but in obedience to the god whom they believe accompanies them on campaign. Certain totems, in fact, and emblems are fetched from groves and carried into battle. The strongest incentive to courage lies in this, that neither chance nor casual grouping makes the squadron or the wedge, but family and kinship. Close at hand, too, are their dearest, so that they hear the wailing voices of women and cries of children. Here are the witnesses who are in each man's eyes most precious; here the praise he covets most. The warriors take their wounds to mother and wife, who do not shrink from counting the hurts and demanding a sight of them: they give to the combatants food and encouragement.

8 Tradition relates that some battles that seemed lost have been restored by the women, by their incessant prayers and by the baring of their breasts; for so it is brought home to the men that slavery, which they dread much more keenly on their women's account, is close at hand. It follows that the loyalty of those tribes is more effectively guaranteed if you hold, among other hostages, girls of noble birth.

Further, they conceive that in women is a certain uncanny and prophetic sense: they neither scorn to consult them nor slight their answers. In the reign of Vespasian of happy memory we saw Velaeda treated as a deity by many during a long period; but in ancient times they also reverenced Albruna and many other women—in no spirit of flattery, nor for the manufacture of goddesses.

9 Of the gods they most worship Mercury, to whom on certain days they count even the sacrifice of human life lawful. Hercules and Mars they appease with such animal life as is permissible. A section of the Suebi sacrifices also to Isis:[1] the cause and origin of this foreign worship I have not succeeded in discovering, except that the emblem itself, which takes the shape of a Liburnian galley, shows that the ritual is imported.

Apart from this they deem it incompatible with the majesty of the heavenly host to confine the gods within walls, or to mold them into any likeness of the human face. They consecrate groves and thickets, and they give divine names to that mysterious presence which is visible only to the eyes of faith.

10 To divination and casting lots they pay as much attention as any one. The method of drawing lots is uniform. A bough is cut from a nut-bearing tree and divided into slips. These are distinguished by certain runes and spread casually and at random over white cloth. Afterwards, should the inquiry be official the priest of the state, if private the father of the family in person, after prayers to the gods and with eyes turned to heaven takes up one slip at a time till he has done this on three separate occasions. After taking the three he interprets them according to the runes which have already been stamped on them. If the message is a prohibition, no inquiry on the same matter is made during the same day; if the message gives permission, further confirmation is required by means of divination. Among the Germans divination by consultation of the cries and flight of birds is well known. Another form of divination peculiar to them is to seek the omens and warnings furnished by horses.

In the same groves and thickets are fed certain white horses, never soiled by mortal use. These are yoked to a

---

[1] Egyptian mother goddess widely worshiped in the Roman Empire.

sacred chariot and accompanied by the priest and king, or other chief of the state, who then observe their neighing and snorting. On no other form of divination is more reliance placed, not merely by the people but also by their leaders. The priests they regard as the servants of the gods, but the horses are their confidants.

They have another method of taking divinations, by means of which they probe the issue of serious wars. A member of the tribe at war with them is somehow or other captured and pitted against a selected champion of their own countrymen, each in his tribal armor. The victory of one or the other is taken as a presage.

11 On small matters the chiefs consult, on larger questions the community; but with this limitation: even when the decision rests with the people, the matter is considered first by the chiefs. They meet, unless there is some unforeseen and sudden emergency, on days set apart—when the moon is either new or full. They regard these times as the most auspicious for the transaction of business. They count not days as we do, but by nights and their decisions and proclamations are subject to this principle; the night, that is, seems to take precedence over the day.

It is a foible of their freedom that they do not meet at once and when commanded, but waste two or three days by dilatoriness in assembling. When they are finally ready to begin, they take their seats carrying arms. Silence is called for by the priests, who then have the power to force obedience. Then a king or a chief is listened to, in order of age, birth, glory in war, or eloquence. Such figures command attention through the prestige which belongs to their counsel rather than any prescriptive right to command. If the advice tendered is displeasing, the people reject it with groans; if it pleases them, they clash their spears. The most complimentary expression of assent is this martial approbation.

12 At this assembly it is also permissible to lay accusations and to bring capital charges. The nature of the death penalty differs according to the offense: traitors and deserters are hung from trees; cowards, poor fighters, and notorious evil-livers are plunged in the mud of marshes with a hurdle on their heads. These differences of punishment follow the principle that crime should be blazoned abroad by its retribution, but shameful actions hidden. Lighter offenses have also a measured punishment. Those convicted are fined a certain number of horses or cattle. Part of the fine goes to the king or the state; part is paid to the person who has brought the charge or to his relatives. At the same gatherings are selected chiefs, who administer law through the cantons and villages: each of them

has one hundred assessors from the people to act as his responsible advisors.

13 They do no business, public or private, without arms in their hands; yet the custom is that no one takes arms until the state has endorsed this competence. Then in the assembly itself one of the chiefs or his father or his relatives equip the young man with shield and spear. This corresponds with them to the toga, and is youth's first public distinction; before that he was merely a member of the household, now he becomes a member of the state. Conspicuously high birth, or great services on the part of their ancestors may win the chieftain's approval even for the very young men. They mingle with the others, men of maturer strength and tested by long years and have no shame to be seen among the chief's retinue. In the retinue itself degrees are observed at the chief's discretion; there is great rivalry among the retainers to decide who shall have the first place with the chief, and among the chieftains as to who shall have the largest and most enthusiastic retinue. It is considered desirable to be surrounded always with a large band of chosen youths—glory in peace, in war protection. Nor is this only so with a chief's own people; with neighboring states also it means name and fame for a man that his retinue be conspicuous for number and character. Such men are in demand for embassies, and are honored with gifts; often, by the mere terror of their name, they are able to break the back of opposition in war.

14 When the battlefield is reached it is a reproach for a chief to be surpassed in prowess and a reproach for his retinue not to equal the prowess of its chief. Much worse, though, is to have left the field and survived one's chief; this means lifelong infamy and shame. To protect and defend the chief and to devote one's own feats to his glorification is the gist of their allegiance. The chief fights for victory, but the retainers for the chief.

Should it happen that the community where they are born has been drugged with long years of peace and quiet, many of the high-born youth voluntarily seek those tribes which are at the time engaged in some war; for rest is unwelcome to the race, and they distinguish themselves more readily in the midst of uncertainties: besides, you cannot keep up a great retinue except by war and violence. It is the generous chief that the warriors expect to give them a particular war-horse or murderous and masterful spear. Banquetings and a certain rude but lavish outfit take the place of salary. The material for this generosity comes through war and foray. You will not so readily persuade a German to plow the land and wait for the year's returns as to challenge the enemy and earn wounds. Besides, it seems limp and slack to get with the sweating of your brow what you can gain with the shedding of your blood.

15 When they are not warring, they spend much time hunting, but more in idleness—creatures who eat and sleep, the best and bravest warriors doing nothing, having handed over the charge of their home, hearth and estate to the women and the old men and the weakest members of the family. For themselves they vegetate by that curious incongruity of temperament which makes of the same men such lovers of slumber and such haters of quiet.

It is the custom in their states for each man to bestow upon the chief unasked some portion of his cattle or crops. It is accepted as a compliment, but also serves the chief's needs. The chiefs appreciate still more the gifts of neighboring tribes, which are sent not merely by individuals but by the community—selected horses, heavy armor, bosses and bracelets; by this time we have taught them to accept money also.

16 It is well known that none of the German tribes live in cities, that individually they do not permit houses to touch each other. They live separated and scattered, according as spring-water, meadow, or grove appeals to each man. They lay out their villages not, after our fashion, with buildings contiguous and connected; everyone keeps a clear space round his house, whether it be a precaution against the chances of fire or just ignorance of building. They have not even learned to use quarry-stone or tiles: the timber they use for all purposes is unshaped, and stops short of all ornament or attraction. Certain buildings are smeared with a stucco bright and glittering enough to be a substitute for paint and frescoes. They are in the habit also of opening pits in the earth and piling dung in quantities on the roof, as a refuge from the winter or a root-house, because such places lessen the harshness of frost. If an enemy comes, he lays waste the open, but the hidden and buried houses are either missed outright or escape detection just because they require a search.

17 For clothing all wear a cloak, fastened with a clasp, or, in its absence a thorn. They spend whole days on the hearth round the fire with no other covering. The richest men are distinguished by the wearing of underclothes—not loose, like those of Parthians and Sarmatians, but drawn tight, throwing each limb into relief.

They wear also the skins of wild beasts: the tribes adjoining the river-bank in casual fashion, the inland tribes with more attention, since they cannot depend on traders for clothing. The beasts for this purpose are selected, and the hides so taken are checkered with the pied skins of the creatures native to the outer ocean and its unknown waters.

The women have the same dress as the men, except that very often long linen garments, striped with purple, are in use for the women. The upper part of this costume does not widen into sleeves; their arms and shoulders are therefore bare, as is the adjoining portion of the breast.

18 None the less the marriage tie with them is strict; you will find nothing in their character to praise more highly. They are almost the only barbarians who are content with a wife apiece. The very few exceptions have nothing to do with passion, but consist of those with whom polygamous marriage is eagerly sought for the sake of their high birth.

As for the dowry, it is not the wife who brings it to the husband, but the husband to the wife. The parents and relations are present to approve these gifts—gifts not devised for ministering to female fads, nor for the adornment of the person of the bride, but oxen, a horse and bridle, a shield and spear or sword. It is to share these things that the wife is taken by the husband, and she in turn brings some piece of armor to her husband. Here is the gist of the bond between them, here in their eyes its mysterious sacrament, the divinity which hedges it. Thus the wife may not imagine herself released from the practice of heroism, released from the chances of war; she is warned by the very rites with which her marriage begins that she comes to share with her husband hard work and peril. Her fate will be the same as his in peace and in panic, her risks the same. This is the moral of the yoked oxen, of the bridled horse, of the exchange of arms; so she must live and so she must die. The things she takes she is to hand over inviolate to her children, fit to be taken by her daughters-in-law and passed on again to her grandchildren.

19 So their life is one of fenced-in chastity. There is no arena with its seductions, no dinner-tables with their provocations to corrupt them. Of the exchange of secret letters men and women alike are innocent. Adultery is very rare among these people. Punishment is prompt and is the husband's prerogative: the wife's hair is close-cropped, she is stripped of her clothes, her husband drives her from his house in the presence of his relatives and pursues her with blows through the length of the village. For lost chastity there is no pardon; neither beauty nor youth nor wealth will find the sinner a husband. No one laughs at vice there; no one calls seduction the spirit of the age. Better still are those tribes where only maids marry and where a woman makes an end, once and for all, with the hopes and vows of a wife. So they take one

husband only, just as one body and one life, in order that there may be no second thoughts, no belated fancies, and in order that their excessive desire may be not for the man, but for marriage. To limit the number of their children or to put to death any of the later children is considered abominable. Good habits have more force with them than good laws elsewhere.

20 The children in every house grow up amid nakedness and squalor into that girth of limb and frame which is to our people a marvel. Its own mother suckles each at her breast; children are not passed on to nursemaids and wet-nurses.

Nor can master be recognized from servant by having been spoiled in his upbringing. Master and servant live in the company of the same cattle and on the same mud floor till years separate the free-born and character claims her own.

The virginity of young men is long preserved, and their powers are therefore inexhaustible. Nor for the girls is there any hothouse forcing; they pass their youth in the same way as the boys. Their stature is as tall; when they reach the same strength they are mated, and the children reproduce the vigor of the parents. Sisters' children mean as much to their uncle as to their father: some tribes regard this blood-tie as even closer and more sacred than that between son and father, and in taking hostages make it the basis of their demand, as though they thus secure loyalty more surely and have a wider hold on the family.

However, so far as succession is concerned, each man's children are his heirs, and there is no will. If there are no children, the nearest degrees of relationship for the holding of property are brothers, paternal uncles, and maternal uncles. The more relations a man has and the larger the number of his connections by marriage, the more influence has he in his age; it does not pay to have no ties.

21 It is incumbent to take up the feuds of one's father or kinsman no less than his friendships. But such feuds do not continue unappeasable; even homicide may be atoned for by a fixed number of cattle and sheep. The whole family thereby receives satisfaction to the public advantage, for feuds are more dangerous among a free people.

No race indulges more lavishly in hospitality and entertainment. To close the door against any human being is a crime. Everyone according to his means welcomes guests generously. Should there not be enough, he who is your host goes with you next door, without an invitation, but it makes no difference; you are received with the same courtesy. Stranger or acquaintance, no one

distinguishes them where th[...]
cerned. It is customary to [...]
anything he fancies. There [...]
to ask of him: gifts are [...]
neither count upon wha[...]
by what they have rece[...]

22 On waking from s[...] long in the day, they wash, usuall[...] winter bulks so large in their lives. After [...] take a meal, seated apart, each at his own table. Th[...] arms in hand, they proceed to business, or, just as often, to revelry. To drink heavily day and night is a reproach to no man. Brawls are frequent, as you would expect among heavy drinkers: these seldom terminate with abuse, more often in wounds and bloodshed. Nevertheless the mutual reconciliation of enemies, the forming of family alliances, the appointment of chiefs, the question even of war or peace, are usually debated at these banquets; as though at no other time were the mind more open to obvious, or better warmed to larger, thoughts. The people are without craft or cunning, and expose in the freedom of revelry the heart's secrets; so every mind is bared to nakedness. On the next day the matter is handled afresh. So the principle of each debating season is justified: deliberation comes when people are incapable of pretense, but decision when they are secure from illusion.

23 For drink they use a liquid distilled from barley or wheat, after fermentation has given it a certain resemblance to wine. The tribes nearest the river also buy wine. Their diet is simple: wild fruit, fresh venison, curdled milk. They banish hunger without sauce or ceremony, but there is not the same temperance in facing thirst: if you humor their drunkenness by supplying as much as they crave, they will be vanquished through their vices as easily as on the battlefield.

24 Their shows are all of one kind, and the same whatever the gathering may be: naked youths, for whom this is a form of professional acting, jump and bound between swords and upturned spears. Practice has made them dexterous and graceful. Yet they do not perform for hire or gain: however daring be the sport, the spectator's pleasure is the only price they ask.

Gambling, one may be surprised to find, they practise in all seriousness in their sober hours, with such recklessness in winning or losing that, when all else has failed, they stake personal liberty on the last and final throw.

The loser faces voluntary slavery; though he may be the younger and the stronger man, he will still allow himself to be bound and sold. Such is the Germans' persistence in wrongdoing, or their good faith, as they

ves style it. Slaves so acquired they trade, in order
ver themselves as well as the slave from the humili-
n involved in such victory.

25 Their other slaves are not organized in our fashion: that is, by a division of the services of life among
them. Each of them remains master of his own house and
home: the master requires from the slave as serf a certain
quantity of grain or cattle or clóthing. The slave so far is
subservient; but the other services of the household are
discharged by the master's wife and children. To beat a
slave or coerce him with hard labor and imprisonment is
rare. If slaves are killed, it is not usually to preserve strict
discipline, but in a fit of fury like an enemy, except that
there is no penalty to be paid.

Freedmen are not much above slaves. Rarely are they
of any weight in the household, never in politics, except
in those states which have kings. Then they climb above
the free-born and above the nobles; in other states the
disabilities of the freedman are the evidence of freedom.

26 To charge interest, let alone interest at high rates, is
unknown and the principle of avoiding usury is accordingly better observed than if there had been actual
prohibition.

Land is taken up by a village as a whole, in quantity
according to the number of cultivators. They then distribute it among themselves on the basis of rank, such
distribution being made easy by the amount of land
available. They change the arable land yearly, and there
is still land to spare, for they do not strain the fertility and
resources of the soil by tasking them, through the plant-
ing of vineyards, the setting apart of water-meadows,
or the irrigation of vegetable gardens. Grain is the only
harvest required of the land. Accordingly the year itself is
not divided into as many parts as with us: winter, spring,
summer have a meaning and a name; the gifts of autumn
and its name are alike unknown.

27 In burial there is no ostentation. The only ceremony is to burn the bodies of their notables with special kinds of wood. They build a pyre, but do not load
it with palls or spices. The man's armor and some of his
horse also is added to the fire. The tomb is a mound of
turf: the difficult and tedious tribute of a monument
they reject as too heavy on the dead. Weeping and wailing they put away quickly; sorrow and sadness linger.
Lamentation becomes women: men must restrain their
emotion.

So much in general we have ascertained concerning
the origin of the undivided Germans and their customs.
I shall now set forth the habits and customs of the several nations, and the extent to which they differ from

each other; and explain what tribes have migrated from
Germany to the Gallic provinces.

28 That the fortunes of Gaul were once higher than
those of Germany is recorded on the supreme authority
of Julius of happy memory. Therefore it is easy to believe
that the Gauls at one time crossed over into Germany;
small chance there was of the river preventing each tribe,
as it became powerful, from seizing new land, which had
not yet been divided into powerful kingdoms. Accordingly the country between the Hercynian forest and the
rivers Rhine and Moenus was occupied by the Helvetii,
and the country beyond by the Boii, both Gallic races.
The name Boihaemum still testifies to the old traditions
of the place, though here has been a change of occupants.

Whether, however, the Aravisci migrated into Pannonia from the Osi, or the Osi into Germany from the
Aravisci, must remain uncertain, since their speech, habits, and type of character are still the same. Originally, in
fact, there was the same misery and the same freedom
on either bank of the river, the same advantages and the
same drawbacks.

The Treveri and Nervi conversely go out of their way
in their ambition to claim a German origin, as though
this illustrious ancestry delivers them from any affinity
with the indolent Gaul.

On the river bank itself are planted certain peoples
who are unquestionably German: Vangiones, Triboci,
Nemetes. Not even the Ubii, though they have earned the
right to be a Roman colony and prefer to be called "Agrip-
pinenses" after the name of their founder, blush to own
their German origin. They originally came from beyond
the river. After they had given proof of their loyalty, they
were placed in charge of the bank itself, in order to block
the way to others, not in order to be under supervision.

29 Of all these races the most manly are the Batavi,
who occupy only a short stretch of the river bank, but
with it the island in the stream. They were once a tribe
of the Chatti, and on account of a rising at home they
crossed the river onto lands which later became part of the
Roman Empire. Their distinction persists and the emblem
of their ancient alliance with us; they are not insulted, that
is, by the exaction of tribute, and there is no tax-farmer to
oppress them. Immune from burdens and contributions,
and set apart for fighting purposes only, they are reserved
for war to be, as it were, our arms and weapons. Equally
loyal are the tribe of the Mattiaci; for the greatness of the
Roman nation has projected the awe felt for our empire
beyond the Rhine, and beyond the long-established frontier. So by site and territory they belong to their own bank,
but by sentiment and thought they act with us, and are

similar in all respects to the Batavi, except that hitherto both the soil and the climate of their land make them more lively.

I should not count among the people of Germany, though they have established themselves beyond the Rhine and Danube, the tribes who cultivate "the tithe-lands." All the wastrels of Gaul, plucking courage from misery, took possession of that disputed land. Later, since the frontier line has been drawn and the garrisons pushed forward, these lands have been counted as an outlying corner of the empire and a part of the Roman province.

30 Beyond these people are the Chatti. The front of their settlements begins with the Hercynian forest. The land is not so low and marshy as the other states of the level German plain; yet even where the hills cover a considerable territory they gradually fade away, and so the Hercynian forest, after escorting its Chatti to the full length of their settlement, drops them in the plain. This tribe has hardier bodies than the others, close-knit limbs, a forbidding expression, and more strength of the intellect. There is much method in what they do, for Germans at least, and much shrewdness. They elect magistrates and listen to the man elected; know their place in the ranks and recognize opportunities; reserve their attack; have a time for everything; entrench at night; distrust luck, but rely on courage; and—the rarest thing of all, and usually attained only through Roman discipline—depend on the initiative of the general rather than on that of the soldier. Their whole strength lies in their infantry, whom they load with iron tools and baggage, in addition to their arms. Other Germans may be seen going to battle, but the Chatti go to war. Forays and casual fighting are rare with them. The latter method no doubt is part of the strength of cavalry—to win suddenly, that is, and as suddenly to retire. For the speed of cavalry is near allied to panic, but the deliberate action of infantry is more likely to be resolute.

31 One ceremony that is practised by other German peoples only occasionally, depending on preference, has with the Chatti become a convention: to let the hair and beard grow when a youth has attained manhood, and to remove this manly facial garb only after an enemy has been slain. Standing above the bloody spoil, they dismantle their faces again, and advertise that then and not before have they paid the price of their birthpangs, and are worthy of their kin and country. Cowards and weaklings remain unkempt. The bravest also wear a ring of iron—the badge of shame on other occasions among this people—as a symbolic band from which each man frees himself by the slaughter of an enemy. This symbolism is very popular, and men already growing gray still wear this uniform for the pointing finger of friend and foe. Every battle begins with these men: the front rank is made up of them and is a curious sight. But, even in peace they do not allow a tamer life to enervate them. None of them has a house or land or any business. Wherever they go they are entertained; they waste the possessions of others and are indifferent to their own, until age and loss of blood make them unequal to such demanding heroism.

32 Next to the Chatti come the Usipi and Tencteri, on the Rhine banks where the river has ceased to shift its bed and has become fit to serve as a boundary. The Tencteri, in addition to the general reputation as the race of warriors, excel in the accomplishments of trained horsemen. Even the fame of the Chattan infantry is not greater than that of their cavalry. Their ancestors established the precedent, and succeeding generations vie with them. Horsemanship is the diversion of children, the center of competition for youth, and the abiding interest of age. Horses descend with servants, house, and regular inheritance. The heir to the horse, however, is not as in other things the eldest son but the confident soldier and the better man.

33 Next to the Tencteri one originally came across the Bructeri. The Chamavi and Angrivarii are said to have trekked there recently, after the Bructeri had been expelled or cut to pieces by the joint action of neighboring peoples. Whether this was from disgust at their arrogance or from the attractions of plunder, or because Heaven leans to the side of Rome cannot be said. But Heaven did not grudge us a dramatic battle; over sixty thousand men fell, not before the arms and spears of Rome, but—what was even a greater triumph for us—merely to delight our eyes. Long may such behavior last, I pray, and persist among the German nations—if they feel no love for us, at least may they feel hatred for each other. Now that the destinies of the empire have passed their zenith, Fortune can guarantee us nothing better than discord among our foes.

34 The Angrivarii and Chamavi are surrounded to the south by the Dulgubnii and the Chasuarii and other tribes not so well known to history. To the north follow the Frisii: they are called the Greater or Lesser Frisii according to the measure of their strength. These two tribes border the Rhine down to the ocean, and also fringe the great lakes which the fleets of Rome navigate. In that quarter we have even reached the ocean itself, and beyond our range are rumored to stand the pillars of Hercules. Did Hercules really visit those shores, or is it only that we have agreed to credit all marvels everywhere

to him? Nor did Drusus Germanicus lack audacity as an explorer but Ocean vetoed inquiry into either itself or Hercules. Soon the attempt was abandoned, and it came to be judged more reverent to believe in the works of deities than to comprehend them.

35 Thus far we have been enquiring into Western Germany. At this point the country falls away with a great bend towards the north. First in this area come the Chauci. Though they start next to the Frisii and occupy part of the seaboard, they also border on all of the tribes just mentioned, and finally edge away south as far as the Chatti. This vast block of territory is not merely held by the Chauci but filled by them. They are the noblest of the German tribes, and prefer to protect their vast domain by justice alone. They are neither grasping nor lawless; in peaceful seclusion they provoke no wars and despatch no raiders on marauding forays. The special proof of their great strength is, indeed, just this, that they do not depend for their superior position on injustice. Yet they are ready with arms, and, if circumstances should require, with armies, men and horse in abundance. So, even though they keep the peace, their reputation does not suffer.

36 Bordering the Chauci and the Chatti are the Cherusci. For long years they have been unassailed and have encouraged an abnormal and languid peacefulness. It has been a pleasant rather than a sound policy. With lawlessness and strength on either side of you, you will find no true peace; where might is right, self-control and righteousness are titles reserved for the stronger. Accordingly, the Cherusci, who were once styled just and generous, are now described as indolent and shortsighted, while the good luck of the victorious Chatti has been credited to them as wisdom. The fall of the Cherusci dragged down the Fosi also, a neighboring tribe. They share the adversity of the Cherusci on even terms, though they have only been dependents in their prosperity.

37 This same "sleeve" or peninsula of Germany is the home of the Cimbri, who dwell nearest the ocean. They are a small state today, but rich in memories. Broad traces of their ancient fame are still extant—a spacious camp on each bank (of the Rhine), by the circuit of which you can even today measure the size and skill of the nation and get some sense of that mighty trek.

Our city was in its six hundred and fortieth year when the Cimbrian armies were first heard of, in the consulship of Caecilius Metellus and Papirius Carbo. If we count from that date to the second consulship of the Emperor Trajan, the total amounts to about two hundred and ten years. For that length of time the conquest of Germany

has been in process. Between the beginning and end of that long period there have been many mutual losses. Neither Samnite nor Carthaginian, neither Spain nor Gaul, nor even the Parthians have taught us more lessons. The German fighting for liberty has been a keener enemy than the absolutism of Arsaces. What has the East to taunt us with, apart from the overthrow of Crassus—the East which itself fell at the feet of a Ventidius and lost Pacorus?

But the Germans routed or captured Carbo and Cassius and Aurelius Scaurus and Servilius Caepio and Gnaeus Mallius, and wrested five consular armies in one campaign from the people of Rome, and even from a Caesar wrested Varus and three legions with him. Nor was it without paying the price that Marius smote them in Italy, and Julius of happy memory in Gaul, and Drusus, Nero, and Germanicus in their own homes. Soon after that the great tragedy threatened by Gaius Caesar turned into a farce. Then came peace until, on the opportunity offered by our own dissensions and by civil war, the Germans carried the legions' winter quarters by storm and even aspired to the Gallic provinces. Finally they were repulsed, and they have in recent years gratified us with more triumphs than victories.

38 Now I must speak of the Suebi, who do not comprise only one tribe, as with the Chatti and the Tencteri. Rather they occupy the greater part of Germany, and are still distinguished by special national names, though styled in general Suebi. One mark of the race is to comb the hair back over the side of the face and tie it low in a knot behind. This distinguishes the Suebi from other Germans, and the free-born of the Suebi from the slave. In other tribes, whether from some relationship to the Suebi or, as often happens, from imitation, the same thing may be found, but it is rare and confined to the period of youth. Among the Suebi, even till the hair is gray they twist the rough locks backward, and often knot them on the very crown. The chieftains wear theirs somewhat more ornamentally, and are to this extent interested in appearances, but innocently so. It is not for making love or being made love to, but rather that men who are to face battle are—in the eyes of their foes—more terrifying with these adornments heightening their stature.

39 The Semnones are described as the most ancient and best-born tribe of the Suebi; this is confirmed by religious rite. At fixed seasons all the tribes of the same blood gather with their delegations at a certain forest that is hallowed by visions beheld by their ancestors and by the awe of the ages. After publicly offering up a human life, they celebrate the grim "initiation" of their barbarous worship. There is a further tribute which they pay

to the grove; no one enters it until he has been bound with a chain. He puts off his freedom, and advertises in his person the might of the deity. If he chances to fall, he must not be lifted up or rise—he must writhe along the ground until he is out again. The whole superstition comes to this, that it was here where the race arose, here where dwells the god who is lord of all things; everything else is subject to him. The prosperity of the Semnones enforces the idea; they occupy one hundred cantons, and their magnitude leads them to consider themselves the head of the Suebi.

40 The Langobardi, conversely, are distinguished by lack of number. Set in the midst of numberless and powerful tribes, they find safety not in submissiveness, but in peril and pitched battle. Then come the Reudigni and the Aviones, and the Anglii and the Varini, the Eudoses and Suardones and Nuithones. These tribes are protected by forests and rivers. There is nothing noteworthy about them individually, except that they worship in common Nerthus, or Mother Earth, and conceive her as intervening in human affairs, and riding in procession through the cities of men. In an island of the ocean is a holy grove, and in it a consecrated chariot, covered with robes. A single priest is permitted to touch it; he interprets the presence of the goddess in her shrine, and follows with deep reverence as she rides away, drawn by cows. Then come days of rejoicing, and all places keep holiday, as many as she thinks worthy to receive and entertain her. They make no war, take no arms. Every weapon is put away; peace and quiet rules until the same priest returns the goddess to her temple, when she has had her fill of the society of mortals. After this the chariot and the robes, and, if you are willing to credit it, the deity in person, are washed in a sequestered lake. Slaves perform this duty and are then straightaway swallowed by the same lake. Hence a mysterious terror and ignorance full of piety as to what it may be which men only behold to die.

41 These sections on the Suebi extend into the more secluded parts of Germany. Nearer to us—to follow the course of the Danube, as before I followed the Rhine—comes the state of the Hermunduri. They are loyal to Rome, and with them alone among Germans business is transacted not on the river bank, but far within the frontier in the most thriving colony of the province of Rhaetia. They cross the river everywhere without supervision, and while we let other peoples see only our fortified camps, to them we have thrown open our houses and homes because they do not covet them. Among the Hermunduri rises the River Albis—a river once famous, now a name only.

42 Next to the Hermunduri are the Naristi and then the Marcomani and the Quadi. The fame and strength of the Marcomani are outstanding; their very home was won by their bravery, through the expulsion in ancient times of the Boii. Nor are the Naristi and Quadi inferior to them. These tribes are, so to speak, the brow of Germany, so far as Germany is wreathed by the Danube. The Marcomani and the Quadi retained kings of their own race down to our time—the noble houses of Maroboduus and Tudrus. Now they submit to foreign kings also, but the force and power of their kings rest on the influence of Rome. Occasionally they are assisted by our armed intervention: more often by subsidies, out of which they get as much help.

43 Behind them are the Marsigni, Cotini, Osi, and Buri, enclosing the Marcomani and Quadi from the rear. Among these the Marsigni and Buri in language and culture recall the Suebi. As for the Cotini and Osi, the Gallic tongue of the first and the Pannonian of the second prove not to be Germans; so does their submission to tribute. This tribute is imposed upon them as foreigners in part by the Sarmatae, in part by the Quadi. The Cotini, to their shame, even have iron-mines to work. All these peoples have little level land, but occupy the summits and ridges of mountains. In fact, a continuous range parts and cuts Suebia in two.

Beyond the range are many races. The most widely diffused name is that of the Lugii, which extends over several states. It will be sufficient to have named the strongest: Harii, Helvecones, Manimi, Elisii, Nahanarvali. Among the Nahanarvali one is shown a grove, the seat of a prehistoric ritual. A priest presides in female dress; but according to the Roman interpretation the gods recorded in this fashion are Castor and Pollux. That at least is the spirit of the godhead here recognized, whose name is the Alci. No images are in use; there is no sign of foreign superstition. Nevertheless they worship these deities as brothers and as youths.

But to return. The Harii, apart from the strength in which they surpass the peoples just enumerated, are fierce in nature, and augment this natural ferocity by the help of art and season. They blacken their shields and dye their bodies; they choose pitchy nights for their battles; by sheer panic and darkness they strike terror like an army of ghosts. No enemy can face this novel and, as it were, phantasmagorical vision. In every battle, after all, the eye is conquered first.

Beyond the Lugii is the monarchy of the Gotones. The hand upon the reins closes somewhat tighter here than among the other tribes of Germans, but not so tight yet as to destroy freedom. Then immediately following them and on the ocean are the Rugii and the Lemovii. The distinguishing features of all these tribes are round shields, short swords, and a submissive bearing before their kings.

44 Beyond these tribes the states of the Suiones, on the ocean, possess not merely arms and men but powerful fleets. The style of their ships differs in this respect: there is a prow at each end, with a beak ready to be driven forwards. They neither work a ship with sails, nor add oars in banks to the side; the gearing of the oars is detached as on certain rivers, and reversible as occasion demands for movement in either direction.

Among these peoples respect is paid to wealth, and one man is accordingly supreme, with no restrictions and with an unchallenged right to obedience. Nor is there any general carrying of arms here, as among the other Germans. Rather they are locked up in charge of a custodian, who is a slave. The ocean forbids sudden inroads from enemies; and, besides, bands of armed men, with nothing to do, easily become riotous: it is not in the king's interest to put a noble or a freemen or even a freedman in charge of the arms.

45 Beyond the Suiones is another sea, sluggish and almost motionless, with which the earth is girdled and bounded. Evidence for this is furnished by the brilliance of the last rays of the sun, which remain so bright from his setting to his rising again as to dim the stars. Faith adds further that the sound of the sun's emergence is audible and the forms of his horses visible, with the spikes of his crown.

So far (and here rumor speaks the truth), and so far only, does Nature reach.

We must now turn to the right-hand shore of the Suebic Sea. Here it washes the tribes of the Aestii; there customs and dress are Suebic, but their language is nearer British.

They worship the mother of the gods. As an emblem of that superstition they wear the figures of wild boars; this boar takes the place of arms or of any other protection, and guarantees to the votary of the goddess a mind at rest even in the midst of foes. They use swords rarely, clubs frequently. Grain and other products of the earth they cultivate with a patience out of keeping with the lethargy customary to Germans. They ransack the sea also, and are the only people who gather in the shallows and on the shore itself amber, which they call in their tongue "glaesum."

Nor have they, being barbarians, inquired or learned what substance or process produces it. It lay there long among the rest of the flotsam and jetsam of the sea, until Roman luxury gave it a name. To the natives it is useless.

It is gathered crude and is forwarded to Rome unshaped; the barbarians are astonished to be paid for it. Yet you may infer that it is the gum of trees; certain creeping and even winged creatures are continually found embedded in it. They have been entangled in its liquid form, and, as the material hardens, are imprisoned. I should suppose therefore that just as in the secluded places in the East, where frankincense and balsam are exuded, so in the islands and lands of the West there are groves and glades more than ordinarily luxuriant. These are tapped and liquefied by the rays of the sun as it approached, and ooze into the nearest sea, whence by the force of tempests they are stranded on the shores opposite. If you try the qualities of amber by setting fire to it, it kindles like a torch, feeds an oily and odorous flame, and soon dissolves into something like pitch and resin.

Adjacent to the Suiones come the tribes of the Sitones, resembling them in all other respects, and differing only in this, that among them the woman rules. To this extent they have fallen lower not merely than freemen but even than slaves.

46 Here Suebia ends. As for the tribes of the Peucini, Venedi, and Fenni, I am in doubt whether to count them as Germans or Sarmatians. Though the Peucini, whom some men call Bastarnae, in language, culture, fixity of habitation, and house-building, conduct themselves as Germans, all are dirty and lethargic. The faces of the chiefs, too, owing to intermarriage, wear to some extent the degraded aspect of Sarmatians while the Venedi have contracted many Sarmatian habits; they are caterans [robbers], infesting all the hills and forests which lie between the Peucini and the Fenni.

And yet these peoples are preferably entered as Germans, since they have fixed abodes, and carry shields, and delight to use their feet and to run fast, all of which are traits opposite to those of the Sarmatians, who live in wagons and on horseback.

The Fenni live in astonishing barbarism and disgusting misery: no arms, no horses, no fixed homes; herbs for their food, skins for their clothing, earth for their bed. Arrows are all their wealth and for want of iron they tip them with bone. This same hunting is the support of the women as well as of the men, for they accompany the men freely and claim a share of the spoil. Nor have their infants any shelter against wild beasts and rain, except the covering afforded by a few intertwined branches. To these the hunters return: these are the refuge of age; and yet the people think it happier so than to groan over field labor, be encumbered with house-service, and be forever exchanging their own and their neighbors' goods with alternate hopes and fears. Unconcerned towards men, unconcerned towards Heaven, they have achieved a consummation very difficult: they have nothing even to ask for.

Beyond this all else that is reported the Hellusii and Oxiones have human the limbs and bodies of beasts. It has tained, and I shall leave it an open qu

5. JORDANES

HISTORY OF THE GOTHS

Jordanes was a sixth-century Goth or Alan who had been notary to Gunthigis-Baza, a Gothic chieftain, but who spent part of his later life in Constantinople, where in 551 he composed his *History of the Goths*, largely a summary of Cassidorus's now lost work of the same name. It combines genuine Gothic oral traditions into the traditional framework of classical ethnography to present the Goths within the broader perspective of Roman and Christian history.

Source: The Gothic History of Jordanes, trans. Charles C. Mierow (Princeton, NJ: Princeton University Press, 1915).
Further Reading: James J. O'Donnell, "The Aims of Jordanes," *Historia: Zeitschrift für Alte Geschichte* 31 (1982): 223–40.

The United Goths

IV Now from this island of Scandza, as from a hive of races or a womb of nations, the Goths are said to have come forth long ago under their king, Berig by name. As soon as they disembarked from their ships and set foot on the land, they straightway gave their name to the place. And even today it is said to be called Gothiscandza. Soon they moved from here to the abodes of the Ulmerugi, who then dwelt on the shores of Ocean, where they pitched camp, joined battle with them and drove them from their homes. Then they subdued their neighbors, the Vandals, and thus added to their victories. But when the number of the people increased greatly and Filimer, son of Gadaric, reigned as king—about the fifth since Berig—he decided that the army of the Goths with their families should move from that region. In search of suitable homes and pleasant places they came to the land of Scythia, called *Oium* in that tongue. Here they were delighted with the great richness of the country, and it is said that when half the army had been brought over, the bridge whereby they had crossed the river fell in utter ruin, nor could anyone thereafter pass to or fro. For the place is said to be surrounded by quaking bogs and an encircling abyss, so that by this double obstacle nature has made it inaccessible. And even to-day one may hear in that neighborhood the lowing of cattle and may find traces of men, if we are to believe the stories of travelers, although we must grant that they hear these things from afar.

This part of the Goths, which is said to have crossed the river and entered with Filimer into the country of Oium, came into possession of the desired land, and there they soon came upon the race of the Spali, joined battle with them and won the victory. Thence the victors hastened to the farthest part of Scythia, which is near the sea of Pontus; for so the story is generally told in their early songs, in almost historic fashion. Ablabius also, a famous chronicler of the Gothic race, confirms this in his most trustworthy account. Some of the ancient writers also agree with the tale. Among these we may mention Josephus, a most reliable relator of annals, who everywhere follows the truth and unravels from the beginning the origin of things;—but why he has omitted the beginnings of the race of the Goths, of which I have spoken, I do not know. He barely mentions Magog of that stock, and says they were Scythians by race and were called so by name.

Before we enter on our history, we must describe the boundaries of this land, as it lies.

V Now Scythia borders on the land of Germany as far as the source of the river Ister and the expanse of the Morsian Swamp. It reaches even to the rivers Tyra, Danaster, and Vagosola, and the great Danaper, extending to the Taurus range—not the mountains in Asia but our own, that is, the Scythian Taurus—all the way to Lake Maeotis. Beyond Lake Maeotis it spreads on the other side of the straits of Bosphorus to the Caucasus Mountains and the river Araxes. Then it bends back to the left behind the Caspian Sea, which comes from the northeastern ocean in the most distant parts of Asia, and so is formed like a mushroom, at first narrow and then broad and round in shape. It extends as far as the Huns, Albani, and Seres. This land, I say—namely, Scythia, stretching far and spreading wide—has on the east the Seres, a race that dwelt at the very beginning of their history on the shore of the Caspian Sea. On the west are the Germans and the river Vistula; on the arctic side, namely the north, it is surrounded by Ocean; on the south by Persis, Albania, Hiberia, Pontus, and the farthest channel of the Ister, which is called the Danube all the way from the mouth to the source. But in that region where Scythia touches the Pontic coast it is dotted with towns of no mean fame:—Borysthenis, Olbia, Callipolis, Cherson, Theodosia, Careon, Myrmicion, and Trapezus. These towns the wild Scythian tribes allowed the Greeks to build to afford them the means of trade. In the midst of Scythia is the place that separates Asia and Europe, I mean the Rhipaeian mountains, from which the mighty Tanais flows. This river enters Maeotis, a marsh having circuit of one hundred and four miles and never subsiding to a depth of less than eight cubits.

In the land of Scythia to the westward dwells, first of all, the race of the Gepidae, surrounded by great and famous rivers. For the Tisia flows through it on the north and northwest, and on the southwest is the great Danube. On the east it is cut by the Flutausis, a swiftly eddying stream that sweeps whirling into the Ister's waters. Within these rivers lies Dacia, encircled by the lofty Alps as by a crown. Near their left ridge, which inclines toward the north, and beginning at the source of the Vistula, the populous race of the Venethi dwell, occupying a great expanse of land. Though their names are now dispersed amid various clans and places, yet they are chiefly called Sclaveni and Antes. The abode of the Sclaveni extends from the city of Noviodunum and the lake called Mursianus to the Danaster, and northward as far as the Vistula. They have swamps and forests for their cities. The Antes, who are the bravest of these peoples dwelling in the curve of the sea of Pontus, spread from the Danaster to the Danaper, rivers that are many days' journey apart. But on the shore of Ocean, where the floods of the river Vistula empty from three mouths, the Vidivarii dwell, a people gathered out of various tribes. Beyond them the Aesti, a subject race, likewise hold the shore of Ocean. To the south dwell the Acatziri, a very brave tribe ignorant of agriculture, who subsist on their flocks and by hunting. Farther away and above the Sea of Pontus are the abodes of the Bulgares, well known from the disasters our neglect has brought upon us. From this region the Huns, like a fruitful root of bravest races, sprouted into two hordes of people. Some of these are called Altziagiri, others Sabiri; and they have different dwelling places. The Altziagiri are near Cherson, where the avaricious traders bring in the goods of Asia. In summer they range the plains, their broad domains, wherever the pasturage for their cattle invites them, and betake themselves in winter beyond the sea of Pontus. Now the Hunuguri are known to us from the fact that they trade in marten skins. But they have been cowed by their bolder neighbors.

We read that in their first abode the Goths dwelt in the land of Scythia near Lake Maeotis; in their second in Moesia, Thrace, and Dacia, and in their third they dwelt again in Scythia, above the sea of Pontus. Nor do we find anywhere in their written records legends which tell of their subjection to slavery in Britain or in some other island, or of their redemption by a certain man at the cost of a single horse. Of course if anyone in our city says that the Goths had an origin different from that I have related, let him object. For myself, I prefer to believe what I have read, rather than put trust in old wives' tales.

To return, then, to my subject. The aforesaid race of which I speak is known to have had Filimer as king while they remained in their first home in Scythia near Maeotis. In their second home, that is, in the countries of Dacia, Thrace, and Moesia, Zalmoxes reigned, whom many annals mention as a man of remarkable learning in philosophy. Yet even before this they had a learned man Zeuta, and after him Dicineus; and the third was Zalmoxes of whom I have made mention above. Nor did they lack teachers of wisdom. Wherefore the Goths have ever been wiser than other barbarians and were nearly like the Greeks, as Dio relates, who wrote their history and annals with a Greek pen. He says that those of noble birth among them, from whom their kings and priests were appointed, were called first Tarabostesei and then Pilleati. Moreover so highly were the Getae praised that Mars, whom the fables of poets call the god of war, was reputed to have been born among them. Hence Virgil says:

Father Gradivus rules the Getic fields.[2]

Now Mars has always been worshipped by the Goths with cruel rites, and captives were slain as his victims. They thought that he who is lord of war ought to be appeased by the shedding of human blood. To him they devoted the first share of the spoil, and in his honor arms stripped from the foe were suspended from trees. And they had more than all other races a deep spirit of religion, since the worship of this god seemed to be really bestowed upon their ancestor.

In their third dwelling place, which was above the Sea of Pontus, they had now become more civilized and, as I have said before, were more learned. Then the people were divided under ruling families. The Visigoths served the family of the Balthi and the Ostrogoths served the renowned Amali. They were the first race of men to string the bow with cords, as Lucan, who is more of a historian than a poet, affirms:

They string Armenian bows with Getic cords.[3]

In earliest times they sang of the deeds of their ancestors in strains of song accompanied by the cithara; chanting of Eterpamara, Hanala, Fritigern, Vidigoia, and others whose fame among them is great; such heroes as admiring antiquity scarce proclaims its own to be. Then, as the story goes, Vesosis waged a war disastrous to himself against the Scythians, whom ancient tradition asserts to have been the husbands of the Amazons. Concerning these female warriors Orosius speaks in convincing language. Thus we can clearly prove that Vesosis then fought with the Goths, since we know surely that he waged war with the husbands of the Amazons. They dwelt at that time along a bend of Lake Maeotis, from the river Borysthenes, which the natives call the Danaper, to the stream of the Tanais. By the Tanais I mean the river which flows down from the Rhipaeian mountains and rushes with so swift a current that when the neighboring streams or Lake Maeotis and the Bosphorus are frozen fast, it is the only river that is kept warm by the rugged mountains and is never solidified by the Scythian cold. It is also famous as the boundary of Asia and Europe. For the other Tanais is the one which rises in the mountains of the Chrinni and flows into the Caspian Sea. The Danaper begins in a great marsh and issues from it as from its mother. It is sweet and fit to drink as far as half-way down its course. It also produces fish of a fine flavor and without bones, having only cartilage as the frame-work of their bodies. But as it approaches the Pontus it receives a little stream called Exampaeus, so very bitter that although the river is navigable for the length of a forty days' voyage, it is so altered by the water of this scanty stream as to become tainted and unlike itself, and flows thus tainted into the sea between Greek towns of Callipidae and Hypanis. At its mouth there is an island named Achilles. Between these two rivers is a vast land filled with forests and treacherous swamps.

VI This was the region where the Goths dwelt when Vesosis, king of the Egyptians, made war upon them. Their king at that time was Tanausis. In a battle at the river Phasis (whence come the birds called pheasants, which are found in abundance at the banquets of the great all over the world), Tanausis, king of the Goths, met Vesosis, king of the Egyptians, and there inflicted a severe defeat upon him, pursuing him even to Egypt. Had he not been restrained by the waters of the impassable Nile and the fortifications which Vesosis had long ago ordered to be made against the raids of the Ethiopians, he would have slain him in his own land. But finding he had no power to injure him there, he returned and conquered almost all Asia and made it subject and tributary to Sornus, king of the Medes, who was then his dear friend. At that time some of his victorious army, seeing that the subdued provinces were rich and fruitful, deserted their companies and of their own accord remained in various parts of Asia. From their name or race Pompeius Trogus says the stock of the Parthians had its origin. Hence even to-day in the Scythian tongue they are called Parthi, that is, Deserters. And in consequence of their descent they are archers—almost alone among the nations of Asia—and are very valiant warriors. Now in regard to the name, though I have said they were called Parthi because they were deserters, some have traced the derivation of the word otherwise, saying that they were called Parthi because they fled from their kinsmen. Now when this Tanausis, king of the Goths, was dead, his people worshipped him as one of their gods.

VII After his death, while the army under his successors was engaged in an expedition in other parts, a neighboring tribe attempted to carry off women of the

---

[2] *Aeneid* 3.5.
[3] Lucan, *Pharsalla* 8.221.

Goths as booty. But they made a brave resistance, as they had been taught to do by their husbands, and routed in disgrace the enemy who had come upon them. When they had won this victory, they were inspired with greater daring. Mutually encouraging each other, they took up arms and chose two of the bolder, Lampeto and Marpesia, to act as their leaders. While they were in command, they cast lots both for the defense of their own country and the devastation of other lands. So Lampeto remained to guard their native land and Marpesia took a company of women and led this novel army into Asia. After conquering various tribes in war and making others their allies by treaties, she came to the Caucasus. There she remained for some time and gave the place the name Rock of Marpesia, of which also Virgil makes mention:

Like to hard flint or the Marpesian Cliff.[4]

It was here Alexander the Great afterwards built gates and named them the Caspian Gates, which now the tribe of the Lazi guard as a Roman outpost. Here, then the Amazons remained for some time and were much strengthened. Then they departed and crossed the river Halys, which flows near the city of Gangra, and with equal success subdued Armenia, Syria, Cilicia, Galatia, Pisidia, and all the places of Asia. Then they turned to Ionia and Aeolia, and made provinces of them after their surrender. Here they ruled for some time and even founded cities and camps bearing their name. At Ephesus also they built a very costly and beautiful temple for Diana, because of her delight in archery and the chase—arts to which they were themselves devoted. Then these Scythian-born women, who had by such a chance gained control over the kingdoms of Asia, held them for almost a hundred years, and at last came back to their own kinsfolk in the Marpesian rocks I have mentioned above, namely in the Caucasus mountains. . . .

VIII Fearing their race would fail, they sought marriage with neighboring tribes. They appointed a day for meeting once in every year, so that when they should return to the same place on that day in the following year each mother might give over to the father whatever male child she had borne, but should herself keep and train for warfare whatever children of the female sex were born. Or else, as some maintain, they exposed the males, destroying the life of the ill-fated child with a hate like that of a stepmother. Among them childbearing was detested,

though everywhere else it is desired. The terror of their cruelty was increased by common rumor; for what hope, pray, would there be for a captive, when it was considered wrong to spare even a son? Hercules, they say fought against them and overcame Menalippe, yet more by guile than by valor. Theseus, moreover, took Hippolyte captive, and of her he begat Hippolytus. And in later times the Amazons had a queen named Penthesilea, famed in the tales of the Trojan war. These women are said to have kept their power even to the time of Alexander the Great.

IX But say not "Why does a story which deals with the men of the Goths have so much to say of their women?" Hear, then, the tale of the famous and glorious valor of the men. Now Dio, the historian and diligent investigator of ancient times, who gave to his work the title "Getica" (and the Getae we have proved in a previous passage to be Goths, on the testimony of Orosius Paulus)—this Dio, I say, makes mention of a later king of theirs named Telefus. Let no one say that this name is quite foreign to the Gothic tongue, and let no one who is ignorant cavil at the fact that the tribes of men make use of many names, even as the Romans borrow from the Macedonians, the Greeks from the Romans, the Sarmatians from the Germans, and the Goths frequently from the Huns. This Telefus, then, a son of Hercules by Auge, and the husband of a sister of Priam, was of towering stature and terrible strength. He matched his father's valor by virtues of his own and also recalled the traits of Hercules by his likeness in appearance. Our ancestors called his kingdom Moesia. This province has on the east the mouths of the Danube, on the south Macedonia, on the west Histria, and on the north the Danube. Now this king we have mentioned carried on wars with the Greeks, and in their course he slew in battle Thesander, the leader of Greece. But while he was making a hostile attack upon Ajax and was pursuing Ulysses, his horse became entangled in some vines and fell. He himself was thrown and wounded in the thigh by a javelin of Achilles, so that for a long time he could not be healed. Yet, despite his wound, he drove the Greeks from his land. Now when Telefus died, his son Eurypylus succeeded to the throne, being a son of the sister of Priam, king of the Phrygians. For love of Cassandra he sought to take part in the Trojan war, that he might come to the help of her parents and his own father-in-law; but soon after his arrival he was killed. . . .

XI Then when Buruista was king of the Goths, Dicineus came to Gothia at the time when Sulla ruled the Romans. Buruista received Dicineus and gave him almost royal power. It was by his advice that the Goths ravaged the lands of the Germans, which the Franks now possess. Then came Caesar, the first of all the Romans to assume imperial power and to subdue almost the whole world, who conquered all kingdoms and even seized islands lying beyond our world, reposing in the bosom of Ocean. He made tributary to the Romans those that knew not the Roman name even by hearsay, and yet was unable to prevail against the Goths, despite his frequent attempts. Soon Gaius Tiberius reigned as third emperor of the Romans, and yet the Goths continued in their kingdom unharmed. Their safety, their advantage, their one hope lay in this, that whatever their counselor Dicineus advised should by all means be done; and they judged it expedient that they should labor for its accomplishment. And when he saw that their minds were obedient to him in all things and that they had natural ability, he taught them almost the whole of philosophy, for he was a skilled master of this subject. Thus by teaching them ethics he restrained their barbarous customs; by imparting a knowledge of physics he made them live naturally under laws of their own, which they possess in written form to this day and call *belagines.* He taught them logic and made them skilled in reasoning beyond all other races; he showed them practical knowledge and so persuaded them to abound in good works. By demonstrating theoretical knowledge he urged them to contemplate the courses of the twelve signs and the planets passing through them, and the whole of astronomy. He told them how the disc of the moon gains increase or suffers loss, and showed them how much the fiery globe of the sun exceeds in size our earthly planet. He explained the names of the three hundred and forty-six stars and told through what signs in the arching vault of the heavens they glide swiftly from their rising to their setting. Think, I pray you, what pleasure it was for these brave men, when for a little space they had leisure from warfare, to be instructed in the teachings of philosophy! You might have seen one scanning the position of the heavens and another investigating the nature of plants and bushes. Here stood one who studied the waxing and waning of the moon, while still another regarded the labors of the sun and observed how these bodies which were hastening to go toward the east are whirled around and borne back to the west by the rotation of the heavens. When they had learned the reason, they were at rest. These and various other matters Dicineus taught the Goths in his wisdom and gained marvelous repute among them, so that he ruled not only the common men but their kings. He chose from among them those that were at that time of noblest birth and superior wisdom and taught them theology, bidding them worship certain divinities and

holy places. He gave the name of Pilleati to the priests he ordained, I suppose because they offered sacrifice having their heads covered with tiaras, which we otherwise call *pillei.* But he bade them call the rest of their race Capillati. This name the Goths accepted and prized highly, and they retain it to this day in their songs.

After the death of Dicineus, they held Comosicus in almost equal honor, because he was not inferior in knowledge. By reason of his wisdom he was accounted their priest and king, and he judged the people with the greatest uprightness.

XII When he too had departed from human affairs, Coryllus ascended the throne as king of the Goths and for forty years ruled his people in Dacia. I mean ancient Dacia, which the race of the Gepidae now possesses. This country lies across the Danube within sight of Moesia, and is surrounded by a crown of mountains. It has only two ways of access, one by way of Boutae and the other by Tapae. This Gothia, which our ancestors called Dacia and now, as I have said, is called Gepidia, was then bounded on the east by the Roxolani, on the west by the Iazygres, on the north by the Sarmatians and Basternae, and on the south by the river Danube. The Iazyges are separated from the Roxolani by the Aluta river only.

And since mention has been made of the Danube, I think it not out of place to make brief notice of so excellent a stream. Rising in the fields of the Alamanni, it receives sixty streams which flow into it here and there in the twelve hundred miles from its source to its mouths in the Pontus, resembling a spine interwoven with ribs like a basket. It is indeed a most vast river. In the language of the Bessi it is called the Hister, and it has profound waters in its channel to a depth of quite two hundred feet. This stream surpasses in size all other rivers, except the Nile. Let this much suffice for the Danube. But let us now with the Lord's help return to the subject from which we have digressed.

XIII Now after a long time, in the reign of the Emperor Domitian, the Goths, through fear of his avarice, broke the truce they had long observed under other emperors. They laid waste the bank of the Danube, so long held by the Roman Empire, and slew the soldiers and their generals. Oppius Sabinus was then governor of that province, after Agrippa, while Dorpaneus held command over the Goths. Thereupon the Goths made war and conquered the Romans, cut off the head of Oppius Sabinus and invaded and boldly plundered many castles and cities belonging to the emperor. In this plight of his countrymen Domitian hastened with all his might to Illyricum, bringing with him the troops of almost the entire empire.

He sent Fuscus before him as his general with picked soldiers. Then joining boats together like a bridge, he made his soldiers cross the river Danube above the army of Dorpaneus. But the Goths were on the alert. They took up arms and presently overwhelmed the Romans in the first encounter. They slew Fuscus, the commander, and plundered the soldiers' camp of its treasure. And because of the great victory they had won in this region, they thereafter called their leaders, by whose good fortune they seemed to have conquered, not mere men, but demigods, that is *Ansis*. Their genealogy I shall run through briefly, telling the lineage of each and the beginning and the end of this line. And do thou, O reader, hear me without repining; for I speak truly.

XIV Now the first of these heroes, as they themselves relate in their legends, was Gapt, who begat Hulmul. And Hulmul begat Augis; and Augis begat him who was called Amal, from whom the name of Amali comes. This Amal begat Hisarnis. Hisarnis moreover begat Ostrogotha, and Ostrogotha begat Hunuil, and Hunuil likewise begat Athal. Athal begat Achiulf and Oduulf. Now Achiulf begat Ansila and Ediulf, Vultuulf and Hermanaric. And Vultuulf begat Valaravans, and Valaravans begat Vandalarius; Vandalarius begat Thiudimer and Valamir and Vidimer; and Thiudimer begat Theodoric. Theodoric begat Amalasuentha; Amalasuentha bore Athalaric and Mathesuentha to her husband Eutharic, whose race was thus joined to hers in kinship. For the aforesaid Hermanaric, the son of Achiulf, begat Hunimund, and Hunimund begat Thorismud. Now Thorismud begat Beremud, Beremud begat Veteric, and Veteric likewise begat Eutharic, who married Amalasuentha and begat Athalaric and Mathesuentha. Athalaric died in the years of his childhood, and Mathesuentha married Vitiges, to whom she bore no child. Both of them were taken together by Belisarius to Constantinople. When Vitiges passed from human affairs, Germanus the patrician, a nephew of the Emperor Justinian, took Mathesuentha in marriage and made her a Patrician Ordinary.[5] And of her he begat a son, also called Germanus. But upon the death of Germanus, she determined to remain a widow. Now how and in what wise the kingdom of the Amali was overthrown we shall keep to tell in its proper place, if the Lord help us. . . .

XVII From this city [Marcianople], as we were saying, the Getae returned after a long siege to their own land, enriched by the ransom they had received. Now the race

of the Gepidae was moved with envy when they saw them laden with booty and so suddenly victorious everywhere, and made war on their kinsmen. Should you ask how the Getae and Gepidae are kinsmen, I can tell you in a few words. You surely remember that in the beginning I said the Goths went forth from the bosom of the island of Scandza with Berig, their king, sailing in only three ships toward the hither shore of Ocean, namely to Gothiscandza. One of these three ships proved to be slower than the others, as is usually the case, and thus is said to have given the tribe their name, for in their language *gepanta* means slow. Hence it came to pass that gradually and by corruption the name Gepidae was coined for them by way of reproach. For undoubtedly they too trace their origin from the stock of the Goths, but because, as I have said, *gepanta* means something slow and stolid, the word Gepidae arose as a gratuitous name of reproach. I do not believe this is very far wrong, for they are slow of thought and too sluggish for quick movement of their bodies.

These Gepidae were then smitten by envy while they dwelt in the province of Spesis on an island surrounded by the shallow waters of the Vistula. This island they called, in the speech of their fathers, Gepedoios; but it is now inhabited by the race of the Vividarii, since the Gepidae themselves have moved to better lands. The Vividarii are gathered from various races into this one asylum, if I may call it so, and thus they form a nation. So then, as we were saying, Fastida, king of the Gepidae, stirred up his quiet people to enlarge their boundaries by war. He overwhelmed the Burgundians, almost annihilating them, and conquered a number of other races also. He unjustly provoked the Goths, being the first to break the bonds of kinship by unseemly strife. He was greatly puffed up with vain glory, but in seeking to acquire new lands for his growing nation, he only reduced the numbers of his own countrymen. For he sent ambassadors to Ostrogotha, to whose rule Ostrogoths and Visigoths alike, that is, the two peoples of the same tribe, were still subject. Complaining that he was hemmed in by rugged mountains and dense forests, he demanded one of two things, that Ostrogotha should either prepare for war or give up part of his lands to them. Then Ostrogotha, king of the Goths, who was a man of firm mind, answered the ambassadors that he did indeed dread such a war and that it would be a grievous and infamous thing to join battle with his kin—but he would not give up his lands. And why say more? The Gepidae hastened to take arms and Ostrogotha likewise moved his forces against them, lest he should seem a coward. They met at the town of Galtis, near which the river Auha flows, and there both sides

---

[5] A high Roman dignity.

fought with great valor; indeed the similarity of their arms and of their manner of fighting turned them against their own men. But the better cause and their natural alertness aided the Goths. Finally night put an end to the battle as a part of the Gepidae were giving way. Then Fastida, king of the Gepidae, left the field of slaughter and hastened to his own land, as much humiliated with shame and disgrace as formerly he had been elated with pride. The Goths returned victorious, content with the retreat of the Gepidae, and dwelt in peace and happiness in their own land as long as Ostrogotha was their leader.

XVIII After his death, Cniva divided the army into two parts and sent some to waste Moesia, knowing that it was undefended through the neglect of the emperors. He himself with seventy thousand men hastened to Euscia, that is, Novae. When driven from this place by the general Gallus, he approached Nicopolis, a very famous town situated near the Iatrus river. This city Trajan built when he conquered the Sarmatians and named it the City of Victory. When the Emperor Decius drew near, Cniva at last withdrew to the regions of Haemus, which were not far distant. Thence he hastened to Philippopolis, with his forces in good array. When the Emperor Decius learned of his departure, he was eager to bring relief to his own city and, crossing Mount Haemus, came to Beroa. While he was resting his horses and his weary army in that place, all at once Cniva and his Goths fell upon him like a thunderbolt. He cut the Roman army to pieces and drove the emperor, with a few who had succeeded in escaping, across the Alps again to Euscia in Moesia, where Gallus was then stationed with a large force of soldiers as guardian of the frontier. Collecting an army from this region as well as from Oescus, he prepared for the conflict of the coming war. But Cniva took Philippopolis after a long siege and then, laden with spoil, allied himself to Priscus, the commander in the city, to fight against Decius. In the battle that followed they quickly pierced the son of Decius with an arrow and cruelly slew him. His father saw it, and although he is said to have exclaimed, to cheer the hearts of his soldiers: "Let no one mourn; the death of one soldier is not a great loss to the republic," he was yet unable to endure it, because of his love for his son. So he rode against the foe, demanding either death or vengeance, and when he came back to Abrittus, a city of Moesia, he was himself cut off by the Goths and slain, thus making an end of his dominion and of his life. This place is to-day called the Altar of Decius, because he there offered strange sacrifices to idols before the battle.

XIX Then upon the death of Decius, Gallus and Volusianus succeeded to the Roman Empire. At this time a destructive plague, almost like death itself, such as we suffered nine years ago, blighted the face of the whole earth and especially devastated Alexandria and all the land of Egypt. The historian Dionysius[6] gives a mournful account of it and Cyprian,[7] our own bishop and venerable martyr in Christ, also describes it in his own book entitled "On Mortality." At this time the Goths frequently ravaged Moesia, through the neglect of the emperors. When a certain Aemilianus saw that they were free to do this, and that they could not be dislodged by anyone without great cost to the republic, he thought that he too might be able to achieve fame and fortune. So he seized the rule in Moesia and, taking all the soldiers he could gather, began to plunder cities and people. In the next few months, while an armed host was being gathered against him, he wrought no small harm to the state. Yet he died almost at the beginning of his evil attempt, thus losing at once his life and the power he coveted. Now though Gallus and Volusianus, the emperors we have mentioned, departed this life after remaining in power for barely two years, yet during this space of two years which they spent on earth they reigned amid universal peace and favor. Only one thing was laid to their charge, namely the great plague. But this was an accusation made by ignorant slanderers, whose custom it is to wound the lives of others with their malicious bite. Soon after they came to power they made a treaty with the race of the Goths. When both rulers were dead, it was no long time before Gallienus usurped the throne.

XX While he was given over to luxurious living of every sort, Respa, Veduc, and Thuruar, leaders of the Goths, took ship and sailed across the strait of the Hellespont to Asia. There they laid waste many populous cities and set fire to the renowned temple of Diana at Ephesus, which, as we have said before, the Amazons built. Being driven from the neighborhood of Bithynia, they destroyed Chalcedon, which Cornelius Avitus afterwards restored to some extent. Yet even to-day, though it is happily situated near the royal city, it still shows some traces of its ruin as a witness to posterity. After their success, the Goths recrossed the strait of the Hellespont, laden with booty and spoil, and returned along the same route by which they had entered Asia, sacking Troy and Ilium on the way. These cities, which had scarce recovered a little from the famous war with Agamemnon, were thus destroyed anew by the hostile sword. After the Goths had

---

[6] Dionysius of Alexandria, third-century Egyptian bishop.

[7] Cyprian, Bishop of Carthage (d. 258).

thus devastated Asia, Thrace next felt their ferocity. For they went thither and presently attacked Anchiali, a city at the foot of Haemus and not far from the sea. Sardanapalus, king of the Parthians, had built this city long ago between an inlet of the sea and the base of Haemus. There they are said to have stayed for many days, enjoying the baths of the hot springs which are situated about twelve miles from the city of Anchiali. There they gush from the depths of their fiery source, and among the innumerable hot springs of the world they are particularly famous and efficacious to heal the sick.

XXI After these events, the Goths had already returned home when they were summoned at the request of the Emperor Maximian to aid the Romans against the Parthians. They fought for him faithfully, serving as auxiliaries. But after Caesar Maximian by their aid had routed Narseus, king of the Persians, the grandson of Sapor the Great, taking as spoil all his possessions, together with his wives and his sons, and when Diocletian had conquered Achilles in Alexandria and Maximianus Herculius had broken the Quinquegentiani in Africa, thus winning peace for the empire, they began rather to neglect the Goths.

Now it had been a hard matter for the Roman army to fight against any nations whatsoever without them. This is evident from the way in which the Goths were so frequently called upon. Thus they were summoned by Constantine to bear arms against his kinsman Licinius. Later, when he was vanquished and shut up in Thessalonica and deprived of his power, they slew him with the sword of Constantine the victor. In like manner it was the aid of the Goths that enabled him to build the famous city that is named after him, the rival of Rome, inasmuch as they entered into a truce with the emperor and furnished him forty thousand men to aid him against various peoples. This body of men, namely, the Allies, and the service they rendered in war are still spoken of in the land to this day. Now at that time they prospered under the rule of their kings Ariaric and Aoric. Upon their death Geberich appeared as successor to the throne, a man renowned for his valor and noble birth.

XXII For he was the son of Hilderith, who was the son of Ovida, who was the son of Nidada; and by his illustrious deeds he equaled the glory of his race. Soon he sought to enlarge his country's narrow bounds at the expense of the race of the Vandals and Visimar, their king. This Visimar was of the stock of the Asdingi, which is eminent among them and indicates a most warlike descent, as Dexippus the historian relates. He states furthermore that by reason of the great extent of their country they could

scarcely come from Ocean to our frontier in a year's time. At that time they dwelt in the land where the Gepidae now live, near the rivers Marisia, Miliare, Gilpil, and the Grisia, which exceeds in size all previously mentioned. They then had on the east the Goths, on the west the Marcomanni, on the north the Hermunduli, and on the south the Hister, which is also called the Danube. At the time when the Vandals were dwelling in this region, war was begun against them by Geberich, king of the Goths, on the shore of the river Marisia which I have mentioned. Here the battle raged for a little while on equal terms. But soon Visimar himself, the king of the Vandals, was overthrown, together with the greater part of his people. When Geberich, the famous leader of the Goths, had conquered and spoiled the Vandals, he returned to his own place whence he had come. Then the remnant of the Vandals who had escaped, collecting a band of their unwarlike folk, left their ill-fated country and asked Emperor Constantine for Pannonia. Here they made their home for about sixty years and obeyed the commands of the emperors like subjects. A long time afterward they were summoned thence by Stilicho, Master of the Soldiery, Ex-Consul and Patrician, and took possession of Gaul. Here they plundered their neighbors and had no settled place of abode.

XXIII Soon Geberich, king of the Goths, departed from human affairs and Hermanaric, noblest of the Amali, succeeded to the throne. He subdued many warlike peoples of the north and made them obey his laws, and some of our ancestors have justly compared him to Alexander the Great. Among the tribes he conquered were the Golthescytha, Thiudos, Inaunxis, Vasinabroncae, Merens, Mordens, Imniscaris, Rogas, Tadzans, Athaul, Navego, Bubegenae, and Coldae. But though famous for his conquest of so many races, he gave himself no rest until he had slain some in battle and then reduced to his sway the remainder of the tribe of the Heruli, whose chief was Alaric. Now the aforesaid race, as the historian Ablabius tells us, dwelt near Lake Maeotis in swampy places which the Greeks call *hele*; hence they were named Heluri. They were a people swift of foot, and on that account were the more swollen with pride, for there was at that time no race that did not choose from them its light-armed troops for battle. But though their quickness often saved them from others who made war upon them, yet they were overthrown by the slowness and steadiness of the Goths; and the lot of fortune brought it to pass that they, as well as the other tribes, had to serve Hermanaric, king of the Getae. After the slaughter of the Heruli, Hermanaric also took arms against the Venethi. This people, though despised in war, was strong in numbers and tried to resist him. But a multitude of cowards is of no avail, particularly when God permits an armed multitude to attack them. These people, as we started to say at the beginning of our account or catalogue of nations, though off-shoots from one stock, have now three names, that is, Venethi, Antes, and Sclaveni. Though they now rage in war far and wide, in consequence of our neglect, yet at that time they were all obedient to Hermanaric's commands. This ruler also subdued by his wisdom and might the race of the Aesti, who dwell on the farthest shore of the German Ocean, and ruled all the nations of Scythia and Germany by his own prowess alone.

XXIV But after a short space of time, as Orosius relates, the race of the Huns, fiercer than ferocity itself, flamed forth against the Goths. We learn from old traditions that their origin was as follows: Filimer, king of the Goths, son of Gadaric the Great, who was the fifth in succession to hold the rule of the Getae after their departure from the island of Scandza—and who, as we have said, entered the land of Scythia with his tribe—found among his people certain witches, whom he called in his native tongue *Haliurunnae*. Suspecting these women, he expelled them from the midst of his race and compelled them to wander in solitary exile afar from his army. There the unclean spirits, who beheld them as they wandered through the wilderness, bestowed their embraces upon them and begat this savage race, which dwelt at first in the swamps, a stunted, foul and puny tribe, scarcely human and having no language save one which bore but slight resemblance to human speech. Such was the descent of the Huns who came to the country of the Goths.

This cruel tribe, as Priscus the historian relates, settled on the farther bank of the Maeotic swamp. They were fond of hunting and had no skill in any other art. After they had grown to a nation, they disturbed the peace of neighboring races by theft and rapine. At one time, while hunters of their tribe were as usual seeking for game on the farthest edge of Maeotis, they saw a doe unexpectedly appear to their sight and enter the swamp, acting as guide of the way; now advancing and again standing still. The hunters followed and crossed on foot the Maeotic swamp, which they had supposed was impassable as the sea. Presently the unknown land of Scythia disclosed itself and the doe disappeared. Now in my opinion the evil spirits, from whom the Huns are descended, did this from envy of the Scythians. And the Huns, who had been wholly ignorant that there was another world beyond Maeotis, were now filled with admiration for the Scythian land. As they were quick of mind, they believed that this path,

utterly unknown to any age of the past, had been divinely revealed to them. They returned to their tribe, told them what had happened, praised Scythia and persuaded the people to hasten thither along the way they had found by the guidance of the doe. As many as they captured, when they thus entered Scythia for the first time, they sacrificed to Victory. The remainder they conquered and made subject to themselves. Like a whirlwind of nations they swept across the great swamp and at once fell upon the Alpidzuri, Alcildzuri, Itimari, Tuncarsi, and Boisci, who bordered on that part of Scythia. The Alani also, who were their equals in battle, but unlike them in civilization, manners, and appearance, they exhausted by their incessant attacks and subdued. For by the terror of their features they inspired great fear in those whom perhaps they did not really surpass in war. They made their foes flee in horror because their swarthy aspect was fearful, and they had, if I may call it so, a sort of shapeless lump, not a head, with pin-holes rather than eyes. Their hardihood is evident in their wild appearance, and they are beings who are cruel to their children on the very day they are born. For they cut the cheeks of the males with a sword, so that before they receive the nourishment of milk they must learn to endure wounds. Hence they grow old beardless and their young men are without comeliness, because a face furrowed by the sword spoils by its scars the natural beauty of a beard. They are short in stature, quick in bodily movement, alert horsemen, broad shouldered, ready in the use of bow and arrow, and have firm-set necks which are ever erect in pride. Though they live in the form of men, they have the cruelty of wild beasts.

When the Getae beheld this active race that had invaded many nations, they took fright and consulted with their king how they might escape from such a foe. Now although Hermanaric, king of the Goths, was the conqueror of many tribes, as we have said above, yet while he was deliberating on this invasion of the Huns, the treacherous tribe of the Rosomoni, who at that time were among those who owed him their homage, took this chance to catch him unawares. For when the king had given orders that a certain woman of the tribe I have mentioned, Sunilda by name, should be bound to wild horses and torn apart by driving them at full speed in opposite directions (for he was roused to fury by her husband's treachery to him), her brothers Sarus and Ammius came to avenge their sister's death and plunged a sword into Hermanaric's side. Enfeebled by this blow, he dragged out a miserable existence in bodily weakness. Balamber, king of the Huns, took advantage of his ill health to move an army into the country of the

Ostrogoths, from whom the Visigoths had already separated because of some dispute. Meanwhile Hermanaric, who was unable to endure either the pain of his wound or the inroads of the Huns, died full of days at the great age of one hundred and ten years. The fact of his death enabled the Huns to prevail over those Goths who, as we have said, dwelt in the east and were called Ostrogoths.

The Divided Goths: Visigoths

XXV The Visigoths, who were their other allies and inhabitants of the western country, were terrified as their kinsmen had been, and knew not how to plan for their safety against the race of the Huns. After long deliberation by common consent they finally sent ambassadors into Romania to the Emperor Valens, brother of Valentinian, the elder emperor, to say that if he would give them part of Thrace or Moesia to keep, they would submit themselves to his laws and commands. That he might have greater confidence in them, they promised to become Christians, if he would give them teachers who spoke their language. When Valens learned this, he gladly and promptly granted what he had himself intended to ask. He received the Getae into the region of Moesia and placed them there as a wall of defense for his kingdom against other tribes. And since at that time the Emperor Valens, who was infected with the Arian perfidy, had closed all the churches of our party, he sent as preachers to them those who favored his sect. They came and straightway filled a rude and ignorant people with the poison of their heresy. Thus the Emperor Valens made the Visigoths Arians rather than Christians. Moreover, from the love they bore them, they preached the Gospel both to the Ostrogoths and to their kinsmen the Gepidae, teaching them to reverence the heresy, and they invited all people of their speech everywhere to attach themselves to this sect. They themselves, as we have said, crossed the Danube and settled Dacia Ripensis, Moesia, and Thrace by permission of the emperor.

XXVI Soon famine and want came upon them, as often happens with a people not yet well settled in a country. Their princes and the leaders who ruled them in place of kings, that is Fritigern, Alatheus, and Safrac, began to lament the plight of their army and begged Lupicinus and Maximus, the Roman commanders, to open a market. But to what will not the "cursed lust for gold" compel men to assent? The generals, swayed by avarice, sold them at a high price not only the flesh of sheep and oxen, but even the carcasses of dogs and unclean animals, so that a slave would be bartered for a loaf of bread or ten pounds of meat. When their goods and chattels failed, the greedy trader demanded their sons in return for the necessities of life. And the parents consented even to this, in order to provide for the safety of their children, arguing that it was better to lose liberty than life; and indeed it is better that one be sold, if he will be mercifully fed, than that he should be kept free only to die.

Now it came to pass in that troublous time that Lupicinus, the Roman general, invited Fritigern, a chieftain of the Goths, to a feast and, as the event revealed, devised a plot against him. But Fritigern, thinking no evil, came to the feast with a few followers. While he was dining in the praetorium he heard the dying cries of his ill-fated men, for, by order of the general, his soldiers were slaying his companions who were shut up in another part of the house. The loud cries of the dying fell upon ears already suspicious, and Fritigern at once perceived the treacherous trick. He drew his sword and with great courage dashed quickly from the banqueting-hall, rescued his men from their threatening doom and incited them to slay the Romans. Thus these valiant men gained the chance they had longed for—to be free to die in battle rather than to perish of hunger—and immediately took arms to kill the generals Lupicinus and Maximus. Thus that day put an end to the famine of the Goths and the safety of the Romans, for the Goths no longer as strangers and pilgrims, but as citizens and lords, began to rule the inhabitants and to hold in their own right all the northern country as far as the Danube.

When the Emperor Valens heard of this at Antioch, he made ready an army at once and set out for the country of Thrace. Here a grievous battle took place and the Goths prevailed. The emperor himself was wounded and fled to a farm near Hadrianople. The Goths, not knowing that an emperor lay hidden in so poor a hut, set fire to it (as is customary in dealing with a cruel foe), and thus he was cremated in royal splendor. Plainly it was a direct judgment of God that he should be burned with fire by the very men whom he had perfidiously led astray when they sought the true faith, turning them aside from the flame of love into the fire of hell. From this time the Visigoths, in consequence of their glorious victory, possessed Thrace and Dacia Ripensis as if it were their native land.

XXVII Now in the place of Valens, his uncle, the Emperor Gratian established Theodosius the Spaniard in the eastern empire. Military discipline was soon restored to a high level, and the Goths, perceiving that the cowardice and sloth of former princes had ended, became afraid. For the emperor was famed alike for his acuteness and discretion. By stern commands and by generosity and kindness he encouraged a demoralized army to deeds of daring. But when the soldiers, who had obtained a better leader by the change, gained new confidence, they sought to attack the Goths and drive them from the borders of Thrace. But as Emperor Theodosius fell so sick at this time that his life was almost despaired of, the Goths were again inspired with courage. Dividing the Gothic army, Fritigern set out to plunder Thessaly, Epirus, and Achaia, while Alatheus and Safrac with the rest of the troops made for Pannonia. Now the Emperor Gratian had at this time retreated from Rome to Gaul because of the invasions of the Vandals. When he learned that the Goths were acting with greater boldness because Theodosius was in despair of his life, he quickly gathered an army and came against them. Yet he put no trust in arms, but sought to conquer them by kindness and gifts. So he entered on a truce with them and made peace, giving them provisions.

XXVIII When the Emperor Theodosius afterwards recovered and learned that the Emperor Gratian had made a compact between the Goths and the Romans, as he had himself desired, he was very well pleased and gave his assent. He gave gifts to King Athanaric, who had succeeded Fritigern, made an alliance with him and in the most gracious manner invited him to visit him in Constantinople. Athanaric very gladly consented and as he entered the royal city exclaimed in wonder, "Lo, now I see what I have often heard of with unbelieving ears," meaning the great and famous city. Turning his eyes hither and thither, he marveled as he beheld the situation of the city, the coming and going of the ships, the splendid walls, and the people of diverse nations gathered like a flood of waters streaming from different regions into one basin. So too, when he saw the army in array, he said, "Truly the emperor is a god on earth, and whoso raises a hand against him is guilty of his own blood." In the midst of his admiration and the enjoyment of even greater honors at the hand of the emperor, he departed this life after the space of a few months. The emperor had such affection for him that he honored Athanaric even more when he was dead than during his lifetime, for he not only gave him a worthy burial, but himself walked before the bier at the funeral. Now when Athanaric was dead, his whole army continued in the service of the Emperor Theodosius and submitted to the Roman rule, forming as it were one body with the imperial soldiery. The former service

of the Allies under the Emperor Constantine was now renewed and they were again called Allies. And since the emperor knew that they were faithful to him and his friends, he took from their number more than twenty thousand warriors to serve against the tyrant Eugenius who had slain Gratian and seized Gaul. After winning the victory over this usurper, he wreaked his vengeance upon him.

XXIX But after Theodosius, the lover of peace and of the Gothic race, had passed from human cares, his sons began to ruin both empires by their luxurious living and to deprive their Allies, that is to say the Goths, of the customary gifts. The contempt of the Goths for the Romans soon increased, and for fear their valor would be destroyed by long peace, they appointed Alaric king over them. He was of famous stock, and his nobility was second only to that of the Amali, for he came from the family of the Balthi, who because of their daring valor had long ago received among their race the name *Baltha*, that is, The Bold. Now when this Alaric was made king, he took counsel with his men and persuaded them to seek a kingdom by their own exertions rather than serve others in idleness. In the consulship of Stilicho and Aurelian he raised an army and entered Italy, which seemed to be bare of defenders, and came through Pannonia and Sirmium along the right side. Without meeting any resistance, he reached the bridge of the river Candidianus at the third milestone from the royal city of Ravenna.

This city lies amid the streams of the Po between swamps and the sea, and is accessible only on one side. Its ancient inhabitants, as our ancestors relate, were called *a vero*, that is "Laudable." Situated in a corner of the Roman Empire above the Ionian Sea, it is hemmed in like an island by a flood of rushing waters. On the east it has no sea, and one who sails straight to it from the region of Corcyra and those parts of Hellas sweeps with his oars along the right hand coast, first touching Epirus, then Dalmatia, Liburnia and Histria, and at last the Venetian Isles. But on the west it has swamps through which a sort of door has been left by a very narrow entrance. To the north is an arm of the Po, called the Fossa Asconis. On the south likewise is the Po itself, which they call the King of the rivers of Italy; and it has also the name Eridanus. This river was turned aside by the Emperor Augustus into a very broad canal which flows through the midst of the city with a seventh part of its stream, affording a pleasant harbor at its mouth. Men believed in ancient times, as Dio relates, that it would hold a fleet of two hundred and fifty vessels in its safe anchorage. Fabius[8] says that this, which was once a harbor, now displays itself like a spacious garden full of trees; but from them hang not sails but apples. The city boasts of three names and is happily placed in its three-fold location. I mean to say the first is called Ravenna and the most distant part Classis; while midway between the city and the sea is Caesarea, full of luxury. The sand of the beach is fine and suited for riding.

XXX But as I was saying, when the army of the Visigoths had come into the neighborhood of the city, they sent an embassy to the Emperor Honorius, who dwelt within. They said that if he would permit the Goths to settle peaceably in Italy, they would so live with the Roman people that men might believe them both to be of one race; but if not, whoever prevailed in war should drive out the other, and the victor should henceforth rule unmolested. But the Emperor Honorius feared to make either promise. So he took counsel with his senate and considered how he might drive them from the Italian borders. He finally decided that Alaric and his race, if they were able to do so, should be allowed to seize for their own home the provinces farthest away, namely Gaul and Spain. For at this time he had almost lost them, and moreover they had been devastated by the invasion of Gaiseric, king of the Vandals. The grant was confirmed by an imperial rescript, and the Goths, consenting to the arrangement, set out for the country given them.

When they had gone away without doing any harm in Italy, Stilicho, the Patrician and father-in-law of the Emperor Honorius—for the emperor had married both his daughters, Maria and Thermantia, in succession, but God called both from this world in their virgin purity—this Stilicho, I say, treacherously hurried to Pollentia, a city in the Cottian Alps. There he fell upon the unsuspecting Goths in battle, to the ruin of all Italy and his own disgrace. When the Goths suddenly beheld him, at first they were terrified. Soon regaining their courage and arousing each other by brave shouting, as is their custom, they turned to flight the entire army of Stilicho and almost exterminated it. Then forsaking the journey they had undertaken, the Goths with hearts full of rage returned again to Liguria whence they had set out. When they had plundered and spoiled it, they also laid waste Aemilia, and then hastened toward the city of Rome along the Flaminian Way, which runs between Picenum and Tuscia, taking as booty whatever they found on either

hand. When they finally entered Rome, by Alaric's express command they merely sacked it and did not set the city on fire, as wild peoples usually do, nor did they permit serious damage to be done to the holy places. Thence they departed to bring like ruin upon Campania and Lucania, and then came to Bruttii. Here they remained a long time and planned to go to Sicily and thence to the countries of Africa.

Now the land of the Bruttii is at the extreme southern bound of Italy, and a corner of it marks the beginning of the Apennine mountains. It stretches out like a tongue into the Adriatic Sea and separates it from the Tyrrhenian waters. It chanced to receive its name in ancient times from a Queen Bruttia. To this place came Alaric, king of the Visigoths, with the wealth of all Italy which he had taken as spoil, and from there, as we have said, he intended to cross over by way of Sicily to the quiet land of Africa. But since man is not free to do anything he wishes without the will of God, that dread strait sunk several of his ships and threw all into confusion. Alaric was cast down by his reverse and, while deliberating what he should do, was suddenly overtaken by an untimely death and departed from human cares. His people mourned for him with the utmost affection. Then turning from its course the river Busentus near the city of Consentia—for this stream flows with its wholesome waters from the foot of a mountain near that city—they led a band of captives into the midst of its bed to dig out a place for his grave. In the depths of the pit they buried Alaric, together with many treasures, and then turned the waters back into their channel. And that none might ever know the place, they put to death all the diggers. They bestowed the king-dom of the Visigoths on Athavulf his kinsman, a man of imposing beauty and great spirit; for though not tall of stature, he was distinguished for beauty of face and form.

XXXI When Athavulf became king, he returned again to Rome, and whatever had escaped the first sack his Goths stripped bare like locusts, not merely despoiling Italy of its private wealth, but even of its public resources. The Emperor Honorius was powerless to resist even when his sister Placidia, the daughter of the Emperor Theodosius by his second wife, was led away captive from the city. But Athavulf was attracted to her nobility, beauty, and chaste purity, and so he took her to wife in lawful marriage at Forum Julii, a city of Aemilia. When the barbarians learned of this alliance, they were the more effectually terrified, since the empire and the Goths now seemed to be made one. Then Athavulf set out for Gaul, leaving Honorius Augustus stripped of his wealth, to be sure, yet pleased at heart because he was now a sort of

___
[8] Possibly a reference to Fabius Rusticus, a first-century Roman historian.

kinsman of his. Upon his arrival the neighboring tribes who had long made cruel raids into Gaul—Franks and Burgundians alike—were terrified and began to keep within their own borders. Now the Vandals and the Alani, as we have said before, had been dwelling in both Pannonias by permission of the Roman emperors. Yet fearing they would not be safe even here if the Goths should return, they crossed over into Gaul. But no long time after they had taken possession of Gaul they fled thence and shut themselves up in Spain, for they still remembered from the tales of their forefathers what ruin Geberich, king of the Goths, had long ago brought on their race, and how by his valor he had driven them from their native land. And thus it happened that Gaul lay open to Athavulf when he came. Now when the Goth had established his kingdom in Gaul, he began to grieve for the plight of the Spaniards and planned to save them from the attacks of the Vandals. So Athavulf left with a few faithful men at Barcelona his treasures and those who were unfit for war, and entered the interior of Spain. Here he fought frequently with the Vandals and, in the third year after he had subdued Gaul and Spain, fell pierced through the groin by the sword of Euervulf, a man whose short stature he had been wont to mock. After his death Segeric was appointed king, but he too was slain by the treachery of his own men and lost both his kingdom and his life even more quickly than Athavulf.

XXXII Then Valia, the fourth from Alaric, was made king, and he was an exceeding stern and prudent man. The Emperor Honorius sent an army against him under Constantius, who was famed for his achievements in war and distinguished in many battles, for he feared that Valia would break the treaty long ago made with Athavulf and that, after driving out the neighboring tribes, he would again plot evil against the empire. Moreover Honorius was eager to free his sister Placidia from the disgrace of servitude, and made an agreement with Constantius that if by peace or war or any means soever he could bring her back to the kingdom, he should have her in marriage. Pleased with this promise, Constantius set out for Spain with an armed force and in almost royal splendor. Valia, king of the Goths, met him at a pass in the Pyrenees with as great a force. Hereupon embassies were sent by both sides and it was decided to make peace on the following terms, namely that Valia should give up Placidia, the emperor's sister, and should not refuse to aid the Roman Empire when occasion demanded.

Now at that time a certain Constantine usurped imperial power in Gaul and appointed as Caesar his son Constans, who was formerly a monk. But when he had

held for a short time the empire he had seized, he was himself slain at Arelate and his son at Vienne. Jovinus and Sebastian succeeded them with equal presumption and thought they might seize the imperial power; but they perished by a like fate.

Now in the twelfth year of Valia's reign the Huns were driven out of Pannonia by the Romans and Goths, almost fifty years after they had taken possession of it. Then Valia found that the Vandals had come forth with bold audacity from the interior of Galicia, whither Athavulf had long ago driven them, and were devastating and plundering everywhere in his own territories, namely in the land of Spain. So he made no delay but moved his army against them at once, at about the time when Hierius and Ardabures had become consuls.

XXXIII But Gaiseric, king of the Vandals, had already been invited into Africa by Boniface, who had fallen into a dispute with the Emperor Valentinian and was able to obtain revenge only by injuring the empire. So he invited them urgently and brought them across the narrow strait known as the Strait of Gades, scarcely seven miles wide, which divides Africa from Spain and unites the mouth of the Tyrrhenian Sea with the waters of Ocean. Gaiseric, still famous in the City for the disaster of the Romans, was a man of moderate height and lame in consequence of a fall from his horse. He was a man of deep thought and few words, holding luxury in disdain, furious in his anger, greedy for gain, shrewd in winning over the barbarians and skilled in sowing the seeds of dissension to arouse enmity. Such was he who, as we have said, came at the solicitous invitation of Boniface to the country of Africa. There he reigned for a long time, receiving authority, as they say, from God Himself. Before his death he summoned the band of his sons and ordained that there should be no strife among them because of desire for the kingdom, but that each should reign in his own rank and order as he survived the others; that is, the next younger should succeed his elder brother, and he in turn should be followed by his junior. By giving heed to this command they ruled their kingdom in happiness for the space of many years and were not disgraced by civil war, as is usual among other nations; one after another receiving the kingdom and ruling the people in peace.

Now this is their order of succession: first, Gaeseric who was the father and lord, next Huneric, the third Gunthamund, the fourth Thrasamund, and the fifth Ilderich. He was driven from his throne and slain by Gelimer, who destroyed his race by disregarding his ancestor's advice and setting up a tyranny. But what he had done did not remain unpunished, for soon the vengeance of the

Emperor Justinian was manifested against him. With his whole family and that wealth over which he gloated like a robber, he was taken to Constantinople by that most renowned warrior Belisarius, Master of the Soldiery of the East, Ex-Consul Ordinary[9] and Patrician. Here he afforded a great spectacle to the people in the Circus.[10] His repentance, when he cast himself down from his royal state, came too late. He died as a mere subject and in retirement, though he had formerly been unwilling to private life. Thus after a century Africa, which in the division of the earth's surface is regarded as the third part of the world, was delivered from the yoke of the Vandals and brought back to the liberty of the Roman Empire. The country which the hand of the heathen had long ago cut off from the body of the Roman Empire, by reason of the cowardice of emperors and the treachery of generals, was now restored by a wise prince and a faithful leader and to-day is happily flourishing. And though, even after this, it had to deplore the misery of civil war and the treachery of the Moors, yet the triumph of the Emperor Justinian, vouchsafed him by God, brought to a peaceful conclusion what he had begun. But why need we speak of what the subject does not require? Let us return to our theme.

Now Valia, king of the Goths, and his army fought so fiercely against the Vandals that he would have pursued them even into Africa, had not such a misfortune recalled him as befell Alaric when he was setting out for Africa. So when he had won great fame in Spain, he returned after a bloodless victory to Tolosa, turning over to the Roman Empire, as he had promised, a number of provinces which he had rid of his foes. A long time after this he was seized with sickness and departed this life. Just at that time Beremud, the son of Thorismud, whom we have mentioned above in the genealogy of the family of the Amali, departed with his son Veteric from the Ostrogoths, who still submitted to the oppression of the Huns in the land of Scythia, and came to the kingdom of the Visigoths. Well aware of his valor and noble birth, he believed that the kingdom would be more readily bestowed upon him by his kinsmen, inasmuch as he was known to be the heir of many kings. And who would hesitate to choose one of the Amali, if there were an empty throne? But he was not himself eager to make known who he was, and so upon the death of Valia the

Visigoths made Theodorid his successor. Beremud came to him and, with the strength of mind for which he was noted, concealed his noble birth by prudent silence, for he knew that those of royal lineage are always distrusted by kings. So he suffered himself to remain unknown, that he might not bring the established order into confusion. King Theodorid received him and his son with special honor and made him partner in his counsels and a companion at his board; not for his noble birth, which he knew not, but for his brave spirit and strong mind, which Beremud could not conceal.

XXXIV And what more? Valia (to repeat what we have said) had but little success against the Gauls, but when he died the more fortunate and prosperous Theodorid succeeded to the throne. He was a man of the greatest moderation and notable for vigor of mind and body. In the consulship of Theodosius and Festus the Romans broke the truce and took up arms against him in Gaul, with the Huns as their auxiliaries. For a band of the Gallic Allies, led by Count Gaina, had aroused the Romans by throwing Constantinople into a panic. Now at that time the Patrician Aëtius was in command of the army. He was of the bravest Moesian stock, the son of Gaudentius and born in the city of Durostorum. He was a man fitted to endure the toils of war, born expressly to serve the Roman state; and by inflicting crushing defeats he had compelled the proud Suavi and barbarous Franks to submit to Roman sway. So then, with the Huns as allies under their leader Litorius, the Roman army moved in array against the Goths. When the battle lines of both sides had been standing for a long time opposite each other, both being brave and neither side the weaker, they struck a truce and returned to their ancient alliance. And after the treaty had been confirmed by both and an honest peace was established, they both withdrew.

During this peace Attila was lord over all the Huns and almost the sole earthly ruler of all the tribes of Scythia; a man marvelous for his glorious fame among all nations. The historian Priscus, who was sent to him on an embassy by the younger Theodosius, says this among other things: "Crossing mighty rivers—namely, the Tisia and Tibisia and Dricca—we came to the place where long ago Vidigoia, bravest of the Goths, perished by the guile of the Sarmatians. At no great distance from that place we arrived at the village where King Attila was dwelling, a village, I say, like a great city, in which we found wooden walls made of smooth-shining boards, whose joints so counterfeited solidity that the union of the boards could scarcely be distinguished by close scrutiny. There you might see dining halls of large extent and

---

[9] The consulship was the highest office in the Roman state; a consul ordinary distinguishes one who actually exercised this office from others given honorary consul status.

[10] The hippodrome of Constantinople.

porticoes planned with great beauty, while the courtyard was bounded by so vast a circuit that its very size showed it was the royal palace." This was the abode of Attila, the king of all the barbarian world; and he preferred this as a dwelling to the cities he captured.

XXXV Now this Attila was the son of Mundiuch, and his brothers were Octar and Ruas who are said to have ruled before Attila, though not over quite so many tribes as he. After their death he succeeded to the throne of the Huns, together with his brother Bleda. In order that he might first be equal to the expedition he was preparing, he sought to increase his strength by murder. Thus he proceeded from the destruction of his own kindred to the menace of all others. But though he increased his power by this shameful means, yet by the balance of justice he received the hideous consequences of his own cruelty. Now when his brother Bleda, who ruled over a great part of the Huns, had been slain by his treachery, Attila united all the people under his own rule. . . .

XXXVI Now when Gaiseric, king of the Vandals, whom we mentioned shortly before, learned that his mind was bent on the devastation of the world, he incited Attila by many gifts to make war on the Visigoths, for he was afraid that Theodorid, king of the Visigoths, would avenge the injury done to his daughter. She had been joined in wedlock with Huneric, the son of Gaiseric, and at first was happy in this union. But afterwards he was cruel even to his own children, and because of the mere suspicion that she was attempting to poison him, he cut off her nose and mutilated her ears. He sent her back to her father in Gaul thus despoiled of her natural charms. So the wretched girl presented a pitiable aspect ever after, and the cruelty which would stir even strangers still more surely incited her father to vengeance. Attila, therefore, in his efforts to bring about the wars long ago instigated by the bribe of Gaiseric, sent ambassadors into Italy to the Emperor Valentinian to sow strife between the Goths and the Romans, thinking to shatter by civil discord those whom he could not crush in battle. He declared that he was in no way violating his friendly relations with the empire, but that he had a quarrel with Theodorid, king of the Visigoths. As he wished to be kindly received, he filled the rest of the letter with the usual flattering salutations, striving to win credence for his falsehood. In like manner he despatched a message to Theodorid, king of the Visigoths, urging him to break his alliance with the Romans and reminding him of the battles to which they had recently provoked him. Beneath his great ferocity he was a subtle man, and fought with craft before he made war.

Then the Emperor Valentinian sent an embassy to the Visigoths and their king Theodorid, with this message: "Bravest of nations, it is the part of prudence for us to unite against the lord of the earth who wishes to enslave the whole world; who requires no just cause for battle, but supposes whatever he does is right. He measures his ambition by his might. License satisfies his pride. Despising law and right, he shows himself an enemy to Nature herself. And thus he, who clearly is the common foe of each, deserves the hatred of all. Pray remember—what you surely cannot forget—that the Huns do not overthrow nations by means of war, where there is an equal chance, but assail them by treachery, which is a greater cause for anxiety. To say nothing about ourselves, can you suffer such insolence to go unpunished? Since you are mighty in arms, give heed to your own danger and join hands with us in common. Bear aid also to the empire, of which you hold a part. If you would learn how such an alliance should be sought and welcomed by us, look into the plans of the foe."

By these and like arguments the ambassadors of Valentinian prevailed upon King Theodorid. He answered them, saying: "Romans, you have attained your desire; you have made Attila our foe also. We will pursue him wherever he summons us, and though he is puffed up by his victories over diverse races, yet the Goths know how to fight this haughty foe. I call no war dangerous save one whose cause is weak; for he fears no ill on whom Majesty has smiled." The nobles shouted assent to the reply and the multitude gladly followed. All were fierce for battle and longed to meet the Huns, their foe. And so a countless host was led forth by Theodorid, king of the Visigoths, who sent home four of his sons, namely Friderich and Eurich, Retemer and Himnerith, taking with him only the two elder sons, Thorismud and Theodorid, as partners of his toil. O brave array, sure defense and sweet comradeship, having the aid of those who delight to share in the same dangers!

On the side of the Romans stood the Patrician Aëtius, on whom at that time the whole empire of the west depended; a man of such wisdom that he had assembled warriors from everywhere to meet them on equal terms. Now these were his auxiliaries: Franks, Sarmatians, Armoricians, Liticians, Burgundians, Saxons, Riparians, Olibriones (once Roman soldiers and now the flower of the allied forces), and some other Celtic or German tribes. And so they met in the Catalaunian Plains, which are also called Mauriacian, extending in length one hundred *leuva*, as the Gauls express it, and seventy in width. Now a Gallic *leuva* measures a distance of fifteen hundred paces. That portion of the earth accordingly became the threshing-floor of countless races. The two hosts bravely joined battle. Nothing was done under cover, but they contended in open fight. What just cause can be found for the encounter of so many nations, or what hatred inspired them all to take arms against each other? It is proof that the human race lives for its kings, for it is at the mad impulse of one mind a slaughter of nations takes place, and at the whim of a haughty ruler that which nature has taken ages to produce perishes in a moment.

XXXVII But before we set forth the order of the battle itself, it seems needful to relate what had already happened in the course of the campaign, for it was not only a famous struggle but one that was complicated and confused. Well then, Sangiban, king of the Alani, smitten with fear of what might come to pass, had promised to surrender to Attila, and to give into his keeping Aureliani, a city of Gaul wherein he dwelt. When Theodorid and Aëtius learned of this, they cast up great earthworks around that city before Attila's arrival and kept watch over the suspected Sangiban, placing him with his tribe in the midst of their auxiliaries. Then Attila, king of the Huns, was taken aback by this event and lost confidence in his own troops, so that he feared to begin the conflict. While he was meditating on flight—a greater calamity than death itself—he decided to inquire into the future through soothsayers. So, as was their custom, they examined the entrails of cattle and certain streaks in bones that had been scraped, and foretold disaster to the Huns. Yet as a slight consolation they prophesied that the chief commander of the foe they were to meet should fall and mar by his death the rest of the victory and the triumph. Now Attila deemed the death of Aëtius a thing to be desired even at the cost of his own life, for Aëtius stood in the way of his plans. So although he was disturbed by this prophecy, yet inasmuch as he was a man who sought counsel of omens in all warfare, he began the battle with anxious heart at about the ninth hour of the day, in order that the impending darkness might come to his aid if the outcome should be disastrous.

XXXVIII The armies met, as we have said, in the Catalaunian Plains. The battle field was a plain rising by a sharp slope to a ridge, which both armies sought to gain; for advantage of position is a great help. The Huns with their forces seized the right side, the Romans, the Visigoths and their allies the left, and then began a struggle for the yet untaken crest. Now Theodorid with the Visigoths held the right wing and Aëtius with the Romans the left. They placed in the center Sangiban (who, as said before, was in command of the Alani), thus

contriving with military caution to surround by a host of faithful troops the man in whose loyalty they had little confidence. For one who has difficulties placed in the way of his flight readily submits to the necessity of fighting. On the other side, however, the battle line of the Huns was arranged so that Attila and his bravest followers were stationed in the center. In arranging them thus the king had chiefly his own safety in view, since by his position in the very midst of his race he would be kept out of the way of threatening danger. The innumerable peoples of the diverse tribes, which he had subjected to his sway, formed the wings. Amid them was conspicuous the army of the Ostrogoths under the leadership of the brothers Valamir, Thiudimer, and Vidimer, nobler even than the king they served, for the might of the family of the Amali rendered them glorious. The renowned king of the Gepidae, Ardaric, was there also with a countless host, and because of his great loyalty to Attila, he shared his plans. For Attila, comparing them in his wisdom, prized him and Valamir, king of the Ostrogoths, above all the other chieftains. Valamir was a good keeper of secrets, bland of speech and skilled in wiles, and Ardaric, as we have said, was famed for his loyalty and wisdom. Attila might well feel sure that they would fight against the Visigoths, their kinsmen. Now the rest of the crowd of kings (if we may call them so) and the leaders of various nations hung upon Attila's nod like slaves, and when he gave a sign even by a glance, without a murmur each stood forth in fear and trembling, or at all events did as he was bid. Attila alone was king of all kings over all and concerned for all.

So then the struggle began for the advantage of position we have mentioned. Attila sent his men to take the summit of the mountain, but was outstripped by Thorismud and Aëtius, who in their effort to gain the top of the hill reached higher ground and through this advantage of position easily routed the Huns as they came up.

XXXIX Now when Attila saw his army was thrown into confusion by this event, he thought it best to encourage them by an extemporaneous address on this wise: "Here you stand, after conquering mighty nations and subduing the world. I therefore think it foolish for me to goad you with words, as though you were men who had not been proved in action. Let a new leader or an untried army resort to that. It is not right for me to say anything common, nor ought you to listen. For what is war but your usual custom? Or what is sweeter for a brave man than to seek revenge with his own hand? It is a right of nature to glut the soul with vengeance. Let us then attack the foe eagerly; for they are ever the bolder who make the attack. Despise this union of discordant races! To defend oneself by alliance is proof of cowardice. See, even before our attack they are smitten with terror. They seek the heights, they seize the hills and, repenting too late, clamor for protection against battle in the open fields. You know how slight a matter the Roman attack is. While they are still gathering in order and forming in one line with locked shields, they are checked, I will not say by the first wound, but even by the dust of battle. Then on to the fray with stout hearts, as is your wont. Despise their battle line. Attack the Alani, smite the Visigoths! Seek swift victory in that spot where the battle rages. For when the sinews are cut the limbs soon relax, nor can a body stand when you have taken away the bones. Let your courage rise and your own fury burst forth! Now show your cunning, Huns, now your deeds of arms! Let the wounded exact in return the death of his foe; let the unwounded revel in the slaughter of the enemy. No spear shall harm those who are sure to live; and those who are sure to die Fate overtakes even in peace. And finally, why should Fortune have made the Huns victorious over so many nations, unless it were to prepare them for the joy of this conflict. Who was it revealed to our sires the path through the Maeotian swamp, for so many ages a closed secret? Who, moreover, made armed men yield to you, when you were as yet unarmed? Even a mass of federated nations could not endure the sight of the Huns. I am not deceived in the issue; here is the field so many victories have promised us. I shall hurl the first spear at the foe. If any can stand at rest while Attila fights, he is a dead man." Inflamed by these words, they all dashed into battle.

XL And although the situation was itself fearful, yet the presence of their king dispelled anxiety and hesitation. Hand to hand they clashed in battle, and the fight grew fierce, confused, monstrous, unrelenting—a fight whose like no ancient time has ever recorded. There such deeds were done that a brave man who missed this marvelous spectacle could not hope to see anything so wonderful all his life long. For, if we may believe our elders, a brook flowing between low banks through the plain was greatly increased by blood from the wounds of the slain. It was not flooded by showers, as brooks usually rise, but was swollen by a strange stream and turned into a torrent by the increase of blood. Those whose wounds drove them to slake their parching thirst drank water mingled with gore. In their wretched plight they were forced to drink what they thought was the blood they had poured from their own wounds.

Here King Theodorid, while riding by to encourage his army, was thrown from his horse and trampled under foot by his own men, thus ending his days at a ripe old age. But others say he was slain by the spear of Andag of the host of the Ostrogoths, who were then under the sway of Attila. This was what the soothsayers had told to Attila in prophecy, though he understood it of Aëtius. Then the Visigoths, separating from the Alani, fell upon the horde of the Huns and nearly slew Attila. But he prudently took flight and straightway shut himself and his companions within the barriers of the camp, which he had fortified with wagons. A frail defense indeed; yet there they sought refuge for their lives, whom but a little while before no walls of earth could withstand. But Thorismud, the son of King Theodorid, who with Aëtius had seized the hill and repulsed the enemy from the higher ground, came unwittingly to the wagons of the enemy at night, thinking he had reached his own lines. As he was fighting bravely, someone wounded him in the head and dragged him from his horse. Then he was rescued by the watchful care of his followers and withdrew from the fierce conflict. Aëtius also became separated from his men in the confusion of night and wandered about in the midst of enemy. Fearing disaster had happened, he went about in search of the Goths. At last he reached the camp of his allies and passed the remainder of the night in the protection of their shields.

At dawn on the following day, when the Romans saw the fields were piled high with bodies and that the Huns did not venture forth, they thought the victory was theirs, but knew that Attila would not flee from the battle unless overwhelmed by a great disaster. Yet he did nothing cowardly, like one that is overcome, but with clash of arms sounded the trumpets and threatened an attack. He was like a lion pierced by hunting spears, who paces to and fro before the mouth of his den and dares not spring, but ceases not to terrify the neighborhood by his roaring. Even so this warlike king at bay terrified his conquerors. Therefore the Goths and Romans assembled and considered what to do with the vanquished Attila. They determined to wear him out by a siege, because he had no supply of provisions and was hindered from approaching by a shower of arrows from the bowmen placed within the confines of the Roman camp. But it was said that the king remained supremely brave even in this extremity and had heaped up a funeral pyre of horse saddles, so that if the enemy should attack him, he was determined to cast himself into the flames, that none might have the joy of wounding him and that the lord of so many races might not fall into the hands of his foes.

XLI Now during these delays in the siege, the Visigoths sought their king and the king's sons their father, wondering at his absence when success had been attained. When, after a long search, they found him where the dead lay thickest, as happens with brave men, they honored him with songs and bore him away in the sight of the enemy. You might have seen bands of Goths shouting with dissonant cries and paying honor to the dead while the battle still raged. Tears were shed, but such as they were accustomed to devote to brave men. It was death indeed, but the Huns are witness that it was a glorious one. It was a death whereby one might well suppose the pride of the enemy would be lowered, when they beheld the body of so great a king borne forth with fitting honors. And so the Goths, still continuing the rites due to Theodorid, bore forth the royal majesty with sounding arms, and valiant Thorismud, as befitted a son, honored the glorious spirit of his dear father by following his remains.

When this was done, Thorismud was eager to take vengeance for his father's death on the remaining Huns, being moved to this both by the pain of bereavement and the impulse of that valor for which he was noted. Yet he consulted with the Patrician Aëtius (for he was an older man and of more mature wisdom) with regard to what he ought to do next. But Aëtius feared that if the Huns were totally destroyed by the Goths, the Roman Empire would be overwhelmed, and urgently advised him to return to his own dominions to take up the rule which his father had left. Otherwise his brothers might seize their father's possessions and obtain the power over the Visigoths. In this case Thorismud would have to fight fiercely and, what is worse, disastrously with his own countrymen. Thorismud accepted the advice without perceiving its double meaning, but followed it with an eye toward his own advantage. So he left the Huns and returned to Gaul. Thus while human frailty rushes into suspicion, it often loses an opportunity of doing great things.

In this most famous war of the bravest tribes, one hundred and sixty-five thousand are said to have been slain on both sides, leaving out of account fifteen thousand of the Gepidae and Franks, who met each other the night before the general engagement and fell by wounds mutually received, the Franks fighting for the Romans and the Gepidae for the Huns.

Now when Attila learned of the retreat of the Goths, he thought it a ruse of the enemy—for so men are wont to believe when the unexpected happens—and remained for some time in his camp. But when a long silence followed the absence of the foe, the spirit of the mighty king was aroused to the thought of victory and the anticipation of pleasure, and his mind turned to the old oracles of his destiny.

Thorismud, however, after the death of his father on the Catalaunian Plains where he had fought, advanced in royal state and entered Tolosa. Here although the throng of his brothers and brave companions were still rejoicing over the victory he yet began to rule so mildly that no one strove with him for the succession to the kingdom.

XLII But Attila took occasion from the withdrawal of the Visigoths, observing what he had often desired—that his enemies were divided. At length feeling secure, he moved forward his array to attack the Romans. As his first move he besieged the city of Aquileia, the metropolis of Venetia, which is situated on a point or tongue of land by the Adriatic Sea. On the eastern side its walls are washed by the river Natissa, flowing from Mount Piccis. The siege was long and fierce, but of no avail, since the bravest soldiers of the Romans withstood him from within. At last his army was discontented and eager to withdraw. Attila chanced to be walking around the walls, considering whether to break camp or delay longer, and noticed that the white birds, namely, the storks, who build their nests in the gables of houses, were bearing their young from the city and, contrary to their custom, were carrying them out into the country. Being a shrewd observer of events, he understood this and said to his soldiers: "You see the birds foresee the future. They are leaving the city sure to perish and are forsaking strongholds doomed to fall by reason of imminent peril. Do not think this a meaningless or uncertain sign; fear, arising from the things they foresee, has changed their custom." Why say more? He inflamed the hearts of his soldiers to attack Aquileia again. Constructing battering rams and bringing to bear all manner of engines of war, they quickly forced their way into the city, laid it waste, divided the spoil and so cruelly devastated it as scarcely to leave a trace to be seen. Then growing bolder and still thirsting for Roman blood, the Huns raged madly through the remaining cities of the Veneti. They also laid waste Mediolanum, the metropolis of Liguria, once an imperial city, and gave over Ticinum to a like fate. Then they destroyed the neighboring country in their frenzy and demolished almost the whole of Italy.

Attila's mind had been bent on going back to Rome. But his followers, as the historian Priscus relates, took him away, not out of regard for the city to which they were hostile, but because they remembered the case of Alaric, the former king of the Visigoths. They distrusted the good fortune of their own king, inasmuch as Alaric did not live long after the sack of Rome, but straightway departed this life. Therefore while Attila's spirit was wavering in doubt between going and not going, and he still lingered to ponder the matter, an embassy came to him from Rome to seek peace. Pope Leo himself came to meet him in the Ambuleian district of the Veneti at the well-traveled ford of the river Mincius. Then Attila quickly put aside his usual fury, turned back on the way he had advanced from beyond the Danube and departed with the promise of peace. But above all he declared and avowed with threats that he would bring worse things upon Italy, unless they sent him Honoria, the sister of the Emperor Valentinian and daughter of Augusta Placidia, with her due share of the royal wealth. For it was said that Honoria, although bound to chastity for the honor of the imperial court and kept in constraint by command of her brother, had secretly despatched a eunuch to summon Attila that she might have his protection against her brother's power; a shameful thing, indeed, to get license for her passion at the cost of the public weal.

XLIII So Attila returned to his own country, seeming to regret the peace and to be vexed at the cessation of war. For he sent ambassadors to Marcian, emperor of the east, threatening to devastate the provinces, because that which had been promised him by Theodosius, a former emperor, was in no wise performed, and saying that he would show himself more cruel to his foes than ever. But as he was shrewd and crafty, he threatened in one direction and moved his army in another; for in the midst of these preparations he turned his face towards the Visigoths who had yet to feel his vengeance. But here he had not the same success as against the Romans. Hastening back by a different way than before, he decided to reduce to his sway that part of the Alani which was settled across the river Loire, in order that by attacking them, and thus changing the aspect of the war, he might become a more terrible menace to the Visigoths. Accordingly he started from the provinces of Dacia and Pannonia, where the Huns were then dwelling with various subject peoples, and moved his array against the Alani. But Thorismud, king of the Visigoths, with like quickness of thought perceived Attila's trick. By forced marches he came to the Alani before him, and was well prepared to check the advance of Attila when he came after him. They joined battle in almost the same way as before at the Catalaunian Plains, and Thorismud dashed his hopes of victory, for he routed him and drove him from the land without a triumph, compelling him to flee to his own country. Thus while Attila, the famous leader and lord of many victories, sought to blot out the fame of his destroyer and in this way to annul what he had suffered

at the hands of the Visigoths, he met a second defeat and retreated ingloriously. Now after the bands of the Huns had been repulsed by the Alani, without any hurt to his own men, Thorismud departed for Tolosa. There he established a settled peace for his people and in the third year of his reign he fell sick. While letting blood from a vein, he was betrayed to his death by Ascalc, a client, who told his foes that his weapons were out of reach. Yet grasping a foot-stool in the one hand he had free, he became the avenger of his own blood by slaying several of those that were lying in wait for him.

XLIV After his death, his brother Theodorid succeeded to the kingdom of the Visigoths and soon found that Riciarius his kinsman, the king of the Suavi, was hostile to him. For Riciarius, presuming on his relationship to Theodorid, believed that he might seize almost the whole of Spain, thinking the disturbed beginning of Theodorid's reign made the time opportune for this trick. The Suavi formerly occupied as their country Galicia and Lusitania, which extend on the right side of Spain along the shore of Ocean. To the east is Austrogonia, to the west, on a promontory, is the sacred monument of the Roman general Scipio, to the north Ocean, and to the south Lusitania and the Tagus river, which mingles golden grains in its sands and thus carries wealth in its worthless mud. So then Riciarius, king of the Suavi, set forth and strove to seize the whole of Spain. Theodorid, his kinsman, a man of moderation, sent ambassadors to him and told him quietly that he must not only withdraw from the territories that were not his own, but furthermore that he should not presume to make such an attempt, as he was becoming hated for his ambition. But with arrogant spirit he replied: "If you murmur here and find fault with my coming, I shall come to Tolosa where you dwell. Resist me there, if you can." When he heard this, Theodorid was angry and, making a compact with all the other tribes, moved his array against the Suavi. He had as his close allies Gundiuch and Hilperic, kings of the Burgundians. They came to battle near the river Ulbius, which flows between Asturica and Hiberia, and in the engagement Theodorid with the Visigoths, who fought for the right, came off victorious, overthrowing the entire tribe of the Suavi and almost exterminating them. Their king Riciarius fled from the dread foe and embarked upon a ship. But he was beaten back by another foe, the adverse wind of the Tyrrhenian Sea, and so fell into the hands of the Visigoths. Thus though he changed from sea to land, the wretched man did not avert his death.

When Theodorid had become the victor, he spared the conquered and did not suffer the rage of conflict to continue, but placed over the Suavi whom he had conquered one of his own retainers, named Agrivulf. But Agrivulf soon treacherously changed his mind, through the persuasion of the Suavi, and failed to fulfill his duty. For he was quite puffed up with tyrannical pride, believing he had obtained the province as a reward for the valor by which he and his lord had recently subjugated it. Now he was a man born of the stock of the Varni, far below the nobility of Gothic blood, and so was neither zealous for liberty nor faithful toward his patron. As soon as Theodorid heard of this, he despatched a force to cast him out from the kingdom he had usurped. They came quickly and conquered him in the first battle, inflicting a punishment befitting his deeds. For he was captured, taken from his friends, and beheaded. Thus at last he was made aware of the wrath of the master he thought might be despised because he was kind. Now when the Suavi beheld the death of their leader, they sent priests of their country to Theodorid as suppliants. He received them with the reverence due their office and not only granted the Suavi exemption from punishment, but was moved by compassion and allowed them to choose a ruler of their own race for themselves. The Suavi did so, taking Rimismund as their prince. When this was done and peace was everywhere assured, Theodorid died in the thirteenth year of his reign.

XLV His brother Eurich succeeded him with such eager haste that he fell under dark suspicion. Now while these and various other matters were happening among the people of the Visigoths, the Emperor Valentinian was slain by the treachery of Maximus, and Maximus himself, like a tyrant, usurped the rule. Gaiseric, king of the Vandals, heard of this and came from Africa to Italy with ships of war, entered Rome and laid it waste. Maximus fled and was slain by a certain Ursus, a Roman soldier. After him Majorian undertook the government of the western empire at the bidding of Marcian, emperor of the east. But he too ruled but a short time. For when he had moved his forces against the Alani who were harassing Gaul, he was killed at Dertona near the river named Ira. Severus succeeded him and died at Rome in the third year of his reign. When the Emperor Leo, who had succeeded Marcian in the eastern empire, learned of this, he chose as emperor his Patrician Anthemius and sent him to Rome. Upon his arrival he sent against the Alani his son-in-law Ricimer, who was an excellent man and almost the only one in Italy at that time fit to command

the army. In the very first engagement he conquered and destroyed the host of the Alani, together with their king, Beorg.

Now Eurich, king of the Visigoths, perceived the frequent change of Roman emperors and strove to hold Gaul by his own right. The Emperor Anthemius heard of it and asked the Brittones for aid. Their King Riotimus came with twelve thousand men into the state of the Bituriges by the way of Ocean, and was received as he disembarked from his ships. Eurich, king of the Visigoths, came against them with an innumerable army, and after a long fight he routed Riotimus, king of the Brittones, before the Romans could join him. So when he had lost a great part of his army, he fled with all the men he could gather together, and came to the Burgundians, a neighboring tribe then allied to the Romans. But Eurich, king of the Visigoths, seized the Gallic city of Arverna; for the Emperor Anthemius was now dead. Engaged in fierce war with his son-in-law Ricimer, he had worn out Rome and was himself finally slain by his son-in-law and yielded the rule to Olybrius.

At that time Aspar, first of the Patricians and a famous man of the Gothic race was wounded by the swords of the eunuchs in his palace at Constantinople and died. With him were slain his sons Ardabures and Patriciolus, the one long a Patrician, and the other styled a Caesar and son-in-law of the Emperor Leo. Now Olybrius died barely eight months after he had entered upon his reign, and Glycerius was made Caesar at Ravenna, rather by usurpation than by election. Hardly had a year been ended when Nepos, the son of the sister of Marcellinus, once a Patrician, deposed him from his office and ordained him bishop at the Port of Rome.

When Eurich, as we have already said, beheld these great and various changes, he seized the city of Arverna, where the Roman general Ecdicius was at that time in command. He was a senator of most renowned family and the son of Avitus, a recent emperor who had usurped the reign for a few days—for Avitus held the rule for a few days before Olybrius, and then withdrew of his own accord to Placentia, where he was ordained bishop. His son Ecdicius strove for a long time with the Visigoths, but had not the power to prevail. So he left the country and (what was more important) the city of Arverna to the enemy and betook himself to safer regions. When the Emperor Nepos heard of this, he ordered Ecdicius to leave Gaul and come to him, appointing Orestes in his stead as Master of the Soldiery. This Orestes thereupon received the army, set out from Rome against the enemy and came to Ravenna. Here he tarried while he made his son Romulus Augustulus emperor. When Nepos learned of this, he fled to Dalmatia and died there, deprived of his throne, in the very place where Glycerius, who was formerly emperor, held at that time the bishopric of Salona.

XLVI Now when Augustulus had been appointed emperor by his father Orestes in Ravenna, it was not long before Odoacer, king of the Torcilingi, invaded Italy, as leader of the Sciri, the Heruli, and allies of various races. He put Orestes to death, drove his son Augustulus from the throne and condemned him to the punishment of exile in the Castle of Lucullus in Campania. Thus the western empire of the Roman race, which Octavianus Augustus, the first of the Augusti, began to govern in the seven hundred and ninth year from the founding of the city, perished with this Augustulus in the five hundred and twenty-second year from the beginning of the rule of his predecessors and those before them, and from this time onward kings of the Goths held Rome and Italy. Meanwhile Odoacer, king of nations, subdued all Italy and then at the very outset of his reign slew Count Bracila at Ravenna that he might inspire a fear of himself among the Romans. He strengthened his kingdom and held it for almost thirteen years, even until the appearance of Theodoric, of whom we shall speak hereafter.

XLVII But first let us return to that order from which we have digressed and tell how Eurich, king of the Visigoths, beheld the tottering of the Roman Empire and reduced Arelate and Massilia to his own sway. Gaiseric, king of the Vandals, enticed him by gifts to do these things, to the end that he himself might forestall the plots which Leo and Zeno had contrived against him. Therefore he stirred the Ostrogoths to lay waste the eastern empire and the Visigoths the western, so that while his foes were battling in both empires, he might himself reign peacefully in Africa. Eurich perceived this with gladness and, as he already held all of Spain and Gaul by his own right, proceeded to subdue the Burgundians also. In the nineteenth year of his reign he was deprived of his life at Arelate, where he then dwelt. He was succeeded by his own son Alaric, the ninth in succession from the famous Alaric the Great to receive the kingdom of the Visigoths. For even as it happened to the line of the Augusti, as we have stated above, so too it appears in the line of the Alarici, that kingdoms often come to an end in kings who bear the same name as those at the beginning. Meanwhile let us leave this subject, and weave together the whole story of the origin of the Goths, as we promised.

The Divided Goths: Ostrogoths

XLVIII Since I have followed the stories of my ancestors and retold to the best of my ability the tale of the period when both tribes, Ostrogoths and Visigoths, were united, and then clearly treated of the Visigoths apart from the Ostrogoths, I must now return to those ancient Scythian abodes and set forth in like manner the ancestry and deeds of the Ostrogoths. It appears that at the death of their king, Hermanaric, they were made a separate people by the departure of the Visigoths, and remained in their country subject to the sway of the Huns; yet Vinitharius of the Amali retained the insignia of his rule. He rivaled the valor of his grandfather Vultuulf, although he had not the good fortune of Hermanaric. But disliking to remain under the rule of the Huns, he withdrew a little from them and strove to show his courage by moving his forces against the country of the Antes. When he attacked them, he was beaten in the first encounter. Thereafter he did valiantly and, as a terrible example, crucified their king, named Boz, together with his sons and seventy nobles, and left their bodies hanging there to double the fear of those who had surrendered. When he had ruled with such license for barely a year, Balamber, king of the Huns, would no longer endure it, but sent for Gesimund, son of Hunimund the Great. Now Gesimund, together with a great part of the Goths, remained under the rule of the Huns, being mindful of his oath of fidelity. Balamber renewed his alliance with him and led his army up against Vinitharius. After a long contest, Vinitharius prevailed in the first and in the second conflict, nor can any say how great slaughter he made of the army of the Huns. But in the third battle, when they met each other unexpectedly at the river named Erac, Balamber shot an arrow and wounded Vinitharius in the head, so that he died. Then Balamber took to himself in marriage Vadamerca, the granddaughter of Vinitharius, and finally ruled all the people of the Goths as his peaceful subjects, but in such a way that one ruler of their own number always held the power over the Gothic race, though subject to the Huns.

And later, after the death of Vinitharius, Hunimund ruled them, the son of Hermanaric, a mighty king of yore; a man fierce in war and of famous personal beauty, who afterwards fought successfully against the race of the Suavi. And when he died, his son Thorismud succeeded him, in the very bloom of youth. In the second year of his rule he moved an army against the Gepidae and won a great victory over them, but is said to have been killed by falling from his horse. When he was dead, the Ostrogoths mourned for him so deeply that for forty years no other king succeeded in his place, and during all this time they had ever on their lips the tale of his memory. Now as time went on, Valamir grew to man's estate. He was the son of Thorismud's cousin Vandalarius. For his son Beremud, as we have said before, at last grew to despise the race of the Ostrogoths because of the overlordship of the Huns, and so had followed the tribe of the Visigoths to the western country, and it was from him Veteric was descended. Veteric also had a son Eutharic, who married Amalasuentha, the daughter of Theodoric, thus uniting again the stock of the Amali which had divided long ago. Eutharic begat Athalaric and Mathesuentha. But since Athalaric died in the years of his boyhood, Mathesuentha was taken to Constantinople by her second husband, namely Germanus, a nephew of the Emperor Justinian, and bore a posthumous son, whom she named Germanus.

But that the order we have taken for our history may run its due course, we must return to the stock of Vandalarius, which put forth three branches. This Vandalarius, the great grandnephew of Hermanaric and cousin of the aforesaid Thorismud, vaunted himself among the race of the Amali because he had begotten three sons, Valamir, Thiudimer, and Vidimer. Of these Valamir ascended the throne after his parents, though the Huns as yet held the power over the Goths in general as among other nations. It was pleasant to behold the concord of these three brothers; for the admirable Thiudimer served as a soldier for the empire of his brother Valamir, and Valamir bade honors be given him, while Vidimer was eager to serve them both. Thus regarding one another with common affection, not one was wholly deprived of the kingdom which two of them held in mutual peace. Yet, as has often been said, they ruled in such a way that they respected the dominion of Attila, king of the Huns. Indeed they could not have refused to fight against their kinsmen the Visigoths, and they must even have committed parricide at their lord's command. There was no way whereby any Scythian tribe could have been wrested from the power of the Huns, save by the death of Attila—an event the Romans and all other nations desired. Now his death was as base as his life was marvelous. . . .

We shall not omit to say a few words about the many ways in which his shade was honored by his race. His body was placed in the midst of a plain and lay in state in a silken tent as a sight for men's admiration. The best horsemen of the entire tribe of the Huns rode around in circles, after the manner of circus games, in the place to which he had been brought and told of his deeds in a funeral dirge in the following manner: "The chief of the Huns, King Attila, born of his sire Mundiuch, lord of bravest tribes, sole possessor of the Scythian and German realms—powers unknown before—captured cities and terrified both empires of the Roman world and, appeased by their prayers, took annual tribute to save the rest from plunder. And when he had accomplished all this by the favor of fortune, he fell not by wound of the foe, nor by treachery of friends, but in the midst of his nation at peace, happy in his joy and without sense of pain. Who can rate this as death, when none believes it calls for vengeance?" When they had mourned him with such lamentations, a *strava*, as they call it, was celebrated over his tomb with great reveling. They gave way in turn to the extremes of feeling and displayed funereal grief alternating with joy. Then in the secrecy of night they buried his body in the earth. They bound his coffins, the first with gold, the second with silver and the third with the strength of iron, showing by such means that these three things suited the mightiest of kings; iron because he subdued the nations, gold and silver because he received the honors of both empires. They also added the arms of foemen won in the fight, trappings of rare worth, sparkling with various gems, and ornaments of all sorts whereby princely state is maintained. And that so great riches might be kept from human curiosity, they slew those appointed to the work—a dreadful pay for their labor; and thus sudden death was the lot of those who buried him as well as of him who was buried.

L . . . When Ardaric, king of the Gepidae, learned this, he became enraged because so many nations were being treated like slaves of the basest condition, and was the first to rise against the sons of Attila. Good fortune attended him, and he effaced the disgrace of servitude that rested upon him. For by his revolt he freed not only his own tribe, but all the others who were equally oppressed; since all readily strive for that which is sought for the general advantage. They took up arms against the destruction that menaced all and joined battle with the Huns in Pannonia, near a river called Nedao. There an encounter took place between the various nations Attila had held under his sway. Kingdoms with their peoples were divided, and out of one body were made many members not responding to a single impulse. Being deprived of their head, they madly strove against each other. They never found their equals ranged against them without harming each other by wounds mutually given. And so the bravest nations tore themselves to pieces. For then, I think, must have occurred a most remarkable spectacle, where one might see the Goths fighting with pikes, the Gepidae raging with the sword, the Rugi breaking off the spears in their own wounds, the Suavi fighting on foot, the Huns with bows, the Alani drawing up a battle-line of heavy-armed and the Heruli of light-armed warriors.

Finally, after many bitter conflicts, victory fell unexpectedly to the Gepidae. For the sword and conspiracy of Ardaric destroyed almost thirty thousand men, Huns as well as those of the other nations who brought them aid. In this battle fell Ellac, the elder son of Attila, whom his father is said to have loved so much more than all the rest that he preferred him to any child or even to all the children in his kingdom. But fortune was not in accord with his father's wish. For after slaying many of the foe, it appears that he met his death so bravely that if his father had lived, he would have rejoiced at his glorious end. When Ellac was slain, his remaining brothers were put to flight near the shore of the Sea of Pontus, where we have said the Goths first settled. Thus did the Huns give way, a race to which men thought the whole world must yield. So baneful a thing is division, that they who used to inspire terror when their strength was united, were overthrown separately. The cause of Ardaric, king of the Gepidae, was fortunate for the various nations who were unwillingly subject to the rule of the Huns, for it raised their long downcast spirits to the glad hope of freedom. Many sent ambassadors to the Roman territory, where they were most graciously received by Marcian, who was then emperor, and took the abodes allotted them to dwell in. But the Gepidae by their own might won for themselves the territory of the Huns and ruled as victors over the extent of Dacia, demanding of the Roman Empire nothing more than peace and an annual gift as a pledge of their friendly alliance. This the emperor freely granted at the time, and to this day that race receives its customary gifts from the Roman emperor.

Now when the Goths saw the Gepidae defending for themselves the territory of the Huns, and the people of the Huns dwelling again in their ancient abodes, they preferred to ask for lands from the Roman Empire, rather than invade the lands of others with danger to themselves. So they received Pannonia, which stretches in a long plain, being bounded on the east by Upper Moesia, on the south by Dalmatia, on the west by Noricum, and on the north by the Danube. This land is adorned with many cities, the first of which is Sirmium and the last Vindobona. But the Sauromatae, whom we call Sarmatians, and the Cemandri and certain of the Huns dwelt in Castra Martis, a city given them in the region of Illyricum. Of this race was Blivila, Duke of Pentapolis, and his brother Froila and also Bessa, a Patrician in our time. The Sciri, moreover, and the Sadagarii and certain of the Alani with their leader, Candac by name, received Scythia Minor and Lower Moesia. Paria, the father of my father Alanoviiamuth (that is to say, my grandfather), was secretary to this Candac as long as he lived. To his sister's son Gunthigis, also called Baza, the Master of the Soldiery, who was descended from the stock of the Amali, I also, Jordanes, although an unlearned man before my conversion, was secretary. The Rugi, however, and some other races asked that they might inhabit Bizye and Arcadiopolis. Hernac, the younger son of Attila, with his followers, chose a home in the most distant part of Lesser Scythia. Emnetzur and Ultzindur, kinsmen of his, won Oescus and Utus and Almus in Dacia on the banks of the Danube, and many of the Huns, then swarming everywhere, betook themselves into Romania, and from them the Sacromontisi and the Fossatisii of this day are said to be descended.

LI There were other Goths also, called the Lesser, a great people whose priest and primate was Vulfila, who is said to have taught them to write. And to-day they are in Moesia, inhabiting the Nicopolitan region as far as the base of Mount Haemus. They are a numerous people, but poor and unwarlike, rich in nothing save flocks of various kinds and pasture-lands for cattle and forests for wood. Their country is not fruitful in wheat and other sorts of grain. Some of them do not know that vineyards exist elsewhere, and they buy their wine from neighboring countries. But most of them drink milk.

LII Let us now return to the tribe with which we started, namely the Ostrogoths, who were dwelling in Pannonia under their king Valamir and his brothers Thiudimer and Vidimer. Although their territories were separate, yet their plans were one. For Valamir dwelt between the rivers Scarniunga and Aqua Nigra, Thiudimer near Lake Pelso, and Vidimer between them both. Now it happened that the sons of Attila, regarding the Goths as deserters from their rule, came against them as though they were seeking fugitive slaves, and attacked Valamir alone, when his brothers knew nothing of it. He sustained their attack, though he had but few supporters, and after harassing them a long time, so utterly overwhelmed them that scarcely any portion of the enemy remained. The remnant turned in flight and sought the parts of Scythia which border on the stream of the river Danaper, which the Huns call in their own tongue the Var. Thereupon he sent a messenger of good tidings to his brother Thiudimer, and on the very day the messenger arrived he found even greater joy in the house of Thiudimer. For on that day his son Theodoric was born, of a concubine Erelieva indeed, and yet a child of good hope.

Now after no great time King Valamir and his brothers Thiudimer and Vidimer sent an embassy to the Emperor Marcian, because the usual gifts which they received like a New Year's present from the emperor, to preserve the compact of peace, were slow in arriving. And they found that Theodoric, son of Triarius, a man of Gothic blood also, but born of another stock, not of the Amali, was in great favor, together with his followers. He was allied in friendship with the Romans and obtained an annual bounty, while they themselves were merely held in disdain. Thereat they were aroused to frenzy and took up arms. They roved through almost the whole of Illyricum and laid it waste in their search for spoil. Then the emperor quickly changed his mind and returned to his former state of friendship. He sent an embassy to give them the past gifts, as well as those now due, and furthermore promised to give these gifts in future without any dispute. From the Goths the Romans received as a hostage of peace Theodoric, the young child of Thiudimer, whom we have mentioned above. He had now attained the age of seven years and was entering upon his eighth. While his father hesitated about giving him up, his uncle Valamir besought him to do it, hoping that peace between the Romans and the Goths might thus be assured. Therefore Theodoric was given as a hostage by the Goths and brought to the city of Constantinople to the Emperor Leo and, being a goodly child, deservedly gained the imperial favor.

LIII Now after firm peace was established between Goths and Romans, the Goths found that the possessions they had received from the emperor were not sufficient for them. Furthermore, they were eager to display their wonted valor, and so began to plunder the neighboring races around them, first attacking the Sadagis who held the interior of Pannonia. When Dintzic, king of the Huns, a son of Attila, learned this, he gathered to him the few who still seemed to have remained under his sway, namely, the Ultzinzures, the Angisciri, the Bittugures, and the Bardores. Coming to Bassiana, a city of Pannonia, he beleaguered it and began to plunder its territory. Then the Goths at once abandoned the expedition they had planned against the Sadagis, turned upon the Huns and drove them so ingloriously from their own land that those who remained have been in dread of the arms of the Goths from that time even down to the present day.

When the tribe of the Huns was at last subdued by the Goths, Hunimund, chief of the Suavi, who was crossing over to plunder Dalmatia, carried off some cattle of the Goths which were straying over the plains; for Dalmatia was near Suavia and not far distant from the territory of Pannonia, especially that part where the Goths were then staying. So then, as Hunimund was returning with the Suavi to his own country, after he had devastated Dalmatia, Thiudimer the brother of Valamir, king of the Goths, kept watch on their line of march. Not that he grieved so much over the loss of his cattle, but he feared that if the Suavi obtained this plunder with impunity, they would proceed to greater license. So in the dead of night, while they were asleep, he made an unexpected attack on them, near Lake Pelso. Here he so completely crushed them that he took captive and sent into slavery under the Goths even Hunimund, their king, and all of his army who had escaped the sword. Yet as he was a great lover of mercy, he granted pardon after taking vengeance and became reconciled to the Suavi. He adopted as his son the same man whom he had taken captive, and sent him back with his followers into Suavia. But Hunimund was unmindful of his adopted father's kindness. After some time he brought forth a plot he had contrived and aroused the tribe of the Sciri, who then dwelt above the Danube and abode peaceably with the Goths. So the Sciri broke off their alliance with them, took up arms, joined themselves to Hunimund and went out to attack the race of the Goths. Thus war came upon the Goths who were expecting no evil, because they relied upon both of their neighbors as friends. Constrained by necessity they took up arms and avenged themselves and their injuries by recourse to battle. In this battle, as King Valamir rode on his horse before the line to encourage his men, the horse was wounded and fell, overthrowing its rider. Valamir was quickly pierced by his enemies' spears and slain. Thereupon the Goths proceeded to exact vengeance for the death of their king, as well as for the injury done them by the rebels. They fought in such wise that there remained of all the race of the Sciri only a few who bore the name, and they with disgrace. Thus were all destroyed.

LIV The kings [of the Suavi], Hunimund and Alaric, fearing the destruction that had come upon the Sciri, next made war upon the Goths, relying upon the aid of the Sarmatians, who had come to them as auxiliaries with their kings Beuca and Babai. They summoned the last remnants of the Sciri, with Edica and Hunuulf, their chieftains, thinking they would fight the more desperately to avenge themselves. They had on their side the Gepidae also, as well as no small reinforcements from the race of the Rugi and from others gathered here and there. Thus they brought together a great host at the river Bolia in Pannonia and encamped there. Now when Valamir was dead, the Goths fled to Thiudimer, his brother. Although he had long ruled along with his brothers, yet he took the insignia of increased authority and summoned his younger brother Vidimer and shared with him the cares of war, resorting to arms under compulsion. A battle was fought and the party of the Goths was found to be so much the stronger that the plain was drenched in the blood of their fallen foes and looked like a crimson sea. Weapons and corpses, piled up like hills, covered the plain for more than ten miles. When the Goths saw this, they rejoiced with joy unspeakable, because by this great slaughter of their foes they had avenged the blood of Valamir their king and the injury done themselves. But those of the innumerable and motley throng of the foe who were unable to escape, though they got away, nevertheless came to their own land with difficulty and without glory.

LV After a certain time, when the wintry cold was at hand, the river Danube was frozen over as usual. For a river like this freezes so hard that it will support like a solid rock an army of foot-soldiers and wagons and sledges and whatsoever vehicles there may be—nor is there need of skiffs and boats. So when Thiudimer, king of the Goths, saw that it was frozen, he led his army across the Danube and appeared unexpectedly to the Suavi from the rear. Now this country of the Suavi has on the east the Baiovari, on the west the Franks, on the south the Burgundians, and on the north the Thuringians. With the Suavi there were present the Alamanni, then their confederates, who also ruled the Alpine heights, whence several streams flow into the Danube, pouring in with a great rushing sound. Into a place thus fortified King Thiudimer led his army in the winter-time and conquered, plundered, and almost subdued the race of the Suavi as well as the Alamanni, who were mutually banded together. Thence he returned as victor to his own home in Pannonia and joyfully received his own son Theodoric, once given as hostage to Constantinople and now sent back by the Emperor Leo with great gifts. Now Theodoric had reached man's estate, for he was eighteen years of age and his boyhood was ended. So he summoned certain of his father's adherents and took to himself from the people his friends and retainers—almost six thousand men. With these he crossed the Danube, without his father's knowledge, and marched against Babai, king of the Sarmatians, who had just won a victory over Camundus, a general of the Romans, and was ruling with insolent pride. Theodoric came upon him and slew him, and taking as booty his slaves and treasure, returned victorious to his father. Next he invaded the city of Singidunum, which the Sarmatians themselves had seized, and did not return to the Romans, but reduced it to his own sway.

LVI Then as the spoil taken from one and another of the neighboring tribes diminished, the Goths began to lack food and clothing, and peace became distasteful to men for whom war had long furnished the necessaries of life. So all the Goths approached their king Thiudimer and, with great outcry, begged him to lead forth his army in whatsoever direction he might wish. He summoned his brother and, after casting lots, bade him go into the country of Italy, where at this time Glycerius ruled as emperor, saying that he himself as the mightier would go to the east against a mightier empire. And so it happened. Thereupon Vidimer entered the land of Italy, but soon paid the last debt of fate and departed from earthly affairs, leaving his son and namesake Vidimer to succeed him. The Emperor Glycerius bestowed gifts upon Vidimer and persuaded him to go from Italy to Gaul, which was then harassed on all sides by various races, saying that their own kinsmen, the Visigoths, there ruled a neighboring kingdom. And what more? Vidimer accepted the gifts and, obeying the command of the Emperor Glycerius, pressed on to Gaul. Joining with his kinsmen the Visigoths, they again formed one body, as they had been long ago. Thus they held Gaul and Spain by their own right and so defended them that no other race won the mastery there.

But Thiudimer, the elder brother, crossed the river Savus with his men, threatening the Sarmatians and their soldiers with war if any should resist him. From fear of this they kept quiet; moreover they were powerless in the face of so great a host. Thiudimer, seeing prosperity everywhere awaiting him, invaded Naissus, the first city of Illyricum. He was joined by his son Theodoric and the Counts Astat and Invilia, and sent them to Ulpiana by way of Castrum Herculis. Upon their arrival the town surrendered, as did Stobi later; and several places of Illyricum, inaccessible to them at first, were thus made easy of approach. For they first plundered and then ruled by right of war Heraclea and Larissa, cities of Thessaly. But Thiudimer the king, perceiving his own good fortune and that of his son, was not content with this alone, but set forth from the city of Naissus, leaving only a few men behind as a guard. He himself advanced to Thessalonica, where Hilarianus the Patrician, appointed by the emperor, was stationed with his army. When Hilarianus beheld Thessalonica surrounded by an entrenchment and saw that he could not resist attack, he sent an embassy to Thiudimer the king and by the offer of gifts turned him aside from destroying the city. Then the Roman general entered upon a truce with the Goths and of his own accord handed over to them those places they inhabited, namely Cyrrhus, Pella, Europus, Methone, Pydna, Beroea, and another which is called Dium. So the Goths and their king laid aside their arms, consented to peace and became quiet. Soon after these events, King Thiudimer was seized with a mortal illness in the city of Cyrrhus. He called the Goths to himself, appointed Theodoric his son as heir of the kingdom and presently departed this life.

LVII When the Emperor Zeno heard that Theodoric had been appointed king over his own people, he received the news with pleasure and invited him to come and visit him in the city, sending an escort of honor. Receiving Theodoric with all due respect, he placed him among the princes of his palace. After some time Zeno increased his dignity by adopting him as his son-in-arms and gave him a triumph in the city at his expense. Theodoric was made Consul Ordinary also, which is well known to be the supreme good and highest honor in the world. Nor was this all, for Zeno set up before the royal palace an equestrian statue to the glory of this great man.

Now while Theodoric was in alliance by treaty with the empire of Zeno and was himself enjoying every comfort in the city, he heard that his tribe, dwelling as we have said in Illyricum, was not altogether satisfied or content. So he chose rather to seek a living by his own exertions, after the manner customary to his race, rather than to enjoy the advantages of the Roman Empire in luxurious ease while his tribe lived apart. After pondering these matters, he said to the emperor: "Though I lack nothing in serving your empire, yet if Your Piety deem it worthy, be pleased to hear the desire of my heart." And when as usual he had been granted permission to speak freely, he said: "The western country, long ago governed by the rule of your ancestors and predecessors, and that city which was the head and mistress of the world—wherefore is it now shaken by the tyranny of the Torcilingi and the Rugi? Send me there with my race. Thus if you but say the word, you may be freed from the burden of expense here, and, if by the Lord's help I shall conquer, the fame of Your Piety shall be glorious there. For it is better that I, your servant and your son, should rule that kingdom, receiving it as a gift from you if I conquer, than that one whom you do not recognize should oppress your Senate with his tyrannical yoke and a part of the republic with slavery. For if I prevail, I shall retain it as your grant and gift; if I am conquered, Your Piety will lose nothing—nay, as I have said, it will save the expense I now entail." Although the emperor was grieved that he should go, yet when he heard this he granted what Theodoric asked, for he was unwilling to cause him sorrow. He sent him forth enriched by great gifts and commended to his charge the Senate and the Roman people.

Therefore Theodoric departed from the royal city and returned to his own people. In company with the whole tribe of the Goths, who gave him their unanimous consent, he set out for Hesperia. He went in straight march through Sirmium to the places bordering on Pannonia and, advancing into the territory of Venetia as far as the bridge of the Sontius, encamped there. When he had halted there for some time to rest the bodies of his men and pack-animals, Odoacer sent an armed force against him, which he met on the plains of Verona and destroyed with great slaughter. Then he broke camp and advanced through Italy with greater boldness. Crossing the river Po, he pitched camp near the royal city of Ravenna, about the third milestone from the city in the place called Pineta. When Odoacer saw this, he fortified himself within the city. He frequently harassed the army of the Goths at night, sallying forth stealthily with his men, and this not once or twice, but often; and thus he struggled for almost three whole years. But he labored in vain, for all Italy at last called Theodoric its lord and the empire obeyed his nod. But Odoacer, with his few adherents and the Romans who were present, suffered daily from war and famine in Ravenna. Since he accomplished nothing, he sent an embassy and begged for mercy. Theodoric first granted it and afterwards deprived him of his life.

It was in the third year after his entrance into Italy, as we have said, that Theodoric, by advice of the Emperor Zeno, laid aside the garb of a private citizen and the dress of his race and assumed a costume with a royal mantle, as he had now become the ruler over both the Goths and Romans. He sent an embassy to Lodoin, king of the Franks, and asked for his daughter Audefleda in marriage. Lodoin freely and gladly gave her, and also his sons Celdebert and Heldebert and Thiudebert, believing that by this alliance a league would be formed and that they would be associated with the race of the Goths. But that union was of no avail for peace and harmony, for they fought fiercely with each other again and again for the lands of the Goths; but never did the Goths yield to the Franks while Theodoric lived.

LVIII Now before he had a child from Audefleda, Theodoric had children of a concubine, daughters begotten in Moesia, one named Thiudigoto and another Ostrogotho. Soon after he came to Italy, he gave them in marriage to neighboring kings, one to Alaric, king of the Visigoths, and the other to Sigsimund, king of the Burgundians. Now Alaric begat Amalaric. While his grandfather Theodoric cared for and protected him—for he had lost both parents in the years of childhood—he found that Eutharic, the son of Veteric, grandchild of Beremud and of Thorismud, and a descendant of the race of the Amali, was living in Spain, a young man strong in wisdom and valor and health of body. Theodoric sent for him and gave him his daughter Amalasuentha in marriage. And that he might extend his family as much as possible, he sent his sister Amalafrida (the mother of Theodahad, who was afterwards king) to Africa as wife of Thrasamund, king of the Vandals, and her daughter Amalaberga, who was his own niece, he united with Herminefred, king of the Thuringians.

Now he sent his Count Pitza, chosen from among the chief men of his kingdom, to hold the city of Sirmium. He got possession of it by driving out its king Thrasaric, son of Thraustila, and keeping his mother captive. Thence he came with two thousand infantry and five hundred horsemen to aid Mundo against Sabinian, Master of the Soldiery of Illyricum, who at that time had made ready to fight with Mundo near the city named Margoplanum, which lies between the Danube and Margus rivers, and destroyed the Army of Illyricum. For this Mundo, who traced his descent from the Attilani of old, had fled from the tribe of the Gepidae and was roaming around beyond the Danube in waste places where no man tilled the soil. He had gathered around him many outlaws and ruffians and robbers from all sides and had seized a tower called Herta, situated on the bank of the Danube. There he plundered his neighbors in wild license and made himself king over his vagabonds. Now Pitza came upon him when he was nearly reduced to desperation and was already thinking of surrender. So he rescued him from the hands of the Sabinian and made him a grateful subject of his king Theodoric.

Theodoric won an equally great victory over the Franks through his Count Ibba in Gaul, when more than thirty thousand Franks were slain in battle. Moreover, after the death of his son-in-law Alaric, Theodoric appointed Thiudis, his armor-bearer, guardian of his grandson Amalaric in Spain. But Amalaric was ensnared by the plots of the Franks in early youth and lost at once his kingdom and his life. Then his guardian Thiusis, advancing from the same kingdom, assailed the Franks and delivered the Spaniards from their disgraceful treachery. So long as he lived he kept the Visigoths united. After him Thiudigisclus obtained the kingdom and, ruling but a short time, met his death at the hands of his own followers. He was succeeded by Agil, who holds the kingdom to the present day. Athanagild has rebelled against him and is even now provoking the might of the Roman Empire. So Liberius the Patrician is on the way with an army to oppose him. Now there was not a tribe in the west that did not serve Theodoric while he lived, either in friendship or by conquest.

LIX When he had reached old age and knew that he should soon depart this life, he called together the Gothic counts and chieftains of his race and appointed Athalaric as king. He was a boy scarce ten years old, the son of his daughter Amalasuentha, and he had lost his father Eutharic. As though uttering his last will and testament, Theodoric adjured and commanded them to honor their king, to love the Senate and Roman people and to make sure of the peace and good will of the emperor of the east, as next after God.

They kept this command fully so long as Athalaric their king and his mother lived, and ruled in peace for almost eight years. But as the Franks put no confidence in the rule of a child and furthermore held him in contempt, and were also plotting war, he gave back to them those parts of Gaul which his father and grandfather had seized. He possessed all the rest in peace and quiet. Therefore when Athalaric was approaching the age of manhood, he entrusted to the emperor of the east both his own youth and his mother's widowhood. But in a short time the ill-fated boy was carried off by an untimely death and departed from earthly affairs. His mother feared she might be despised by the Goths on account of the weakness of her sex. So after much thought she decided, for the sake of relationship, to summon her cousin Theodahad from Tuscany, where he led a retired life at home, and thus she established him on the throne. But he was unmindful of their kinship and, after a little time, had her taken from the palace at Ravenna to an island of the Bulsinian lake where he kept her in exile. After spending a very few days there in sorrow, she was strangled in the bath by his hirelings.

LX When Justinian, the emperor of the east, heard this, he was aroused as if he had suffered personal injury in the death of his wards. Now at that time he had won a triumph over the Vandals in Africa, through his most faithful Patrician Belisarius. Without delay he sent his army under this leader against the Goths at the very time when his arms were yet dripping with the blood of the Vandals. This sagacious general believed he could not overcome the Gothic nation, unless he should first seize Sicily, their nursing-mother. Accordingly he did so. As soon as he entered Trinacria, the Goths, who were besieging the town of Syracuse, found that they were not succeeding and surrendered of their own accord to Belisarius, with their leader Sinderith. When the Roman general reached Sicily, Theodahad sought out Evermud, his son-in-law, and sent him with an army to guard the strait which lies between Campania and Sicily and sweeps from a bend of the Tyrrhenian Sea into the vast tide of the Adriatic. When Evermud arrived, he pitched his camp by the town of Rhegium. He soon saw that his side was the weaker. Coming over with a few close and faithful followers to the side of the victor and willingly casting himself at the feet of Belisarius, he decided to serve the rulers of the Roman Empire. When the army of the Goths perceived this, they distrusted Theodahad and clamored for his expulsion from the kingdom and for the appointment as king of their leader Vitiges, who had been his armor-bearer. This was done; and presently Vitiges was raised to the office of king on the Barbarian Plains. He entered Rome and sent on to Ravenna the men most faithful to him to demand the death of Theodahad. They came and executed his command. After King Theodahad was slain, a messenger came from the king—for he was already king in the Barbarian Plains—to proclaim Vitiges to the people.

Meanwhile the Roman army crossed the strait and marched toward Campania. They took Naples and pressed on to Rome. Now a few days before they arrived, King Vitiges had set forth from Rome, arrived at Ravenna and married Mathesuentha, the daughter of Amalasuentha and granddaughter of Theodoric, the former king. While he was celebrating his new marriage and holding court at Ravenna, the imperial army advanced from Rome and attacked the strongholds in both parts of Tuscany. When Vitiges learned of this through messengers, he sent a force under Hunila, a leader of the Goths, to Perusia which was beleaguered by them. While they were endeavoring by a long siege to dislodge Count Magnus, who was holding the place with a small force, the Roman army came upon them, and they themselves were driven away and utterly exterminated. When Vitiges heard the news, he raged like a lion and assembled all the host of the Goths. He advanced from Ravenna and harassed the walls of Rome with a long siege. But after fourteen months his courage was broken and he raised the siege of the city of Rome and prepared to overwhelm Ariminum. Here he was baffled in like manner and put to flight; and so he retreated to Ravenna. When besieged there, he quickly and willingly surrendered himself to the victorious side, together with his wife Mathesuentha and the royal treasure.

And thus a famous kingdom and most valiant race, which had long held sway, was at last overcome in almost its two thousand and thirtieth year by that conqueror of many nations, the Emperor Justinian, through his most faithful consul Belisarius. He gave Vitiges the title of Patrician and took him to Constantinople, where he dwelt for more than two years, bound by ties of affection to the emperor, and then departed this life. But his consort Mathesuentha was bestowed by the emperor upon the Patrician Germanus, his nephew. And of them was born a son (also called Germanus) after the death of his father Germanus. This union of the race of the Anicii with the stock of the Amali gives hopeful promise, under the Lord's favor, to both peoples.

Conclusion

And now we have recited the origin of the Goths, the noble line of the Amali and the deeds of brave men. This glorious race yielded to a more glorious prince and surrendered to a more valiant leader, whose fame shall be silenced by no ages or cycles of years; for the victorious and triumphant Emperor Justinian and his consul Belisarius shall be named and known as Vandalicus, Africanus, and Geticus.

Thou who readest this, know that I have followed the writings of my ancestors, and have culled a few flowers from their broad meadows to weave a chaplet for him who cares to know these things. Let no one believe that to the advantage of the race of which I have spoken—though indeed I trace my own descent from it—I have added aught besides what I have read or learned by inquiry. Even thus I have not included all that is written or told about them, nor spoken so much to their praise as to the glory of him who conquered them.

6. HILDEBRANDSLIED

The fragmentary *Song of Hildebrand and Hadubrand*, the oldest extant continental Germanic heroic poem, was copied into a manuscript in the monastery of Fulda around 800. The current scholarly opinion is that the poem was composed in the eighth century in Lombardy, drawing on a much older Gothic tradition of the fifth and sixth centuries concerning the family of the Brandings: Heribrand, Hildebrand, and Hadubrand. Versions of the legend spread throughout the Germanic and Celtic worlds from Germany to Scandinavia to Ireland. The poem presents the complex world of late antiquity from the perspective of the barbarians as well as the tragic conflict between honor and kindred.

Source: Von Hildebrand und Hadubrand: Lied—Sage—Mythos, trans. Sigfried Gutenbrunner (Heidelberg: Winter, 1976).

Further Reading: Cyril Edwards, *The Beginnings of German Literature: Comparative and Interdisciplinary Approaches to Old High German* (Rochester: Camden House, 2002).

THE SONG OF HILDEBRAND AND HADUBRAND

That I heard it said . . .[11]
that two warriors encountered each other
Hildebrand and Hadubrand, between their two
   armies.
Son and father looked to their armor,
They prepared their battle-dress, their swords the
   heroes belted fast
Over their ring-armor, and then they rode to the
   battle.
Hildebrand spoke, Heribrand's son; he was the
   older man,
Experienced in the world. He began to ask
With few words, who his father was
From among the heroes of the people . . .
. . . "or of what ancestry are you?
Name but one, the others I will know,
Youth, in the kingdoms all the kindreds are known
   to me."
Hadubrand spoke, Hildebrand's son:
"Long ago our people told me,
The elders and sages who had lived long,
That my father was called Hildebrand, I am called
   Hadubrand.
Long ago he went east, fled the anger of Odoacer,
With Dietrich [Theoderic] and his many
   swordsmen.
He established misery in the land
The woman in the home, the small child,
He robbed of their inheritance, and then rode east.
Therefore my father was and remained for Dietrich
Indispensable, he was such a reliable man.

He was a great enemy of Odoacer But he was the
   best of the swords with Dietrich;
He was always at the head of the army; swordplay
   was always dear to him.
He was known to many brave men.
I do not imagine that he still wanders the earth."
Hildebrand spoke, Heribrand's son:
"The Father of All above in heaven knows
That never before have you exchanged speech with
   so close a kinsman."
Then he took from his arm a twisted ring,
Made from Emperor's gold, as the king had given it
   to him,
The lord of the Huns: "This I give to you as a gift!"
Hadubrand spoke, Hildebrand's son:
"With the spear should one receive gifts,
Point against point.
You old Hun, outrageous trickster,
You entice me with your words, you want to cast me
   down with the spear,
You have become so old that you intend only
   treachery.
This men have told me who have traveled to
   the sea
And westward over the earth-encircling sea: War
   took him away,
Hildebrand is dead, Heribrand's son."
Hildebrand spoke, Heribrand's son:
"In truth I hear it and see it in your war-gear,
That you have at home a lord so good
That under this prince you would never be exiled."
   . . .
"Now sorrow, ruling god, the destiny of woe fulfills
   itself!
I have traveled through sixty summers and winters,
Always I was counted among the most forward
But before none of the cities did I come to die;
Now my child must kill me with the sword,

---

[11] Ellipses indicate lost portions of the poem.

Must lay me low with the death-ax, or else I must
    become his killer!
Now you lightly wish, if you have the power,
To win the armor of so old a hero,
To capture the spoils if you have the right to them!"
He would be the most repulsive of all the East
    people (said Hildebrand)
Who would refuse you battle, now he gladly desires
Hand to hand battle with you! May the encounter
    decide
Which of us must today lose his armor
Or possess both coats of mail.
Then first they sprang at each other with spears

In hard attacks; the shields protect them.
Then they rush together to bitter swordplay,
The bright shields strike sorrowfully
Until the linden wood became light to them
Ground away by the weapons . . .

Questions for Study

"Barbarian" was a label used by the Romans to refer to their non-Roman neighbors and to emphasize their difference. To what extent do these texts reflect Roman culture, barbarian culture, or the intermixture of the two? Does barbarian identity appear fixed in these texts?

The Early Franks

7. THE TOMB OF CHILDERIC, FATHER OF CLOVIS

In 1653 the tomb of the Frankish chieftain Childeric (d. 481 or 482) was discovered at Tournai, Belgium. Most of the extremely precious objects from the tomb were stolen and destroyed in the nineteenth century. However, descriptions and sketches of them, as well as objects recently discovered in the area surrounding the tomb, have made it possible to reconstruct the multiethnic and multicultural world of such Germanic chieftains.

These objects include a lance and an ax typical of northern Gaul and particularly of "Frankish" warriors. Childeric's cruciform broach or fibula is of Roman origin, and similar pieces have been found in Hungary and the former Czechoslovakia. His signet ring with its inscription "Childirici regis" is also typically Roman, although the inscription itself, indicating that he is a king, is a barbarian title granted perhaps but not carried by Romans. Another fibula found recently near the tomb appears to be Anglo-Saxon. Childeric's long sword and shorter sword with a single blade resemble others found in Pannonia, and the cloisonné enamels of bees and other zoomorphic motifs indicate a strong oriental influence although they were probably produced in northern Gaul. Finally, the form of burial itself, although difficult to interpret, apparently was a tumulus or mound in which the chieftain and at least one horse were buried, while a herd of at least 30 horses were killed and buried around his tomb. Such a burial is much more typical of Alans and Sarmats from Iran than of western Germanic peoples.

Source: Patrick Périn and Laure-Charlotte Feffer, *Les Francs*, vol. I: *À la conquête de la Gaule*, trans. Joelle Favreau (Paris: Colin, 1987), 119–33.
Further Reading: Bonnie Effros, *Merovingian Mortuary Archaeology and the Making of the Early Middle Ages* (Berkeley: University of California Press, 2003).

Childeric's tomb was discovered on May 27, 1653, at 3 PM by a deaf-mute mason, Adrien Quinquin, during the Saint-Brice hospice reconstructions in Tournai. At 2.50 m deep, Quinquin brought to light the remnants of a leather bag full of gold coins, then a gold bracelet, fragments of iron and, most importantly, a large quantity of jewelry cloisonné with garnet. Among these objects was a gold signet ring with the inscription

CHILDIRICI REGIS. In fact it was the tomb of Childeric, Clovis's father.

Exceptional in its value, the funeral artifacts found in Childeric's tomb are also remarkable for their precise dating. It was in 481 or 482 that Clovis succeeded his father. The date of his father's death is corroborated by the signet ring. Indeed, this date constitutes an exact *terminus ante quem* for the dating of the objects gathered in Tournai in 1653, corroborated by the period of issue of the most recent coins found in the royal grave (bearing the effigy of the Emperor Zeno).

Dated to the third quarter of the fifth century, these funeral artifacts still raise two problems: first, the identification of some of their components because of the almost total ignorance of their original sites in the tomb; second, the appreciation of the circumstances that led to the accumulation of all these objects, modest or precious.

While it is possible to allocate precisely the cloisonné ornaments which belonged to the long sword and to the scramasax,[1] and to attribute to the royal costume some accessories (belt and shoe buckles, cruciform buckle, purse clasp) and jewels (bracelets, signet ring, ring), archeologists still remain divided as to the identification of other objects, considered by some as clothing accessories and by others as ornaments for the harness of the royal horse. It is the same for the possibility of an adjacent woman's burial place, granted to Basina[2] (second skullcap, sphere of rock crystal characteristic of a woman's costume). The apparent presence of the tomb of a horse (whose head was found) also divides the archeologists: was the entire horse buried, or the head only, or merely the harness? The three possibilities are all plausible, taking into account other similar discoveries.

As controversial is the question of influences reflected by the components of Childeric's funeral artifacts. In a schematic manner, one can try to isolate several lines of influence. The spear and the ax, classic during that era in northern Gaul, must be attributed to the "Frankish" warlike style. The gold cruciform buckle of Roman origin (similar to those found in the tombs of Barbarian princes of Apahida, in Hungary, and of Blucina, in the former Czechoslovakia), as well as the signet ring (also present in Apahida), illustrate in an eloquent way that the "Roman"

style was adopted by Barbarian princes in contact with the Empire. Childeric's tomb also reveals the style then common to the Germans as a whole and even to other Barbarians such as the Alani-Sarmatians (Iranians): the actual funeral pomp (possibly completed by the presence of an adjacent tomb for a horse, with the collective sacrifice of a herd of domestic horses); the presence on the right wrist of a permanently fixed solid gold bracelet which, as in the Apahida, Blucina, and Pouan (Aube) tombs, showed the princely status of these wealthy warriors.

Of other influences, perhaps the most spectacular can be termed "Danubian." Parallels between the tombs of Tournai and Pouan and those of wealthy warriors from the oriental Germanic world (more precisely of the Danubian regions such as the Gepide burial places of Apahida and the Lombard or Skire tombs of Blucina), were identified long ago. In all these cases the tomb has held a long sword and a straight sword with a narrow blade and only one cutting edge; clothing accessories such as massive belt buckles equipped with tongues with large shields; and the ornaments of cloisonné jewelry. These parallels suggest that Childeric's tomb must be directly related to the Germanic tombs which were part of the contemporary Germanic culture that survived the fall of the Hunnic Empire in 455. The parallels should not be assumed to result from Attila and the Huns' raid in Gaul in 451. Indeed, at the end of the fourth century and during the first half of the fifth century, some rare discoveries in occidental Europe (men's tombs at Wolfsheim, Altussheim, and Mundolsheim, in the Middle Rhine or vicinity; Béja in Portugal; women's tombs of Hochfelden in Alsace and of Airan in Calvados) testify that there were already contacts with the Danubian regions. These contacts were broadened during the second half of the fifth century and facilitated the adoption and imitation by the occidental Barbarian courts of some styles popular in the oriental Germanic world.

While the cloisonné enamel objects of Childeric's tomb, and in particular the sword and scramasax sword, testify to the remarkable work of several workshops or of several goldsmiths, it does not seem possible today to try to separate those that could have been imported from the Danubian regions or fabricated at the Frankish court by goldsmiths who were native to these regions from those that were produced by local craftsmen imitating the oriental productions. The most plausible hypothesis, supported by the presence of decorated designs that

---

[1] Single-edged short sword.

[2] Wife of the Thuringian king Bisinus.

were totally foreign to the oriental world, is that all of Childeric's funeral artifacts were made in northern Gaul by goldsmiths who were either of oriental origin or were working largely according to the traditions of oriental goldsmiths (among which some probably were not "Barbarians," but, for example, Greeks).

Recent excavations in Tournai around the Saint-Brice church have shed some new light on the archeological environment of Childeric's tomb. For example, until 1983 it was thought that this royal burial, established on the site of an old Roman necropolis of the first and second centuries, was isolated. While the recent research had not been able to date this graveyard to the late Empire, it nonetheless has revealed the presence of a series of Merovingian burial places dating from the second half of the fifth century to the seventh century.

However, it has not been possible to determine whether the oldest ones among them were prior or contemporary to Childeric's tomb. Therefore it is now established that the royal grave was part of an original core of a Merovingian necropolis and may have marked its beginning.

Several Merovingian burial places have been found to contain rich funeral artifacts: proof that Tournai remained an important town at the beginning of the early Middle Ages, even though it was no longer a Merovingian capital. Also significant has been the discovery of three collective burial places of horses, each containing a dozen animals, most of them stallions. These burial places, which lacked artifacts, have been dated to the second half of the fifth century or to the beginning of the sixth century (Carbon 14 dating, between 430 and 560

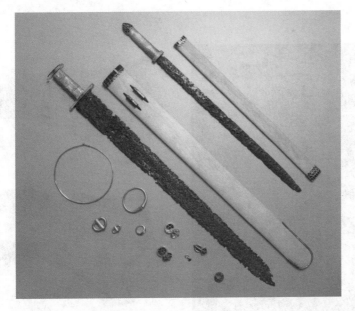

"Treasure of Pouan." The sword and the scramasax.

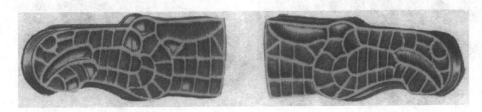

Childeric's tomb. Zoomorphic purse clasps.

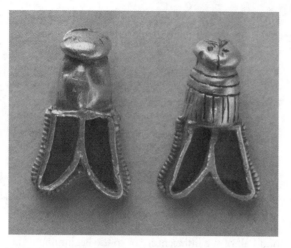

(a) Two gold bees cloisonné with garnet from the "Childeric's treasure."

(b) The signet ring of Childeric I.

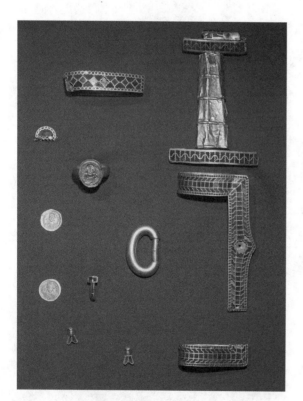

Childeric's tomb. Reconstruction of the scramasax sheath. Knob of button and scramasax appliqués of cloisonné goldsmith work.

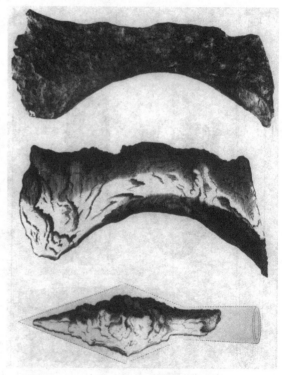

Childeric's tomb. Frankish battle-ax. Spear.

A selection of items from the Treasure of Childeric.

Hilt and mouth of the sheath of Childeric's sword.

Childeric's tomb. Signet ring and gold bracelet. Belt and shoe buckles and appliqués.

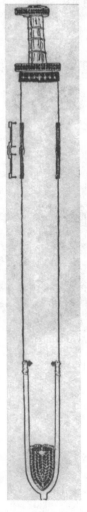

Reconstruction of the sheath of the sword.

Anglo-Saxon–type buckle with zoomorphic and anthropomorphic design, sixth century.

and more probably 440 and 540). Taking into consideration that their location was around 20 m from Childeric's tomb, it is likely that they bear some direct relation to the royal burial. Thus a new detail may be added to our picture of the funeral splendor of Clovis's father: the collective sacrifice of a whole herd of domestic horses. There are no precise parallels for this exceptional ritual in the occidental Germanic world; indeed, in Westphalia as well as in Thuringia, such burials involved only two or three horses.

8. SALIC LAW

The first codification of Salic law took place under King Clovis (481–511) and represents the shift from oral tradition to a literary one for the Franks. The laws were drawn up with the assistance of Gallo-Romans trained in the Roman legal tradition. However, they also contain much that may date from Frankish customs from as early as the fourth century. The Salic Franks, from which these laws derive their name, were originally members of a single tribe, the *Salii*, who eventually became the most dominant group within the Frankish confederation. These laws would have been applicable throughout Clovis's kingdom, except for the Gallo-Romans still following Roman legal precedents.

Source: E.F. Henderson (ed.), *Select Historical Documents of the Middle Ages* (London: George Bell, 1892), 176–89.

Further Reading: Patrick Wormald, "Lex Scripta and Verbum Regis: Legislation and Germanic Kinship, from Euric to Cnut," in P.H. Sawyer and I.N. Wood (eds.), *Early Medieval Kingship* (Leeds: The School of History, University of Leeds, 1977), 105–38.

Title I. Concerning Summonses.

1. If any one be summoned before the "Thing"[3] by the king's law, and do not come, he shall be sentenced to 600 denars, which make 15 shillings (solidi).

2. But he who summons another, and does not come himself, shall, if a lawful impediment have not delayed him, be sentenced to 15 shillings, to be paid to him whom he summoned.

3. And he who summons another shall walk with witnesses to the home of that man, and, if he be not at home, shall bid the wife or any one of the family to make known to him that he has been summoned to court.

4. But if he be occupied in the king's service he can not summon him.

5. But if he shall be inside the hundred[4] seeing about his own affairs, he can summon him in the manner explained above.

Title II. Concerning Thefts of Pigs, etc.

1. If any one steal a suckling pig, and it be proved against him, he shall be sentenced to 120 denars, which make 3 shillings.

2. If any one steal a pig that can live without its mother, and it be proved on him, he shall be sentenced to 40 denars—that is, 1 shilling.

3. If any one steal 25 sheep where there were no more in that flock, and it be proved on him, he shall be sentenced to 2,500 denars—that is, 62 shillings.

---

[3] Germanic legislative assembly or meeting, sometimes advisory in nature.

[4] A small territorial subdivision that may have corresponded to the land sufficient to sustain 100 families.

Title III. Concerning Thefts of Cattle.

. . . 4. If any one steal that bull which rules the herd and never has been yoked, he shall be sentenced to 1,800 denars, which make 45 shillings.

5. But if that bull is used for the cows of three villages in common, he who stole him shall be sentenced to three times 45 shillings.

6. If any one steal a bull belonging to the king he shall be sentenced to 3,600 denars, which make 90 shillings.

Title IV. Concerning Damage Done among Crops or in Any Enclosure.

1. If any one finds cattle or a horse, or flocks of any kind in his crops, he shall not at all mutilate them.

2. If he do this and confess it, he shall restore the worth of the animal in place of it, and shall himself keep the mutilated one.

3. But if he have not confessed it, and it have been proved on him, he shall be sentenced, besides the value of the animal and the fines for delay, to 600 denars, which make 15 shillings. . . .

Title XI. Concerning Thefts or Housebreakings of Freemen.

1. If any freeman steal, outside of the house, something worth 2 denars, he shall be sentenced to 600 denars, which make 15 shillings.

2. But if he steal, outside of the house, something worth 40 denars, and it be proved on him, he shall be sentenced, besides the amount and the fines for delay, to 1,400 denars, which make 35 shillings.

3. If a freeman break into a house and steal something worth 2 denars, and it be proved on him, he shall be sentenced to 15 shillings.

4. But if he shall have stolen something worth more than 5 denars, and it have been proved on him, he shall be sentenced, besides the worth of the object and the fines for delay, to 1,400 denars, which make 35 shillings.

5. But if he have broken, or tampered with, the lock, and thus have entered the house and stolen anything from it, he shall be sentenced, besides the worth of the object and the fines for delay, to 1,800 denars, which make 45 shillings.

6. And if he have taken nothing, or have escaped by flight, he shall, for the housebreaking alone, be sentenced to 1,200 denars, which make 30 shillings.

Title XII. Concerning Thefts or Housebreakings on the Part of Slaves.

1. If a slave steal, outside of the house, something worth 2 denars, he shall, besides paying the worth of the object and the fines for delay, be stretched out and receive 120 blows.

2. But if he steal something worth 40 denars, he shall either be castrated or pay 6 shillings. But the lord of the slave who committed the theft shall restore to the plaintiff the worth of the object and the fines for delay.

Title XIII. Concerning Rape Committed by Freemen.

1. If three men carry off a free-born girl, they shall be compelled to pay 30 shillings.

2. If there are more than three, each one shall pay 8 shillings.

3. Those who shall have been present with boats shall be sentenced to 3 shillings.

4. But those who commit rape shall be compelled to pay 2,500 denars, which make 63 shillings.

5. But if they have carried off that girl from behind lock and key, or from the spinning room, they shall be sentenced to the above price and penalty.

6. But if the girl who is carried off be under the king's protection, then the "frith" [peace money] shall be 2,500 denars, which make 63 shillings.

7. But if a bondsman of the king, or a leet, should carry off a free woman, he shall be sentenced to death.

8. But if a free woman have followed a slave of her own will, she shall lose her freedom.

9. If a free-born man shall have taken an alien bondswoman, he shall suffer similarly.

10. If any body take an alien spouse and join her to himself in matrimony, he shall be sentenced to 2,500 denars, which make 63 shillings.

Title XIV. Concerning Assault and Robbery.

1. If any one have assaulted and plundered a free man, and it be proved on him, he shall be sentenced to 2,500 denars, which make 63 shillings.

2. If a Roman have plundered a Salian Frank, the above law shall be observed.

3. But if a Frank have plundered a Roman, he shall be sentenced to 35 shillings.

4. If any man should wish to migrate, and has permission from the king, and shall have shown this in the public "Thing": whoever, contrary to the decree of the king, shall presume to oppose him, shall be sentenced to 8,000 denars, which make 200 shillings.

Title XV. Concerning Arson.

If any one shall set fire to a house in which men were sleeping, as many freemen as were in it can make complaint before the "Thing"; and if any one shall have been burned in it, the incendiary shall be sentenced to 2,500 denars, which make 63 shillings. . . .

Title XVII. Concerning Wounds.

1. If any one have wished to kill another person, and the blow have missed, he on whom it was proved shall be sentenced to 2,500 denars, which make 63 shillings.

2. If any person have wished to strike another with a poisoned arrow, and the arrow have glanced aside, and it shall be proved on him, he shall be sentenced to 2,500 denars, which make 63 shillings.

3. If any person strike another on the head so that the brain appears, and the three bones which lie above the brain shall project, he shall be sentenced to 1,200 denars, which make 30 shillings.

4. But if it shall have been between the ribs or in the stomach, so that the wound appears and reaches to the entrails, he shall be sentenced to 1,200 denars—which make 30 shillings—besides 5 shillings for the physician's pay.

5. If any one shall have struck a man so that blood falls to the floor, and it be proved on him, he shall be sentenced to 600 denars, which make 15 shillings.

6. But if a freeman strike a freeman with his fist so that blood does not flow, he shall be sentenced for each blow—up to 3 blows—to 120 denars, which make 3 shillings.

Title XVIII. Concerning Him Who, Before the King, Accuses an Innocent Man.

If any one, before the king, accuse an innocent man who is absent, he shall be sentenced to 2,500 denars, which make 63 shillings.

Title XIX. Concerning Magicians.

1. If any one have given herbs to another so that he die, he shall be sentenced to 200 shillings (or shall surely be given over to fire).

2. If any person have bewitched another, and he who was thus treated shall escape, the author of the crime, who is proved to have committed it, shall be sentenced to 2,500 denars, which make 63 shillings. . . .

Title XXIV. Concerning the Killing of Little Children and Women.

1. If any one have slain a boy under 10 years—up to the end of the tenth—and it shall have been proved on him, he shall be sentenced to 24,000 denars, which make 600 shillings. . . .

3. If any one have hit a free woman who is pregnant, and she dies, he shall be sentenced to 28,000 denars, which make 700 shillings. . . .

6. If any one have killed a free woman after she has begun bearing children, he shall be sentenced to 24,000 denars, which make 600 shillings.

7. After she can have no more children, he who kills her shall be sentenced to 8,000 denars, which make 200 shillings. . . .

Title XXX. Concerning Insults.

. . . 3. If any one, man or woman, shall have called a woman harlot, and shall not have been able to prove it, he shall be sentenced to 1,800 denars, which make 45 shillings.

4. If any person shall have called another "fox," he shall be sentenced to 3 shillings.

5. If any man shall have called another "hare," he shall be sentenced to 3 shillings.

6. If any man shall have brought it up against another that he have thrown away his shield, and shall not have been able to prove it, he shall be sentenced to 120 denars, which make 3 shillings.

7. If any man shall have called another "spy" or "perjurer," and shall not have been able to prove it, he shall be sentenced to 600 denars, which make 15 shillings. . . .

Title XXXIII. Concerning the Theft of Hunting Animals.

. . . 2. If any one have stolen a tame marked stag[-hound?] trained to hunting, and it shall have been proved through witnesses that his master had him for hunting, or had killed him with two or three beasts, he shall be sentenced to 1,800 denars, which make 45 shillings.

Title XXXIV. Concerning the Stealing of Fences.

1. If any man shall have cut 3 staves by which a fence is bound or held together, or have stolen or cut the heads of 3 stakes, he shall be sentenced to 600 denars, which make 15 shillings.

2. If any one shall have drawn a harrow through another's harvest after it has sprouted, or shall have gone through it with a wagon where there was no road, he shall be sentenced to 120 denars, which make 3 shillings.

3. If any one shall have gone, where there is no way or path, through another's harvest which has already become thick, he shall be sentenced to 600 denars, which make 15 shillings. . . .

Title XLI. Concerning the Murder of Free Men.

1. If any one shall have killed a free Frank, or a barbarian living under the Salic law, and it have been proved on him, he shall be sentenced to 8,000 denars.

2. But if he shall have thrown him into a well or into the water, or shall have covered him with branches or anything else, to conceal him, he shall be sentenced to 24,000 denars, which make 600 shillings.

3. But if any one has slain a man who is in the service of the king, he shall be sentenced to 24,000 denars, which make 600 shillings.

4. But if he have put him in the water or a well, and covered him with anything to conceal him, he shall be sentenced to 72,000 denars, which make 1,800 shillings.

5. If any one have slain a Roman who eats in the king's palace, and it have been proved on him, he shall be sentenced to 12,000 denars, which make 300 shillings.

6. But if the Roman shall not have been a landed proprietor and table companion of the king, he who killed him shall be sentenced to 4,000 denars, which make 100 shillings.

7. But if he shall have killed a Roman who was obliged to pay tribute, he shall be sentenced to 63 shillings. . . .

9. If any one have thrown a free man into a well, and he have escaped alive, he (the criminal) shall be sentenced to 4,000 denars, which make 100 shillings. . . .

Title XLV. Concerning Migrators.

1. If any one wish to migrate to another village and if one or more who live in that village do not wish to receive him,—if there be only one who objects, he shall not have leave to move there.

2. But if he shall have presumed to settle in that village in spite of his rejection by one or two men, then some one shall give him warning. And if he be unwilling to go away, he who gives him warning shall give him warning, with witnesses, as follows: I warn thee that thou may'st remain here this next night as the Salic law demands, and I warn thee that within 10 nights thou shalt go forth from this village. After another 10 nights he shall again come to him and warn him again within 10 nights to go away. If he still refuse to go, again 10 nights shall be added to the command, that the number of 30 nights may be full. If he will not go away even then, then he shall summon him to the "Thing," and present his witnesses as to the separate commands to leave. If he who has been warned will not then move away, and no valid reason detains him, and all the above warnings which we have mentioned have been given according to law: then he who gave him warning shall take the matter into his own hands and request the "comes"[5] to go to that place and expel him. And because he would not listen to the law, that man shall relinquish all that he has earned there, and, besides, shall be sentenced to 1,200 denars, which make 30 shillings.

3. But if anyone have moved there, and within 12 months no one have given him warning, he shall remain as secure as the other neighbors.

Title XLVI. Concerning Transfers of Property.

1. The observance shall be that the Thunginus or Centenarius[6] shall call together a "Thing," and shall have his shield in the "Thing," and shall demand three men as witnesses for each of the three transactions. He (the owner of the land to be transferred) shall seek a man who has no connection with himself, and shall throw a stalk into his lap. And to him into whose lap he has thrown the stalk he shall tell, concerning his property, how much of it—or whether the whole or a half—he wishes to give. He in whose lap he threw the stalk shall remain in his (the owner's) house, and shall collect three or more guests, and shall have the property—as much as is given him—in his power. And, afterwards,

he to whom that property is entrusted shall discuss all these things with the witnesses collected afterwards, either before the king or in the regular "Thing," he shall give the property up to him for whom it was intended. He shall take the stalk in the "Thing," and, before 12 months are over, shall throw it into the lap of him whom the owner has named heir; and he shall restore not more nor less, but exactly as much as was entrusted to him.

2. And if any one shall wish to say anything against this, three sworn witnesses shall say that they were in the "Thing" which the Thunginus or Centenarius called together, and that they saw that man who wished to give his property throw a stalk into the lap of him whom he had selected. They shall name by name him who threw his property into the lap of the other, and, likewise, shall name him whom he named his heir. And three other sworn witnesses shall say that he in whose lap the stalk was thrown had remained in the house of him who gave his property, and had there collected three or more guests, and that they had eaten porridge at table, and that he had collected those who were bearing witness, and that those guests had thanked him for their entertainment. All this those other sworn witnesses shall say, and that he who received that property in his lap in the "Thing" held before the king, or in the regular public "Thing," did publicly, before the people, either in the presence of the king or in the public "Thing"—namely on the Mallberg, before the "Thunginus"—throw the stalk into the lap of him whom the owner had named as heir. And thus nine witnesses shall confirm all this. . . .

Title L. Concerning Promises to Pay.

1. If any freeman or leet have made to another a promise to pay, then he to whom the promise was made shall, within 40 days or within such term as was agreed when he made the promise, go to the house of that man with witnesses, or with appraisers. And if he (the debtor) be unwilling to make the promised payment, he shall be sentenced to 15 shillings above the debt which he had promised.

2. If he then be unwilling to pay, he (the creditor) shall summon him before the "Thing" and thus accuse him: "I ask thee, 'Thunginus,' to bann[7] my opponent who

---

[5] A royal official responsible for an administrative area later known as a county.

[6] Royal officials with judicial powers subordinate to the count.

---

[7] I.e., command.

made me a promise to pay and owes me a debt." And he shall state how much he owes and promised to pay. Then the "Thunginus" shall say: "I bann thy opponent to what the Salic law decrees." Then he to whom the promise was made shall warn him (the debtor) to make no payment or pledge of payment to any body else until he have fulfilled his promise to him (the creditor). And straightway on that same day, before the sun sets, he shall go to the house of that man with witnesses, and shall ask if he will pay that debt. If he will not, he (the creditor) shall wait until after sunset; then, if he shall have waited until after sunset, 120 denars, which make 3 shillings shall be added on to the debt. And this shall be done up to 3 times in 3 weeks. And if at the third time he will not pay all this, it (the sum) shall increase to 360 denars, or 9 shillings: so, namely, that, after each admonition or waiting until after sunset, 3 shillings shall be added to the debt.

3. If any one be unwilling to fulfill his promise in the regular assembly,—then he to whom the promise was made shall go to the count of that place, in whose district he lives, and shall take the stalk and shall say: oh count, that man made me a promise to pay, and I have lawfully summoned him before the court according to the Salic law on this matter; I pledge thee myself and my fortune that thou may'st safely seize his property. And he shall state the case to him, and shall tell how much he (the debtor) had agreed to pay. Then the count shall collect seven suitable bailiffs, and shall go with them to the house of him who made the promise and shall say: thou who art here present pay voluntarily to that man what thou didst promise, and choose any two of these bailiffs who shall appraise that from which thou shalt pay; and make good what thou dost owe, according to a just appraisal. But if he will not hear, or be absent, then the bailiffs shall take from his property the value of the debt which he owes. And, according to the law, the accuser shall take two thirds of that which the debtor owes, and the count shall collect for himself the other third as peace money; unless the peace money shall have been paid to him before in this same matter.

4. If the count have been appealed to, and no sufficient reason, and no duty of the king, have detained him—and if he have put off going, and have sent no substitute to demand law and justice: he shall answer for it with his life, or shall redeem himself with his "wergeld." . . .

Title LIV. Concerning the Slaying of a Count.

1. If any one slay a count, he shall be sentenced to 24,000 denars, which make 600 shillings.

Title LV. Concerning the Plundering of Corpses.

. . . 2. If any one shall have dug up and plundered a corpse already buried, and it shall have been proved on him, he shall be outlawed until the day when he comes to an agreement with the relatives of the dead man, and they ask for him that he be allowed to come among men. And whoever, before he come to an arrangement with the relative, shall give him bread or shelter—even if they are his relations or his own wife—shall be sentenced to 600 denars, which make 15 shillings.

3. But he who is proved to have committed the crime shall be sentenced to 8,000 denars, which make 200 shillings.

Title LVI. Concerning Him Who Shall Have Scorned to Come to Court.

1. If any man shall have scorned to come to court, and shall have put off fulfilling the injunction of the bailiffs, and shall have not been willing to consent to undergo the fine, or the kettle ordeal,[8] or anything prescribed by law: then he (the plaintiff) shall summon him to the presence of the king. And there shall be 12 witnesses who—3 at a time being sworn—shall testify that they were present when the bailiff enjoined him (the accused) either to go to the kettle ordeal, or to agree concerning the fine; and that he had scorned the injunction. Then 3 others shall swear that they were there on the day when the bailiffs enjoined that he should free himself by the kettle ordeal or by composition; and that 40 days after that, in the "mallberg," he (the accuser) had again waited until after sunset, and that he (the accused) would not obey the law. Then he (the accuser) shall summon him before the king for a fortnight thence; and 3 witnesses shall swear that they were there when he summoned him and when he waited for

[8] I.e., ordeal by hot water.

sunset. If he does not then come, those 9, being sworn, shall give testimony as we have above explained. On that day likewise, if he do not come, he (the accuser) shall let the sun go down on him, and shall have 3 witnesses who shall be there when he waits till sunset. But if the accuser shall have fulfilled all this, and the accused shall not have been willing to come to any court, then the king, before whom he has been summoned, shall withdraw his protection from him. Then he shall be guilty, and all his goods shall belong to the fisc, or to him to whom the fisc may wish to give them. And whoever shall have fed or housed him—even if it were his own wife—shall be sentenced to 600 denars, which make 15 shillings; until he (the debtor) shall have made good all that has been laid to his charge.

Title LVII. Concerning the "Chrenecruda."[9]

1. If any one have killed a man, and, having given up all his property, has not enough to comply with the full terms of the law, he shall present 12 sworn witnesses to the effect that, neither above the earth nor under it, has he any more property than he has already given. And he shall afterwards go into his house, and shall collect in his hand dust from the four corners of it, and shall afterwards stand upon the threshold, looking inwards into the house. And then, with his left hand, he shall throw over his shoulder some of that dust on the nearest relative that he has. But if his father and (his father's) brothers have already paid, he shall then throw that dust on their (the brothers') children—that is, over three (relatives) who are nearest on the father's and three on the mother's side. And after that, in his shirt, without girdle and without shoes, a staff in his hand, he shall spring over the hedge. And then those three shall pay half of what is lacking of the compounding money or the legal fine; that is, those others who are descended in the paternal line shall do this.

2. But if there be one of those relatives who has not enough to pay his whole indebtedness, he, the poorer one, shall in turn throw the "chrenecruda" on him of them who has the most, so that he shall pay the whole fine.

3. But if he also have not enough to pay the whole, then he who has charge of the murderer shall bring him before the "Thing," and afterwards to 4 Things, in order that they (his friends) may take him under their protection. And if no one have taken him under his protection—that is, so as to redeem him for what he can not pay—then he shall have to atone with his life. . . .

Title LIX. Concerning Private Property.

1. If any man die and leave no sons, if the father and mother survive, they shall inherit.

2. If the father and mother do not survive, and he leave brothers or sisters, they shall inherit.

3. But if there are none, the sisters of the father shall inherit.

4. But if there are no sisters of the father, the sisters of the mother shall claim that inheritance.

5. If there are none of these, the nearest relatives on the father's side shall succeed to that inheritance.

6. But of Salic land no portion of the inheritance shall come to a woman; but the whole inheritance of the land shall come to the male sex. . . .

Title LXII. Concerning Wergeld.

1. If any one's father have been killed, the sons shall have half the compounding money (wergeld); and the other half the nearest relatives, as well on the mother's as on the father's side, shall divide among themselves.

2. But if there are no relatives, paternal or maternal, that portion shall go to the fisc.

---

[9] A ceremony performed by an individual too poor to pay his debt or fine.

9. BISHOPS REMIGIUS OF REIMS AND AVITUS OF VIENNE

LETTERS TO CLOVIS

The following two letters are the only contemporary records directly addressed to Clovis. Remigius of Reims (ca. 437–533) wrote to Clovis shortly after he succeeded his father Childeric in 481/482 and well before his victory over Syagrius at Soissons in 486 or his conversion. The letter of Avitus (ca. 470–517/519) was written after Clovis's conversion to Orthodox Christianity. From the letter it is unclear whether Clovis was converted from paganism, as Gregory of Tours asserts, or from Arianism.

Source: *Christianity and Paganism, 350–750*, trans. J.N. Hillgarth (Philadelphia: University of Pennsylvania Press, 1986).
Further Reading: Ian Wood, *The Merovingian Kingdoms: 450–751* (London: Longman, 1994).

Bishop Remigius of Reims to Clovis (ca. 481).

To the celebrated and rightly magnificent Lord, King Clovis, Bishop Remigius.

A strong report has come to us that you have taken over the administration of the Second Belgic Province. There is nothing new in that you now begin to be what your parents always were. First of all, you should act so that God's Judgment may not abandon you and that your merits should maintain you at the height where you have arrived by your humility. For, as the proverb says, man's acts are judged. You ought to associate with yourself counselors who are able to do honor to your reputation. Your deeds should be chaste and honest. You should defer to your bishops and always have recourse to their advice. If you are on good terms with them your province will be better able to stand firm. Encourage your people, relieve the afflicted, protect widows, nourish orphans, so shine forth that all may love and fear you. May justice proceed from your mouth. Ask nothing of the poor or of strangers, do not allow yourself to receive gifts from them. Let your tribunal be open to all men, so that no man may leave it with the sorrow [of not having been heard]. You possess the riches your father left you. Use them to ransom captives and free them from servitude. If someone is admitted to your presence let him not feel he is a stranger. Amuse yourself with young men, deliberate with the old. If you wish to reign, show yourself worthy to do so.

Bishop Avitus to King Clovis.

The followers of [Arian] error have in vain, by a cloud of contradictory and untrue opinions, sought to conceal from your extreme subtlety the glory of the Christian name. While we committed these questions to eternity and trusted that the truth of each man's belief would appear at the Future Judgment, the ray of truth has shone forth even among present shadows. Divine Providence has found the arbiter of our age. Your choice is a general sentence. Your Faith is our victory. Many others, in this matter, when their bishops or friends exhort them to adhere to the True Faith, are accustomed to oppose the traditions of their race and respect for their ancestral cult; thus they culpably prefer a false shame to their salvation. While they observe a futile reverence for their parents [by continuing to share their] unbelief, they confess that they do not know what they should choose to do. After this marvelous deed guilty shame can no longer shelter behind this excuse. Of all your ancient genealogy you have chosen to keep only your own nobility, and you have willed that your race should derive from you all the glories which adorn high birth. Your ancestors have prepared a great destiny for you; you willed to prepare better things [for those who will follow you]. You follow your ancestors in reigning in this world; you have opened the way to your descendants to a heavenly reign. Let Greece indeed rejoice it has elected an emperor who shares our Faith; it is no longer alone in deserving such a favor. Your sphere also burns with its own brilliance, and, in the person of a king, the light of a rising sun shines over the western lands. It is right that this light began at the Nativity of Our Redeemer, so that the waters of rebirth have brought you forth to salvation the very day that the world received the birth of its Redemption, the Lord of Heaven. The day celebrated as the Lord's Nativity is also yours, in which you have consecrated your soul to God, your life to your contemporaries, your glory to posterity.

What should be said of the glorious solemnity of your regeneration? If I could not assist in person among the ministers [of the rite] I shared in its joy. Thanks to God, our land took part in the thanksgiving, for, before your Baptism, a messenger of Your Most Subtle Humility informed us that you were a "competens."[10] Therefore the sacred night [of Christmas] found us sure of what you would do. We saw (with the eyes of the spirit) that great sight, when a crowd of bishops around you, in the ardor of their holy ministry, poured over your royal limbs the waters of life; when that head feared by the peoples bowed down before the servants of God; when your royal locks, hidden under a helmet, were steeped in holy oil; when your breast, relieved of its cuirass, shone with the same whiteness as your baptismal robes. Do not doubt, most flourishing of kings, that this soft clothing will give more force to your arms: whatever Fortune has given up to now, this Sanctity will bestow.

I would wish to add some exhortations to your praises if anything escaped either your knowledge or your attention. Should we preach the Faith to the convert who perceived it without a preacher; or humility, which you have long shown toward us [bishops], although you only owe it to us now, after your profession of Faith; or mercy, attested, in tears and joy to God and men, by a people once captive, now freed by you? One wish remains for me to express. Since God, thanks to you, will make of your people His own possession, offer a part of the treasure of Faith which fills your heart to the peoples living beyond you, who, still living in natural ignorance, have not been corrupted by the seeds of perverse doctrines.[11] Do not fear to send them envoys and to plead with them the cause of God, who has done so much for your cause. So that the other pagan peoples, at first being subject to your empire for the sake of religion, while they still seem to have another ruler, may be distinguished rather by their race than by their prince. [End of letter missing.]

10. GREGORY OF TOURS

THE TEN BOOKS OF HISTORIES

Gregory of Tours (ca. 540–594) was a member of an illustrious Gallo-Roman family that for centuries had dominated the episcopal see of Tours, where he himself was bishop beginning in 573. His *Ten Books of Histories* is the most important source for early Frankish history. Gregory was primarily concerned in his history with Orthodox Christianity, with his community of Tours, and with his Gallo-Roman aristocratic colleagues. He worked closely with the Frankish kings, whom he saw as instruments of divine providence. These concerns are evident in the following passages. The first is his account of Clovis. Written almost a century after the events it describes, it is largely unreliable as a detailed account of Clovis but essential for understanding the meaning of Clovis to later Frankish history. The other selections show Gregory's activities as peacemaker in Tours and his involvement with his contemporary kings of the Franks.

Source: The History of the Franks by Gregory of Tours, vol. II, trans. with an introduction by O.M. Dalton (Oxford: Clarendon Press, 1927), slightly revised and updated.
Further Reading: Kathleen Mitchell and Ian Wood (eds.), *The World of Gregory of Tours* (Leiden: Brill, 2002).

---

[10] I.e., to be baptized within 40 days.

[11] I.e., Arianism.

Excerpts from Book II

12. But Childeric, who reigned over the Franks, was sunk in debauchery, and began to dishonor their daughters. For which cause they were angry, and expelled him from the kingdom. And when he learned that they intended to slay him, he fled into Thuringia, leaving behind a friend who should try to soothe their fury by smooth words, and send him a token when he might return to his country. For this purpose they divided a gold coin. Childeric took one half with him, and his friend kept the other, saying: "Whenever I send you this part, and by joining the two halves you make a single *solidus*, then with a mind free from anxiety you may return to thine own land." Childeric therefore departed into Thuringia and took refuge with King Bisinus and Basina his queen. And after his expulsion, the Franks unanimously chose for their king Aegidius, who, as I stated above, had been sent from Rome as master of the soldiery. But in the eighth year of his reign over them the faithful friend, who had succeeded in secretly pacifying the Franks, sent a messenger to Childeric bearing the half of the divided *solidus* which he had kept. Then Childeric, receiving it as a sure sign that the Franks wished him back, returned from Thuringia at their invitation and was restored to his kingdom. The two being now joint kings, the above-mentioned Basina left her lord and came to Childeric. To his anxious question why she had come to him from so great a distance, she is said to have replied: "I know you capable and strenuous in action, therefore am I come to dwell with you. For be sure that if in the parts beyond the sea I were acquainted with one more capable than you, I should in like manner have sought him for my husband." At which answer he rejoiced, and was united with her in wedlock. And she conceived, and bore a son, and called him Clovis. And he was a great man and a famous warrior.

13. In Auvergne, after the death of the holy Artemius, Venerandus, a man of senatorial family, was consecrated bishop. Paulinus bears witness what manner of man this bishop was when he says: "If you were at this present time to see those worthy priests of the Lord Exsuperius of Toulouse, Simplicius of Vienne, Amandus of Bordeaux, Diogenianus of Albi, Dynamius of Angoulême, Venerandus of Clermont, Alithius of Cahors, or Pegasius of Périgueux, however great the evils of the age, you would behold the most excellent guardians of all our faith and religion." Venerandus is said to have died on Christmas Eve, and the next morning the procession of the feast was his funeral train. After his death a disgraceful contest arose among the citizens with regard to the succession to the episcopate. Parties were divided, one wishing to elect one man and one another, and there was great strife among the people. While the bishops were seated together one Sunday, a certain woman, veiled and dedicated to God, approached them boldly and said: "Hearken to me, priests of the Lord. Know that none of those whom the citizens have selected for the bishopric finds favor in the sight of God. Behold today the Lord Himself shall provide a bishop. Therefore do not excite the people or set them at variance, but have patience little while for the Lord even now sends the man who shall govern this church." While they were marveling at her words, suddenly one Rusticus approached, a priest of the diocese of Clermont, and the very man revealed to the woman in a vision. As soon as she saw him, she said: "Behold him whom the Lord has chosen for your chief priest! Let him be consecrated bishop." Upon these words, the whole people, abandoning all their dispute, cried out that this was a worthy and just man. He was therefore set on the bishop's throne, and amid the joy of the people he received the honor of the bishopric, being the seventh to occupy the throne of Clermont.

14. In the city of Tours, upon the death of Eustochius in the seventeenth year of his episcopate, Perpetuus was consecrated as fifth in succession from the blessed Martin. Now when he saw the continual wonders wrought at the tomb of the saint, and observed how small was the chapel erected over him he judged it unworthy of such miracles. He caused it to be removed, and built on the spot the great basilica which has endured until our day, standing five hundred and fifty paces from the city. It is one hundred and sixty feet long by sixty broad; its height to the ceiling is forty-five feet. It has thirty-two windows in the sanctuary and twenty in the nave, with forty-one columns. In the whole structure there are fifty-two windows, a hundred and twenty columns, and eight doors, three in the sanctuary, five in the nave. The great festival of the church has a threefold significance: it is at once a feast of the dedication, of the translation of the saint's body, and of his consecration as bishop. This festival you shall keep on the fourth day of July; the day of the saint's burial you shall find to fall on the eleventh of November. They who keep these celebrations in faith shall deserve the protection of the holy bishop both in this world and the next. As the ceiling of the earlier chapel was fashioned with delicate workmanship, Perpetuus deemed it unseemly that such work should perish; so he built another basilica in honor of the blessed apostles Peter and Paul, and in it

he fixed the ceiling. He built many other churches, which are still standing to-day in the name of Christ.

15. At this time also the church of the blessed Symphorian, the martyr of Autun, was built by the priest Eufronius, who himself afterwards became bishop of this city. He it was who, in his great devotion, sent the marble which covers the holy sepulchre of the blessed Martin.

16. After the death of Bishop Rusticus, the holy Namatius became in these days eighth bishop of Clermont. By his own efforts he built the church which still exists, and is deemed the older of those within the town walls. It is a hundred and fifty feet long, sixty feet broad, that is across the nave, and fifty feet high to the ceiling: it ends in a rounded apse, and has on either side walls of skilled construction; the whole building is disposed in the form of a cross. It has forty-two windows, seventy columns, and eight doors.

There is felt the dread of God, and the great brightness of His glory, and truly there often the devout are aware of a most sweet odor as of spices wafted to them. The walls of the sanctuary are adorned with a lining of many kinds of marble. The building being completed in the twelfth year, the blessed bishop sent priests to the city of Bologna in Italy to bring him relics of the saints Vitalis and Agricola, crucified, as is known of all men, for the name of Christ our Lord.

17. The wife of Namatius built the church of the holy Stephen outside the walls. As she wished it to be adorned with paintings, she used to hold a book upon her knees, in which she read the story of deeds done of old time, and pointed out to the painters what subjects should be represented on the walls. It happened one day, as she was sitting reading in the church, that a certain poor man came in to pray. And when he saw her clad in black, for she was advanced in years, he deemed her one of the needy, and producing a piece of bread, put it in her lap, and went his way. She did not despise the gift of the poor man who did not perceive her quality, but took it and thanked him, and put it by, afterwards preferring it to her costlier food and receiving a blessing from it every day until it was all consumed.

18. Childeric fought at Orleans. Odovacar, with his Saxons, came to Angers. At that time a great pestilence ravaged the population. Aegidius died, leaving a son named Syagrius. After his death, Odovacar took hostages from Angers and other places. The Bretons were driven from Bourges by the Goths, and lost many men at Bourg-de-Déols. Count Paul, with Roman and Frankish forces, made war on the Goths and carried off booty. Odovacar having come to Angers, King Childeric arrived

the following day; and the king took the city, after Count Paul had been slain. On that day the church house was burned in a great fire.

19. After these events, there was war between the Saxons and the Romans; but the Saxons turned their backs, and abandoned many of their men to the sword of the pursuing Romans. Their islands were taken and ravaged by the Franks, and much people were slain. In the ninth month of that year there was an earthquake. Odovacar made a treaty with Childeric, and they subdued the Alamanni, who had overrun a part of Italy.

20. Euric, king of the Goths, set Victorius as duke over the seven cities in the fourteenth year of his reign. Victorius went forthwith to Clermont and sought to win over the city. From his time date the subterranean chapels, which survive to this day. He ordered to be brought to the church of the holy Julian the columns which still stand in the church. He also ordered the building of the church of the holy Laurence and the church of the holy Germanus in the township of Ligne. He remained nine years in Auvergne. He poured out calumnies against Eucherius the senatorial; first he imprisoned him, then had him dragged forth by night, and bound against an ancient wall which he ordered to be thrown down upon him. He was licentious in his passion for women; and in dread of being slain by the Arvernians, he fled to Rome. But there, attempting the same debaucheries, he was stoned. After his death, Euric ruled for four years, but died in the twenty-seventh year of his reign. There again occurred a great earthquake.

21. On the decease of Namatius in Auvergne, Eparchius, a man of holy and religious life, succeeded him. Now as at this time the Church had only a small property within the walls of the city, the bishop had his lodging in the part of the church called the sacristy, and was wont to rise at night to give thanks to God before the altar. It befell that one night as he entered the church, he found it full of devils, whose chief, in the guise of a woman richly bedecked, was seated upon his throne. The bishop said to him: "O execrable whore, is it not enough for you to infect other places with your pollutions, but you must needs defile this seat, consecrated of the Lord, by the loathsome contact of your body? Go forth from the house of God, and let it no longer be polluted by your presence." The demon answered: "And do you call me whore? I will prepare many a snare for you through desire of women." As he spoke these words, he vanished like a smoke. And the bishop was indeed tempted by the stirring of fleshly lusts, but he was protected by the sign of the holy Cross, and the enemy could in no wise do him harm. He is said

to have built a monastery on the summit of the hill of Chantoin, where the oratory now is, and there he went into retreat during the holy days of Lent. But on the day of the Lord's Supper, escorted by citizens and clerics with great chanting, he returned to his church. On his death, he was succeeded by Sidonius, the ex-prefect, a man of most noble birth as the world counts distinction, and among the first of the senatorial rank in Gaul, so that the emperor Avitus gave him his daughter in marriage. In his time, when the above-mentioned Victorius was still at Clermont, there was in the monastery of the blessed Cyricus in the same city an abbot named Abraham, who shone with the faith and works of the patriarch his namesake, as we have written in the book recording his life.

22. The holy Sidonius was of such eloquence that often he could speak most luminously without preparation on any subject that he chose. It happened that one day he was invited to the festival of the church belonging to the monastery which I have mentioned above, where some malicious person removed the book of which he habitually made use in conducting the sacred office. But he was so well prepared beforehand that he went through the whole service of the festival in such a way that all wondered, and those present seemed to hear an angel, rather than a man. This I have more fully related in the preface to the book which I wrote on the Masses composed by him. As he was eminent in holiness and, as I have said, was one of the first senatorial families, he would often take from his home vessels of silver unknown to his wife, and give them to the poor. When she heard of it she was offended with him, whereupon he would restore the plate to his home, giving the needy its value in money.

23. After his admission to the Lord's service, while he was already living as a saint in this world, there rose up against him two priests, who deprived him of all authority over the property of the Church, left him narrow and stinted means of life, and subjected him to the greatest indignity. But the divine clemency did not long suffer the wrongdoers to go unpunished. One of these most vile men, all unworthy of the priestly rank, who had threatened the night before to drag the bishop from the church, rose the next morning at the sound of the bell calling to matins, full of spite against the holy man of God, pondering in his unjust heart the plan which he had devised on the preceding day. But visiting the lavatory, he gave up the ghost while he sought to purge the body. A servant with a candle waited without for his master to come forth. Dawn was now come, and his satellite, the other priest, sent him a messenger to say: "Come, make no delay, that we may execute the plan which we agreed upon

yesterday." The dead man giving no answer, the slave lifted the curtain before the door and found his master lifeless upon the seat. Whence it may not be doubted that this man was guilty of a crime not less than that of the vile Arius, who in like manner perished by the issue of his bowels through the draught. For this too is heretical belief, that in the Church man may disobey the bishop of God to whom the sheep are entrusted to be fed, and that authority may be usurped by one to whom none has been entrusted, either by God or man. Thereafter the saintly bishop, though one foe was yet left to him, was restored to his authority. But it befell, at a later time, that he fell ill of an attack of fever, and asked his people to carry him into the church. And when he was carried in, there came about him a multitude of men and women, yea, and of children, weeping and saying: "Wherefore do you abandon us, O good shepherd, or to whom would you leave us, abandoned even as orphans? Shall life be nothing to us after your passing? Shall there be any one in the time to come to preserve us with the like salt of wisdom, or with like far-seeing reason persuade us to the fear of God's name?" These things, and others like to them, the people uttered with great lamentation; to whom at length the bishop answered, the power of the Holy Spirit moving him: "Fear not, my people, for behold Aprunculus my brother lives, and he shall be your bishop." But they understood him not, deeming that he spoke in an ecstasy. After the passing of the holy man, that evil priest who yet survived his fellow forthwith, in his blind greed, laid usurping hands on the whole property of the Church, as if he were already bishop, and proclaimed: "God has at length looked down to me, perceiving in me one more just than Sidonius; it is he that has bestowed on me this authority." He rode in his pride through the whole city, and on the Sunday next after the saint's passing, he made ready a feast in the church house, and invited all the citizens. And slighting the senior among them, he reclined first upon the couch. Then the cup-bearer, offering him a cup, said: "My lord, I have seen vision in a dream, which, if you permit me, I will relate to you. I saw it on this Sunday night, and behold, there was a great dwelling, and in the dwelling was set a throne, whereon one sat like unto a judge, more excellent in power than all. And about him were many priests in white raiment, and also multitudes of people without order in uncounted numbers. While I gazed on these things in fear, I beheld the blessed Sidonius standing forth in a high place among them, hotly contending with that priest so very dear to you who a few years since departed out of this world. This priest was vanquished, whereupon that king commanded that he be thrust into the narrowest and lowest prison cell. After he had been removed, I saw the saint once more arise in accusation, this time against you, as confederate in the crime for which that other had just been condemned. The judge began to make earnest inquiry whom he might send to you, and I began to hide myself among the rest, and stood at the back, considering with myself that he might send me, as being known to the man in question. While I was secretly revolving these things everyone else vanished, and I was left standing alone. The judge called to me, and I came nearer, but at the sight of his might and splendor I was stupefied and tottered for very dread. Then he said: "My servant, have no fear, but go and say to that priest: 'Come and answer to the charge, for Sidonius has requested that you be summoned.' Do you, therefore, delay not in going, for with great threatenings that king bade me tell you all these things, saying to me: 'If you do not tell them, you shall die the worst death.'" At these words, the priest in terror let fall the cup from his hand, and gave up the ghost; he was borne away dead from the couch and committed to the grave, to share in hell with that his accomplice. Such judgment upon these unruly priests did the Lord pass in this world: that the one should meet the fate of Arius, that the other, like Simon Magus at the prayer of a holy apostle, should be dashed headlong from the high summit of his pride. None may doubt that both, have their part in hell, who together did wickedness against their holy bishop.

In the meantime the rumor of Frankish might already echoed in these regions, and all men longed for their dominion with a passionate desire. For this reason the holy Aprunculus, bishop of Langres, had fallen under suspicion with the Burgundians; their hatred towards him grew from day to day, and the order went forth that he should be slain secretly with the sword. But tidings of his danger reaching him, he was let down by night from the walls of Dijon and so came to Clermont, where, in accordance with the Lord's word placed in the mouth of Sidonius, he was made eleventh bishop of the city.

24. In the time of Bishop Sidonius a great famine afflicted the Burgundians. The people scattered themselves through all parts, and there was none to give food to the poor. Then Ecdicius, a man of senatorial family, and a relative of Sidonius, putting his trust in God, is said to have done a great thing. For when the famine reached its height, he sent out his servants through neighboring towns with horses and wagons to bring in all who were suffering under this privation. And they went out and brought all the poor whom they could find to his house, where he fed them through the whole time of

barrenness, saving them from death by starvation. Many assert that there were more than four thousand persons of both sexes. But when a time of plenty returned, he arranged for their transport home again, and sent back each one of them to his own place. But after all were gone a voice came down to him from above, saying: "Ecdicius, Ecdicius, because you have done this thing, bread shall not fail you or your offspring for ever; for you have hearkened to My words, and in nourishing the poor you have satisfied My hunger also." This Ecdicius is commemorated by many as a man wondrously swift in action; for it is related that once he put to flight a multitude of Goths with ten men. But the holy Patiens, bishop of Lyons, is said to have done like service to the people during the same famine. There is preserved a letter of Sidonius giving him eloquent praise.

25. In Sidonius's time also Euric, king of the Goths, passing the frontiers of Spain, began a grievous persecution of the Christians in Gaul. Everywhere he beheaded those who would not conform to his perverse doctrine; he cast priests into prison; some of the bishops he exiled, others he slew with the sword. The doors of the holy churches he ordered to be blocked with briers, that only a few might enter and the faith might pass into oblivion. It was chiefly the cities of Novempopulana and Aquitaine that were wasted by this storm; there is to-day extant a letter on this subject written by the noble Sidonius to Bishop Basilius, in which these facts are recorded. But not long afterwards, smitten by the divine vengeance, the persecutor himself perished.

26. After these events the blessed Perpetuus, bishop of Tours, after completing thirty years in his episcopate, went to his rest. Volusianus, a man of senatorial family, was appointed in his place. But he was regarded with suspicion by the Goths, and in the seventh year of his episcopate was taken captive into Spain, where he soon ended his days. Verus, succeeding to his place, was consecrated as seventh bishop after the blessed Martin.

27. After this, Childeric died, and Clovis his son reigned in his stead. In the fifth year of his reign, Syagrius, king of the Romans, son of Aegidius, had his residence in the city of Soissons, which had before been the home of the above-mentioned Aegidius. Clovis marched against him, with his relation Ragnachar, himself also a king, and called upon him to fix a field of battle. Syagrius did not seek delay nor did he fear to stand his ground. And so when the battle was joined between them, Syagrius, seeing his army crushed, turned to flight and escaped as fast as he could to Alaric at Toulouse. But Clovis sent to Alaric calling upon him to surrender the fugitive, else

he must look to be himself invaded for giving him refuge. Then Alaric, lest he should incur the wrath of the Franks for his sake, was afraid, after the craven habit of the Goths, and handed him over to the messengers in bonds. When Clovis received his prisoner, he ordered him to be imprisoned, had him put to the sword in secret, while he took possession of his kingdom.

At this time many churches were plundered by the troops of Clovis, because he was yet fast held in pagan errors. Thus it happened that a ewer of great size and beauty had been taken, with other ornaments used in the service of the church. But the bishop of that church sent messengers to the king, asking that if no other of the sacred vessels might be restored, his church might at least receive back this ewer. When the king heard this he said to the envoy: "Follow us to Soissons, for there all the booty is to be divided, and if the lot gives me the vessel, I will fulfill the desire of the bishop." When they were at Soissons and all the spoil was laid out in open view, the king said: "I ask you, most valiant warriors, not to refuse to cede me that vessel" (he meant the ewer of which I have spoken) "over and above my share." After this speech all the men of sense replied: "All that is before our eyes, most glorious king, is thine; we ourselves are submitted to your power. Do now that which seems good to you, for none is so strong as to say you nay." At the words a soldier of a vain, jealous, and unstable temper raised his ax and smote the ewer, crying with a loud voice: "You shalt receive nothing of this but that which your own lot gives you." While all stood astounded at this act, the king suppressed his resentment at the wrong under a show of patient mildness; he then took the ewer and restored it to the bishop's envoy. But the wound remained hidden in his heart. After the lapse of a year, he commanded the whole army to assemble with full equipment, and to exhibit their arms in their brightness on the field of March. The king went round inspecting them all; but when he came to the man who struck the ewer he said: "None has appeared with his arms so ill-kept as you; neither your lance, nor your sword, nor your ax is fit for use." He then seized the ax, and threw it on the ground. As the man bent down a little to take it up, the king swung his own ax high and cleft his skull, saying as he did it, "Thus did you treat the ewer at Soissons." The man lying dead, he dismissed the rest, having put great fear of him into their hearts by his act. Clovis waged many wars and won many victories. For in the tenth year of his reign he invaded the Thuringians and subjected them to this rule.

28. At that time the king of the Burgundians was Gundioc, of the race of the royal persecutor Athanaric whom I have before mentioned. He had four sons, Gundobad, Godigisel, Chilperic, and Gundomar. Gundobad put his brother Chilperic to the sword, and drowned his wife by tying a stone to her neck. Her two daughters he condemned to exile, the elder of whom, Chrona, had adopted the habit of a nun, while the younger was called Clotild. It happened that Clovis used often to send envoys into Burgundy, and they discovered the young Clotild. Observing her grace and understanding, and learning that she was of the blood royal, they spoke of these things to Clovis, who straightway sent an embassy to Gundobad, asking her in marriage. Gundobad was afraid to refuse, and handed her over to the men, who received her, and with all speed brought her before the king. At the sight of her he greatly rejoiced and was united to her in wedlock, having already by a concubine one son named Theuderic.

29. Of Queen Clotild the king had a firstborn son whom the mother wished to be baptized; she therefore persistently urged Clovis to permit it, saying: "The gods whom you worship are naught; they cannot aid either themselves or others, seeing that they are images carved of wood or stone, or metal. Moreover the names which you have given them are the names of men and not of gods. Saturn was a man, fabled to have escaped by flight from his son to avoid being thrust from his kingdom; Jupiter also, the lewdest practiser of all debaucheries and of unnatural vice, the abuser of the women of his own family, who could not even abstain from intercourse with his own sister, as she herself admitted in the words 'sister and spouse of Jove.'[12] What power had Mars and Mercury? They may have been endowed with magical arts; they never had the power of the divine name. But you should rather serve Him, who at His word created out of nothing the heaven and earth, the sea and all therein; who made the sun to shine and adorned the heaven with stars who filled the waters with fish, the earth with animals, the air with birds; at whose nod the lands are made fair with fruits, the trees with apples, the vines with grapes; by whose hand the race of man was created; by whose largess every creature was made to render homage and service to the man whom he created." Though the queen ever argued thus, the king's mind was nowise moved towards belief, but he replied: "It is by command of our gods that all things are created and come forth; it is manifest that your god can do nothing; moreover, he

_____

[12] *Aeneid* 1.46–47.

is not even proven to belong to the race of gods." But the queen, true to her faith, presented her son for baptism; she ordered the church to be adorned with hangings and curtains, that the king, whom no preaching could influence, might by this ceremony be persuaded to belief. The boy was baptized and named Ingomer, but died while yet clothed in the white raiment of his regeneration. Thereupon the king was moved to bitter wrath, nor was he slow to reproach the queen, saying: "If the child had been dedicated in the name of my gods, surely he would have survived, but now, baptized in the name of your God, he could not live a day." The queen replied: "I render thanks to Almighty God, Creator of all things, who has not judged me all unworthy, and deigns to take into His kingdom this child born of my womb. My mind is untouched by grief at this event, since I know that they which are called from this world in the white robes of baptism shall be nurtured in the sight of God." Afterwards she bore another son, who was baptized with the name of Chlodomer. When he too began to ail, the king said: "It cannot but befall that this infant like his brother shall straightway die, being baptized in the name of your Christ." But the mother prayed, and God ordained that the child should recover.

30. Now the queen without ceasing urged the king to confess the true God, and forsake his idols; but in no wise could she move him to this belief, until at length he made war upon a time against the Alamanni, when he was driven of necessity to confess what of his free will he had denied. It befell that when the two hosts joined battle there was grievous slaughter, and the army of Clovis was being swept to utter ruin. When the king saw this he lifted up his eyes to heaven, and knew compunction in his heart, and, moved to tears, cried aloud: "Jesus Christ, You who are proclaimed by Clotild Son of the living God, You that are said to give aid to those in stress, and to grant victory to those that hope in You, I entreat from a devout heart the glory of your aid. If You grant me victory over these enemies, and experience confirm that power which the people dedicated to Your name claims to have proved, then will I also believe on You and be baptized in Your name. I have called upon my own gods, but here is proof that they have withdrawn themselves from helping me; wherefore I believe that they have no power, since they come not to the succor of their servants. You do I now invoke, on You am I fain to believe, if but I may be plucked out of the hands of my adversaries." And as he said this, lo, the Alamanni turned their backs, and began to flee. And when they saw that their king was slain, they yielded themselves to Clovis, saying: "No

longer, we entreat you, let the people perish; we are now your men." Then the king put an end to the war, and having admonished the people, returned in peace, relating to the queen how he had called upon the name of Christ and had been found worthy to obtain the victory. This happened in the fifteenth year of his reign.

31. Then the queen commanded the holy Remigius, bishop of Reims, to be summoned secretly, entreating him to impart the word of salvation to the king. The bishop, calling the king to him in private, began to instill into him faith in the true God, Maker of heaven and earth, and urged him to forsake his idols, which were unable to help either himself or others. But Clovis replied: "I myself, most holy father, will gladly hearken to you; but one thing yet remains. The people that follow me will not allow that I forsake their gods; yet will I go, and reason with them according to your word." But when he came before the assembled people, or ever he opened his mouth, the divine power had gone forth before him, and all the people cried with one voice: "O gracious king, we drive forth our gods that perish, and are ready to follow that immortal God whom Remigius preaches." News of this was brought to the bishop, who was filled with great joy, and commanded the font to be prepared. The streets were overshadowed with colored hangings, the churches adorned with white hangings, the baptistery was set in order, smoke of incense spread in clouds, perfumed tapers gleamed, the whole church about the place of baptism was filled with the divine fragrance. And now the king first demanded to be baptized by the bishop. Like a new Constantine, he moved forward to the water, to blot out the former leprosy, to wash away in this new stream the foul stains borne from old days. As he entered to be baptized the saint of God spoke these words with eloquent lips: "Meekly bow your proud head, Sicamber; adore that which you have burned, burn that which you have adored." For the holy Remigius, the bishop, was of excellent learning, and above all skilled in the art of rhetoric, and so exemplary in holiness that his miracles were equal to those of the holy Silvester; there is preserved to us a book of his life, in which it is related how he raised a man from the dead. The king therefore, confessing Almighty God, three in one, was baptized in the name of the Father, the Son, and the Holy Ghost, and anointed with holy chrism, with the sign of the Cross of Christ. Of his army were baptized more than three thousand; and his sister Albofled, who not long after was taken to the Lord, was likewise baptized. And when the king was sorrowing for her death, the holy Remigius sent him a letter of consolation, beginning after this fashion:

"The cause of your sadness does afflict me with a great affliction, for that your sister of fair memory has passed away. But this shall console us, that she has in such wise left the world as that we should rather lift up our eyes to her than mourn her." And another of his sisters was converted, by name Lanthechild, who had fallen into the heresy of the Arians; she also received the holy chrism, having confessed the Son and the Holy Ghost equal to the Father.

32. At this time two brothers, Gundobad and Godigisel, possessed their kingdom about the Rhône and Saône with the territory of Marseilles. They and their people were in the bondage of the Arian sect. And as the brothers were on terms of hostility, Godigisel, who had heard of the victories won by King Clovis, sent envoys to him by stealth, saying: "If you afford me aid to pursue my brother, so that I may either slay him in battle, or drive him from the kingdom, I will pay you every year such tribute as you may impose yourself." This offer Clovis received gladly, and promised him aid whenever his necessity should demand it. At a time appointed between them he marched an army against Gundobad, who, ignorant of his brother's guile, sent to him upon this news, saying: "Come you to my deliverance, for the Franks have risen against us, and are come up against our territory to take it. Let us therefore be of one mind against a people that hates us, for if we hold apart we shall undergo the fate suffered by other peoples." Godigisel made answer: "I will come with my army, and will bring you succor." So all three kings set their forces in movement together, Clovis marching against Gundobad and Godigisel; they came to Dijon with all the armaments of war. But when they joined battle on the Ouche, Godigisel joined Clovis and their united armies crushed the force of Gundobad. But he, perceiving the treachery of his brother which till that hour he never suspected, turned his back and fled along the Rhône, until he entered the city of Avignon. After his victory thus gained, Godigisel promised Clovis a part of his kingdom, and went home in peace, entering Vienne in triumph, as though he were master of the entire kingdom. But Clovis reinforced his troops, and followed Gundobad with intent to take him from Avignon and slay him. When Gundobad heard this, he was grievously afraid, dreading to be overtaken by a sudden death. Now he had with him Aridius, a man of rank, who was both strenuous and astute. Him he summoned and thus addressed: "I am hemmed in by straits upon every side, and know not what to do, for these barbarians are fallen upon me with intent to slay us and lay waste all the land." Aridius answered: "You had best assuage the savagery of this man, and so preserve your life. Now therefore, if it be pleasing in your sight, I will pretend to forsake you and desert to him; once with him, I will bring it about that he neither ruin you nor this country. You must only take care to satisfy all the demands which by my advice he shall make of you, till the Lord of His goddness deign to make your cause triumph." Gundobad made answer: "I will do all that you shalt demand." Thereupon Aridius bade him farewell and departed, and came to King Clovis, to whom he said: "Behold in me, most pious king, your humble slave, who has forsaken the miserable Gundobad to serve your mightiness. If now your piety deign to look on me, you and your posterity shall find in me an honest and faithful follower." Clovis forthwith took him to himself, and kept him near his person; for he could tell lively tales, was active in counsel, just in judgment, and faithful in every trust. Clovis then continuing to invest the city with his army, Aridius said: "O king, if in the majesty of your high estate you deign to hear from me a few words of humble advice, though indeed you have small need of counsel, I will offer them in all loyalty; and it shall be useful to you and to the cities through which it is your intent to pass. Wherefore do you keep afoot this army, when your foe resides in an impregnable place? You lay waste the fields and destroy the meadows, you cut the vines, you hew down the olives, all the fruits of this region you utterly destroy, and yet you fail to harm him. Send rather envoys to him and impose a yearly tribute, that this region be saved from ruin, and you be always lord over your vassal. If he should refuse, then do according to your pleasure." The king hearkened to this counsel, and bade his army return home. And he sent an embassy to Gundobad, commanding him yearly to pay the tribute now to be laid upon him. And he paid it immediately, and pledged himself to pay it hereafter.

33. But later, when he had recovered strength, he disdained to pay the promised tribute to King Clovis, and marched an army against Godigisel his brother, besieging him in the city of Vienne. As soon as provisions began to run short among the common people, Godigisel feared the famine might extend even to him, and ordered them to be driven outside the city. It was done; but among the rest was expelled the engineer who had charge of the aqueduct. This man, indignant at his expulsion with the others, went in a fury to Gundobad, and showed him how he might break into the city and take vengeance on his brother. Under his guidance armed men were led along the aqueduct, preceded by men with iron crowbars. For there was an outlet covered by a great stone, which was moved away by the crowbars under

the direction of the engineer, and so they entered the city, taking in the rear the garrison who were discharging their arrows from the walls. Then at a signal given by a trumpet from the center of the city, the besiegers seized the gates, threw them open, and crowded in. The inhabitants were caught between two forces and cut to pieces, but Godigisel took refuge in a church of the heretics, and was there put to death with the Arian bishop. The Franks who were with him held together in a tower; Gundobad commanded that none of them should be harmed, and when they were taken, sent them into banishment to King Alaric at Toulouse; but the Gallo-Romans of senatorial family and the Burgundians who had taken part with Godigisel he slew. He restored to his dominion the whole region now known as Burgundy, and instituted milder laws among the Burgundians that there should be no undue oppression of the Romans.

34. Gundobad, perceiving the doctrines of the heretics to be worthless, confessed that Christ, the Son of God, and the Holy Ghost are both equal to the Father, and asked secret baptism of the holy bishop of Vienne. But the bishop replied: "If you truly believe, it is your duty to follow the teaching of our Lord Himself, when He said: 'If any man will confess Me before men, him will I also confess before My Father which is in heaven; but whosoever shall deny Me before men, him will I also deny before My Father which is in heaven.'[13] This also did our Lord urge even upon His holy and beloved, the blessed apostles, when He said: 'But beware of men; for they will deliver you up to councils, and in their synagogues they will scourge you; yea, and before governors and kings shall you be brought for My sake, for a testimony to them and to the Gentiles.'[14] But you that art a king, and need not to fear that any shall lay hands on you, see how you dread revolt among the people, not daring to confess in public the Creator of all men. Forsake this foolishness, and that which you profess to believe in your heart declare with your lips before the people. For according to the word of the blessed apostle: 'With the heart man believes unto righteousness, and with the mouth confession is made unto salvation.'[15] Likewise also the prophet says: 'I will give You thanks in the great congregation, I will praise You among much people.'[16] And again: 'I will give thanks unto You, O Lord, among the peoples; I will

sing praises unto You among the nations.'[17] You fear the people, O king; but do you not perceive that it is more fitting for the people to follow your belief, than for you to indulge their weakness? For you are the head of the people; the people is not your head. If you go to war, it is you that goes before the troops of your host, which follow wherever you lead. Therefore it is better that you should lead them to the knowledge of the truth than that you should perish and leave them in their error. 'For God is not mocked,'[18] nor does He love the man who for an earthly kingdom refuses to confess Him before the world." Though troubled by these arguments, Gundobad persisted to his dying day in this madness, nor ever would publicly confess that the three Persons of the Trinity are equal. The blessed Avitus was at this time of great eloquence; for heresy springing up in Constantinople, both that taught by Eutyches and that of Sabellius, to the effect that our Lord Jesus Christ had in Him nothing of the divine nature, and at the request of King Gundobad he wrote against them. There are today extant among us his admirable letters, which, as they once quelled heresy, so now they edify the Church of God. He wrote a book of Homilies, six metrical books on the creation of the world and on various other subjects, and nine books of Letters, including those just mentioned. In a homily composed on the Rogations, he relates that these solemnities which we celebrate before the triumph of our Lord's Ascension were instituted by Mamertus, bishop of Vienne (his own see when he wrote), at a time when the city was alarmed by many portents. For it was frequently shaken by earthquakes, and wild creatures, stags and wolves, entered the gates, wandering without fear through the whole city. These things befell through the circle of the year, till at the approach of the Easter festival the whole people looked devoutly for the mercy of God, that at last this day of great solemnity might set a term to all their terror. But on the very vigil of that glorious night, while the holy rite of the Mass was being celebrated, on a sudden the royal palace within the walls was set ablaze by fire from heaven. All the congregation, stricken with fear, rushed from the church, believing that the whole city would be consumed in this fire, or that the earth would open and swallow it up. The holy bishop, prostrate before the altar, with groans and tears implored the mercy of God. What need for me to say more? The prayer of the illustrious bishop penetrated to the height of heaven; the river of

---

[13] Matthew 10:32–33.

[14] Matthew 10:17–18.

[15] Romans 10:10.

[16] Psalm 35:18.

---

[17] Psalm 57:9.

[18] Galatians 6:7.

his flowing tears extinguished the burning palace. When, after these events, the day of the Lord's Ascension drew near, he imposed a fast upon the people, instituted the form of prayer, the order of their repasts, and the manner of their joyful almsgiving to the poor. Thereupon all these terrors ceased; the fame of this deed spread through all the provinces, putting all the bishops in mind to follow the example of his faith. And down to our day these rites are celebrated in all churches in Christ's name, in compunction of the heart and a contrite spirit.

35. Now when Alaric, king of the Goths, beheld the manner in which King Clovis kept steadily subduing his neighbors in war, he sent envoys to him with this message: "If it please you, O my brother, I am minded that we two meet by God's grace." Clovis did not refuse, but came to him. They met on an island in the Loire near the village of Amboise in the territory of the city of Tours. There they conversed, ate and drank together, swore mutual friendship, and parted in peace. Many people in Gaul at this time ardently desired to live under the dominion of the Franks.

36. This was the reason why Quintianus, bishop of Rodez, incurred hatred and was driven from the city. Men said to him: "It is because you desire the Franks to become masters and possess this land." A few days afterwards there was a quarrel between him and the citizens. Those of the Gothic nation dwelling in the town were suspicious of him, and the citizens accused him of wishing to bring them under the Frankish rule. They took counsel together, and planned to put him to the sword. But the man of God was warned, and rising in the night with the most faithful of his attendants, left Rodez and came to Clermont. There he was kindly received by the holy Bishop Eufrasius, successor to Aprunculus of Dijon, who kept him with him, and bestowed on him houses, lands, and vineyards, saying: "The riches of this church suffice to support us both; only let the brotherly love preached by the blessed apostle continue among the priests of God." The bishop of Lyons also presented him with possessions of his church in Auvergne. The remaining history of the holy Quintianus, both the treachery which he endured, and the works which the Lord deigned to perform by his hands, is written in the book containing his life.

37. Now King Clovis said to his men: "It bothers me greatly that these Arians hold a part of Gaul. Let us go forth, then, and with God's aid bring the land under our own sway." This speech finding favor with all, he assembled his army, and marched on Poitiers, where King Alaric then happened to be. Part of the troops had to traverse the territory of Tours, and out of reverence for the blessed Martin the king issued an edict that none should take anything from that region but water and hay. Now a certain soldier, finding some hay belonging to a poor man, said: "Was it not the king's order that we should take grass and nothing besides? Well, this is grass, and if we take it we shall not transgress his bidding." So he took the hay from the poor man by force, taking advantage of his own strength, The matter came to the ears of the king, who straightway cut the man down with his own sword, saying: "Where shall be our hope of victory, if we offend the blessed Martin?" And the army was content to take nothing more from this region. Moreover the king sent messengers to the church of the saint, with these words: "Go now, and perhaps bring some good news of victory from that sacred house." He entrusted them with offerings to be set in the holy place, saying: "If You, O Lord, are my helper, and if You have determined to deliver into my hands this unbelieving people, ever set against You, deign of Your favor to give me a sign at the going in to the basilica of the blessed Martin, that I may know that You will deign to show Your servant Your favor." His men, setting forth on their journey, reached Tours according to the king's command. And as they were entering the church, the cantor chanced to lead this antiphon: "You have girded me, O Lord, with strength unto the battle; You have subdued under me those that rose up against me. You have also made mine enemies turn their backs upon me, and You have destroyed them that hate me." The messengers, hearing these words chanted, gave thanks to God, and vowing gifts to the blessed confessor, joyfully returned with their news to the king. But when Clovis had reached the Vienne with his army he was wholly at a loss where to cross the stream, for it was swollen by heavy rains. That night he besought the Lord that He would show him where he might pass, and lo! at dawn a deer of wondrous size entered the river at God's bidding, and where she forded the host saw that it could cross. When the king came to the neighborhood of Poitiers, but was abiding at some distance in his tents, he saw a fiery beacon issue from the church of the holy Hilary and come over above his head; it signified that aided by the light of the blessed confessor Hilary he might more surely overcome the host of those heretics against whom the saint himself had so often done battle for the faith. He commanded the whole army to despoil no man, either there or upon the way, and to rob none of his goods.

In those days the abbot Maxentius, a man laudable in holiness lived recluse for the fear of God in his monastery in the territory of Poitiers. I give no particular name to the monastery, since to our own day the place is always known as the cell of the holy Maxentius. Now when the monks beheld a dense body of soldiers drawing near the monastery, they besought the abbot to come forth out of his cell for their encouragement. He delayed to come. Then, stricken with panic, they opened the cell door and brought him out, whereupon he went forth fearlessly to meet the enemy as if to ask peace of them. One of their number unsheathed his sword to strike the abbot on the head, when lo! he found his hand held rigid at the level of his ear, while the sword fell backwards; he then fell at the feet of the holy man, and besought his pardon. When the rest saw what was done, they returned to the army in great dread, fearing that they might all perish. But the blessed confessor rubbed the man's arm with consecrated oil, and making the sign of the Cross, restored him to health; thus by his protection the monastery remained unharmed. He performed many other miracles, which whoso seeks diligently will find as he reads the history of the abbot's life. This took place in the twenty-fifth year of Clovis.

In the meantime King Clovis encountered Alaric, king of the Goths, on the field of Vouillé at the tenth milestone out of Poitiers. Part of the combatants fought with missiles from a distance, another part hand to hand. But when, as their habit is, the Goths turned to fly, King Clovis by God's aid obtained the victory. He had with him as an ally Chloderic, son of Sigibert the Lame. This Sigibert, in the fight at Zülpich against the Alamanni, was wounded in the knee so that he limped. When the Goths were put to flight, and the king had slain Alaric, two of the enemy suddenly came up and struck at him with their spears on each side; the cuirass which he wore and the speed of his horse preserved him from death. There perished on this field a great number of the people of Auvergne who had come with Apollinaris, and the chief men of senatorial family fell. From this battle Amalaric, son of Alaric, fled into Spain and ruled with prudence his father's kingdom. Clovis sent his own son Theuderic through Albi and Rodez to Clermont. Traversing these cities he subdued beneath his father's sway the whole country from the Gothic to the Burgundian frontier. Alaric had reigned twenty-two years. Clovis, after wintering in Bordeaux, carried off all Alaric's treasures from Toulouse and came to Angoulême. And the Lord showed him such favor that the walls fell down of themselves before his eyes; he drove out the Goths and subjected the city to his own rule. Then, his victory being complete, he returned to Tours and made many offerings to the holy shrine of the holy Martin.

38. Clovis received letters from the emperor Anastasius conferring the consulate, and in the church of the blessed Martin he was vested in the purple tunic, and in a mantle, and set the diadem upon his head. Then, mounting his horse, he showered with his own hand in the generosity of his heart pieces of gold and silver among the people all along the road between the gate of the atrium of the holy Martin's church, and the church of the city. From that day he was hailed as consul or Augustus. He left Tours and came to Paris, where he established the seat of his government. There he was joined by Theuderic.

39. After the death of Eustochius, bishop of Tours, Licinius was consecrated as eighth bishop after Martin. In his time was waged the war which I have above described, and it was in his time that King Clovis came to Tours. He is said to have been in the East, to have visited the holy places, and to have even entered Jerusalem; it is related that he often saw the places of the Passion and Resurrection of our Lord, of which we read in the Gospels.

40. While Clovis was sojourning at Paris, he sent secretly to the son of Sigibert, saying: "Your father is grown old, and is lame of one foot. If he were to die, his kingdom would fall to you of right, together with our friendship." The prince, seduced through his ambition, plotted his father's death. One day Sigibert left Cologne and crossed the Rhine, to walk in the forest of Buchau. He was enjoying a midday repose in his tent when his son compassed his death by sending assassins against him, intending so to get possession of his kingdom. But by the judgment of God he fell himself into the pit which he had treacherously dug for his father. He sent messengers to King Clovis announcing his father's death in these terms: "My father has perished, and his kingdom and treasures are in my power. Come to me, and right gladly will I hand over to you whatever things may please you from his treasure." Clovis answered: "I thank you for your goodwill, and request of you that you show all to my envoys; but you shalt keep the whole." On the arrival of the envoys, the prince displayed his father's treasure, and while they were inspecting its various contents, said to them: "In this coffer my father used to amass pieces of gold." They answered: "Plunge in your hand to the bottom, to make sure of all." He did so; but as he was stooping, one of them raised his two-edged ax and buried it in his brain; so was his guilt towards his father requited on himself. When Clovis heard that Sigibert was slain, and his son also, he came to Cologne and called all the people together, addressing them in these words: "Hear what has befallen. While I was sailing the Scheldt, Chloderic, son of my cousin, was harassing his father, and telling him

that I desired his death. When his father fled through the forest of Buchau, he set bandits upon him, delivering him over to death. But he in his turn has perished, stricken I know not by whom, while he was showing his father's treasure. To all these deeds I was in no wise privy; for I could not bear to shed the blood of my kindred, holding it an impious deed. But since things have so fallen out, I offer you this counsel, which take, if it seems good to you: turn to me, and live under my protection." At these words the clash of shields vied with their applause; they raised Clovis upon a shield, and recognized him as their king. Thus he became possessed of the kingdom of Sigibert and of his treasures, and submitted the people also to his dominion. For daily the Lord laid his enemies low under his hand, and increased his kingdom, because he walked before Him with an upright heart, and did that which was pleasing in His sight.

41. After this he marched, against King Chararic.[19] For during his war with Syagrius, this Chararic, summoned to his aid, stood aloof, joining neither side, but awaiting the issue in order to ally himself with the victor, for which cause Clovis marched against him full of wrath. And he cunningly circumvented him and took him, together with his son; he then bound them, and cut off their hair, commanding that Chararic should be ordained priest, and his son deacon. Chararic lamented his humiliation and wept; but they say that his son replied: "These branches have been cut from a green tree, nor are they all withered, but shall soon shoot forth, and grow again. May he who has done these things as swiftly perish!" This saying reached the ears of Clovis, who thought that they threatened to let their hair grow again and compass his death. He therefore ordered both of their heads to be cut off. After their death, he took possession of their kingdom, together with their treasure and their people.

42. There was at that time in Cambrai a king named Ragnachar, whose wantonness was so unbridled that he hardly spared his own near kindred. He had as counselor a certain Farron, defiled by the same foul taint, in regard to whom it was alleged that when any one brought the king a gift of food or a present, or any other kind of thing, the king would say that the gift was sufficient for him and his Farron. On this account the hearts of the Franks were swollen with the utmost indignation. Thereupon Clovis presented armlets and baldrics of spurious gold to the

leudes[20] of Ragnachar in order that they might call him in against their lord; the supposed gold was only copper, cunningly gilded. When he had set his army on foot against him, Ragnachar kept sending out scouts to bring in intelligence. These men were asked on their return in what strength the enemy was. They answered: "Abundant force for you and for your Farron." But Clovis came, and drew up his battle array. And when Ragnachar saw his army vanquished, he made ready to escape in flight, but he was caught by his own men, and brought before Clovis with his arms bound behind his back; so likewise was Ricchar his brother. Clovis said to him: "Why have you disgraced our race by suffering yourself to be bound? It had been better for you to die"; he then raised his ax and buried it in his head. Afterwards he turned to his brother, and said: "If you had stood by your brother, he would not have been thus bound," and slew him in the same way with a blow of his ax, After their death, their betrayers for the first time discovered that the gold which Clovis had given them was false. But when they remonstrated with the king, men say that he replied: "This is the kind of gold deserved by the man who of set mind lures his lord to his death"; adding that they ought to be content to have escaped with their lives, not expiating the betrayal of their lords by a death amid torments. When they heard this, they chose to sue for grace, declaring that it sufficed them if they were judged worthy to live. The two kings of whom I have spoken were kinsmen of Clovis. Their brother, Rignomer, was slain at Le Mans by his command, and the kingdom and treasures of all three passed into his possession. He caused many other kings to be slain and the near relatives whom he suspected of usurping his kingdom; in this way he extended his dominion over all Gaul. Upon a day when he had assembled his own people, he is said to have spoken as follows of the kinsmen whom he had destroyed: "Woe unto me who remain as a traveler among strangers, and have none of my kin to help me in the evil day." But he did not thus allude to their death out of grief, but craftily, to see if he could bring to light some new relative to kill.

43. After these events Clovis died at Paris, and was buried in the church of the Holy Apostles which he had himself built, with Clotild his queen. It was the fifth year

---

[19] King of the Salian Franks.

[20] The personal following of a Frankish king or magnate who had sworn a special oath of loyalty and from whom his personal bodyguard was formed.

after the battle of Vouillé that he passed away. And all the days of his reign were thirty years, and of his own age forty-five. From the passing of the holy Martin to the passing of Clovis, which was in the eleventh year of the episcopate of Licinius, bishop of Tours, there are counted one hundred and twelve years. After the death of her lord, Queen Clotild came to Tours, and, save for rare visits to Paris, here she remained all the days of her life, distinguished for her great modesty and kindliness.

Excerpt from Book VII

47. A cruel feud now arose between citizens of Tours. While Sichar, the son of one John, deceased, was celebrating the feast of Christmas in the village of Manthelan, with Austregisel and other people of the district, the local priest sent a servant to invite several persons to drink wine with him at his house. When the servant came, one of the invited drew his sword and was brutal enough to strike, so that the man fell dead upon the spot. Sichar was bound by ties of friendship to the priest; and as soon as he heard of the servant's murder he seized his weapons and went to the church to wait for Austregisel. He in his turn, hearing of this, took up his arms and equipment and went out against him. There was an encounter between the two parties; in the general confusion Sichar was brought safely away by some clerics, and escaped to his country estate, leaving behind in the priest's house money and clothing, with four wounded servants. After his flight, Austregisel burst into the house, slew the servants, and carried off the gold and silver and other property. The two parties afterwards appeared before a tribunal of citizens, who found Austregisel guilty as a homicide who had murdered the servants, and without any right or sanction seized the property. A few days after the case had been before the court, Sichar heard that the stolen effects were in the hands of Auno, his son, and his brother Eberulf. He set the tribunal at naught, and taking Audinus with him, lawlessly attacked these men by night with an armed party. The house where they were sleeping was forced open, the father, brother, and son were slain, the slaves murdered, and the movable property and herds carried off. The matter coming to my ears, I was deeply troubled, and acting in conjunction with the judge, sent messengers bidding them come before us to see if the matter could be reasonably settled so that the parties might separate in amity and the quarrel go no farther. They came, and the citizens assembled,

whereupon I said: "Desist, O men, from further crime, lest the evil spread more widely. We have already lost sons of the Church, and now we fear that by this same feud we may be deprived of others. Be you peacemakers, I beseech you; let him who did the wrong make composition for the sake of brotherly love, that you be children of peace, and worthy, by the Lord's grace, to possess the kingdom of heaven. For He Himself has said: 'Blessed are the peacemakers, for they shall be called the children of God.' And behold, now, if he who is liable to the penalty have not the means of paying, the Church shall redeem the debt from her own moneys; meanwhile let no man's soul perish." Saying thus, I offered money belonging to the Church. But the party of Chramnesind, who demanded justice for the death of his father and his uncle, refused to accept it. When they were gone, Sichar made preparations for a journey, intending to proceed to the king, and with this in mind set out for Poitiers to see his wife first. But while he was there admonishing a slave to work, he struck him several times with a rod, whereupon the man drew the sword from his master's baldric and did not fear to wound him with it. He fell to the ground; but friends ran up and caught the slave, whom they first beat cruelly; then they cut off his hands and feet and condemned him to the gibbet. Meanwhile the rumor reached Tours that Sichar was dead. As soon as Chramnesind heard it, he warned his relations and friends, and went with all speed to Sichar's house. He plundered it and slew some of the servants, burned down all the houses, not only that of Sichar, but also those belonging to other landholders on the estate. He then took off with him the cattle, and all the movable effects. The parties were now summoned by the count to the city, and pleaded their own causes. The judges decided that he who had already refused a composition and then burned houses down should forfeit half of the sum formerly awarded to him, wherein they acted illegally, to ensure the restoration of peace; they further ordered that Sichar should pay the other moiety of the composition. The Church then provided the sum named in the judgment; the parties gave security, and the composition was paid, both sides promising each other upon oath that they would never make further trouble against each other. So the feud came to an end.

Excerpts from Book IX

19. The feud between the citizens of Tours, which I above described as ended, broke out afresh with revived

fury. After the murder of the kinsfolk of Chramnesind, Sichar formed a great friendship with him; so fond of one another did they grow that often they shared each other's meals and slept in the same bed. One evening Chramnesind made ready a supper, and invited Sichar. His friend came, and they sat down together to the feast. But Sichar, letting the wine go to his head, kept making boastful remarks against Chramnesind, and is reported at last to have said: "Sweet brother, you owe me great thanks for the slaying of your relations; for the composition made to you for their death has caused gold and silver to abound in your house. But for this cause, which enriched you greatly, you would be today poor and destitute." Chramnesind heard these words with bitterness of heart, and said within himself: "If I do not avenge the death of my kinsmen, I deserve to lose the name of man, and to be called weak woman." And straightway he put out the lights and cleft the head of Sichar with his dagger. The man fell and died, uttering but a faint sound as the last breath left him. The servants who had accompanied him fled away. Chramnesind stripped the body of its garments, and hung it from a post of his fence; he then rode away to the king. Entering the church, he prostrated himself at the king's feet, and said: "I ask of you my life, most glorious king, for I have slain men who secretly did to death my kinsmen and plundered all their possessions." He then set forth the whole matter in due order. But Queen Brunhild took it exceeding ill that Sichar, who was under her protection, should have thus been slain, and broke into a fury against Chramnesind, who, seeing that she was set against him, gained the village of Bouges in the territory of Bourges, where his kinsmen lived, because it counted to the kingdom of Guntram. Tranquilla, wife of Sichar, left her children and her husband's property in Tours and Poitiers and withdrew to her own kinsfolk in the village of Mauriopes where she married again. Sichar was about twenty years of age when he died. In life he was a light fellow, a wine-bibber and man-slayer, who did violence to many in his drunkenness. Chramnesind sought the king once more, and was sentenced to prove that he had slain Sichar for his honor: this he was able to do. But Queen Brunhild ordered his property to be confiscated because she had taken Sichar under her protection; afterwards, however, it was restored by Flavianus, the domestic. Proceeding at the time to Agen, he obtained a safe-conduct from Flavianus, to whom his property had been granted by the queen.

20. In this year, the thirteenth of Childebert, I had journeyed to Metz to meet that king, when I was commanded to proceed as envoy to King Guntram. I found him at Chalon, and spoke as follows: "Illustrious king, your most glorious nephew Childebert sends you his fullest greeting, rendering you thanks beyond measure, for your perpetual admonishment do that which is pleasing in God's sight, acceptable to you, and fitting his people's need. He promises to fulfill all that was agreed upon between you, and to break no clauses in the pact signed by you both." The king answered: "No like thanks can I return, seeing that the promise made to me is so clearly broken. He withholds from me my part in the city of Senlis. He has not surrendered my enemy whom, for my safety, I wished to have removed from his kingdom. How say you, then, that my very dear nephew desires in no way to transgress the provisions of the pact drawn up between us?" To this I replied: "It is not his will to contravene any provision; he promises to fulfill them all, in such wise that if you desire to send with regard to the division of Senlis, you shall forthwith receive that which is due to you. As to the men of whom you complain, let their names be written down and sent to him, and every pledge shall be redeemed." After this statement of mine, the king commanded the agreement to be read over again before all present.

Copy of the Pact.

When in the name of Christ the most excellent lords King Guntram and King Childebert and the right glorious lady the Queen Brunhild met together at Andelot for loving-kindness' sake, that they might take full counsel to end whatsoever causes of offense might arise between them, it was settled, approved, and agreed between them with the concourse of their bishops and chief men, the grace of God being their help and mutual love their care, that as long as Almighty God shall grant them life in this present world they shall preserve mutual faith and loving-kindness in purity and singleness of heart.

Likewise that since King Guntram, in accordance with the treaty which he made with King Sigibert of good memory, claimed all the portion of the said lord Sigibert in the kingdom of Charibert, and since King Childebert sought to recover the whole part which his father had possessed; it is hereby after final deliberation decided between the parties as hereinafter follows. All that the lord Sigibert obtained by treaty from the kingdom of Charibert, namely, the third part of the city of Paris, with its territory and its inhabitants, the castles of Châteaudun, Vendôme, and all that the said king had possessed in the territory of Étampes towards those regions, and in Chartres, with their territories and their inhabitants, shall remain in perpetuity under the lawful rule and dominion of King Guntram, in addition to all that he previously possessed of the kingdom of Charibert while the lord Sigibert was yet alive.

In like manner the lord King Childebert shall from this day forward hold under his dominion the city of Meaux, two-thirds of Senlis, the cities of Tours, Poitiers, Avranches, Aire, Saint-Lizier, Bayonne, and Albi, with their territories; but on this condition, that whichever of the two kings God shall cause to survive the other, if that other pass childless from the light of this present world, shall inherit his kingdom in its entirety and forever, and by God's aid hand it down to his descendants.

It is especially determined, and through all things inviolably to be observed, that whatsoever the lord King Guntram has resented to his daughter Clotild or by God's favor shall yet present to her in all kinds of property, or in men, in cities, lands or revenues, shall remain under her power and control; and if she should be fain to dispose of any part of the domain lands assigned to her, or of costly objects, or money, or to bestow them upon any person, these gifts shall with the aid of the Lord be preserved to the possessors forever, nor shall they at any time or by any man be taken from them; and she herself, under the guardianship and protection of King Childebert, shall hold in undisturbed possession, with all honor and dignity, everything of which she shall stand possessed at the death of her sire.

Likewise the lord King Guntram promise that if, through the frailty of our human flesh, that should befall which he would fain not live to see, and which he trusts that God's goodness may forbid, namely, that King Childebert should depart first from the light of this world, leaving him behind, he will receive as a true father under his guardianship and protection the said king's sons, Theudebert and Theuderic as kings, and any other sons which God may have willed to give him, and will see that in all

security they possess their father's kingdom; and that he will receive under his guardianship and defense in all spiritual affection the lady Queen Brunhild, mother of the lord King Childebert, and her daughter Chlodosind, sister of the lord King Childebert, as long as she shall remain in the Frankish dominions, and likewise his queen Faileuba, as it were his own dear sister, with her daughters, and shall grant them to possess in all security and quietness, with all honor and dignity, all their goods, their cities, lands, revenues, and rights, all their property, both such as they hold at this present time, and such as, with Christ's guidance, they may lawfully add hereafter, so that if of their free will they shall desire to dispose of any part of that which was given them out of the domain lands, or of their several effects, or of their moneys, or to confer such property on any person, it shall be secured to him in safe possession in perpetuity, and their wish shall at no time and by no man whatsoever be annulled.

As to the cities of Bordeaux, Limoges, Cahors, Lescar, and Cieutat, which were given, whether as dowry, or as *morgengabe*, which is to say morning-gift, to Galswinth, sister of the lady Brunhild, on her coming into Francia, and which the lady Brunhild, in the lifetime of kings Chilperic and Sigibert, acquired by decision of the lord King Guntram and of the Franks, it is agreed that the lady Brunhild shall forthwith receive in her own possession the city of Cahors with its territory and all its inhabitants, and that all the other cities named above in this relation shall belong to the lord Guntram during his life, but by God's furthering grace shall revert after his death, undiminished in extent, into the possession of the lady Brunhild and her heirs; meanwhile, so long as the lord Guntram lives, they shall at no time and under no pretext be claimed by the lady Brunhild, or by her son King Childebert, or by his sons.

It is likewise agreed that the lord Childebert shall hold Senlis in its entirety, and that the said lord Childebert shall compensate the lord Guntram for the third part of it of right belonging to him, by adding to his possessions the third part of Ressons now in the lord Childebert's possession.

It is further agreed that in accordance with the compacts made between the lord Guntram and the lord Sigibert of blessed memory, those *leudes* who upon the death of King Clothar first took oaths of loyalty to the lord Guntram, and are shown thereafter to have transferred their allegiance elsewhere, shall be brought back from the places where they now dwell. Likewise those who after the death of the lord King Clothar are proved to have first taken oaths of fealty to the lord Sigibert, and then transferred their allegiance elsewhere, shall in like manner be sent back.

Likewise whatsoever the above-mentioned kings have conferred upon churches and upon their own trusty adherents, or may yet by God's propitious grace decide lawfully to confer upon them, shall be preserved to them in security.

And whatsoever any trusty subject of the kings in either kingdom shall of law and justice possess, he shall suffer no prejudice, but shall be permitted to hold these things which are his due. And if, during an interregnum, anything be lost to any man without any fault of his, an inquiry shall be held and it shall be restored. And that which each man has possessed through the munificence of preceding kings down to the death of the lord King Clothar of glorious memory, let him continue to possess it in security. And that which has thereafter been taken from our trusty subjects, let it be forthwith returned.

And since the aforesaid kings are now united in the name of God in a pure and single concord, it is agreed that at no time shall a free passage through the kingdom of either be refused to their respective *leudes*, whether a man would travel upon public or upon private affairs. In like manner it is agreed that neither shall invite to him the *leudes* of the other, or receive them if they come to him of their own accord. And if haply, on the ground of some offense, a subject of one king shall deem it well to seek the territory of the other, he shall be delivered up, but treated with such lenience as the nature of the offend allows.

Further, it was resolved to add this article to the present treaty: if either party shall by any subtle pretext, or at any time, transgress these its provisions, he shall forfeit all the benefits, as well those promised for the future as those straightway conferred, and these benefits shall profit him only who shall have observed all the above conditions; he shall be in all respects absolved from the obligation of keeping his oaths.

These points being thus decided, the contracting parties swear by the name of Almighty God and the indivisible Trinity, by all things divine, and by the tremendous day of Judgment, that without any treachery or fraud they will inviolably observe all that is hereinbefore set down.

This treaty was made on the fourth day of the kalends of December [i.e., November 28], in the twenty-sixth year of the reign of the lord King Guntram, and in the twelfth year of the lord Childebert.

When therefore it had all been read through, the king said: "May God's judgment strike me, if I transgress aught of the provisions herein contained." Then, turning to Felix who had come with us as an envoy, he said: "Tell me, Felix, have you not joined in the fullest friendship my sister Brunhild and Fredegund, the enemy of God and man?" Felix denying the charge, I said: "Let not the king doubt that the same kind of friendship which has bound them these many years is still maintained. For know certainly that the hatred which long ago was between them, far from being withered, is still in vigorous growth. Would that you, most glorious king, were less kindly disposed towards that queen! For as I have myself often perceived, you do receive her embassies with greater honor than ours." To this the king: "Know, O bishop, that I receive her envoys in such fashion as never to fall short in my affection for King Childebert my nephew. How could I establish friendship with one who has often sent forth assassins to take my life?" When he had thus spoken, Felix said: "I suppose that your majesty has heard that Recared has sent an embassy to your nephew to demand in marriage your niece Chlodosind, the daughter of your brother. But King Childebert is not minded to make any promise without your sanction." The king answered: "It is by no means good that my niece should go to the same land where her sister was slain; nor can I accept it as right that the death of my niece Ingund should go unavenged." Felix replied: "They of Spain much desire to clear themselves, by taking oaths, or by any other means which you mayst impose; only give your consent that Chlodosind be betrothed as they desire." The king said: "If my nephew shall fulfill all the conditions written at his own wish in this treaty, then I on my side will gratify his wishes in this matter." We thereupon promised that he would fulfill them all, and Felix added: "He further beseeches you of loyalty to kin to lend him aid against the Lombards, that they may be driven out of Italy and that the territory which his sire claimed in his lifetime may come back to him; the remainder he would fain see, by your aid and his own, restored to the dominions of the emperor." The king replied: "Nay, I cannot send my army into Italy, to give it over to destruction without need, for Italy is now devastated by a most grievous pestilence." Then I said: "You have made known to your nephew your desire that all the bishops in his kingdom be assembled, on the ground that there be many matters calling for investigation. But following our canonical use, your most glorious nephew prefers that each metropolitan should meet together with the bishops of his province, and amend by decree of such councils the disorders occurring in his own region. And what reason should there be for assembling such a multitude in a single place? The faith of the Church is unshaken by any peril; no new heresy shows its head. Where, then, is the necessity that all these bishops should meet together?" The king answered: "There be many points calling for decision: many acts of injustice have been committed; there is much impurity of life; there are also the matters to be discussed between us. First and above all, there is that which concerns God Himself; you are to inquire how it befell that Bishop Praetextatus was slain by the sword in his cathedral church. But there should also be discussion with regard to those accused of immorality, that they may either amend their lives after yielding to your sanctions, or else, if proved innocent be publicly acquitted of a false charge." He then commanded this council to be put off until the kalends of the fourth month. When he had spoken we proceeded to the church, for that day was the festival of our Lord's Resurrection. After the Mass he summoned us to his table, at which the abundance of the dishes was not greater than our own good cheer. For the king without ceasing talked of God, of building new churches, or of protecting the poor. But at times he would be merry, delighting us with jests harmless to religion, that we too might share in his happy mood. He said this, among other things: "Heaven grant that my nephew keep his promises, for all that I have is his. But if he take offense because I receive envoys from my nephew Clothar, am I in such wise a fool as not to be able to mediate between them and prevent the cause of dispute from spreading? Well do I know that it is better to end it than allow it to drag a weary length. I shall give Clothar, if I formally recognize him as my nephew, two or three cities in some part of my dominions, that he may not feel himself disinherited; thus may Childebert be easy

as to the inheritance which his cousin shall receive." This he said, with much else; and after using us right lovingly, and loading us with presents, he dismissed us, bidding us ever give King Childebert such counsel as should further his prosperity.

21. King Guntram, as I have often said, was great in charity and disposed to fasting and vigils. At this time it was reported that Marseilles was ravaged by a plague affecting the groin, which had rapidly spread to a village called Octavus near Lyons. The king, like some good bishop providing the remedies to heal the scars of a people that had sinned, commanded everyone to assemble in the great church and Rogations to be celebrated with the utmost devotion; nothing was to be taken by way of nourishment but barley bread and pure water; all were to be constant in keeping the vigils. His orders were obeyed. For three days the largess of his alms much exceeded his wonted amount, and he was so anxious for the whole people that he might have been taken not merely for their king but also for one of the Lord's bishops. All his hope was now set on the Lord's mercy; all the thoughts that came to him he threw upon God, through whose power he believed with a whole and perfect faith they should be brought to good effect. It was commonly told by the faithful that a certain woman, whose son was sick of a quartan ague[21] and lay uneasily upon his bed, came up through the crowd immediately behind the king, and tore off by stealth some particles of the fringe upon his royal mantle. These she steeped in water, which she gave her son to drink; and immediately the fever was quenched, and he was made whole. I cannot doubt the story, since I myself have often heard evil spirits in the hour of their possession invoking the king's name, and confessing their crimes, compelled by his miraculous power.

22. The city of Marseilles being afflicted, as I have just said, by a most grievous pestilence, I deem it well to unfold from the beginning how much it endured. At that time Bishop Theodore had journeyed to the king to make some complaint against the patrician Nicetius. King Childebert would scarce give ear to the matter, so he prepared to return home. In the meantime a ship had put into the port with the usual merchandise from Spain, unhappily bringing the tinder which kindled this disease. Many citizens purchased various objects from the cargo, and soon a house inhabited by eight people was left empty, every one of them being carried off by the contagion. The fire of this plague did not spread immediately

---

[21] A fever, probably malarial, that occurs every fourth day.

through all the houses in the place; but there was a certain interval, and then the whole city blazed with the pest, like a cornfield set aflame. Nevertheless the bishop came back, and abode within the walls of the church of the holy Victor with the few who remained beside him; there throughout the whole calamity he gave himself up to prayers and vigils, imploring God's mercy, that at last the destruction might have end, and peace and quiet be granted to the people. After two months the affliction ceased, and the people returned, thinking the danger past. But the plague began once more, and all who had returned perished. On several other occasions Marseilles was afflicted by this death.

23. Ageric, bishop of Verdun, fell seriously ill, through the sore grief that afflicted him day by day because Guntram Boso, for whom he had stood surety, had been slain, and through an added bitterness, because Berthefred had been killed in the oratory of the church house; yet more, through his daily lamentation for Guntram's sons, whom he still kept in his dwelling. For he would say: "On account of the hatred felt for me you are now left orphans." Excited by reason of these things, and oppressed, as I have said, by bitterness of heart, but above all worn down by the rigor of his fasting, he died and was laid in the tomb. The abbot Buccovald contended for his bishopric, but had no success. For the citizens agreed in the choice of Charimer, the referendary, who was appointed bishop by royal decree, while Buccovald was passed over. They say that this man was overweening in his pride, for which cause some gave him the nickname "Big Cheek." Licerius, bishop of Arles, likewise died, to whose place succeeded Virgilius, abbot of Autun, with the support of Bishop Syagrius. . . .

30. Now King Childebert, at the request of Maroveus, bishop of Poitiers, sent thither Florentianus, his mayor of the household, and Romulf, count of the palace, to prepare new tax-lists, that the people might pay the taxes as in his father's time. For many on the lists had died, and the weight of the tribute pressed heavily upon their widows and the orphans and upon the infirm. The king's representatives examined the cases in due order, relieving the poor and feeble, and making all those pay this public tax to the state who were justly liable. In due course they came to Tours. But when they proposed to tax our people, saying that they had in their hands the book with lists of taxpayers made

in the time of former kings, we answered them: "It is clear that a register of taxpayers for the city of Tours was made in the reign of King Clothar, and that the books were taken away to be submitted to the king. But smitten with fear of the holy bishop Martin, he caused them to be burned. After the death of King Clothar our people took the oath of loyalty to King Charibert, who likewise solemnly swore not to make new laws or customs binding on our people, but to secure to them the same conditions under which they had lived in his father's reign; he further promised to inflict no new ordinances upon them which would cause them loss. But Gaiso, then count, took the lists, made, as I have said, by former assessors, and began to exact the tax. He was opposed by Bishop Eufronius, but took the amounts which he had wrongfully collected, and went to the king, to whom he showed the capitulary in which the sums due were set down. The king, sighing, yet fearing the power of the holy Martin, threw the capitulary into the fire and returned the pieces of gold already extorted to the church of the saint, declaring that no citizen of Tours should pay any tax to the royal treasury. After his death King Sigibert possessed this city, but laid no burden of tribute upon it. And Childebert, now in the fourteenth year of his reign, has likewise exacted nothing, nor has the city had to groan under the pressure of any taxation. It lies in your power to assess this tax or not; but be you aware of the harm that shall ensue if you prepare to go against the oath of the king." To this speech of mine they replied: "Here in our hands is the book in which is entered the tax imposed on the people of Tours." I retorted: "This book has not issued from the royal treasury, nor has it been valid throughout all these years. There is no reason for surprise if, through the enmities of the citizens, it has been preserved in the house of some private person. But God shall judge those who, to despoil our city, have produced it after so great a tract of time." Meanwhile the son of Audinus, who had actually produced the book, caught a fever that very day, and died the next day but one. We then dispatched a mission to the king, petitioning him to send us notice of his commands with regard to this matter. Forthwith a letter was sent confirming the immunity of the people of Tours from all assessment in veneration of the holy Martin. After it had been read, the men who had been sent for this purpose returned home.

11. *LIFE OF SAINT BALTHILD*

Balthild, wife of King Clovis II (639–657) rose from Anglo-Saxon slave to Frankish queen and regent for her son Clothar III. Her *Life* was written shortly after her death, probably by a nun of Chelles (near modern-day Paris), the monastery she was forced to enter after a palace coup overthrew her regency. The account presents, although in veiled manner, both the possibilities and dangers facing a Frankish queen who, lacking the support of powerful family members, looked to ecclesiastical institutions to protect her position and that of her son.

Source: Sainted Women of the Dark Ages, ed. and trans. Jo Ann McNamara and John E. Halborg, with E. Gordon Whatley (Durham, NC: Duke University Press, 1992).
Further Reading: Janet L. Nelson, "Queens as Jezebels: The Careers of Brunhild and Balthild in Merovingian History," in D. Baker (ed.), *Medieval Women* (Oxford: Blackwell, 1978), 31–77.

Here Begins the Prologue to the Life of Lady Balthild the Queen

1. Most beloved brothers, I have been commanded by the prelate Christ, to accomplish a simple and pious work. My lack of skill and experience prevents me from setting forth an exquisite narrative in learned language. But the power of heartfelt love more strongly commands us not to be puffed up with vain glory and simply bring the truth to light. For we know that the lord Jesus Christ asked for fruit from the fig tree, not leaves. And likewise we have determined that the fruit of truth shall not be hidden but shine forth upon a candlestick for the advancement and edification of many. Though less skilled in scholarship, we are all the more eager to cultivate a plain and open style so as to edify the many people who, like prudent bees seeking sweet nectar from the flowers, seek from simple words the burgeoning truth that edifies but does not flatter and puff up the one who hears it. Thus may the compendium of piety be thrown open to those who desire to imitate her. Therefore in what follows we have shown forth the truth as best we can, not for detractors but rather for the faithful.

Here Begins the Life of the Blessed Queen Balthild

2. The blessed Lord, "who will have all men to be saved, and to come unto the knowledge of the truth,"[22] works "all in all"[23] both "to will and to do."[24] By the same token, among the merits and virtues of the saints, praise should first be sung of Him Who made the humble great and raised the pauper from the dunghill and seated him among the princes of his people. Such a one is the woman present to our minds, the venerable and great lady Balthild the queen. Divine Providence called her from across the seas. She, who came here as God's most precious and lofty pearl, was sold at a cheap price. Erchinoald,[25] a Frankish magnate and most illustrious man, acquired her and in his service the girl behaved most honorably. And her pious and admirable manners pleased this prince and all his servants. For she was kindhearted and sober and prudent in all her ways, careful and plotting evil for none. Her speech was not frivolous nor her words presumptuous but in every way she behaved with utmost propriety. And since she was of the Saxon race, she was graceful in form with refined features, a most seemly woman with a smiling face and serious gait. And she so showed herself just as she ought in all things, that she pleased her master and found favor in his eyes. So he determined that she should set out the drinking cup for him in his chamber and, honored above all others as his housekeeper, stand at his side always ready to serve him. She did not allow this dignity to make her proud but rather kept her humility. She was all obedience to her companions and amiable,

---

[22] 1 Timothy 2:4.

[23] 1 Corinthians 15:28.
[24] Philippians 2:3–4.
[25] Neustrian mayor of the palace.

ministering with fitting honor to her elders, ready to draw the shoes from their feet and wash and dry them. She brought them water to wash themselves and prepared their clothing expeditiously. And she performed all these services with good spirits and no grumbling.

3. And from this noble conduct, the praise and love of her comrades for her increased greatly. She gained such happy fame that, when the said lord Erchinoald's wife died, he hoped to unite himself to Balthild, that faultless virgin, in a matronal bed. But when she heard of this, she fled and most swiftly took herself out of his sight. When she was called to the master's chamber she hid herself secretly in a corner and threw some vile rags over herself so that no one could guess that anyone might be concealed there. Thus for the love of humility, the prudent and astute virgin attempted to flee as best she could from vain honors. She hoped that she might avoid a human marriage bed and thus merit a spiritual and heavenly spouse. But doubtless, Divine Providence brought it about that the prince, unable to find the woman he sought, married another wife. Thereafter it happened, with God's approval, that Balthild, the maid who escaped marriage with a lord, came to be espoused to Clovis, son of the former king Dagobert. Thus by virtue of her humility she was raised to a higher rank. Divine dispensation determined to honor her in this station so that, having scorned the king's servant, she came to be coupled with the king himself and bring forth royal children. And these events are known to all for now her royal progeny rule the realm.

4. She upon whom God conferred the grace of prudence obeyed the King with vigilant care as her lord, acted as a mother to the princes, as a daughter to priests, and as a most pious nurse to children and adolescents. And she was amiable to all, loving priests as fathers, monks as brothers, a pious nurse to the poor. And she distributed generous alms to everyone. She guarded the princes' honor by keeping their intimate counsels secret. She always exhorted the young to strive for religious achievement and humbly and assiduously suggested things to the king for the benefit of the church and the poor. For, desiring to serve Christ in the secular habit at that time, she frequented daily prayers commending herself with tears to Christ, the King of heaven. The pious king, impressed by her faith and devotion, delegated his faithful servant the abbot Genesius as her helper. Through his hands, she ministered to priests and poor alike, feeding the needy and clothing the naked and taking care to order the burial of the dead, funneling large amounts of gold and silver

through him to convents of men and virgins. Afterwards that servant of Christ, Genesius, by Christ's order, was ordained bishop of Lyon in Gaul. But at that time, he was busy about the palace of the Franks. And as we have said, by King Clovis's order, Lady Balthild followed the servant of God's advice in providing alms through him to every poor person in many places.

5. What more? In accordance with God's will, her husband King Clovis migrated from the body and left his sons with their mother. Immediately after him her son Clothar took up the kingdom of the Franks, maintaining peace in the realm, with the most excellent princes, Chrodebert, Bishop of Paris, Lord Ouen, and Ebroin, Mayor of the Palace, with the rest of the elders and many others. Then to promote peace, by command of Lady Balthild with the advice of the other elders, the people of Austrasia accepted her son Childeric as their king and the Burgundians were united with the Franks. And we believe, under God's ordinance, that these three realms then held peace and concord among themselves because of Lady Balthild's great faith.

6. Then following the exhortations of good priests, by God's will working through her, Lady Balthild prohibited the impious evil of the simoniac heresy, a depraved custom which stained the church of God, whereby episcopal orders were obtained for a price. She proclaimed that no payment could be exacted for receipt of a sacred rank. Moreover, she, or God acting through her, ordained that yet another evil custom should cease, namely, that many people determined to kill their children rather than nurture them, for they feared to incur the public exactions which were heaped upon them by custom, which caused great damage to their affairs. In her mercy, that lady forbade anyone to do these things. And for all these deeds, a great reward must surely have awaited her.

7. Who can count how many and how great her services were to religious communities? She showered great estates and whole forests upon them for the construction of their cells and monasteries. And at Chelles, in the region of Paris, she built a great community of virgins as her own special house of God. There she established the maiden Bertilla, God's serving girl, as the first to hold the place of their mother. And there in turn the venerable Lady Balthild had determined she would finally go to live under the rule of religion and to rest in peace and in truth she fulfilled her desire with willing devotion. Whatever wonders God works through His saints and His chosen ones should not be passed over, for they contribute to His praise. For, as Scripture says, "God does wonders in

his saints."[26] For His Holy Spirit, the Paraclete,[27] dwells within and cooperates with the benevolent heart as it is written: "All things work together for good to them that love God."[28] And thus it was spoken truly of this great woman. As we said, neither our tongue nor any others, however learned as I believe, can give voice to all the good she did. How much consolation and help did she lavish on the houses of God and on the poor for the love of Christ and how many advantages and comforts did she confer on them? And what of the monastery called Corbie in the parish of Amiens that she built at her own expense? There the venerable man, Lord Theofredus, now a bishop but then the abbot, ruled a great flock of brothers whom Lady Balthild had requested from the most saintly Lord Waldebert, then abbot of the monastery of Luxeuil, who wondrously had them sent to that same convent which all agree in praising to this very day.

8. What more? At Jumièges, the religious man Lord Philibert was given a great wood from the fisc where his community has settled and other gifts and pastures were also conceded from the fisc for the building of this same monastery. And how many great farms and talents of gold and silver did she give to Lord Lagobert at Curbio? She took off a girdle from her regalia, which had encircled her own holy loins, and gave it to the brothers to devote to alms. And she dispensed all this with a benign and joyous soul, for as the scripture says: "The Lord loveth a cheerful giver."[29] And likewise to Fontanelle and Logium, she conceded many things. As to Luxeuil and the monasteries in Burgundy, who can tell how many whole farms and innumerable gifts of money she gave? And what did she do for Jouarre, whence she gathered the Lady Bertilla abbess of Chelles and other sacred virgins? How many gifts of wealth and land? And similarly she often directed gifts to holy Fara's monastery. And she granted many great estates to the basilicas of the saints and monasteries of the city of Paris, and enriched them with many gifts. What more? As we have said, we cannot recount these things one by one, not even half of them, and to give an account of all the blessings she conferred is utterly beyond our powers.

9. We should not pass over, however, what she did in her zealous love of God for the older basilicas of the saints, Lord Denis and Lord Germanus and Lord Médard

and Saint Peter or the Lord Anianus, and Saint Martin, or wherever something came to her notice. She would send orders and letters warning bishops and abbots that the monks dwelling in those places ought to live according to their holy rule and order. And that they might agree more freely, she ordered their privileges confirmed and granted immunities that it might please them all the more to beseech Christ the highest King to show mercy to the king and give peace. And let it be remembered, since it increases the magnitude of her own reward, that she prohibited the sale of captive Christian folk to outsiders and gave orders through all the lands that no one was to sell captive Christians within the borders of the Frankish realm. What is more, she ordered that many captives should be ransomed, paying the price herself. And she installed some of the captives she released and other people in monasteries, particularly as many men and women of her own people as possible and cared for them. For as many of them as she could persuade thereto, she commended to holy communities and bade that they might pray for her. And even to Rome, to the basilicas of Peter and Paul, and the Roman poor, she directed many and large gifts.

10. And as we have said before, it was her own holy intention to convert to this monastery of religious women which she had built at Chelles. But the Franks delayed much for love of her and would not have permitted this to happen except that there was a commotion made by the wretched Bishop Sigobrand whose pride among the Franks earned him his mortal ruin. Indeed, they formed a plan to kill him against her will. Fearing that the lady would act heavily against them, and wish to avenge him, they suddenly relented and permitted her to enter the monastery. There can be no doubt that the princes' motives were far from pure. But the lady, considering the will of God rather than their counsel, thought it a dispensation from God so that, whatever the circumstances, she might have the chance to fulfill her holy plan under Christ's rule. And conducted by several elders, she came to her aforesaid monastery of Chelles and there she was received into the holy congregation by the holy maidens, as was fitting, honorably and with sufficient love. But at first she had no small complaint against those whom she had so sweetly nurtured. For they suspected her of false motives or else simply attempted to return evil for good. Hastily conferring with the priests about this, she mercifully indulged them in the delay and begged that they would forgive the commotion in her heart. And afterwards by the largesse of God, peace was fully restored between them.

---

[26] Psalm 67:36.

[27] The Holy Spirit (from the Greek *parakletos*).

[28] Romans 8:28.

[29] 2 Corinthians 9:7.

11. And indeed, she loved her sisters with the most pious affection as her own daughters and she obeyed their most holy abbess as a mother. She showed herself as a servant and lowliest bondwoman to them from holy devotion, even while she still ruled over the public palace, and had often visited the community. One example of her great humility was the way she would valiantly take care of the dirtiest cleaning jobs for the sisters in the kitchen, personally cleaning up the dung from the latrine. And she did all this gladly and in perfect joy of spirit, doing such humble service for Christ's sake. For who would believe that one so sublime in power would take care of things so vile? Only if she were driven by the fullest love of Christ could it be expected. And she prayed constantly, persistently, devoutly, tearfully. She frequently attended divine reading and gave constant comfort to the sick through holy exhortation and frequent visits. Through the achievement of charity, she grieved with the sorrowful, rejoiced with the joyful and, that all might be comforted, she often made suggestions for their improvement humbly to the lady abbess. And that lady amiably gave heed to her petitions for truly in them as in the apostles, there was but one heart and one soul, and they loved each other tenderly in Christ.

12. Then the Lady Balthild became physically ill of body and suffered wearily from pain in the bowels caused by a serious infection, and but for the doctors' efforts she would have died. But she always had more confidence in celestial medicine for her health. So, with a holy and pious conscience, she never ceased to thank God for chastising. She gave her astute advice at all times and—example of great humility—she provided a pattern of piety in her service to her sisters. She often consulted with the mother of the monastery as to how they might always call on the king and queen and their honored nobles with gifts, as was customary, that the house of God might continue to enjoy the good fame with which it began. Thus it would not lose but always remain in loving affection with all its friends and grow stronger in the name of God, as it is written: "It is fitting to have good report of them which are without."[30] Particularly, she urged them always to care for the poor and for guests with the utmost zeal, out of love and mercy and the mother of the monastery heard her salutary admonitions willingly for love of Christ and did all with gladness of heart. Nor did she ever cease to carry out all this and to increase the rewards of her community.

13. And as her glorious death approached, a clear vision was shown to her. Before holy Mary's altar, a ladder stood upright whose height reached the heavens. Angels of God were going up and down and there the Lady Balthild made her ascent. Through this revelation, she was clearly given to understand that her sublime merit, patience and humility, would take her to the heights of the eternal King who would swiftly reward her with an exalted crown. The lady knew, from this clear vision, that it would not be long before she would migrate from her body and come where she had already laid up her best treasures. And she ordered that this be concealed from her sisters so that until her passing the vision was not revealed lest it cause painful grief to the sisters or the mother of the monastery. But she on her part devoted herself with ever greater piety and good spirits to holy prayer, commending herself ever more zealously, humbly, and in contrition of heart to the celestial king, the Lord Jesus Christ. As much as she could, she concealed the weight of her pain and consoled Lady Bertilla and the rest of the sisters saying that her illness was not serious, that she was convalescent, dissimulating what was to come so that afterwards they took comfort in believing that the blow fell suddenly and she went unexpectedly from life.

14. And when the lady felt her end to be truly near, she raised her holy mind to Heaven. And having made certain that she would be awarded the great prize that the blessed receive, she vehemently forbade her attendants to say how sick she was to the other sisters or to the abbess who was ill herself lest she be distracted by a multitude of even heavier sorrows. At the time there was an infant, her goddaughter whom she wished to take with her. And she was suddenly snatched from her body and preceded her to the tomb. Then full of faith, she crossed herself. Raising pious eyes and holy hands to heaven, the saint's soul was released from the chains of her flesh in peace. And immediately her chamber glittered brightly with the light of divine splendor. And no doubt with that light, a chorus of angels and her faithful old friend Bishop Genesius came to receive that most holy soul as her great merits deserved.

15. For a little while, the sisters attending her, stifled their sorrowful groans. They said nothing of her death and, as she had ordered, remained silent and told only those priests who commended her most blessed soul to the Lord. But when the abbess and all the congregation learned what had happened they asked tearfully how this universally desired jewel could have been snatched away so suddenly without warning, without knowing the hour of her departure. And stupefied, they all prostrated

---

[30] 1 Timothy 3:7.

themselves on the ground in grief and with profuse tears and fearful groans, gave thanks to the pious Lord and praised Him together. Then they commended her holy soul to Christ, the pious King, that He might escort her to holy Mary in the chorus and company of the saints. Then they buried her with great honor and much reverence as was proper. And Lady Bertilla the abbess, with solicitous striving for piety, earnestly commended her to the holy priests in several churches that her holy name be carefully commemorated in the sacred oblations. And they still celebrate her merits in many places.

16. To her followers, she left a holy example of humility and patience, mildness and overflowing zest for loving; nay more, infinite mercy, astute and prudent vigilance, pure confessions. She showed that everything should be done as a result of consultation and that nothing should be done without consent but that all actions should be temperate and rational. She left this rule of piety as a model to her companions and now for her holy virtues and many other merits she has received the prize of the crown that the Lord set aside for her long ago. So she is happy among the angels in the Lord's sight and as His spouse rejoices forever among the white-garbed flock of virgins enjoying the immense and everlasting joy she had always desired. And in order to make known her sublime merits to the faithful, God in his goodness has effected many miracles at her holy tomb. For whoever came there seized by fever, or vexed with demons, or worn with toothache, if they had faith, was immediately cured through divine virtue and her holy intercession from whatever plague or illness. Safe and sound, they went out in the Lord's name as was manifested not long ago in the case of a certain boy.

17. A certain venerable man, Bishop Leudegund, came from Provence, a faithful friend to the monastery of Chelles. His son was possessed by a demon so violent that his companions could only control him if his hands and feet were bound, for with great cruelty he tore apart all he could reach. But when they brought him into the place of her holy sepulcher and laid him half-alive on the pavement, the ferocious demon grew stiff and terrified with fear of God and fell silent. Divine power made him flee from the boy forthwith. And the boy rose up confidently, crossed himself and, giving thanks to God, returned to his own unharmed and in his right mind.

18. Now let us recall that there have been other noble queens in the realm of the Franks who worshipped God: Clothild, King Clovis's queen of old, niece of King Gundobad. Her husband was a mighty pagan but she drew him, with many other Frankish leaders, to Christianity and the Catholic faith by holy exhortations. She led them to construct a church in honor of Saint Peter at Paris, and she built the original community of virgins for Saint George at Chelles and in honor of the saints and to store up her future reward she founded many others which she endowed with much wealth. And likewise we are told of Queen Ultragotha of the most Christian king Childebert, that she was a comforter of the poor and helper of the monks who served God. And also, there was the most faithful handmaid Radegund, King Clothar's queen of elder time, whom the grace of the Holy Spirit enkindled so that she relinquished her husband during his life and consecrated herself to the Lord Christ under the holy veil. And we may read in her acts of all the good she did for Christ her spouse.

19. But it is only right that we meditate instead on her who is our subject here, Lady Balthild whose many good deeds have been done in our time and whose acts are best known to us. We have commemorated a few of these many acts and cannot think her merits inferior to those who came before her for we know she surpassed them in zealous striving for what is holy. For after performing many good deeds to the point of evangelical perfection, she at last surrendered herself freely to holy obedience and happily ended her life as a religious, a true *monacha*.[31] Her sacred obit and holy feast are celebrated on the third kalends of February. She lies entombed in Chelles, her monastery, while truly she reigns gloriously with Christ in Heaven in perpetual joy never, we trust, to forget her faithful friends. And as well as we could, if not as much as we ought, in fervent charity we have striven to follow your orders. Forgive our lack of skill and for our sins of negligence we pray for charity's sake that you ask the good Lord to exonerate us. May the peace of the Lord be with you to Whom be glory from everlasting to everlasting. Amen.

Questions for Study

While in many ways an heir to the Roman Empire, the Frankish kingdoms had a markedly different political landscape from that of the Empire. What are some of the major characteristics of Frankish political life as revealed by these sources?

---

[31] Female monk.

Early Italy

12. ST. BENEDICT

RULE FOR MONASTERIES

Benedict of Nursia (ca. 480–547) began his religious life as a hermit near Subiaco, a small town near Rome. He went on to found 12 monasteries, the most important being Monte Cassino. His *Rule*, derived largely from an earlier anonymous *Rule of the Master*, first became widely known in the middle of the seventh century. By the ninth century it had become the dominant monastic rule in the West, a position that it holds to the present day.

Source: The Rule of Saint Benedict, trans. Francis Gasquet (London: Chatto and Windus, 1909); rev. Julian Hendrix.
Further Reading: Adalbert de Vogüé, *Saint Benedict: The Man and His Work* (Petersham, MA: St. Bebe's Publications, 2006).

The Prologue

Listen, my son, and turn the ear of your heart to the precepts of your master.[1] Receive readily, and faithfully carry out the advice of a loving father, so that by the work of obedience you may return to him, whom you have left by the sloth of disobedience. For you, therefore, whosoever you be, my words are intended, who, giving up your own will, takes up the all-powerful and excellent arms of obedience to fight under the Lord Christ, the true king.

First, beg of him with most earnest prayer to finish the good work begun; that he who now has deigned to count us among his children may never be grieved by our evil deeds. For at all times we must so serve him with the good things he has given us, that he may not, as an angry father, disinherit his children, nor as a terrifying lord, provoked by our evil deeds, deliver us to everlasting punishment as wicked servants who refuse to follow him to glory.

Let us, therefore, arise at once, the scripture stirring us up, saying, "It is now the hour for us to rise from sleep."[2] And, our eyes now open to the divine light, let us with wondering ears attend to the divine voice, daily calling to

---

[1] The beginning of this Prologue suggests that St. Benedict had before him in writing the Latin translation of St. Basil's *Admonitio ad filium spiritualem,* which commences with the words "Audi fili admonitionem patris tui, et inclina aurem tuam." The invitation in the Prologue to the *Rule* is considerably longer than that of St. Basil's tract.

[2] Romans 13:11.

us and warning us, "Today if you should hear his voice, harden not your hearts;"[3] and again, "He that has ears, let him hear what the Spirit says to the Churches."[4] And what does he say? "Come, children, and listen to me: I will teach you the fear of the Lord."[5] "Run while you have the light of life, that the darkness of death may not overtake you."[6]

And our Lord, seeking his workman among the multitude of those to whom he thus speaks, says again, "Who is the man that will have life, and desires to see good days?"[7] And if you, hearing this, reply, "I am he": God says to you, If you desire to possess true and everlasting life "restrain your tongue from evil, and your lips so that they do not speak deceptively. Turn from evil and do good; seek after peace and pursue it."[8] And when you have done this my eyes shall be on you, and my ears shall be open to your prayers. And before you can call upon me, I will say to you, "Behold, I am present."[9] What can be more agreeable, dearest brothers, than this voice of our Lord inviting us? Behold how in his loving kindness he shows us the way of life.

Therefore, with our loins girded by faith, and by the practice of good works under the guidance of his gospel, let us walk in the path he has marked out for us, that we may deserve to see him who has called us into his kingdom.[10]

If we would live in the shelter of this kingdom, we can reach it only by speeding on the way of good works (by this path alone is it to be attained). But let us, with the prophet, ask our lord, and say to him, "Lord, who shall dwell in your tabernacle? Or who shall rest on your holy hill?"[11] And when we have so asked, let us hear our lord's answer, pointing out to us the way to this his dwelling, and saying, "He that walks without stain and works for justice; he that speaks truth in his heart; that has not created deceit with his tongue; he that has not done evil to his neighbor, and has not accepted dishonor against him."[12] He that, casting out of the innermost thoughts of

his heart the suggestions of the evil-minded devil trying to lead him astray, has brought them all to nothing; he that taking hold of such thoughts while in their birth has dashed them against the rock, which is Christ. They who, fearing the lord, are not lifted up by their good observance, but knowing that all that is good in them comes not from themselves but from the lord, extol his work in them, saying with the prophet, "Not to us, oh lord, not to us, but to your name give glory."[13] Thus the apostle Paul imputed nothing of his preaching to himself, saying, "By the grace of God I am what I am."[14] And again he says, "He that glories, let him glory in the lord."[15]

Hence also our lord in the gospel says, "He that hears these words of mine and does them, I will compare him to a wise man who has built his house upon a rock. The floods came, the winds blew and beat against that house, and it did not fall, because it was founded upon a rock."[16] In fulfilling this our lord daily looks for deeds by us that comply with his holy admonitions. Therefore are the days of this life of ours lengthened for a while so that we can make amends for our evil deeds, according to the words of the apostle, "Do you not know that the patience of God will lead you to repentance?"[17] For our loving lord says, "I do not wish for the death of the sinner, but that he be converted and live."[18]

So questioning the lord, brethren, we have heard on what conditions we may dwell in his temple; and if we fulfill these we shall be heirs of the kingdom of heaven. Therefore must our hearts and bodies be prepared to fight under the holy obedience of his orders, and we must beg our lord to supply by the help of his grace what by nature is not possible to us. And if, fleeing from the pains of hell, we wish to attain life everlasting, we must, while we yet live in the flesh and the light is still on our path, hurry to do now what will profit us for all eternity.

We are, therefore, now about to institute a school for the service of God, in which we hope nothing harsh nor burdensome will be ordained. But if we proceed in certain things with some little severity, sound reason so advising for the amendment of vices or the preserving of charity, do not, for fear of this, in that very place flee

---

[3] Psalm 94:8.

[4] Revelation 2:7.

[5] Psalm 33:12.

[6] John 12:35.

[7] Psalm 33:13.

[8] Psalm 33:14, 15.

[9] Isaiah 65:24.

[10] Ephesians 6:14, 15.

[11] Psalm 14:4.

[12] Psalm 14:2, 3.

---

[13] Psalm 13:1.

[14] 1 Corinthians 15:10.

[15] 2 Corinthians 10:47.

[16] Romans 2:4.

[17] Romans 2:4.

[18] Ezekiel 18:23.

from the way of salvation, which is always narrow in the beginning.[19] In living our life, however, and by the growth of faith, when the heart has been enlarged, the path of God's commandments is run with unspeakable loving sweetness; so that never leaving his school, but persevering in the monastery in his teaching until death, we share by our patience in the sufferings of Christ, and so merit to be participants in his kingdom.[20]

Chapter I—Of the Several Kinds of Monks and Their Lives

It is recognized that there are four kinds of monks. The first are the Cenobites: that is, those who live in a monastery under a rule or an abbot. The second kind is that of the Anchorites or Hermits, who not in the first heat of conversion, but after long trial in the monastery, and already taught by the example of many others, have learned to fight against the devil, are well prepared to go forth from the ranks of the brotherhood to the single combat of the desert. They can now, by God's help, safely fight against the vices of their flesh and against evil thoughts alone, with their own hand and arm and without the encouragement of a companion. The third and worst kind of monks is that of the Sarabites, who have not been tried under any rule nor schooled by an experienced master, as gold is proved in the furnace, but soft as lead and still in their works sticking fast to the world, are known to lie to God with their tonsure.

These in twos or threes, or more frequently alone, are shut away, without a shepherd; not in our lord's fold, but in their own. The pleasure of carrying out their particular desires is their law, and whatever they dream of or choose, this they call holy; but what they do not like, that they consider to be unlawful.

The fourth class of monks is called Gyrovites (or Wanderers). These move about all their lives through various countries, staying as guests for three or four days at different monasteries. They are always on the move and never settle down, and are slaves to their own wills and to the enticements of gluttony. In every way they are worse than the Sarabites, and of their wretched way of life it is better to be silent than to speak.

Leaving these, therefore, aside, let us by God's help set down a rule for Cenobites, who are the best kind of monks.

Chapter II—What the Abbot Should Be

In order to be fit to rule a monastery, an abbot should always remember what he is called, and in his acts illustrate his high calling. For in a monastery he is considered to take the place of Christ, since he is called by his name as the apostle says, "You have received the spirit of the adoption of sons, by which we cry, Abba, Father."[21] Therefore the abbot should neither teach, ordain, nor require anything against the command of our lord (God forbid!), but in the minds of his disciples let his orders and teaching be mingled with the leavening of divine justice.

The abbot should always be mindful that at the dreaded judgment of God there will be an inquiry into both his teaching and the obedience of his disciples. Let the abbot know that any lack of goodness, which the master of the family shall find in his flock, will be accounted the shepherd's fault. On the other hand, he shall be acquitted in so far as he shall have shown all the watchfulness of a shepherd over a restless and disobedient flock; and if as their pastor he shall have employed every care to cure their corrupt manners, he shall be declared guiltless in the Lord's judgment, and he may say with the prophet, "I have not hidden your justice in my heart; I have told your truth and your salvation;[22] but they condemned and despised me."[23] And then in the end shall death be inflicted as a suitable punishment upon the sheep which have not responded to his care. When, therefore, any one shall receive the name of abbot, he ought to rule his disciples with a twofold teaching: that is, he should first show them in deeds rather than words all that is good and holy. To such as are understanding, indeed, he may expound the lord's commands by words; but to the hard-hearted and to the simpleminded he must manifest the divine precepts in his life. Thus, what he has taught his disciples to be contrary to God's law, let him show in his own deeds that such things are not to be done, or else by preaching to others "he himself becomes a castaway,"[24] and God says to him about his sins, "Why do you declare my justices, and take my testament in your mouth? You have hated discipline, and cast my

---

[19] Matthew 17:13.

[20] 2 Corinthians 1:7.

[21] Romans 8:15.

[22] Psalm 39:11.

[23] Isaiah 1:2.

[24] 1 Corinthians 9:27.

speeches behind you."[25] And, "You, who saw the speck in your brother's eye, have you not seen the beam that is in your own?"[26]

Let him make no distinction of persons in the monastery. Let not one be loved more than another, save such as are found to excel in obedience or good works. Do not put the free-born before the serf-born in religion, unless there is another reasonable cause for it. If, upon due consideration, the abbot shall see such cause he may place him where he pleases; otherwise let all keep their own places, because "whether bound or free we are all one in Christ,"[27] and bear an equal burden of service under one Lord: "for with God there is no regard for persons."[28] For one thing only are we preferred by him, which is if we are found better than others in good works and more humble. Let the abbot therefore have equal love for all, and let all, according to their merits, be under the same discipline.

The abbot in his teaching should always observe that apostolic rule which says, "Reprove, entreat, rebuke."[29] That is to say, as occasions require he ought to mingle encouragement with rebukes. Let him manifest the sternness of a master and the loving affection of a father. He must severely reprove the undisciplined and restless, but he should exhort such as are obedient, quiet and patient, for their better profit. We charge him, however, to reprove and punish the stubborn and negligent. Let him not shut his eyes to the sins of offenders; but, directly they begin to show themselves and to grow, he must use every means to root them up utterly, remembering the fate of Heli, the priest of Silo.[30] To the more virtuous and apprehensive, indeed, he may for the first or second time use words of warning; but in dealing with the stubborn, the hard-hearted, the proud, and the disobedient, even at the very beginning of their sin, let him chastise them with whipping and with bodily punishment, knowing that it is written, "The fool is not corrected with words."[31] And again, "Strike your son with a rod and you shall deliver his soul from death."[32]

The abbot ought ever to bear in mind what he is and what he is called; he ought to know that to whom more is entrusted, from him more is exacted. Let him recognize how difficult and how hard a task he has undertaken, to rule souls and to make himself a servant to the temperaments of many. One, indeed, must be led by gentle words, another by rebuke, another by persuasion; and thus shall he so shape and adapt himself to the character and intelligence of each, that he not only suffers no loss in the flock entrusted to his care, but may even rejoice in its good growth. Above all things let him not slight nor make little of the souls committed to his care, heeding more fleeting, worldly and frivolous things; but let him remember always that he has undertaken the guidance of souls, of which he shall also have to give an account. And that he may not complain of the lack of temporal means, let him remember that it is written, "Seek first the kingdom of God, and his justice, and all things shall be given to you."[33] And again, "Nothing is wanting to those that fear him."[34]

He should know that whoever undertakes the government of souls must prepare himself to account for them. And however great the number of the brethren under him may be, let him understand for certain that at the Day of Judgment he will have to give an account to our lord of all their souls as well as of his own. In this way, by fearing the inquiry concerning his flock which the shepherd will hold, he is anxious on account of others' souls as well as of his own, and thus while reclaiming other men by his corrections, he frees himself also from all vice.

Chapter III—On Taking Counsel of the Brethren

Whenever any weighty matters have to be transacted in the monastery, let the abbot call together all the community and himself propose the matter for discussion. After hearing the advice of the brethren, let him consider it in his own mind, and then do what he judges most expedient. Often the Lord reveals to a younger member what is best. And let the brethren give their advice with all humble subjection, and not presume to boldly defend their own opinion. Let them rather leave the matter to the abbot's discretion, so that all submit to what he shall deem best. As it becomes disciples to obey

[25] Psalm 49:16, 17.
[26] Matthew 8:3.
[27] 1 Corinthians 12:13.
[28] Ephesians 6:9.
[29] 2 Timothy 4:2.
[30] 1 Samuel 2:12–17.
[31] Proverbs 23:13.
[32] Proverbs 23:14.
[33] Matthew 6:33.
[34] Psalm 33:19.

their master, so does it becomes the master to dispose of all things with forethought and justice.

In all things, therefore, everyone shall follow the Rule as their master, and let no one rashly depart from it. In the monastery no one is to be led by the desires of his own heart, nor shall anyone within or outside of the monastery presume to argue recklessly with his abbot. If he presumes to do so let him be subjected to punishment according to the Rule.

The abbot, however, must himself do all things in the fear of God and according to the Rule, knowing that he shall undoubtedly have to give an account of his whole government to God, the most just Judge.

If anything minor has to be done in the monastery, let the abbot take the advice of the seniors only, as it is written, "Do all things with counsel, and you shall not afterwards repent of it."[35]

Chapter IV—The Instruments of Good Works

First of all, to love the lord God with all our heart, with all our soul, with all our strength.[36]

2. Then, to love our neighbor as ourself.[37]
3. Then, not to kill.[38]
4. Not to commit adultery.[39]
5. Not to steal.[40]
6. Not to be covetous.[41]
7. Not to bear false witness.[42]
8. To respect all men.[43]
9. Not to do to another what one would not have done to oneself.[44]
10. To deny oneself in order to follow Christ.[45]
11. To chastise the body.[46]

12. Not to be fond of pleasures.[47]
13. To love fasting.[48]
14. To give refreshment to the poor.[49]
15. To clothe the naked.[50]
16. To visit the sick.[51]
17. To bury the dead.[52]
18. To come to the help of those in trouble.[53]
19. To comfort those in sadness.[54]
20. To become a stranger to the ways of the world.[55]
21. To prefer nothing to the love of Christ.[56]
22. Not to give way to wrath.[57]
23. Not to harbor anger for any time.[58]
24. Not to foster deceit in the heart.[59]
25. Not to make a false peace.[60]
26. Not to depart from charity.[61]
27. Not to swear at all, lest one swear falsely.[62]
28. To speak the truth with heart and lips.[63]
29. Not to return evil for evil.[64]
30. Not to do an injury, but patiently to suffer one when done.[65]
31. To love one's enemies.[66]
32. Not to speak ill of those who speak ill of one, but instead to speak well of them.[67]
33. To suffer persecution for justice's sake.[68]
34. Not to be proud.[69]

[35] Ecclesiasticus 32:24.
[36] Deuteronomy 6:5.
[37] Luke 10:27.
[38] Luke 18:20.
[39] Matthew 19:18.
[40] Exodus 20:15.
[41] Deuteronomy 6:21.
[42] Mark 10:19.
[43] 1 Peter 2:17.
[44] Tobit 4:16.
[45] Luke 9:23.
[46] 1 Corinthians 9:27.

[47] 2 Peter 2:13.
[48] Joel 1:14.
[49] Tobit 4:7.
[50] Isaiah 18:7.
[51] Matthew 25:36.
[52] Tobit 1:21.
[53] Isaiah 1:17.
[54] 1 Thessalonians 5:14.
[55] James 1:27.
[56] Matthew 10:38.
[57] Matthew 5:22.
[58] Ephesians 4:26.
[59] Psalm 14:3.
[60] Romans 12:18.
[61] 1 Peter 4:8.
[62] Matthew 5:33–37.
[63] Psalm 14:3.
[64] 1 Thessalonians 5:15.
[65] 1 Corinthians 6:7.
[66] Luke 6:27.
[67] 1 Peter 3:9.
[68] Matthew 5:10.
[69] Tobit 4:14.

35. Not to be a wine drinker.[70]
36. Not to be a great eater.[71]
37. Not to be given to sleep.[72]
38. Not to be slothful.[73]
39. Not to be a murmurer.[74]
40. Not to be a detractor.[75]
41. To put one's trust in God.[76]
42. When one sees any good in oneself to attribute it to God, not to oneself.[77]
43. That a man recognize that it is he who does evil, and so let him attribute it to himself.[78]
44. To fear the day of judgment.[79]
45. To be afraid of hell.[80]
46. To desire life everlasting with complete spiritual longing.[81]
47. To have the vision of death before one's eyes daily.[82]
48. To watch over the actions of one's life every hour of the day.[83]
49. To know for certain that God sees one everywhere.[84]
50. To smash at once against Christ (as if against a rock) evil thoughts which rise up in the mind.[85]
51. And to reveal all such thoughts to one's spiritual Father.[86]
52. To guard one's lips from uttering evil or wicked words.[87]
53. Not to be fond of too much talking.[88]
54. Not to speak idle words, or those that move others to laughter.[89]

55. Not to love much or boisterous laughter.[90]
56. Willingly to hear holy reading.[91]
57. Often to devote oneself to prayer.[92]
58. Daily with tears and sighs to confess to God in prayer one's past offenses, and to avoid them for the future.[93]
59. Not to give way to the desires of the flesh;[94] and to hate one's own will.[95]
60. In all things to obey the abbot's commands, even though he himself (which God forbid) should act otherwise, remembering our lord's precept, "What they say, you should do, but what they do, you should not do."[96]
61. Not to wish to be called holy before one is so; but to be holy first so as to be called such with truth.[97]
62. Daily in one's acts to keep God's commandments.[98]
63. To love chastity.[99]
64. To hate no man.[100]
65. Not to be jealous or envious.[101]
66. Not to love strife.[102]
67. To not have an arrogant spirit.[103]
68. To revere the old.[104]
69. To love the young.[105]
70. To pray for one's enemies for the love of Christ.[106]
71. To make peace with an adversary before the sun sets.[107]
72. And, never to despair of God's mercy.[108]

Behold these are the tools of our spiritual craft; when we shall have made use of them constantly day and night,

---

[70] 1 Timothy 3:3.
[71] Ecclesiasticus 31:17.
[72] Proverbs 20:13.
[73] Romans 12:11.
[74] 1 Corinthians 10:10.
[75] Proverbs 1:11.
[76] Psalm 72:28.
[77] 1 Corinthians 4:7.
[78] Hosea 12:9.
[79] Job 31:14.
[80] Matthew 10:28.
[81] Philippians 1:23.
[82] Matthew 24:42.
[83] Deuteronomy 4:9.
[84] Proverbs 5:21.
[85] Psalm 136:9.
[86] Ecclesiasticus 8:11.
[87] Psalm 33:13.
[88] Proverbs 10:19.
[89] Matthew 12:36.

[90] Ecclesiasticus 21:23.
[91] Luke 11:28.
[92] Colossians 4:2.
[93] Psalm 6:7.
[94] Galatians 5:16.
[95] Ecclesiasticus 18:30.
[96] Matthew 23:30.
[97] Matthew 6:1.
[98] Ecclesiasticus 6:37.
[99] 1 Timothy 5:22.
[100] Leviticus 19:17.
[101] James 3:14–16.
[102] 2 Timothy 2:24.
[103] Psalm 130:1.
[104] Leviticus 19:32.
[105] 1 Timothy 6:1.
[106] Matthew 5:44.
[107] Ephesians 4:26.
[108] Psalm 51:10.

and shall have proved them at the day of judgment, that reward, which He has promised, shall be given to us by our lord, "Which eye has not seen, nor ear heard, nor has it entered into the heart of man to conceive what God has prepared for those that love him."[109] Steadfastly abiding in the community, the workshop where all these instruments are made use of is the cloister of the monastery.

Chapter V—On Obedience

The first degree of humility is prompt obedience. This is required of all who, whether by reason of the holy servitude to which they are pledged, or through fear of hell, or to attain to the glory of eternal life, hold nothing more dear than Christ. Such disciples delay not in doing what is ordered by their superior, just as if the command had come from God. Of such people our lord says, "At the hearing of the ear he has obeyed me."[110] And to the teachers, he likewise says, "He that hears you, hears me."[111]

For this reason such disciples, immediately surrendering all they possess, and giving up their own will, leave unfinished what they were working at, and with the ready foot of obedience in their acts follow the word of command. Thus, as it were, at the same moment comes the order of the master and the finished work of the disciple: with the speed of the fear of God both go jointly forward and are quickly effected by such as ardently desire to walk in the way of eternal life. These take the narrow way, of which the Lord says, "Narrow is the way which leads to life."[112] That is, they live not as they themselves will, nor do they obey their own desires and pleasures, but following the command and direction of another and remaining in their monasteries, their desire is to be ruled by an abbot. Without doubt such as these carry out that saying of our lord, "I came not to do my own will, but the will of him who sent me."[113]

This kind of obedience will be both acceptable to God and pleasing to men, when what is ordered is not done out of fear, or slowly and coldly, grudgingly, or with reluctant protest. Obedience shown to superiors is indeed given to God, who himself has said, "He that hears you, hears me."[114] What is commanded should be done by those under obedience, with a good will, since God loves

a cheerful giver.[115] If the disciple obey unwillingly and murmur in word as well as in heart, it will not be accepted by God, who considers the heart of a murmurer, even if he does what was ordered. For work done in this spirit shall have no reward; rather shall the doer receive the penalty appointed for murmurers if he does not amend and does not make satisfaction.

Chapter VI—On Silence

Let us do as the prophet says, "I have said: I will keep my ways, that I do not offend with my tongue. I have been watchful over my mouth; I held my peace and humbled myself and was silent from speaking even good things."[116] Here the prophet shows that, for the sake of silence, we are at times to abstain even from good talk. If this is so, how much more needful is it that we refrain from evil words, on account of the penalty of the sin! Because of the importance of silence, therefore, let permission to speak be seldom given, even to perfect disciples, although their talk be of good and holy matters and tending to edification, since it is written, "In much speaking, you shall not escape sin."[117] The master, indeed, should speak and teach: the disciple should hold his peace and listen.

Whatever, therefore, has to be asked of the prior, let it be done with all humility and with reverent submission. But as to coarse, idle words, or such as move to laughter, we utterly condemn and ban them in all places. We do not allow any disciple to speak them.

Chapter VII—On Humility

Brethren, Holy Scripture cries out to us, saying, "Everyone who exalts himself shall be humbled, and he who humbles himself shall be exalted."[118] In this it tells us that every form of self-exaltation is a kind of pride, which the prophet declares he carefully avoided, where he says, "Lord, my heart is not exalted, neither are my eyes lifted up, nor have I walked in great things, nor in wonders above myself." And why? "If I did not think humbly, but exalted my soul: as a child weaned from his mother, so will you reward my soul."[119]

[109] 1 Corinthians 2:9.
[110] Psalm 17:45.
[111] Luke 10:16.
[112] Matthew 7:14.
[113] John 5:30.
[114] Luke 10:16.

[115] 2 Corinthians 9:7.
[116] Psalm 38:2, 3.
[117] Proverbs 18:21.
[118] Luke 14:2.
[119] Psalm 130:1, 2.

Therefore, brethren, if we would scale the summit of humility, and swiftly gain the heavenly height which is reached by our lowliness in this present life, we must set up a ladder of climbing deeds like that which Jacob saw in his dream, on which angels were descending and ascending. Without doubt that descending and ascending is to be understood by us as signifying that we descend by exalting ourselves and ascend by humbling ourselves. But the ladder itself thus set up is our life in this world, which by humility of heart is lifted by our Lord to heaven. Our body and soul we may indeed call the sides of the ladder in which our divine vocation has set the diverse steps of humility and discipline we have to ascend.

The first step of humility, then, is reached when a man, with the fear of God always before his eyes, does not allow himself to forget, but is ever mindful of all God's commandments. He remembers, moreover, that such as condemn God fall into hell for their sins, and that life eternal awaits such as fear him. And warding off at each moment all sin and defect in thought and word, of eye, hand or foot, of self-will, let such a one rouse himself to prune away the lusts of the flesh.

Let him think that he is seen at all times by God from heaven; and that wheresoever he may be, all his actions are visible to the eye of God and at all times are reported by the angels. The prophet shows us this when he says that God is ever present to our thoughts: "God searches the hearts and minds."[120] And again, "The Lord knows the thoughts of men that they are vain."[121] He also says, "You have understood my thoughts from afar";[122] and again, "The thought of man shall confess to you."[123] In order, then, that the humble brother may be careful to avoid wrong thoughts, let him always say in his heart, "Then shall I be without stain before him, if I shall keep myself from my iniquity."[124]

We are forbidden to do our own will, since Scripture tells us, "Leave your own will and desire."[125] And again, "We beg of God in prayer that his will may be done in us."[126]

Rightly are we taught, therefore, not to do our own will, if we take heed of what the Scripture teaches: "There

are ways which to men seem right, the end of which plunges into the deep pit of hell."[127] And again, when we fear what is said about the negligent, "They are corrupted, and made abominable in their pleasures."[128] But in regard to the desires of the flesh we ought to believe that God is present with us; as the prophet says, speaking to the Lord, "Oh Lord, all my desire is before you."[129]

We have therefore to beware of evil desires, since death stands close at the door of pleasure. It is for this reason that Scripture bids us, "Follow not your desires."[130] If, therefore, the eyes of the Lord see both the good and the bad, if he is always looking down from heaven upon the sons of men to find one who thinks of God or seeks him, and if day and night what we do is made known to him—for these reasons, by the angels appointed to watch over us, we should always take heed, brethren, lest God may sometime or other see us, as the prophet says in the psalm, "inclined to evil and becoming unprofitable servants."[131] Even though he spares us for a time, because he is loving and waits for our conversion to better ways, let us fear that he may say to us in the future, "These things you have done and I held my peace."[132]

The second step of humility is reached when anyone not loving self-will takes no heed to satisfy his own desires, but copies in his life what our lord said, "I came not to do my own will, but the will of him who sent me."[133] Scripture likewise proclaims that self-will engenders punishment, and necessity purchases a crown.

The third step of humility is reached when a man, for the love of God, submits himself with all obedience to a superior, imitating our lord, of whom the apostle says, "He was made obedient even up to death."[134]

The fourth step of humility is reached when anyone in the exercise of his obedience patiently and with a quiet mind bears all that is inflicted on him, things contrary to nature, and even at times unjust, and in suffering all these he neither tires nor gives up the work, since the Scripture says, "Only he that persists to the end shall be saved";[135] also "Let your heart be comforted, and await

---

[120] Psalm 7:10.

[121] Psalm 93:2.

[122] Psalm 138:3.

[123] Psalm 75:11.

[124] Psalm 17:24.

[125] Ecclesiasticus 18:30.

[126] Matthew 6:10.

[127] Proverbs 16:25.

[128] Psalm 52:2.

[129] Psalm 37:10.

[130] Ecclesiasticus 18:30.

[131] Psalm 52:4.

[132] Psalm 49:21.

[133] John 6:38.

[134] Philippians 2:8.

[135] Matthew 24:13.

the Lord."[136] And in order to show that for our Lord's sake the faithful man ought to bear all things, no matter how contrary to nature they may be (the psalmist), in the person of the sufferers, says, "For you we suffer death all the day long; we are valued as sheep for the slaughter."[137] Secure in the hope of divine reward they rejoice, saying, "But in all things we overcome by the help of him who has loved us."[138]

Elsewhere also Scripture says, "You have protected us, Lord; you have tried us, as silver is tried, with fire. You have brought us into the snare; you have laid tribulation upon our backs."[139] And to show that we ought to be subject to a prior (or superior) it goes on, "You have placed men over our heads."[140] And, moreover, they fulfill the Lord's command by patience in adversity and injury, who, "when struck on one cheek, offer the other"; when someone "takes away their coat let go of their cloak as well," and who being compelled to carry a burden one mile, go two; who, with Paul the apostle, suffer false brethren, and bless those who speak ill of them.[141]

The fifth step of humility is reached when a monk manifests to his abbot, by humble confession, all the evil thoughts of his heart and his secret faults. The Scripture urges us to do this where it says, "Reveal your way to the Lord and hope in him."[142] It also says, "Confess to the Lord, because he is good, because his mercy endures forever."[143] And the prophet also says, "I have made known to you my offenses, and my injustices I have not hidden. I have said, I will declare openly to the Lord my injustices against myself; and you have pardoned the wickedness of my heart."[144]

The sixth step of humility is reached when a monk is content with all that is lowly and vile; and in regard to everything enjoined to him accounts himself a poor and worthless workman, saying with the prophet, "I have been brought to nothing, and knew it not. I have become like a beast before you, and I am always with you."[145]

The seventh step of humility is reached when a man not only confesses with his tongue that he is most lowly and inferior to others, but in his innermost heart believes so. Such a one, humbling himself, exclaims with the prophet, "I am a worm and no man, the reproach of men and the outcast of the people."[146] "I have been exalted and am humbled and confounded."[147] And again, "It is good for me that you have humbled me, that I may learn your commandments."[148]

The eighth step of humility is reached when a monk does nothing but what the common rule of the monastery, or the example of his seniors, enforces.

The ninth step of humility is reached when a monk restrains his tongue from talking, and, practicing silence, does not speak until a question is asked of him, since Scripture says, "In many words you shall not avoid sin,"[149] and "a talkative man moves aimlessly upon the earth."[150]

The tenth step of humility is attained to when one is not easily and quickly moved to laughter, for it is written, "The fool lifts his voice in laughter."[151]

The eleventh step of humility is reached when a monk, in speaking, does so quietly and without laughter, humbly, gravely and in a few words and not with a loud voice, for it is written, "A wise man is known by a few words."[152]

The twelfth step of humility is reached when a monk not only has humility in his heart, but even shows it also externally to all who see him. Thus, whether he is in the oratory at the "Work of God," in the monastery, or in the garden, on a journey, or in the fields, or wherever he is, sitting, standing or walking, always let him, with head bent and eyes fixed on the ground, think of his sins and imagine that he is arraigned before the dreaded judgment of God. Let him always be saying to himself, with the publican in the gospel, "Lord, I, a sinner, am not worthy to lift my eyes to heaven";[153] and with the prophet, "I am bowed down and humbled on every side."[154]

When all these steps of humility have been mounted the monk will presently attain to that love of God which

[136] Psalm 26:14.
[137] Psalm 43:22.
[138] Romans 8:37.
[139] Psalm 65:10, 11.
[140] Psalm 65:12.
[141] 2 Corinthians 11:26.
[142] Psalm 36:5.
[143] Psalm 105:1.
[144] Psalm 31:5.
[145] Psalm 72:22, 23.

[146] Psalm 21:7.
[147] Psalm 87:16.
[148] Psalm 118:7.
[149] Proverbs 10:19.
[150] Psalm 139:12.
[151] Ecclesiasticus 21:23.
[152] Ecclesiasticus 10:14.
[153] Luke 18:13.
[154] Psalm 118:107.

is perfect and casts out fear. By means of this love everything which before he had not observed without fear, he shall now begin to do by habit, without any trouble and, as it were, naturally. He acts now not through fear of hell, but for the love of Christ, out of a good habit and a delight in virtue. All this our Lord will vouchsafe to work by the Holy Ghost in his servant, now cleansed from vice and sin.

Chapter VIII—Of the Divine Office[155] at Night

In the winter time—that is, from the first of November until Easter—the brethren shall get up at the eighth hour of the night by reasonable calculation, so that having rested until a little after midnight they may rise refreshed. Let the time that remains after the Night Office be used, by those brethren who need it, for the study of the Psalter or the readings. From Easter to the aforesaid first of November, let the hour for saying the Night Office be so arranged that after a brief interval, during which the brethren may go forth for the necessities of nature, Lauds, which are to be said at daybreak, may presently follow.

Chapter IX—How Many Psalms Are to Be Said in the Night Office

In the winter season, having first said the verse, "Oh God, incline unto my aid; Oh Lord, make haste to help me,"[156] the words, "Oh Lord, you shall open my lips and my mouth shall declare your praise"[157] are then to be said three times. After this Psalm 3 is to be said with a *Gloria*; after which Psalm 94, with an antiphon, is to be recited or sung, followed by a hymn, and then six psalms with their antiphons. When these are ended and a versicle is said, let the abbot give a blessing; and then, all being seated, let three lessons from the book placed on the lectern be read by the brethren in turns. Between

these lessons, three responsories are to be sung, two without a *Gloria*. After the third lesson, however, let the cantor add the *Gloria* to the responsory, and as soon as he begins it let all rise from their seats out of honor and reverence for the Holy Trinity.

Let the divinely inspired books of the Old and New Testament be read at the Night Office, together with their commentaries from the best-known, orthodox, and catholic fathers.

After these three lessons, with their responsories, let six other psalms be sung with the *Alleluia*. A lesson from the apostle is then to be said by heart, and a verse with the petition of the Litany—that is, *Kyrie eleison*—and so let the Night Office end.

Chapter X—How the Night Office Is to Be Said in the Summer Season

From Easter to the first day of November the same number of psalms as indicated above are to be said. On account of the short nights, however, the lessons are not to be read from the book, but in place of the three lessons let one out of the Old Testament be said by heart and followed by a short responsory. Let all the rest be done as we have arranged above, so that, without counting Psalms 3 and 94, there may never be less than twelve psalms at Matins.

Chapter XI—How the Night Office Is to Be Celebrated on Sundays

On Sunday let the brethren rise earlier for the Night Office, in which the following order is to be observed: when six psalms and the versicle have been sung, as we have before arranged, let all sit down in proper order and let four lessons be read from the book with their responsories, in the manner before prescribed. To the fourth responsory only let the cantor add the *Gloria*, and when he begins it let all rise at once out of reverence. After these lessons six other psalms follow in order with their antiphons and a versicle as before. Then let four other lessons be read with their responsories in the same way as the former, and then three canticles out of the prophets, chosen by the abbot; these canticles are to be sung with *Alleluia*.

When the versicle has been said, and the abbot has given the blessing, four more lessons from the New Testament are to be read, in the same order as before. After the fourth responsory let the abbot begin the hymn

---

[155] The Divine Office refers to the monastic liturgies—Matins, Lauds, Prime, Terce, Sext, None, Vespers, and Compline—which are celebrated at specific times of day or night: Matins around midnight; Lauds at dawn; Prime in the early morning; Terce mid-morning; Sext midday; None mid-afternoon; Vespers in the evening; and Compline at night.

[156] Psalm 69:2.

[157] Psalm 50:17.

Te Deum laudamus, and when that is finished he shall read a lesson from the gospel, with reverence and fear, while all stand. At the conclusion of this let all answer Amen, and let the abbot immediately go on with the hymn *Te decet laus*; after the blessing let them begin Lauds.

This method of singing Matins on Sundays is to be observed always, both in summer and in winter, unless perhaps (which God forbid) they get up late, and the lessons or responsories have to be somewhat shortened. Let great care be taken that this does not happen; but if it does, let him to whose carelessness it is due make full satisfaction to God in the oratory.

Chapter XII—How Lauds Are to Be Solemnized

At Lauds on Sunday let Psalm 66 be first said straight on and without an antiphon. After this Psalm 50 is to be said with *Alleluia*, with Psalm 117 and 62. Then follow the "Blessings" (or *Benedicite*) and the "Praises" (or *Laudate* psalms), a lesson from the Apocalypse [or book of Revelation], said by heart, a responsory and hymn, the versicle and the canticle from the gospel (or *Benedictus*) with the litanies (or *Kyrie*), and so conclude.

Chapter XIII—How Lauds Are to Be Celebrated on Ordinary Days

On ordinary weekdays let Lauds be celebrated as follows: Psalm 66 is to be said, as on Sunday, straight on without any antiphon, and somewhat slowly, to allow for all to be in their places for Psalm 50, which is to be said with an antiphon. After this come two other psalms according to custom: that is, on Monday, Psalm 5 and 36; on Tuesday, Psalm 42 and 56; on Wednesday, Psalm 63 and 64; on Thursday, Psalm 87 and 89; on Friday, Psalm 75 and 91; on Saturday, Psalm 142 and the Canticle of Deuteronomy, which must be divided into two *Glorias*. But on other days let a canticle out of the Prophets be said, each on its proper day, according to the custom of the Roman Church. After these let the Praises (or *Laudate* psalms) follow, then a lesson of the apostle, said by heart, the responsory, hymn and versicle, the canticle from the gospel (or *Benedictus*), the litanies (or *Kyrie eleison*), and the office is completed.

Lauds and Evensong are never to be finished without the Lord's prayer at the end. This is said by the prior (that is, the superior) aloud, so that all may hear, because of the thorns of scandal which are always cropping up: that the community, by reason of the pledge given in this prayer, in the words, "Forgive us our trespasses as we forgive those that trespass against us," may purge themselves from this kind of vice. In saying the other Hours, however, only the last part of the prayer is said aloud that all may answer, "But deliver us from evil."

Chapter XIV—How the Night Office Is to Be Said on the Feast Days of Saints

On Saints' feast days and on all solemnities let the Night Office be said in the manner we have ordered for Sunday, except that the psalms, antiphons, and lessons are said which are proper to the day itself. The method of saying them, however, shall remain as before prescribed.

Chapter XV—During Which Seasons Alleluia Is to Be Said

From the holy feast of Easter until Pentecost *Alleluia* is always to be said both with the psalms and in the responsories. From Pentecost until the beginning of Lent let it be said every night at the Night Office only with the last six psalms. On every Sunday not in Lent let the Canticles, Lauds, Prime, Terce, Sext, and None be said with *Alleluia*, but Vespers with antiphons. Responsories, however, except from Easter until Pentecost, are never to be said with *Alleluia*.

Chapter XVI—How the Divine Office Is to Be Said During the Day

The prophet says, "Seven times I have sung your praises."[158] This sacred number of seven will be kept by us if we perform the duties of our service in the Hours of Lauds, Prime, Terce, Sext, None, Vespers, and Compline. It was of these daytime Hours that the prophet said, "Seven times a day I have sung your praises," for the same prophet says of the Night Office, "At midnight I arose to confess to you."[159] At these times, therefore, let us give praise to our creator for his just judgments, that

---

[158] Psalm 118:164.

[159] Psalm 18:62.

is, at Lauds, Prime, Terce, Sext, None, Vespers, and Compline, and at night let us rise to confess to him.

Chapter XVII—How Many Psalms Are to Be Said in These Hours

We have already settled the order of the psalmody for the Night Office and for Lauds, let us now arrange for the Hours which follow. At Prime, three psalms are to be said separately, that is, not under one *Gloria*. After the verse, "Oh God, make haste to help me," and before the psalms are begun, the hymn of each Hour is to be said. At the end of the three psalms a lesson is recited, then with the versicle and *Kyrie eleison* the Hour is concluded. The Hours of Terce, Sext, and None are to be said in the same way, that is, the verse ("Oh God, incline," etc.), the hymns of these Hours, three psalms, the lesson and versicle, and with *Kyrie eleison* they are concluded.

If the community is large, the Hours shall be sung with antiphons, but if it is small they are to be sung without. Vespers shall be said with four psalms and antiphons, after which a lesson is to be recited, then a responsory, hymn, versicle, canticle from the gospel (i.e. *Magnificat*), and it is concluded by the litanies (or *Kyrie*) and the Lord's Prayer. Compline shall consist in the saying of three psalms straight through and without antiphons, followed by the hymn of the Hour, a lesson, versicle, *Kyrie eleison*, and shall conclude with the blessing.

Chapter XVIII—The Order in Which the Psalms Are to Be Said

Let the verse, "Oh God, make haste to deliver me, Oh Lord, make haste to help me," with a *Gloria*, always come first, followed by the hymn of each Hour. Then, on Sundays, at Prime, four divisions of Psalm 118 are to be said; and at the other Hours of Terce, Sext, and None three divisions of the same. On Monday, at Prime, Psalm 1, 2, and 3 are recited, and so on each day until Sunday, three other psalms are to be recited in order up to Psalm 19; Psalm 9 and 17 are each divided in two by a *Gloria*. In this way the Sunday Night Office will always begin with Psalm 20.

On Mondays, at Terce, Sext, and None, let the remaining nine divisions of Psalm 118 be said, three at each Hour. Psalm 118 is finished on the two days, Sunday and Monday, therefore on Tuesday, at Terce, Sext, and None the three psalms at each Hour shall be the nine from Psalm 119 to 127. And these same psalms are to be repeated at the

Hours until the Sunday. A uniform order of the hymns, lessons, and versicles is to be likewise observed, so that Psalm 118 is always begun on the Sunday.

Four psalms are to be sung each day at Vespers. These begin with Psalm 109 and conclude with Psalm 147, omitting those already set apart for the various other Hours, that is to say, from Psalm 117 to Psalm 127; Psalm 133 and 142. All the rest are to be said at Vespers, and because this leaves three psalms short, the longest of them, namely, Psalms 138, 143, and 144, are to be divided. Psalm 116, however, since it is brief, is to be joined to Psalm 115.

The order of the psalms for Vespers being thus arranged, let the other parts, such as the lessons, responsories, hymns, versicles, and canticles be used as discussed before. At Compline the same psalms are repeated every day, namely, Psalms 4, 90, and 133.

The order of the psalmody for the day office being thus settled, all the rest of the psalms are to be equally divided among the seven night hours (or the Night Office). Those that are too long are to be divided into two; and twelve psalms are to be arranged for each night. If this distribution of the psalms displeases anyone we especially desire him to arrange them otherwise, if he thinks of something better, provided that care be taken that every week the whole Psalter of one hundred and fifty psalms are sung, and that at the Night Office on Sunday the cycle is begun again. Monks, indeed, show themselves in their service to be too negligent and undevout when they sing less than the Psalter, with the usual canticles, once in the week, when we read that our holy Fathers courageously performed in one day what I resolve that we, who are tepid, may do in a whole week.

Chapter XIX—Of the Manner of Singing the Office

We believe that the divine presence is everywhere, and that the eyes of the lord see both the good and the bad in all places. Especially do we believe without any doubt that this is so when we stand for the Divine Office. Let us, therefore, always be mindful of what the prophet says, "Serve you the lord in fear";[160] and again, "Sing you his praises with understanding";[161] and, "In the sight of the angels I will sing praise to you."[162] Therefore let us consider how it is proper for us to be in the sight of God

---

[160] Psalm 2:11.

[161] Psalm 46:8.

[162] Psalm 137:1.

and the angels, and so let us take our part in the psalmody so that our mind agrees with our voice.

Chapter XX—On Reverence in Prayer

If, when we wish to obtain some favor from those who have the power to help us, we dare not ask except with humility and reverence, how much more reason is there that we should present our petitions to the Lord God of the universe in all lowliness of heart and purity of devotion. We may know for certain that we shall be heard, not because we use many words, but on account of the purity of our hearts and our tears of sorrow. Our prayer, therefore, should be short and pure, unless by some inspiration of divine grace it is prolonged. All prayer made by the community in common, however, should be short; and when the prior (that is, the superior) has given the sign, let all rise together.

Chapter XXI—The Deans of the Monastery

If the community is large, let brethren of good repute and holy lives be chosen from among them and appointed deans. These shall carefully watch over their deaneries in all things relating to the commandments of God and the injunctions of the abbot. Deans are to be chosen on whom the abbot may safely rely to share his burdens, and the choice is not to be determined by their order (in the community) but by the worthiness of their lives and their proved learning. And if perhaps any one of these deans, being puffed up by pride, is found blameworthy, and after being corrected three times will not amend, then let him be put out of office and another more worthy be substituted. We direct the same in the case of the Provost.

Chapter XXII—How the Monks Are to Sleep

All shall sleep in separate beds and each shall receive, according to the appointment of his abbot, bedclothes, fitted to the condition of his life. If it is possible, let them all sleep in a common dormitory, but if their great numbers will not allow this they may sleep in tens or twenties, with seniors to have charge of them. Let a candle be constantly burning in the room until morning, and let the monks sleep clothed and girded with girdles or cords, but they are not to have knives by their sides in their beds, lest perhaps they are injured while sleeping. In this way the monks shall always be ready to rise quickly when the signal is given and hasten each one to come before his brother to the Divine Office, and yet with all gravity and modesty.

The younger brethren are not to have their beds next to each other, but among those of the elders. When they rise for the Divine Office let them gently encourage one another, because of the excuses made by those that are drowsy.

Chapter XXIII—Of Excommunication for Offenses

If any brother is found to be stubborn, disobedient, proud, murmuring, or in any way acting contrary to the holy rule, or disdaining the orders of his seniors, let him, according to the precept of our lord, be secretly admonished by those seniors, once or twice. If he will not amend let him be publicly reproached before all. But if even then he does not correct his faults, let him, if he understands the nature of the punishment, be subject to excommunication. But if he be obstinate he is to undergo corporal punishment.

Chapter XXIV—What the Manner of Excommunication Should Be

The mode of excommunication or punishment should be proportionate to the fault, and the gravity of the fault shall depend on the judgment of the abbot. If any brother is detected in small faults let him be excluded from eating at table with the rest. The punishment of one thus separated from the common table shall be of this kind: in the oratory he shall not lead either psalm or antiphon; nor shall he read any lesson until he has made satisfaction. He shall take his portion of food alone, after the brethren have had their meal, and in such quantity and at such time as the abbot shall think fit. So that if, for example, the brethren take their meal at the sixth hour let him take his at the ninth; if the brethren take theirs at the ninth, let him have his in the evening, until such time as by due satisfaction he obtains pardon.

Chapter XXV—Of Graver Faults

Let the brother who is guilty of some graver fault be excluded both from the common table and from the oratory. None of the brethren shall talk to him or keep company with him. Let him be alone at the work which is set for him; let him remain in penance and sorrow, and keep before his mind that terrible sentence of the apostle where he says, "Such a one is delivered over to Satan for the destruction of the flesh, that his spirit may be saved in the day of our lord."[163] Let him take his food alone, in such quantity and at such time as the abbot shall think fit. Let no one bless him as he passes by, nor ask a blessing on the food that is given him.

Chapter XXVI—Of Those Who Keep Company with the Excommunicated without the Abbot's Order

If any brother shall presume, without the abbot's order, to have interaction in any way with an excommunicated brother, to talk with him or send him any message, let him suffer the same penalty of excommunication.

Chapter XXVII—What Care the Abbot Should Have of the Excommunicated

Let the abbot take every possible care of the offending brethren, for "They that are well need not the physician, but they that are sick."[164] Like a wise physician, therefore, he ought to make use of every remedy; he should send some of the older and wiser brethren as comforters, to console, as it were, in secret their wayward brother, and convince him to make humble satisfaction. And let them comfort him so that he is not overwhelmed by too great a sorrow, but as the apostle says, "Let charity be confirmed in him and let all pray for him."[165]

The abbot ought to take the greatest care and to use all prudence and industry to lose none of the sheep entrusted to him. Let him know that he has undertaken the care of souls that are sick, and not act like a tyrant over such as are well. Let him fear the reproach of the prophet in which God speaks thus, "What you saw to be fat, you took for yourselves, and what was diseased you threw away."[166] Let him copy the loving example of the good shepherd, who, leaving ninety-nine sheep in the mountains, went to seek the one that had gone astray, and on whose frailty he took such compassion that he deigned to lay it on his shoulders and carry it back to the flock.[167]

Chapter XXVIII—Of Those Who, Being Often Corrected, Do Not Amend

If any brother does not amend after being often corrected for any fault, and even excommunicated, let a sharper punishment be administered to him, that is, let him be punished with flogging. And if even after this he shall not correct himself, or being puffed up by pride (which God forbid) shall attempt to defend his doings, then let the abbot act like a wise physician. If after applying the poultices and ointments of exhortation, the medicine of the holy Scriptures and the final cauterizing of excommunication and scourging, he find that his labors have had no effect, then let him try what is more than all this, his own prayer and those of the brethren for him, that the Lord, who can do all things, may work the cure of the sick brother. If he is not healed by this means then let the abbot use the severing knife, according to that saying of the apostle, "Put away the evil one from among you";[168] and again, "If the faithless one depart, let him depart,"[169] lest one diseased sheep infects the whole flock.

Chapter XXIX—Whether Brethren Who Leave Their Monastery Must Be Allowed to Return

If the brother, who through his own bad conduct leaves or is expelled from the monastery, desires to return, he must first promise full correction of the fault for which he left it. He may then be received back at the lowest position, so that by this his humility may be tested. If he again leaves he may be received back until the third time, but he should know that after this all possibility of returning will be denied to him.

---

[163] 1 Corinthians 5:5.

[164] Matthew 9:12.

[165] 2 Corinthians 2:8.

[166] Ezekiel 34:3.

[167] Luke 15:4.

[168] 1 Corinthians 5:13.

[169] 1 Corinthians 7:15.

Chapter XXX—How Young Children Are to Be Corrected

Every age and state of intelligence ought to be governed in the way suitable to it. Thus the faults of those who are children or adolescents, or who cannot understand the seriousness of the penalty of excommunication, shall be punished by rigorous fasting or corrected by harsh floggings.

Chapter XXXI—What Manner of Man the Cellarer of the Monastery Ought to Be

Let one of the community be chosen as cellarer of the monastery, who is wise, mature in character, temperate, not a great eater, not arrogant nor quarrelsome, nor insolent, and not a dawdler, nor wasteful, but one who fears God and is as a father to the community. Let him have the charge of everything; do nothing without the abbot's order; see to what is commanded; and not make the brethren sad. If any of them shall perhaps ask something unreasonable he must not vex him by contemptuously rejecting his request, but humbly and reasonably refuse what he wrongly asks.

Let him look after his own soul, mindful of the apostolic principle, that "they that ministered well, shall purchase for themselves a good degree."[170] Let him take every care of the sick, of children, of guests, and of the poor, knowing that without doubt he shall have to render an account of all these on judgment day.

Let him look upon all the vessels and goods of the monastery as if they were the consecrated chalices of the altar. He must not think anything can be neglected; he must not be covetous, nor prodigal by wasting the goods of the monastery; but let him do everything with forethought and according to the direction of his abbot.

Above all things let him have humility and give a gentle answer to those to whom he can give nothing else, for it is written, "A good word is better than the best gift."[171] Let him take charge of all that the abbot shall commit to him, but let him not meddle with anything which is forbidden to him. Let him provide the brethren with their appointed allowance of food without impatience or delay, so that they are not driven to offend, being mindful of the divine word which declares the punishment he deserves, "Who shall scandalize one of these little ones. It were better for him that a millstone should be hung about his neck, and that he should be drowned in the depth of the sea."[172] If the community is large let him be given helpers, by whose aid he may without worry perform the office committed to him. What is given let it be given, and what is asked for let it be asked for at suitable times, so that no one be troubled or distressed in the house of God.

Chapter XXXII—Concerning the Iron Tools or Other Goods of the Monastery

Let the abbot appoint brethren, of whose life and moral conduct he is sure, to keep the iron tools, the clothes, or other property of the monastery. To these he shall allot the various things to be kept and collected, as he deems expedient. The abbot shall hold a list of these things that, as the brethren succeed each other in their appointed work, he may know what he gives each and what he receives back from them. If anyone shall treat the property of the monastery in a slovenly or careless way let him be corrected; if he does not amend let him be subjected to regular discipline.

Chapter XXXIII—Ought Monks to Have Anything of Their Own?

Above all others, let this vice be extirpated in the monastery. No one, without leave of the abbot, shall presume to give, or receive, or keep as his own, anything whatsoever: neither book, nor tablets, nor pen, nothing at all. For monks are men who can claim no dominion over even their own bodies or wills. All that is necessary, however, they may hope from the father of the monastery, but they shall keep nothing which the abbot has not given or allowed. All things are to be common to all, as it is written, "Neither did anyone say or think that anything was his own."[173] Hence if anyone shall be found given to this most wicked vice let him be admonished once or twice, and if he does not amend let him be subjected to correction.

---

[170] 1 Timothy 3:13.

[171] Ecclesiasticus 18:17.

[172] Matthew 18:6.

[173] Acts 4:32.

Chapter XXXIV—Whether All Ought to Receive Necessary Things Uniformly

It is written, "Distribution was made to everyone, according to his need."[174] By this we do not mean that there is to be a personal preference (which God forbid), but a consideration for infirmities. In this regard let him who needs less thank God and not be distressed, and let him who requires more be humbled because of his infirmity, and not puffed up by the mercy that is shown him, so that all the members shall be in peace. Above all things do not let the pest of murmuring, for whatever cause, by any word or sign, be manifested. If anyone shall be found faulty in this let him be subjected to the most severe punishment.

Chapter XXXV—Of the Weekly Servers in the Kitchen

The brethren are so to serve each other that no one be excused from the work of the kitchen unless on account of health, or because he is occupied in some matter of great utility, for thence great reward is obtained and charity is exercised. Let the weaker brethren, however, have help that they may not do their work in sadness; and let all generally be helped according to the circumstances of the community or the position of the place (i.e., kitchen). If the community is large the cellarer may be relieved from the service of the kitchen, and any others who (as we have said) are engaged in matters of greater utility. Let the rest serve one another in charity. On Saturday, he who ends his weekly service must clean up everything. He must wash the towels with which the brethren wipe their hands and feet; and he who finishes his service, and he who enters on it, are to wash the feet of all. He shall give back to the cellarer all the vessels used in his ministry, cleaned and unbroken, and the cellarer shall hand them to the one entering into the office, so that he may know what he gives and what he receives.

An hour before the meal these weekly servers may receive a drink of water and a piece of bread over and above the appointed allowance, so that they may serve the brethren at meal time without murmuring or too much fatigue. On solemn days, however, let them wait until after Mass. Immediately after Lauds on Sunday both the incoming and outgoing servers for the week shall cast themselves on their knees in the presence of all and ask for their prayers. Let him who finishes his week say this verse, "Blessed are you, Lord God, who helped me and consoled me";[175] and when this has been said three times let him receive a blessing. He who enters on his office shall then follow and say, "Oh God, incline to my aid; Oh Lord, make haste to help me";[176] and this also shall be repeated three times by all, and having received his blessing let him enter into his service.

Chapter XXXVI—Of the Sick Brethren

Before all things and above all things special care must be taken of the sick, so that in truth they are looked after as if it was Christ himself who was served. He himself has said, "I was sick, and you visited me; and what you did to one of these, my least brethren, you did to me."[177]

But let the sick themselves bear in mind that they are served for the honor of God, and should not grieve their brethren, who serve them, by their superfluous demands. These, nevertheless, must be tolerated with patience, since from such requests a more abundant reward is obtained. Let the abbot, therefore, take the greatest care that the sick suffer no neglect.

Let a separate cell for them be set apart with an attendant who is God-fearing, diligent, and painstaking. Let baths be granted to the sick as often as it shall be expedient, but to those in health, and especially to the young, they shall be seldom permitted. Also for the recovery of their strength the use of meat may be allowed to the sick and those of very weak health. As soon, however, as they mend they must all in the accustomed manner abstain from meat. Let the abbot take special care that the sick are not neglected by the cellarer or the attendants, because he is responsible for what is done amiss by his disciples.

Chapter XXXVII—Concerning Old Men and Children

Although human nature itself inclines us to show pity and consideration to age, to the old, that is, and to children, still it is proper that the authority of the rule should provide for them. Let their weakness be always taken into account, and let the full rigor of the rule as regards food

---

[174] Acts 4:35.

[175] Psalm 85:18.

[176] Psalm 69:2.

[177] Matthew 25:36–40.

be in no way maintained in their regard. There is to be a kind consideration for them, and permission is to be given them to anticipate the regular hours.

Chapter XXXVIII—The Weekly Reader

There ought always to be reading while the brethren eat at table. Yet no one shall presume to read there from any book taken up haphazardly; but whoever is appointed to read for the whole week is to enter into his office on the Sunday. Let the brother when beginning his service after Mass and Communion ask all to pray for him, that God may preserve him from the spirit of pride. And let the following verse be repeated three times by all in the oratory, he, the reader, first beginning: "Oh Lord, open my lips, and my mouth shall declare your praise,"[178] then, having received a blessing, let the reader enter into his office. The greatest silence shall be kept, so that no whispering, nor noise, save the voice of the reader alone, is heard there.

Whatever is required for eating and drinking the brethren shall minister to each other so that no one need ask for anything. Yet should anything be wanted it ought to be demanded by sign rather than by word. Let no one ask any question there about what is being read or about anything else, lest opportunity be given to the evil one; unless, perhaps, the prior shall wish to say something briefly for the purpose of edification. The brother who is reader for the week may take some porridge before beginning to read, on account of holy communion, and in case, perhaps, it may be too long for him to fast. He shall eat afterwards with the weekly servers and kitchen helpers. The brethren, however, are not all to read or sing in turn, but only such as may edify the hearers.

Chapter XXXIX—Of the Amount of Food

We believe that it is enough to satisfy just requirement if in the daily meals, at both the sixth and ninth hours, there is at all seasons of the year two cooked dishes, so that he who cannot eat one may make his meal of the other. Therefore two dishes of cooked food must suffice for all the brethren, and if there is any fruit or young vegetables these may be added to the meal as a third dish. Let a pound of bread suffice for each day, whether there

be one meal or two, that is, for both dinner and supper. If there is to be supper, a third of the pound is to be kept back by the cellarer and given to the brethren at that meal.

If, however, the community has been occupied in any great labor it shall be at the will, and in the power of the abbot, if he thinks it fit, to increase the allowance, so long as every care be taken to guard against excess, and that no monk be incapacitated by overindulging. For nothing is more contrary to the Christian spirit than gluttony, as our Lord declares, "Take heed to yourselves lest perhaps your hearts be over-charged with overindulgence."[179] And the same quantity shall not be given to young children, but a lesser amount than to those older; frugality being maintained in everything. All, save the very weak and sick, are to abstain wholly from eating the flesh of quadrupeds.

Chapter XL—Of the Measure of Drink

"Everyone has his proper gift from God, one thus, another thus."[180] For this reason the amount of other people's food cannot be determined without some misgiving. Still, having regard to the weak state of the sick, we think that a pint of wine a day is sufficient for anyone. But let those to whom God gives the gift of abstinence know that they shall receive their proper reward. If either local circumstances, the amount of labor, or the heat of summer require more, it can be allowed at the will of the prior, care being taken in all things that gluttony and drunkenness do not creep in.

Although we read that "wine is not the drink of monks at all," yet, since in our days they cannot be persuaded of this, let us at least agree not to drink to satiety, but sparingly, "Because wine makes even the wise to fall away."[181]

Chapter XLI—The Hours at Which the Brethren Are to Take Their Meals

From the holy feast of Easter until Pentecost the brethren shall have their first meal at the sixth hour and their supper at night. But from Pentecost, throughout the summer, if the monks do not have to work in the fields, nor are oppressed by any great heat, let them fast on

[178] Psalm 50:17.

[179] Luke 21:34.
[180] 1 Corinthians 7:7.
[181] Ecclesiasticus 19:2.

Wednesdays and Fridays until None; on the other days they may dine at the sixth hour. Dinner at the sixth hour shall be the rule at the discretion of the abbot, if they have work in the fields, or the heat of the summer is great. Let the abbot so temper and arrange everything that souls may be saved, and that what the brethren do may be done without just complaint.

From the Ides of September until the beginning of Lent, the brethren shall always take their meal at the ninth hour. During Lent, however, until Easter their meal shall be at dusk; but this evening meal shall be so arranged that they shall not need lamps while eating, and all things are finished in daylight. Indeed, at all times of the year let the hour of meals, whether of dinner or supper, be so arranged that all things are done by daylight.

Chapter XLII—That No One Shall Speak after Compline

Monks should practice silence at all times, but especially during the night hours. On all days, therefore, whether it is a fast day or otherwise (this shall be the practice). If it is not a fast day, as soon as they shall have risen from supper let all sit together while one of them reads the *Collations*, or *Lives of the Fathers*, or some other book to edify the hearers. He shall not, however, read the *Heptateuch*, or *Book of Kings*, for at that hour it will not benefit weak understandings to listen to this part of Scripture; at other times, however, they may be read. If it is a fast day, let the brethren, when Vespers is over, and after a brief interval, come to the reading of the *Collations*, as we have said. Four or five pages are to be read, or as many as time will allow, that during the reading all may come together, even those that have had some work given them to do. When all, therefore, are gathered together let them say Compline, and on coming out from Compline no one shall be permitted to speak at all. If anyone shall be found breaking this rule of silence he shall be punished severely, unless the needs of a guest require it, or the abbot shall order something of someone. But even this shall be done with the greatest gravity and moderation.

Chapter XLIII—Of Those Who Come Late to the Divine Office or to the Table

As soon as the signal for the Divine Office shall be heard each one must lay aside whatever work he may be engaged upon and hasten to it, with all speed, but still with gravity, so as not to cause any light behavior. Nothing, therefore, shall be put before the Divine Office. If anyone shall come to the Night Office after the *Gloria* of Psalm 94, which on this account we wish to be said slowly and leisurely, he shall not take his place in the choir, but go last of all, or to some place apart which the abbot may appoint for those that so fail in his sight, and of all the brethren, until the Divine Office is ended and he shall have done penance and made public satisfaction.

We have judged it fitting that these should stand last, or in some place apart, in order that, being seen by all, for very shame they may amend. For if they remain outside the oratory someone will, perhaps, return to sleep, or at least sit outside by himself, or setting himself to idle talk give an occasion to the evil one. Let such a one, therefore, come inside, so that he may not lose all, but make amends during the rest of the Office. At the day Hours, one who does not come to the "Work of God" until after the verse (*Deus in adjutorium*), and the *Gloria* of the first Psalm said after the verse, shall stand last, according to the rule laid down above. He is not to presume to join the choir of singers until he has made satisfaction, unless, indeed, the abbot, by his permission, allows him to do so; but even then on the condition that he shall afterward make satisfaction for his omission.

He who does not come to table before the verse, so that all may say it, and praying together sit down to table at the same time, must be corrected once or twice if this is through his own fault or bad habit. If he does not after this amend he is not to be allowed to share in the common table, but he is to be separated from the company of all the rest and eat alone. Until he makes satisfaction and mends his ways let his portion of wine be taken away from him. He is to undergo the same punishment who is not present at the verse which is said after meals. Let no one presume to take food or drink before or after the regular time; but if something is offered to anyone by the prior, and he refuse it, and afterward wishes to have what he had rejected, or some other thing, let him get neither this nor anything else until he makes proper satisfaction.

Chapter XLIV—How Those Who Are Excommunicated Are to Make Satisfaction

He who has been excluded from the oratory and the table for grievous offenses is to prostrate himself before the door of the oratory, in silence, at the time when the Divine Office is being celebrated; with his face to the ground let him lie at the feet of all who leave the place. This he shall continue to do until the abbot shall judge that he has made satisfaction. Then, when the abbot ordains, let him cast himself first at the feet of the abbot and then at those of the brethren, that they may pray for him.

Afterward, if the abbot shall so direct, let him be received into the choir and into the place he shall appoint for him. Even so he may not presume to lead a psalm or to read a lesson, or to do anything else in the oratory, unless the abbot again orders it. Moreover, after each Hour, when the Divine Office is ended, let him cast himself on the ground in his place, and in this way make satisfaction until such time as the abbot tells him to stop. Those who are excluded from the table only shall make satisfaction in the oratory, as long as the abbot shall direct, and shall continue to do this until he blesses them and declares it to be sufficient.

Chapter XLV—On Those Who Blunder in the Oratory

If anyone, while reciting a psalm, responsory, antiphon, or lesson, makes any mistake, and does not at once make humble satisfaction for it before all, let him be subjected to greater punishment, as being one who is unwilling to correct by humility what he has done amiss through negligence. For such a fault let children be whipped.

Chapter XLVI—Of Those Who Offend in Other Ways

If anyone while engaged in any work, either in the kitchen, in the cellar, in serving others, in the bakehouse, in the garden, or in any other occupation or place, shall do anything amiss, break or lose anything, or offend in any way whatsoever, and does not come at once to the abbot and community of his own accord to confess his offense and make satisfaction, if afterward it shall become known by another he shall be more severely punished. If, however, it be a secret sin let him reveal it only to the abbot, or to his spiritual seniors, who know how to heal their own wounds and not to disclose and make public those of others.

Chapter XLVII—On Letting the Hour of Divine Office Be Known

Let the duty of giving warning of the time of the Divine Office, both night and day, be that of the abbot. Either he himself shall give the signal or he shall assign this task to some careful brother, so that all things be done at their fixed time. After the abbot those appointed are to lead the psalms and antiphons in turns. No one, however, shall presume either to sing or read except such as can do so to the edification of the hearers. Let him to whom the abbot shall enjoin this duty do it with humility, gravity, and fear.

Chapter XLVIII—Of Daily Manual Labor

Idleness is an enemy of the soul. Because this is so the brethren ought to be occupied at specified times in manual labor, and at other fixed hours in holy reading. We, therefore, think that both these may be arranged as follows: from Easter to the first of October, on coming out from Prime, let the brethren labor until about the fourth hour. From the fourth until close upon the sixth hour, let them occupy themselves in reading. On rising from table after the sixth hour let them rest on their beds in strict silence; but if anyone wishes to read, let him do so in such a way as not to disturb anyone else.

Let None be said somewhat before the time, about the middle of the eighth hour, and after this all shall work at what they have to do until evening. If, however, the nature of the place or poverty requires them to labor at gathering in the harvest, let them not grieve at that, for then are they truly monks when they live by the labor of their hands, as our fathers and the apostles did. Let everything, however, be done with moderation for the sake of the faint-hearted.

From the first of October until the beginning of Lent let the brethren be occupied in reading until the end of the second hour. At that time Terce shall be said, after which they shall labor at the work enjoined to them until None. At the first signal for the Hour of None all shall cease to work, so as to be ready when the second signal is given. After their meal they shall be occupied with reading or the psalms.

On the days of Lent, from the morning until the end of the third hour, the brethren are to have time for reading, after which let them work at what is set them to do until the close of the tenth hour. During these Lenten days let each one have some book from the library which he shall read through carefully. These books are to be given out at the beginning of Lent.

It is very important that one or two seniors be appointed to go about the monastery at such times as the brethren are free to read, in order to see that no one is slothful, given to idleness or foolish talking instead of reading, and so not only makes no profit himself but also distracts others. If any such be found (which God forbid) let him be corrected once or twice, and if he amend not let him be subjected to regular discipline of such a character that the rest may take warning. Moreover one brother shall not associate with another at unsuitable hours.

On Sunday also, all, save those who are assigned to various offices, shall have time for reading. If, however, anyone be so negligent and slothful as to be unwilling or unable to read or meditate, he must have some work given him, so as not to be idle. For weak brethren, or those of delicate constitutions, some work or craft shall be found to keep them from idleness, and yet not such as to crush them by heavy labor or to drive them away. The weakness of such brethren must be taken into consideration by the abbot.

Chapter XLIX—The Observance of Lent

The mode of a monk's life ought at all times to favor that of Lenten observance. Since few, however, are capable of this we exhort everyone in these days of Lent to guard their lives in all purity, and during this holy season to wash away every negligence of other times. This we shall worthily accomplish if we restrain ourselves from every vice, and give ourselves to tearful prayer, to reading, to heartfelt sorrow, and to abstinence. In these days of Lent, therefore, let us of our own accord add something to our usual yoke of service, such as private prayer, or abstinence from food and drink. Let everyone of his own will with the joy of the Holy Spirit offer to God something above the allotted measure, that is, let him deny his body in food, drink, sleep, talking or laughter, and with spiritual joy await the holy feast of Easter. On this condition, however, that each one inform his abbot what it is that he is offering, for what is done without leave of the spiritual father will be reckoned presumptious and vainglorious, and merit no reward. All things, therefore, must be done with the approval of the abbot.

Chapter L—Of the Brethren Who Work at a Distance from the Oratory or Are on a Journey

Those brethren who work at a distance and cannot come to the oratory at the appointed hours, and the abbot judges that this is so, shall say the Divine Office where they are working, kneeling in the fear of God. In the same way, those who are sent on a journey shall not omit the customary hours, but keep them as best they may, and fail not to accomplish this duty of their service.

Chapter LI—Of Brethren Who Go Only a Short Distance

The brother who is sent on an errand and expects to return to his monastery the same day shall not presume to eat outside his house, even if he is asked to do so by anyone, unless he is so ordered by his abbot. If he does otherwise let him be excommunicated.

Chapter LII—Concerning the Oratory of the Monastery

Let the oratory be what its name signifies, and let nothing else be done or discussed there. When the "Work of God" is ended let all depart in strict silence, in reverence of God, so that the brother who wishes to pray privately may not be hindered by the misconduct of another. If any brother wishes to pray privately let him go into the oratory, without ostentation, and say his prayers, not with a loud voice, but with tears and an earnest heart. Therefore, as has been said, no one is allowed to remain in the oratory after the Divine Office is ended, unless for the purpose of prayer, lest some other brother is hindered by him.

Chapter LIII—On the Reception of Guests

Let all guests who come be received as Christ would be, because he will say, "I was a stranger, and you took me in."[182] And let appropriate honor be shown to all, especially to those who are of the servants of the faith, and to pilgrims. As soon, therefore, as a guest is announced let him be met by the prior or the brethren, with all marks of charity. And let them first pray together, so that they may associate in peace. The kiss of peace, however, is not to be given until after prayer, on account of the deceptions practiced by the devil. And in the salutation itself let true humility be shown to all guests coming and going. By bowed head, or body prostrate on the ground,

---

[182] Matthew 25:35.

all shall adore Christ in them, who, indeed, is received in their persons.

Let guests, after their reception, be conducted to prayer, and then the prior, or anyone he may order, shall sit with them. Let the divine law be read in the presence of the guest for his edification, and after this let all courtesy be shown to him. For the guest's sake the prior may break his fast, unless it is a major day of fasting, when the fast may not be broken. The brethren, however, shall keep the accustomed fasts. Let the abbot pour water on the hands of the guests, and let him and all the community wash their feet. After this let them say the verse, "We have received your mercy, oh God, in the midst of your temple."[183] Let special care be taken of the poor and pilgrims, because in them Christ is more truly received, for the very awe of the rich secures respect for them.

Let the kitchen of the abbot and the guests be apart, so that strangers, who are never absent from a monastery, coming in at irregular hours, may not disturb the community. Let two of the brethren, who can perform their duties well, take charge of this kitchen for a year at a time. When they need it they shall be given assistance, so that they may serve without murmuring. In like manner, when they have lighter work, let them labor where they are told. And, indeed, not only in their regard, but also in respect to all the other officers of the monastery let this consideration always be given; when they need help let them have it, and when, on the other hand, they are free they shall do what they are ordered. Also, let the charge of the guesthouse be assigned to a brother whose soul is possessed by the fear of God. A sufficient number of beds are to be prepared there, and let the house of God be wisely ruled by wise men.

No one, unless ordered, may associate with or speak to the guests. If any one shall meet or see them, after such humble salutation as we have above enjoined, having asked their blessing, let him pass on, saying he is not permitted to talk with any guest.

Chapter LIV—Whether a Monk May Receive Letters or Presents

It is by no means lawful, without the abbot's permission, for any monk to receive or give letters, presents, and gifts of any kind to anyone, whether parent or other, and not even to one of the brethren. If anything is sent to a monk from his parents he shall not venture to receive it unless the abbot is first told. If he orders it to be accepted he may appoint the person to whom it shall be given. And let not the brother, to whom perhaps it was sent, be grieved, lest an opening be given to the devil. He who shall dare to do otherwise shall be subjected to regular discipline.

Chapter LV—Of the Clothes and Shoes of the Brethren

Let clothing suitable to the locality and the temperature be given to the brethren, for in cold regions more is needed, and less in warm. The determination of all these things is in the hands of the abbot. We believe, however, that in ordinary places it will be enough for each monk to have a cowl and tunic; in winter the cowl being of thicker stuff, in summer of finer or old cloth. He should have also a scapular for working purposes, and shoes and stockings for the feet.

Monks must not grumble at the color or coarseness of these things; they shall be such as can be procured in the district where they live, or such as can be bought at the cheapest price.

Let the abbot see to their dimensions, that they are not too short, but of the proper length for those who use them. When receiving new clothes the monks shall always give back the old ones at the same time, to be put away in the clothes-room for the poor. For it is sufficient that a monk have two tunics and two cowls, both for night wear as well as for the convenience of washing. Anything beyond this is superfluous, and must be cut off. Their shoes also, and whatever is worn out, they shall return on getting new things. Those who are sent on a journey shall get hose from the wardrobe, which, on their return when washed, they shall restore. Let their cowls and tunics on such occasions be somewhat better than those in ordinary use. These they shall receive from the wardrobe when starting and restore on their return.

A mattress, blanket, coverlet, and pillow are to be sufficient for bedding. The beds shall be frequently searched by the abbot to guard against the vice of hoarding. And if anyone is found in possession of something not allowed by the abbot let him be subjected to the severest punishment. And to uproot this vice of appropriation let all that is necessary be furnished by the abbot, that is, cowl, tunic, shoes, stockings, girdle, knife, pen, needle, handkerchief, and tablets. By this every pretext of necessity will be taken away. The abbot, however, should always

---

[183] Psalm 47:10.

bear in mind that sentence in the Acts of the Apostles, "And distribution was made to everyone according to his need."[184] He should, therefore, consider the infirmities of such as need something, and not regard the ill will of the envious. In all his decisions let him consider the retribution of God.

Chapter LVI—The Abbot's Table

The abbot shall always take his meals with the guests and strangers. But when there are few guests, he may invite any of the brethren he may choose. Let him see, however, that one or two of the seniors are always left with the community, for the sake of discipline.

Chapter LVII—Of the Craftsmen of the Monastery

Let such craftsmen as be in the monastery ply their trade in all lowliness of mind, if the abbot allow it. But if any are puffed up by his skill in his craft, and think the monastery indebted to him for it, such a one shall be shifted from his handicraft, and not attempt it again until such time as, having learned a low opinion of himself, the abbot shall bid him to resume. If anything of the fruit of their labors be sold let them that have the handling of the affair see to it that they do not dare to practice any fraud therein.

Let them remember Ananias and Saphira,[185] lest they, or any who practice any fraud in regard to the possessions of the monastery, suffer the death of their souls as did they of their bodies. In setting the prices, however, do not let the vice of greed creep in, but let the things be sold somewhat cheaper than they can be by laymen, that in all things God may be glorified.

Chapter LVIII—The Manner of Receiving the Brethren

Anyone on first coming to the religious life should not find the entrance made easy, but as the apostle says, "Try the spirits, if they are of God."[186] If, however, the newcomer continues to knock, and for four or five days shows a patient bearing, both of the harshness shown him and of the difficulty made about admitting him, and persists in his petition he shall then be allowed to enter the guesthouse for a few days. After that let him be in the novitiate, where he shall meditate and eat and sleep.

And let a senior, such as has the skill of winning souls, be appointed to watch carefully over him, to discover whether he truly seeks God and is eager for the Divine Office, for obedience and humiliations. Let all the rigor and austerity of our journey to God be put clearly before him. If he promises to continue in a steadfast perseverance, at the end of two months the entire rule shall be read to him, and let him be told, "See the law under which you wish to fight, if you can observe it enter into the life; if you cannot you are free to depart."

If he still perseveres let him be brought back to the novitiate and again tried in all patience. And after the passing of six months let the rule be read to him again, that he may fully know the kind of life he is entering into. If he still perseveres, after four months the rule shall be read to him once more. If after due deliberation he then promises to keep the whole law and to do whatever is commanded of him, let him be received into the community, knowing that he is now under the law of the rule, so that he can henceforth neither leave the monastery nor withdraw his neck from the yoke of the rule which after so long a deliberation he was free to have taken or refused.

When he is to be admitted into the community let him in the oratory, and in the presence of all, promise before God and his saints stability, amendment of manners and obedience, in order that if at any time he shall act otherwise he may know that he shall be condemned by him whom he mocks. He shall draw up the form of his promise in the name of the saints, whose relics are reposing there, and of the abbot there present. Let him write out this form himself, or at least, if he is uneducated another at his request must write it for him, and to this the novice himself shall set his mark and with his own hand lay it upon the altar.

After he has placed it there, let the novice immediately begin the verse, "Uphold me, oh Lord, according to your word, and I shall live, and let me not be confounded in my expectation."[187] The community shall repeat this verse three times, adding at the end, "Glory be to the Father," etc. Then the brother novice shall cast himself at the feet of all, asking their prayers, and from that time he shall be counted as one of the community. If he has

---

[184] Psalm 47:10.

[185] Acts 5:1–10.

[186] 1 John 4:1.

[187] Psalm 118:116.

any property, he must first either give it to the poor, or by formal gift make it over to the monastery without any reservation for himself, since he must know that he has henceforth no power even over his own body. Let him, therefore, immediately be divested in the oratory of his own garments and be clothed in those of the monastery. The clothes he has taken off, however, are to be kept in the wardrobe, so that if (which God forbid) he resolves, by the persuasion of the devil, to leave the monastery, he may be stripped of his monastic dress and expelled. The form of profession which the abbot took from him at the altar he shall not receive back, but it shall be kept in the monastery.

Chapter LIX—Of the Sons of Nobles or of the Poor Who Are Offered to God

If any nobleman shall offer his son to God in the monastery, let the parents, if the child himself is under age, make the petition for him, and together with the oblation wrap the formal promise and the hand of the boy in the altar cloth and thus dedicate him to God. With regard to any property let the parents promise in the document under oath that they will never either give or furnish him with the means of obtaining anything whatever, either themselves or by any other person or by any means. Or, if they will not do this, and desire to give some alms to the monastery, as a free gift, let them hand over to the place what they wish, reserving, if they please, the income for themselves. Let all these matters be so managed that the child have no expectations by which he may be deceived and perish (which God forbid), as by experience we have learned is sometimes the case. In the same way let those who are poorer act. But such as have nothing whatever shall simply make the promise and offer their son before witnesses with the oblation.

Chapter LX—Of Priests Who Wish to Dwell in the Monastery

If anyone in the ranks of the priesthood asks to be received into the monastery let him not obtain permission too quickly. If, however, he persists in his request he shall understand that he will have to keep the rule in all rigor, and that no mitigation will be allowed to him, according to what is written, "Friend, for what have you

come?" Nevertheless let him be allowed to stand next after the abbot, to give the blessing or to say Mass, provided the abbot orders him. If not, he may not presume to do anything, knowing that he is subject to the discipline of regular life, and is especially obliged to set an example of humility to all. If perhaps his position in the monastery is given him because of his orders, or for any other reason, he should remember that his proper place is what he has according to the time of his entry to the monastery, not that which is given to him out of respect for the priesthood. But if any clerics manifest the same desire to be admitted into the monastery let them be put into a middle rank, but only if they give promise of observance of the rule and of their stability to it.

Chapter LXI—Of Monks Who Are Strangers, How They Are to Be Received

If any stranger monk, coming from a distant place, desires to dwell in the monastery as a guest and, content with the customs he finds there, does not trouble the house by superfluous wants, but is simply content with what he finds, let him be received for as long a time as he desires to remain. And if he reasonably and with loving humility blames something, or points out anything amiss, let the abbot prudently consider it, lest perhaps the Lord has sent him there for that purpose. If, also, after a time he wish to make his stay permanent, such a desire should not be refused, particularly since during the time he has lived as a guest his manner of life could be known.

If in that period he shall have been found troublesome or vicious, not only should he not be incorporated within the community, but he should even be told frankly to leave, lest others be corrupted by his ill doing. But if he does not deserve to be sent away, not only if he ask, shall he be received into the ranks of the community, but he should even be induced to stay, that others may be taught by his example, because in every place we serve a common lord, and fight under the same king.

And if the abbot finds such a monk deserving he may even put him into a somewhat higher rank. And the abbot may raise above the rank of his entry into religion, not only any monk, but also any of the aforesaid priests or clerics, if he considers that their lives deserve it. Let the abbot, however, beware never to receive permanently any monk of a known monastery without the consent of his own abbot, or without letters of recommendation from him, for it is written, "What you will not have done to yourself, do not do to another."[188]

Chapter LXII—The Priests of the Monastery

If any abbot desires to have a priest or deacon ordained let him choose from his monks one who is worthy to fill the office of priesthood. Let the monk, however, who is ordained beware of haughtiness and pride, and let him not presume to do anything except what is ordered by the abbot, remembering that he is now much more subject to regular discipline. Let him not make his priesthood an excuse for forgetting obedience and the rigor of the rule, rather he should strive on account of it to draw more and more toward God.

He shall, moreover, always keep the place he had when he came to the monastery, except in his service at the altar, or if on account of the holiness of his life by the wish of the community and the will of the abbot, he is moved up to a higher place. Even then let him understand that he must keep the rules prescribed for him by the deans or provosts, and if he presumes to act otherwise he shall be judged not as a priest but as a rebel. If after frequent warnings he does not amend his ways, even the bishop shall be brought in to witness to the fact. And if after this he does not amend, and his faults become notorious, let him be expelled from the monastery, if his contempt is such that he will not submit and obey the rule.

Chapter LXIII—The Order of the Community

The brethren shall take their places according to the date of their conversion, the merit of their lives, or the appointment of their abbot. And the abbot must not disturb the flock committed to him, nor, as it were, by any arbitrary use of his power, ordain anything unjustly. But let him always remember that he will have to render an account to God of all his judgments and of all his works.

Accordingly, in the order he shall appoint, or in that which they hold among themselves, let the brethren receive the Pax,[189] approach Communion, lead a psalm, and stand in choir. In all places, without exception, order shall not be decided by age, for this shall not be

a prejudice to anyone, since Samuel and Daniel, though children, were judges of the priests.[190] With the exception, therefore, of those who, as we have said, for some weighty reason, the abbot advances, or for certain reasons puts in a lower place, let all the rest remain in the order of their conversion. For example, one who comes to the monastery at the second hour of the day shall know that he is junior to him who has come at the first hour, no matter what his age or dignity may be. In regard to children, let them be kept by all under discipline in every way.

Let the juniors, therefore, honor their seniors, and the seniors love the juniors. In addressing each other in person no one shall call another by his mere name, but let the senior call the junior, Brother, and the junior call the senior, Father. But, because the abbot is held to take the place of Christ, he shall be called Sir and Abbot, not out of consideration for himself, but for the honor and love of Christ. He, however, should remember and so conduct himself in order to be worthy of such an honor.

Wherever the brethren meet each other, the junior shall ask a blessing from the senior. When a senior passes by let the junior rise and make a place for him to sit down; neither shall the junior presume to sit unless the senior bid him so to do, in order to fulfill what is written, "In honor preventing one another."[191]

Little children or adolescents shall keep their respective places in the oratory and at table, under discipline. Outside watch shall be kept over them, everywhere indeed, until they come to an age of understanding.

Chapter LXIV—The Election of the Abbot

In the election of an abbot let the following points be always borne in mind: that he is made abbot whom the whole community, in the fear of God, make a choice of, or a part of it, however small, acting with greater wisdom. Let him who is made abbot be chosen because of his virtuous life and his wisdom, even if he is the last in the community. And if the whole community (which God forbid) shall unanimously choose one who supports them in their evil practices, and their vicious lives become known to the bishop (to whose diocese the monastery belongs), or to the abbots or Christians of the neighborhood, they shall annul the choice of these bad men and

[188] Matthew 7:12.
[189] I.e., kiss of peace.
[190] 1 Kings 7:15; cf. Daniel 13:51 ff.
[191] Romans 13:10.

appoint a worthy steward of God's House, knowing that for this they shall receive a good reward, provided they do it with pure intention and through zeal for God, just as, on the other hand, they sin if they neglect to do it.

Let him who has been made abbot always reflect upon the weighty burden he has taken up and remember to whom he shall give an account of his stewardship. Let him know also that it is better for him to profit others than to rule over them. He must therefore be learned in the divine law that he may know when to "bring forth new things and old."[192] He must be chaste, sober, merciful, and always exalt mercy above justice, that he may obtain mercy. He shall hate vice and love the brethren. Even in his correction he shall act with prudence and not try too much, lest while too violently scouring off the rust the vessel itself is broken. Let him always bear in mind his own frailty, and remember that "the bruised reed must not be broken."[193]

In saying this we do not propose that he should allow vices to spring up, but, as we have declared before, he should seek to root them out prudently and with charity, in the way he thinks proper in each case. Let him aim at being loved rather than feared. He must not be worried nor anxious, neither should he be too exacting or obstinate, or jealous, or oversuspicious, for then he will never be at rest. Even in what he orders, whether it relates to God or to worldly matters, let him be prudent and considerate. In all that he enjoins he should be discreet and moderate, meditating on the prudence of holy Jacob, who says, "If I shall cause my flocks to be overdriven, they will all die in one day."[194] Accordingly adopting these and like principles of discretion, the mother of virtues, let him so temper all things that the strong may have their scope and the weak are not scared. And especially let him keep the present rule in all things, so that when he has administered it well he may hear from our Lord what the good servant heard who gave corn to his fellow servants in due season: "Amen, I say to you, over all his goods will he place him."[195]

Chapter LXV—The Provost of the Monastery

It often happens that by the appointment of a provost, grave scandals arise in monasteries. There are some who, puffed up by the evil spirit of pride, and esteeming themselves to be like abbots, take on themselves to act the tyrant, to foster scandals, and promote discord in the community. This is especially the case in places where the provost is appointed by the same priests or abbots who appoint the abbot of the monastery. How foolish this custom is may easily be seen. From the very beginning of the appointment a pretext for pride is given to the provost, since his imagination suggests to him that he is now released from the power of his abbot, for (as it seems to say) "You are appointed by those who created the abbot." Hence arises envy, quarrels, detractions, rivalries, and disorders. And while the abbot and the provost are at variance it must of necessity follow that their souls are endangered by the quarrel, and that those under them, by taking sides, are going to destruction. The guilt of this danger chiefly weighs on those who were the authors of such appointments.

Therefore we anticipate that for the preservation of peace and charity it is expedient that the ordering of his monastery depend on the will of the abbot. And, as we have indicated before, if it is possible, let all the work of the monastery be managed by deans, as we have directed, in order that where many are entrusted with the work no one may become proud.

But if the circumstances of the place require a provost, or the community shall with reason and humility ask for one, and the abbot thinks it is expedient, with the advice of the brethren who have the fear of God, let him nominate whomsoever he chooses himself as provost. Let this provost, moreover, reverently do whatever is enjoined him by his abbot, never acting against his will or directions, because the higher he is raised above the others the more careful he must be to keep the precepts of the rule. If this provost is found viciously inclined, or carried away by the haughtiness of pride, or a proven despiser of the holy rule, let him be warned four times; if he does not amend let him fall under the punishment of regular discipline. If even then he is not corrected he shall be deposed from his position of provost, and another who is worthy shall be put in his place. If after this he shall not be quiet and obedient in the community let him even be put out of the monastery. The abbot nevertheless shall bear in mind that he will have to give an account of all his judgments to God, lest perhaps his soul burns with the flame of envy and jealousy.

Chapter LXVI—The Porter of the Monastery

Let there be stationed at the gate of the monastery some wise old man who knows how to give and receive an

---

[192] Matthew 13:52.

[193] Isaiah 42:3.

[194] Genesis 33:13.

[195] Matthew 24:47.

answer, and whose age will not allow him to wander from his post. This porter should have his cell near the door, that those who arrive may always find him there to give an answer.

As soon as anyone knocks, or some poor man calls for help, let him reply, "Thanks be to God," or invoke a blessing. And let him in the meekness of God's fear hurry to reply with zealous charity. If the porter is in need of help let him have a junior brother with him. The monastery, however, itself ought, if possible, to be so constructed as to contain within it all necessities, that is, water, mill, garden, and [places for] the various crafts which are exercised within a monastery, so that there is no occasion for monks to wander outside, since this is in no way expedient for their souls. We wish this rule to be read frequently in the community so that no brother may plead ignorance as an excuse.

Chapter LXVII—Of Brethren Sent on a Journey

When brethren are about to be sent on a journey let them commend themselves to the prayers of all the brethren and of the abbot, and at the closing prayer of the Divine Office let a commemoration be made of all the absent brethren. When they come back from a journey, on the day of their return, at all the canonical hours when the Divine Office is finished, the brethren shall prostrate themselves on the ground and beg the prayers of all for any faults they may have fallen into on the road, by the sight or hearing of evil things, or by idle discourse. And let no one dare to relate to another what he has seen or heard outside the monastery, because this is most detrimental. If anyone shall presume to do this he must be subjected to the punishment prescribed in the rule. In like manner shall he be punished who presumes to break the enclosure of the monastery, or go anywhere, or do anything, however trifling, without the abbot's permission.

Chapter LXVIII—When a Brother Is Ordered to Do the Impossible

If anything hard or impossible is enjoined on a brother let him receive the injunctions of him who orders him in all mildness and obedience. If he sees that the burden altogether exceeds the measure of his strength let him patiently and at the proper time state, without show of pride, resistance, or contradiction, the reason of this

impossibility. If after his suggestion the will of the prior still remains unchanged, let the young monk know that it is best for him; and trusting in God's help, through love of him, let him obey.

Chapter LXIX—That in the Monastery No One Presume to Defend Another

Special care must be taken that under no pretext should one monk presume to defend or uphold another in a monastery, even though they may be very close kin. In no way whatsoever let monks dare to do this, because from it an occasion of the gravest scandal may arise. If anyone shall transgress in this way he shall be severely punished.

Chapter LXX—That No One Presume to Strike Another

In the monastery every occasion of presumption should be avoided. We ordain that no one is allowed to excommunicate or strike any of his brethren unless the abbot has given him authority to do so. Those who offend in this matter shall be rebuked before all, that the rest may be inspired with fear. But over children, until they are fifteen years old, let all exercise strict discipline and care, yet this also must be done with moderation and discretion. He, however, who presumes to do so to those above this age, without the abbot's order, or is severe to children beyond discretion, shall be subjected to regular discipline, since it is written, "What you would not have done to yourself, do not do to another."[196]

Chapter LXXI—That the Brethren Be Obedient to Each Other

The excellent virtue of obedience is to be shown by all, not to the abbot only, but to the brethren who shall also mutually obey each other, knowing that by this path of obedience they go to God. The commands of the abbot, or other superiors constituted by him, having the first place (for to these we do not allow any private orders to be preferred) the juniors shall obey their seniors with all charity and diligence. If anyone be found contentious let him be punished.

---

[196] Tobit 4:16.

...uked for even the least thing by the ...r (i.e., superior), or if he perceives ...uperior is, however slightly, moved ...er with him, let him without delay ...feet, and remain offering satisfac-...removed and he receives a bless-...anyone is found too proud to do this let him be expelled from the monastery.

Chapter LXXII—Of the Good Zeal Monks Should Have

As there is an evil and bitter emulation which separates from God and leads to hell, so there is a good spirit of emulation which frees from vices and leads to God and life everlasting. Let monks, therefore, practice this emulation with the most fervent love; that is to say, let them "in honor prevent one another,"[197] let them bear most patiently with each other's infirmities, whether of body or of manner. Let them contend with one another in their obedience. Let no one follow what he thinks most profitable to himself, but rather what is best for another. Let them show brotherly charity with a chaste love. Let them fear God and love their abbot with sincere and humble affection, and set nothing whatsoever before Christ, who can bring us into eternal life.

Chapter LXXIII—That All Perfection Is Not Contained in This Rule

We have written this rule, so that, by its observance in monasteries, we may show that we have in some measure uprightness of manners or the beginning of religious life. But for such as hasten onward to the perfection of a holy life there are the teachings of the holy fathers, the observance of which leads a man to the heights of perfection. For what page or what passage of the divinely inspired books of the Old and the New Testament is not a most perfect rule for man's life? Or what book is there of the holy catholic fathers that does not proclaim this, that by a direct course we may come to our creator? Also, what else are the *Collations* of the fathers, their *Institutes*, their *Lives*, and the rule of our holy father St. Basil, but examples of the virtues, of the good living and obedience of monks? But to us who are slothful, and lead bad and negligent lives, they are matter for shame and confusion.

Do, therefore, whosoever you are who hastens forward to the heavenly country, accomplish first, by the help of Christ, this little rule written for beginners, and then at length shall you come, under God's guidance, to the lofty heights of doctrine and virtue, which we have spoken of above.

---

13. GREGORY THE GREAT

DIALOGUES

The book of *Dialogues* traditionally attributed to Pope Gregory the Great (589–604) spread the fame of Benedict across Europe and was one of the most important hagiographical texts (relating the life and miracles of a saint) of the Middle Ages. The second book, *A Life of Benedict of Nursia*, became a model for lives of monastic saints. In this text, the discussion between a master and his student describes Benedict's life and presents him as a model for ascetic devotional practices.

> *Source:* Odo John Zimmerman (ed. and trans.), *Saint Gregory the Great, Dialogues* (New York: The Fathers of the Church, 1959), 55–110.
>
> *Further Reading:* R. Markus, *Gregory the Great and His World* (Cambridge: Cambridge University Press, 1997).

---

[197] Romans 12:10.

Book II

Life and Miracles of St. Benedict Founder and Abbot of the Monastery Which Is Known as the Citadel of Campania.

There was a man of saintly life; blessed Benedict was his name, and he was blessed also with God's grace. Even in boyhood he showed mature understanding, for he kept his heart detached from every pleasure with a strength of character far beyond his years. While still living in the world, free to enjoy its earthly advantages, he saw how barren it was with its attractions and turned from it without regret.

He was born in the district of Norcia[198] of distinguished parents, who sent him back to Rome for a liberal education. But when he saw many of his fellow students falling headlong into vice, he stepped back from the threshold of the world in which he had just set foot. For he was afraid that if he acquired any of its learning, he, too, would later plunge, body and soul, into the dread abyss. In his desire to please God alone, he turned his back on further studies, gave up home and inheritance and resolved to embrace the religious life. He took this step, well aware of his ignorance, yet wise, uneducated though he was.

I was unable to learn about all his miraculous deeds. But the few that I am going to relate I know from the lips of four of his own disciples: Constantine, the holy man who succeeded him as abbot; Valentinian, for many years superior of the monastery at the Lateran; Simplicius, Benedict's second successor; and Honoratus, who is still abbot of the monastery where the man of God first lived.

(1) When Benedict abandoned his studies to go into solitude, he was accompanied only by his nurse, who loved him dearly. As they were passing through Affile, a number of devout men invited them to stay there and provided them with lodging near the Church of St. Peter. One day, after asking her neighbors to lend her a tray for cleaning wheat, the nurse happened to leave it on the edge of the table and when she came back found it had slipped off and broken in two. The poor woman burst into tears; she had only borrowed this tray and now it was ruined. Benedict, who had always been a devout and thoughtful boy, felt sorry for his nurse when he saw her

weeping. Quietly picking up both the pieces, he knelt down by himself and prayed earnestly to God, even to the point of tears. No sooner had he finished his prayer than he noticed that the two pieces were joined together again, without even a mark to show where the tray had been broken. Hurrying back at once, he cheerfully reassured his nurse and handed her the tray in perfect condition.

News of the miracle spread to all the country around Affile and stirred up so much admiration among the people that they hung the tray at the entrance to their church. Ever since then it has been a reminder to all of the great holiness Benedict had acquired at the very outset of his monastic life. The tray remained there many years for everyone to see, and it is still hanging over the doorway of the church in these days of Lombard rule.[199] Benedict, however, preferred to suffer ill-treatment from the world rather than enjoy its praises. He wanted to spend himself laboring for God, not to be honored by the applause of men. So he stole away secretly from his nurse and fled to a lonely wilderness about thirty-five miles from Rome called Subiaco. A stream of cold, clear water running through the region broadens out at this point to form a lake, then flows off and continues on its course. On his way there Benedict met a monk named Romanus, who asked him where he was going. After discovering the young man's purpose, Romanus kept it secret and even helped him carry it out by clothing him with the monastic habit and supplying his needs as well as he could.

At Subiaco, Benedict made his home in a narrow cave and for three years remained concealed there, unknown to anyone except the monk Romanus, who lived in a monastery close by under the rule of Abbot Deodatus. With fatherly concern this monk regularly set aside as much bread as he could from his own portion; then from time to time, unnoticed by his abbot, he left the monastery long enough to take the bread to Benedict. There was no path leading from the monastery down to his cave because of a cliff that rose directly over it. To reach him Romanus had to tie the bread to the end of a long rope and lower it over the cliff. A little bell attached to the rope let Benedict know when the bread was there, and he would come out to get it. The ancient Enemy of mankind grew envious of the kindness shown by the older monk in supplying Benedict with food, and one day, as the bread was being lowered, he threw a stone at

---

[198] A little town about 70 miles northeast of Rome. The saint was born around 480.

[199] The Lombards, a Germanic people, left their homes along the upper Danube and invaded Italy in 568, establishing a kingdom there which lasted until 774.

the bell and broke it. In spite of this, Romanus kept on with his faithful service.

At length the time came when almighty God wished to grant him rest from his toil and reveal Benedict's virtuous life to others. Like a shining lamp his example was to be set on a lampstand to give light to everyone in God's house. The Lord therefore appeared in a vision to a priest some distance away, who had just prepared his Easter dinner. "How can you prepare these delicacies for yourself," He asked, "while my servant is out there in the wilds suffering from hunger?"

Rising at once, the priest wrapped up the food and set out to find the man of God that very day. He searched for him along the rough mountainsides, in the valleys, and through the caverns, until he found him hidden in the cave. They said a prayer of thanksgiving together and then sat down to talk about the spiritual life. After a while the priest suggested that they take their meal. "Today is the great feast of Easter," he added.

"It must be a great feast to have brought me this kind visit," the man of God replied, not realizing after his long separation from men that it was Easter Sunday.

"Today is really Easter," the priest insisted, "the feast of our Lord's Resurrection. On such a solemn occasion you should not be fasting. Besides, I was sent here by almighty God so that both of us could share in His gifts."

After that they said grace and began their meal. When it was over they conversed some more and then the priest went back to his church.

At about the same time some shepherds also discovered Benedict's hiding place. When they first looked through the thickets and caught sight of him clothed in rough skins, they mistook him for some wild animal. Soon, however, they recognized in him a servant of God, and many of them gave up their sinful ways for a life of holiness. As a result, his name became known to all the people in that locality and great numbers visited his cave, supplying him with the food he needed and receiving from his lips in return spiritual food for their souls.

(2) One day, while the saint was alone, the Tempter came in the form of a little blackbird, which began to flutter in front of his face. It kept so close that he could easily have caught it in his hand. Instead, he made the sign of the cross and the bird flew away. The moment it left, he was seized with an unusually violent temptation. The evil spirit recalled to his mind a woman he had once seen, and before he realized it his emotions were carrying him away. Almost overcome in the struggle, he was on the point of abandoning the lonely wilderness, when suddenly with the help of God's grace he came to himself.

He then noticed a thick patch of nettles and briers next to him. Throwing his garment aside he flung himself into the sharp thorns and stinging nettles. There he rolled and tossed until his whole body was in pain and covered with blood. Yet, once he had conquered pleasure through suffering, his torn and bleeding skin served to drain the poison of temptation from his body. Before long, the pain that was burning his whole body had put out the fires of evil in his heart. It was by exchanging these two fires that he gained the victory over sin. So complete was his triumph that from then on, as he later told his disciples, he never experienced another temptation of this kind.

Soon after, many forsook the world to place themselves under his guidance, for now that he was free from these temptations he was ready to instruct others in the practice of virtue. That is why Moses commanded the Levites to begin their service when they were twenty-five years old or more and to become guardians of the sacred vessels only at the age of fifty.

Peter: The meaning of the passage you quote is becoming a little clearer to me now. Still, I wish you would explain it more fully.

Gregory: It is a well-known fact, Peter, that temptations of the flesh are violent during youth, whereas after the age of fifty concupiscence dies down. Now, the sacred vessels are the souls of the faithful. God's chosen servants must therefore obey and serve and tire themselves out with strenuous work as long as they are still subject to temptations. Only when full maturity has left them undisturbed by evil thoughts are they put in charge of the sacred vessels, for then they become teachers of souls.

Peter: I like the way you interpreted that passage. Now that you have explained what it means, I hope you will continue with your account of the holy man's life.

Gregory: (3) With the passing of this temptation, Benedict's soul, like a field cleared of briers, soon yielded a rich harvest of virtues. As word spread of his saintly life, the renown of his name increased. One day the entire community from a nearby monastery[200] came to see him. Their abbot had recently died, and they wanted the man of God to be their new superior. For some time he tried to discourage them by refusing their request, warning them that his way of life would never harmonize with theirs. But they kept insisting, until in the end he gave his consent.

At the monastery he watched carefully over the religious spirit of the monks and would not tolerate any of

---

[200] Usually identified as Vicovaro, about 20 miles farther down the Anio.

their previous disobedience. No one was allowed to turn from the straight path of monastic discipline either to the right or to the left. Their waywardness, however, clashed with the standards he upheld, and in their resentment they started to reproach themselves for choosing him as abbot. It only made them the more sullen to find him curbing every fault and every evil habit. They could not see why they should have to force their settled minds into new ways of thinking.

At length, proving once again that the very life of the just is a burden to the wicked, they tried to find a means of doing away with him and decided to poison his wine. A glass pitcher containing this poisoned drink was presented to the man of God during his meal for the customary blessing. As he made the sign of the cross over it with his hand, the pitcher was shattered, even though it was well beyond his reach at the time. It broke at his blessing as if he had struck it with stone.

Then he realized it had contained a deadly drink which could not bear the sign of life. Still calm and undisturbed, he rose at once and, after gathering the community together, addressed them. "May almighty God have mercy on you," he said. "Why did you conspire to do this? Did I not tell you at the outset that my way of life would never harmonize with yours? Go and find yourselves an abbot to your liking. It is impossible for me to stay here any longer." Then he went back to the wilderness he loved, to live alone with himself in the presence of his heavenly Father.

Peter: I am not quite sure I understand what you mean by saying "to live with himself."

Gregory: These monks had an outlook on religious life entirely unlike his own and were all conspiring against him. Now, if he had tried to force them to remain under his rule, he might have forfeited his own fervor and peace of soul and even turned his eyes from the light of contemplation. Their persistent daily faults would have left him almost too weary to look to his own needs, and he would perhaps have forsaken himself without finding them. For, whenever anxieties carry us out of ourselves unduly, we are no longer with ourselves even though we still remain what we are. We are too distracted with other matters to give any attention whatever to ourselves.

Surely we cannot describe as "with himself" the young man who traveled to a distant country where he wasted his inheritance and then, after hiring himself out to one of its citizens to feed swine, had to watch them eat their fill of pods while he went hungry. Do we not read in Scripture that, as he was considering all he had lost, "he came to himself and said, 'how many hired servants there are in my father's house that have more bread than they can eat'"? If he was already "with himself," how could he have come "to himself"?

Blessed Benedict, on the contrary, can be said to have lived "with himself" because at all times he kept such close watch over his life and actions. By searching continually into his own soul he always beheld himself in the presence of his Creator. And this kept his mind from straying off to the world outside.

Peter: But what of Peter the Apostle when he was led out of prison by an angel? According to the Scriptures, he, too, "came to himself." "Now I can tell for certain," he said, "that the Lord has sent his angel, to deliver me out of Herod's hands, and from all that the people of the Jews hoped to see."

Gregory: There are two ways in which we can be carried out of ourselves, Peter. Either we fall below ourselves through sins of thought or we are lifted above ourselves by the grace of contemplation. The young man who fed the swine sank below himself as a result of his shiftless ways and his unclean life. The Apostle Peter was also out of himself when the angel set him free and raised him to a state of ecstasy, but he was above himself. In coming to themselves again, the former had to break with his sinful past before he could find his true and better self, whereas the latter merely returned from the heights of contemplation to his ordinary state of mind.

Now, the saintly Benedict really lived "with himself" out in that lonely wilderness by always keeping his thoughts recollected. Yet he must have left his own self far below each time he was drawn heavenward in fervent contemplation.

Peter: I am very grateful to you for that explanation. Do you think it was right, though, for him to forsake this community, once he had taken it under his care?

Gregory: In my opinion, Peter, a superior ought to bear patiently with a community of evil men as long as it has some devout members who can benefit from his presence. When none of the members is devout enough to give any promise of good results, his efforts to help such a community will prove to be a serious mistake, especially if there are opportunities nearby to work more fruitfully for God. Was there anyone the holy man could have hoped to protect by staying where he was, after he saw that they were all united against him?

In this matter we cannot afford to overlook the attitude of the saints. When they find their work producing no results in one place, they move on to another where it can do some good. This explains the action of the blessed Apostle Paul. In order to escape from Damascus, where he was being persecuted, he secured a basket and a rope and had himself secretly lowered over the wall. Yet this outstanding preacher of the Gospel longed to depart and be with Christ, since for him life meant Christ, and death was a prize to be won. Besides being eager for the trials of persecution himself, he even inspired others to endure them. Can we say that Paul feared death, when he expressly declared that he longed to die for the love of Christ? Surely not. But, when he saw how little he was accomplishing at Damascus in spite of all his toil, he saved himself for more fruitful labors elsewhere. God's fearless warrior refused to be held back inside the walls and sought the open field of battle.

Peter: I am sure your conclusion is correct, after the simple proof you gave and that striking example from sacred Scripture. Would you be good enough to return now to the story of this great abbot's life?

Gregory: As Benedict's influence spread over the surrounding countryside because of his signs and wonders, a great number of men gathered round him to devote themselves to God's service. Christ blessed his work and before long he had established twelve monasteries there, with an abbot and twelve monks in each of them. There were a few monks whom he kept with him, since he felt that they still needed his personal guidance.

It was about this time that pious noblemen from Rome first came to visit the saint and left their sons with him to be schooled in the service of God. Thus, Euthicius brought his son Maurus; and Senator Tertullus, Placid—both very promising boys. Maurus, in fact, who was a little older, had already acquired solid virtue and was soon very helpful to his saintly master. But Placid was still only a child.

(4) In one of the monasteries Benedict had founded in that locality, there was a monk who would never remain with the rest of the community for silent prayer. Instead, he left the chapel as soon as they knelt down to pray, and passed the time aimlessly at whatever happened to interest him. His abbot corrected him repeatedly and at length sent him to the man of God. This time the monk received a stern rebuke for his folly and after his return took the correction to heart for a day or two, only to fall back the third day into his old habit of wandering off during the time of prayer. On learning of this from the abbot, the man of God sent word that he was coming over himself to see that the monk mended his ways.

Upon his arrival at the monastery, Benedict joined the community in the chapel at the regular hour. After they had finished chanting the psalms and had begun their silent prayer, he noticed that the restless monk was drawn outside by a little black boy who was pulling at the edge of his habit.

"Do you see who is leading that monk out of the chapel?" he whispered to Abbot Pompeianus and Maurus.

"No," they replied.

"Let us pray, then," he said, "that you may see what is happening to him."

They prayed for two days, and after that Maurus also saw what was taking place, but Abbot Pompeianus still could not. The next day, when prayers were over, Benedict found the offender loitering outside and struck him with his staff for being so obstinate of heart. From then on the monk remained quietly at prayer like the rest, without being bothered again by the Tempter. It was as if that ancient Enemy had been struck by the blow himself and was afraid to domineer over the monk's thoughts any longer.

(5) Three of the monasteries the saint had built close by stood on the bare rocky heights. It was a real hardship for these monks always to go down to the lake to get water for their daily needs. Besides, the slope was steep and they found the descent very dangerous. The members of the three communities therefore came in a body to see the servant of God. After explaining how difficult it was for them to climb down the mountainside every day for their water supply, they assured him that the only solution was to have the monasteries moved somewhere else.

Benedict answered them with fatherly words of encouragement and sent them back. That same night, in company with the little boy Placid, he climbed to the rocky heights and prayed there for a long time. On finishing his prayer, he placed three stones together to indicate the spot where he had knelt and then went back to his monastery, unnoticed by anyone.

The following day, when the monks came again with their request, he told them to go to the summit of the mountain. "You will find three stones there," he said, "one on top of the other. If you dig down a little, you will see that almighty God has the power to bring forth water even from that rocky summit and in His goodness relieve you of the hardship of such a long climb."

Going back to the place he had described, they noticed that the surface was already moist. As soon as they had dug the ground away, water filled the hollow and welled up in such abundance that today a full stream is still flowing from the top of the mountain into the ravine below.

(6) At another time a simple, sincere Goth came to Subiaco to become a monk, and blessed Benedict was very happy to admit him. One day he had him take a brush hook and clear away the briers from a place at

the edge of the lake where a garden was to be planted. While the Goth was hard at work cutting down the thick brush, the iron blade slipped off the handle and flew into a very deep part of the lake, where there was no hope of recovering it.

At this the poor man ran trembling to Maurus and, after describing the accident, told him how sorry he was for his carelessness. Maurus in turn informed the servant of God, who on hearing what had happened went down to the lake, took the handle from the Goth and thrust it in the water. Immediately the iron blade rose from the bottom of the lake and slipped back onto the handle. Then he handed the tool back to the Goth and told him, "Continue with your work now. There is no need to be upset."

(7) Once while blessed Benedict was in his room, one of his monks, the boy Placid, went down to the lake to draw water. In letting the bucket fill too rapidly, he lost his balance and was pulled into the lake, where the current quickly seized him and carried him about a stone's throw from the shore. Though inside the monastery at the time, the man of God was instantly aware of what had happened and called out to Maurus: "Hurry, Brother Maurus! The boy who just went down for water has fallen into the lake, and the current is carrying him away."

What followed was remarkable indeed, and unheard of since the time of Peter the Apostle! Maurus asked for the blessing and on receiving it hurried out to fulfill his abbot's command. He kept on running even over the water till he reached the place where Placid was drifting along helplessly. Pulling him up by the hair, Maurus rushed back to shore, still under the impression that he was on dry land. It was only when he set foot on the ground that he came to himself and looking back realized that he had been running on the surface of the water. Overcome with fear and amazement at a deed he would never have thought possible, he returned to his abbot and told him what had taken place.

The holy man would not take any personal credit for the deed, but attributed it to the obedience of his disciple. Maurus, on the contrary, claimed that it was due entirely to his abbot's command. He could not have been responsible for the miracle himself, he said, since he had not even known he was performing it. While they were carrying on this friendly contest of humility, the question was settled by the boy who had been rescued. "When I was being drawn out of the water," he told them, "I saw the abbot's cloak over my head; he is the one I thought was bringing me to shore."

Peter: What marvelous deeds these are! They are sure to prove inspiring to all who hear of them. Indeed, the more you tell me about this great man, the more eager I am to keep on listening.

Gregory: (8) By this time the people of that whole region for miles around had grown fervent in their love for Christ, and many of them had forsaken the world in order to bring their hearts under the light yoke of the Savior. Now, in a neighboring church there was a priest named Florentius, the grandfather of our subdeacon Florentius. Urged on by the bitter Enemy of mankind, this priest set out to undermine the saint's work. And envious as the wicked always are of the holiness in others which they are not striving to acquire themselves, he denounced Benedict's way of life and kept everyone he could from visiting him.

The progress of the saint's work, however, could not be stopped. His reputation for holiness kept on growing, and with it the number of vocations to a more perfect state of life. This infuriated Florentius all the more. He still longed to enjoy the praise the saint was receiving, yet he was unwilling to lead a praiseworthy life himself. At length, his soul became so blind with jealousy that he decided to poison a loaf of bread and send it to the servant of God as though it was a sign of Christian fellowship.

Though aware at once of the deadly poison it contained, Benedict thanked him for the gift.

At mealtime a raven used to come out of the nearby woods to receive food from the saint's hands. On this occasion he set the poisoned loaf in front of it and said, "In the name of our Lord Jesus Christ, take this bread and carry it to a place where no one will be able to find it." The raven started to caw and circled round the loaf of bread with open beak and flapping wings as if to indicate that it was willing to obey, but found it impossible to do so. Several times the saint repeated the command. "Take the bread," he said, "and do not be afraid! Take it away from here and leave it where no one will find it." After hesitating a long while, the raven finally took the loaf in its beak and flew away. About three hours later, when it had disposed of the bread, it returned and received its usual meal from the hands of the man of God.

The saintly abbot now realized how deep the resentment of his enemy was, and he felt grieved not so much for his own sake as for the priest's. But Florentius, after his failure to do away with the master, determined instead to destroy the souls of the disciples and for this purpose sent seven depraved women into the garden of Benedict's monastery. There they joined hands and danced together for some time within sight of his followers, in an attempt to lead them into sin.

When the saint noticed this from his window, he began to fear that some of his younger monks might go astray. Convinced that the priest's hatred for him was the real cause of this attack, he let envy have its way, and, taking only a few monks with him, set out to find a new home. Before he left, he reorganized all the monasteries he had founded, appointing priors to assist in governing them, and adding some new members to the communities.

Hardly had the man of God made his humble escape from all this bitterness when almighty God struck the priest down with terrible vengeance. As he was standing on the balcony of his house congratulating himself on Benedict's departure, the structure suddenly collapsed, crushing him to death, though the rest of the building remained undamaged. This accident occurred before the saint was even ten miles away. His disciple Maurus immediately decided to send a messenger with the news and ask him to return, now that the priest who had caused him so much trouble was dead. Benedict was overcome with sorrow and regret on hearing this, for not only had his enemy been killed, but one of his own disciples had rejoiced over his death. And for showing pleasure in such a message he gave Maurus a penance to perform.

Peter: This whole account is really amazing. The water streaming from the rock reminds me of Moses, and the iron blade that rose from the bottom of the lake, of Eliseus. The walking on the water recalls St. Peter, the obedience of the raven, Elias, and the grief at the death of an enemy, David. This man must have been filled with the spirit of all the just.

Gregory: Actually, Peter, blessed Benedict possessed the Spirit of only one Person, the Savior who fills the hearts of all the faithful by granting them the fruits of His Redemption. For St. John says of Him, "There is one who enlightens every soul born into the world; he was the true light."[201] And again, "we have all received something out of his abundance."[202] Holy men never were able to hand on to others the miraculous powers which they received from God. Our Savior was the only one to give His followers the power to work signs and wonders, just as He alone could assure His enemies that He would give them the sign of the prophet Jonas. Seeing this sign fulfilled in His death, the proud looked on with scorn. The humble, who saw its complete fulfillment in His rising from the

dead, turned to Him with reverence and love. In this mystery, then, the proud beheld Him dying in disgrace, whereas the humble witnessed His triumph over death.

Peter: Now that you have finished explaining this, please tell me where the holy man settled after his departure. Do you know whether he performed any more miracles?

Gregory: Although he moved to a different place, Peter, his enemy remained the same. In fact, the assaults he had to endure after this were all the more violent, because the very Master of evil was fighting against him in open battle.

The fortified town of Cassino lies at the foot of a towering mountain that shelters it within its slope and stretches upward over a distance of nearly three miles.[203] On its summit stood a very old temple, in which the ignorant country people still worshipped Apollo as their pagan ancestors had done, and went on offering superstitious and idolatrous sacrifices in groves dedicated to various demons.

When the man of God arrived at this spot, he destroyed the idol, overturned the altar and cut down the trees in the sacred groves.[204] Then he turned the temple of Apollo into a chapel dedicated to St. Martin,[205] and where Apollo's altar had stood, he built a chapel in honor of St. John the Baptist. Gradually, the people of the countryside were won over to the true faith by his zealous preaching.

Such losses the ancient Enemy could not bear in silence. This time he did not appear to the saint in a dream or under a disguise, but met him face to face and objected fiercely to the outrages he had to endure. His shouts were so loud that the brethren heard him, too, although they were unable to see him. According to the saint's own description, the Devil had an appearance utterly revolting to human eyes. He was enveloped in

---

[201] John 1:9.

[202] John 1:16.

---

[203] St. Gregory is referring to the winding path that led up the mountain. The altitude of Monte Cassino is 1,500 feet.

[204] Monte Cassino is about 75 miles southeast of Rome. St. Benedict arrived there in 529. In addition to the pagan shrines mentioned by St. Gregory, there was also a very ancient fortress on the summit for the defense of the townspeople below and the surrounding plains. The Abbey of Monte Cassino was built entirely within the walls of the fortress and was for that reason known at first as the Citadel of Campania, as we learn from the full title of this book.

[205] St. Martin of Tours.

fire and, when he raged against the man of God, flames darted from his eyes and mouth. Everyone could hear what he was saying. First he called Benedict by name. Then, finding that the saint would not answer, he broke out in abusive language. "Benedict, Benedict, blessed Benedict!" he would begin, and then add, "You cursed Benedict! Cursed, not blessed! What do you want with me? Why are you tormenting me like this?"

From now on, Peter, as you can well imagine, the Devil fought against the man of God with renewed violence. But, contrary to his plans, all these attacks only supplied the saint with further opportunities for victory.

(9) One day while the monks were constructing a section of the abbey, they noticed a rock lying close at hand and decided to use it in the building. When two or three did not succeed in lifting it, others joined in to help. Yet it remained fixed in its place as though it was rooted to the ground. Then they were sure that the Devil himself was sitting on this stone and preventing them from moving it in spite of all their efforts. Faced with this difficulty, they asked Abbot Benedict to come and use his prayers to drive away the Devil who was holding down the rock. The saint began to pray as soon as he got there, and after he had finished and made the sign of the cross, the monks picked up the rock with such care that it seemed to have lost all its previous weight.

(10) The abbot then directed them to spade up the earth where the stone had been. When they had dug a little way into the ground they came upon a bronze idol, which they threw into the kitchen for the time being. Suddenly the kitchen appeared to be on fire and everyone felt that the entire building was going up in flames. The noise and commotion they made in their attempt to put out the blaze by pouring on buckets of water brought Benedict to the scene. Unable to see the fire which appeared so real to his monks, he quietly bowed his head in prayer and soon had opened their eyes to the foolish mistake they were making. Now, instead of the flames the evil spirit had devised, they once more saw the kitchen standing intact.

(11) On another occasion they were working on one of the walls that had to be built a little higher. The man of God was in his room at the time, praying, when the Devil appeared to him and remarked sarcastically that he was on his way to visit the brethren at their work. Benedict quickly sent them word to be on their guard against the evil spirit who would soon be with them. Just as they received his warning, the Devil overturned the wall, crushing under its ruins the body of a very young monk who was the son of a tax collector.

Unconcerned about the damaged wall in their grief and dismay over the loss of their brother, the monks hurried to Abbot Benedict to let him know of the dreadful accident. He told them to bring the mangled body to his room. It had to be carried in on a blanket, for the wall had not only broken the boy's arms and legs but had crushed all the bones in his body. The saint had the remains placed on the reed matting where he used to pray and after that told them all to leave. Then he closed the door and knelt down to offer his most earnest prayers to God. That very hour, to the astonishment of all, he sent the boy back to his work as sound and healthy as he had been before. Thus, in spite of the Devil's attempt to mock the man of God by causing this tragic death, the young monk was able to rejoin his brethren and help them finish the wall.

Meanwhile, Benedict began to manifest the spirit of prophecy by foretelling future events and by describing to those who were with him what they had done in his absence.

(12) It was a custom of the house, strictly observed as a matter of regular discipline, that monks away on business did not take food or drink outside the monastery. One day, a few of them went out on assignment which kept them occupied till rather late. They stopped for a meal at the house of a devout woman they knew in the neighborhood. On their return, when they presented themselves to the abbot for the usual blessing, he asked them where they had taken their meal.

"Nowhere," they answered.

"Why are you lying to me?" he said. "Did you not enter the house of this particular woman and eat these various foods and have so many cups to drink?"

On hearing him mention the woman's hospitality and exactly what she had given them to eat and drink, they clearly recalled the wrong they had done, fell trembling at his feet, and confessed their guilt. The man of God did not hesitate to pardon them, confident that they would do no further wrong in his absence, since they now realized he was always present with them in spirit.

(13) The monk Valentinian, mentioned earlier in our narrative, had a brother who was a very devout layman. Every year he visited the abbey in order to get Benedict's blessing and see his brother. On the way he always used to fast. Now, one time as he was making this journey he was joined by another traveler who had brought some food along.

"Come," said the stranger after some time had passed, "let us have something to eat before we become too fatigued."

"I am sorry," the devout layman replied. "I always fast on my way to visit Abbot Benedict."

After that the traveler was quiet for a while. But when they had walked along some distance together, he repeated his suggestion. Still mindful of his good resolve, Valentinian's brother again refused. His companion did not insist and once more agreed to accompany him a little further without eating.

Then, after they had covered a great distance together and were very tired from the long hours of walking, they came upon a meadow and a spring. The whole setting seemed ideal for a much needed rest. "Look," said the stranger, "water and a meadow! What a delightful spot for us to have some refreshments! A little rest will give us strength to finish our journey without any discomfort."

It was such an attractive sight and this third invitation sounded so appealing that the devout layman was completely won over and stopped there to eat with his companion. Toward evening he arrived at the monastery and was presented to the abbot. As soon as he asked for the blessing, however, the holy man reproved him for his conduct on the journey. "How is it," he said, "that the evil spirit who spoke with you in the person of your traveling companion could not persuade you to do his will the first and second time he tried, but succeeded on his third attempt?" At this Valentinian's brother fell at Benedict's feet and admitted the weakness of his will. The thought that even from such a distance the saint had witnessed the wrong he had done filled him with shame and remorse.

Peter: This proves that the servant of God possessed the spirit of Eliseus. He, too, was present with one of his followers who was far away.

Gregory: If you will listen a little longer, Peter, I have an incident to tell you that is even more astonishing. (14) Once while the Goths were still in power, Totila their king happened to be marching in the direction of Benedict's monastery.[206] When still some distance away, he halted with his troops and sent a messenger ahead to announce his coming, for he had heard that the man of God possessed the gift of prophecy. As soon as he received word that he would be welcomed, the crafty king decided to put the saint's prophetic powers to a test. He had Riggo, his sword-bearer, fitted out with royal robes and riding boots and directed him to go in this disguise to the man of God. Vul, Ruderic, and Blidin, three men from his own bodyguard, were to march at his side as if he really were king of the Goths. To supplement these marks of kingship, Totila also provided him with a sword-bearer and other attendants.

As Riggo entered the monastery grounds in his kingly robes and with all his attendants, Benedict caught sight of him and as soon as the company came within hearing called out from where he sat, "Son, lay aside the robes you are wearing," he said. "Lay them aside. They do not belong to you." Aghast at seeing what a great man he had tried to mock, Riggo sank to the ground, and with him all the members of his company. Even after they had risen to their feet they did not dare approach the saint, but hurried back in alarm to tell their king how quickly they had been detected.

(15) King Totila then went to the monastery in person. The moment he noticed the man of God sitting at a distance, he was afraid to come any closer and fell down prostrate where he was. Two or three times Benedict asked him to rise. When Totila still hesitated to do so in his presence, the servant of Christ walked over to him and with his own hands helped him from the ground. Then he rebuked the king for his crimes and briefly foretold everything that was going to happen to him. "You are the cause of many evils," he said. "You have caused many in the past. Put an end now to your wickedness. You will enter Rome and cross the sea. You will have nine more years to rule, and in the tenth year you will die."

Terrified at these words, the king asked for a blessing and went away. From that time on he was less cruel. Not long after, he went to Rome and then crossed over to Sicily. In the tenth year of his reign he lost his kingdom and his life as almighty God had decreed.

There is also a story about the bishop of Canosa,[207] who made regular visits to the abbey and stood high in Benedict's esteem because of his saintly life. Once while they were discussing Totila's invasion and the downfall of Rome, the bishop said, "The city will be destroyed by this king and left without a single inhabitant."

"No," Benedict assured him, "Rome will not be destroyed by the barbarians. It will be shaken by tempests

---

[206] The Ostrogoths were a Germanic people from eastern Europe who had established their kingdom in Italy under Theodoric in 493. King Totila (541–552) was fighting to re-establish Gothic power there after it had virtually been broken by Emperor Justinian's armies during the previous decade. The following events probably took place when Totila was marching on Naples, which he captured in 543. See doc. 5, above, for more on the Ostrogoths.

[207] In southeastern Italy, about 120 miles from Monte Cassino.

and lightnings, hurricanes and earthquakes, until finally it lies buried in its own ruins."

The meaning of this prophecy is perfectly clear to us now. We have watched the walls of Rome crumble and have seen its homes in ruins, its churches destroyed by violent storms, and its dilapidated buildings surrounded by their own debris.

Benedict's disciple Honoratus, who told me about the prophecy, admits he did not hear it personally, but he assures me that some of his brethren gave him this account of it.

(16) At about the same time there was a cleric from the church at Aquino[208] who was being tormented by an evil spirit. Constantius, his saintly bishop, had already sent him to the shrines of various martyrs in the hope that he would be cured. But the holy martyrs did not grant him this favor, preferring instead to reveal the wonderful gifts of the servant of God.

As soon as the cleric was brought to him, Benedict drove out the evil spirit with fervent prayers to Christ. Before sending him back to Aquino, however, he told him to abstain from meat thereafter and never to advance to sacred orders. "If you ignore this warning," he added, "and present yourself for ordination, you will find yourself once more in the power of Satan."

The cleric left completely cured, and as long as his previous torments were still fresh in his mind he did exactly as the man of God had ordered. Then with the passing of years, all his seniors in the clerical state died, and he had to watch newly ordained young men moving ahead of him in rank. Finally, he pretended to have forgotten about the saint's warning and, disregarding it, presented himself for ordination. Instantly he was seized by the Devil and tormented mercilessly until he died.

Peter: The servant of God must even have been aware of the hidden designs of Providence, to have realized that this cleric had been handed over to Satan to keep him from aspiring to holy orders.

Gregory: Is there any reason why a person who has observed the commandments of God should not also know God's secret designs? "The man who unites himself to the Lord becomes one spirit with him,"[209] we read in sacred Scripture.

Peter: If everyone who unites himself to the Lord becomes one spirit with him, what does the renowned apostle mean when he asks, "Who has ever understood the Lord's thoughts, or been his counselor?"[210] It hardly seems possible to be one spirit with a person without knowing his thoughts.

Gregory: Holy men do know the Lord's thoughts, Peter, in so far as they are one with Him. This is clear from the apostle's words, "Who else can know a man's thoughts, except the man's own spirit that is within him? So no one else can know God's thoughts but the Spirit of God."[211] To show that he actually knew God's thoughts, St. Paul added: "And what we have received is no spirit of worldly wisdom; it is the Spirit that comes from God."[212] And again: "No eye has seen, no ear has heard, no human heart conceived, the welcome God has prepared for those who love him. To us, then, God has made a revelation of it through his Spirit."[213]

Peter: If it is true that God's thoughts are revealed to the apostle by the Holy Spirit, how could he introduce his statement with the words, "How deep is the mine of God's wisdom, of his knowledge; how inscrutable are his judgments, how undiscoverable his ways!"[214] Another difficulty just occurred to me now as I was speaking. In addressing the Lord, David the Prophet declares, "With my lips I have pronounced all the judgments of thy mouth."[215] Surely it is a greater achievement to express one's knowledge than merely to possess it. How is it, then, that St. Paul calls the judgments of God inscrutable, whereas David says he knows them all and has even pronounced them with his lips?

Gregory: I already gave a brief reply to both of these objections when I told you that holy men know God's thoughts in so far as they are one with Him. For all who follow the Lord wholeheartedly are living in spiritual union with Him. As long as they are still weighed down with a perishable body, however, they are not actually united to Him. It is only to the extent that they are one with God that they know His hidden judgments. In so far as they are not yet one with Him, they do not know them. Since even holy men cannot fully grasp the secret designs of God during this present life, they call His judgments inscrutable. At the same time, they understand His judgments and can even pronounce them with their lips; for they keep their hearts united to God by dwelling

[208] About five miles from Monte Cassino.

[209] 1 Corinthians 6:17.

[210] 1 Corinthians 2:16.

[211] 1 Corinthians 2:11.

[212] 1 Corinthians 2:13.

[213] 1 Corinthians 2:9.

[214] Romans 11:33.

[215] Psalm 119:13.

continually on the words of holy Scripture and on such private revelations as they may receive, until they grasp His meaning. In other words, they do not know the judgments which God conceals but only those which He reveals. That is why, after declaring, "With my lips I have pronounced all the judgments," the Prophet immediately adds the phrase, "of thy mouth," as if to say, "I can know and pronounce only the judgments You have spoken to me. Those You leave unspoken must remain hidden from our minds."[216] So the Prophet and the apostle are in full agreement. God's decisions are truly unfathomable. But, once His mouth has made them known, they can also be proclaimed by human lips. What God has spoken man can know. Of the thoughts He has kept secret man can know nothing.

Peter: That is certainly a reasonable solution to the difficulties that I raised. If you know any other miraculous events in this man's life, would you continue with them now?

Gregory: (17) Under the direction of Abbot Benedict a nobleman named Theoprobus had embraced monastic life. Because of his exemplary life he enjoyed the saint's personal friendship and confidence. One day, on entering Benedict's room, he found him weeping bitterly. After he had waited for some time and there was still no end to the abbot's tears, he asked what was causing him such sorrow, for he was not weeping as he usually did at prayer, but with deep sighs and lamentation.

"Almighty God has decreed that this entire monastery and everything I have provided for the community shall fall into the hands of the barbarians," the saint replied. "It was only with the greatest difficulty that I could prevail upon Him to spare the lives of its members."

This was the prophecy he made to Theoprobus, and we have seen its fulfillment in the recent destruction of his abbey by the Lombards.[217] They came at night while the community was asleep and plundered the entire monastery, without capturing a single monk. In this way God fulfilled His promise to Benedict, His faithful servant. He allowed the barbarians to destroy the monastery, but safeguarded the lives of the religious. Here you can see how the man of God resembled St. Paul, who had the consolation of seeing everyone with him escape alive from the storm, while the ship and all its cargo were lost.

(18) Exhilaratus, a fellow Roman who, as you know, later became a monk was once sent by his master to Abbot Benedict with two wooden flasks of wine. He delivered only one of them, however; the other he hid along the way. Benedict, who could observe even what was done in his absence, thanked him for the flask, but warned him as he turned to go: "Son, be sure not to drink from the flask you have hidden away. Tilt it carefully and you will see what is inside."

Exhilaratus left in shame and confusion and went back to the spot, still wishing to verify the saint's words. As he tilted the flask a serpent crawled out, and at the sight of it he was filled with horror for his misdeed.

(19) Not far from the monastery was a village largely inhabited by people the saintly Benedict had converted from the worship of idols and instructed in the true faith. There were seven nuns living there too, and he used to send one of his monks down to give them spiritual conferences.

After one of these instructions they presented the monk with a few handkerchiefs, which he accepted and hid away in his habit. As soon as he got back to the abbey he received a stern reproof. "How is it," the abbot asked him, "that evil has found its way into your heart?" Taken completely by surprise, the monk did not understand why he was being rebuked, for he had completely forgotten about the handkerchiefs. "Was I not present," the saint continued, "when you accepted those handkerchiefs from the handmaids of God and hid them away in your habit?" The offender instantly fell at Benedict's feet, confessed his fault, and gave up the present he had received.

(20) Once when the saintly abbot was taking his evening meal, a young monk whose father was a high-ranking official happened to be holding the lamp for him. As he stood at the abbot's table the spirit of pride began to stir in his heart. "Who is this," he thought to himself, "that I should have to stand here holding the lamp for him while he is eating? Who am I to be serving him?"

Turning to him at once, Benedict gave the monk a sharp reprimand. "Brother," he said, "sign your heart with the sign of the cross. What are you saying? Sign your heart!" Then, calling the others together, he had one of them take the lamp instead, and told the murmurer to sit down by himself and be quiet. Later, when asked what he had done wrong, the monk explained how he had given in to the spirit of pride and silently murmured against the man of God. At this the brethren all realized that nothing could be kept secret from their holy abbot, since he could hear even the unspoken sentiments of the heart.

---

[216] Psalm 119:13.

[217] Monte Cassino was destroyed by Duke Zotto in 589 and was not rebuilt until 720, under Abbot Petronax.

(21) During a time of famine the severe shortage of food was causing a great deal of suffering in Campania. At Benedict's monastery the entire grain supply had been used up and nearly all the bread was gone as well. In fact, when mealtime came, only five loaves could be found to set before the community. Noticing how downcast they were, the saint gently reproved them for their lack of trust in God and at the same time tried to raise their dejected spirits with a comforting assurance. "Why are you so depressed at the lack of bread!" he asked. "What if today there is only a little? Tomorrow you will have more than you need."

The next day 200 measures of flour were found in sacks at the gate of the monastery, but no one ever discovered whose services almighty God had employed in bringing them there. When they saw what had happened, the monks were filled with gratitude and learned from this miracle that even in their hour of need they must not lose faith in the bountiful goodness of God.

Peter: Are we to believe that the spirit of prophecy remained with the servant of God at all times, or did he receive it only on special occasion?

Gregory: The spirit of prophecy does not enlighten the minds of the prophets constantly, Peter. We read in sacred Scripture that the Holy Spirit breathes where He pleases, and we should also realize that He breathes when He pleases. For example, when King David asked whether he could build a temple, the Prophet Nathan gave his consent, but later had to withdraw it. And Eliseus once found a woman in tears without knowing the reason for her grief. This is why he told his servant who was trying to interfere, "Let her alone, for her soul is in anguish and the Lord has hidden it from me and has not told me."

All this reflects God's boundless wisdom and love. By granting these men the spirit of prophecy He raises their minds above the world, and by withdrawing it again He safeguards their humility. When the spirit of prophecy is with them they learn what they are by God's mercy. When the spirit leaves them they discover what they are of themselves.

Peter: This convincing argument leaves no room for doubt about the truth of what you say. Please resume your narrative now, if you recall any other incidents in the life of the blessed Benedict.

Gregory: (22) A Catholic layman once asked him to found a monastery on his estate at Terracina. The servant of God readily consented and, after selecting several of his monks for this undertaking, appointed one of them abbot and another his assistant. Before they left he specified a day on which he would come to show them where to build the chapel, the refectory, a house for guests, and the other buildings they would need. Then he gave them his blessing.

After their arrival at Terracina they looked forward eagerly to the day he had set for his visit and prepared to receive the monks who would accompany him. Before dawn of the appointed day, Benedict appeared in a dream to the new abbot as well as to his prior and showed them exactly where each section of the monastery was to stand. In the morning they told each other what they had seen, but, instead of putting their entire trust in the vision, they kept waiting for the promised visit. When the day passed without any word from Benedict, they returned to him disappointed. "Father," they said, "we were waiting for you to show us where to build, as you assured us you would, but you did not come."

"What do you mean?" he replied. "Did I not come as I promised?"

"When?" they asked.

"Did I not appear to both of you in a dream as you slept and indicate where each building was to stand? Go back and build as you were directed in the vision."

They returned to Terracina, filled with wonder, and constructed the monastery according to the plans he had revealed to them.

Peter: I wish you would explain how Benedict could possibly travel that distance and then in a vision give these monks directions which they could hear and understand while they were asleep.

Gregory: What is there in this incident that should raise a doubt in your mind, Peter? Everyone knows that the soul is far more agile than the body. Yet we have it on the authority of holy Scripture that the Prophet Habacuc was lifted from Judea to Chaldea in an instant, so that he might share his dinner with the Prophet Daniel, and presently found himself back in Judea again. If Habacuc could cover such a distance in a brief moment to take a meal to his fellow Prophet, is it not understandable that Abbot Benedict could go in spirit to his sleeping brethren with the information they required? As the Prophet came in body with food for the body, Benedict came in spirit to promote the life of the soul.

Peter: Your words seem to smooth away all my doubts. Could you tell me now what this saint was like in his everyday speech?

Gregory: (23) There was a trace of the marvelous in nearly every thing he said, Peter, and his words never failed to take effect because his heart was fixed in God. Even when he uttered a simple threat that was indefinite and conditional, it was just as decisive as a final verdict.

Some distance from the abbey two women of noble birth were leading the religious life in their own home. A God-fearing layman was kind enough to bring them what they needed from the outside world. Unfortunately, as is sometimes the case, their character stood in sharp contrast to the nobility of their birth, and they were too conscious of their former importance to practice true humility toward others. Even under the restraining influence of religious life they still had not learned to control their tongues, and the good layman who served them so faithfully was often provoked at their harsh criticisms. After putting up with their insults for a long time, he went to blessed Benedict and told him how inconsiderate they were. The man of God immediately warned them to curb their sharp tongues and added that he would have to excommunicate them if they did not. This sentence of excommunication was not actually pronounced, therefore, but only threatened.

A short time afterward the two nuns died without any sign of amendment and were buried in their parish church. Whenever Mass was celebrated, their old nurse, who regularly made an offering for them, noticed that each time the deacon announced, "The non-communicants must now leave," the nuns rose from their tombs and went outside.[218] This happened repeatedly, until one day she recalled the warning Benedict had given them while they were still alive, when he threatened to deprive them of communion with the Church if they kept on speaking so uncharitably.

The grief-stricken nurse had Abbot Benedict informed of what was happening. He sent her messengers back with an oblation and said, "Have this offered up for their souls during the Holy Sacrifice, and they will be freed from the sentence of excommunication." The offering was made and after that the nuns were not seen leaving the church any more at the deacon's dismissal of the non-communicants. Evidently, they had been admitted to communion with our blessed Lord in answer to the prayers of His servant Benedict.

Peter: Is it not extraordinary that souls already judged at God's invisible tribunal could be pardoned by a man who was still living in the mortal flesh, however holy and revered he may have been?

Gregory: What of Peter the Apostle? Was he not still living in the flesh when he heard the words, "Whatever thou shalt bind on earth shall be bound in heaven, and whatever thou shalt loose on earth shall be loosed in heaven"? All those who govern the Church in matters of faith and morals exercise the same power of binding and loosing that he received. In fact, the Creator's very purpose in coming down from heaven to earth was to impart to earthly man this heavenly power. It was when God was made flesh for man's sake that flesh received its undeserved prerogative of sitting in judgment even over spirits. What raised our weakness to these heights was the descent of an almighty God to the depths of our own helplessness.

Peter: Your lofty words are certainly in harmony with these mighty deeds.

Gregory: (24) One time, a young monk who was too attached to his parents left the monastery without asking for the abbot's blessing and went home. No sooner had he arrived there he died. The day after his burial his body was discovered lying outside the grave. His parents had him buried again, but on the following day found the body unburied as before. In their dismay they hurried to the saintly abbot and pleaded with him to forgive the boy for what he had done. Moved by their tears, Benedict gave them a consecrated Host with his own hands. "When you get back," he said, "place this sacred Host upon his breast and bury him once more."[219] They did so, and thereafter his body remained in the earth without being disturbed again.

Now, Peter, you can appreciate how pleasing this holy man was in God's sight. Not even the earth would retain the young monk's body until he had been reconciled with blessed Benedict.

Peter: I assure you I do. It is really amazing.

Gregory: (25) One of Benedict's monks had set his fickle heart on leaving the monastery. Time and again the man of God pointed out how wrong this was and tried to reason with him but without any success. The monk persisted obstinately in his request to be released. Finally, Benedict lost patience with him and told him to go.

Hardly had he left the monastery grounds when he noticed to his horror that a dragon with gaping jaws was

---

[218] The deacon's words applied to the unbaptized and the excommunicated, who were not allowed to remain for the Mass of the Faithful. Their dismissal took place after the Gospel and sermon.

[219] During the first centuries laypeople were permitted to handle the Blessed Sacrament and even keep it in their homes. The practice of placing a consecrated Host on the bodies of those who died in union with the Church was quite common in St. Benedict's time.

blocking his way. "Help! Help!" he cried out, trembling, "or the dragon will devour me." His brethren ran to the rescue, but could see nothing of the dragon. Still breathless with fright, the monk was only too glad to accompany them back to the abbey. Once safe within its walls, he promised never to leave again. And this time he kept his word, for Benedict's prayers had enabled him to see with his own eyes the invisible dragon that had been leading him astray.

(26) I must tell you now of an event I heard from the distinguished Anthony. One of his father's servants had been seized with a severe case of leprosy. His hair was already falling out and his skin growing thick and swollen. The fatal progress of the disease was unmistakable. In this condition he was sent to the man of God, who instantly restored him to his previous state of health.

(27) Benedict's disciple Peregrinus tells of a Catholic layman who was heavily burdened with debt and felt that his only hope was to disclose the full extent of his misfortune to the man of God. So he went to him and explained that he was being constantly tormented by a creditor to whom he owed twelve gold pieces.

"I am very sorry," the saintly abbot replied. "I do not have that much money in my possession." Then, to comfort the poor man in his need, he added, "I cannot give you anything today, but come back again the day after tomorrow."

In the meantime the saint devoted himself to prayer with his accustomed fervor. When the debtor returned, the monks, to their surprise, found thirteen gold pieces lying on top of a chest that was filled with grain. Benedict had the money brought down at once. "Here, take these," he told him. "Use twelve to pay your creditor and keep the thirteenth for yourself."

I should like to return now to some other events I learned from the saint's four disciples who were mentioned at the beginning of this book.

There was a man who had become so embittered with envy that he tried to kill his rival by secretly poisoning his drink. Though the poison did not prove fatal, it produced horrible blemishes resembling leprosy, which spread over the entire body of the unfortunate victim. In this condition he was brought to the servant of God, who cured the disease with a touch of his hand and sent him home in perfect health.

(28) While Campania was suffering from famine, the holy abbot distributed the food supplies of his monastery to the needy until there was nothing left in the storeroom but a little oil in a glass vessel. One day, when Agapitus, a subdeacon, came to beg for some oil, the man of God

ordered the little that remained to be given to him, for he wanted to distribute everything he had to the poor and thus store up riches in heaven.

The cellarer listened to the abbot's command, but did not carry it out. After a while, Benedict asked him whether he had given Agapitus the oil. "No," he replied, "I did not. If I had, there would be none left for the community." This angered the man of God, who wanted nothing to remain in the monastery through disobedience, and he told another monk to take the glass with the oil in it and throw it out the window. This time he was obeyed.

Even though it struck against the jagged rocks of the cliff just below the window, the glass remained intact as if it had not been thrown at all. It was still unbroken and none of the oil had spilled. Abbot Benedict had the glass brought back and given to the subdeacon. Then he sent for the rest of the community and in their presence rebuked the disobedient monk for his pride and lack of faith.

(29) After that the saint knelt down to pray with his brethren. In the room where they were kneeling there happened to be an empty oil-cask that was covered with a lid. In the course of his prayer the cask gradually filled with oil and the lid started to float on top of it. The next moment the oil was running down the sides of the cask and covering the floor. As soon as he was aware of this, Benedict ended his prayer and the oil stopped flowing. Then, turning to the monk who had shown himself disobedient and wanting in confidence, he urged him again to strive to grow in faith and humility.

This wholesome reprimand filled the cellarer with shame. Besides inviting him to trust in God, the saintly abbot had clearly shown by his miracle what marvelous power such trust possesses. In the future who could doubt any of his promises? Had he not in a moment's time replaced the little oil still left in the glass with a cask that was full to overflowing?

(30) One day, on his way to the Chapel of St. John at the highest point of the mountain, Benedict met the ancient Enemy of mankind, disguised as a veterinarian with medicine horn and triple shackle.

"Where are you going?" the saint asked him.

"To your brethren," he replied with scorn. "I am bringing them some medicine."

Benedict continued on his way and after his prayer hurried back. Meanwhile, the evil spirit entered one of the older monks whom he found drawing water and had thrown him to the ground in a violent convulsion. When the man of God caught sight of this old brother in such torment, he merely struck him on the cheek, and the evil spirit was promptly driven out, never to return.

Peter: I should like to know whether he always obtained these great miracles through fervent prayer. Did he ever perform them at will?

Gregory: It is quite common for those who devoutly cling to God to work miracles in both of these ways, Peter, either through their prayers or by their own power, as circumstances may dictate. Since we read in St. John that "all those who did welcome him he empowered to become the children of God," why should we be surprised if those who are the children of God use this power to work signs and wonders? Holy men can undoubtedly perform miracles in either of the ways you mentioned, as is clear from the fact that St. Peter raised Tabitha to life by praying over her, and by a simple rebuke brought death to Ananias and Saphira for their lies. Scripture does not say that he prayed for their death, but only that he reprimanded them for the crime they had committed. Now, if St. Peter could restore to life by a prayer and deprive of life by a rebuke, is there any reason to doubt that the saints can perform miracles by their own power as well as through their prayers?

I am now going to consider two instances in the life of God's faithful servant Benedict. One of them shows the efficacy of his prayer; the other, the marvelous powers that were his by God's gift.

(31) In the days of King Totila one of the Goths, the Arian heretic Zalla, had been persecuting devout Catholics everywhere with the utmost cruelty. No monk or cleric who fell into his hands ever escaped alive. In his merciless brutality and greed he was one day lashing and torturing a farmer whose money he was after. Unable to bear it any longer, the poor man tried to save his life by telling Zalla that all his money was in Abbot Benedict's keeping. He only hoped his tormentor would believe him and put a stop to his brutality. When Zalla heard this, he did stop beating him, but immediately bound his hands together with a heavy cord. Then, mounting his horse, he forced the farmer to walk ahead of him and lead the way to this Benedict who was keeping his money.

The helpless prisoner had no choice but to conduct him to the abbey. When they arrived, they found the man of God sitting alone in front of the entrance reading. "This is the Abbot Benedict I meant," he told the infuriated Goth behind him.

Imagining that this holy man could be frightened as readily as anyone else, Zalla glared at him with eyes full of hate and shouted harshly, "Get up! Do you hear? Get up and give back the money this man left with you!" At the sound of this angry voice the man of God looked up from his reading and, as he glanced toward Zalla, noticed the farmer with his hands bound together. The moment he caught sight of the cord that held them, it fell miraculously to the ground. Human hands could never have unfastened it so quickly.

Stunned at the hidden power that had set his prisoner free, Zalla fell trembling to his knees and, bending his stubborn, cruel neck at the saint's feet, begged for his prayers. Without rising from his place, Benedict called for his monks and had them take Zalla inside for some food and drink. After that he urged him to give up his heartless cruelty. Zalla went away thoroughly humbled and made no more demands on this farmer who had been freed from his bonds by a mere glance from the man of God.

So you see, Peter, what I said is true. Those who devote themselves wholeheartedly to the service of God can sometimes work miracles by their own power. Blessed Benedict checked the fury of a dreaded Goth without even rising to his feet, and with a mere glance unfastened the heavy cord that bound the hands of an innocent man. The very speed with which he performed this marvel is proof enough that he did it by his own power.

And now, here is a remarkable miracle that was the result of his prayer. (32) One day, when he was out working in the fields with his monks, a farmer came to the monastery carrying in his arms the lifeless body of his son. Broken-hearted at his loss, he begged to see the saintly abbot and, on learning that he was at work in the fields, left the dead body at the entrance of the monastery and hurried off to find him. By then the abbot was already returning from his work. The moment the farmer caught sight of him he cried out, "Give me back my son! Give me back my son!"

Benedict stopped when he heard this. "But I have not taken your son from you, have I?" he asked.

The boy's father only replied, "He is dead. Come! Bring him back to life."

Deeply grieved by his words, the man of God turned to his disciples. "Stand back, brethren!" he said. "Stand back! Such a miracle is beyond our power. The holy apostles are the only ones who can raise the dead. Why are you so eager to accept what is impossible for us?"

But overwhelming sorrow compelled the man to keep on pleading. He even declared with an oath that he would not leave until Benedict restored his son to life. The saint then asked him where the body was. "At the entrance to the monastery," he answered.

When Benedict arrived there with his monks, he knelt down beside the child's body and bent over it. Then, rising, he lifted his hands to heaven in prayer. "O Lord," he said, "do not consider my sins but the faith of this man who is asking to see his son alive again, and restore to this body the soul You have taken from it."

His prayer was hardly over when the child's whole body began once more to throb with life. No one present there could doubt that this sudden stirring was due to a heavenly intervention. Benedict then took the little boy by the hand and gave him back to his father alive and well.

Obviously, Peter, he did not have the power to work this miracle himself. Otherwise he would not have begged for it prostrate in prayer.

Peter: The way facts bear out your words convinces me that everything you have said is true. Will you please tell me now whether holy men can always carry out their wishes, or at least obtain through prayer whatever they desire?

Gregory: (33) Peter, will there ever be a holier man in this world than St. Paul? Yet he prayed three times to the Lord about the sting in his flesh and could not obtain his wish. In this connection I must tell you how the saintly Benedict once had a wish he was unable to fulfill.

His sister Scholastica, who had been consecrated to God in early childhood, used to visit with him once a year. On these occasions he would go down to meet her in a house belonging to the monastery, a short distance from the entrance.

For this particular visit he joined her there with a few of his disciples and they spent the whole day singing God's praises and conversing about the spiritual life. When darkness was setting in, they took their meal together and continued their conversation at table until it was quite late. Then the holy nun said to him, "Please do not leave me tonight, brother. Let us keep on talking about the joys of heaven till morning."

"What are you saying, sister?" he replied. "You know I cannot stay away from the monastery."

The sky was so clear at the time that there was not a cloud in sight. At her brother's refusal Scholastica folded her hands on the table and rested her head upon them in earnest prayer. When she looked up again, there was a sudden burst of lightning and thunder, accompanied by such a downpour that Benedict and his companions were unable to set a foot outside the door.

By shedding a flood of tears while she prayed, this holy nun had darkened the cloudless sky with a heavy rain. The storm began as soon as her prayer was over. In fact, the two coincided so closely that the thunder was already resounding as she raised her head from the table. The very instant she ended her prayer the rain poured down.

Realizing that he could not return to the monastery in this terrible storm, Benedict complained bitterly, "God forgive you, sister!" he said. "What have you done?"

Scholastica simply answered, "When I appealed to you, you would not listen to me. So I turned to my God and He heard my prayer. Leave now if you can. Leave me here and go back to your monastery."

This, of course, he could not do. He had no choice now but to stay, in spite of his unwillingness. They spent the entire night together and both of them derived great profit from the holy thoughts they exchanged about the interior life.

Here you have my reason for saying that this holy man was once unable to obtain what he desired. If we consider his point of view, we can readily see that he wanted the sky to remain as clear as it was when he came down from the monastery. But this wish of his was thwarted by a miracle almighty God performed in answer to a woman's prayer. We need not be surprised that in this instance she proved mightier than her brother; she had been looking forward so long to this visit. Do we not read in St. John that God is love? Surely it is no more than right that her influence was greater than his, since hers was the greater love.

Peter: I find this discussion very enjoyable.

Gregory: (34) The next morning Scholastica returned to her convent and Benedict to his monastery. Three days later as he stood in his room looking up toward the sky, he beheld his sister's soul leaving her body and entering the court of heaven in the form of a dove.

Overjoyed at her eternal glory, he gave thanks to God in hymns of praise. Then, after informing his brethren of her death, he sent some of them to bring her body to the monastery and bury it in the tomb he had prepared for himself. The bodies of these two were now to share a common resting place, just as in life their souls had always been one in God.

(35) At another time, the deacon Servandus came to see the servant of God on one of his regular visits. He was abbot of the monastery in Campania that had been built by the late Senator Liberius, and always welcomed an opportunity to discuss with Benedict the truths of eternity, for he, too, was a man of deep spiritual understanding. In speaking of their hopes and longings they were able to taste in advance the heavenly food that was not yet fully theirs to enjoy. When it was time to retire for the night, Benedict went to his room on the second floor of the tower, leaving Servandus in the one below, which was connected with his own by a stairway. Their disciples slept in the large building facing the tower.

Long before the night office began, the man of God was standing at his window, where he watched and prayed while the rest were asleep. In the dead of night he suddenly beheld a flood of light shining down from above more brilliant than the sun, and with it every trace of darkness cleared away. Another remarkable sight followed. According to his own description, the whole world was gathered up before his eyes in what appeared to be a single ray of light. As he gazed at all this dazzling display, he saw the soul of Germanus, the Bishop of Capua, being carried by angels up to heaven in a ball of fire.

Wishing to have someone else witness this great marvel, he called out for Servandus, repeating his name two or three times in a loud voice. As soon as he heard the saint's call, Servandus rushed to the upper room and was just in time to catch a final glimpse of the miraculous light. He remained speechless with wonder as Benedict described everything that had taken place. Then without any delay the man of God instructed the devout Theoprobus to go to Cassino and have a messenger sent to Capua that same night to find out what had happened to Germanus. In carrying out these instructions the messenger discovered that the revered bishop was already dead. When he asked for further details, he learned that his death had occurred at the very time blessed Benedict saw him carried into heaven.

Peter: What an astounding miracle! I hardly know what to think when I hear you say that he saw the whole world gathered up before his eyes in what appeared to be a single ray of light. I have never had such an experience. How is it possible for anyone to see the whole universe at a glance?

Gregory: Keep this well in mind, Peter. All creation is bound to appear small to a soul that sees the Creator. Once it beholds a little of His light, it finds all creatures small indeed. The light of holy contemplation enlarges and expands the mind in God until it stands above the world. In fact, the soul that sees Him rises even above itself, and as it is drawn upward in His light all its inner powers unfold. Then, when it looks down from above, it sees how small everything is that was beyond its grasp before.

Now, Peter, how else was it possible for this man to behold the ball of fire and watch the angels on their return to heaven except with light from God? Why should it surprise us, then, that he could see the whole world gathered up before him after this inner light had lifted him so far above the world? Of course, in saying that the world was gathered up before his eyes I do not mean that heaven and earth grew small, but that his spirit was enlarged. Absorbed as he was in God, it was now easy for him to see all that lay beneath God. In the light outside

that was shining before his eyes, there was a brightness which reached into his mind and lifted his spirit heavenward, showing him the insignificance of all that lies below.

Peter: My difficulty in understanding you has proved of real benefit, the explanation it led to was so thorough. Now that you have cleared up this problem for me, would you return once more to your account of blessed Benedict's life?

Gregory: (36) I should like to tell you much more about this saintly abbot, but I am purposely passing over some of his miraculous deeds in my eagerness to take up those of others. There is one more point, however, I want to call to your attention. With all the renown he gained by his numerous miracles, the holy man was no less outstanding for the wisdom of his teaching. He wrote a Rule for Monks that is remarkable for its discretion and its clarity of language. Anyone who wishes to know more about his life and character can discover in his Rule exactly what he was like as an abbot, for his life could not have differed from his teaching.

(37) In the year that was to be his last, the man of God foretold the day of his holy death to a number of his disciples. In mentioning it to some who were with him in the monastery, he bound them to strict secrecy. Some others, however, who were stationed elsewhere he only informed of the special sign they would receive at the time of his death.

Six days before he died he gave orders for his tomb to be opened. Almost immediately he was seized with a violent fever that rapidly wasted his remaining strength. Each day his condition grew worse until finally, on the sixth day, he had his disciples carry him into the chapel, where he received the Body and Blood of our Lord to gain strength for his approaching end. Then, supporting his weakened body on the arms of his brethren, he stood with his hands raised to heaven and as he prayed he breathed his last.

That day two monks, one of them at the monastery, the other some distance away, received the very same revelation. They both saw a magnificent road covered with rich carpeting and glittering with thousands of lights. From his monastery it stretched eastward in a straight line until it reached up into heaven. And there in the brightness stood a man of majestic appearance, who asked them, "Do you know who passed this way?"

"No," they replied.

"This," he told them, "is the road taken by blessed Benedict, the Lord's beloved, when he went to heaven."

Thus, while the brethren who were with Benedict witnessed his death, those who were absent knew about it through the sign he had promised them. His body was laid to rest in the Chapel of St. John the Baptist, which he had built to replace the altar of Apollo.

(38) Even in the cave at Subiaco, where he had lived before, this holy man still works numerous miracles for people who turn to him with faith and confidence. The incident I am going to relate happened only recently.

A woman who had completely lost her mind was roaming day and night over hills and valleys, through forests and fields, resting only when she was utterly exhausted. One day, in the course of her aimless wanderings, she strayed into the saint's cave and rested there without the least idea of where she was. The next morning she woke up entirely cured and left the cave without even a trace of her former affliction. After that she remained free from it for the rest of her life.

Peter: How is it that, as a rule, even the martyrs in their care for us do not grant the same great favors through their bodily remains as they do through their other relics? We find them so often performing more outstanding miracles away from their burial places.

Gregory: There is no doubt, Peter, that the holy martyrs can perform countless miracles where their bodies rest. And they do so in behalf of all who pray there with a pure intention. In places where their bodies do not actually lie buried, however, there is danger that those whose faith is weak may doubt their presence and their power to answer prayers. Consequently, it is in these places that they must perform still greater miracles. But faith in God is strong earns all the more m faith, for he realizes that the martyrs are prese his prayers even though their bodies happen to elsewhere.

It was precisely to increase the faith of His disciples that the eternal Truth told them, "If I do not go, the Advocate will not come to you." Now certainly the Holy Spirit, the Advocate, is ever proceeding from the Father and the Son. Why, then, should the Son say He will go in order that the Spirit may come, when, actually, the Spirit never leaves Him? The point is that as long as the disciples could see our Lord in His human flesh they would want to keep on seeing Him with their bodily eyes. With good reason, therefore, did He tell them, "If I do not go, the Advocate will not come." What He really meant was, "I cannot teach you spiritual love unless I remove my body from your sight; as long as you continue to see me with your bodily eyes you will never learn to love me spiritually."

Peter: That is a very satisfying explanation.

Gregory: Let us interrupt our discussion for a while. If we are going to take up the miracles of other holy men, we shall need a short period of silence to rest our voices.

Question for Study

Monasticism can be broadly defined as a movement to dedicate one's entire life to the service of God. To what extent does the account of Benedict's life illustrate the rule for monasteries?

Anglo-Saxon England

14. *LAWS OF ETHELBERT*

Ethelbert of Kent (560–616) was the Anglo-Saxon ruler whose hegemony extended over all Britain south of the Humber. He received Augustine of Canterbury and allowed him to begin his mission of the conversion of the Anglo-Saxons. His law code, written in Old English, was probably compiled around 602 and is the earliest Anglo-Saxon legal compilation. Furthermore, it set a precedent in England, and many later Anglo-Saxon kings promulgated their own codes.

Source: Dorothy Whitelock (ed.), *English Historical Documents 500–1042*, vol. 1 (London: Eyre & Spottiswoode, 1955), 391–94.
Further Reading: A.W.B. Simpson, "The Laws of Ethelbert," in M.S. Arnold (ed.), *On the Laws and Customs of England: Essays in Honor of Samuel E. Thorne* (Chapel Hill: University of North Carolina Press, 1981).

1. The property of God and the Church [is to be paid for] with a twelve-fold compensation; a bishop's property with an eleven-fold compensation; a priest's property with a nine-fold compensation; a deacon's property with a six-fold compensation; a cleric's property with a three-fold compensation; the peace of the Church with a two-fold compensation; the peace of a meeting with a two-fold compensation.

2. If the king calls his people to him, and anyone does them injury there, [he is to pay] a two-fold compensation and 50 shillings to the king.

3. If the king is drinking at a man's home, and anyone commits any evil deed there, he is to pay two-fold compensation.

4. If a freeman steal from the king, he is to repay nine-fold.

5. If anyone kills a man in the king's estate, he is to pay 50 shillings compensation.

6. If anyone kills a freeman, [he is to pay] 50 shillings to the king as "lord-ring."[1]

7. If [anyone] kills the king's own smith or his messenger, he is to pay the ordinary wergeld.

8. The [breach of the] king's protection,[2] 50 shillings.

---

[1] Presumably what is called elsewhere a *manbot*. The term used here is obviously ancient, belonging to a time when payments were more often in rings than in currency. Several of the words in this code are either unique or used only in poetry, which was conservative in its vocabulary.

[2] Offenses against anyone or any place under the king's protection, but also including various acts showing lack of respect. Other persons than the king had their *mund(byrd)*, or "(right of giving) protection."

9. If a freeman steals from a freeman, he is to pay three-fold, and the king is to have the fine or all the goods.

10. If anyone lies with a maiden belonging to the king, he is to pay 50 shillings compensation.

11. If it is a grinding slave, he is to pay 25 shillings compensation; [if a slave of] the third [class], 12 shillings.

12. The king's *fedesl*[3] is to be paid for with 20 shillings.

13. If anyone kills a man in a nobleman's estate, he is to pay 12 shillings compensation.

14. If anyone lies with a nobleman's serving-woman, he is to pay 20 shillings compensation.

15. The [breach of a] *ceorl*'s[4] protection: six shillings.

16. If anyone lie with a *ceorl*'s serving-woman, he is to pay six shillings compensation; [if] with a slave-woman of the second [class], 50 *sceattas*;[5] [if with one of] the third [class], 30 *sceattas*.

17. If a man is the first to force his way into a man's homestead, he is to pay six shillings compensation; he who enters next, three shillings; afterwards each [is to pay] a shilling.

18. If anyone provides a man with weapons, when a quarrel has arisen, and [yet] no injury results, he is to pay six shillings compensation.

19. If highway-robbery is committed, he[6] is to pay six shillings compensation.

20. If, however, a man is killed, he is to pay 20 shillings compensation.

21. If anyone kills a man, he is to pay as an ordinary wergeld 100 shillings.

22. If anyone kills a man, he is to pay 20 shillings at the open grave, and within 40 days the whole wergeld.

23. If the slayer departs from the land, his kinsmen are to pay half the wergeld.

24. If anyone binds a free man, he is to pay 20 shillings compensation.

25. If anyone kills a *ceorl*'s dependant, he is to pay six shillings compensation.

26. If [anyone] kills a *l[æ]t*,[7] he is to pay for one of the highest class 80 shillings; if he kills one of the second class, he is to pay 60 shillings; if one of the third class, he is to pay 40 shillings.

27. If a freeman breaks an enclosure, he is to pay six shillings compensation.

28. If anyone seizes property inside, the man is to pay three-fold compensation.

29. If a freeman enters the enclosure, he is to pay four shillings compensation.

30. If anyone kill a man, he is to pay with his own money and unblemished goods, whatever their kind.

31. If a freeman lies with the wife of another freeman, he is to atone with his wergeld, and to obtain another wife with his own money, and bring her to the other's home.

32. If anyone thrusts through a true *hamseyld*,[8] he is to pay for it with its value.

33. If hair-pulling occur, 50 *sceattas* [are to be paid] as compensation. . . .

73. If a freewoman, with long hair,[9] commits any misconduct, she is to pay 30 shillings compensation.

74. The compensation for [injury to] a maiden is to be as for a freeman.

75. [Breach of] guardianship over a noble-born widow of the highest class is to be compensated for with 50 shillings.

75.1. That over one of the second class, with 20 shillings; over one of the third class, with 12 shillings; over one of the fourth, with 6 shillings.

76. If a man takes a widow who does not belong to him, the [penalty for breach of the] guardianship is to be doubled.

77. If anyone buys a maiden, she is to be bought with a [bride] payment, if there is no fraud.

77.1. If, however, there is any fraud, she is to be taken back home, and he is to be given back his money.

78. If she bears a living child, she is to have half the goods, if the husband dies first.

79. If she wishes to go away with the children, she is to have half the goods.

80. If the husband wishes to keep [the children], [she is to have the same share] as a child.

81. If she does not bear a child, [her] paternal kinsmen are to have [her] goods and the "morning-gift."[10]

---

[3] Boarder.

[4] Though modern English "churl" is the direct descendant of this word, the sense has changed so much that to use it would be misleading. Its normal Old English meaning is a peasant proprietor.

[5] A type of silver coin.

[6] The man who provided the weapon.

[7] Only in Kent is there reference to this class, lower than the *ceorl*, but above the slave.

---

[8] Possibly a fence around a dwelling.

[9] This is generally taken to be a distinguishing feature of a free, as opposed to a bond, woman.

[10] The gift made by the husband to the bride on the morning after the consummation of the marriage.

82. If anyone carries off a maiden by force, [he is to pay] to the owner 50 shillings, and afterward buy from the owner his consent [to the marriage].

83. If she is betrothed to another man at a [bride] price, he[11] is to pay 20 shillings compensation.

84. If a return [of the woman] takes place, [he is to pay] 35 shillings and 15 shillings to the king.

85. If anyone lies with the woman of a servant while her husband is alive, he is to pay a two-fold compensation.

86. If one servant kills another without cause, he is to pay the full value.

87. If a servant's eye or foot is destroyed, the full value is to be paid for him.

88. If anyone binds a man's servant, he is to pay six shillings compensation.

89. Highway robbery of [or by?] a slave is to be three shillings.

90. If a slave steals, he is to pay two-fold compensation.

---

15. BEDE

HISTORY OF THE ENGLISH CHURCH AND PEOPLE

Bede (ca. 672–735) spent almost all of his life as a monk in the Northumbrian monastery of St. Paul at Jarrow. His writing included exegetical works, chronology, rhetoric, metrics, natural history, and hagiography, as well as history. His *History of the English Church and People* is the most important narrative source for English history up to 731. Bede was extremely careful in his selection and use of sources, although he carefully molded his work in order to present his own vision of the growth of English Christianity. The following selections present Augustine's mission to England, the life of Bishop Aidan, and the Synod of Whitby.

Source: Bede's Ecclesiastical History of England, trans. A.M. Sellar (London: George Bell and Sons, 1907).
Further Reading: James Campbell, *Essays in Anglo-Saxon History: 400–1200* (London: Hambledon Press, 1986).

Book One

Chapter XXIII: How the holy Pope Gregory sent Augustine, with other monks, to preach to the English nation, and encouraged them by a letter of exhortation, not to desist from their labor. [596 CE]

In the year of our Lord 582, Maurice, the fifty-fourth from Augustus, ascended the throne, and reigned twenty-one years. In the tenth year of his reign, Gregory, a man eminent in learning and the conduct of affairs, was promoted to the Apostolic see of Rome, and presided over it thirteen years, six months, and ten days. He, being moved by Divine inspiration, in the fourteenth year of the same emperor, and about the one hundred and fiftieth after the coming of the English into Britain, sent the servant of God, Augustine, and with him diverse other monks, who feared the Lord, to preach the Word of God to the English nation. They having, in obedience to the pope's commands, undertaken that work, when they had gone but a little way on their journey, were seized with craven terror, and began to think of returning home, rather than proceed to a barbarous, fierce, and unbelieving nation, to whose very language they were strangers; and by common consent they decided that this was the safer course. At once Augustine, who had been appointed to be consecrated bishop, if they should be received by the English, was sent back, that he might, by humble entreaty, obtain of the blessed Gregory, that they should not be compelled to undertake so dangerous, toilsome, and uncertain a journey. The pope, in reply, sent them a letter of exhortation, persuading them to set forth to the work of the Divine Word, and rely on the help of God. The purport of which letter was as follows:

Gregory, the servant of the servants of God, to the servants of our Lord. Forasmuch as it had been

---

[11] The man who ran off with her.

better not to begin a good work, than to think of desisting from one which has been begun, it behooves you, my beloved sons, to fulfill with all diligence the good work, which, by the help of the Lord, you have undertaken. Let not, therefore, the toil of the journey, nor the tongues of evil-speaking men, discourage you; but with all earnestness and zeal perform, by God's guidance, that which you have set about; being assured, that great labor is followed by the greater glory of an eternal reward. When Augustine, your Superior, returns, whom we also constitute your abbot, humbly obey him in all things; knowing, that whatsoever you shall do by his direction, will, in all respects, be profitable to your souls. Almighty God protect you with His grace, and grant that I may, in the heavenly country, see the fruits of your labor, inasmuch as, though I cannot labor with you, I shall partake in the joy of the reward, because I am willing to labor. God keep you in safety, my most beloved sons.

Given the twenty-third of July, in the fourteenth year of the reign of our most religious lord, Mauritius Tiberius Augustus, the thirteenth year after the consulship of our lord aforesaid, and the fourteenth indiction.

Chapter XXIV: How he wrote to the bishop of Arles to entertain them. [596 CE]

The same venerable pope also sent at the same time a letter to Aetherius, archbishop of Arles, exhorting him to give favorable entertainment to Augustine on his way to Britain; which letter was in these words:

To his most reverend and holy brother and fellow bishop Aetherius, Gregory, the servant of the servants of God.

Although religious men stand in need of no recommendation with priests who have the charity which is pleasing to God; yet because an opportunity of writing has occurred, we have thought fit to send this letter to you, Brother, to inform you, that with the help of God we have directed thither, for the good of souls, the bearer of these presents, Augustine, the servant of God, of whose zeal we are assured, with other servants of God, whom it is requisite that your Holiness readily assist with priestly zeal, affording him all the comfort in your power. And to the end that you may be the more ready in your help, we have enjoined him to inform you particularly of the occasion of his coming; knowing, that when you are acquainted with it, you will, as the matter requires, for the sake of God, dutifully dispose yourself to give him comfort. We also in all things recommend to your charity, Candidus, the priest, our common son, whom we have transferred to the administration of a small patrimony in our Church. God keep you in safety, most reverend brother.

Given the twenty-third day of July, in the fourteenth year of the reign of our most religious lord, Mauritius Tiberius Augustus, the thirteenth year after the consulship of our lord aforesaid, and the fourteenth indiction.

Chapter XXV: How Augustine, coming into Britain, first preached in the Isle of Thanet to the King of Kent, and having obtained license from him, went into Kent, in order to preach therein. [597 CE]

Augustine, thus strengthened by the encouragement of the blessed Father Gregory, returned to the work of the Word of God, with the servants of Christ who were with him, and arrived in Britain. The powerful Ethelbert was at that time king of Kent; he had extended his dominions as far as the boundary formed by the great river Humber, by which the Southern Saxons are divided from the Northern. On the east of Kent is the large Isle of Thanet, containing, according to the English way of reckoning, 600 families, divided from the mainland by the river Wantsum, which is about three furlongs in breadth, and which can be crossed only in two places; for at both ends it runs into the sea. On this island landed the servant of the Lord, Augustine, and his companions, being, as is reported, nearly forty men. They had obtained, by order of the blessed Pope Gregory, interpreters of the nation of the Franks, and sending to Ethelbert, signified that they were come from Rome, and brought a joyful message, which most undoubtedly assured to those that hearkened to it everlasting joys in heaven, and a kingdom that would never end, with the living and true God. The king hearing this gave orders that they should stay in the island where they had landed, and be furnished with necessaries, till he should consider what to do with them. For he had before heard of the Christian religion, having a Christian wife of the royal family of the Franks, called Bertha; whom he had received from her parents, upon condition that she should be permitted to preserve inviolate the rites of her religion with the Bishop Liud-hard, who was sent with her to support her in the faith. Some days after, the king came into the island, and sitting in the open air, ordered Augustine and his companions to come and hold a conference with him. For he had taken precaution that they should not come to him in any house, lest, by so coming, according to an ancient superstition, if they practiced any magical arts, they might impose upon him, and so get the better of him. But they came endued with Divine, not with magic power, bearing a silver cross for their banner, and the image of our Lord and Savior painted on a board; and chanting litanies, they offered up their prayers to the Lord for the eternal salvation both of themselves and of those to whom and for whom they had come. When they had sat down, in obedience to the king's commands, and preached to him and his attendants there present the Word of life, the king answered thus: "Your words and promises are fair, but because they are new to us, and of uncertain import, I cannot consent to them so far as to forsake that which I have so long observed with the whole English nation. But because you are come from far as strangers into my kingdom, and, as I conceive, are desirous to impart to us those things which you believe to be true, and most beneficial, we desire not to harm you, but will give you favorable entertainment, and take care to supply you with all things necessary to your sustenance; nor do we forbid you to preach and gain as many as you can to your religion." Accordingly he gave them an abode in the city of Canterbury, which was the metropolis of all his dominions, and, as he had promised, besides supplying them with sustenance, did not refuse them liberty to preach. It is told that, as they drew near to the city, after their manner, with the holy cross, and the image of our sovereign Lord and King, Jesus Christ, they sang in concert this litany: "We beseech thee, O Lord, for Thy great mercy, that Thy wrath and anger be turned away from this city, and from Thy holy house, for we have sinned. Hallelujah."

Chapter XXVI: How St. Augustine in Kent followed the doctrine and manner of life of the primitive Church, and settled his episcopal see in the royal city. [597 CE]

As soon as they entered the dwelling-place assigned to them, they began to imitate the Apostolic manner of life in the primitive Church; applying themselves to constant prayer, watchings, and fastings; preaching the Word of life to as many as they could; despising all worldly things, as in nowise concerning them; receiving only their necessary food from those they taught; living themselves in all respects conformably to what they taught, and being always ready to suffer any adversity, and even to die for that truth which they preached. In brief, some believed and were baptized, admiring the simplicity of their blameless life, and the sweetness of their heavenly doctrine. There was on the east side of the city, a church dedicated of old to the honor of St. Martin, built whilst the Romans were still in the island, wherein the queen, who, as has been said before, was a Christian, was wont to pray. In this they also first began to come together, to chant the psalms, to pray, to celebrate Mass, to preach, and to baptize, till when the king had been converted to the faith, they obtained greater liberty to preach everywhere and build or repair churches.

When he, among the rest, believed and was baptized, attracted by the pure life of these holy men and their gracious promises, the truth of which they established by many miracles, greater numbers began daily to flock together to hear the Word, and, forsaking their heathen rites, to have fellowship, through faith, in the unity of Christ's Holy Church. It is told that the king, while he rejoiced at their conversion and their faith, yet compelled none to embrace Christianity, but only showed more affection to the believers, as to his fellow citizens in the kingdom of Heaven. For he had learned from those who had instructed him and guided him to salvation, that the service of Christ ought to be voluntary, not by compulsion. Nor was it long before he gave his teachers a settled residence suited to their degree in his metropolis of Canterbury, with such possessions of diverse sorts as were necessary for them. . . .

Chapter XXIX: How the same Pope sent to Augustine the Pall[12] and a letter, along with several ministers of the Word. [601 CE]

Moreover, the same Pope Gregory, hearing from Bishop Augustine, that the harvest which he had was great and the laborers but few, sent to him, together with his aforesaid envoys, certain fellow laborers and ministers of the Word, of whom the chief and foremost were Mellitus, Justus, Paulinus, and Rufinianus, and by them all things in general that were necessary for the worship and service of the Church, to wit, sacred

---

[12] The symbol of his archiespiscopal office.

vessels and altar-cloths, also church-furniture, and vestments for the bishops and clerks, as likewise relics of the holy Apostles and martyrs; besides many manuscripts. He also sent a letter, wherein he signified that he had dispatched the *pallium* to him, and at the same time directed how he should constitute bishops in Britain. The letter was in these words:

> *To his most reverend and holy brother and fellow bishop, Augustine; Gregory, the servant of the servants of God.*

Though it be certain, that the unspeakable rewards of the eternal kingdom are reserved for those who labor for Almighty God, yet it is requisite that we bestow on them the benefit of honors, to the end that they may by this recompense be encouraged the more vigorously to apply themselves to the care of their spiritual work. And, seeing that the new Church of the English is, through the bounty of the Lord, and your labors, brought to the grace of God, we grant you the use of the pall in the same, only for the celebration of the solemn service of the Mass; that so you may ordain twelve bishops in different places, who shall be subject to your jurisdiction. But the bishop of London shall, for the future, be always consecrated by his own synod, and receive the pall, which is the token of his office, from this holy and Apostolic see, which I, by the grace of God, now serve. But we would have you send to the city of York such a bishop as you shall think fit to ordain; yet so, that if that city, with the places adjoining, shall receive the Word of God, that bishop shall also ordain twelve bishops, and enjoy the honor of a metropolitan; for we design, if we live, by the help of God, to bestow on him also the pall; and yet we would have him to be subject to your authority, my brother; but after your decease, he shall so preside over the bishops he shall have ordained, as to be in no way subject to the jurisdiction of the bishop of London. But for the future let there be this distinction as regards honor between the bishops of the cities of London and York, that he who has been first ordained have the precedence. But let them take counsel and act in concert and with one mind dispose whatsoever is to be done for zeal of Christ; let them judge rightly, and carry out their judgment without dissension.

But to you, my brother, shall, by the authority of our God and Lord Jesus Christ, be subject not only those bishops whom you shall ordain, and those that shall be ordained by the bishop of York, but also all the prelates in Britain; to the end that from the words and manner of life of your Holiness they may learn the rule of a right belief and a good life, and fulfilling their office in faith and righteousness, they may, when it shall please the Lord, attain to the kingdom of Heaven. God preserve you in safety, most reverend brother.

Given the twenty-second of June, in the nineteenth year of the reign of our most religious lord, Mauritius Tiberius Augustus, the eighteenth year after the consulship of our said lord, and the fourth indiction.

Chapter XXX: A copy of the letter which Pope Gregory sent to the Abbot Mellitus, then going into Britain. [601 CE]

The aforesaid envoys having departed, the blessed Father, Gregory, sent after them a letter worthy to be recorded, wherein he plainly shows how carefully he watched over the salvation of our country. The letter was as follows:

> *To his most beloved son, the Abbot Mellitus; Gregory, the servant of the servants of God.*

We have been much concerned, since the departure of our people that are with you, because we have received no account of the success of your journey. Howbeit, when Almighty God has led you to the most reverend Bishop Augustine, our brother, tell him what I have long been considering in my own mind concerning the matter of the English people; to wit, that the temples of the idols in that nation ought not to be destroyed; but let the idols that are in them be destroyed; let water be consecrated and sprinkled in the said temples, let altars be erected, and relics placed there. For if those temples are well built, it is requisite that they be converted from the worship of devils to the service of the true God; that the nation, seeing that their temples are not destroyed, may remove error from their hearts, and knowing and adoring the true God, may they more freely resort to the places to which they have been accustomed. And because they are used to slaughter many oxen in sacrifice to devils, some solemnity must be given them in exchange for this, as that on the day of the dedication, or the nativities of the holy martyrs, whose relics are there deposited, they should build themselves huts of the boughs of trees about those churches which have been turned to that use from being temples, and celebrate the solemnity with religious feasting, and no more offer animals to the Devil, but kill cattle and glorify God in their feast, and return thanks to the Giver of all things for their abundance; to the end that, whilst some outward gratifications are retained, they may the more easily consent to the inward joys. For there is no doubt that it is impossible to cut off everything at once from their rude natures; because he who endeavors to ascend to the highest place rises by degrees or steps, and not by leaps. Thus the Lord made Himself known to the people of Israel in Egypt; and yet He allowed them the use, in His own worship, of the sacrifices which they were wont to offer to the Devil, commanding them in His sacrifice to kill animals, to the end that, with changed hearts, they might lay aside one part of the sacrifice, whilst they retained another; and although the animals were the same as those which they were wont to offer, they should offer them to the true God, and not to idols; and thus they would no longer be the same sacrifices. This then, dearly beloved, it behooves you to communicate to our aforesaid brother, that he, being placed where he is at present, may consider how he is to order all things. God preserve you in safety, most beloved son.

Given the seventeenth of June, in the nineteenth year of the reign of our most religious lord, Mauritius Tiberius Augustus, the eighteenth year after the consulship of our said lord, and the fourth indiction.

Chapter XXXI: How Pope Gregory, by letter, exhorted Augustine not to glory in his miracles. [601 CE]

At which time he also sent Augustine a letter concerning the miracles that he had heard had been wrought by him; wherein he admonishes him not to incur the danger of being puffed up by the number of them. The letter was in these words:

I know, dearly beloved brother, that Almighty God, by means of you, shows forth great miracles to the nation which it was His will to choose. Wherefore you must needs rejoice with fear, and fear with joy concerning that heavenly gift; for you will rejoice because the souls of the English are by outward miracles drawn to inward grace; but you will fear, lest, amidst the wonders that are wrought, the weak mind may be puffed up with self-esteem, and that whereby it is outwardly raised to honor cause it inwardly to fall through vain glory. For we must call to mind, that when the disciples returned with joy from preaching, and said to their Heavenly Master, "Lord, even the devils are subject to us through Thy Name";[13] forthwith they received the reply, "In this rejoice not; but rather rejoice, because your names are written in heaven."[14] For their minds were set on private and temporal joys, when they rejoiced in miracles; but they are recalled from the private to the common joy, and from the temporal to the eternal, when it is said to them, "Rejoice in this, because your names are written in heaven." For all the elect do not work miracles, and yet the names of all are written in heaven. For those who are disciples of the truth ought not to rejoice, save for that good thing which all men enjoy as well as they, and in which their joy shall be without end.

It remains, therefore, most dear brother, that amidst those outward actions, which you perform through the power of the Lord, you should always carefully judge yourself in your heart, and carefully understand both what you are yourself, and how much grace is bestowed upon that same nation, for the conversion of which you have received even the gift of working miracles. And if you remember that you have at any time sinned against our Creator, either by word or deed, always call it to mind, to the end that the remembrance of your guilt may crush the vanity which rises in your heart. And whatsoever gift of

---

[13] Luke 10:17.
[14] Luke 10:20.

working miracles you either shall receive, or have received, consider the same, not as conferred on you, but on those for whose salvation it has been given you.

Chapter XXXII: How Pope Gregory sent letters and gifts to King Ethelbert. [601 CE]

The same blessed Pope Gregory, at the same time, sent a letter to King Ethelbert, with many gifts of diverse sorts; being desirous to glorify the king with temporal honors, at the same time that he rejoiced that through his own labor and zeal he had attained to the knowledge of heavenly glory. The copy of the said letter is as follows:

To the most glorious lord, and his most excellent son, Ethelbert, king of the English, Bishop Gregory.

Almighty God advances good men to the government of nations, that He may by their means bestow the gifts of His loving-kindness on those over whom they are placed. This we know to have come to pass in the English nation, over whom your Highness was placed, to the end, that by means of the blessings which are granted to you, heavenly benefits might also be conferred on your subjects. Therefore, my illustrious son, do you carefully guard the grace which you have received from the Divine goodness, and be eager to spread the Christian faith among the people under your rule; in all uprightness increase your zeal for their conversion; suppress the worship of idols; overthrow the structures of the temples; establish the manners of your subjects by much cleanness of life, exhorting, terrifying, winning, correcting, and showing forth an example of good works, that you may obtain your reward in Heaven from Him, Whose Name and the knowledge of Whom you have spread abroad upon earth. For He, Whose honor you seek and maintain among the nations, will also render your Majesty's name more glorious even to posterity.

For even so the most pious emperor, Constantine, of old, recovering the Roman commonwealth from the false worship of idols, brought it with himself into subjection to Almighty God, our Lord Jesus Christ, and turned to Him with his whole mind, together with the nations under his rule. Whence it followed, that his praises transcended the fame of former princes; and he excelled his predecessors in renown as much as in good works. Now, therefore, let your Highness hasten to impart to the kings and peoples that are subject to you, the knowledge of one God, Father, Son, and Holy Ghost; that you may surpass the ancient kings of your nation in praise and merit, and while you cause the sins of others among your own subjects to be blotted out, become the more free from anxiety with regard to your own sins before the dread judgment of Almighty God.

Willingly hear, devoutly perform, and studiously retain in your memory, whatsoever counsel shall be given you by our most reverend brother, Bishop Augustine, who is trained up in the monastic rule, full of the knowledge of Holy Scripture, and, by the help of God, endued with good works; for if you give ear to him when he speaks on behalf of Almighty God, the sooner will Almighty God hear his prayers for you. But if (which God forbid!) you slight his words, how shall Almighty God hear him on your behalf, when you neglect to hear him on behalf of God? Unite yourself, therefore, to him with all your mind, in the fervor of faith, and further his endeavors, by that virtue which God has given you, that He may make you partaker of His kingdom, Whose faith you cause to be received and maintained in your own.

Besides, we would have your Highness know that, as we find in Holy Scripture from the words of the Almighty Lord, the end of this present world, and the kingdom of the saints, which will never come to an end, is at hand. But as the end of the world draws near, many things are about to come upon us which were not before, to wit, changes in the air, and terrors from heaven, and tempests out of the order of the seasons, wars, famines, pestilences, earthquakes in diverse places; which things will not, nevertheless, all happen in our days, but will all follow after our days. If, therefore, you perceive that any of these things come to pass in your country, let not your mind be in any way disturbed; for these signs of the end of the world are sent before, for this reason, that we may take heed to our souls, and be watchful for the hour of death, and may be found prepared with good works to meet our Judge. Thus much, my illustrious son, I have said in few words, with intent that when the Christian faith is spread abroad in your kingdom, our discourse to you may also be more copious, and we may desire to say the more, as joy for the full conversion of your nation is increased in our mind.

I have sent you some small gifts, which will not appear small to you, when received by you with the blessing of the blessed Apostle, Peter. May Almighty God, therefore, perfect in you His grace which He has begun, and prolong your life here through a course of many years, and in the fullness of time receive you into the congregation of the heavenly country. May the grace of God preserve you in safety, my most excellent lord and son.

Given the twenty-second day of June, in the nineteenth year of the reign of our most religious lord, Mauritius Tiberius Augustus, in the eighteenth year after his consulship, and the fourth indiction.

Book Two

Chapter II: How Augustine admonished the bishops of the Britons on behalf of Catholic peace, and to that end wrought a heavenly miracle in their presence; and of the vengeance that pursued them for their contempt.
[ca. 603 CE]

In the meantime, Augustine, with the help of King Ethelbert, drew together to a conference the bishops and doctors of the nearest province of the Britons, at a place which is to this day called, in the English language, Augustine's Ác, that is, Augustine's Oak, on the borders of the Hwiccas and West Saxons; and began by brotherly admonitions to persuade them to preserve Catholic peace with him, and undertake the common labor of preaching the Gospel to the heathen for the Lord's sake. For they did not keep Easter Sunday at the proper time, but from the fourteenth to the twentieth moon; which computation is contained in a cycle of eighty-four years. Besides, they did many other things which were opposed to the unity of the church. When, after a long disputation, they did not comply with the entreaties, exhortations, or rebukes of Augustine and his companions, but preferred their own traditions before all the Churches which are united in Christ throughout

the world, the holy father, Augustine, put an end to this troublesome and tedious contention, saying, "Let us entreat God, who maketh men to be of one mind in His Father's house, to vouchsafe, by signs from Heaven, to declare to us which tradition is to be followed; and by what path we are to strive to enter His kingdom. Let some sick man be brought, and let the faith and practice of him, by whose prayers he shall be healed, be looked upon as hallowed in God's sight and such as should be adopted by all." His adversaries unwillingly consenting, a blind man of the English race was brought, who having been presented to the British bishops, found no benefit or healing from their ministry; at length, Augustine, compelled by strict necessity, bowed his knees to the Father of our Lord Jesus Christ, praying that He would restore his lost sight to the blind man, and by the bodily enlightenment of one kindle the grace of spiritual light in the hearts of many of the faithful. Immediately the blind man received sight, and Augustine was proclaimed by all to be a true herald of the light from Heaven. The Britons then confessed that they perceived that it was the true way of righteousness which Augustine taught; but that they could not depart from their ancient customs without the consent and sanction of their people. They therefore desired that a second time a synod might be appointed, at which more of their number should be present.

This being decreed, there came, it is said, seven bishops of the Britons, and many men of great learning, particularly from their most celebrated monastery, which is called, in the English tongue, Bancornaburg, and over which the Abbot Dinoot is said to have presided at that time. They that were to go to the aforesaid council, betook themselves first to a certain holy and discreet man, who was wont to lead the life of a hermit among them, to consult with him, whether they ought, at the preaching of Augustine, to forsake their traditions. He answered, "If he is a man of God, follow him."—"How shall we know that?" said they. He replied, "Our Lord saith, Take My yoke upon you, and learn of Me, for I am meek and lowly in heart; if therefore, Augustine is meek and lowly of heart, it is to be believed that he bears the yoke of Christ himself, and offers it to you to bear. But, if he is harsh and proud, it is plain that he is not of God, nor are we to regard his words." They said again, "And how shall we discern even this?"—"Do you contrive," said the anchorite, "that he first arrive with his company at the place where the synod is to be held; and if at your approach he rises up to you, hear him submissively, being assured that he is the servant of Christ; but if he despises you, and does not rise up to you, whereas you are more in number, let him also be despised by you." They did as he directed; and it happened, that as they approached, Augustine was sitting on a chair. When they perceived it, they were angry, and charging him with pride, set themselves to contradict all he said. He said to them, "Many things ye do which are contrary to our custom, or rather the custom of the universal Church, and yet, if you will comply with me in these three matters, to wit, to keep Easter at the due time; to fulfill the ministry of Baptism, by which we are born again to God, according to the custom of the holy Roman Apostolic Church; and to join with us in preaching the Word of God to the English nation, we will gladly suffer all the other things you do, though contrary to our customs." They answered that they would do none of those things, nor receive him as their archbishop; for they said among themselves, "if he would not rise up to us now, how much more will he despise us, as of no account, if we begin to be under his subjection?" Then the man of God, Augustine, is said to have threatened them, that if they would not accept peace with their brethren, they should have war from their enemies; and, if they would not preach the way of life to the English nation, they should suffer at their hands the vengeance of death. All which, through the dispensation of the Divine judgment, fell out exactly as he had predicted.

For afterward the warlike king of the English, Ethelfrid, of whom we have spoken, having raised a mighty army, made a very great slaughter of that heretical nation, at the city of Legions, which by the English is called Legacaestir [Chester], but by the Britons more rightly Carlegion. Being about to give battle, he observed their priests, who were come together to offer up their prayers to God for the combatants, standing apart in a place of greater safety; he inquired who they were, and what they came together to do in that place. Most of them were of the monastery of Bangor, in which, it is said, there was so great a number of monks, that the monastery being divided into seven parts, with a superior set over each, none of those parts contained less than 300 men, who all lived by the labor of their hands. Many of these, having observed a fast of three days, had come together along with others to pray at the aforesaid battle, having one Brocmail for their protector, to defend them, whilst they were intent upon their prayers, against the swords of the barbarians. King Ethelfrid being informed of the occasion of their coming, said, "If then they cry to their God against us, in truth, though they do not bear arms, yet they fight against us, because they assail us with their curses." He, therefore, commanded them to be attacked first, and then destroyed the rest of the impious army, not without great loss of his own forces. About 1,200 of those that came to pray are said to have been killed, and only fifty to have escaped by flight. Brocmail, turning his back with his men, at the first approach of the enemy, left those whom he ought to have defended unarmed and exposed to the swords of the assailants. Thus was fulfilled the prophecy of the holy Bishop Augustine, though he himself had been long before taken up into the heavenly kingdom, that the heretics should feel the vengeance of temporal death also, because they had despised the offer of eternal salvation.

Chapter III: How St. Augustine made Mellitus and Justus bishops; and of his death. [604 CE]

In the year of our Lord 604, Augustine, Archbishop of Britain, ordained two bishops, to wit, Mellitus and Justus; Mellitus to preach to the province of the East-Saxons, who are divided from Kent by the river Thames, and border on the Eastern sea. Their metropolis is the city of London, which is situated on the bank of the aforesaid river, and is the mart of many nations resorting to it by sea and land. At that time, Sabert, nephew to Ethelbert through his sister Ricula, reigned over the nation, though he was under subjection to Ethelbert, who, as has been said above, had command over all the nations of the English as far as the river Humber. But when this province also received the word of truth, by the preaching of Mellitus, King Ethelbert built the church of St. Paul the Apostle, in the city of London, where he and his successors should have their episcopal see. As for Justus, Augustine ordained him bishop in Kent, at the city of Dorubrevis, which the English call Hrofaescaestrae [Rochester], from one that was formerly the chief man of it, called Hrof. It is about twenty-four miles distant from the city of Canterbury to the westward, and in it King Ethelbert dedicated a church to the blessed Apostle Andrew, and bestowed many gifts on the bishops of both those churches, as well as on the Bishop of Canterbury, adding lands and possessions for the use of those who were associated with the bishops.

After this, the beloved of God, our father Augustine, died, and his body was laid outside, close by the church of the blessed Apostles, Peter and Paul, above spoken of, because it was not yet finished, nor consecrated, but as soon as it was consecrated, the body was brought in, and fittingly buried in the north chapel thereof; wherein also were interred the bodies of all the succeeding archbishops, except two only, Theodore and Bertwald, whose bodies are in the church itself, because the aforesaid chapel could contain no more. Almost in the midst of this chapel is an altar dedicated in honor of the blessed Pope Gregory, at which every Saturday memorial Masses are celebrated for the archbishops by a priest of that place. On the tomb of Augustine is inscribed this epitaph:

"Here rests the Lord Augustine, first Archbishop of Canterbury, who, being of old sent hither by the blessed Gregory, Bishop of the city of Rome, and supported by God in the working of miracles, led King Ethelbert and his nation from the worship of idols to the faith of Christ, and having ended the days of his office in peace, died the 26th day of May, in the reign of the same king."

Book Three

Chapter VII: How the West Saxons received the Word of God by the preaching of Birinus; and of his successors, Agilbert and Leutherius. [635–670 CE]

At that time, the West Saxons, formerly called Gewissae, in the reign of Cynegils [ca. 611–643], received the faith of Christ, through the preaching of Bishop Birinus, who came into Britain by the counsel of Pope Honorius; having promised in his presence that he would sow the seed of the holy faith in the farthest inland regions of the English, where no other teacher had been before him. Hereupon at the bidding of the pope he received episcopal consecration from Asterius, bishop of Genoa; but on his arrival in Britain, he first came to the nation of the Gewissae, and finding all in that place confirmed pagans, he thought it better to preach the Word there, than to proceed further to seek for other hearers of his preaching.

Now, as he was spreading the Gospel in the aforesaid province, it happened that when the king himself, having received instruction as a catechumen, was being baptized together with his people, Oswald, the most holy and victorious king of the Northumbrians, being present, received him as he came forth from baptism, and by an honorable alliance most acceptable to God, first adopted as his son, thus born again and dedicated to God, the man whose daughter he was about to receive in marriage. The two kings gave to the bishop the city called Dorcic [Dorchester], there to establish his episcopal see; where having built and consecrated churches, and by his pious labors called many to the Lord, he departed to the Lord,

and was buried in the same city; but many years after, when Haedde was bishop, he was translated thence to the city of Venta [Winchester], and laid in the church of the blessed Apostles, Peter and Paul.

When the king died, his son Coinwalch succeeded him on the throne, but refused to receive the faith and the mysteries of the heavenly kingdom; and not long after he lost also the dominion of his earthly kingdom; for he put away the sister of Penda, king of the Mercians, whom he had married, and took another wife; whereupon a war ensuing, he was by him deprived of his kingdom, and withdrew to Anna, king of the East Angles, where he lived three years in banishment, and learned and received the true faith; for the king, with whom he lived in his banishment, was a good man, and happy in a good and saintly offspring, as we shall show hereafter.

But when Coinwalch was restored to his kingdom, there came into that province out of Ireland, a certain bishop called Agilbert, a native of Gaul, but who had then lived a long time in Ireland, for the purpose of reading the Scriptures. He attached himself to the king, and voluntarily undertook the ministry of preaching. The king, observing his learning and industry, desired him to accept an episcopal see there and remain as the bishop of his people. Agilbert complied with the request, and presided over that nation as their bishop for many years. At length the king, who understood only the language of the Saxons, weary of his barbarous tongue, privately brought into the province another bishop, speaking his own language, by name Wini, who had also been ordained in Gaul; and dividing his province into two dioceses, appointed this last his episcopal see in the city of Venta, by the Saxons called Wintancaestir. Agilbert, being highly offended, that the king should do this without consulting him, returned into Gaul, and being made bishop of the city of Paris, died there, being old and full of days. Not many years after his departure out of Britain, Wini was also expelled from his bishopric by the same king, and took refuge with Wulfhere, king of the Mercians, of whom he purchased for money the see of the city of London, and remained bishop thereof till his death. Thus the province of the West Saxons continued no small time without a bishop.

During which time, the aforesaid king of that nation, sustaining repeatedly very great losses in his kingdom from his enemies, at length bethought himself, that as he had been before expelled from the throne for his unbelief, he had been restored when he acknowledged the faith of Christ; and he perceived that his kingdom, being deprived of a bishop, was justly deprived also of the Divine protection. He, therefore, sent messengers into Gaul to Agilbert, with humble apologies entreating him to return to the bishopric of his nation. But he excused himself, and protested that he could not go, because he was bound to the bishopric of his own city and diocese; notwithstanding, in order to give him some help in answer to his earnest request, he sent thither in his stead the priest Leutherius, his nephew, to be ordained as his bishop, if he thought fit, saying that he thought him worthy of a bishopric. The king and the people received him honorably, and asked Theodore, then Archbishop of Canterbury, to consecrate him as their bishop. He was accordingly consecrated in the same city, and many years diligently governed the whole bishopric of the West Saxons by synodical authority. . . .

Chapter XXV: How the question arose about the due time of keeping Easter, with those that came out of Scotland. [664 CE]

In the meantime, Bishop Aidan being taken away from this life, Finan, who was ordained and sent by the Scots, succeeded him in the bishopric, and built a church in the Isle of Lindisfarne, fit for the episcopal see; nevertheless, after the manner of the Scots, he made it, not of stone, but entirely of hewn oak, and covered it with reeds; and it was afterwards dedicated in honor of the blessed Peter the Apostle, by the most reverend Archbishop Theodore. Eadbert, also bishop of that place, took off the thatch, and caused it to be covered entirely, both roof and walls, with plates of lead.

At this time, a great and frequently debated question arose about the observance of Easter; those that came from Kent or Gaul affirming, that the Scots celebrated Easter Sunday contrary to the custom of the universal Church. Among them was a most zealous defender of the true Easter, whose name was Ronan, a Scot by nation, but instructed in the rule of ecclesiastical truth in Gaul or Italy. Disputing with Finan, he convinced many, or at least induced them to make a more strict inquiry after the truth; yet he could not prevail upon Finan, but, on the contrary, embittered him the more by reproof, and made him a professed opponent of the truth, for he was of a violent temper. James, formerly the deacon of the venerable Archbishop Paulinus, as has been said above, observed the true and Catholic Easter, with all those that he could instruct in the better way. Queen Eanfled and her followers also observed it as she had seen it practiced in Kent, having with her a Kentish priest who followed the Catholic observance, whose name was Romanus. Thus it is said to have sometimes happened in those times that Easter was twice celebrated in one year; and that when the king, having ended his fast, was keeping Easter, the queen and her followers were still fasting, and celebrating Palm Sunday. Whilst Aidan lived, this difference about the observance of Easter was patiently tolerated by all men, for they well knew, that though he could not keep Easter contrary to the custom of those who had sent him, yet he industriously labored to practice the works of faith, piety, and love, according to the custom of all holy men; for which reason he was deservedly beloved by all, even by those who differed in opinion concerning Easter, and was held in veneration, not only by less important persons, but even by the bishops, Honorius of Canterbury, and Felix of the East Angles.

But after the death of Finan, when Colman, who succeeded him, who was also sent from Scotland, came to be bishop, a greater controversy arose about the observance of Easter, and other rules of ecclesiastical life. Whereupon this question began naturally to influence the thoughts and hearts of many who feared, lest haply, having received the name of Christians, they might run, or have run, in vain. This reached the ears of the rulers, King Oswy and his son Alchfrid. Now Oswy, having been instructed and baptized by the Scots, and being very perfectly skilled in their language, thought nothing better than what they taught; but Alchfrid, having for his teacher in Christianity the learned Wilfrid, who had formerly gone to Rome to study ecclesiastical doctrine, and spent much time at Lyons with Dalfinus, archbishop of Gaul, from whom also he had received the crown of ecclesiastical tonsure, rightly thought that this man's doctrine ought to be preferred before all the traditions of the Scots. For this reason he had also given him a monastery of forty families, at a place called Inhrypum [Ripon]; which place, not long before, he had given for a monastery to those that were followers of the Scots; but forasmuch as they afterwards, being left to their choice, preferred to quit the place rather than alter their custom, he gave it to him, whose life and doctrine were worthy of it.

Agilbert, bishop of the West Saxons, above-mentioned, a friend of King Alchfrid and of Abbot Wilfrid, had at that time come into the province of the Northumbrians, and was staying some time among them; at the request of Alchfrid, he made Wilfrid a priest in his aforesaid monastery. He had in his company a priest, whose name was Agatho. The question being raised there concerning Easter and the tonsure and other ecclesiastical matters, it was arranged, that a synod should be held in the monastery of Streanaeshalch, which signifies the Bay of the Lighthouse, where the Abbess Hilda, a woman devoted to the service of God, then ruled; and that there this question should be decided. The kings, both father and son, came thither, and the bishops, Colman with his Scottish clerks, and Agilbert with the priests Agatho and Wilfrid. James and Romanus were on their side; but the Abbess Hilda and her followers were for the Scots, as was also the venerable Bishop Cedd, long before ordained by the Scots, as has been said above, and he acted in that council as a most careful interpreter for both parties.

King Oswy first made an opening speech, in which he said that it behooved those who served one God to observe one rule of life; and as they all expected the same kingdom in heaven, so they ought not to differ in the celebration of the heavenly mysteries; but rather to inquire which was the truer tradition, that it might be followed by all in common; he then commanded his bishop, Colman, first to declare what the custom was which he observed, and whence it derived its origin. Then Colman said, "The Easter which I keep, I received from my elders, who sent me hither as bishop; all our forefathers, men beloved of God, are known to have celebrated it after the same manner; and that it may not seem to any contemptible and worthy to be rejected, it is the same which the blessed John the Evangelist, the disciple specially beloved of our Lord, with all the churches over which he presided, is recorded to have celebrated." When he had said thus much, and more to the like effect, the king commanded Agilbert to make known the manner of his observance and to show whence it was derived, and on what authority he followed it. Agilbert answered, "I beseech you, let my disciple, the priest Wilfrid, speak in my stead; because we both concur with the other followers of the ecclesiastical tradition that are here present, and he can better and more clearly explain our opinion in the English language, than I can by an interpreter."

Then Wilfrid, being ordered by the king to speak, began thus:—"The Easter which we keep, we saw celebrated by all at Rome, where the blessed Apostles, Peter and Paul, lived, taught, suffered, and were buried; we saw the same done by all in Italy and in Gaul, when we traveled through those countries for the purpose of study and prayer. We found it observed in Africa, Asia, Egypt, Greece, and all the world, wherever the Church of Christ is spread abroad, among diverse nations and tongues, at one and the same time; save only among these and their accomplices in obstinacy, I mean the Picts and the Britons, who foolishly, in these two remote islands of the ocean, and only in part even of them, strive to oppose all the rest of the world." When he had so said, Colman answered, "It is strange that you choose to call our efforts foolish, wherein we follow the example of so great an Apostle, who was thought worthy to lean on our Lord's bosom, when all the world knows him to have lived most wisely." Wilfrid replied, "Far be it from us to charge John with folly, for he literally observed the precepts of the Mosaic Law, whilst the Church was still Jewish in many points, and the Apostles, lest they should give cause of offense to the Jews who were among the Gentiles, were not able at once to cast off all the observances of the Law which had been instituted by God, in the same way as it is necessary that all who come to the faith should forsake the idols which were invented by devils. For this reason it was, that Paul circumcized Timothy, that he offered sacrifice in the temple, that he shaved his head with Aquila and Priscilla at Corinth; for no other advantage than to avoid giving offense to the Jews. Hence it was, that James said to the same Paul, 'Thou seest, brother, how many thousands of Jews there are which believe; and they are all zealous of the Law.' And yet, at this time, when the light of the Gospel is spreading throughout the world, it is needless, nay, it is not lawful, for the faithful either to be circumcized, or to offer up to God sacrifices of flesh. So John, according to the custom of the law, began the celebration of the feast of Easter, on the fourteenth day of the first month, in the evening, not regarding whether the same happened on a Saturday, or any other week-day. But when Peter preached at Rome, being mindful that our Lord arose from the dead, and gave to the world the hope of resurrection, on the first day of the week, he perceived that Easter ought to be kept after this manner: he always awaited the rising of the moon on the fourteenth day of the first month in the evening, according to the custom and precepts of the Law, even as John did. And when that came, if the Lord's day, then called the first day of the week, was the next day, he began that very evening to celebrate Easter, as we all do at the present time. But if the Lord's day did not fall the next morning after the fourteenth moon, but on the sixteenth, or the seventeenth, or any other moon till the twenty-first, he waited for that, and on the Saturday before, in the evening, began to observe the holy solemnity of Easter. Thus it came to pass, that Easter Sunday was only kept from the fifteenth moon to the twenty-first. Nor does this evangelical and apostolic tradition abolish the Law, but rather fulfill it; the command being to keep the Passover from the fourteenth moon of the first month in the evening to the twenty-first moon of the same month in the evening; which observance all the successors of the blessed John in Asia, since his death, and all the Church throughout the world, have since followed; and that this is the true Easter, and the only one to be celebrated by the faithful, was not newly decreed by the council of Nicaea, but only confirmed afresh; as the history of the Church informs us.

"Thus it is plain, that you, Colman, neither follow the example of John, as you imagine, nor that of Peter, whose tradition you oppose with full knowledge, and that you neither agree with the Law nor the Gospel in the keeping of your Easter. For John, keeping the Paschal time according to the decree of the Mosaic Law, had no regard to the first day of the week, which you do not practice, seeing that you celebrate Easter only on the first day after the Sabbath. Peter celebrated Easter Sunday between the fifteenth and the twenty-first moon, which you do not practice, seeing that you observe Easter Sunday from the fourteenth to the twentieth moon; so that you often begin Easter on the thirteenth moon in the evening, whereof neither the Law made any mention, nor did our Lord, the Author and Giver of the Gospel, on that day either eat the old Passover in the evening, or deliver the Sacraments of the New Testament, to be celebrated by the Church, in memory of His Passion, but on the fourteenth. Besides, in your celebration of Easter, you utterly exclude the twenty-first moon, which the Law ordered to be specially observed. Thus, as I have said before, you agree neither with John nor Peter, nor with the Law, nor the Gospel, in the celebration of the greatest festival."

To this Colman rejoined: "Did the holy Anatolius, much commended in the history of the Church, judge contrary to the Law and the Gospel, when he wrote, that Easter was to be celebrated from the fourteenth to the twentieth moon? Is it to be believed that our most reverend Father Columba and his successors, men beloved by God, who kept Easter after the same manner, judged or acted contrary to the Divine writings? Whereas there were many among them, whose sanctity was attested by heavenly signs and miracles which they wrought; whom I, for my part, doubt not to be saints, and whose life, customs, and discipline I never cease to follow."

"It is evident," said Wilfrid, "that Anatolius was a most holy, learned, and commendable man; but what have you to do with him, since you do not observe his decrees? For he undoubtedly, following the rule of truth in his Easter, appointed a cycle of nineteen years, which either you are ignorant of, or if you know it, though it is kept by the whole Church of Christ, yet you despise it as a thing of naught. He so computed the fourteenth moon in our Lord's Paschal Feast, that according to the custom of the Egyptians, he acknowledged it to be the fifteenth moon on that same day in the evening; so in like manner he assigned the twentieth to Easter-Sunday, as believing that to be the twenty-first moon, when the sun had set. That you are ignorant of the rule of this distinction is proved by this, that you sometimes manifestly keep Easter before the full moon, that is, on the thirteenth day. Concerning your Father Columba and his followers, whose sanctity you say you imitate, and whose rule and precepts confirmed by signs from Heaven you say that you follow, I might answer, then when many, in the day of judgment, shall say to our Lord, that in His name they have prophesied, and have cast out devils, and done many wonderful works, our Lord will reply, that He never knew them. But far be it from me to speak thus of your fathers, for it is much more just to believe good than evil of those whom we know not. Wherefore I do not deny those also to have been God's servants, and beloved of God, who with rude simplicity, but pious intentions, have themselves loved Him. Nor do I think that such observance of Easter did them much harm, as long as none came to show them a more perfect rule to follow; for assuredly I believe that, if any teacher, reckoning after the Catholic manner, had come among them, they would have as readily followed his admonitions, as they are known to have kept those commandments of God, which they had learned and knew.

"But as for you and your companions, you certainly sin, if, having heard the decrees of the Apostolic see, nay, of the universal Church, confirmed, as they are, by Holy Scripture, you scorn to follow them; for, though your fathers were holy, do you think that those few men, in a corner of the remotest island, are to be preferred before the universal Church of Christ throughout the world? And if that Columba of yours, (and, I may say, ours also, if he was Christ's servant,) was a holy man and powerful in miracles, yet could he be preferred before the most blessed chief of the Apostles, to whom our Lord said, 'Thou art Peter, and upon this rock I will build my Church, and the gates of hell shall not prevail against it, and I will give unto thee the keys of the kingdom of Heaven?'"

When Wilfrid had ended thus, the king said, "Is it true, Colman, that these words were spoken to Peter by our Lord?" He answered, "It is true, O king!" Then said he, "Can you show any such power given to your Columba?" Colman answered, "None." Then again the king asked, "Do you both agree in this, without any controversy, that these words were said above all to Peter, and that the keys of the kingdom of Heaven were given to him by our Lord?" They both answered, "Yes." Then the king concluded, "And I also say unto you, that he is the doorkeeper, and I will not gainsay him, but I desire, as far as I know and am able, in all things to obey his laws, lest haply when I come to the gates of the kingdom of Heaven, there should be none to open them, he being my adversary who is proved to have the keys." The king having said this, all who were seated there or standing by, both great and small, gave their assent, and renouncing the less perfect custom, hastened to conform to that which they had found to be better.

16. KING ALFRED

The following texts relate to King Alfred of Wessex (849–899). Alfred led the Anglo-Saxon resistance to Danish invasions, united all of England not under Danish rule, and fostered a reform of English political and cultural life.

Alfred's laws (*Dooms*) were prepared between 871 and 899. Asser, who originally had been a monk and bishop, lived and worked with Alfred and assisted him with his translation of Gregory the Great's *Pastoral Care*; Asser used the Anglo-Saxon Chronicle as a source and Einhard's *Life of Charlemagne* as a model for his *Life of King Alfred*, which survived in only one copy but provides more information about Alfred than any other source and makes him the Anglo-Saxon king for whose reign we have the most information. The letter to Edward the Elder shows the importance of Alfred's legal program.

Source: Dorothy Whitelock (ed.), *English Historical Documents 500–1042*, vol. 1 (London: Eyre & Spottiswoode, 1955), 176–91, 264–76, 408–17.
Further Reading: Richard P. Abels, *Alfred the Great: War, Kingship, and Culture in Anglo-Saxon England* (London: Longman, 1998).

DOOMS

Introduction

I, then, King Alfred, have collected these [dooms] and ordered them to be written down, many of those which our predecessors observed and which were also pleasing to me. And those which were not pleasing to me, by the advice of my *witan*,[15] I have rejected, ordering them to be observed only as amended. I have not ventured to put in writing much of my own, being uncertain what might please those who shall come after us. So I have here collected the dooms that seemed to me the most just, whether they were from the time of Ine, my kinsman, from that of Offa, king of the Mercians, or from that of Aethelbert, the first of the English to receive baptism; the rest I have discarded. I then, Alfred, king of the West Saxons, have shown these to all my *witan* who have declared it is the will of all that they be observed . . .

1. First we direct, what is most necessary, that each man keep carefully his oath and pledge.
1.1. If anyone is wrongfully compelled to either of these, [to promise] treachery against his lord or any illegal aid, then it is better to leave it unfulfilled than to perform it.
1.2. [If, however, he pledges what it is right for him to perform,] and leaves it unfulfilled, let him with humility give his weapons and his possessions into his friends' keeping and be 40 days in prison at a king's estate; let him endure there what penance the bishop prescribes for him, and his kinsmen are to feed him if he has no food himself.
1.3. If he has no kinsmen and has not the food, the king's reeve is to feed him.
1.4. If he has to be forced thither, and will not go otherwise, and he is bound, he is to forfeit his weapons and his possessions.

---

[15] An advisory council to the Saxon English king.

1.5. If he is killed, he is to lie unpaid for.

1.6. If he escapes before the end of the period, and he is caught, he is to be 40 days in prison, as he should have been before.

1.7. If he gets clear, he is to be outlawed, and to be excommunicated from all the churches of Christ.

1.8. If, however, there is secular surety for him, he is to pay for the breach of surety as the law directs him, and for the breach of pledge as his confessor prescribes for him.

2. If anyone for any guilt flees to any one of the monastic houses to which the king's food-rent belongs, or to some other privileged community which is worthy of honor, he is to have a respite of three days to protect himself, unless he wishes to be reconciled.

2.1. If during that respite he is molested with slaying or binding or wounding, each of those [who did it] is to make amends according to the legal custom, both with wergeld and with fine, and to pay to the community 120 shillings as compensation for the breach of sanctuary, and is to have forfeited his own [claim against the culprit].

3. If anyone violates the king's surety, he is to pay compensation for the charge as the law directs him, and for the breach of the surety with five pounds of pure pennies. The breach of the archbishop's surety or of his protection is to be compensated with three pounds; the breach of the surety or protection of another bishop or an ealdorman is to be compensated with two pounds.

4. If anyone plots against the king's life, directly or by harboring his exiles or his men, he is liable to forfeit his life and all that he owes.

4.1. If he wishes to clear himself, he is to do it by [an oath equivalent to] the king's wergeld.

4.2. Thus also we determine concerning all ranks, both *ceorl* and noble: he who plots against his lord's life is to be liable to forfeit his life and all that he owns, or to clear himself by his lord's wergeld.

5. Also we determine this sanctuary for every church which a bishop has consecrated: if a man exposed to a vendetta reaches it running or riding, no one is to drag him out for seven days, if he can live in spite of hunger, unless he himself fights [his way] out. If however anyone does so, he is liable to [pay for breach of] the king's protection and of the church's sanctuary—more, if he seizes more from there.

5.1. If the community have more need of their church, he is to be kept in another building, and it is to have no more doors than the church.

5.2. The head of that church is to take care that no one give him food during that period.

5.3. If he himself will hand out his weapons to his foes, they are to keep him for 30 days, and send notice about him to his kinsmen.

5.4. Further sanctuary of the church: if any man has recourse to the church on account of any crime which has not been discovered, and there confesses himself in God's name, it is to be half remitted.

5.5. Whoever steals on Sunday or at Christmas or Easter or on the Holy Thursday in Rogation days; each of those we wish to be compensated doubly, as in the Lenten fast.

6. If anyone steals anything in church, he is to pay the simple compensation and the fine normally belonging to that simple compensation, and the hand with which he did it is to be struck off.

6.1. And if he wishes to redeem the hand, and that is allowed to him, he is to pay in proportion to his wergeld.

7. If anyone fights or draws his weapon in the king's hall, and he is captured, it is to be at the king's judgment, whether he will grant him death or life.

7.1. If he escapes, and is afterward captured, he shall always pay for himself with his wergeld, and compensate for the crime, with wergeld as with fine, according to what he has done.

8. If anyone brings a nun out of a nunnery without the permission of the king or the bishop, he is to pay 120 shillings, half to the king and half to the bishop and the lord of the church which has the nun.

8.1. If she outlives him who brought her out, she is to have nothing of his inheritance.

8.2. If she bears a child, it is not to have any of that inheritance, any more than the mother.

8.3. If her child is killed, the share of the maternal kindred is to be paid to the king; the paternal kindred are to be given their share.

9. If a woman with child is slain when she is bearing the child, the woman is to be paid for with full payment, and the child at half payment according to the wergeld of the father's kin.

9.1. The fine is always to be 60 shillings until the simple compensation rises to 30 shillings; when the simple compensation has risen to that, the fine is afterwards to be 120 shillings.

9.2. Formerly, [the fine] for the stealer of gold, the stealer of stud-horses, the stealer of bees, and many fines, were greater than others; now all are alike, except for the stealer of a man: 120 shillings.

10. If anyone lies with the wife of a man of a twelve-hundred wergeld, he is to pay to the husband 120 shillings; to a man of a six-hundred wergeld 100 shillings is to be paid; to a man of the *ceorl* class 40 shilling one ands is to be paid. . . .

12. If a man burns or fells the wood of another, without permission, he is to pay for each large tree with 5 shillings, and afterward for each, no matter how many there are, with fivepence; and 30 shillings as a fine.

13. If at a common task a man unintentionally kills another [by letting a tree fall on him] the tree is to be given to the kinsmen, and they are to have it from that estate within 30 days, or else he who owns the wood is to have the right to it.

14. If anyone is born dumb, or deaf, so that he cannot deny sins or confess them, the father is to pay compensation for his misdeeds.

15. If anyone fights or draws a weapon in the presence of the archbishop, he is to pay 150 shillings as compensation; if this happens in the presence of another bishop or of an ealdorman, he is to pay 100 shillings compensation.

16. If anyone steals a cow or a brood-mare and drives off a foal or a calf, he is to pay a shilling compensation [for the latter], and for the mothers according to their value.

17. If anyone entrusts to another one of his helpless dependents, and he dies during that time of fostering, he who reared him is to clear himself of guilt, if anyone accuses him of any.

18. If anyone in lewd fashion seizes a nun either by her clothes or her breast without her leave, the compensation is to be double that we have established for a lay person.

18.1. If a betrothed maiden commits fornication, if she is of *ceorl* birth, 60 shillings compensation is to be paid to the surety; and it is to be paid in livestock, cattle [only], and one is not to include in it any slave.

18.2. If she is a woman of a six-hundred wergeld, 100 shillings are to be given to the surety.

18.3. If she is a woman of a twelve-hundred wergeld, 120 shillings are to be paid to the surety.

19. If anyone lends his weapon to another that he may kill a man with it, they may, if they wish, join him to pay the wergeld.

19.1. If they do not join, he who lent the weapon is to pay a third part of the wergeld and a third part of the fine.

19.2. If he wishes to clear himself, that in making the loan he was aware of no evil intent, he may do so.

19.3. If a sword-polisher receives another man's weapon to polish it, or a smith a man's tool, they both are to give it back unstained,[16] just as either of them had received it; unless either of them had stipulated that he need not be liable to compensation for it.

20. If anyone entrusts property to another man's monk, without the permission of the monk's lord, and it is lost to him, he who owned it before is to bear the loss.

21. If a priest slays another man, he is to be handed over, and all of the [minster] property which he bought for himself, and the bishop is to unfrock him, when he is to be delivered up out of the minster, unless the lord is willing to settle the wergeld on his behalf.

22. If anyone brings up a charge in a public meeting before the king's reeve, and afterward wishes to withdraw it, he is to make the accusation against a more likely person, if he can; if he cannot, he is to forfeit his compensation.

23. If a dog rends or bites a man to death, [the owner] is to pay 6 shillings at the first offense; if he gives it food, he is to pay on a second occasion 12 shillings, on a third 30 shillings.

23.1. If in any of these misdeeds the dog is destroyed, nevertheless this compensation is still to be paid.

23.2. If the dog commits more offenses, and the owner retains it, he is to pay compensation for such wounds as the dog inflicts, according to the full wergeld.

24. If a neat[17] wounds a man, [the owner] is to hand over the neat, or make terms.

25. If anyone rapes a *ceorl*'s slave-woman, he is to pay 5 shillings compensation to the *ceorl*, and 60 shillings fine.

25.1. If a slave rape a slave-woman, he is to pay by suffering castration.

26 (29).[18] If anyone with a band of men kills an innocent man of a two-hundred wergeld, he who admits

---

[16] Without it having been used to commit a crime.

[17] Domestic cow or ox.

[18] The figures in parentheses derive from earlier editors who rearranged the manuscript order.

the slaying is to pay the wergeld and the fine, and each man who was in that expedition is to pay 30 shillings as compensation for being in that band.

27 (30). If it is a man of a six-hundred wergeld, each man [is to pay] 60 shillings as compensation for being in that band, and the slayer the wergeld and full fine.

28. (31). If he is a man of a twelve-hundred wergeld, each of them [is to pay] 120 shillings, and the slayer the wergeld and the fine.

28.1. (31.1). If a band of men does this and afterward wishes to deny it[19] on oath, they are all to be accused; and then they are all collectively to pay the wergeld, and all one fine, as is accordant to the wergeld.

29. (26). If anyone rapes a girl not of age, that is to be the same compensation as for an adult.

30. (27). If a man without paternal kinsmen fights and kills a man, and if then he has maternal kinsmen, those are to pay a third share of the wergeld, [and the associates a third; for the third part] he is to flee.[20]

30.1. (27.1). If he has no maternal kinsmen, the associates are to pay half, and for half he is to flee.

31. (28). If anyone kills a man so placed, if he has no kinsmen, he is to pay half to the king, half to the associates.

32. If anyone is guilty of public slander, and it is proved against him, it is to be compensated for with no lighter penalty than the cutting off of his tongue, with the proviso that it be redeemed at no cheaper rate than it is valued in proportion to the wergeld.

33. If anyone charges another about a pledge sworn by God, and wishes to accuse him that he did not carry out any of those [promises] which he gave him, he [the plaintiff] is to pronounce the preliminary oath in four churches, and the other, if he wishes to clear himself, is to do it in twelve churches.

34. Moreover, it is prescribed for traders; they are to bring before the king's reeve in a public meeting the men whom they take up into the country with

them, and it is to be established how many of them there are to be; and they are to take with them men whom they can afterward bring to justice at a public meeting; and whenever it may be necessary for them to have more men out with them on their journey, it is always to be announced, as often as it is necessary for them, to the king's reeve in the witness of the meeting.

35. If anyone binds an innocent *ceorl*, he is to pay him 10 shillings compensation.

35.1. If anyone scourges him, he is to pay him 20 shillings compensation.

35.2. If he places him in the stocks, he is to pay him 30 shillings compensation.

35.3. If in insult he disfigures him by cutting his hair, he is to pay him 10 shillings compensation.

35.4. If, without binding him, he cuts his hair like a priest's, he is to pay him 30 shillings compensation.

36. Moreover, it is established; if anyone has a spear over his shoulder, and a man is transfixed on it, the wergeld is to be paid without the fine.

36.1. If he transfixed before his eyes, he is to pay the wergeld; if anyone accuses him of intention in this act, he is to clear himself in proportion to the fine, and by that [oath] do away with the fine.

36.2. If the point is higher than the butt end of the shaft. If they are both level, the point and the butt end, that is to be [considered] without risk.

37. If anyone from one district wishes to seek a lord in another district, he is to do so with the witness of the ealdorman, in whose shire he previously served.

37.1. If he do it without his witness, he who accepts him as his man is to pay 120 shillings compensation; he is, however, to divide it, half to the king in the shire in which the man served previously, half in that into which he has come.

37.2. If he has committed any wrong where he was before, he who now receives him as his man is to pay compensation for it, and 120 shillings to the king as fine.

38. If anyone fights in a meeting in the presence of the king's ealdorman, he is to pay wergeld and fine, as it is the law, and before that, 120 shillings to the ealdorman as a fine.

38.1. If he disturbs a public meeting by drawing a weapon, [he is to pay] 120 shillings to the ealdorman as a fine.

38.2. If any of this takes place in the presence of the deputy of the king's ealdorman, or of the king's priest, 30 shillings [is to be paid] as a fine.

---

[19] I.e., each wishes to deny being the actual slayer.

[20] This shows that the payment of their proper share frees the kinsmen from the dangers of a vendetta, even if the whole wergeld is not paid. The slayer himself remains exposed if his own third is unpaid.

39. If anyone fights in the house of a *ceorl*, he is to pay 6 shillings compensation to the *ceorl*.

39.1. If he draws a weapon and does not fight, it is to be half as much.

39.2. If either of these things happens to a man of a six-hundred wergeld, it is to amount to threefold the compensation to a *ceorl*; [if] to a man of a twelve-hundred wergeld, to double that of the man of the six-hundred wergeld.

40. Forcible entry into the king's residence shall be 120 shillings; into the archbishop's, 90 shillings; into another bishop's or an ealdorman's, 60 shillings; into that of a man of a twelve-hundred wergeld, 30 shillings; into that of a man of a six-hundred wergeld, 15 shillings; forcible entry into a *ceorl*'s enclosure, 5 shillings.

40.1. If any of this happens when the army has been called out, or in the Lenten fast, the compensations are to be doubled.

40.2. If anyone openly neglects the rules of the Church in Lent without permission, he is to pay 120 shillings compensation.

41. The man who holds bookland, which his kinsmen left to him—then we establish that he may not alienate it from his kindred if there is a document or witness [to show] that he was prohibited from doing so by those men who acquired it in the beginning and by those who gave it to him; and that is then to be declared[21] in the witness of the king and of the bishop, in the presence of his kinsmen.

42. Moreover we command: that the man who knows his opponent[22] to be dwelling at home is not to fight before he asks justice for himself.

42.1. If he has sufficient power to surround his opponent and besiege him there in his house, he is to keep him seven days inside and not fight against him, if he will remain inside; and then after seven days, if he will surrender and give up his weapons, he is to keep him unharmed for 30 days, and send notice about him to his kinsmen and his friends.

42.2. If, however, he reaches a church, it is then to be [dealt with] according to the privilege of the church, as we have said before.

42.3. If he [the attacker] has not sufficient power to besiege him in his house, he is to ride to the ealdorman and ask him for support; if he will not give him support, he is to ride to the king, before having recourse to fighting.

42.4. Likewise, if a man run across his opponent, and did not previously know him to be at home, if he will give up his weapons, he is to be kept for 30 days and his friends informed; if he will not give up his weapons, then he may fight against him. If he is willing to surrender, and to give up his weapons, and after that anyone fights against him, he [who does] is to pay wergeld or compensation for wounds according to what he has done, and a fine, and is to have forfeited [the right to avenge] his kinsman.

42.5. Moreover we declare that a man may fight on behalf of his lord, if the lord is being attacked, without incurring a vendetta. Similarly the lord may fight on behalf of his man.

42.6. In the same way, a man may fight on behalf of his born kinsman, if he is being wrongfully attacked, except against his lord; that we do not allow.

42.7. And a man may fight without incurring a vendetta if he finds another man with his wedded wife, within closed doors or under the same blanket, or with his legitimate daughter or his legitimate sister, or with his mother who was given as a lawful wife to his father.

43. These days are to be given to all free men, but not to slaves or unfree laborers: 12 days at Christmas, and the day on which Christ overcame the Devil, and the anniversary of St. Gregory, and seven days at Easter and seven days after, and one day at the feast of St. Peter and St. Paul, and in harvest-time the whole week before the feast of St. Mary, and one day at the feast of All Saints. And the four Wednesdays in the four Ember weeks[23] are to be given to all slaves, to sell to whomsoever they choose anything of what anyone has given them in God's name, or of what they can earn in any of their leisure moments.[24]

THE TREATY BETWEEN ALFRED AND GUTHRUM (886–890)

PROLOGUE. This is the peace which King Alfred and King Guthrum and the councilors of all the English race and all the people which is in East Anglia have all agreed

---

[21] By whoever is contesting the alienation of the land.

[22] A man against whom he has a legitimate blood-feud.

[23] The weeks in which occur four sets of three days of fasting, spaced through the year.

[24] The rest of the code consists of a tariff of the compensations to be paid for wounds of various kinds and for other injuries.

on and confirmed with oaths, for themselves and for their subjects, both for the living and those yet unborn, who care to have God's grace or ours.

1. First concerning our boundaries: up the Thames, and then up the Lea, and along the Lea to its source, then in a straight line to Bedford, then up the Ouse to the Watling Street.[25]

2. This is next, if a man is slain, all of us estimate Englishmen and Dane at the same amount, at eight half-marks[26] of refined gold, except the *ceorl* who occupies rented land, and their [the Danes'] freedmen; these also are estimated at the same amount, both at 200 shillings.

3. And if anyone accuses a king's thegn[27] of manslaughter, if he dares to clear himself by oath, he is to do it with 12 king's thegns; if anyone accuses a man who is less powerful than a king's thegn, he is to clear himself with 12 of his equals and with one king's thegn—and so in every suit which involves more than four mancuses[28]— and if he dare not [clear himself], he is to pay three-fold compensation, according as it is valued.

4. And that each man is to know his warrantor at [the purchase of] men or horses or oxen.

5. And we all agreed on the day when the oaths were sworn, that no slaves nor freemen might go without permission into the army of the Danes, any more than any of theirs to us. But if it happens that from necessity any one of them wishes to have traffic with us, or we with them, for cattle or goods, it is to be permitted on condition that hostages shall be given as a pledge of peace and as evidence so that one may know no fraud is intended.

---

[25] An ancient roadway from Canterbury and St. Albans.

[26] A mark was a Scandinavian weight, by the end of the next century, and perhaps already, about 3,440–3,520 grains. The amount here stated may represent a recognized Scandinavian wergeld, but, if the ratio of gold to silver was approximately 10:1 at this time, it would not be very far from the wergeld of the highest English class.

[27] An aristocratic retainer of a king.

[28] A gold coin or a unit of accounting equal to 30 pennies.

LETTER TO KING EDWARD THE ELDER EXPLAINING THE HISTORY OF AN ESTATE AT FONTHILL, WILTSHIRE (899–924, PROBABLY EARLY IN THE REIGN)

Sire, I will inform you what happened about the land at Fonthill, the five hides which Æthelhelm Higa is claiming. When Helmstan committed the crime of stealing Æthelred's belt, Higa at once began to bring a charge against him, along with other claimants, and wished to win the land from him by litigation. Then he came to me and begged me to intercede for him, because I had stood sponsor to him at his confirmation before he committed that crime. Then—may God repay his soul—he allowed him to be entitled to prove his right against Æthelhelm as regards the land, because of my advocacy and true account. Then he ordered that they should be brought to agreement, and I was one of the men appointed to do it, and Wihtbord and Ælfric, who was then keeper of the wardrobe, and Brihthelm and Wulfhun the Black of Somerton, and Strica and Ubba and more men than I can now name. Then each of them gave his account, and it then seemed to us all that Helmstan should be allowed to come forward with the title-deeds and prove his right to the land, that he had it as Æthelthryth had sold it into Oswulf's possession at a suitable price; and she had told Oswulf that she was entitled to sell it to him because it was her "morning-gift" when she married Æthelwulf. And Helmstan included all this in the oath. And King Alfred had given his signature to Oswulf, when he bought the land from Æthelthryth, that it might thus remain valid, and Edward gave his and Æthelnoth his and Deormod his, and so did each of the men whom one then wished to have. And when we were reconciling them at Wardour, the deed was produced and read, and the signatures were all written on it. Then it seemed to all of us who were at that arbitration that Helmstan was the nearer to the oath on that account.

Then Æthelhelm would not fully assent until we went in to the king and told exactly how we had decided it and why we had decided it; and Æthelhelm stood himself in there with us. And the king stood in the chamber at Wardour—he was washing his hands. When he had finished, he asked Æthelhelm why what we had decided for him did not seem just to him; he said that he could think of nothing more just then than that Helmstan should be allowed to give the oath if he could. I then said that he wished to attempt it, and asked the king to appoint a day for it, and he then did so. And on that appointed day he performed the oath fully. He asked me to help him, and said that he would rather give [the land to me] than that the oath should fail or it ever. . . . Then I said that I would help him to obtain justice, but never to any wrong, on condition that he granted it to me; and he gave me a pledge to that.

And then we rode on that appointed day, I—and Wihtbord rode with me, and Brihthelm rode there with Æthelhelm; and we all heard that he gave the oath in full. Then we all said that it was a closed suit when the sentence had been fulfilled. And, Sire, when will any suit be ended if one can end it neither with money nor with an oath? And if one wishes to change every judgment which King Alfred gave, when shall we have finished disputing? And he then gave me the title-deed just as he had pledged to do, as soon as the oath was given; and I promised him that he might use the land as long as he lived, if he would keep himself out of disgrace.

Then on top of that—I do not know whether it was a year and a half or two years later—he stole the untended oxen at Fonthill, by which he was completely ruined, and drove them to Chicklade, and there he was discovered, and the man who tracked him rescued the traced cattle [?]. Then he fled, and a bramble scratched him in the face; and when he wished to deny it, that was brought in evidence against him. Then Eanwulf, Peneard's son, who was the reeve, intervened, and took from him all the property that he owned at Tisbury. I then asked him why he did so, and he said that he was a thief, and the property was adjudged to the king, because he was the king's man. And Ordlaf succeeded to his land; because what he was occupying was held on lease from him, he could not forfeit it. And you then pronounced him an outlaw. Then he sought your father's body, and brought a seal[29] to me, and I was with you at Chippenham. Then I gave the seal to you, and you removed his outlawry and gave him the estate to which he still has withdrawn [?]. And I succeeded to my land, and then in your witness and that of your councilors I gave it to the bishop, five hides in exchange for the land of five hides at Lyddiard. And the bishop and all the community granted me the four hides, and the fifth was subject to tithe. Now, Sire, it is very necessary for me that it may remain as it is now arranged and was before. If it shall be otherwise, then I must and will be satisfied with what seems right to you as a charitable gift.

Endorsement

And Æthelhelm Higa retired from the dispute when the king was at Warminster, in the witness of Ordlaf and Osferth and Odda and Wihtbord and Ælfstan the Bald and Æthelnoth.

ASSER'S *LIFE OF KING ALFRED*

To my venerable and most pious lord, ruler of all the Christians of the island of Britain, Alfred, king of the Anglo-Saxons, Asser, lowest of all the servants of God, wishes thousandfold prosperity in both the present and future life, according to his prayers and desires.

Chapter 1. In the year of our Lord's incarnation 849, Alfred, king of the Anglo-Saxons, was born in the royal residence called Wantage, in the shire which is named Berkshire; which shire is thus called from the wood *Berroc*, where box grows very abundantly. . . .[30]

Chapter 2. His mother was called Osburh, a very religious woman, noble in character, noble also by birth; for she was the daughter of Oslac, the renowned cupbearer of King Æthelwulf. This Oslac was by race a Goth, for he was sprung from the Goths and Jutes, namely from the stock of Stuf and Wihtgar, two brothers, and also ealdormen, who received the rule over the Isle of Wight from their uncle King Cerdic and his son Cynric, their cousin. They killed the few British inhabitants of the island whom they could find on it at the place called *Wihtgarabyrig*; for the rest of the inhabitants of the island had either already been killed or had fled as exiles. . . .

Chapter 12. But meanwhile,[31] King Æthelwulf was lingering beyond the sea for some little time, a certain disgraceful thing, contrary to the practice of all Christians, arose to the west of Selwood. For King Æthelbald, son of King Æthelwulf, and Ealhstan, bishop of the church of Somerset, are said to have plotted that King Æthelwulf should not be received again into the kingship when he returned from Rome. This unhappy business, unheard of in all previous ages, very many persons ascribe to the bishop and the ealdorman alone, by whose counsel it is said this deed was done. But there are also many who impute it solely to the royal pride, because that king was stubborn in this affair and in many other wrong acts,

---

[29] Probably a document authenticated by a seal, to show that he had taken an oath at the king's tomb.

[30] Here follows his genealogy.

[31] I.e., while Æthelwulf was away on his visit to Rome in 855.

as we have heard from certain men's accounts; and this was proved by the outcome of the affair. For as King Æthelwulf was returning from Rome, his son aforesaid, with all his counselors, or rather conspirators, tried to commit so great a crime as to keep the king out of his own kingdom; but God did not allow it to happen, neither did the nobles of all the Saxon land consent. For, in order that the irremediable danger to the Saxon land from civil war, with father and son at war, or rather with the whole people fighting against one or the other of them, might not grow more fierce and cruel from day to day, the kingdom previously united was by the indescribable forbearance of the father and the assent of all the nobles divided between father and son; and the eastern districts were assigned to the father, the western, on the other hand, to the son. Thus, where the father ought to have reigned by rights, the wicked and stubborn son reigned; for the western part of the Saxon land has always been more important than the eastern.

Chapter 13. When therefore King Æthelwulf arrived from Rome, all the people, as was fitting, rejoiced so greatly at the coming of their lord, that, if he had allowed it, they wished to deprive his stubborn son Æthelbald, with all his counselors, of any share in the kingdom. But he, as we have said, exercising great forbearance and prudent counsel, lest danger should befall the kingdom, would not have it done thus. And without any opposition or illfeeling on his nobles' part, he ordered that Judith, daughter of King Charles, whom he had received from her father, was to sit beside him on the royal throne as long as he lived, contrary to the wrongful custom of that nation. For the people of the West Saxons did not allow the queen to sit next the king, or even to be called queen, but "wife of the king." . . . [32]

Chapter 16. Thus King Æthelwulf lived two years after he came back from Rome. During these years, among many other good endeavors in this present life, meditating on his departure on the way of all flesh, he ordered to be written a testamentary, or rather an advisory, letter, so that his sons should not dispute unduly among themselves after their father's death; in this he took care to command in writing in due form, a division of the kingdom between his sons, that is to say the two eldest, of his own inheritance between his sons and daughter and his relations also, and of the money, which he should

leave, between the needs of the soul and his sons and also his nobles. Concerning this prudent policy we have decided to record a few examples out of many, for posterity to imitate, namely such as are understood to belong particularly to the necessities of the soul. It is unnecessary to insert the rest, which belong to human dispensation, in this little book, lest by its length it should arouse disgust in the readers and also in those desiring to hear it. For the benefit of his soul then, which he had been zealous to promote in all things from the first flower of his youth, he enjoined that his successors after him until the Day of Judgment were always to supply with food, drink and clothing, one poor man, whether a native or foreigner, from every ten hides throughout all his hereditary land, provided that that land was occupied by men and herds, and had not become waste land. He gave orders also that a great sum of money was every year to be taken to Rome for his soul, namely 300 mancuses, which were to be divided there thus: 100 mancuses in honor of St. Peter, especially for the purchase of oil to fill all the lamps of that apostolic church on Easter eve and likewise at cockcrow, and 100 mancuses in honor of St. Paul on the same terms, for the purchase of oil to fill the lamps on Easter eve and at cockcrow, and 100 mancuses also for the universal apostolic pope.

Chapter 17. But when King Æthelwulf was dead, his son Æthelbald, contrary to God's prohibition and Christian dignity, and also against the usage of all pagans, ascending the bed of his father, married Judith, daughter of Charles, king of the Franks, earning much infamy from all who heard of it; and ruled the government of the kingdom of the West Saxons for two and a half years after his father's death. . . .

Chapter 21. . . . I think that we should return to what specially incited me to this work; that is to say, that I consider that I should insert briefly in this place the little that has come to my knowledge concerning the character of my revered lord, Alfred, king of the Anglo-Saxons, during his childhood and boyhood.

Chapter 22. Now, he was loved by his father and mother, and indeed by everybody, with a united and immense love, more than all his brothers, and was always brought up in the royal court, and as he passed through his childhood and boyhood he appeared fairer in form than all his brothers, and more pleasing in his looks, his words, and his ways. And from his cradle a longing for wisdom before all things and among all the pursuits of this present life, combined with his noble birth, filled the noble temper of his mind; but alas, by the unworthy carelessness of his parents and tutors, he remained ignorant

---

[32] Here follows a story that this custom arose from the evil behavior of Offa's daughter, Eadburh, wife of Brihtric of Wessex, part of which Asser tells on Alfred's authority.

of letters until his twelfth year, or even longer. But he listened attentively to Saxon poems day and night, and hearing them often recited by others committed them to his retentive memory. A keen huntsman, he toiled unceasingly in every branch of hunting, and not in vain; for he was without equal in his skill and good fortune in that art, as also in all other gifts of God, as we have ourselves often seen.

Chapter 23. When, therefore, his mother one day was showing him and his brothers a certain book of Saxon poetry which she held in her hand, she said: "I will give this book to whichever of you can learn it most quickly." And moved by these words, or rather by divine inspiration, and attracted by the beauty of the initial letter of the book, Alfred said in reply to his mother, forestalling his brothers, his elders in years though not in grace: "Will you really give this book to one of us, to the one who can soonest understand and repeat it to you?" And, smiling and rejoicing, she confirmed it, saying: "To him will I give it." Then taking the book from her hand he immediately went to his master, who read it. And when it was read, he went back to his mother and repeated it.

Chapter 24. After this he learnt the daily course, that is, the services of the hours, and then certain psalms and many prayers. He collected these into one book and carried it about with him everywhere in his bosom (as I have myself seen) day and night, for the sake of prayer, through all the changes of this present life, and was never parted from it. But alas, what he principally desired, the liberal arts, he did not obtain according to his wish, because, as he was wont to say, there were at that time no good scholars in all the kingdom of the West Saxons.

Chapter 25. He often affirmed with frequent laments and sighs from the bottom of his heart, that among all his difficulties and hindrances in this present life this was the greatest; that, during the time when he had youth and leisure and aptitude for learning, he had no teachers; but when he was more advanced in years, he did have teachers and writers to some extent, when he was not able to study, because he was harassed, nay, rather disturbed, day and night both with illnesses unknown to all the physicians of this island, and with the cares of the royal office at home and abroad, and also with the invasions of pagans by land and sea. Yet, among all the difficulties of this present life, from infancy unto the present day, he has never abandoned that same insatiable longing, and even now still yearns for it. . . .

Chapter 75. Sons and daughters were born to him by the aforesaid wife, namely Æthelflæd, the firstborn, and after her Edward, then Æthelgifu, next Ælfthryth, then Æthelweard, besides those who were snatched away in infancy by an early death. . . . Æthelflæd, when she reached marriageable age, was joined in matrimony to Æthelred, ealdorman of the Mercians. Æthelgifu, devoted to God as a virgin, subjected and consecrated to the rules of the monastic life, entered the service of God. Æthelweard, the youngest, was given over by the divine counsel and the admirable prudence of the king to the pleasures of literary studies, along with almost all the children of noble birth of the whole country, and also many of humble birth, under the diligent care of masters. In that school, books of both languages, Latin, that is, and English, were assiduously read, and they had leisure for writing; so that before they had the strength for manly pursuits, namely hunting and other pursuits which are fitting for noblemen, they were zealous and skilled in the liberal arts. Edward and Ælfthryth were always brought up in the royal court, with great care from their tutors and nurses, and indeed, with great affection from all; and until this day they continue there, showing humility, affability, and gentleness to all, whether their countrymen or foreigners, and great obedience to their father. Nor, indeed, are they allowed to live idly and carelessly without a liberal education among the other occupations of this present life which are fitting for nobles; for they have learnt carefully psalms and Saxon books, and especially Saxon poems, and they frequently make use of books.

Chapter 76. Meanwhile the king, in the midst of wars and frequent hindrances of this present life, and also of the raids of the pagans and his daily infirmities of body did not cease, single-handed, assiduously, and eagerly with all his might, to govern the kingdom, to practice every branch of hunting, to instruct his goldsmiths and aid his craftsmen, and his falconers, hawkers and dog-keepers, to erect buildings to his own new design more stately and magnificent than had been the custom of his ancestors, to recite Saxon books, and especially to learn by heart Saxon poems, and command others to do so. He also was in the habit of hearing daily the divine office, the Mass, and certain prayers and psalms, and of observing both the day and the night hours, and of visiting churches at night-time, as we have said, in order to pray without his followers knowing. Moreover, he showed zeal for almsgiving, and generosity both to his countrymen and to strangers from all nations, and very great and matchless kindness and pleasantness toward all men, and skill in searching into things unknown. And many Franks, Frisians, men of Gaul, pagans, Welsh, Scots, and Bretons willingly submitted to his lordship, both noblemen and men of humble rank; and he ruled them all in accordance with his own honorable nature just like his own people, and loved and honored them, and enriched them with money and rights. Also he was accustomed to listen to the Holy Scripture recited by native clergy, but also, if by chance someone had come from elsewhere, to listen with equal earnestness and attention to prayers along with foreigners. He also loved his bishops and all the ecclesiastical order, his ealdormen and his nobles, his officials and all members of his household, with a wonderful affection. And he himself never ceased among other occupations, day and night, to train their sons, who were being brought up in the royal household, in all good behavior, and to educate them in letters, loving them no less than his own sons. Yet, as if he had no comfort in all these things and as if he suffered no disquiet from within or without, he complained in anxious sadness by day and night to God and to all who were bound to him in close affection, and lamented with repeated sighs, that Almighty God had not made him skilled in divine wisdom and the liberal arts; emulating in this the pious and most illustrious and rich Solomon, king of the Hebrews, who, despising all present glory and riches, sought first wisdom from God, and also found both, wisdom and present glory, as it is written: "Seek therefore first the kingdom of God and his justice, and all these things shall be granted unto you."[33] But God, who always sees into the inmost thoughts, and prompts our designs and all good desires, and also most amply ordains that good desires may be obtained, and who never prompts anyone to desire well without also ordaining what each man well and justly desires to have, stirred up the king's mind from within, not without; as it is written: "I will hear what the Lord God will speak in me."[34] Whenever he could, he would acquire assistants in his good design, who could help him to the desired wisdom, that he might obtain what he longed for. Forthwith, like the prudent bee, which arises in the summer-time at dawn from its beloved cells and, directing its course in swift flight through the unknown ways of the air, alights upon many and various blossoms of herbs, plants, and fruits, and finds and carries home what pleases it most, he turned afar the gaze of his mind, seeking abroad what he had not at home, that is, in his own kingdom.

Chapter 77. And then God, suffering no longer his so good and just complaint, sent for the king's good-will some consolations, certain lights, as it were, namely Wærferth, bishop of the church of Worcester, a man well

versed in the divine Scriptures, who at the king's command first translated clearly and beautifully from Latin into the Saxon language the books of the "Dialogues" of Pope Gregory and his disciple Peter, sometimes giving a paraphrase; and then Plegmund, a Mercian by race, archbishop of the church of Canterbury, a venerable man, endowed with wisdom; also Æthelstan and Wærwulf, priests and chaplains, learned men, of Mercian race. King Alfred summoned these four to him from Mercia, and advanced them with great honors and authority in the kingdom of the West Saxons, in addition to those which Archbishop Plegmund and Bishop Wærferth possessed in Mercia. By the teaching and wisdom of all these men, the king's desire was ceaselessly increased and fulfilled. For by day and night, whenever he had any free time, he ordered books to be read before him by such men, nor indeed did he allow himself to be without any of them. Therefore he obtained a knowledge of almost all books, although he could not as yet by himself understand anything from books, for he had not yet begun to read anything.

Chapter 78. But, since in this matter the royal avarice, praiseworthy as it was, was still unsatisfied, he sent messengers across the sea to Gaul to acquire teachers. From there he summoned Grimbald, priest and monk, a venerable man, an excellent singer, most learned in every way in ecclesiastical studies and the divine Scriptures and adorned with all good qualities; and also John, likewise a priest and monk, a man of very keen intelligence and most learned in all branches of the art of literature, enriched and skilled in many other arts. By their teaching the king's mind was much enriched; he endowed and honored them with great authority.

Chapter 79. At that time I also was summoned by the king, and came to the Saxon land from the western and farthest parts of Wales, and when I had decided to come to him through great tracts of country. I reached the province of the South Saxons, which is called Sussex in the Saxon language, led by guides of that race. There I first saw the king in the royal residence which is called Dean. And when I had been kindly received by him, among other topics of conversation, he asked me pressingly to devote myself to his service and to be a member of his court, and to give up for his sake all that I possessed to the north and west of the Severn; and he promised also to give me a greater recompense. And this he did. I replied that I could not make such a promise carelessly and rashly. For it seemed wrong to me to desert for the sake of any worldly honor and power those so holy places in which I had been reared and educated, tonsured, and finally ordained, unless by force and compulsion. To

---

[33] Luke 12:31.
[34] Psalm 85:8.

which he said: "If you cannot accede to this, at least grant to me half of your service, so that you may be six months with me and as many in Wales." To which I replied thus: "I cannot promise this easily and rashly without the counsel of my friends." But indeed, since I realized that he desired my services, though I knew not why, I promised that I would return to him six months later, if my life were spared, with such a reply as might be advantageous for me and mine, and acceptable to him. And when this reply seemed good to him, and I had given a pledge to return at the appointed time, on the fourth day we rode away from him and returned to our own land. But when we had left him, a violent fever laid hold of me in the city of Caer and I was grievously afflicted with it day and night for 12 months and a week without any hope of life. And when I did not come to him at the appointed time, as I had promised, he sent letters to me, which urged me to ride to him and inquired the cause of the delay. But as I could not ride to him, I sent another letter to him, which explained to him the reason for my delay and declared that I would perform what I had promised if I could recover from that sickness. Therefore, when the sickness left me, I devoted myself, as I had promised the king, to his service, by the advice and permission of all our people, for the benefit of that holy place and all dwelling in it, on this condition, that I should spend six months of every year with him, either, if I could, six months at a time, or otherwise by turns spend three months in Wales and three in the Saxon land, and that land should be benefited by the teaching of St. David, yet in every case in proportion to our strength. For our brethren hoped that they would suffer fewer tribulations and injuries from King Hyfaidd—who often plundered that monastery and the diocese of St. David's, sometimes by driving out the bishops who were in charge of it, as he at one time among these drove out Archbishop Nobis, my kinsman, and me myself—if I were to come to the notice and friendship of that king by any kind of agreement.

Chapter 80. For at that time, and for a long time before, all the districts of the southern part of Wales belonged to King Alfred, and still belong to him; for Hyfaidd with all the inhabitants of the region of Dyfed, compelled by the power of the six sons of Rhodri, had submitted to the royal overlordship; also Hywel, son of Rhys, king of Glywyssing, and Brochwel and Ffernfael, the sons of Merwig, kings of Gwent, compelled by the might and tyranny of Ealdorman Æthelred and the Mercians, of their own accord besought the same king that he would be their lord and protector against their enemies. Also Elise, son of Tewdwr, king of Brecknock, forced by the power of the same sons of Rhodri, with his brothers, finally deserted the friendship of the Northumbrians, from which they had no good, but only injury, and came to the king's presence earnestly beseeching his friendship. And when he had been honorably received by the king, and been accepted by him as his son from the hands of the bishop at confirmation, and been enriched by great gifts, he submitted with all his followers to the king's overlordship, on such terms that he would be obedient to the king in all things, just like Æthelred with the Mercians.

Chapter 81. Nor did they all obtain the king's friendship in vain. For those who desired to increase their earthly power, obtained this; those who desired money, obtained money; those who desired friendship, gained friendship; those who desired both, received both. And all had love and guardianship and protection from every side, in as far as the king with his people could defend himself. When, therefore, I came to him at the royal residence which is called *Leonaford*, I was honorably received by him, and remained with him in his court on that occasion for eight months, during which I read to him whatever books he wished and which we had at hand. For it is his most usual habit either himself to read books aloud or to listen to others who read them, day and night, in the midst of all other occupations of mind and body. And when I had frequently asked his permission to return, and could by no means obtain it, at length when I had made up my mind absolutely to demand his permission, I was summoned to him in the early morning of the eve of our Lord's Nativity, and he delivered to me two letters, in which there was a detailed list of all the things belonging to two monasteries, which in Saxon are called Congresbury and Banwell, and on that same day he delivered to me those two monasteries with everything that was in them, and a very costly silk robe, and a strong man's load of incense, adding these words, that he did not give me these small things because he was unwilling to give greater later on. Indeed at a later time he unexpectedly gave me Exeter, with all the diocese belonging to it, in Saxon territory and in Cornwall, besides innumerable daily gifts of all kinds of earthly riches, which it would be tedious to enumerate here lest it should cause weariness to the readers. But do not let anyone think that I have mentioned such gifts in this place out of any vain-glory or in flattery, or for the sake of gaining greater honor; for I call God to witness that I have not done so, but only to make clear to those who do not know, how profuse is his generosity. Then at once he gave me leave to ride to those two monasteries, which were filled with all good things, and thence to return to my own country.

Chapter 87. Also in that same year (887) the oft-mentioned Alfred, king of the Anglo-Saxons, first began by the divine inspiration both to read (Latin) and translate on one and the same day. But, that this may be made clear to those ignorant of it, I will take care to explain the reason for this late start.

Chapter 88. For when we were both sitting one day in the royal chamber talking as was our wont, on all sorts of subjects, it happened that I read to him a passage from a certain book. And when he had listened to it intently with both his ears, and pondered it carefully in the depths of this mind, he suddenly showed me a little book, which he constantly carried in the depths of his bosom, in which were contained the daily course and certain psalms and prayers which he had read in his youth, and he ordered me to write that passage in the same little book. And I, hearing this and perceiving in part his eagerness of mind and also his devout wish to study the divine wisdom, gave great thanks to Almighty God, although silently, with hands outstretched to heaven, who had planted so great devotion for the study of wisdom in the king's heart. But when I found no vacant space in that little book, in which I could write the passage—for it was completely filled with various matters—I hesitated for a little while, principally that I might provoke the king's fine understanding to a greater knowledge of the divine testimonies. And when he urged me to write it as quickly as possible I said to him: "Are you willing that I should write this passage on a separate leaf? For we do not know whether we may not at some time find one or more such passages which may please you; and if this happens unexpectedly, we shall be glad to have kept it apart." And hearing this, he said that it was a good plan. When I heard this I was glad, and hastened to prepare a quire, at the beginning of which I wrote the passage he had commended; and on the same day I wrote by his command no fewer than three other passages which pleased him, in the same quire, as I had foretold. And henceforth as we daily talked together, and searching to this end found other equally pleasing passages, that quire became full; and rightly, as it is written: "The just man builds upon a small foundation and by degrees passes to greater things." Like a most productive bee, traveling far and wide over the marshes in its quest, he eagerly and unceasingly collected many various flowers of Holy Scripture, with which he densely stored the cells of his mind.

Chapter 89. Now, once that passage had been written, he straightway was eager to read and to translate into the Saxon language, and hence to instruct many others. And just as we should learn from that happy thief, who knew the Lord Jesus Christ, his Lord, and indeed the Lord of all, hanging beside him on the venerable gallows of the Holy Cross; for with humble prayers, bending on him his bodily eyes, because he could do nothing else, being all fixed with nails, he called with a lowly voice: "Christ, remember me when thou shalt come into thy kingdom," and on the gallows first began to learn the rudiments of the Christian faith; the king likewise, though in a different way, for he was set with royal power, presumed by the instigation of God to begin his first lessons in holy writings on the festival of St. Martin and he [began] to learn those flowers, which had been gathered from various masters, and to bring them all into the compass of one book although in no order, as they came to hand, until it grew almost to the size of a psalter. This book he used to call his "enchiridion," that is, "hand-book," because he was most careful to have it at hand by day and night. And he found, as he then said, no little comfort in it. . . .

Chapter 91. The king was pierced by many nails of tribulation, although placed in royal power. For, from his twentieth till his forty-fifth year, in which he now is, he has been constantly afflicted with a most severe attack of an unknown malady, so that he has not a single hour's peace, in which he is not either suffering that infirmity or driven almost to despair by apprehension of it. Moreover he was troubled, and with good reason, by the constant inroads of foreign peoples, which he constantly sustained by land and sea without any peaceful interval. What shall I say of his frequent expeditions and battles against the pagans and the incessant cares of government? What of his daily [solicitude] for the nations, which dwell from the Tyrrhenian Sea to the farthest end of Ireland? Indeed, we have even seen and read letters sent to him along with gifts by the patriarch Elias. What of the cities and towns he restored, and the others, which he built where none had been before? Of the buildings made by his instructions with gold and silver, beyond compare? Of the royal halls and chambers constructed admirably in stone and timber at his command? Of the royal residences in stone, moved at the royal command from their ancient sites and beautifully erected in more suitable places? And what of the great trouble and vexation (besides his illness) he had with his own people, who would voluntarily submit to little or no labor for the common needs of the kingdom? Yet, just as a skillful pilot strives to bring his ship, laden with great riches, to the longed-for safe harbor of his native land, though nearly all his sailors are worn out; he, upheld by divine aid, would not allow the helm of the kingdom he had once received to totter or waver, though set alone in the midst of the raging and manifold whirlpools of this present life. For he most wisely brought over and bound to his own will and to the common profit of the whole kingdom his bishops and ealdormen and nobles, and the thegns who were dearest to him, and also his reeves, to whom, after God and the king, the control of the kingdom seems rightly to belong, by gently instructing, flattering, urging, commanding them, and, after long patience, by punishing sharply the disobedient, and by showing in every way hatred of vulgar folly and obstinacy. But if among these exhortations of the king, his orders were not carried out because of the slackness of the people, or things begun late in time of need were unfinished and of no profit to those who undertook them—for I may tell of fortresses ordered by him and still not begun, or begun too late to be brought to completion—and enemy forces broke in by land or sea, or, as often happened, on every side, the opponents of the royal ordinances then were ashamed with a vain repentance when on the brink of ruin. For by the witness of Scripture I call that repentance vain, by which numberless men sorrow when afflicted with grievous loss for the many ill-deeds they have committed. But though—alas, the pity of it—they are sadly afflicted through this, and moved to tears by the loss of their fathers, wives, children, servants, slaves, handmaids, their labors, and all their goods, what help is hateful repentance, when it cannot succor their slain kinsmen, nor redeem captives from odious captivity, nor even can it help themselves, who have escaped, seeing that they have nought with which to sustain their own lives? Grievously afflicted, they then repent with too late repentance, and regret that they have carelessly neglected the king's orders, and with one voice praise the king's wisdom, and promise to fulfill with all their strength what they have before refused, that is, with regard to the building of fortresses and the other things for the common profit of the whole kingdom.

Chapter 92. I do not consider it profitable to pass over in this place his vow and most well thought-out scheme, which he was never able to put aside by any means either in prosperity or adversity. For when in his usual manner he was meditating on the needs of his soul, among other good acts in which he was actively engaged by day and night, he ordered the foundation of two monasteries; one for monks in the place which is called Athelney, which is surrounded on all sides by very great swampy and impassable marshes, so that no one can approach it by any means except in punts or by a bridge which has been made with laborious skill between two fortresses. At the western end of this bridge a very strong fort has been placed of most beautiful workmanship by the king's

command. In this monastery he collected monks of various races from every quarter, and set them therein.

Chapter 93. For at first he had no noble or freeman of his nation who would of his own accord enter the monastic life—apart from children, who by reason of their tender age could not yet choose good or refuse evil—for indeed for many years past the desire for the monastic life had been utterly lacking in all that people, and also in many other nations, although there still remains many monasteries founded in that land, but none properly observing the rule of this way of life, I know not why; whether on account of the onslaughts of foreigners, who very often have invaded by land or sea, or on account of the nation's too great abundance of riches of every kind, which I am much more inclined to think the reason for that contempt of the monastic life. For this reason he sought to gather together monks of different race in that monastery.

Chapter 94. First, he appointed John, priest and monk, by race an Old Saxon, as abbot, and then some priests and deacons from across the sea. But when he still had not with these the number he wanted, he also procured many of that same Gallic race, some of whom, being children, he ordered to be educated in that same monastery, and to be raised to the monastic order at a later time. In that monastery I also saw one of pagan race, brought up there and wearing the monastic habit, quite a young man, and not the lowest among them. . . .

Chapter 98. The aforesaid king also ordered to be built another monastery by the east gate of Shaftesbury, as a habitation for nuns, over which he appointed as abbess his own daughter, Æthelgifu, a virgin dedicated to God. And along with her dwell many other noble nuns serving God in the monastic life in the same monastery. He richly endowed these two monasteries with estates and wealth of all kinds.

Chapter 99. When all this was thus settled, he meditated according to his usual practice what he could still add that would further his pious intentions. Things wisely begun and profitably conceived were profitably continued. For long ago he had heard that it was written in the law that the Lord had promised to repay His tithe many times over, and had faithfully kept his promise. Inspired by this example and wishing to excel the practice of his predecessors, the pious thinker promised that he would faithfully and devoutly with all his heart give to God a half part of his service, both by day and night, and also the half part of all the riches which reached him every year by moderate and just acquisition; and this resolve he strove to carry out skillfully and wisely in as far as human discernment can observe and keep it. But, as was his habit, in order that he might carefully avoid what we are warned against in another place in Holy Scripture: "If thou offer aright, but dost not divide aright, thou sinnest," he considered how he might rightly divide what he willingly devoted to God, and, as Solomon says: "The heart of the king"—that is his counsel—"is in the hand of the Lord." Taking counsel from on high, he ordered his officers first to divide into two equal parts all his annual revenue.

Chapter 100. When this was done, he adjudged that the first part should be devoted to secular uses, and ordered that this should be further divided into three parts. The first of these shares he bestowed annually on his fighting men, and also on his noble thegns who dwelt by turns in his court, serving him in many offices. Now the royal household was always managed in three relays; for the followers of the aforesaid king were prudently divided into three companies, so that the first company resided one month in the royal court on duty day and night, and when the month was over and another company arrived, the first went home and remained there for two months, each seeing to his own affairs. So also the second company, when its month was over and the third company arrived, returned home and stayed there for two months. And also the third, having finished one month of service, went home when the first company arrived, to remain there for two months. And by this arrangement the administration of the royal court is taken in turn at all times of this present life.

Chapter 101. Thus, then, did he grant the first of the three aforesaid shares to such men, to each, however, according to his rank and also to his office; and the second to the craftsmen, whom he had with him in almost countless number, collected and procured from many races, who were men skilled in every kind of earthly craft; and the third share to strangers from every race, who flocked to him from places far and near asking him for money, and even to those who did not ask, to each according to his rank. He gave in a praiseworthy manner with a wonderful liberality, and cheerfully, since it is written: "The Lord loveth a cheerful giver."

Chapter 102. But the second part of all his wealth, which came to him every year from revenue of every kind, and was paid into his treasury, he devoted, as we said a little while back, with all his will, to God, and ordered his officials to divide it most carefully into four equal parts, in such a way, that the first part of this division was to be prudently dispended on the poor of every race who came to him. He used to say in this connexion, that as far as

human discretion could ensure it, the saying of the holy Pope Gregory ought to be observed, in which he made a wise observation about the division of alms, saying thus: "Do not give little to whom you should give much, nor much to whom you should give little, nor nothing to whom you should give something, nor anything to whom you should give nothing." And the second part he gave to the two monasteries which he himself had built, and to those serving in them, about which we spoke more fully a little way back; and the third to a school which he had collected very zealously from many nobles of his own race and also boys not of noble birth; and the fourth part to the neighboring monasteries throughout the Saxon kingdom and Mercia. And in some years he also either made gifts, according to his means, to the churches in Wales and Cornwall, Old Brittany, Northumbria, and sometimes even in Ireland, in turn, and to the servants of God dwelling in them, or else he proposed to give them later on, provided his life and prosperity continued. . . .

Chapter 105. When these things had been completely set in order, since he desired as he had vowed to God, to preserve half his service, and to increase it further, in as far as his capacity and his means, and indeed his infirmity, permitted, he showed himself a minute inquirer into the truth of judgments, and this especially because of his care for the poor, on whose behalf he exerted himself wonderfully by day and by night in the midst of his other duties in this present life. For except for him alone, the poor had no helpers throughout that kingdom, or indeed very few; since almost all the magnates and nobles of that land had turned their minds more to the things of this world than to the things of God; indeed, in the things of this world each regarded more his own private advantage than the common good.

Chapter 106. Also he gave attention to judgments for the benefit of his nobles and common people, for in the assemblies of the ealdormen and the reeves they disagreed among themselves, so that hardly one of them would allow to be valid whatever had been judged by the ealdormen or reeves. And compelled by this perverse and obstinate dissension, all desired to submit to the king's judgment, and both parties quickly hastened to do so. But yet anyone who knew that on his side some injustice had been committed in that suit, was unwilling to approach the judgment of such a judge of his own accord, but only against his will, though compelled to come by force of law and covenant. For he knew that there he could not quickly conceal any part of his ill-doing, and no wonder, since the king was in truth a most skilled investigator into the exercise of justice, as in all other matters. For he shrewdly looked into almost all the judgments of his whole country which were made in his absence, to see whether they were just or unjust, and if truly he could discover any wrong in those judgments, he would on his own authority mildly inquire of those judges, either in person or by some of his faithful followers, why they had given so wrong a judgment, whether from ignorance or out of any kind of ill-will, that is, for love or fear of one party, or hatred of the other, or even for greed of anyone's money. And then, if those judges admitted that they had given such judgments because they knew no better in those cases, he wisely and moderately reproved their inexperience and folly, saying thus: "I am amazed at your presumption, that you have by God's favor and mine assumed the office and status of wise men, but have neglected the study and practice of wisdom. I command you therefore either to resign on the spot the exercise of the worldly authority you hold, or to apply yourselves much more zealously to the study of wisdom." When they had heard these words, the ealdormen and reeves hastened to turn themselves with all their might to the task of learning justice, for they were terrified and as if they had been severely punished; so that in a marvelous fashion almost all the ealdormen, reeves, and thegns, who had been untaught from their childhood, gave themselves to the study of letters, preferring thus toilsomely to pursue this unaccustomed study rather than resign the exercise of their authority. But if anyone were unable to make progress in learning to read, either by reason of his age or the too great slowness of an unpracticed mind, he ordered his son, if he had one, or some other kinsman, or even, if he had no one else, his own man, free man or slave, whom he had long before made to learn to read, to read Saxon books to him day and night whenever he had any leisure. And, greatly sighing from the bottom of their hearts that they had not applied themselves to such studies in their youth, they considered the youth of this age happy, who could have the good fortune to be trained in the liberal arts, accounting themselves unhappy indeed, since they had neither learnt in their youth, nor were able to learn in their old age, though they ardently desired it. But we have dealt on this quickness of old and young to learn to read to add to knowledge of the aforesaid king.

ANGLO-SAXON CHRONICLE

865 In this year the heathen army encamped on Thanet and made peace with the people of Kent. And the people of Kent promised them money for that peace. And under cover of that peace and promise of money the army stole away inland by night and ravaged all east Kent.

866 In this year Ethelbert's brother Æthelred succeeded to the kingdom of the West Saxons. And the same year a great heathen army came into England and took up winter quarters in East Anglia; and there they were supplied with horses, and the East Angles made peace with them.

867 In this year the army went from East Anglia to Northumbria, across the Humber estuary to the city of York. And there was great civil strife going on in that people, and they had deposed their king Osbert and taken a king with no hereditary right, Æella. And not until late in the year did they unite sufficiently to proceed to fight the raiding army; and nevertheless they collected a large army and attacked the enemy in York, and broke into the city; and some of them got inside, and an immense slaughter was made of the Northumbrians, some inside and some outside, and both kings were killed, and the survivors made peace with the enemy. And the same year Bishop Ealhstan died, and he had held the bishopric of Sherborne for 50 years, and his body is buried in the cemetery there.

868 In this year the same army went into Mercia to Nottingham and took up winter quarters there. And Burgred, king of the Mercians, and his councilors asked Æthelred, king of the West Saxons, and his brother Alfred to help him to fight against the army. They then went with the army of the West Saxons into Mercia to Nottingham, and came upon the enemy in that fortress and besieged them there. There occurred no serious battle there, and the Mercians made peace with the enemy.

869 In this year the raiding army returned to the city of York, and stayed there one year.

870 In this year the raiding army rode across Mercia into East Anglia, and took up winter quarters at Thetford. And that winter King Edmund fought against them, and the Danes had the victory, and killed the king, and conquered all the land. And the same year Archbishop Ceolnoth died.

871 In this year the army came into Wessex to Reading, and three days later two Danish earls rode farther inland. Then Ealdorman Æthelwulf encountered them at Englefield, and fought against them there and had the victory, and one of them, whose name was Sidroc, was killed there. Then four days later King Æthelred and his brother Alfred led a great army to Reading and fought against the army; and a great slaughter was made on both sides and Ealdorman Æthelwulf was killed, and the Danes had possession of the battlefield.

And four days later King Æthelred and his brother Alfred fought against the whole army at Ashdown; and the Danes were in two divisions: in the one were the heathen kings Bagsecg and Healfdene, and in the other were the earls. And then King Æthelred fought against the kings' troop, and King Bagsecg was slain there; and Æthelred's brother Alfred fought against the earls' troop, and there were slain Earl Sidroc the Old, and Earl Sidroc the Younger and Earl Osbearn, Earl Fræna and Earl Harold; and both enemy armies were put to flight and many thousands were killed, and they continued fighting until night.

And a fortnight later King Æthelred and his brother Alfred fought against the army at Basing, and there the Danes had the victory. And two months later, King Æthelred and his brother Alfred fought against the army at *Meretun*, and they were in two divisions; and they put both to flight and were victorious far on into the day; and there was a great slaughter on both sides; and the Danes had possession of the battlefield. And Bishop Heahmind was killed there and many important men. And after this battle a great summer army came to Reading. And afterward, after Easter, King Æthelred died, and he had reigned five years, and his body is buried at Wimborne minster.

Then his brother Alfred, the son of Æthelwulf, succeeded to the kingdom of the West Saxons. And a month later King Alfred fought with a small force · against the whole army at Wilton and put it to flight far on into the day; and the Danes had possession of the battlefield. And during that year nine general engagements were fought against the Danish army in the kingdom south of the Thames, besides the expeditions which the king's brother Alfred and [single] ealdormen and king's thegns often rode on, which were not counted. And that year nine [Danish] earls were killed and one king. And the West Saxons made peace with the enemy that year.

872 In this year the army went from Reading to London, and took up winter quarters there; and then the Mercians made peace with the army.

873 In this year the army went into Northumbria, and it took up winter quarters at Torksey in Lindsey; and then the Mercians made peace with the army.

In this year the army took up winter quarters at Torksey.

874 In this year the army went from Lindsey to Repton and took up winter quarters there, and drove King Burgred across the sea, after he had held the kingdom twenty-two years. And they conquered all that land. And he went to Rome and settled there; and his body is buried in the church of St. Mary in the English quarter. And the same year they gave the kingdom of the Mercians to be held by Ceolwulf, a foolish king's thegn; and he swore oaths to them and gave hostages, that it should be ready for them on whatever day they wished to have it, and he would be ready, himself and all who would follow him, at the enemy's service.

875 In this year the army left Repton: Healfdene went with part of the army into Northumbria and took up winter quarters by the River Tyne. And the army conquered the land and often ravaged among the Picts and the Strathclyde Britons; and the three kings, Guthrum, Oscetel, and Anwend, went from Repton to Cambridge with a great force, and stayed there a year. And that summer King Alfred went out to sea with a naval force, and fought against the crews of seven ships, and captured one ship and put the rest to flight.

876 In this year the enemy army slipped past the army of the West Saxons into Wareham; and then the king made peace with the enemy and they gave him hostages, who were the most important men next to their king in the army, and swore oaths to him on the holy ring[35]—a thing which they would not do before for any nation—that they would speedily leave his kingdom. And then under cover of that, they—the mounted army—stole by night away from the English army to Exeter. And that year Healfdene shared out the land of the Northumbrians, and they proceeded to plow and to support themselves.

877 In this year the enemy army from Wareham came to Exeter; [and the naval force sailed west along the

---

[35] A sacred ring, normally kept in the inner sanctuary of the heathen temples and worn by the chief at assemblies, is mentioned in the saga literature of Iceland.

coast] and encountered a great storm at sea, and 120 ships were lost at Swanage. And King Alfred rode after the mounted army with the English army as far as Exeter, but could not overtake them [before they were in the fortress where they could not be reached]. And they gave him hostages there, as many as he wished to have, and swore great oaths and then kept a firm peace. Then in the harvest season the army went away into Mercia and shared out some of it, and gave some to Ceolwulf.

878 In this year in midwinter after twelfth night the enemy army came stealthily to Chippenham, and occupied the land of the West Saxons and settled there, and drove a great part of the people across the sea, and conquered most of the others; and the people submitted to them, except King Alfred. He journeyed in difficulties through the woods and fen-fastnesses[36] with a small force.

And the same winter the brother of Ivar and Healfdene was in the kingdom of the West Saxons [in Devon], with 23 ships. And he was killed there and 840 men of his army with him. And there was captured the banner which they called "Raven."

And afterward at Easter, King Alfred with a small force made a stronghold at Athelney, and he and the section of the people of Somerset which was nearest to it proceeded to fight from that stronghold against the enemy. Then in the seventh week after Easter he rode to "Egbert's stone" east of Selwood, and there came to meet him all the people of Somerset and of Wiltshire and of that part of Hampshire which was on this side of the sea, and they rejoiced to see him. And then after one night he went from that encampment to Iley, and after another night to Edington, and there fought against the whole army and put it to flight, and pursued it as far as the fortress, and stayed there a fortnight. And then the enemy gave him preliminary hostages and great oaths that they would leave his kingdom, and promised also that their king should receive baptism, and they kept their promise. Three weeks later King Guthrum with 30 of the men who were the most important in the army came [to him] at Aller, which is near Athelney, and the king stood sponsor to him at his baptism there; and the unbinding of the chrism[37] took place at Wedmore. And

he was twelve days with the king, and he honored him and his companions greatly with gifts.

879 In this year the army went from Chippenham to Cirencester, and stayed there for one year. And the same year a band of vikings assembled and encamped at Fulham by the Thames. And the same year there was an eclipse of the sun for one hour of the day.

880 In this year the army went from Cirencester into East Anglia, and settled there and shared out the land. And the same year the army which had encamped at Fulham went overseas into the Frankish empire to Ghent and stayed there for a year.

881 In this year the army went farther inland into the Frankish empire, and the Franks fought against them; and the Danish army provided itself with horses after that battle.

882 In this year the army went farther into the Frankish empire along the Meuse, and stayed there a year. And the same year King Alfred went out with ships to sea and fought against four crews of Danish men, and captured two of the ships—and the men were killed who were on them—and two crews surrendered to him. And they had great losses in killed or wounded before they surrendered.

883 In this year the army went up the Scheldt to Condé, and stayed there for a year. And Pope Marinus sent some wood of the Cross to King Alfred. And that same year Sigelm and Athelstan took to Rome the alms [which King Alfred had promised thither], and also to India to St. Thomas and St. Bartholomew, when the English were encamped against the enemy army at London; and there, by the grace of God, their prayers were well answered after that promise.

884 In this year the army went up the Somme to Amiens, and stayed there a year.

885 In this year the aforesaid army divided into two [one part going east], the other part to Rochester, where they besieged the city and made other fortifications round themselves. And nevertheless the English defended the city until King Alfred came up with his army. Then the enemy went to their ships and abandoned their fortification, and they were deprived of their horses there, and immediately that same summer they went back across

[36] Alkaline wetlands usually fed by underground water sources.
[37] For eight days after baptism, white robes were worn and a white cloth was bound round the head after the anointment with the chrism. The ceremony of its removal is what is meant here.

the sea. That same year King Alfred sent a naval force from Kent into East Anglia. Immediately they came into the mouth of the Stour and they encountered 16 ships of vikings and fought against them, and seized all the ships and killed the men. When they turned homeward with the booty, they met a large naval force of vikings and fought against them on the same day, and the Danes had the victory.

That same year before Christmas, Charles, king of the Franks, died. He was killed by a boar, and a year previously his brother, who had also held the western kingdom, had died. They were both sons of Louis, who died in the year of the eclipse of the sun. He was the son of that Charles[38] whose daughter Æthelwulf, king of the west Saxons, had married. That same year a large naval force assembled among the Old Saxons and twice in the year there occurred a great battle, and the Saxons had the victory, and with them there were the Frisians.

That same year Charles[39] succeeded to the western kingdom and to all the kingdom on this side of the Mediterranean and beyond this sea, as his great-grandfather[40] had held it, except for Brittany. This Charles was the son of Louis,[41] the brother of the Charles who was the father of Judith whom King Æthelwulf married; and they were sons of Louis.[42] This Louis was the son of the old Charles.[43] This Charles was Pippin's son.

That same year there died the good pope, Marinus, who had freed from taxation the English quarter at the request of Alfred, king [of the West Saxons]. And he had sent him great gifts, including part of the Cross on which Christ suffered.

And that same year the Danish army in East Anglia violated their peace with King Alfred.

886 In this year the Danish army which had gone east went west again, and then up the Seine, and made their winter quarters there at the town of Paris.

That same year King Alfred occupied London; and all the English people that were not under subjection to

the Danes submitted to him. And he then entrusted the borough to the control of Ealdorman Æthelred.[44]

887 In this year the Danish army went up past the bridge at Paris, then up along the Seine to the Marne, and then up the Marne as far as Chézy, and stayed there and in the Yonne area, spending two winters in those two places.

And the same year Charles,[45] king of the Franks, died; and six weeks before he died his brother's son Arnulf had deprived him of the kingdom. The kingdom was then divided into five, and five kings were consecrated to it. It was done, however, with Arnulf's consent and they said that they would hold it under him, for not one of them was born to it in the male line but him alone. Arnulf then lived in the land east of the Rhine, and Rudolf[46] succeeded to the middle kingdom and Odo[47] to the western portion; and Berengar[48] and Guido[49] to Lombardy and the lands on that side of the Alps; and they held it with much discord and fought two general engagements, and ravaged the land again and again, and each repeatedly drove out the other.

And the same year in which the army went up beyond the bridge at Paris, Ealdorman Æthelhelm took to Rome the alms of King Alfred and the West Saxons.

888 In this year Ealdorman Beocca took to Rome the alms of the West Saxons and of King Alfred. And Queen Æthelswith, who was King Alfred's sister, died, and her body is buried in Pavia. And the same year Archbishop Æthelred and Ealdorman Æthelwold died in the same month.

889 There was no expedition to Rome in this year, but King Alfred sent two couriers with letters.

890 In this year Abbot Beornhelm took to Rome the alms of the West Saxons and of King Alfred. And the northern king, Guthrum, whose baptismal name was Athelstan, died. He was King Alfred's godson, and he lived in East Anglia and was the first[50] to settle that land.

---

[38] Charles the Bald (823–877).

[39] Charles the Fat (839–888, deposed in 887).

[40] Charles the Great (742–814).

[41] Louis the German (806–876).

[42] Louis the Pious (778–840).

[43] Charles the Great.

[44] The lord of the Mercians, who married Alfred's daughter, Æthelflæd. Under their rule, Mercia preserved its autonomy.

[45] Charles the Fat, who died in January 888.

[46] Count of Upper Burgundy.

[47] Count of Paris.

[48] Margrave of Friuli.

[49] Duke of Spoleto.

[50] I.e., of the Danes.

And the same year the Danish army went from the Seine to St. Lô, which lies between Brittany and France; and the Bretons fought against them and had the victory, and drove them into a river and drowned many of them.

891 In this year the Danish army went east, and King Arnulf with the East Franks, the Saxons, and Bavarians fought against the mounted force before the ships arrived, and put it to flight.

And three Scots came to King Alfred in a boat without any oars from Ireland, which they had left secretly, because they wished for the love of God to be in foreign lands, they cared not where. The boat in which they traveled was made of two and a half hides, and they took with them enough food for seven days. And after seven days they came to land in Cornwall, and went immediately to King Alfred. Their names were as follows: Dubslane, Machbethu, and Maelinnum. And Swifneh, the best scholar among the Scots, died.

And the same year after Easter, at the Rogation days or before, there appeared the star which is called in Latin *cometa*. Some men say that it is in English the long-haired star, for there shines a long ray from it, sometimes on one side, sometimes on every side.

892 In this year the great Danish army, which we have spoken about before, went back from the eastern kingdom westward to Boulogne, and they were provided with ships there, so that they crossed in one journey, horses and all, and then came up into the estuary of the Lympne with 200 [and 50] ships. That estuary is in East Kent, at the east end of that great wood which we called *Andred*. The wood is from east to west 120 miles long, or longer, and 30 miles broad. The river, of which we spoke before, comes out of the Weald. They rowed their ships up the river as far as the Weald, four miles from the mouth of the estuary, and there they stormed a fortress. Inside that fortification there were a few peasants, and it was only half made.

Then immediately afterward Hæsten[51] came with 80 ships up the Thames estuary and made himself a fortress at Milton, and the other army made one at Appledore.

---

[51] Old Norse Hæsteinn (*Hastingus*), a viking leader first heard of on the Loire in 866, who afterward had an active career on the Continent.

893 In this year, that was twelve months after the Danes had built the fortress in the eastern kingdom, the Northumbrians and East Angles had given King Alfred oaths, and the East Angles had given six preliminary hostages; and yet, contrary to those pledges, as often as the other Danish armies went out in full force, they went either with them or on their behalf. And then King Alfred collected his army, and advanced to take up a position between the two enemy forces, where he had the nearest convenient site with regard both to the fort in the wood and the fort by the water, so that he could reach either army, if they chose to come into the open country. Then they went afterward along the Weald in small bands and mounted companies, by whatever side it was then undefended by the English army. And also they were sought by other bands, almost every day, either by day or by night, both from the English army and from the boroughs. The king had divided his army into two, so that always half its men were at home, half on service, apart from the men who guarded the boroughs. The enemy did not all come out of those encampments more than twice: once when they first landed, before the English force was assembled, and once when they wished to leave those encampments. Then they captured much booty, and wished to carry it north across the Thames into Essex, to meet the ships. Then the English army intercepted them and fought against them at Farnham, and put the enemy to flight and recovered the booty. And the Danes fled across the Thames where there was no ford, and up along the Colne on to an islet. Then the English force besieged them there for as long as their provisions lasted; but they had completed their term of service and used up their provisions, and the king was then on the way there with the division which was serving with him. When he was on his way there and the other English army was on its way home, and the Danes were remaining behind there because their king had been wounded in the battle, so that they could not move him, those Danes who lived in Northumbria and East Anglia collected some hundred ships, and went south around the coast [and some 40 ships went north around the coast] and besieged a fortress on the north coast of Devon, and those who had gone south besieged Exeter.

When the king heard that, he turned west toward Exeter with the whole army, except for a very inconsiderable portion of the people [who continued] eastward. They went on until they came to London, and then with the citizens and with the reinforcements which came to them from the west, they went east to Benfleet. Hæsten had then come there with his army which had been at Milton, and the large army which had been at Appledore on the estuary of the Lympne had then also come there. Hæsten had previously built that fortress at Benfleet; and he was then out on a raid, and the large army was at home. Then the English went there and put the enemy to flight, and stormed the fortress and captured all that was within, both goods, and women and also children, and brought all to London; and they either broke up or burnt all the ships, or brought them to London or to Rochester. And Hæsten's wife and two sons were brought to the king; and he gave them back to him, because one of them was his godson, and the other the godson of Ealdorman Æthelred. They had stood sponsor to them before Hæsten came to Benfleet, and he had given the king oaths and hostages, and the king had also made him generous gifts of money, and so he did also when he gave back the boy and the woman. But immediately they came to Benfleet and had made that fortress, Hæsten ravaged his kingdom, that very province which Æthelred, his son's godfather, was in charge of; and again, a second time, he had gone on a raid in that same kingdom when his fortress was stormed.

When the king had turned west with the army toward Exeter, as I have said before, and the Danish army had laid siege to the borough, they went to their ships when he arrived there. When he was occupied against the army there in the west, and the [other] two Danish armies were assembled at Shoebury in Essex, and had made a fortress there, they went both together up along the Thames, and a great reinforcement came to them both from the East Angles, and the Northumbrians. [They then went up along the Thames until they reached the Severn, then up along the Severn.] Then Ealdorman Æthelred and Ealdorman Æthelhelm and Ealdorman Æthelnoth and the king's thegns who then were at home at the fortresses assembled from every borough east of the Parret, and both west and east of Selwood, and also north of the Thames and west of the Severn, and also some portion of the Welsh people. When they were all assembled, they overtook the Danish army at Buttington on the bank of the Severn, and besieged it on every side in a fortress. Then when they had encamped for many weeks on the two sides of the river, and the king was occupied in the west in Devon against the naval force, the besieged were oppressed by famine, and had eaten the greater part of their horses and the rest had died of starvation. They then came out

against the men who were encamped on the east side of the river, and fought against them, and the Christians had the victory. And the king's thegn Ordheah and also many other king's thegns were killed, and a very great [slaughter] of the Danes was made, and the part that escaped were saved by flight.

When they came to Essex to their fortress and their ships, the survivors collected again before winter a large army from the East Angles and Northumbrians, placed their women and ships and property in safety in East Anglia, and went continuously by day and night till they reached a deserted city in Wirral, which is called Chester. Then the English army could not overtake them before they were inside that fortress. However, they besieged the fortress for some two days, and seized all the cattle that was outside, and killed the men whom they could cut off outside the fortress, and burnt all the corn, or consumed it by means of their horses, in all the surrounding districts. And that was twelve months after they had come hither across the sea.

894 And then in this year, immediately after that, the Danish went into Wales from Wirral, because they could not stay there. That was because they were deprived both of cattle and the corn which had been ravaged. When they turned back from Wales with the booty they had captured there, they went, so that the English army could not reach them, across Northumbria and into East Anglia, until they came into east Essex on to an island called Mersea, which is out in the sea.

And when the Danish army which had besieged Exeter turned homewards, they ravaged up in Sussex near Chichester, and the citizens put them to flight and killed many hundreds of them, and captured some of their ships.

Then that same year in early winter the Danes who were encamped on Mersea rowed their ships up the Thames and up the Lea. That was two years after they came hither across the sea.

895 And in the same year the aforesaid army made a fortress by the Lea, 20 miles above London. Then afterward in the summer a great part of the citizens and also of other people marched till they arrived at the fortress of the Danes, and there they were put to flight and four king's thegns were slain. Then later, in the autumn, the king encamped in the vicinity of the borough while they were reaping their corn, so that the Danes could not deny them that harvest. Then one day the king rode up along the river, and examined where the river could be obstructed, so that they could not bring the ships out. And when this was carried out, two fortresses were made on the two sides of the river. When they had just begun that work [and had encamped for that purpose], the enemy perceived that they could not bring the ships out. Then they abandoned the ships and went overland till they reached Bridgnorth on the Severn and built that fortress. Then the English army rode after the enemy, and the men from London fetched the ships, and broke up all which they could not bring away, and brought to London those which were serviceable. And the Danes had placed their women in safety in East Anglia before they left that fortress. Then they stayed the winter at Bridgnorth. That was three years after they had come hither across the sea into the estuary of the Lympne.

896 And afterward in the summer of this year the Danish army divided, one force going into East Anglia and one into Northumbria; and those that were moneyless got themselves ships and went south across the sea to the Seine.

By the grace of God, the army had not on the whole afflicted the English people very greatly; but they were much more seriously afflicted in those three years by the mortality of cattle and men, and most of all in that many of the best king's thegns who were in the land died in those three years. Of those, one was Swithwulf, bishop of Rochester, and Ceolmund, ealdorman of Kent, and Brihtwulf, ealdorman of Essex [and Wulfred, ealdorman of Hampshire], and Ealhheard, bishop of Dorchester, and Eadwulf, a king's thegn in Sussex, and Beornwulf, the town-reeve of Winchester, and Ecgwulf, the king's marshal, and many besides them, though I have named the most distinguished.

In the same year the armies in East Anglia and Northumbria greatly harassed Wessex along the south coast with marauding bands, most of all with the warships which they had built many years before. Then King Alfred had "long ships" built to oppose the Danish warships. They were almost twice as long as the others. Some had 60 oars, some more. They were both swifter and steadier and also higher than the others. They were built neither on the Frisian nor the swifter and steadier Danish pattern, but as it seemed to him himself that they could be most useful. Then on a certain occasion of the same year, six ships came to the Isle of Wight and did great harm there, both in Devon and everywhere along the coast. Then the king ordered [a force] to go

thither with nine of the new ships, and they blocked the estuary from the seaward end. Then the Danes went out against them with three ships, and three were on dry land farther up the estuary; the men from them had gone up on land. Then the English captured two of those three ships at the entrance to the estuary, and killed the men, and the one ship escaped. On it also the men were killed except five. These got away because the ships of their opponents ran aground. Moreover, they had run aground very awkwardly; three were aground on that side of the channel on which the Danish ships were aground, and all [the others] on the other side, so that none of them could get to the others. But when the water had ebbed many furlongs from the ships, the Danes from the remaining three ships went to the other three which were stranded on their side, and they then fought there. And there were killed the king's reeve Lucuman, Wulfheard the Frisian, Æbba the Frisian, Æthelhere the Frisian, Æthelfrith the king's *geneat*,[52] and in all 62 Frisians and English and 120 of the Danes. Then, however, the tide reached the Danish ships before the Christians could launch theirs, and therefore they rowed away out. They were then so wounded that they could not row past Sussex, but the sea cast two of them on to the land, and the men were brought to Winchester to the king, and he ordered them to be hanged. And the men who were on the one ship reached East Anglia greatly wounded. That same summer no fewer than 20 ships, men and all, perished along the south coast. That same year died Wulfric, the king's marshal, who was [also] the Welsh-reeve.

897 In this year, nine days before midsummer, Æthelhelm, ealdorman of Wiltshire, died; and in this year died Heahstan, who was bishop of London.

900 In this year Alfred the son of Æthelwulf died, six days before All Saints' Day. He was king over the whole English people except for that part which was under Danish rule, and he had held the kingdom for one and a half years less than thirty; and then his son Edward succeeded to the kingdom.

In this year King Alfred died on 26 October; and he had held the kingdom twenty-eight years and half a year; then his son Edward succeeded to the kingdom.

---

[52] Companion.

Then the atheling Æthelwold, his father's brother's son,[53] rode and seized the residence at Wimborne and at *Twinham*, against the will of the king and his councilors. Then the king rode with the army till he encamped at Badbury near Wimborne, and Æthelwold stayed inside the residence with the men who had given allegiance to him; and he had barricaded all the gates against him, and said that he would either live there or die there.

Then meanwhile the atheling rode away by night, and went to the Danish army in Northumbria, and they accepted him as king and gave allegiance to him. Then the woman was seized whom he had taken without the king's permission and contrary to the bishops' orders—for she had been consecrated a nun.

And in this same year Æthelred, who was ealdorman of Devon, died four weeks before King Alfred....

17. THEODORE

PENITENTIAL

Handbooks of penance were important texts in insular spirituality, designed to direct sinners toward the proper course of penance and prayer. In the course of the seventh and eighth centuries, they spread to the Continent and had deep and lasting influence on the development of medieval ethics and spirituality. The penitential attributed to Theodore of Tarsus, Archbishop of Canterbury (ca. 668–690), was one of the most widely disseminated of these handbooks both in England and on the Continent.

Source: John McNeill and Helena M. Gamer, *Medieval Handbooks of Penance: A Translation of the* Principal Libri Poenitentiales *and Selections from Related Documents* (New York: Columbia University Press, 1938).
Further Reading: Allen J. Frantzen, *The Literature of Penance in Anglo-Saxon England* (New Brunswick, NJ: Rutgers University Press, 1983).

Preface

In the name of Christ. Here begins the preface of the booklet which Father Theodore, having been inquired of by different persons, prepared for the remedy of penance. A pupil of the [North]umbrians, to all Catholics of the English, especially to the physicians of souls, as a suppliant [sends] blessing and greeting in the Lord Christ.

First, then, beloved, from love of your blessedness, I thought it fitting, to set forth whence I have collected the penitential remedies which follow, in order that the law may not, on account of the age or negligence of copyists, be perpetuated in a confused and corrupted state, as is usual—that law which of old time God gave figuratively by its first promulgator and then later committed to the Fathers, that they should make it known to their sons that another generation should be acquainted with it; to

wit, the [law of] penance, which the Lord Jesus, when he was baptized before us all, proclaimed as the instrument of his teaching for those who had no means of healing; saying: "Do penance," etc. For the increase of your felicity, He deigned to send from the blessed see of him to whom it is said, "Whatsoever thou shalt loose on earth shall be loosed also in heaven," one by whom this most wholesome treatment of wounds is to be controlled; "for I," says the apostle, "have received of the Lord," and I, beloved, have received of you, by God's favor, that which, in turn, I have handed over to you. For the greater part of these [decisions] the presbyter Eoda, of blessed memory, whose surname was "Christian," is said, by true report, to have received in answer to his questions from the venerable prelate Theodore. Supplementing these also is that element which the divine grace has in like manner provided to our unworthy hands, the things which that man is likewise reported to have searched out, from a booklet of the Irish. Concerning this book, the aged [Theodore] is said to have expressed the opinion that the author was an ecclesiastic.

---

[53] He was son of King Æthelred, Alfred's elder brother and predecessor. An atheling was a male member of a royal house and presumed heir to the throne.

Further, not only many men but also women, enkindled by him through these [decisions] with inextinguishable fervor, burning with desire to quench the thirst, made haste in crowds to visit a man undoubtedly of extraordinary knowledge for our age. Hence there has been found in diverse quarters that conflicting and confused digest of those rules of the second book compiled with the cases adjudged. For which reason I implore, brethren, the most kind indulgence of your favor, through Him who was crucified and [who] by the shedding of His blood in life mightily confirmed what He had preached, that, if for the interests of the practical service I have committed any sin of rashness or ignorance, you will defend me before Him with the support of your intercession. For I call to witness the Maker of all things, that so far as I know my own heart, I have done these things for the sake of that kingdom of which He has preached; and if, as I fear, I undertake something beyond my talents, then, you thus assisting me, let your good will toward a work so necessary implore the pardon of my sin before Him. For in all these things equally and without invidious discrimination, according as I am able, I carefully select out of the whole the more useful things I have been able to find, and I have collected them, prefixing headings to them one by one. For I believe that men of good spirit give attention to these things, of whom it is said: "On earth peace to men of good will."

Book One

I. Of Excess and Drunkenness

1. If any bishop or deacon or any ordained person has had by custom the vice of drunkenness, he shall either desist or be deposed.

2. If a monk vomits on account of drunkenness, he shall do penance for thirty days.

3. If a presbyter or a deacon [does this] on account of drunkenness, he shall do penance for forty days.

4. If [the offense is] due to weakness or because he has been a long time abstinent and is not accustomed to drink or eat much; or if it is for gladness at Christmas or Easter or for any festival of a saint, and he then has imbibed no more than is commanded by his seniors, no offense is committed. If a bishop commands it no offense is committed, unless he himself does likewise.

5. If a lay Christian vomits because of drunkenness, he shall do penance for fifteen days.

6. Whoever is drunk against the Lord's command, if he has taken a vow of sanctity, shall do penance for seven days on bread and water, or twenty days without fat; or laymen, without beer.

7. Whoever in wickedness makes another drunk, shall do penance for forty days.

8. Whoever vomits from excess shall do penance for three days.

9. If with the sacrifice of communion, he shall do penance for seven days; if on account of weakness, he is without guilt.

II. Of Fornication

1. If anyone commits fornication with a virgin he shall do penance for one year. If with a married woman, for four years, two of these entire, and in the other two during the three forty-day periods[54] and three days a week.

2. He judged that he who often commits fornication with a man or with a beast should do penance for ten years.

3. Another judgment is that he who is joined to beasts shall do penance for fifteen years.

4. He who after his twentieth year defiles himself with a male shall do penance for fifteen years.

5. A male who commits fornication with a male shall do penance for ten years.

6. Sodomites shall do penance for seven years, and the effeminate man as an adulteress.

7. Likewise he who commits this sexual offense once shall do penance for four years. If he has been in the

---

54 Probably by the "three forty-day periods" frequently assigned in this penitential, those mentioned in Book II, xiv, 1, below, are to be understood. Some modern writers habitually call these "the three lents."

habit of it, as Basil says, fifteen years; but if not, one year less[?] as a woman. If he is a boy, two years for the first offense; if he repeats it, four years.

8. If he does this between the thighs, one year, or the three forty-day periods.

9. If he defiles himself, forty days.

10. He who desires to commit fornication, but is not able, shall do penance for forty or twenty days.

11. As for boys who mutually engage in vice, he judged that they should be whipped.

12. If a woman practices vice with a woman, she shall do penance for three years.

13. If she practices solitary vice, she shall do penance for the same period.

14. The penance of a widow and of a girl is the same. She who has a husband deserves a greater penalty if she commits fornication.

15. He who ejaculates into the mouth of another shall do penance for seven years; this is the worst of evils. Elsewhere it was his judgment that both [participants in the offense] shall do penance to the end of life; or twelve years, or as above seven.

16. If one commits fornication with his mother, he shall do penance for fifteen years and never change except on Sundays. But this so impious incest is likewise spoken of by him in another way—that he shall do penance for seven years, with perpetual pilgrimage.

17. He who commits fornication with his sister shall do penance for fifteen years in the way which it is stated above of his mother. But this [penalty] he also elsewhere established in a canon as twelve years. Whence it is not unreasonable that the fifteen years that are written apply to the mother.

18. The first canon determined that he who often commits fornication should do penance for ten years; a second canon, seven; but on account of the weakness of man, on deliberation they said he should do penance for three years.

19. If a brother commits fornication with a natural brother, he shall abstain from all kinds of flesh for fifteen years.

20. If a mother imitates acts of fornication with her little son, she shall abstain from flesh for three years and fast one day in the week, that is until Vespers.

21. He who amuses himself with libidinous imagination shall do penance until the imagination is overcome.

22. He who loves a woman in his mind shall seek pardon from God; but if he has spoken [to her], that is, of love and friendship, but is not received by her, he shall do penance for seven days.

III. Of Thieving Avarice

1. If any layman carries off a monk from the monastery by stealth, he shall either enter a monastery to serve God or subject himself to human servitude.

2. Money stolen or robbed from churches is to be restored fourfold; from secular persons, twofold.

3. Whoever has often committed theft, seven years is his penance, or such a sentence as his priest shall determine, that is, according to what can be arranged with those whom he has wronged. And he who used to steal, when he becomes penitent, ought always to be reconciled to him against whom he has offended and to make restitution according to the wrong he has done to him; and [in such case] he shall greatly shorten his penance. But if he refuses, or is unable, let him do penance scrupulously for the prescribed time.

4. And he who gives notice of stolen goods shall give a third part to the poor; and whoever treasures up goods in excess through ignorance, shall give a third part to the poor.

5. Whoever has stolen consecrated things shall do penance for three years without fat and then [be allowed to] communicate.

IV. Of Manslaughter

1. If one slays a man in revenge for a relative, he shall do penance as a murderer for seven or ten years. However, if he will render to the relatives the legal price, the

penance shall be lighter, that is, [it shall be shortened] by half the time.

2. If one slays a man in revenge for a brother, he shall do penance for three years. In another place it is said that he should do penance for ten years.

3. But a murderer, ten or seven years.

4. If a layman slays another with malice aforethought, if he will not lay aside his arms, he shall do penance for seven years; without flesh and wine, three years.

5. If one slays a monk or a cleric, he shall lay aside his arms and serve God, or he shall do penance for seven years. He is in the judgment of his bishop. But as for one who slays a bishop or presbyter, it is for the king to give judgment in this case.

6. One who slays a man by command of his lord shall keep away from the church for forty days; and one who slays a man in public war shall do penance for forty days.

7. If through anger, he shall do penance for three years; if by accident, for one year; if by a potion or any trick, seven years or more; if as a result of a quarrel, ten years.

V. Of Those Who Are Deceived by Heresy

1. If one has been ordained by heretics, if he was without blame [in the matter] he ought to be reordained; but if not, he ought to be deposed.

2. If one goes over from the Catholic Church to heresy and afterward returns, he cannot be ordained except after a long probation and in great necessity. Pope Innocent claimed that such a person is not permitted by the authority of the canons to become a cleric [even] after penance. Therefore if Theodore says this: "only in great necessity," as has been said, he permitted the procedure, who often used to say that he wished that the decrees of the Romans should never be changed by him.

3. If one flouts the Council of Nicea and keeps Easter with the Jews on the fourteenth of the moon, he shall be driven out of every church unless he does penance before his death.

4. If one prays with such a person as if he were a Catholic cleric, he shall do penance for a week; if indeed he neglects this, he shall the first time do penance for forty days.

5. If one seeks to encourage the heresy of these people and does not do penance, he shall be likewise driven out; as the Lord saith: "He that is not with me is against me."

6. If one is baptized by a heretic who does not rightly believe in the Trinity, he shall be rebaptized. This we do not believe Theodore to have said [since it is] in opposition to the Nicene council and the decrees of the synod; as is confirmed in connection with the Arian converts who did not rightly believe in the Trinity.[55]

7. If one gives the communion to a heretic or receives it from his hand, and does not know that the Catholic Church disapproves it, when he afterward becomes aware [of this] he shall do penance for an entire year. But if he knows and [yet] neglects [the rule] and afterward does penance, he shall do penance for ten years. Others judge that he should do penance for seven years and, more leniently, for five.

8. If one, without knowing it, permits a heretic to celebrate the Mass in a Catholic church, he shall do penance for forty days. If [he does this] out of veneration for him [i.e., for the heretic], he shall do penance for an entire year.

9. If [he does this] in condemnation of the Catholic Church and the customs of the Romans, he shall be cast out of the Church as a heretic, unless he is penitent; if he is, he shall do penance for ten years.

10. If he departs from the Catholic Church to the congregation of the heretics and persuades others and afterward performs penance, he shall do penance for twelve years; four years outside the church, and six among the "hearers," and two more out of communion. Of these it is said in a synod: They shall receive the communion or oblation in the tenth year.

---

[55] The writer has mistaken the canons of Constantinople (381) for those of Nicaea. The council of Constantinople admitted Arians without rebaptism.

11. If a bishop or an abbot commands a monk to sing a mass for dead heretics, it is not proper or expedient to obey him.

12. If a presbyter is present where he has sung a mass, and another recites the names of dead persons and names heretics together with Catholics, and after the mass he is aware of it, he shall do penance for a week. If he has done it frequently, he shall do penance for an entire year.

13. But if anyone orders a mass for a dead heretic and preserves his relics on account of his piety, because he fasted much, and he does not know the difference between the Catholic faith and that of the Quatrodecimans, and [if he] afterward understands and performs penance, he ought to burn the relics with fire, and he shall do penance for a year. If one knows, however, and is indifferent, when he is moved to penance he shall do penance for ten years.

14. If anyone departs from God's faith without any necessity and afterward receives penance with his whole heart, he shall do penance among the "hearers"; according to the Nicene council, three years without the church among the penitents, and two years in addition out of communion.

VI. Of Perjury

1. He who commits perjury in a church shall do penance for eleven years.

2. He who [commits perjury] however [because] forced by necessity, for the three forty-day periods.

3. But he who swears on the hand of a man[56]—this is nothing among the Greeks.

4. If, however, he swears on the hand of a bishop or of a presbyter or of a deacon or on an altar or on a consecrated cross and lies, he shall do penance for three years. But if on a cross that is not consecrated, he shall do penance for one year.

5. The penance for perjury is three years.

VII. Of Many and Diverse Evils, and What Necessary Things Are Harmless

1. He who has committed many evil deeds, that is, murder, adultery with a woman and with a beast, and theft, shall go into a monastery and do penance until his death.

2. Of money which has been seized in a foreign province from a conquered enemy, that is, from an alien king who has been conquered, the third part shall be given to the church or to the poor, and penance shall be done for forty days because it was the king's command.[57]

3. He who drinks blood or semen shall do penance for three years.

4. There is pardon for evil imaginations if they are not carried out in action, nor yet by intention.

5. Further, Theodore approved reckoning the twelve three-day periods as the equivalent of a year. Also in the case of sick persons, the value of a man or of a female slave for a year, or to give the half of all his possessions, and if he have defrauded anyone, to restore fourfold, as Christ judged. These are the proofs of what we said in the preface about the booklet of the Irish; in which, as in other matters, sometimes he [the author of the Irish booklet] determined these things therein more leniently, as seemed best to him; it set the measure [of penance] for the week.

6. He who eats unclean flesh or a carcass that has been torn by beasts shall do penance for forty days. But if the necessity of hunger requires it, there is no offense, since a permissible act is one thing and what necessity requires is another.

7. If anyone accidentally touches food with unwashed hands, or [if] a dog, a cat, a mouse, or an unclean animal that has eaten blood [touches it] there is no offense; and if one from necessity eats an animal that seems unclean, whether a bird or a beast, there is no offense.

8. If a mouse falls into a liquid it shall be removed and sprinkled with holy water, and if it is alive it may be

---

[56] Meaning a layman, as indicated by the next canon.

[57] The last clause gives the reason for the lightness of the penalty.

taken [for food]; but if it is dead, all the liquid shall be poured out and not given to man, and the vessel shall be cleansed.

9. Again, if that liquid in which a mouse or a weasel is submerged and dies and contains much food, it shall be purged and sprinkled with holy water and taken if there is need.

10. If birds drop dung into any liquid, the dung shall be removed from it, and it shall be sanctified with [holy] water, and it shall be clean food.

11. Unwittingly to absorb blood with the saliva is not a sin.

12. If without knowing it, one eats what is polluted by blood or any unclean thing, it is nothing; but if he knows, he shall do penance according to the degree of the pollution.

VIII. Of Various Failings of the Servants of God

1. If a priest is polluted in touching or in kissing a woman he shall do penance for forty days.

2. If a presbyter kisses a woman from desire, he shall do penance for forty days.

3. Likewise if a presbyter is polluted through imagination, he shall fast for a week.

4. For masturbation, he shall fast for three weeks.

5. If any presbyter denies penance to the dying, he is answerable for their souls, since the Lord saith, "On whatever day the sinner is converted, he shall live and die." For true conversion is possible in the last hour, since the Lord sees not only the time but the heart; for the thief in his last hour, by a confession of one moment, merited to be in paradise.

6. A monk or a holy virgin who commits fornication shall do penance for seven years.

7. He who often pollutes himself through the violence of his imagination shall do penance for twenty days.

8. He who when asleep in a church pollutes himself shall do penance for three days.

9. For masturbation, the first time he shall do penance for twenty days, on repetition, forty days; for further offenses fasts shall be added.

10. If between the thighs, one year or the three forty-day periods.

11. He who defiles himself shall do penance for forty days; if he is a boy, for twenty days or be flogged. If he is in orders, for the three forty-day periods or a year if he has done it frequently.

12. If anyone renounces the world and afterward resumes a secular habit, if he was a monk and after these things performs penance, he shall do penance for ten years and after the first three years, if he has been approved in all his penance in tears and prayers, the bishop can deal more leniently with him.

13. If he was not a monk when he departed from the Church, he shall do penance for seven years.

14. Basil gave judgment that a boy should be permitted to marry before the age of sixteen if he could not abstain; but that if he is already a monk, [and marries], he is both [classed] among bigamists and shall do penance for one year.

IX. Of Those Who Are Degraded or Cannot Be Ordained

1. A bishop, presbyter, or deacon guilty of fornication ought to be degraded and to do penance at the decision of a bishop; yet they shall take communion. With loss of rank, penance dies, the soul lives.

2. If anyone after he has vowed himself to God takes a secular habit, he assuredly ought not to proceed a second time to any rank.

3. Nor ought a woman [in such case] to take the veil; it is far better that she should not come to prominence in the Church.

4. If any presbyter or deacon marries a strange woman, he shall be deposed before the people.

5. If he commits adultery with her and it comes to the knowledge of the people, he shall be cast out of the Church and shall do penance among the laymen as long as he lives.

6. If anyone has a concubine, he ought not to be ordained.

7. If any presbyter in his own province or in another or wherever he may be found refuses to baptize a sick person who has been committed to him or on account of the exertion of the journey [declines the duty] so that he dies without baptism, he shall be deposed.

8. Likewise he who slays a man or commits fornication, shall be deposed.

9. It is not permitted to ordain a boy brought up in a monastery before the age of twenty-five.

10. If anyone, before or after baptism, marries a twice married woman, as in the case of twice married men, he cannot be ordained.

11. If anyone who is not ordained performs baptism through temerity, he is cut off from the Church and shall never be ordained.

12. If through ignorance anyone has been ordained before he is baptized, those who have been baptized by that pagan ought to be [re]baptized, and he himself shall not be ordained [again].

This, again, is said to have been differently determined by the Roman pontiff of the apostolic see, to the effect that not he who baptizes, even if he is a pagan, but the Spirit of God, ministers the grace of baptism; but also this matter was differently decided in the case of a "pagan" presbyter—he who thinks himself baptized, holding the Catholic faith in his works—these cases are differently decided—that is, that he should have been baptized and ordained.

X. Of Those Who Have Been Baptized Twice; How They Shall Do Penance

1. Those who in ignorance have been twice baptized are not required to do penance for this, except that according to the canons they cannot be ordained unless some great necessity compels it.

2. However, those who have been baptized a second time, not ignorantly, [which is] as if they crucified Christ a second time, shall do penance for seven years on Wednesdays and Fridays and during the forty-day periods, if it was on account of some fault. But if they determined [to be baptized] for the sake of cleanness, they shall do penance in this way for three years.

XI. Of Those Who Despise the Lord's Day, and Neglect the Appointed Fasts of the Church of God

1. Those who labor on the Lord's day, the Greeks reprove the first time; the second, they take something from them; the third time, [they take] the third part of their possessions, or flog them; or they shall do penance for seven days.

2. But if on account of negligence anyone fasts on the Lord's day, he ought to abstain for a whole week. If [he does this] a second time, he shall fast for twenty days; if afterward forty days.

3. If he fasts out of contempt for the day, he shall be abhorred as a Jew by all the Catholic churches.

4. But if he despises a fast appointed in the Church and acts contrary to the decrees of the elders, not in Lent, he shall do penance for forty days. But if it is in Lent, he shall do penance for a year.

5. If he does it frequently and it has become habitual to him, he shall be cast out of the Church, as saith the Lord: "He that shall scandalize one of these little ones," etc.

XII. Of the Communion of the Eucharist, or the Sacrifice

1. The Greeks, clergy, and laymen, communicate every Lord's day, and those who do not communicate for three Lord's days are to be excommunicated, as the canons state.

2. Likewise the Romans who so wish, communicate; however those who do not so wish are not excommunicated.

3. The Greeks and Romans abstain from women for three days before the [feast of] loaves of proposition, as it is written in the law.

4. Penitents according to the canons ought not to communicate before the conclusion of the penance; we, however, out of pity give permission after a year or six months.

5. He who receives the sacrament after food shall do penance for seven days. (It is in the judgment of his bishop. This point, that it is in the judgment of the bishop, is not added in some texts.)

6. If the host has become corrupted with dirt accumulated by time it is always to be burned with fire.

7. Moreover, it shall be permitted if necessary that confession be made to God alone. And this [word] "necessary" is not in some codices.

8. He who mislays the host, [leaving it] for beasts and birds to devour, if by accident, he shall fast for three weeks; if through neglect, for the three forty-day periods.

XIII. Of Reconciliation

1. The Romans reconcile a man within the apse; but the Greeks will not do this.

2. The reconciliation of the penitents in the Lord's Supper is by the bishops only—and the penance is ended.

3. If it is difficult for the bishop, he can, for the sake of necessity, confer authority on a presbyter, to perform this.

4. Reconciliation is not publicly established in this province, for the reason that there is no public penance either.

XIV. Of the Penance for Special Irregularities in Marriage

1. In a first marriage the presbyter ought to perform Mass and bless them both, and afterward they shall absent themselves from church for thirty days. Having done this, they shall do penance for forty days, and absent themselves from the prayer; and afterward they shall communicate with the oblation.

2. One who is twice married shall do penance for a year; on Wednesdays and Fridays and during the three forty-day periods he shall abstain from flesh; however, he shall not put away his wife.

3. He that is married three times, or more, that is a fourth or fifth marriage, or beyond that number, for

seven years on Wednesdays and Fridays and during the three forty-day periods they shall abstain from flesh; yet they shall not be separated. Basil so determined, but in the canon four years [are indicated].

4. If anyone finds his wife to be an adulteress and does not wish to put her away but has had her in the matrimonial relation to that time, he shall do penance for two years on two days in the week and [shall perform] the fasts of religion; or as long as she herself does penance he shall avoid the matrimonial relation with her, because she has committed adultery.

5. If any man or woman who has taken the vow of virginity is joined in marriage, he shall not set aside the marriage but shall do penance for three years.

6. Foolish vows and those incapable of being performed are to be set aside.

7. A woman may not take a vow without the consent of her husband; but if she does take a vow she can be released, and she shall do penance according to the decision of a priest.

8. He who puts away his wife and marries another shall do penance with tribulation for seven years or a lighter penance for fifteen years.

9. He who defiles his neighbor's wife, deprived of his own wife, shall fast for three years two days a week and in the three forty-day periods.

10. If [the woman] is a virgin, he shall do penance for one year without meat and wine and mead.

11. If he defiles a vowed virgin, he shall do penance for three years, as we said above, whether a child is born of her or not.

12. If she is his slave, he shall set her free and fast for six months.

13. If the wife of anyone deserts him and returns to him undishonored, she shall do penance for one year; otherwise for three years. If he takes another wife he shall do penance for one year.

14. An adulterous woman shall do penance for seven years. And this matter is stated in the same way in the canon.

Plate 1 Fifth-century ivory, produced in Constantinople. It represents the arrival of relics, transported by two bishops, into the city where they are welcomed by the emperor, possibly Theodosius II (401–450) and Pulcheria (398/399–453), his mother who ruled as his regent.

See Fergus Miller, *A Greek Roman Empire: Power and Belief under Theodosius II* (Berkeley: University of California Press, 2006).

Plate 2 Seventh-century stone from Hornhausen, which may have formed part of an altar-screen. It shows a Frankish warrior with shield and spear.

See Herbert Schutz, *Tools, Weapons and Ornaments: Germanic Material Culture in Pre-Carolingian Central Europe, 400–750* (Leiden: Brill, 2001).

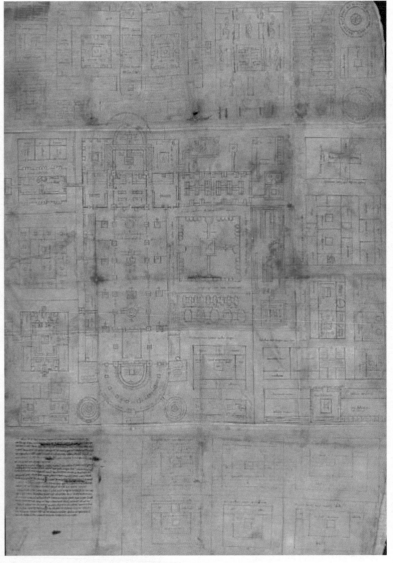

Plate 3 Interior of the Palatine Chapter in Aachen looking toward the royal throne. The inscription reads "When the living stones are linked in peaceful harmony and in even numbers all stand together, the work of the lord who built the whole hall shines brightly and the pious labor of mortal men is crowned with success. Their structure of perpetual beauty will abide if the auctor [i.e., God] protects it in its perfection and holds sway over it. Thus may it be God's will that this entire temple, which the Emperor Charles built, may rest upon a stable foundation." Translation: Günter Bandmann, *Early Medieval Architecture as Bearer of Meaning* (New York: Columbia University Press, 2005), 271.

See Charles McClendon, *The Origins of Medieval Architecture* (New Haven, CT: Yale University Press, 2005).

Plate 4 Plan of St. Gall, ca. 820. This is a visualization of an ideal monastic complex. The Plan is 112 cm × 77.5 cm and includes the ground plans of some 40 structures as well as gardens, fences, walls, a road, and an orchard. Some 333 inscriptions identify the buildings and their uses, including a church, a scriptorium, lodgings for visiting monks, a monastic dormitory, refectory, kitchen, bake and brew house, guest house, abbot's residence, and an infirmary, and numerous fields and industrial out-buildings.

See: http://stgallplan.org/.

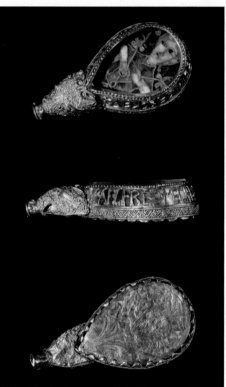

Plate 5 Dedication page of the "San Paolo" bible, created ca. 875 and presented to Pope John VIII at the time of Charles the Bald's coronation as emperor. It represents the emperor enthroned surrounded by his family.

Plate 6 Alfred jewel. This gold, enamel, and quartz jewel, which once was attached to a pointer stick used for helping to follow a line of words in a book, was made in the late ninth century and carries the inscription: "AELFRED MEC HEHT GEWYRCAN" (Alfred ordered me made), and presumably belonged to King Alfred the Great.

Plate 7 Shirt of Queen Balthild. This garment was recovered from the reliquary of Balthild, wife of Clovis II who was buried at the royal monastery of Chelles after her death in 680. The embroidery represents the type of jewelry worn by a queen, jewelry that Balthild, entering religious life, presumably gave up.

Plate 8 Page from the Saint Petersburg Bede. A near-contemporary copy of Bede's *Ecclesiastical History*.

15. A woman who commits adultery shall do penance for three years as a fornicator. So also shall she do penance who makes an unclean mixture of food for the increase of love.

16. A wife who tastes her husband's blood as a remedy shall fast for forty days, more or less.

17. Moreover, women shall not in the time of impurity enter into a church, or communicate—neither nuns nor laywomen; if they presume [to do this] they shall fast for three weeks.

18. In the same way shall they do penance who enter a church before purification after childbirth, that is, forty days.

19. But he who has intercourse at these seasons shall do penance for twenty days.

20. He who has intercourse on the Lord's day shall seek pardon from God and do penance for one or two or three days.

21. In case of unnatural intercourse with his wife, he shall do penance for forty days the first time.

22. For a graver offense of this kind he ought to do penance as one who offends with animals.

23. For intercourse at the improper season he shall fast for forty days.

24. Women who commit abortion before [the fetus] has life, shall do penance for one year or for the three forty-day periods or for forty days, according to the nature of the offense; and if later, that is, more than forty days after conception, they shall do penance for three years as murderesses, that is for three years on Wednesdays and Fridays and in the three forty-day periods. This according to the canons is judged [punishable by] ten years.

25. If a mother slays her child, if she commits homicide, she shall do penance for fifteen years, and never change except on Sunday.

26. If a poor woman slays her child, she shall do penance for seven years. In the canon it is said that if it is a case of homicide, she shall do penance for ten years.

27. A woman who conceives and slays her child in the womb within forty days shall do penance for one year; but if later than forty days, she shall do penance as a murderess.

28. If an infant that is weak and is a pagan has been recommended to a presbyter [for baptism] and dies [unbaptized], the presbyter shall be deposed.

29. If the neglect is on the part of the parents, they shall do penance for one year; and if a child of three years dies without baptism, the father and the mother shall do penance for three years. He gave this decision at a certain time because it happened to be referred to him.

30. In the canon, he who slays his child without baptism [is required to do penance for] ten years, but under advisement he shall do penance for seven years.

XV. Of the Worship of Idols

1. He who sacrifices to demons in trivial matters shall do penance for one year; but he who [does so] in serious matters shall do penance for ten years.

2. If any woman puts her daughter upon a roof or into an oven for the cure of a fever, she shall do penance for seven years.

3. He who causes grains to be burned where a man has died, for the health of the living and of the house, shall do penance for five years.

4. If a woman performs diabolical incantations or divinations, she shall do penance for one year or the three forty-day periods, or forty days, according to the nature of the offense. Of this matter it is said in the canon: He who celebrates auguries,[58] omens from birds, or dreams, or any divinations according to the custom of the heathen, or introduces such people into his houses, in seeking out any trick of the magicians—when these become penitents, if they belong to the clergy they shall be cast out; but if they are secular persons they shall do penance for five years.

5. In the case of one who eats food that has been sacrificed and later confesses, the priest ought to consider the

---

[58] See above, p. 30, n. 52.

person, of what age he was and in what way he had been brought up or how it came about. So also the sacerdotal authority shall be modified in the case of a sick person. And this matter is to be observed with all diligence in all penance always and rigorously in confession, in so far as God condescends to aid.

Book Two

I. Of the Ministry of a Church, or of Its Rebuilding

1. A church may be placed in another place if it is necessary, and it ought not to be sanctified, except that the priest ought to sprinkle it with [holy] water, and in the place of the altar[59] a cross ought to be set.

2. It is acknowledged that two masses may be celebrated in one day on every altar; and he who does not communicate shall not approach the bread nor the kiss [of peace] in the Mass; and he who eats beforehand is not admitted to this kiss.

3. The lumber of a church ought not to be applied to any other work except for another church or for burning with fire or for the benefit of the brethren in a monastery or to bake bread for them; and such things ought not to pass into lay operations.

4. In a church in which the bodies of dead believers are buried, an altar may not be sanctified; but if it seems unsuitable for consecration, when the bodies have been removed and the woodwork of it has been scraped or washed, it[60] shall be re-erected.

5. But if it was previously consecrated, masses may be celebrated in it if religious men are buried there; but if there is a pagan [buried there], it is better to cleanse it and cast [the corpse] out.

6. We ought not to make steps in front of the altar.

7. The relics of saints are to be venerated.

8. If it can be done, a candle should burn near them every night; but if the poverty of the place prevents this, it does them no harm.

9. The incense of the Lord is to be burned on the natal days of saints out of reverence for the day, since they, as lilies, shed an odor of sweetness and asperge [sprinkle] the Church of God as a church is asperged with incense, beginning at the altar.

10. A layman ought not to read a lection in a church nor sing the Alleluia, but only the psalms and responses without the Alleluia.

11. As often as they wish, those who dwell in houses may sprinkle them with holy water; and when thou dost consecrate water thou shalt first offer a prayer.

II. Of the Three Principal Orders of the Church

1. A bishop may confirm in a field if it is necessary.

2. Likewise a presbyter may celebrate masses in a field if a deacon or the presbyter himself holds in his hands the chalice and the oblation.

3. A bishop ought not to compel an abbot to go to a synod unless there is also some sound reason.

4. A bishop determines cases of poor men up to fifty solidi; but the king, if [the amount in litigation] is above that sum.

5. A bishop or an abbot may keep a criminal as a slave if he [the criminal] has not the means of redeeming himself.

6. A bishop may absolve from a vow if he will.

7. Only a presbyter may celebrate masses and bless the people on Good Friday and sanctify a cross.

8. A presbyter is not obliged to give tithes.

9. A presbyter must not reveal the sin of a bishop, since he is set over him.

10. The host is not to be received from the hand of a priest who cannot recite the prayers or the lections according to the ritual.

[59] Meaning, "in the place where the altar formerly stood."
[60] Apparently, the altar.

11. If a presbyter sings the responses in the Mass, or anything [else], he shall not remove his cope;[61] moreover, he lays it on his shoulders even when he is reading the Gospel.

12. In the case of a presbyter who is a fornicator, if before he was found out he baptized, those whom he baptized shall be baptized a second time.

13. If any ordained presbyter perceives that he was not baptized, he shall be baptized and ordained again, and all whom he baptized previously shall be baptized.

14. Among the Greeks, deacons do not break the holy bread; neither do they say the collect or the "Dominus vobiscum" or the Compline.

15. A deacon may not give penance to a layman, but a bishop or a presbyter ought to give it.

16. Deacons can baptize, and they can bless food and drink; they cannot give the bread.

III. Of the Ordination of Various Persons

1. In the ordination of a bishop the mass ought to be sung by the ordaining bishop himself.

2. In the ordination of a presbyter or of a deacon, the bishop ought to celebrate masses as the Greeks are accustomed to do at the election of an abbot or an abbess.

3. In the ordination of a monk, indeed, the abbot ought to perform the mass and complete three prayers over his head; and for seven days he shall veil his head with his cowl, and on the seventh day the abbot shall remove the veil as in baptism the presbyter is accustomed to take away the veil of the infants; so also ought the abbot to do to the monk, since according to the judgment of the fathers it is a second baptism in which, as in baptism, all sins are taken away.

4. A presbyter may consecrate an abbess with the celebration of the mass.

5. In the ordination of an abbot, indeed, the bishop ought to perform the mass and bless him as he bows his head, with two or three witnesses from among his brethren, and give him the staff and shoes.

6. Nuns, moreover, and churches ought always to be consecrated with a mass.

7. The Greeks bless a widow and a virgin together and choose either as an abbess. The Romans, however, do not veil a widow with a virgin.

8. According to the Greeks a presbyter may consecrate a virgin with the sacred veil, reconcile a penitent, and make the oil for exorcism and the chrism of the sick if it is necessary. But according to the Romans these functions appertain to bishops alone.

IV. Of Baptism and Confirmation

1. In baptism sins are remitted; [but] not loose behavior with women, since the children who were born before the baptism of the parents are in such cases in the same status as those born after their baptism.

2. If indeed she who was married before [her] baptism is not regarded as a wife, it follows that the children who were previously begotten can neither be held to be [true] children nor be called brothers among themselves or sharers of the inheritance.

3. If any pagan gives alms and keeps abstinence and [does] other good works which we cannot enumerate, does he not lose these in baptism? No, for he shall not lose any good, but he shall wash away the evil. This Pope Innocent asserted, taking for example what was done concerning the catechumen Cornelius.

4. Gregory Nazianzen declares that the second baptism is that of tears.

5. We believe no one is complete in baptism without the confirmation of a bishop; yet we do not despair.

6. Chrism was established in the Nicene synod.

7. It is not a breach of order if the chrismal napkin is laid again upon another who is baptized.

---

[61] A liturgical vestment in the form of a long cloak.

8. One person may, if it is necessary, be [god]father to a catechumen both in baptism and in confirmation; however, it is not customary, but [usually] separate persons act as godparents in each [office].

9. No one may act as a godparent who is not baptized or confirmed.

10. However, a man may act as a godparent for a woman in baptism, likewise also a woman may act as a godparent for a man.

11. Baptized persons may not eat with catechumens, nor give them the kiss;[62] how much more [must this regulation be observed] in the case of pagans.

V. The Mass of the Dead

1. According to the Roman Church the custom is to carry dead monks or religious men to the church, to anoint their breasts with the chrism, there to celebrate masses for them and then with chanting to carry them to their graves. When they have been placed in the tomb a prayer is offered for them; then they are covered with earth or stone.

2. On the first, the third, the ninth, and also on the thirtieth day a mass is celebrated for them, and, if they wished it, [a mass] is observed a year later.

3. A mass is celebrated for a dead monk on the day of his burial and on the third day; afterward as often as the abbot decides.

4. It is the custom also for masses to be celebrated for monks each week, and for their names to be recited.

5. Three masses in a year [are sung] for dead seculars, on the third, the ninth, and the thirtieth day, since the Lord rose from the dead on the third day and in the ninth hour "he yielded up the ghost, and the children of Israel bewailed Moses for thirty days."

6. For a good layman there is to be a mass on the third day; for a penitent on the thirtieth day, or on the seventh, after the fast; since his neighbors ought to fast seven days and to make an offering at the altar, as in Jesus Ben Sirach we read: "And the children of Israel fasted for Saul";[63] afterward, as often as the priest decides.

7. Many say that it is not permissible to celebrate masses for infants of less than seven years; but it is permitted, nevertheless.

8. Dionysius the Areopagite[64] says that he who offers masses for a bad man commits blasphemy against God.

9. Augustine says that masses are to be performed for all Christians, since it either profits them or consoles those who offer or those who seek [to have it done].

10. A presbyter or a deacon who is not permitted to, or who will not, take communion, may not celebrate masses.

VI. Of Abbots and Monks, or of the Monastery

1. Out of humility and with the permission of the bishop an abbot may relinquish his office. But the brethren shall elect an abbot for themselves from among their own number, if they have [a suitable man]; if not, from among outsiders.

2. And the bishop shall not keep an abbot in his office by violence.

3. The congregation ought to elect an abbot after the abbot's death, or while he is alive if he has gone away or sinned.

4. He himself cannot appoint anyone from among his own monks, nor from those without, nor can he give [the office] to another abbot without the decision of the brethren.

5. If, indeed, the abbot has sinned, the bishop cannot take away the property of the monastery, albeit the abbot has sinned; but he shall send him to another monastery, into the power of another abbot.

6. Neither an abbot nor a bishop may transfer the land of a church to another [church] although both are

---

[62] That is, "the kiss of peace."

[63] Sirach 46:20.

[64] Anonymous theologian philosopher of the late fifth or early sixth century; known as Pseudo-Dionysius.

under his authority. If he wishes to change the land of a church, he shall do it with the consent of both [parties].

7. If anyone wishes to set his monastery in another place, he shall do it on the advice of the bishop and of his brethren, and he shall release a presbyter for the ministry of the church in the former place.

8. It is not permissible for men to have monastic women, nor women, men; nevertheless, we shall not overthrow that which is the custom in this region.

9. A monk may not take a vow without the consent of his abbot; if he lacks this, the vow is to be annulled.

10. If an abbot has a monk worthy of the episcopate, he ought to grant this, if it is necessary.

11. A boy may not marry when he has already set before him the vow of a monk.

12. Any monk whom a congregation has chosen to be ordained to the rank of presbyter for them, ought not to give up his former habit of life.

13. But if he is afterward found to be either proud or disobedient or vicious, and [if] in a better rank [he] seeks a worse life, he shall be deposed and put in the lowest place, or [he shall] make amends with satisfaction.

14. The reception of infirm persons into a monastery is within the authority and liberty of the monastery.

15. Washing the feet of laymen[65] is also within the liberty of a monastery. Except on the Lord's day, it is not obligatory.

16. It is also a liberty of the monastery to adjudge penance to laymen for this is properly a function of the clergy.

VII. The Rite of the Women, or Their Ministry in the Church

1. It is permissible for the women, that is, the handmaidens of Christ, to read the lections and to perform the ministries which appertain to the confession of the sacred altar, except those which are the special functions of priests and deacons.

[In a minority of manuscripts this canon reads]:

Women shall not cover the altar with the corporal, nor place on the altar the offerings, nor the cup, nor stand among ordained men in the church, nor sit at a feast among priests.

2. According to the canons it is the function of the bishops and priests to prescribe penance.

[For this canon a number of manuscripts have the following:]

No woman may adjudge penance for anyone, since in the canon no one may [do this] except the priests alone.

3. Women may receive the host under a black veil, as Basil decided.

4. According to the Greeks a woman can make offerings, but not according to the Romans.

VIII. Of the Customs of the Greeks and of the Romans

1. On the Lord's Day the Greeks and the Romans sail and ride; they do not make bread, nor proceed in a carriage, except only to church, nor bathe themselves.

2. The Greeks do not write publicly on the Lord's Day; in the case of special necessity, however, they write at home.

3. The Greeks and the Romans give clothing to their slaves, and they work, except on the Lord's Day.

4. Greek monks do not have slaves; Roman monks have them.

5. On the day before the Lord's nativity, at the ninth hour, when Mass is ended, that is, the vigil of the Lord, the Romans eat; but the Greeks take supper [only] when Vespers and Mass have been said.

6. In the case of plague, both the Greeks and the Romans say that the sick ought to be visited, as [are] other persons, as the Lord commands.

---

[65] The "pedilavium," or ceremonial foot washing, usually accompanied baptism in the Celtic Church.

7. The Greeks do not give carrion flesh to swine but allow the skins and leather [of carrion] to be taken for shoes, and the wool and horns may be taken [but] not for any sacred [use].

8. The washing of the head is permitted on the Lord's Day, and it is permitted to wash the feet in a solution of lye; but this washing of the feet is not a custom of the Romans.

IX. Of the Communion of the Irish and Britons Who Are Not Catholic in Respect to Easter and the Tonsure

1. Those who have been ordained by Irish or British bishops who are not Catholic with respect to Easter and the tonsure are not united to the Church, but [they] shall be confirmed again by a Catholic bishop with imposition of hands.

2. Likewise also the churches that have been consecrated by these bishops are to be sprinkled with holy water and confirmed by some collect.

3. Further, we have not the liberty to give them, when they request it, the chrism or the eucharist, unless they have previously confessed their willingness to be with us in the unity of the Church. And likewise a person from among these nations, or anyone who doubts his own baptism, shall be baptized.

X. Of Those Who Are Vexed by the Devil

1. If a man is vexed by the Devil and can do nothing but run about everywhere, and [if he] slays himself, there may be some reason to pray for him if he was formerly religious.

2. If it was on account of despair, or of some fear, or for some unknown reasons, we ought to leave to God the decision of this matter, and we dare not pray for him.

3. In the case of one who of his own will slays himself, masses may not be said for him; but we may only pray and dispense alms.

4. If any Christian goes insane through a sudden seizure, or as a result of insanity slays himself—there are some who celebrate masses for such a one.

5. One who is possessed of a demon may have stones and herbs, without [the use of] incantation.

XI. Of the Use or Rejection of Animals

1. Animals which are torn by wolves or dogs are not to be eaten, nor a stag nor a goat if found dead, unless perchance they were previously killed by a man, but they are to be given to swine and dogs.

2. Birds and other animals that are strangled in nets are not to be eaten by men; nor if they are found dead after being attacked by a hawk, since it is commanded in the fourth chapter[66] of the Acts of the Apostles to abstain from fornication, from blood, from that which is strangled, and from idolatry.

3. Fish, however, may be eaten, since they are of another nature.

4. They do not forbid horse [flesh], nevertheless it is not the custom to eat it.

5. The hare may be eaten, and it is good for dysentery; and its gall is to be mixed with pepper for [the relief of] pain.

6. If bees kill a man, they ought also to be killed quickly, but the honey may be eaten.

7. If by chance swine eat carrion flesh or the blood of a man, we hold that they are not to be thrown away; nor are hens; hence swine that [only] taste the blood of a man are to be eaten.

8. But as for those which tear and eat the corpses of the dead, their flesh may not be eaten until they become feeble and until a year has elapsed.

9. Animals that are polluted by intercourse with men shall be killed, and their flesh thrown to dogs, but their offspring shall be for use, and their hides shall be taken. However, when there is uncertainty, they shall not be killed.

XII. Of Matters Relating to Marriage

1. Those who are married shall abstain from intercourse for three nights before they communicate.

2. A man shall abstain from his wife for forty days before Easter, until the week of Easter. On this account

---

[66] Acts 15:20.

the apostle says: "That ye may give yourselves to prayer."[67]

3. When she has conceived a woman ought to abstain from her husband for three months before the birth, and afterward in the time of purgation, that is, for forty days and nights, whether she has borne a male or a female child.

4. It is also fully permitted to a woman to communicate before she is to bear a child.

5. If the wife of anyone commits fornication, he may put her away and take another; that is, if a man puts away his wife on account of fornication, if she was his first, he is permitted to take another; but if she wishes to do penance for her sins, she may take another husband after five years.

6. A woman may not put away her husband, even if he is a fornicator, unless, perchance, for [the purpose of his entering] a monastery. Basil so decided.

7. A legal marriage may not be broken without the consent of both parties.

8. But either, according to the Greeks, may give the other permission to join a monastery for the service of God, and [as it were] marry it, if he [or she] was in a first marriage; yet this is not canonical. But if such is not the case, [but they are] in a second marriage, this is not permitted while the husband or wife is alive.

9. If a husband makes himself a slave through theft or fornication or any sin, the wife, if she has not been married before, has the right to take another husband after a year. This is not permitted to one who has been twice married.

10. When his wife is dead, a man may take another wife after a month. If her husband is dead, the woman may take another husband after a year.

11. If a woman is an adulteress and her husband does not wish to live with her, if she decides to enter a monastery she shall retain the fourth part of her inheritance. If she decides otherwise, she shall have nothing.

12. Any woman who commits adultery is in the power of her husband if he wishes to be reconciled to an adulterous woman. If he makes a reconciliation, her punishment does not concern the clergy, it belongs to her own husband.

13. In the case of a man and a woman who are married, if he wishes to serve God[68] and she does not, or if she wishes to do so and he does not, or if either of them is broken in health, they may still be completely separated with the consent of both.

14. A woman who vows not to take another husband after her husband's death and when he is dead, false to her word, takes another and is married a second time, when she is moved by penitence and wishes to fulfill her vow, it is in the power of her husband [to determine] whether she shall fulfill it or not.

15. Therefore, to one woman who after eleven years confessed [such] a vow, Theodore gave permission to cohabit with the man.

16. And if anyone in a secular habit takes a vow without the consent of the bishop, the bishop himself has power to change the decision if he wishes.

17. A legal marriage may take place equally in the day and in the night, as it is written, "Thine is the day and thine is the night."[69]

18. If a pagan puts away his pagan wife, after baptism it shall be in his power to have her or not to have her.

19. In the same way, if one of them is baptized, the other a pagan, as saith the apostle, "If the unbeliever depart, let him depart";[70] therefore, if the wife of any man is an unbeliever and a pagan and cannot be converted, she shall be put away.

20. If a woman leaves her husband, despising him, and is unwilling to return and be reconciled to her husband, after five years, with the bishop's consent, he shall be permitted to take another wife.

[67] 1 Corinthians 7:5.

[68] That is, to enter a monastery.
[69] Psalm 74:16.
[70] 1 Corinthians 7:15.

21. If she has been taken into captivity by force and cannot be redeemed, [he may] take another after a year.

22. Again, if she has been taken into captivity her husband shall wait five years; so also shall the woman do if such things have happened to the man.

23. If, therefore, a man has taken another wife, he shall receive the former wife when she returns from captivity, and put away the later one; so also shall she do, as we have said above, if such things have happened to her husband.

24. If an enemy carries away any man's wife, and he cannot get her again, he may take another. To do this is better than acts of fornication.

25. If after this the former wife comes again to him, she ought not to be received by him, if he has another, but she may take to herself another husband, if she has had [only] one before. The same ruling stands in the case of slaves from over sea.

26. According to the Greeks it is permitted to marry in the third degree of consanguinity, as it is written in the Law; according to the Romans, in the fifth degree; however, in the fourth degree they do not dissolve [a marriage] after it has taken place. Hence they are to be united in the fifth degree; in the fourth, if they are found [already married] they are not to be separated; in the third, they are to be separated.

27. Nevertheless, it is not permitted to take the wife of another after his death [if he was related] in the third degree.

28. On the same conditions a man is joined in matrimony to those who are related to him, and to his wife's relatives after her death.

29. Two brothers may also have two sisters in marriage, and a father and a son [respectively] a mother and her daughter.

30. A husband who sleeps with his wife shall wash himself before he goes into a church.

31. A husband ought not to see his wife nude.

32. If anyone has illicit connection or illicit marriage, it is nevertheless permissible to eat the food which they have, for the prophet has said: "The earth is the Lord's and the fullness thereof."[71]

33. If a man and a woman have united in marriage, and afterward the woman says of the man that he is impotent, if anyone can prove that this is true, she may take another [husband].

34. Parents may not give a betrothed girl to another man unless she flatly refuses [to marry the original suitor]; but she may go to a monastery if she wishes.

35. But if she who is betrothed refuses to live with the man to whom she is betrothed, the money which he gave for her shall be paid back to him, and a third part shall be added; if, however, it is he that refuses, he shall lose the money which he gave for her.

36. But a girl of seventeen years has power over her own body.

37. Until he is fifteen years old a boy shall be in the power of his father, then he can make himself a monk; but a girl of sixteen or seventeen years who was before in the power of her parents [can become a nun]. After that age a father may not bestow his daughter in marriage against her will.

XIII. Of Male and Female Slaves

1. If he is compelled by necessity, a father has the power to sell his son of seven years of age into slavery; after that, he has not the right to sell him without his consent.

2. A person of fourteen [years] can make himself a slave.

3. A man may not take away from his slave money which he has acquired by his labor.

4. If the master of a male and female slave joins them in marriage and the male slave or the female slave is afterward set free, and if the one who is in slavery cannot be redeemed, the one who has been set free may marry a free-born person.

---

[71] Psalm 24:1.

5. If any freeman takes a female slave in marriage, he has not the right to put her away if they were formerly united with the consent of both.

6. If anyone acquires [as a slave] a free woman who is pregnant, the child that is born of her is free.

7. If anyone sets free a pregnant slave woman, the child which she brings forth shall be [in a state] of slavery.

XIV. Of Various Matters

1. There are three legitimate fasts in a year for the people; the forty [days] before Easter, when we pay the tithes of the year, and the forty [days] before the Lord's nativity and the forty days and nights after Pentecost.[72]

2. He who fasts for a dead person aids himself. But to God alone belongs knowledge of the dead person.

3. Laymen ought not to be dilatory with respect to their promises, since death does not delay.

4. On no account may the servant of God fight. Let [the matter] be for consultation by many servants of God.

5. One infant may be given to God at a monastery instead of another, even if [the father] has vowed the other; nevertheless it is better to fulfill the vow.

6. Similarly, cattle of equal value may be substituted if it is necessary.

7. If a king holds the territory of another king, he may give it for [the good of] his soul.

8. If anyone converted from the world to the service of God has any royal specie[73] received from a king, that [specie] is in the power of that king; but if it is from a former king, [now] dead, that which he received shall be as his other goods; it is permissible to give it to God with himself.

9. That which is found on a road may be taken away. If the owner is found, it shall be restored to him.

10. Let the tribute of the church be according to the custom of the province; that is, so that the poor may not so greatly [?] suffer violence on this account in tithes or in any matters.

11. It is not lawful to give tithes except to the poor and to pilgrims, or for laymen [to give] to their own churches.

12. Out of reverence for the new birth, prayer is to be made in the fifty days.[74]

13. Prayer may be [made] under a veil if necessity requires it.

14. The sick may take food and drink at all hours when they desire it or when they are able [to take it] if they cannot [do so] at the proper times.

Epilogue[75]

Our [authors], as we said, have written these [canons] in consultation with the venerable Theodore, archbishop of the English. If some suppose they have in their possession in more satisfactory or better form these two rules,[76] we hope they will well use their own [versions] and not neglect ours, in which the parts which seem corrupted are attributed by all to the fault of both scribes and interpreters—pretty barbarous men—so that by some, even [by] those instructed by him, the defective and incorrect passages are rightly said not to be his decisions. Of these, although they are retained by many here and there and in a confused state, in succeeding books we have been able with the aid of Christ the Lord to set in order impartially according to our ability not a few of the chief things out of them. But being still in doubt about this work, we connect with it passages in certain minor works that are necessary to it, especially in the booklet on penance, which I think can be easily perceived by a discerning person.

It therefore remains further in vindication of our father Theodore to make satisfaction as best we can to you, beloved,[77] who, not finding a full exposition in the

---

[72] These are the "three forty-day periods" ("quadragesimae") frequently referred to in this and some other penitentials.

[73] Money in coin.

[74] The period between Easter and Pentecost.

[75] The epilogue has come down in only two manuscripts, and neither one includes both the beginning and the end. The text is unusually obscure.

[76] Probably the two books of the penitential.

[77] Literally, "to your love."

utterances of other Catholics, have therefore had recourse to him. In all these matters, I, not undeservedly, entreat you, beloved, who have been judging the difficulties of these [inquiries] that on this account you defend me by your merits on the right hand and on the left, while I strive on your behalf in the welter of these [difficulties], Christ being the judge of the contest, against the threatening blows of calumniators. It is easier for these [calumniators] to defame the laborers than to sweat in the zeal of labor; for some of our people have given themselves to abuse the wisest men of the Church of God by the volubility of their tongues. I refer to St. Jerome whom they call an evil speaker to men, to Augustine whom they call loquacious, and to Isidore whom they call an arranger of glosses. I say nothing of the others, when they say that Gregory, our apostle, easily uttered what others had earlier expounded, a follower in the beaten paths of other men. From this source I have recently heard (what I shudder to tell) that a certain gross follower of heathen fables is abusing the promulgator of the Law of God and chronicler of the whole history of creation, saying, "What could Moses himself, the magician, either know or say to him?"

What, then, can my defense be, since I, in comparison to those whom I have mentioned, am nothing. Yet, "by the grace of God, I am what I am";[78] may it not have been void in me through him who is able to create all things of nothing and to bring to pass great things from little. On this account, if any Catholic author finds anything anywhere in these canons that he is able to amend, he shall have permission from us to do this reasonably, in view of the fact that unless the parts that are not to be followed are suppressed, when they are held of equal validity they occasion contention to those to whom it is said: "not in contention and envy; But put ye on the Lord Jesus Christ."[79]

Questions for Study

What do the sources suggest are some of the major characteristics of Anglo-Saxon society? How comprehensive do you think this picture is? What (or who) might be missing?

---

[78] 1 Corinthians 15:10.
[79] Romans 13:13.

The Carolingians

18. EINHARD

THE LIFE OF CHARLEMAGNE

Einhard (ca. 770–840), originally from the region of Mainz, was raised in the monastery of Fulda and later educated at the court of Charlemagne (d. 814). He later served Charlemagne and his son Louis the Pious (778–840) in various capacities at court and on diplomatic missions. Displeased with the direction of Louis's reign, he retired from court in the early 820s and wrote his *Life of Charlemagne* ca. 825/826. The text, which is a classic of medieval biography, demonstrates the author's thorough familiarity with his model Suetonius, the Roman historian who wrote biographies of the emperors, but is also an extremely subtle critique of Charlemagne's successor. Like royal biographers after him such as Joinville, the biographer of St. Louis IX (see doc. 48 below), Einhard attacks the faults of the reigning monarch simply by praising the virtues of his predecessor.

Source: Paul Edward Dutton (ed. and trans.), "The Life of Charlemagne," in *Charlemagne's Courtier: The Complete Einhard* (Toronto: University of Toronto Press, 2003), 15–39.

Further Reading: Rosamond McKitterick, *Charlemagne: The Formation of a European Identity* (Cambridge: Cambridge University Press, 2008).

Einhard's Preface

After I decided to describe the life and character, and many of the accomplishments, of my lord and foster father, Charles, that most outstanding and deservedly famous king, and seeing how immense this work was, I have expressed it in as concise a form as I could manage. But I have attempted not to omit any of the facts that have come to my attention, and [yet I also seek] not to irritate those who are excessively critical by supplying a long-winded account of everything new. Perhaps, in a way, it will be possible to avoid angering with a new book [even] those who criticize the old masterpieces composed by the most learned and eloquent of men.

And yet, I am quite sure that there are many people devoted to contemplation and learning who do not believe that the circumstances of the present age should be neglected or that virtually everything that happens these days is not worth remembering and should be condemned to utter silence and oblivion. Some people are so seduced by their love of the distant past, that they would rather insert the famous deeds of other peoples in their

...ous compositions than deny posterity any mention of their own names by writing nothing. Still, I did not see why I should refuse to take up a composition of this sort, since I was aware that no one could write about these things more truthfully than me, since I myself was present and personally witnessed them, as they say, with my own eyes. I was, moreover, not sure that these things would be recorded by anyone else.

I thought it would be better to write these things down [that is, his personal observations], along with other widely known details, for the sake of posterity, than to allow the splendid life of this most excellent king, the greatest of all the men in his time, and his remarkable deeds, which people now alive can scarcely equal, to be swallowed up by the shadows of forgetfulness.

There is still another reason, an understandable one, I believe, which even by itself might explain why I felt compelled to write this account; namely, the foster care [Charlemagne] bestowed on me and the constant friendship [I had] with him and his children after I began living at his court. Through his friendship he so won me over to him and I owed him so much both in life and death, that I might both seem and be fairly criticized as ungrateful if I forgot the many kindnesses he conferred upon me. Could I keep silent about the splendid and exceedingly brilliant deeds of a man who had been so kind to me and could I allow his life to remain without record and proper praise, as if he had never lived? But to write and account [for such a life] what was required was [an almost] Ciceronian[1] eloquence, not my feeble talent, which is poor and small, indeed almost non-existent.

Thus [I present] to you this book containing an account of the most splendid and greatest of all men. There is nothing in it that you should admire but his accomplishments, except perhaps that I, a German with little training in the language of Rome, should have imagined that I could write something correct and even elegant in Latin. Indeed, it might seem [to you] that my headlong impudence is very great and that I have willfully spurned the advice of Cicero [himself], since in the first book of his Tusculan [Disputations], when speaking of Latin authors, he had said: "for people to set their thoughts down in writing when they cannot organize them, make them clear, or charm their readers with any style is a complete waste of time and energy." Indeed, this

opinion of the famous orator might have stopped me from writing [this book, at all], if I had not decided in advance that it was better to risk the criticisms of people and to endanger my own small reputation by writing [this book] than to neglect the memory of so great a man and [instead] save myself.

The Life of Charlemagne

1. The family of the Merovingians, from which the Franks used to make their kings, is thought to have lasted down to King Childeric [III], whom Pope Stephen [II] ordered deposed. His [long] hair was shorn and he was forced into a monastery. Although it might seem that the [Merovingian] family ended with him, it had in fact been without any vitality for a long time and [had] demonstrated that there was nothing of any worth in it except the empty name of "king." For both the [real] riches and power of the kingdom were in the possession of the prefects of the palace, who were called the mayors of the palace [maiores domus], and to them fell the highest command. Nothing was left for the king [to do] except sit on his throne with his hair long and his beard uncut, satisfied [to hold] the name of king only and pretending to rule. [Thus] he listened to representatives who came from various lands and, as they departed, he seemed to give them decisions of his own, which he had [in fact] been taught or rather ordered [to pronounce]. Except for the empty name of "king" and a meager living allowance, which the prefect of the court extended to him as it suited him, he possessed nothing else of his own but one estate with a very small income. On that estate, he had a house and servants who ministered to his needs and obeyed him, but there were few of them. He traveled about on a cart that was pulled by yoked oxen and led, as happens in the countryside, by a herdsman to wherever he needed to go. In this way he used to go to the palace and so also to the public assembly of his people, which was held annually for the good of the kingdom, and in this manner he also returned home. But it was the prefect of the court [the mayor of the palace] who took care of everything, either at home or abroad, that needed to be done and arranged for the administration of the kingdom.

2. When Childeric was deposed, Pepin [III, the Short], the father of King Charles, held the office [of mayor of the palace], as if by hereditary right. For his father Charles [Martel] had brilliantly discharged the same civil office, which had been laid down for him by his

---
[1] Marcus Tullius Cicero (106–43 BCE), Roman rhetorician and statesman.

father Pepin [II, of Herstal]. This Charles overthrew those oppressors who claimed personal control over all of Francia and he so completely defeated the Saracens, who were attempting to occupy Gaul, in two great battles—the first in Aquitaine near the city of Poitiers [in 733] and the second near Narbonne on the River Berre [in 737]—that he forced them to fall back into Spain. For the most part, the people [that is, the Frankish nobles] only granted the office [of mayor of the palace] to those men who stood out above others because of the nobility of their birth and the magnitude of their wealth.

For a few years Pepin, the father of King Charles, had held, as if under that [Merovingian] king, the office [of mayor of the palace], which was left to him and his brother Carloman by his grandfather and father. He shared that office with his brother in splendid harmony. [Then in 747] Carloman walked away from the oppressive chore of governing an earthly kingdom. It is not clear why he did this, but it seems that he was driven by a desire to lead a contemplative life. [Hence] he went to Rome in search of a quiet life and there changed his way [of dress and life] completely and was made a monk. With the brothers who joined him there, he enjoyed for a few years the quiet life he so desired in the monastery [he] built on Mount Soracte near the church of St-Sylvester. But since many nobles from Francia frequently visited Rome in order to fulfill their solemn vows and did not wish to miss [seeing] the man who had once been their lord, they interrupted the peaceful life he so loved by constantly paying their respects and so forced him to move. For when he realized that this parade [of visitors] was interfering with his commitment [to the monastic life], he left Mount [Soracte] and retreated to the monastery of St-Benedict located on Monte Cassino in the province of Samnium. There he spent what was left of his earthly life [until 755] in religious contemplation.

3. Moreover, Pepin, who had been mayor of the palace, was established as king [in 751] by the decision of the Roman pope [Zacharias] and he ruled the Franks by himself for fifteen years or more. When the Aquitainian war, which Pepin waged against Waifar, the duke of Aquitaine, for nine straight years, was over, he died of edema in Paris [in 768]. He was survived by two sons, Charles and Carloman, and upon them, by divine will, fell the succession of the kingdom. Indeed, the Franks at a general assembly solemnly established both of them as their kings, but on the condition, agreed to in advance, that they should divide up the entire territory of

the kingdom equally. Charles was to take up and govern that part [of the kingdom] which their father Pepin had held and Carloman that part which their uncle Carloman had [once] governed. Both of them agreed to these conditions and each of them received the portion of the kingdom allotted to him by the plan. That peaceful agreement of theirs held fast, but with the greatest strain, since many on Carloman's side sought to drive the brothers apart. Some went so far as to plot to turn them [against each other] in war. But the outcome of things proved that the threat [of war] was more suspected than real in this case, and when Carloman died [in 771] his wife and sons, along with some of his chief nobles, took refuge in Italy. For no reason at all, she spurned her husband's brother and placed herself and her children under the protection of Desiderius, the king of the Lombards. In fact, Carloman had died [naturally] from disease after ruling the kingdom for two years with his brother. After his death, Charles was established as king by the agreement of all the Franks.

4. I believe it would be improper [for me] to write about Charles's birth and infancy, or even his childhood, since nothing [about those periods of his life] was ever written down and there is no one still alive who claims to have knowledge of these things. Thus, leaving aside the unknown periods [of his life], I have decided to pass straight to the deeds, habits, and other aspects of his life that should be set forth and explained. Nevertheless, so that I might not skip anything either necessary or worth knowing, I shall first describe his deeds inside and outside [the kingdom], then his habits and interests, and finally his administration of the kingdom and his death.

5. Of all the wars he waged, [Charles] began first [in 769] with the one against Aquitaine, which his father had started, but left unfinished, because he thought that it could be quickly brought to a successful conclusion. His brother [Carloman] was [still] alive at the time and [Charles] even asked for his help. And despite the fact that his brother misled him [by not delivering] the promised help, he pursued the campaign with great energy. He refused to back away from a war already in progress or to leave a job undone, until he had by sheer determination and persistence completely achieved the goal he had set for himself. For he forced Hunold, who had tried to take possession of Aquitaine after Waifar's death and to revive a war that was almost over, to give up Aquitaine and seek [refuge in] Gascony. But [Charles], unwilling to allow him to settle there, crossed

the River Garonne and through messengers commanded Lupus, the duke of the Gascons, to hand over the fugitive. If he did not do this quickly, [Charles] would demand his surrender by waging war. Lupus not only gave way to wiser counsel and returned Hunold, but he even entrusted himself and the territory he governed to [Charles's] power.

6. With things settled in Aquitaine and the war over, and since the co-ruler [of Francia, his brother Carloman] was now also dead, [Charles] took up war against the Lombards [in 773]. Hadrian [I], the bishop of the city of Rome, [had] asked and appealed to him to do this. Indeed, his father had previously taken up this war at the request of Pope Stephen [II], [but] with great trouble, since some of the chief Franks, whom he regularly consulted, were so opposed to his plan that they openly stated that they would abandon the king and return home. Despite that [threat], [Pepin] took up the war against King Haistulf and quickly finished it at that time. But, although [Charles] and his father seem to have had a similar or, rather, identical reason for taking up this war, all agree that the [actual] fighting and conclusion [of the two conflicts] were different. For in fact, after laying siege to King Haistulf for a short time [in 756] in Pavia, Pepin forced him to surrender hostages, to restore the cities and fortified places seized from the Romans, and to swear that he would not try to regain the things he had returned. But Charles after he had begun the war did not stop until he had, by means of a long siege [in 774] worn King Desiderius down and had accepted his complete surrender. He forced [Desiderius's] son Adalgis, on whom the hopes of all [the Lombards] seemed to rest, to depart not only from the kingdom, but also from Italy. [Charles] restored everything that had been seized from the Romans. He also overcame Rotgaud, the duke of Friuli, who was plotting new [uprisings in 776], and brought all Italy under his control. He set up his own son Pepin as the king of this conquered land.

I would relate here how difficult it was for one to enter Italy across the Alps and what a struggle it was for the Franks to overcome unmarked mountain ridges, upthrust rocks, and rugged terrain, were it not my intention in this book to record the manner of his life, rather than the details of the wars which he waged. Nevertheless, the end result of this war [against the Lombards] was that Italy was conquered, King Desiderius was sent into permanent exile, his son Adalgis was driven out of Italy, and the properties stolen by the Lombard kings were returned to Hadrian, the head of the Roman church.

7. At the conclusion of this campaign, the Saxon war, which had seemed merely postponed, was begun again. No war taken up by the Frankish people was ever longer, harder, or more dreadful [than this one], because the Saxons, like virtually all the peoples inhabiting Germany, were naturally fierce, worshiped demons, and were opposed to our religion. Indeed, they did not deem it shameful to violate and contravene either human or divine laws. There were underlying causes that threatened daily to disturb the peace, particularly since our borders and theirs ran together almost everywhere in open land, except for a few places where huge forests or mountain ridges came between our respective lands and established a clear boundary. Murder, theft, and arson constantly occurred along this border. The Franks were so infuriated by these [incidents], that they believed they could no longer respond [incident for incident], but that it was worth declaring open war on the Saxons.

Thus, a war was taken up against them, which was waged with great vehemence by both sides for thirty-three straight years [772–804]. But the damage done to the Saxons was greater than that suffered by the Franks. In fact, the war could have been brought to a close sooner, if the faithlessness of the Saxons had [but] allowed it. It is almost impossible to say how many times they were beaten and pledged their obedience to the king. They promised [on those occasions] to follow his orders, to hand over the hostages demanded without delay, and to welcome the representatives sent to them by the king. At different times, they were so broken and subdued that they even promised to give up their worship of demons and freely submit themselves to Christianity. But though they were on occasion inclined to do this, they were always so quick to break their promises, that it is not possible to judge which of the two ways [of acting] can be said to have come more naturally to them. In fact, since the start of the war with the Saxons there was hardly a single year in which they did not reverse themselves in this way. But the king's greatness [of spirit] and steadfast determination—both in bad times and good— could not be conquered by their fickleness or worn down by the task he had set himself. Those perpetrating anything of this sort were never allowed to go unpunished. He took vengeance on them for their treachery and exacted suitable compensation either by leading the army [against them] himself or by sending it under [the charge of] his counts. Finally, when all those who were in the habit of resisting had been crushed and brought back under his control, he removed ten thousand men who had been living with their wives and children along both sides of the Elbe river and he dispersed them here and there throughout Gaul and Germany in various [small] groups. Thus, that war which had lasted for so many years ended on the terms laid down by the king and accepted by the Saxons, namely that they would reject the worship of demons, abandon their ancestral [pagan] rites, take up the Christian faith and the sacraments of religion, and unite with the Franks in order to form a single people.

8. Although this war had been long and drawn out, [Charles] himself met the enemy in battle no more than twice, once near a mountain called Osning in the place known as Detmold and again at the River Haase. [Both battles occurred] within one month, with only a few days separating them [in 783]. His [Saxon] enemies were so destroyed and conquered in these two battles that they no longer dared to anger the king or to thwart his advance, unless they were protected by some fortified place. Nevertheless, in that war many Frankish and Saxon nobles, men holding high offices, were killed. Finally, that war ended in its thirty-third year [in 804], but in the meantime a great many serious wars had broken out against the Franks in other lands. The king managed these with such skill, that an observer might easily wonder which deserves more praise, [the king's] persistence or his successes under adverse conditions. For [the Saxon] war began two years before the Italian [conflict] and, although it was waged without interruption, no war that needed to be fought elsewhere was abandoned or [even] postponed in any way on account of that equally onerous war [against the Saxons]. For in wisdom and greatness of soul this king was the most surpassing of all the kings who ruled the peoples of his time. He abandoned no war that had been entered into and needed to be fought through to the end, because of the exertion [it demanded] or the danger it presented. But rather he had learned to meet and endure each circumstance as it presented itself. Thus, it was not his nature to give up in bad times or to be seduced by the false flattery of success in good times.

9. While he was vigorously pursuing the Saxon war, almost without a break, and after he had placed garrisons at selected points along the border, [Charles] marched into Spain [in 778] with as large a force as he could [mount]. His army passed through the Pyrenees and [Charles] received the surrender of all the towns and fortified places he encountered. He was returning [to Francia] with his army safe and intact, but high in the Pyrenees on that return trip he briefly experienced the treachery of the Basques. That place is so thoroughly covered with thick forest that it is the perfect spot for an ambush. [Charles's] army was forced by the narrow terrain to proceed in a long line and [it was at that spot], high on the mountain, that the Basques set their ambush. They fell upon the last part of the baggage train and drove the men of the rear guard, who were protecting the troops in front, down into the valley below. In the skirmish that followed, they slaughtered every last one of those men. Once they had looted the baggage train, the Basques, under the cover of darkness, since night was then coming on, quickly dispersed in every direction. The Basques had the advantage in this skirmish because of the lightness of their weapons and the nature of the terrain, whereas the Franks were disadvantaged by the heaviness of their arms and the unevenness of the land. Eggihard, the overseer of the king's table, Anselm, the count of the palace, and Roland, the lord of the Breton March, along with many others died in that skirmish. But this deed could not be avenged at that time, because the enemy had so dispersed after the attack that there was no indication as to where they could be found.

10. [Charles] also conquered the Bretons, who live along the sea in the western most part of Gaul. Since they were not subject to him, he sent a force against them [in 786]. The Bretons were forced to surrender hostages and to promise that they would follow his orders.

Next he himself entered Italy with his army and traveled by way of Rome to Capua, a city in Campania. There [in 787], after securing his camp, he threatened to wage war against the Beneventans, unless they surrendered. Areghis, the duke of that people, sent his sons Rumold and Grimold along with a great amount of money to the king. He asked him to accept his sons as hostages and committed himself and his people to following [all the king's] orders, except for an order that would force him personally to appear before [the king]. The king, more concerned with the best interests of [Areghis's] people than with the stubbornness of the duke, accepted the hostages offered to him and granted that, in exchange for a great gift [of money], the duke would not have to appear before him. He kept the younger of the two sons as a hostage, but sent the older one back to his father. His representatives were sent to extract and receive oaths of fidelity from the Beneventans and from Areghis [himself]. [Charles then] returned to Rome and spent a few days visiting holy places before coming back to Gaul.

11. Then the Bavarian war suddenly broke out, but it was brought to a quick end. That war was a product of the pride and foolishness of Duke Tassilo. His wife, who urged him to it, was the daughter of King Desiderius and she thought that she could take revenge for [Charles's] expulsion of her father [from the kingdom of Lombardy] through her husband. Thus, after Tassilo had struck a deal with the Huns, who lived to the east of the Bavarians, he attempted not only to disobey the king, but to provoke him to war. The king in his fury could not abide [the duke's] defiance, which seemed outrageous [to him], and so he gathered troops from all over [Francia] and prepared to invade Bavaria. He himself led that great force [in 787] to the River Lech, which separates the Bavarians from the Alemannians [or Germans]. Before entering the province [of Bavaria], he set up camp on the bank of the river [Lech] and sent representatives to learn the duke's intentions. But Tassilo [now] realized that holding out would benefit neither himself nor his people and so he humbly surrendered to the king. He submitted the hostages demanded, among whom was his own son Theodo, and he also swore with an oath that he would not [in the future] listen to anyone who advised him to rebel against the king's authority. And so this war, which [had] seemed likely to be the greatest conflict of all, was brought to the quickest end. But a little later [that was in 788] Tassilo was summoned before the king and not allowed to leave. The province, which he had [once] held, was not given to another duke to rule, but to [a series of] counts.

12. After [Tassilo's] insurrection had been settled in this way, [the king] declared war against the Slavs, whom we normally refer to as the Wilzi, but who are properly called the Welatabi in their own language. In that war the Saxons fought as auxiliaries alongside the other peoples who were ordered to march in the king's army, but the obedience [of the Saxons] was insincere and lacking in complete commitment. That war came about because [the Slavs] were constantly harassing and attacking the Abodrites, who had once allied themselves with the Franks. [The Slavs] were not inclined [in this matter] to listen to the [king's] commands.

A certain gulf [the Baltic Sea] with an unknown length and a width no more than a hundred miles wide and in many places [much] narrower runs from the western ocean towards the east. Many peoples live around this sea. In fact, the Danes and Swedes, whom we call Northmen, live along the northern shore [of the Baltic] and on all the islands located there. The Slavs, Estonians, and other peoples live along the southern shore [of the Baltic]. The Welatabi were the most prominent of these peoples and it was against them that the king now took up war. He beat them so [decisively] and brought them under his control in the one and only campaign he personally waged [against them], that from that point on they never thought of refusing to obey his commands.

13. Aside from the war against the Saxons, the greatest of all the wars waged by [Charles] was the one against the Avars or Huns, which came next [in 791]. He managed that war with greater attention and preparation than his other wars. Even then, he still led [only] one campaign himself into Pannonia, a province then occupied by the Avars. He turned the other campaigns over to his son Pepin, to the governors of the provinces, and to the counts and even their representatives. These men very vigorously conducted this war and finally brought it to a close in its eighth year [it actually ended in 803]. How many battles occurred in that war and how much blood was spilled is indicated by the utter depopulation of Pannonia and the desertion of the khan's palace; in fact, there is hardly a trace [now] that people once lived there. All the nobility of the Huns died out in this war and all their glory vanished. All the wealth and treasure they had collected over many years was seized. No one can recall any war against the Franks that left them richer or better stocked with resources. Until then they had seemed almost impoverished. So much gold and silver was found in the [khan's] palace and so many precious objects were taken in this war, that it might be fairly said that the Franks had justly seized from the Huns what the Huns had unjustly seized from other peoples. Only two Frankish leaders died in that war: Eric, the duke of Friuli, who was ambushed by the people of Tersatto, a seaside city in Liburnia, and Gerold, the governor of Bavaria. When Gerold was about to engage in battle with the Huns in Pannonia, he was setting out the line of his troops. [At this point] he was killed, it is not known by whom, along with his two escorts as they inspected the troops and urged them individually on. Besides those deaths, the Franks spilled little of their own blood in this war, which was brought to a successful conclusion; and that despite the length of time it took, which was a reflection of the importance of this war.

Then the Saxon [war] came to a [successful] end [in 804] as was [only] appropriate given its long duration. The Bohemian and Linonian wars [in 805 and 808–811] came next, but did not last long. Both of those wars were brought to quick ends under the leadership of the younger Charles [the eldest son of Charlemagne].

14. Charles's final war was the one taken up against the Northmen who are called Danes. First they had operated as pirates, but then they raided the coasts of Gaul and Germany with larger fleets. Their king, Godefrid, was so filled with vain ambition, that he vowed to take control of all Germany. Indeed, he already thought of Frisia and Saxony as his own provinces and had [first] brought the Abodrites, who were his neighbors, under his power and [then] made them pay tribute to him. He even bragged that he would soon come to Aachen, where king [Charles] held court, with a vast army. Some stock was put in his boast, although it was idle, for it was believed that he was about to start something like this, but was suddenly stopped by death. For he was murdered by one of his own attendants and, thus, both his life and the war he had begun came to a sudden end [at the same time].

15. These [then] were the wars that that mighty king waged with great skill and success in many lands over the forty-seven years he reigned. In those wars he so splendidly added to the Frankish kingdom, which he had received in great and strong condition from his father Pepin, that he nearly doubled its size. Previously the so-called eastern Franks had occupied no more than that part of Gaul bounded by the Rhine, the Loire, the [Atlantic] ocean, and the Balearic Sea and that part of Germany bounded by Saxony, the Danube, Rhine, and Saal (the river that divides the Thuringians and Sorabians). In addition to these areas, the Alemannians and Bavarians fell under the control of the Frankish kingdom. Charles himself, in the wars just described, first added Aquitaine, Gascony, and the whole range of the Pyrenees until the River Ebro, which has its source in Navarre, passes through the fertile fields of Spain, and joins the Balearic Sea under the city walls of Tortosa. Next he conquered all of Italy, which runs more than a thousand miles from Aosta to lower Calabria, which forms the border between the Beneventans and the Greeks. Then, he subdued Saxony, which comprises a large part of Germany and is thought to be twice as wide as the land occupied by the Franks, but similar to it in length. After that he added both [upper and lower] Pannonia, Dacia on the far side of the Danube, and also Istria, Liburnia, and Dalmatia. However, for the sake of [maintaining] friendly relations and [preserving] the pact between them, he allowed the emperor of Constan-

tinople to keep certain coastal cities. Then he subordinated and made tributary all the rough and uncivilized peoples inhabiting Germany between the Rhine and Vistula rivers, the ocean and the Danube. They almost all speak a similar language, but are very different from each other in customs and appearance. Among these peoples the Welatabi, Sorabians, Abodrites, and Bohemians are of special importance, and he came into armed conflict with all of them. Other peoples [living there], who far outnumbered them, simply surrendered.

16. He also increased the glory of his kingdom by winning over kings and peoples through friendly means. In this way he so completely won over Alfonso [II], the king of Galicia and Asturias, that when he sent letters or emissaries to Charles, he ordered that in Charles's presence he was only to be referred to as his subject. By his generosity he had so impressed the Irish kings with his goodwill, that they publicly declared that he was certainly their lord and they were his subjects and servants. Some letters they sent to [Charles] still survive and testify to this sort of feeling toward him.

He had such friendly relations with Harun-al-Raschid, the king of the Persians, who held almost all the east except India, that [Harun] counted the favor of his friendship as more valuable than that of all the kings and rulers in the world and thought that only [Charles] was worthy of receiving his honor and generosity. Indeed, when [Charles's] representatives, whom he had sent loaded with gifts for the most Holy Sepulcher of our Lord and Savior [in Jerusalem] and for the place of his resurrection, came before [Harun] and informed him of their lord's wishes, he not only allowed them to complete their mission, but even handed over that sacred and salvific place, so that it might be considered as under Charles's control. [Harun] sent his own representatives back with [Charles's] and he sent magnificent gifts for him, among which were robes, spices, and other riches of the east. A few years before this he had sent an elephant, the only one he then possessed, to Charles who had asked him [for such an animal].

The emperors of Constantinople, Nicephorus [I], Michael [I], and Leo [V], who were also voluntarily seeking friendship and an alliance with Charles, sent many representatives to him. But when he took up the title of emperor, [it seemed] to them that he might want to seize their empire. Thus, [Charles] struck a very strong treaty [with them], so that no [potential] source of trouble of any sort might remain between them. For the Romans and Greeks were always suspicious of Frankish power;

hence that Greek proverb which still circulates: "Have a Frank as a friend, never as a neighbor."

17. Despite being so committed to increasing the size of the kingdom and to subduing foreign peoples and being so constantly preoccupied with business of this kind, [Charles] still took up many projects in different places to improve and beautify the kingdom. He achieved some of them, but not all. Probably the most outstanding of these [projects] are the church of the Holy Mother of God in Aachen, which is a remarkable edifice, and the bridge spanning the Rhine River at Mainz, which was half a mile long, the width of the river at that point. But that bridge burned down the year before Charles died. Although he thought of rebuilding it, this time in stone rather than wood, his sudden death prevented that. He also began [to build two] splendid palaces, one not far from the city of Mainz, on the [royal] estate of Ingelheim, and the other at Nijmegen on the River Waal, which passes along the south side of the island of the Batavians. Even then, if he learned that sacred churches had fallen into ruin because of their age anywhere in his kingdom, he ordered the bishops and priests responsible for them to repair them and charged his representatives with insuring that his orders had been followed.

He [also] constructed a fleet for use against the Northmen. Ships were built for this purpose near the rivers that flow from Gaul and Germany into the North Sea. Since the Northmen were constantly raiding and ravaging the coasts of Gaul and Germany, fortifications and guards were set up at all the ports and at the mouth of every river that seemed large enough to accommodate ships. With such fortifications he stopped the enemy from being able to come and go [freely]. He took the same [precautions] in the south, along the coasts of the province of Narbonne and Septimania and along the whole coast of Italy up to Rome, where the Moors had recently taken to plundering. Through these measures, Italy suffered no great harm from the Moors while [Charles] lived, nor did Gaul and Germany suffer from the Northmen. The Moors did, however, through betrayal capture and pillage Civitavécchia, a city of Etruria, and the Northmen raided some islands in Frisia not far from the German coastline.

18. It is widely recognized that, in these ways, [Charles] protected, increased the size of, and beautified his kingdom. Now I should begin at this point to speak of the character of his mind, his supreme steadfastness in good times and bad, and those other things that belong to his spiritual and domestic life.

After the death of his father [in 768], when he was sharing the kingdom with his brother [Carloman], he endured the pettiness and jealousy of his brother with such great patience, that it seemed remarkable to all that he could not be provoked to anger by him. Then [in 770], at the urging of his mother [Bertrada], he married a daughter of Desiderius, the king of the Lombards, but for some unknown reason he sent her away after a year and took Hildegard [758–783], a Swabian woman of distinct nobility. She bore him three sons, namely Charles, Pepin, and Louis, and the same number of daughters, Rotrude, Bertha, and Gisela. He had three other daughters, Theoderada, Hiltrude, and Rothaide, two by his wife Fastrada, who was an eastern Frank (that is to say, German), and a third by some concubine, whose name now escapes me. When Fastrada died [in 794], [Charles] married Liutgard, an Alemannian woman, who bore no children. After her death [in 800], he took four concubines: Madelgard, who gave birth to a daughter by the name of Ruothilde; Gersvinda, a Saxon, by whom a daughter by the name of Adaltrude was born; Regina, who bore Drogo and Hugh; and Adallinda who gave him Theoderic.

[Charles's] mother, Bertrada, also spent her old age in great honor with him. He treated her with the greatest respect, to the point that there was never any trouble between them, except over the divorce of King Desiderius's daughter, whom he had married at her urging. She died [in 783], not long after Hildegard's death, but [had lived long enough] to have seen three grandsons and the same number of granddaughters in her son's house. [Charles] saw to it that she was buried with great honor in St-Denis, the same church where his father lay.

He had only one sister, whose name was Gisela. She had devoted herself to the religious life from the time she was a girl. As he had with his mother, he treated her with the greatest affection. She died a few years before him [in 810] in the monastery [that is, the monastery of Chelles where she was abbess] in which she had spent her life.

19. [Charles] believed that his children, both his daughters and his sons, should be educated, first in the liberal arts, which he himself had studied. Then, he saw to it that when the boys had reached the right age they were trained to ride in the Frankish fashion, to fight, and to hunt. But he ordered his daughters to learn how to work with wool, how to spin and weave it, so that they might

not grow dull from inactivity and [instead might] learn to value work and virtuous activity.

Out of all these children he lost only two sons and one daughter before he himself died: Charles, his eldest son [who died in 811], Pepin, whom he had set up as king of Italy [died in 810], and Rotrude, his eldest daughter, who [in 781] was engaged to Constantine, emperor of the Greeks [she died in 810]. Pepin left behind only one surviving son, Bernard [who died in 818], but five daughters: Adelhaid, Atula, Gundrada, Berthaid, and Theoderada. The king displayed a special token of affection toward his [grandchildren], since when his son [Pepin] died he saw to it that his grandson [Bernard] succeeded his father [as king of Italy] and he arranged for his granddaughters to be raised alongside his own daughters. Despite the surpassing greatness [of his spirit], he was deeply disturbed by the deaths of his sons and daughter, and his affection [toward his children], which was just as strong [a part of his character], drove him to tears.

When he was informed [in 796] of the death of Hadrian, the Roman pontiff, he cried so much that it was as if he had lost a brother or a deeply loved son, for he had thought of him as a special friend. [Charles] was, by nature, a good friend, for he easily made friends and firmly held on to them. Indeed, he treated with the greatest respect those he had bound closely to himself in a relationship of this sort.

He was so attentive to raising his sons and daughters, that when he was home he always ate his meals with them and when he traveled he always took them with him, his sons riding beside him, while his daughters followed behind. A special rearguard of his men was appointed to watch over them. Although his daughters were extremely beautiful women and were deeply loved by him, it is strange to have to report that he never wanted to give any of them away in marriage to anyone, whether it be to a Frankish noble or to a foreigner. Instead he kept them close beside him at home until his death, saying that he could not stand to be parted from their company. Although he was otherwise happy, this situation [that is, the affairs of his daughters] caused him no end of trouble. But he always acted as if there was no suspicion of any sexual scandal on their part or that any such rumor had already spread far and wide.

20. Earlier I chose not to mention with the others [Charles's] son Pepin [the Hunchback] who was born to him by a concubine [named Himiltrude]. He was handsome in appearance, but hunchbacked. When his father had taken up the war against the Huns [in 792] and was wintering in Bavaria, [Pepin] pretended to be sick and entered into a conspiracy against his father with certain leading Franks who had enticed him with the false promise of a kingdom [of his own]. After the plot was uncovered and the conspirators were condemned, [Pepin] was tonsured and allowed to pursue the religious life he had always wanted in the monastery of Prüm [where he died in 811].

Another powerful conspiracy against Charles had arisen even earlier [in 785–786] in Germany, but all its perpetrators [led by Hardrad] were sent into exile; some blinded, others unharmed. Only three conspirators lost their lives, since to avoid arrest they had drawn their swords to defend themselves and had even killed some men [in the process]. They were cut down themselves, because there was [simply] no other way to subdue them. But it is [widely] believed that the cruelty of Queen Fastrada was the cause and source of these conspiracies, since in both cases these men conspired against the king because it looked as if [Charles] had savagely departed from his usual kind and gentle ways by consenting to the cruel ways of his wife. Otherwise, [Charles] passed his whole life with the highest love and esteem of everyone, both at home and abroad, and not the least charge of cruelty or unfairness was ever brought against him by anyone.

21. He loved foreigners and took great trouble to welcome them [to his court], but the large number [who came] truly seemed a drain both on his palace [resources] and also on the kingdom. But, because of the greatness of his nature, he considered the burden to be insignificant, since he was [more than] repaid for his great trouble with praise for his generosity and with the reward of a fine reputation.

22. [Charles] had a large and powerful body. He was tall [at slightly over six feet or 1.83 meters], but not disproportionately so, since it is known that his height was seven times the length of his own foot. The crown of his head was round, his eyes were noticeably large and full of life, his nose was a little longer than average, his hair was gray and handsome, and his face was attractive and cheerful. Hence, his physical presence was [always] commanding and dignified, whether he was sitting or standing. Although his neck seemed short and thick and his stomach seemed to stick out, the symmetry of the other parts [of his body] hid these [flaws]. [When he walked] his pace was strong and the entire bearing of his

body powerful. Indeed, his voice was distinct, but not as [strong as might have been] expected given his size. His health was good until four years before he died, when he suffered from constant fevers. Toward the very end [of his life] he also became lame in one foot. Even then he trusted his own judgment more than the advice of his physicians, whom he almost loathed, since they urged him to stop eating roast meat, which he liked, and to start eating boiled meat [which he did not].

He kept busy by riding and hunting frequently, which came naturally to him. Indeed, there is hardly a people on earth who can rival the Franks in this skill. [Charles] also liked the steam produced by natural hot springs and the exercise that came from swimming frequently. He was so good at swimming that no one was considered better than him. For this reason [that is, the existence of the hot springs], he built his palace in Aachen and lived there permanently during the final years of his life until he died. He invited not only his sons to the baths, but also his nobles and friends. Sometimes he invited such a crowd of courtiers and bodyguards, that there might be more than a hundred people bathing together.

23. He normally wore the customary attire of the Franks. [Closest] to his body he put on a linen shirt and underwear, then a silk-fringed tunic and stockings. He wrapped his lower legs with cloth coverings and put shoes on his feet. In winter he covered his shoulders and chest with a vest made of otter or ermine skin, above which he wore a blue cloak. He was always armed with a sword, whose handle and belt were made of gold or silver. On occasion he bore a jeweled sword, but only on special feast days or if the representatives of foreign peoples had come [to see him]. He rejected foreign clothes, however gorgeous they might be, and never agreed to be dressed in them, except once in Rome when Pope Hadrian had requested it and, on another occasion, when his successor Leo had begged him to wear a long tunic, chlamys [a Greek mantle], and shoes designed in the Roman [that is to say, Greek] fashion. On high feast days he normally walked in the procession dressed in clothes weaved with gold, bejeweled shoes, in a cloak fastened by a golden clasp, and also wearing a golden, gem-encrusted crown. But on other days his attire differed little from people's usual attire.

24. [Charles] was moderate when it came to both food and drink, but he was even more moderate in the case of drink, since he deeply detested [seeing] anyone inebriated, especially himself or his men. But he was not able

to abstain from food, and often complained that fasting was bad for his health. He seldom put on [large] banquets, but when he did it was for a great number of people on special feast days. His dinner each day was served in four courses only, not including the roast, which his hunters used to carry in on a spit. He preferred [roast meat] over all other food. While eating, he was entertained or listened to someone read out the histories and deeds of the ancients. He was fond of the books of Saint Augustine, particularly the one called the City of God.

He was so restrained in his consumption of wine and other drinks, that he seldom drank more than three times during a meal. After his midday meal in the summertime, he would eat some fruit and take a single drink. Then, after he had removed his clothes and shoes, just as he did at night, he would lie down for two or three hours. While sleeping at night, he would not only wake four or five times, but would even get up. [In the morning] while putting on his shoes and dressing, he not only saw friends, but if the count of the palace informed him that there was some unresolved dispute that could not be sorted out without his judgment, he would order him to bring the disputing parties before him at once. Then, as if he were sitting in court, he heard the nature of the dispute and rendered his opinion. He not only looked after cases such as this at that time, but also matters of any sort that needed to be handled that day or to be assigned to one of his officials.

25. [Charles] was a gifted and ready speaker, able to express clearly whatever he wished to say. Not being content with knowing only his own native tongue [German], he also made an effort to learn foreign languages. Among those, he learned Latin so well, that he spoke it as well as he did his own native language, but he was able to understand Greek better than he could speak it. Indeed, he was such a fluent speaker, that [at times] he actually seemed verbose.

He avidly pursued the liberal arts and greatly honored those teachers whom he deeply respected. To learn grammar, he followed [the teaching of] Peter of Pisa, an aged deacon. For the other disciplines, he took as his teacher Alcuin of Britain, also known as Albinus, who was a deacon as well, but from the Saxon people. He was the most learned man in the entire world. [Charles] invested a great deal of time and effort studying rhetoric, dialectic, and particularly astronomy with him. He learned the art of calculation [arithmetic] and with deep purpose and great curiosity investigated the movement of the stars. He also attempted to [learn how to] write and, for this reason, used to place wax-tablets and note-books under the pillows on his bed, so that, if he had any free time, he might accustom his hand to forming letters. But his effort came too late in life and achieved little success.

26. With great piety and devotion [Charles] followed the Christian religion, in which he had been reared from infancy. For this reason he constructed a church of stunning beauty at Aachen and adorned it with gold and silver, with lamps, grillwork, and doors made of solid bronze. When he could not obtain the columns and marble for this building from any place else, he took the trouble to have them brought from Rome and Ravenna. As long as his health allowed him to, [Charles] regularly went to church both morning and evening, and also to the night reading and to the morning Mass. He was particularly concerned that everything done in the church should be done with the greatest dignity and he frequently warned the sacristans that nothing foul or unclean should be brought into the church or left there. He made sure that his church was supplied with such an abundance of sacred vessels made of gold and silver and with such a great number of clerical vestments, that, indeed, in the celebration of the Mass not even those looking after the doors, who hold the lowest of all ecclesiastical orders, found it necessary to serve in their normal clothes. He very carefully corrected the way in which the lessons were read and the psalms sung, for he was quite skilled at both. But he himself never read publicly and would only sing quietly with the rest of the congregation.

27. [Charles] was so deeply committed to assisting the poor spontaneously with charity, which the Greeks call alms, that he not only made the effort to give alms in his own land and kingdom, but even overseas in Syria, Egypt, and Africa. When he learned that the Christians in Jerusalem, Alexandria, and Carthage were living in poverty, he was moved by their impoverished condition and used to send money. It was chiefly for this reason that he struck up friendships with kings overseas, so that the poor Christians living under their rule might receive some relief and assistance.

He loved the church of St-Peter the Apostle in Rome more than all other sacred and venerable places and showered its altars with a great wealth of gold, silver, and even gems. He [also] sent a vast number of gifts to the popes. During his whole reign he regarded nothing as more important than to restore through his material help and labor the ancient glory of the city of Rome. Not only did he protect and defend the church of St-Peter, but with his own money he even embellished and enriched it above all other churches. Despite holding it in such high regard, he only traveled there four times during the forty-seven years he reigned [in 774, 781, 787, and 800–801] to fulfill his vows and pray.

28. The reasons for his last visit [to Rome] were not just those [that is, his religious vows and for prayer], but rather because residents of Rome had attacked Pope Leo [III]. They had inflicted many injuries on him, including ripping out his eyes and cutting off his tongue. This [attack] forced him to appeal to the loyalty of the king [in 799 at Paderborn]. Thus, [Charles] traveled to Rome to restore the state of the church, which was extremely disrupted, and he spent the whole winter there [until April 801]. It was at that time that he received the title of emperor and augustus, which at first he disliked so much that he stated that, if he had known in advance of the pope's plan, he would not have entered the church that day, even though it was a great feast day [Christmas 800]. But he bore the animosity that the assumption of this title caused with great patience, for the Roman [that is, Greek] emperors were angry over it. He overcame their opposition through the greatness of his spirit, which was without doubt far greater than theirs, and by often sending representatives to them and by calling them his brothers in his letters.

29. After assuming the imperial title, [Charles] realized that there were many deficiencies in the laws of his own people, for the Franks have two sets of laws that differ tremendously at a number of points. He decided, therefore, to fill in what was lacking, to reconcile the disagreements, and also to set right what was bad and wrongly expressed. He did nothing more about this than to add a few items to these laws, but even those were left in an imperfect state. But he did direct that the unwritten laws of all the peoples under his control should be gathered up and written down.

[Charles] also [ordered] that the very old Germanic poems, in which the deeds and wars of ancient kings were sung, should be written down and preserved for posterity. He began [as well] a grammar of his native language. He even gave [German] names to the months, since before then the Franks were used to referring to them by a mix of Latin and Germanic names. He also assigned individual names to the twelve winds, since until then scarcely more than four of them had been named. About the months, he called them:

January	Wintarmanoth	[winter month]
February	Hornung	[antler-shedding or mud month]
March	Lentzinmanoth	[the month of Lent]
April	Ostarmanoth	[easter month]
May	Winnemanoth	[month of joy]
June	Brachmanoth	[plowing month]
July	Heuuimanoth	[hay month]
August	Aranmanoth	[month of ripening wheat]
September	Windumemanoth	[wind month]
October	Windumemanoth	[wine month]
November	Herbistmanoth	[harvest month]
December	Heilagmanoth	[holy month].

He gave the winds these names:

Subsolanus	Ostroniwint	[the east wind]
Eurus	Ostsundroni	[the east-south wind]
Euroauster	Sundostroni	[the south-east wind]
Auster	Sundroni	[the south wind]
Austro-africus	Sundwestroni	[the south-west wind]
Africus	Westsundroni	[the west-south wind]
Zephyrus	Westroni	[the west wind]
Chorus	Westnordroni	[the west-north wind]
Circius	Nordwestroni	[the north-west wind]
Septentrio	Nordroni	[the north wind]
Aquilo	Nordostroni	[the north-east wind]
Vulturnus	Ostnordroni	[the east-north wind].

30. At the very end of his life, when he was already weighed down by poor health and old age, [Charles] summoned his son Louis [the Pious], the king of Aquitaine and the only one of Hildegard's sons still alive, to come to him. When all the leading Franks from the entire kingdom had solemnly assembled and had given their opinion, he established Louis as the co-ruler of the entire kingdom and the heir to the imperial title. Then [on 11 September 813] he placed a crown upon his [son's] head and ordered that he should [henceforth] be addressed as emperor and augustus. This decision of his was widely approved by all who were present, for it seemed to have been divinely inspired in him for the general good of the kingdom. This act [the elevation of Louis] enhanced his powerful reputation and filled foreign peoples with great fear.

[Charles] then sent his son back to Aquitaine and, despite being slowed down by old age, went hunting, as was his usual habit. But he did not travel far from the palace at Aachen and passed what was left of the autumn hunting. He returned to Aachen around the beginning of November [813]. While spending the winter there, he was overcome by a strong fever and took to his bed in January. He immediately decided to abstain from food, as he usually did when he had a fever, because he thought that he could overcome the sickness by fasting or, at least, relieve [its symptoms]. But on top of the fever he developed a pain in his side, which the Greeks call pleurisy. Still he continued his fast and sustained his body with nothing more than an occasional drink. On the seventh day after taking to his bed, he died after receiving Holy Communion. It was nine o'clock in the morning on 28 January [814]. He died in the seventy-second year of his life and in the forty-seventh year of his reign.

31. His body was washed and looked after in a solemn manner and was [then] carried into the church and interred while everyone there wept. At first there had been some uncertainty about where he should be laid to rest, since when he was alive he had specified nothing about it. Finally everyone agreed that the most honorable place for him to be entombed was, in fact, in the very cathedral that he himself had built out of his own resources in Aachen, for the love of God and our Lord Jesus Christ and to honor his mother, the holy and eternal Virgin. He was buried in that church on the same day on which he died and a gilded arch with an image and inscription was erected above his tomb. That inscription ran as follows:

UNDER THIS TOMB LIES THE BODY OF CHARLES, THE GREAT AND
   CATHOLIC EMPEROR, WHO GLORIOUSLY INCREASED THE
   KINGDOM OF THE FRANKS AND REIGNED WITH GREAT SUCCESS
   FOR FORTY-SEVEN YEARS. HE DIED IN HIS SEVENTIES, IN THE
   SEVENTH INDICTION, ON THE TWENTY-EIGHTH DAY OF
   JANUARY, IN THE YEAR OF THE LORD 814.

32. There were so many signs of his approaching death, that not only other people, but even he himself knew that the end was near. For three straight years near the

end of his life there were frequent eclipses of the sun and moon and a dark mark was seen on [the face of] the sun for a space of seven days. The arcade that he had erected with great effort between the church and palace fell to the ground in unexpected ruin on the day of the Ascension of our Lord. Similarly, the bridge over the Rhine River at Mainz, which he built, had taken ten years to complete. Though it was built out of wood with such great labor and remarkable skill that it seemed that it might last forever, it accidentally caught on fire and burned down in three hours [in May 813]. In fact, not a single piece of the bridge's wood survived, except some that was below water.

He himself, when he was waging his last campaign [in 810] in Saxony against Godefrid, the king of the Danes, was leaving camp before dawn one morning, when he saw a brilliant meteor suddenly fall from the sky. It cut across the open sky from right to left. As everyone pondered what this sign meant, the horse on which [Charles] was sitting suddenly fell down headfirst and threw him to the ground with such a bang that the clasp holding his cloak snapped and his sword belt was ripped off. The attendants who were present rushed to his side and lifted him up without his weapons or mantle. Even the javelin that he had been grasping tightly in his hand had fallen and now lay twenty feet or more distant from him.

Added to these events, the palace at Aachen frequently shook [from earthquakes] and the [wooden] ceilings of the buildings in which he lived constantly creaked. The church in which he was later entombed was hit by lightning and the golden apple that stood at the peak of the roof was struck by lightning and landed on top of the bishop's house next door. In that same church an inscription written in red letters that ran between the upper and lower arches along the inside of the building [the inner octagon] gave the name of the builder of the church. In the last line of that inscription [the words] karolvs princeps were to be read. But it was observed by some people that in the very year he died, a few months before his death, the letters that formed princeps became so faint that they were almost invisible. Yet Charles either rejected all these things or acted as if none of them had anything to do with him.

33. [Charles had] decided to draw up a will, so that he might make his daughters and illegitimate children heirs to some part of his estate. But the will was left too late and could not be completed. Nevertheless, three years before he died, he divided up his precious posses-

sions, money, clothes, and other moveable goods in the presence of his friends and officials. He called on them to insure that, with their support, the division he had made would remain fixed and in force after his death. He described in a charter what he wanted done with the goods he had [so] divided. The terms and text of this [division of properties] are such:

In the name of the Lord God Almighty—the Father, Son, and Holy Spirit—[this] inventory and division [of goods] was made by the most glorious and pious Lord Charles, emperor and augustus, in the eight hundred and eleventh year from the Incarnation of our Lord Jesus Christ [that is, 810], in the forty-third year of his reign in Francia and thirty-sixth in Italy, [and] in the eleventh year of his empire, and in the fourth Indiction.

With pious and prudent reflection he decided to make this inventory and division of his precious possessions and the wealth that was located in his treasury on that day and with God's support he accomplished it. In this division he particularly wanted to insure that not only the gift of alms, which Christians solemnly provide for from their own resources, would be looked after on his behalf out of his own wealth and in an orderly and reasonable manner, but also that his heirs should be in no doubt as to what would come to them and so that they might plainly know and divide without legal strife or dispute those things among themselves in an appropriate partition [of goods].

Therefore, with this intention and purpose in mind, he first divided all the wealth and moveable goods (that is, all the gold, silver, precious stones, and royal vestments), that were found in the treasury on that day into three lots. Then he subdivided two of those [three] lots into twenty-one parts, but kept the other lot whole. He divided those two lots into twenty-one parts because there are twenty-one metropolitan cities in his kingdom. In the name of charity his heirs and friends should pass one of those [twenty-one] parts to each metropolitan city. The archbishop then presiding over that church should receive the part given to his church and divide it among his suffragans in this way: one third should remain with his own church, two thirds should be divided among the suffragans [of his diocese]. Each of these divisions, which was made from the first two lots according to the recognized existence of the twenty-one metropolitan cities, has been separated off from the others and lies individually stored in its own repository under the name of the city to which it should be carried. The names of the metropolitan cities to which these alms or gifts should be given are: Rome, Ravenna, Milan, Cividale del Friuli [Aquiliea], Grado, Cologne, Mainz, Salzburg, Trier, Sens, Besançon, Lyons, Rouen, Rheims, Arles, Vienne, Moutiers-en-Tarantaise, Embrun, Bordeaux, Tours, and Bourges.

He wished the third lot to be kept intact so that, while the [the other] two lots had been stored under seal in the [twenty-one] parts described, this third lot might serve his own daily needs as if it were property which he was under no obligation to part with or see alienated from his direct possession. This [arrangement] should hold for as long as he lived or he deemed the use [of the property] necessary for his well-being. But after his death or voluntary withdrawal from the world [into a monastery], this [third] lot should be divided into four parts and one of them should be added to the already [allotted] twenty-one parts. Another [the second] part should be taken up and divided by his sons and daughters, and by the sons and daughters of his sons in a fair and reasonable partition [of goods]. The third part, in keeping with Christian practice, should be set aside for the poor. The fourth part should, in like charitable fashion, be set aside to support the male and female servants of the palace itself. It was his wish to add to the third lot of his complete wealth, which also consists of gold and silver, everything else that was found in his treasury and wardrobe on the day [of his death]: namely, all the vessels and utensils of bronze, iron, and other metals, along with the arms, garments, and other moveable goods, both precious and ordinary, used for various things, such as curtains, bedspreads, tapestries, woolen goods, leather articles, and saddles. [He hoped] in this way that the size of the parts of the third lot would increase and that the distribution of charity would reach more people.

He arranged that his chapel, that is to say its church property, both that which he himself had provided and gathered together, and that which had come by way of family inheritance, should remain whole and not be divided up in any way. If, however, any vessels, books, or other objects should be found in the chapel which he had not indisputably given to the chapel, these could be purchased and retained by anyone who wished to have them after a fair price was determined. He similarly stipulated that the books that he had collected in great number in his personal library could be sold for a fair price to people who wished to own them and that the money [so raised] should be distributed among the poor.

Among his other possessions and riches, it is known that there are three silver tables and a gold one of great size and weight. He arranged and ordered that one of the silver tables, a square-shaped one containing an outline of the city of Constantinople, was to be sent to Rome to the church of St-Peter the Apostle along with the other gifts assigned to the saint. Another [silver table], this one having a round shape and bearing a likeness of the city of Rome, was to be transported to the episcopal seat of Ravenna. The third [silver table], which far surpasses the others in the beauty of its workmanship and its weight, contains a delicate and fine line drawing of the whole universe set within three linked circles, He stipulated that it and the gold table, which is referred to as the fourth, should be used to increase the third lot among his heirs and to increase the share of charity to be distributed from it.

[Charles] made and established this disposition and arrangement [of his goods] in the presence of the bishops, abbots, and counts who were able to be present at that time. Their names are inscribed here. The bishops [were] Hildebald [archbishop of Cologne], Richolf [archbishop of Mainz], Arn [archbishop of Salzburg], Wolfar [archbishop of Rheims], Bernoin [archbishop of Clermont], Leidrad [archbishop of Lyons], John [archbishop of Arles], Theodulf [bishop of Orléans], Jesse [bishop of Amiens], Heito [bishop of Basel], [and] Waltgaud [bishop of Liège]. The abbots [were] Fridugis [of St-Martin of Tours], Adalung [of Lorsch], Angilbert [of St-Riquier],

Irmino [of St-Germain-des-Prés]. The counts were Wala, Meginher, Otulf, Stephen, Unruoc, Burchard, Meginhard, Hatto, Rihwin, Edo, Ercangar, Gerold, Bero, Hildigern, Hroccolf.

After examining this same charter his son Louis, who succeeded by divine right, saw to it that [this division of properties] was fulfilled as quickly and faithfully as possible after his [father's] death.

19. SELECTED CAPITULARIES

The most important source for understanding Carolingian cultural, administrative, and social-reform programs are the capitularies, directives used by the central administration to communicate with local authorities, although some had kingdom-wide distribution. The following examples show the range of these instruments and the various problems of Frankish society they attempt to address.

Source: H.R. Loyn and John Percival, *The Reign of Charlemagne: Documents on Carolingian Government and Administration* (New York: St. Martin's Press, 1975).
Further Reading: Janet L. Nelson, "Literacy in Carolingian Government," in R. McKitterick (ed.), *The Uses of Literacy in the Early Middle Ages* (Cambridge: Cambridge University Press, 1989), 258–96.

Herstal, 779

In the eleventh auspicious year of the reign of our lord and most glorious king, Charles, in the month of March, there was made a capitulary whereby, there being gathered together in one synod and council the bishops and abbots and illustrious counts, together with our most pious lord, decisions were agreed to concerning certain appropriate matters in accordance with God's will.

1 Concerning the metropolitans, that suffragan bishops[2] should be placed under them in accordance with the canons, and that such things as they see needing correction in their ministry they should correct and improve with willing hearts.

2 Concerning bishops: where at present they are not consecrated they are to be consecrated without delay.

3 Concerning the monasteries that have been based on a rule, that they should live in accordance with that rule; and that convents should preserve their holy order, and each abbess reside in her convent without intermission.

4 That bishops should have authority over the priests and clerks within their dioceses, in accordance with the canons.

5 That bishops should have authority to impose correction on incestuous people, and should have the power of reproving widows within their dioceses.

6 That no one should be allowed to receive another's clerk, or to ordain him to any rank.

7 Concerning tithes, that each man should give his tithe, and that these should be disposed of according to the bishop's orders.

8 Concerning murderers and other guilty men who ought in law to die, if they take refuge in a church they are not to be let off, and no food is to be given to them there.

9 That robbers who are caught within an immunity area should be presented by the justices of that area at the count's court; and anyone who fails to comply with this is to lose his benefice and his office. Likewise a vassal of ours, if he does not carry this out, shall lose his benefice and his office; anyone who has no benefice must pay the fine.

---

[2] Metropolitan bishops are bishops of important cities and have supervisory authority over less important suffragan bishops.

10 Concerning a man who commits perjury, that he cannot redeem if except by losing his hand. But if an accuser wishes to press the charge of perjury they are both to go to the ordeal of the cross; and if the swearer wins, the accuser is to pay the equivalent of his wergeld. This procedure is to be observed in minor cases; in major cases, or in cases involving free status, they are to act in accordance with the law.

11 Concerning the judgment of, and punishment inflicted upon robbers, the synod have ruled that the testimony given by the bishops is probably equivalent to that of the count, provided there is no malice or ill will, and there is no intervention in the case except in the interests of seeing justice done. And if he [the judge] should maim a man through hatred or ill intent and not for the sake of justice, he is to lose his office and is to be subject to the laws under which he acted unjustly and to the penalty which he sought to inflict.

12 The heads of procedure which our father of happy memory decided upon for his hearings and for his synods; these we wish to preserve.

13 Concerning the properties of the churches from which the *census*[3] now comes, the tithes and ninths should be paid along with that *census*; likewise tithes and ninths are to be given for those properties from which they have not so far come—from fifty *casati* one shilling, from thirty *casati* half a shilling, and from twenty a *tremissis* [i.e., fourpence]. And concerning precarial holdings, where they are now they are to be renewed, and where they are not they are to be recorded. And a distinction should be made between the precarial holdings established by our authority and those which they establish of their own volition from the property of the church itself.

14 Concerning the raising of an armed following, let no one dare to do it.

15 Concerning those who give tribute in candles, and those who are free by deed or charter, the long-standing arrangements are to be observed.

16 Concerning oaths entered into by swearing together in a fraternity, that no one should dare to perform them.

Moreover, concerning alms-giving, and fire and shipwreck, even though men enter into fraternities they are not to dare to swear to them.

17 Concerning travelers who are going to the palace or anywhere else, that no one should dare to assault them with an armed band. And let no one presume to take away another's crop when the fields are enclosed, unless he is going to the host or is acting as one of our *missi*; anyone who dares to do otherwise shall make amends for it.

18 Concerning the tolls that have before now been forbidden, let no one exact them except where they have existed from of old.

19 Concerning the sale of slaves, that it should take place in the presence of a bishop or count, or in the presence of an archdeacon or *centenarius*, or in that of a *vicedominus*[4] or a count's justice, or before well-known witnesses; and let no one sell a slave beyond the march. Anyone who does so must pay the fine as many times over as the slaves he sold; and if he does not have the means to pay he must hand himself over in service to the count as a pledge, until such time as he can pay off the fine.

20 Concerning coats of mail, that no one should dare to sell them outside our kingdom.

21 If a count does not administer justice in his district he is to arrange for our *missus* to be provided for from his household until justice has been administered there; and if a vassal of ours does not administer justice, then the count and our *missus* are to stay at his house and live at his expense until he does so.

22 If anyone is unwilling to accept a payment instead of vengeance he is to be sent to us, and we will send him where is likely to do least harm. Likewise, if anyone is unwilling to pay a sum instead of vengeance or to give legal satisfaction for it, it is our wish that he be sent to a place where he can do no further harm.

23 Concerning robbers, our instructions are that the following rules should be observed; for the first offense they are not to die but to lose an eye; for the second

---

[3] A payment owed to monasteries by their tenants.

[4] Administrator acting in the place of a count or bishop.

offense the robber's nose is to be cut off; for the third offense, if he does not mend his ways, he must die.

Mantua, 781

Concerning the various provisions which we have made known to all men at the general assembly held at Mantua.

1 Concerning the administration of justice in God's Church, in the matter of widows and orphans, and others who need protection, it is our wish and our special instruction that all bishops, abbots, and counts shall both give and accept full justice according to the law.

2 This we have decided, that everyone who has a claim shall make it three times to his count, and shall find suitable men to give truthful witness that he made the claim and was unable to secure justice as a result of it; and if anyone does otherwise, and brings his claim prematurely to the palace, he shall pay the legal penalty.

3 Further, the count shall declare before witnesses on their behalf that he was willing to give them justice, and he shall have his notary write everything down, namely, what claim they made and what justice they received; so that when the people have made their claim the counts can have no excuse unless it is abundantly clear that they were willing to give them justice; also, that the count himself or his advocate can testify by an oath that there was no negligence in giving them justice, and we can know through their report whether they made the claim to them or not.

4 Let this be known to all men, that if anyone makes a claim after the case has been legally closed, he must either receive 15 strokes of the rod or be made to pay 15 shillings.

5 Let no one receive another's priest and allow him to celebrate mass before he has been interviewed and examined by the local bishop.

6 When a bishop goes the round of his parishes, let the count or his agent [sculdhais] give him assistance, so that he can perform his ministry in full, according to the canons.

7 Let no one sell Christian or pagan slaves or arms of any kind or stallions outside our kingdom; anyone who

does so must be made to pay our fine, and if he is unable to bring the slaves back he must pay their worth.

8 With regard to tolls; let no one presume to levy a toll except in accordance with ancient custom, and let it be levied only in places recognized by law from of old; anyone who levies it unlawfully must make payment according to the law, and in addition must pay our fine to our *missi*.

9 Concerning the coinage: after the first day of August let no one dare to give or receive the pennies now current; anyone who does so is to pay our fine.

10 Concerning brigands who rarely come before our *missi*: let the counts seek them out, and keep them on bail or in custody until the *missi* return to them. . . .

Paderborn, 785 (Capitulary concerning the parts of Saxony)

1 Decisions were taken first on the more important items. All were agreed that the churches of Christ which are now being built in Saxony and are consecrated to God should have no less honor than the temples of idols had, but rather a greater and more surpassing honor.

2 If anyone takes refuge in a church, let no one presume to drive him out of that church by force; rather let him be in peace until he is brought to plead his case, and in honor of God and in reverence for the saints of the church let his life and all his members be respected. But let him pay for his offense according to his means and according to what is decided; and after this let him be brought to the presence of our lord the king, who shall send him wherever in his mercy he shall decide.

3 If anyone makes forcible entry to a church, and steals anything from it by violence or stealth, or if he sets fire to the church, let him die.

4 If anyone in contempt of the Christian faith should spurn the holy Lenten fast and eat meat, let him die; but let the priest enquire into the matter, lest it should happen that someone is compelled by necessity to eat meat.

5 If anyone kills a bishop or a priest or a deacon, he shall likewise pay with his life.

6 If anyone is deceived by the Devil, and believes after the manner of pagans that some man or some woman is a witch and eats people, and if because of this he burns her or gives her flesh to someone to eat or eats it himself, let him pay the penalty of death.

7 If anyone follows pagan rites and causes the body of a dead man to be consumed by fire, and reduces his bones to ashes, let him pay with his life.

8 If there is anyone of the Saxon people lurking among them unbaptized, and if he scorns to come to baptism and wishes to absent himself and stay a pagan, let him die.

9 If anyone sacrifices a man to the Devil, and after the manner of pagans offers him as a victim to demons, let him die.

10 If anyone takes counsel with pagans against Christians, or wishes to persist with them in hostility to Christians, let him die; and anyone who treacherously approves of this against the king or against Christian people, let him die.

11 If anyone is shown to be unfaithful to our lord the king, let him suffer the penalty of death.

12 If anyone rapes the daughter of his lord, he shall die.

13 If anyone kills his lord or his lady, he shall be punished in the same way.

14 However, if anyone has committed these capital crimes and has gone undetected, and goes of his own accord to a priest and is willing to make his confession and undergo a penance, he shall be excused the death penalty on the priest's testimony.

15 On the lesser items all were agreed. For each and every church the people in the area who attend it are to provide a farmstead and two manses of land; and for every 120 men among them, be they noble or free or lidi, they are to give a male and a female slave to the church.

16 This too was decided, with Christ's blessing, that of any revenue which comes to the royal fisc, whether it be from infringement of the peace or a ban of any kind, or from any other payment due to the king, a tithe is to be given to the churches and the clergy.

17 Likewise, in accordance with God's command, we instruct all men to give a tithe of their substance and labor to their churches and clergy; and let nobles, free men and lidi alike make partial return to God for what he has given to each and every Christian.

18 On Sundays there are to be no assemblies or public gatherings, except in cases of great need or when an enemy is pressing; rather let all attend church to hear the word of God, and give their time to prayers and lawful occupations. Likewise on the greater feast-days they should gather to serve God and his Church, and put off secular business.

19 Likewise it was decided to include in these enactments that all infants should be baptized within the year; we have decided further, that if anyone scorns to offer an infant for baptism before a year has gone by, and does not consult a priest or obtain his permission, he shall, if he is of noble birth, pay 120 shillings to the fisc, if he is a free man, 60 shillings, and if he is a lidus[5] 30.

20 If anyone contracts a forbidden or unlawful marriage, he shall pay 60 shillings if he is a noble, 30 if he is a free man, and 15 if he is a lidus.

21 If anyone offers prayers to springs or trees or groves, or makes an offering after the manner of the gentiles and consumes it in honor of demons, he shall pay 60 shillings if he is a noble, 30 if he is a free man, and 15 if he is a lidus. But if they do not have the means to pay at once, they are to be placed in the service of the church until such time as the shillings are paid.

22 It is our order that the bodies of Christian Saxons shall be taken to the Church's cemeteries and not to the pagan burial grounds.

23 We have decided to hand over the diviners and soothsayers to the churches and the clergy.

24 With regard to robbers and other criminals who flee from one country to another, if anyone receives them into his power, and keeps them with him for seven nights for any purpose other than to bring them

---

[5] A semi-free person of low social status in the Frankish world (pl. lidi).

to justice, let him pay our fine. Likewise, if the count lets such a man abscond, and refuses to bring him to justice, and can give no reason for so doing, let him lose his office.

25 With regard to sureties, let no one, under any circumstances, dare to use another man as a surety; anyone who does this shall pay our fine.

26 Let no one take it upon himself to bar the way to any man coming to us to appeal for justice; if anyone tries to do this he shall pay our fine.

27 If any man is unable to find a surety, his property is to be placed in distraint until he finds one. But if he dares to enter his house in defiance of the ban, let him forfeit 10 shillings or one ox in payment for the ban, and in addition pay in full his original debt. And if the surety does not keep him to the appointed day, let him lose whatever he stood to lose in his capacity as surety; but let him who was debtor to the surety pay back double the loss that he caused his surety to suffer.

28 With regard to payments and rewards: let no one take reward against an innocent person; if anyone dares to do this, he must pay our fine. And if, which God forbid, it should happen that a count does it, let him lose his office.

29 Let all the counts endeavor to be at peace and concord with one another: and if it should happen that some disagreement or quarrel should arise among them, they must not scorn our help in settling it.

30 If anyone kills a count or conspires to kill him, his inheritance shall be made over to the king and he shall be subject to his jurisdiction.

31 We have given authority to the counts, within the areas assigned to them, to impose a fine of up to 60 shillings for feuds or other major crimes; but for minor offenses we have fixed the limits of the count's fine at 15 shillings.

32 If anyone has to give an oath to a man, let him swear that oath in church on the appointed day; and if he scorns to swear, let him give a pledge; and anyone who shows himself negligent must pay 15 shillings and afterwards give full satisfaction in the case.

33 With regard to perjury, the law of the Saxons is to apply.

34 We forbid the Saxons to come together as a body in public gatherings, except on those occasions when our *missus* assembles them on our instructions; rather, let each and every count hold court and administer justice in his own area. And the clergy are to see to it that this order is obeyed.

Concerning the Saxons, 797

1 In the seven hundred and ninety-seventh year of the incarnation of Our Lord Jesus Christ, and in the thirtieth and twenty-fifth years respectively of the reign of our lord and most mighty king, Charles, there being assembled together at the palace at Aix at his bidding on the twenty-eighth day of October the reverend bishops and abbots and the illustrious counts, and there being also gathered together the Saxons from the several regions—from Westphalia, from Angaria, and from Eastphalia—they did all with one mind agree and ordain that for those matters for which the Franks pay 60 shillings if they have offended against the king's ban, the Saxon shall likewise pay, if they have done something contrary to the ban. The matters in question are these: first that the Church, and then that widows, orphans, and humble folk generally, should be left in rightful peace and quiet; that no one should dare to commit rape or violence or arson within the neighborhood; and that no one should presume to hold back from military service in defiance of the king's ban.

2 Those who offend in any of the eight matters mentioned are to pay, Saxons and Franks alike, 60 shillings.

3 It was agreed by all the Saxons that, in all cases where Franks are bound by law to pay 15 shillings, the noble Saxons shall pay 12 shillings, free men 5, and *lidi* 3.

4 This also they decided, that when any case is settled within a district by the local authorities, the people of the district are to receive 12 shillings as a fine [*pro districtione*] in the usual way, and they are to have this concession also in payment of the wergeld which it was their custom to have. But if cases are settled in the presence of the royal *missi*, the people are to have these 12 shillings as wergeld and the royal *missus* is to receive another 12 on the king's behalf, on the grounds that he has been troubled with the matter. If, however, the

case is carried through to the palace for a settlement in the king's presence, then both of the 12 shilling payments, that for wergeld and that owed to the local people, making 24 shillings in all, are to be paid to the king's account, on the grounds that the settlement was not arrived at in the district concerned. And if there is anyone who is unwilling to abide by what his neighbors have decided in his district, and who comes to the palace for this reason, and if it is there decided that the original decision was just, he must on the first occasion, as explained above, pay 24 shillings to the king's account; and if he then goes away and refuses to abide by it or to make a just settlement, and is again brought to the palace for this reason and judged, let him pay the 24 shillings twice over; and if, in spite of this, he is detained and brought to the palace for the same reason a third time, let him pay for it three times over to the king.

5 If any noble is summoned to court and refuses to come, let him pay 4 shillings; free men are to pay 2 shillings and *lidi* 1.

6 In the matter of priests, it was decided that if anyone should presume to do harm to them or to their men, or should take anything from them unlawfully, he should pay back everything to them and make amends twice over.

7 Concerning the king's *missi*, it was decided that if a *missus* should happen to be killed by them [the Saxons], he who dared to do it should pay for him three times over. Likewise, for anything done to their men, they should see that threefold restoration is made and payment given according to their law.

8 Concerning fine-raising, it was decided that no one should dare to do so in his district out of anger or enmity or for any other spiteful motive: there should, however, be an exception if a man is so rebellious that he refuses to accept a court's decision and cannot be otherwise restrained; and if he refuses to come to us and be judged in our presence; in such a case a common hearing should be declared and all the people in the district must come, and if they are unanimous in this court the fine can be raised in order to restrain him. When at this hearing a common course of action is agreed upon, let it be carried out in accordance with their own law, and not through any anger or spiteful intent, but only in order to restrain a man for us. If anyone dares to raise a fine

in any other circumstances, let him, as is said above, pay 60 shillings.

9 Likewise, seeing that our lord the king, for the sake of peace and for [preventing] feuds and for other important reasons, wishes to impose a stronger fine [*bannum*], it was decided, with the consent of the Franks and of his faithful Saxons, according to his decision, as the case demands and as opportunity allows, to double the 60 shilling payment; and if anyone goes against this order, let him pay 100 shillings, or even up to a thousand.

10 Concerning the criminals who should (according to the Saxon law code) incur the death penalty, it was decided by all that whoever of them seeks refuge in the royal prerogative it shall be part of that prerogative either to hand the criminal back for punishment, or with their consent to remove him and his wife and family and all his goods from the district, and settle them inside his kingdom or in the march or wherever he wishes, and to have possession of him as though dead.

11 Note should be taken of the proper equivalents of the Saxon shillings; a yearling calf of either sex, in autumn when it is put to byre, is to count for one shilling; likewise in spring, when it comes out of the byre; but afterward, as it grows older, it should increase in value proportionately. Of oats, the Bortrini must give 40 bushels for a shilling, and of rye 20 bushels; those to the south, however, must give 30 bushels of oats for a shilling and 15 bushels of rye. Of honey, the Bortrini must give one and a half *siccli*[6] for a shilling, while those of the south are to give two *siccli*. Likewise of winnowed barley they are to give the same amount as of rye for one shilling. In silver, 12 pennies make a shilling. And in other media of exchange the values shall be the equivalents in each case.

The Synod of Frankfurt, 794

1 A gathering, under God's blessing, in accordance with the apostolic authority and the order of our most pious lord king, Charles, in the twenty-sixth year of his reign, of all the bishops and priests of the kingdom of the Franks, of Italy, of Aquitaine and Provence in synod and council, among whom, in the holy assembly, was the most gentle king himself. Whereat, under the first

---

[6] A unit of weight varying regionally.

and foremost head, there arose the matter of the impious and wicked heresy of Elipandus, bishop of the see of Toledo, and Felix, bishop of Urgel, and their followers, who in their erroneous belief concerning the Son of God assert adoption: this heresy did all the most holy fathers above mentioned repudiate and with one voice denounce, and it was their decision that it should be utterly eradicated from the Holy Church.

2 There was presented for discussion the matter of the new synod of the Greeks, organized at Constantinople on the subject of the adoration of images, in which it was stated that they regarded as anathema those images of the saints which did not have a bearing on the service or adoration of the Holy Trinity; our most holy fathers aforementioned repudiated it and despised all such adoration and service, and argued in condemning it.

3 After this had been dealt with a decision was reached concerning Tassilo, the cousin of our lord king, Charles, who had formerly been duke of Bavaria. He took his stand in the midst of the most holy council, asking pardon for the sins that he had committed, both for those which he had perpetrated in the time of our lord king, Pippin, against him and against the kingdom of the Franks, and for those later ones committed under our lord and most pious king, Charles, in which he had shown himself to be a breaker of his word. He begged to be thought worthy of indulgence from the king, and appeared to do so in all humility, since he wholeheartedly repudiated all anger and scandalous behavior on his part and all things committed against the king to which he had been party. Moreover, all his rights and properties, everything that should lawfully belong to himself or his sons or daughters in the duchy of Bavaria, he disowned and renounced, and forswearing all claims to it for the future irrevocably surrendered it, and along with his sons and daughters commended it to the mercy of the king. Wherefore our lord [the king], moved with pity, both forgave the said Tassilo graciously for the sins he had committed, restored full favor to him, and with compassion received him in love and affection, so that from henceforth he might be secure in the mercy of God. And so he ordered three copies of this decision to be written to the one effect; one he ordered to be kept in the palace, another to be given to the said Tassilo for him to keep by him in the monastery, and the third to be deposited in the chapel of the sacred palace.

4 Our most pious lord the king, with the consent of the holy synod, gave instructions that no man, whether he be cleric or layman, should ever sell corn in time of abundance or in time of scarcity at a greater price than the public level recently decided upon, that is a *modius*[7] of oats one penny, a *modius* of barley two pennies, a *modius* of rye three pennies, a *modius* of wheat four pennies. If he should wish to sell it in the form of bread, he should give 12 loaves of wheat bread, each weighing two pounds, for 1 penny, and for the same price 15 of equal weight of rye bread, 20 of barley bread of the same weight, and 25 of oat bread of the same weight. For the public corn of our lord the king, if it should be sold, the price is to be two *modii* of oats for a penny, one *modius* of barley for a penny, two pence for a *modius* of rye, and three for a *modius* of wheat. Anyone who holds a benefice of us should take the greatest possible care that, if God but provide, none of the slaves of the benefice should die of hunger; and anything that remains above what is necessary for the household he may freely sell in the manner laid down.

5 Concerning the pennies, you should be fully aware of our edict, that in every place, in every city and in every market these new pennies must be current and must be accepted by everyone. Provided they bear the imprint of our name and are of pure silver and of full weight, if anyone should refuse to allow them in any place, in any transaction of buying and selling, he shall, if he is a free man, pay 15 shillings to the king, and, if he is of servile status and the transaction is his own, shall lose the transaction or be flogged naked at the stake in the presence of the people; but if he has done it on his lord's orders, the lord, if it is proved against him, shall pay the 15 shillings.

6 It was ordained by our lord the king and by the holy synod that bishops should administer justice in their parishes. And if any person from among the abbots, priests, deacons, subdeacons, monks, and other clerics, or anyone else in the parish should refuse to obey his bishop, let them come to their metropolitan, and let him decide the case along with his suffragans. Our counts also are to come to the bishops' courts. And if there is anything which the metropolitan bishop cannot put right or settle, then let the accusers finally

---

[7] A unit of measure, often of grain (pl. *modii*).

come to us, with the accused and with letters from the metropolitan, that we may know the truth of the matter.

7 It was ruled by our lord the king and by the holy synod that a bishop should not move from one city to another, but should stay and take care of his church; likewise a priest or a deacon should stay in his church according to the canons.

8 With regard to the dispute between Ursio, bishop of Vienne, and the advocate of Elifantus, bishop of Arles, there were read letters of St. Gregory, Zosimus, Leo, and Symmachus, which made it clear that the church of Vienne should have four suffragan sees, with itself as the fifth over them, and that the church at Arles should have nine suffragan sees under its authority. As to the question of Tarantaise and Embrun and Aix, an embassy was arranged to the apostolic see; and whatever may be decided by the pontiff of the Church of Rome shall be adhered to.

9 It was ruled also by the same our lord the king and by the holy synod that Peter the bishop [of Verdun] should assert before God and his angels and, in the presence of two or three others, as though he were receiving consecration, or indeed in the presence of his archbishop, should swear that he had not conspired for the death of the king or against his kingdom nor been unfaithful to him. The said bishop, since he could find no one with whom he could swear, decided for himself that he would, as God's man, go before the judgment of God, and testify without relics and without the holy Gospels and solely in the presence of God that he was innocent of these matters, and that in accordance with his innocence God should help this his man, who was bound to submit to his judgement and did so. Yet it was not by order of the king or by the decision of the holy synod but by his own free will that he submitted to God's judgment, and was acquitted by Our Lord and found innocent. Nevertheless, our king in his mercy bestowed his favor on the said bishop and endowed him with his former honors, and would not allow a man whom he perceived to merit nothing harmful to be without honor as a result of the charge alleged against him.

10 It was ruled by our lord the king and decided by the holy synod that Gaerbodus, who said he was a bishop but had no witnesses of his consecration, and yet had sought episcopal insignia from Magnardus the metropolitan bishop (who declared moreover that he was not ordained deacon or priest according to canonical prescription), should be deposed by the said metropolitan or by the other bishops of the province from that rank of bishop which he claimed to have.

11 That monks should not go out for secular business nor to engage in lawsuits, unless they do so in accordance with the precepts of the rule itself.

12 That men should not become recluses unless the bishop of the province and the abbot have previously approved of them, and they are to enter upon their place of retreat according to their arrangements.

13 That an abbot should sleep alongside his monks according to the rule of St. Benedict.

14 That greedy men should not be chosen as cellarers in the monasteries, but that such men should be chosen as the rule of St. Benedict instructs.

15 Concerning a monastery where there are bodies of saints; that it should have an oratory within its cloister where the peculiar and daily office may be done.

16 We have heard that certain abbots, led on by greed, require a payment on behalf of those entering their monastery. Therefore we and the holy synod have decided that under no circumstances shall money be required for receiving brothers into a holy order, but that they should be received in accordance with the rule of St. Benedict.

17 That an abbot should not be chosen, when the king so orders, in the congregation, except by the consent of the local bishop.

18 That whatever sin is committed by the monks, we do not allow the abbots under any circumstances to blind them or inflict the mutilation of members upon them, unless the discipline of the rule provides for it.

19 That priests, deacons, monks and clerks should not go into taverns to drink.

20 That a bishop should not be permitted to be ignorant of the canons and the rule.

21 That the Lord's day should be observed from evening to evening.

22 That it should not be proper to consecrate bishops in small towns and villages.

23 Concerning other men's slaves, that they should not be taken in by anyone, and should not be ordained by bishops without their lords' permission.

24 Concerning clerks and monks, that they should remain steadfast in their chosen way of life.

25 That in general, tithes and ninths (or the *census*) should be paid by all who owe them, in respect of benefices and Church property, according to the earlier enactments of our lord the king; and every man should give the lawful tithe in respect of his property to the Church. For we have been informed that in that year when the severe famine broke out there was an abundance of empty corn eaten by demons, and voices of reproach were heard.

26 That the church buildings and their roofs should be repaired and restored by those who hold benefices dependent on them. And where, on the testimony of trustworthy men, it is found that they have in their own houses any wood or stone or tiles that were previously on the church buildings, they must restore to the church everything that has been taken from it.

27 Concerning clerks, that they should under no circumstances move from one church to another, nor be taken in without the knowledge of the bishop and letters of commendation from the diocese to which they belonged, lest it should happen that discord arise in the Church as a result. And wherever such men are found, they must all return to their own church; and let no one dare to keep such a man by him once his bishop or abbot has indicated his wish to have him back. And if it should happen that the lord does not know where he should look for his clerk, let the man with whom he is staying keep him in custody and not allow him to wander elsewhere, until such time as he is restored to his lord.

28 That men should not be ordained without restriction [*absolute*].

29 That each and every bishop should give good teaching and instruction to those placed in his charge, so that there will always in God's house be found men who are worthy to be chosen according to the canons.

30 Concerning clerks who quarrel among themselves or who act in opposition to their bishop, they are to take all the measures that the canons prescribe. And if it should happen that a quarrel arises between a clerk and a layman, the bishop and the count should meet together and should with one mind decide the case between them according to what is right.

31 Concerning plots and conspiracies, that they should not occur; and where they are discovered they are to be crushed.

32 That monasteries should be guarded according to the provisions of the canons.

33 That the Catholic faith of the Holy Trinity, the Lord's Prayer, and the Creed should be preached and handed on to all men.

34 Concerning the stamping out of greed and covetousness.

35 Concerning the practice of hospitality.

36 Concerning criminals, that they should not be allowed to accuse their superiors or their bishops.

37 Concerning absolution in time of emergency.

38 Concerning priests who have been disobedient towards their bishops; they must under no circumstances communicate with the clerks who live in the king's chapel, unless they have made their peace with their bishop, lest it should happen that excommunication according to the canons should come upon them as a result.

39 If a priest is caught in a criminal act, he should be brought before his bishop and be dealt with according to the ruling of the canons. And if it should happen that he wishes to deny the offense, and his accuser is unable to offer proof of it, and the matter cannot be settled before his bishop, then the decision should be referred to their whole council.

40 Concerning girls who have been deprived of their parents; they should, under the supervision of bishops

and priests, be entrusted to suitably sober women, in accordance with the teachings of canonical authority.

41 That no bishop should abandon his proper see by spending his time elsewhere, nor dare to stay on his own property for more than three weeks. And the relatives or heirs of a bishop should in no circumstance inherit after his death any property which was acquired by him after he was consecrated bishop, either by purchase or by gift; rather, it should go in full to the Church. Such property as he had before then shall, unless he make a gift from it to the Church, pass to his heirs and relatives.

42 That no new saints should be revered or invoked in prayers, nor memorials of them erected by the wayside; only those are to be venerated in church which have been deservedly chosen on the basis of their passions or their lives.

43 Concerning the destruction of trees and groves, let the authority of the canons be observed.

44 That the chosen judges should not be rejected by either side in a dispute.

45 Concerning their witnesses, let the canons be observed. And small children should not be compelled to swear an oath, as the Guntbadingi [Burgundians] do.

46 Concerning young girls, at what time they are to take the veil and what are to be their occupations before the age of twenty-five, the writings of the canons should, if necessary, be consulted.

47 Concerning abbesses who do not live according to the canons or the monastic rule: the bishops are to make inquiries and give notice to the king, so that they may be deprived of their office.

48 Concerning offerings which are made to the Church or for the use of the poor, the provisions of the canons are to be observed; such funds are not to be dispensed except by those appointed by the bishop.

49 Concerning priests, and not ordaining them before their thirtieth year.

50 That when the sacred mysteries are accomplished all men should be peaceable towards one another during the rites of mass.

51 Concerning not reciting names until an oblation is offered.

52 That no one should believe that God cannot be prayed to except in three languages only; since God can be prayed to, and man listened to if his prayers are just, in any language.

53 That no bishop or priest should be allowed to be ignorant of the sacred canons.

54 Concerning churches which are built by free men; it is allowed to bestow them as gifts, or to sell them, provided that no church is destroyed and the daily offices are observed.

55 Our lord the king informed the holy synod that he had permission of the holy see, that is of Pope Hadrian, to keep Angilramnus the archbishop permanently in his palace to deal with ecclesiastical matters. He asked the synod that he might be allowed to have bishop Hildebald there on the same terms as he had Angilramnus, he had the apostolic permission. The whole synod agreed, and decided that he should be in the palace to deal with ecclesiastical matters.

56 He suggested that the holy synod should think it right to accept Alcuin into its fellowship and prayers, since he was a man of learning in the doctrines of the Church. All the synod agreed to the suggestion of our lord the king, and accepted him into their fellowship and their prayers.

Charles the Great on the study of literature [De litteris colendis], end of the eighth century

We, Charles, by the grace of God king of the Franks and Lombards and patrician of the Romans, to Abbot Baugulf and all your congregation and our faithful teachers [oratoribus] entrusted to your charge, send affectionate greeting in the name of Almighty God.

Be it known to your devotion, most pleasing in the sight of God, that we, along with our faithful advisers, have deemed it useful that the bishoprics and monasteries which through the favor of Christ have been entrusted to us to govern should, in addition to the way of life prescribed by their rule and practice of holy religion, devote their efforts to the study of literature and to the teaching of it, each according to his ability, to those on whom God has bestowed the capacity to learn; that, just as the observance of a rule gives soundness to their conduct, so also an attention to teaching and learning may give order and adornment to their words, and those who seek to please God by living aright may not fail to please him also by rightness in their speaking. For it is written, "Either by your words shall you be justified, or by your words shall you be condemned."[8] For although it is better to do what is right than to know it, yet knowledge comes before action. Thus each man must first learn what he wishes to carry out, so that he will know in his heart all the more fully what he needs to do, in order that his tongue may run on without stumbling into falsehood in the praise of Almighty God. For since falsehood is to be shunned by all men, how much more should it be avoided, as far as they are able, by those who have been chosen for this one purpose, that they should give special service to truth. Letters have often been sent to us in these last years from certain monasteries, in which was set out what the brothers there living were striving to do for us in their holy and pious prayers; and we found that in most of these writings their sentiments were sound but their speech uncouth. Inwardly their pious devotions gave them a message of truth, but because of their neglect of learning their unskilled tongues could not express it without fault. And so it came about that we began to fear that their lack of knowledge of writing might be matched by a more serious lack of wisdom in the understanding of holy scripture. We all know well that, dangerous as are the errors of words, yet much more dangerous are the errors of doctrine. Wherefore we urge you, not merely to avoid the neglect of the study of literature, but with a devotion that is humble and pleasing to God to strive to learn it, so that you may be able more easily and more rightly to penetrate the mysteries of the holy scriptures. For since there are figures of speech, metaphors and the like to be found on the sacred pages, there can be no doubt that each man who reads them will understand their spiritual meaning more quickly if he is first of all given full instruction in the study of literature. Let men be chosen for this work who have the will and ability to learn and also the desire to instruct others; and let it be pursued with an eagerness equal to my devotion in prescribing it. For we want you, as befits the soldiers of the Church, to be inwardly devout and outwardly learned, pure in good living and scholarly

in speech; so that whoever comes to see you in the name of God and for the inspiration of your holy converse, just as he is strengthened by the sight of you, so he may be instructed also by your wisdom, both in reading and chanting, and return rejoicing, giving thanks to Almighty God. Therefore, if you wish to keep our favor, do not neglect to send copies of this letter to all your suffragans and fellow bishops, and to all the monasteries.

De Villis, end of the eighth century

1 It is our wish that those of our estates which we have established to minister to our needs shall serve our purposes and not those of other men.

2 That all our people shall be well looked after, and shall not be reduced to penury by anyone.

3 That the stewards shall not presume to put our people to their own service, and shall not compel them to give their labor or to cut wood or to do any other work for them; and they shall accept no gifts from them, neither a horse, nor an ox, nor a cow, nor a pig, nor a sheep, nor a piglet, nor a lamb, nor anything other than bottles of wine, vegetables, fruit, chickens, and eggs.

4 If anyone of our people does harm to our interests through theft or any other neglect of duty, let him make good the damage in full, and in addition let him be punished by whipping according to the law, except in the case of murder or arson, for which a fine may be exacted. As far as concerns other men, let the stewards be careful to give them the justice to which they have a right, as the law directs. Our people, as we have said, are to be whipped in preference to being fined. Free men, however, who live on our crown lands [*fiscis*] and estates shall be careful to pay for any wrong they may have done, according to their law; and whatever they may give as their fine, whether it be cattle or any other form of payment, shall be assigned to our use.

5 Wherever it falls to our stewards to see that our work is done, whether it be sowing or plowing, harvesting, haymaking or gathering of grapes, let each one of them, at the appropriate time and place, supervise the work and give instructions as to how it should be done, so that everything may be successfully carried out. If a steward is not in his district, or cannot get to a particular place, let him send a good messenger from among our people, or some other man who can be trusted, to look after our

---

[8] Matthew 12:27.

affairs and settle them satisfactorily; and the steward shall be especially careful to send a reliable man to deal with this matter.

6 It is our wish that our stewards shall pay a full tithe of all produce to the churches that are on our estates, and that no tithe of ours shall be paid to the church of another lord except in places where this is an ancient custom. And no clerics shall hold these churches except our own or those from our people or from our chapel.

7 That each steward shall perform his service in full, according to his instructions. And if the necessity should arise for his service to be increased, let him decide whether he should add to the manpower or to the days spent in performing it.

8 That our stewards shall take charge of our vineyards in their districts, and see that they are properly worked; and let them put the wine into good vessels, and take particular care that no loss is incurred in shipping it. They are to have purchased other, more special, wine to supply the royal estates. And if they should buy more of this wine than is necessary for supplying our estates they should inform us of this, so that we can tell them what we wish to be done with it. They shall also have slips from our vineyards sent for our use. Such rents from our estates as are paid in wine they shall send to our cellars.

9 It is our wish that each steward shall keep in his district measures for *modii* and *sextaria*, and vessels containing eight *sextaria*, and also baskets of the same capacity as we have in our palace.

10 That our mayors and foresters, our stablemen, cellarers, deans, toll-collectors, and other officials shall perform regular services, and shall give pigs in return for their holdings: in place of manual labor, let them perform their official duties well. And any mayor who has a benefice, let him arrange to send a substitute, whose task it will be to carry out the manual labor and other services on his behalf.

11 That no steward, under any circumstances, shall take lodgings for his own use or for his dogs, either among our men or among those living outside our estates.

12 That no steward shall commend a hostage of ours on our estates.

13 That they shall take good care of the stallions, and under no circumstances allow them to stay for long in the same pasture, lest it should be spoiled. And if any of them is unhealthy, or too old, or is likely to die, the stewards are to see that we are informed at the proper time, before the season comes for sending them in among the mares.

14 That they shall look after our mares well, and segregate the colts at the proper time. And if the fillies increase in number, let them be separated so that they can form a new herd by themselves.

15 That they shall take care to have our foals sent to the winter palace at the feast of St. Martin [November 11].

16 It is our wish that whatever we or the queen may order any steward, or whatever our officials, the seneschal or the butler, may order them in our name or in the name of the queen, they shall carry out in full as they are instructed. And whoever falls short in this through negligence, let him abstain from drinking from the moment he is told to do so until he comes into our presence or the presence of the queen and seeks forgiveness from us. And if a steward is in the army, or on guard duty, or on a mission, or is away elsewhere, and gives an order to his subordinates and they do not carry it out, let them come on foot to the palace, and let them abstain from food and drink until they have given reasons for failing in their duty in this way; and then let them receive their punishment, either in the form of a beating or in any other way that we or the queen shall decide.

17 A steward shall appoint as many men as he has estates in his district, whose task it will be to keep bees for our use.

18 At our mills they are to keep chickens and geese, according to the mill's importance—or as many as possible.

19 In the barns on our chief estates they are to keep not less than 100 chickens and not less than 30 geese. At the smaller farms they are to keep not less than 50 chickens and not less than 12 geese.

20 Every steward is to see that the produce is brought to the court in plentiful supply throughout the year; also, let them make their visitations for this purpose at least three or four times.

21 Every steward is to keep fishponds on our estates where they have existed in the past, and if possible he is to enlarge them. They are also to be established in places where they have not so far existed but where they are now practicable.

22 Those who have vines shall keep not less than three or four crowns of grapes.

23 On each of our estates the stewards are to have as many byres, pigsties, sheepfolds, and goat-pens as possible, and under no circumstances are they to be without them. They are also to have cows provided by our serfs for the performance of their service, so that the byres and plow-teams are in no way weakened by service on our demesne. And when they have to provide meat, let them have lame but healthy oxen, cows, or horses which are not mangy, and other healthy animals; and, as we have said, our byres and plow-teams must not suffer as a result of this.

24 Every steward is to take pains over anything he is to provide for our table, so that everything he gives is good and of the best quality, and as carefully and cleanly prepared as possible. And each of them, when he comes to serve at our table, is to have corn for two meals a day for his service; and any other provisions, whether in flour or in meat, are similarly to be of good quality.

25 They are to report on the first of September whether or not there will be food for the pigs.

26 The mayors are not to have more land in their districts than they can ride through and inspect in a single day.

27 Our houses are to have continuous watch-fires and guards to keep them safe. And when our *missi* and their retinues are on their way to or from the palace, they shall under no circumstances take lodging in the royal manor houses, except on our express orders or those of the queen. And the count in his district, or the men whose traditional custom it has been to look after our *missi* and their retinues, shall continue, as they have done in the past, to provide them with pack-horses and other necessities, so that they may travel to and from the palace with ease and dignity.

28 It is our wish that each year in Lent on Palm Sunday, which is also called Hosanna Sunday, the stewards shall take care to pay in the money part of our revenue according to our instructions, after we have determined the amount of our revenue for the year in question.

29 With regard to these of our men who have cases to plead, every steward is to see to it that they are not compelled to come into our presence to make their plea; and he shall not allow a man to lose, through negligence, the days on which he owes service. And if a serf of ours is involved in a lawsuit outside our estates, his master is to do all he can to see that he obtains justice. And if in a given place the serf has difficulty obtaining it, his master shall not allow him to suffer as a result, but shall make it his business to inform us of the matter, either in person or through his messenger.

30 It is our wish that from all the revenue they shall set aside what is needed for our purposes; and in the same way they are to set aside the produce with which they load the carts that are needed for the army, both those of the householders and those of the shepherds, and they shall keep a record of how much they are sending for this purpose.

31 That in the same way each year they shall set aside what is necessary for the household workers and for the women's workshops; and at the appropriate time they are to supply it in full measure, and must be in a position to tell us how they have disposed of it, and where it came from.

32 That every steward shall make it his business always to have good seed of the best quality, whether bought or otherwise acquired.

33 After all these parts of our revenue have been set aside or sown or otherwise dealt with, anything that is left over is to be kept to await our instructions, so that it can be sold or held in reserve as we shall decide.

34 They are to take particular care that anything which they do or make with their hands—that is, lard, smoked meat, sausage, newly-salted meat, wine, vinegar, mulberry wine, boiled wine, garum, mustard, cheese, butter, malt, beer, mead, honey, wax, and flour—that all these are made or prepared with the greatest attention to cleanliness.

35 It is our wish that tallow shall be made from fat sheep and also from pigs; in addition, they are to keep on each estate not less than two fatted oxen, which can be used for making tallow there or can be sent to us.

36 That our woods and forests shall be well protected; if there is an area to be cleared, the stewards are to have it cleared, and shall not allow fields to become overgrown with woodland. Where woods are supposed to exist they shall not allow them to be excessively cut or damaged. Inside the forests they are to take good care of our game; likewise, they shall keep our hawks and falcons in readiness for our use, and shall diligently collect our dues there. And the stewards, or our mayors or their men, if they send their pigs into our woods to be fattened, shall be the first to pay the tithe for this, so as to set a good example and encourage other men to pay their tithe in full in the future.

37 That they shall keep their fields and arable land in good order, and shall guard our meadows at the appropriate time.

38 That they shall always keep fattened geese and chickens sufficient for our use if needed, or for sending to us.

39 It is our wish that the stewards shall be responsible for collecting the chickens and eggs which the serfs and manse-holders contribute each year; and when they are not able to use them they are to sell them.

40 That every steward, on each of our estates, shall always have swans, peacocks, pheasants, ducks, pigeons, partridges, and turtle doves, for the sake of ornament.

41 That the buildings inside our demesnes, together with the fences around them, shall be well looked-after, and that the stables and kitchens, bakeries and wine-presses, shall be carefully constructed, so that our servants who work in them can carry out their tasks properly and cleanly.

42 That each estate shall have in its storeroom beds, mattresses, pillows, bed-linen, table-cloths, seat-covers, vessels of bronze, lead, iron and wood, fire-dogs, chains, pot-hangers, adzes, axes, augers, knives, and all sorts of tools, so that there is no need to seek them elsewhere or to borrow them. As to the iron tools which they provide for the army, the stewards are to make it their business to see that these are good, and that when they are returned they are put back into the storeroom.

43 They are to supply the women's workshops with materials at the appropriate times, according to their instructions—that is, linen, wood, woad, vermilion, madder, wool-combs, teazles, soap, oil, vessels, and the other small things that are needed there.

44 Two thirds of the Lenten food shall be sent each year for our use—that is, of the vegetables, fish, cheese, butter, honey, mustard, vinegar, millet, panic, dry or green herbs, radishes, turnips, and wax or soap, and other small items; and as we have said earlier, they are to inform us by letter of what is left over, and shall under no circumstances omit to do this, as they have done in the past, because it is through those two thirds that we wish to know about the one third that remains.

45 That every steward shall have in his district good workmen—that is, blacksmiths, gold- and silver-smiths, shoemakers, turners, carpenters, shield-makers, fishermen, falconers, soap-makers, brewers (that is, people who know how to make beer, cider, perry, or any other suitable beverage), bakers to make bread for our use, net-makers who can make good nets for hunting or fishing or fowling, and all the other workmen too numerous to mention.

46 That the stewards shall take good care of our walled parks, which the people call *brogili*, and always repair them in good time, and not delay so long that it becomes necessary to rebuild them completely. This should apply to all buildings.

47 That our hunters and falconers, and the other servants who are in permanent attendance on us at the palace, shall throughout our estates be given such assistance as we or the queen may command in our letters, on occasions when we send them out on an errand or when the seneschal or butler gives them some task to do in our name.

48 That the wine-presses on our estates shall be kept in good order. And the stewards are to see to it that no one dares to crush the grapes with his feet, but that everything is clean and decent.

49 That our women's quarters shall be properly arranged—that is, with houses, heated rooms, and living rooms; and let them have good fences all round, and strong doors, so that they can do our work well.

50 That each steward shall determine how many horses there should be in a single stable, and how many grooms with them. Those grooms who are free men, and have

benefices in the district, shall live off those benefices. Similarly the men of the fisc, who hold manses, shall live off them. And those who have no holding shall receive their food from the demesne.

51 Every steward is to take care that dishonest men do not conceal our seed from us, either under the ground or elsewhere, thus making the harvest less plentiful. Similarly, with the other kinds of mischief, let them see to it that they never happen.

52 It is our wish that the men of the fisc, our serfs, and the free men who live on our crown lands and estates shall be required to give all men the full and complete justice to which they are entitled.

53 That every steward shall take pains to prevent our people in his district from becoming robbers and criminals.

54 That every steward shall see to it that our people work well at their tasks, and do not go wasting time at markets.

55 It is our wish that the stewards should record, in one document, any goods or services they have provided, or anything they have appropriated for our use, and, in another document, what payments they have made; and they shall notify us by letter of anything that is left over.

56 That every steward in his district shall hold frequent hearings and dispense justice, and see to it that our people live a law-abiding life.

57 If any of our serfs should wish to say something to us about his master in connection with our affairs, he is not to be prevented from coming to us. And if a steward should learn that his subordinates wish to come to the palace to lodge a complaint against him, then that steward shall present his arguments against them at the palace, and give reason why we should not be displeased at hearing their complaint. In this way we wish to find out whether they come from necessity or merely on some pretext.

58 When our puppies are entrusted to the stewards they are to feed them at their own expense, or else entrust them to their subordinates, that is, the mayors and deans, or cellarers, so that they in their turn can feed them from their own resources—unless there should be an order from ourselves or the queen that they are to be fed at their own expense. In this case the steward is to send a man to them, to see to their feeding, and is to set aside food for them; and there will be no need for the man to go to the kennels every day.

59 Every steward shall, when he is on service, give three pounds of wax and eight *sextaria* of soap each day; in addition, he shall be sure to give six pounds of wax on St. Andrew's Day [November 30], wherever we may be with our people, and a similar amount in mid-Lent.

60 Mayors are never to be chosen from among powerful men, but from men of more modest station who are likely to be loyal.

61 That each steward, when he is on service, shall have his malt brought to the palace; and with him shall come master-brewers who can make good beer there.

62 That each steward shall make an annual statement of all our income, from the oxen which our plowmen keep, from the holdings which owe plowing services, from the pigs, from rents, judgment-fees and fines, from the fines for taking game in our forests without our permission and from the various other payments; from the mills, forests, fields, bridges, and ships; from the free men and the hundreds which are attached to our fisc; from the markets; from the vineyards, and those who pay their dues in wine; from hay, firewood, and torches, from planks and other timber; from waste land; from vegetables, millet, and panic; from wool, linen, and hemp; from the fruits of trees; from larger and smaller nuts; from the graftings of various trees; from gardens, turnips, fishponds; from hides, skins, and horns; from honey and wax; from oil, tallow, and soap; from mulberry wine, boiled wine, mead, and vinegar; from beer and from new and old wine; from new and old grain; from chickens and eggs and geese; from the fishermen, smiths, shield-makers, and cobblers; from kneading troughs, bins, or boxes; from the turners and saddlers; from forges and from mines, that is, from iron- or lead-workings and from workings of any other kind; from people paying tribute; and from colts and fillies. All these things they shall set out in order under separate headings, and shall send the information to us at Christmas time, so that we may know the character and amount of our income from the various sources.

63 With regard to all the things mentioned so far, our stewards should not think it hard of us to make these

demands, since it is our wish that they likewise should be able to make demands of their subordinates without giving offense. And all the things that a man ought to have in his house or on his estates, our stewards shall have on our estates.

64 That our carts which go to the army as war-carts shall be well constructed; their coverings shall be well-made of skins, and sewn together in such a way that, should the necessity arise to cross water, they can get across rivers with the provisions inside and without any water being able to get in—and, as we have said, our belongings can get across safely. It is also our wish that flour—12 *modii* of it—should be placed in each cart for our use; and in those carts which carry wine they are to place 12 *modii* according to our measurement, and they are also to provide for each cart a shield, a lance, a quiver, and a bow.

65 That the fish from our fishponds shall be sold, and others put in their place, so that there is always a supply of fish; however, when we do not visit the estates they are to be sold, and our stewards are to get a profit from them for our benefit.

66 They are to give an account to us of the male and female goats, and of their horns and skins; and each year they are to bring to us the newly-salted meat of the fattened goats.

67 With regard to vacant manses and newly acquired slaves, if they have any surplus which they cannot dispose of, they are to let us know.

68 It is our wish that the various stewards should always have by them good barrels bound with iron, which they can send to the army and to the palace, and that they should not make bottles of leather.

69 They shall at all times keep us informed about wolves, how many each of them has caught, and shall have the skins delivered to us. And in the month of May they are to seek out the wolf cubs and catch them, with poison and hooks as well as with pits and dogs.

70 It is our wish that they shall have in their gardens all kinds of plants: lily, roses, fenugreek, costmary, sage, rue, southernwood, cucumbers, pumpkins, gourds, kidney-beans, cumin, rosemary, caraway, chick-pea, squill, gladiolus, tarragon, anise, colocynth, chicory, ammi, sesili, lettuces, spider's foot, rocket salad, garden cress, burdock, penny-royal, hemlock, parsley, celery, lovage, juniper, dill, sweet fennel, endive, dittany, white mustard, summer savory, water mint, garden mint, wild mint, tansy, catnip, centaury, garden poppy, beets, hazelwort, marshmallows, mallows, carrots, parsnip, orach, spinach, kohlrabi, cabbages, onions, chives, leeks, radishes, shallots, cibols, garlic, madder, teazles, broad beans, peas, coriander, chervil, capers, clary. And the gardener shall have house-leeks growing on his house. As for trees, it is our wish that they shall have various kinds of apple, pear, plum, sorb, medlar, chestnut, and peach; quince, hazel, almond, mulberry, laurel, pine, fig, nut, and cherry trees of various kinds. The names of apples are: *gozmaringa, geroldinga, crevedella, spirauca*; there are sweet ones, bitter ones, those that keep well, those that are to be eaten straightaway, and early ones. Of pears they are to have three or four kinds, those that keep well, sweet ones, cooking pears, and the late-ripening ones.

General capitulary for the *missi*, spring 802

1 Concerning the commission despatched by our lord the emperor. Our most serene and most Christian lord and emperor, Charles, has selected the most prudent and wise from among his leading men, archbishops and bishops, together with venerable abbots and devout laymen, and has sent them out into all his kingdom, and bestowed through them on all his subjects the right to live in accordance with a right rule of law. Wherever there is any provision in the law that is other than right or just he has ordered them to inquire most diligently into it and bring it to his notice, it being his desire, with God's help, to rectify it. And let no one dare or be allowed to use his wit and cunning, as many do, to subvert the law as it is laid down or the emperor's justice, whether it concerns God's churches, or poor people and widows and orphans, or any Christian person. Rather should all men live a good and just life in accordance with God's commands, and should with one mind remain and abide each in his appointed place or profession: the clergy should live a life in full accord with the canons without regard for base gain, the monastic orders should keep their life under diligent control, the laity and secular people should make proper

use of their laws, refraining from ill-will and deceit, and all should live together in perfect love and peace. And the *missi* themselves, as they wish to have the favor of Almighty God and to preserve it through the loyalty they have promised, are to make diligent inquiry wherever a man claims that someone has done him an injustice; so everywhere, and amongst all men, in God's holy churches, among poor people, orphans, and widows, and throughout the whole people they may administer law and justice in full accordance with the will and the fear of God. And if there be anything which they themselves, together with the counts of the provinces, cannot correct or bring to a just settlement, they should refer it without any hesitation to the emperor's judgment along with their reports. And in no way, whether by some man's flattery or bribery, or by the excuse of blood relationship with someone, or through fear of someone more powerful, should anyone hinder the right and proper course of justice.

2 Concerning the promise of fealty to our lord the emperor. He has given instructions that in all his kingdom all men, both clergy and laity, and each according to his vows and way of life, who before have promised fealty to him as king, should now make the same promise to him as Caesar; and those who until now have not made the promise are all to do so from 12 years old and upwards. And that all should be publicly informed, so that each man may understand how many important matters are contained in that oath—not only, as many have thought until now, the profession of loyalty to our lord the emperor throughout his life, and the undertaking not to bring any enemy into his kingdom for hostile reasons, nor to consent to or be silent about anyone's infidelity towards him, but also that all men may know that the oath has in addition the following meaning within it.

3 First, that everyone on his own behalf should strive to maintain himself in God's holy service, in accordance with God's command and his own pledge, to the best of his ability and intelligence, since our lord the emperor himself is unable to provide the necessary care and discipline to all men individually.

4 Second, that no man, through perjury or any other craft or deceit, or through anyone's flattery or bribery, should in any way withhold or take away or conceal our lord the emperor's serf, or his landmark, or his land, or anything that is his by right of possession; and that no

one should conceal the men of his fisc who run away and unlawfully and deceitfully claim to be free men, nor take them away by perjury or any other craft.

5 That no one should presume to commit fraud or theft or any other criminal act against God's holy churches or against widows or orphans or pilgrims; for the lord emperor himself, after God and his saints, has been appointed their protector and defender.

6 That no one should dare neglect a benefice held of our lord the emperor, and build up his own property from it.

7 That no one should presume to ignore a summons to the host from our lord the emperor, and that no count should be so presumptuous as to dare to excuse any of those who ought to go with the host, either on the pretext of kinship or through the enticement of any gift.

8 That no one should presume to subvert in any way any edict or any order of our lord the emperor, nor trifle with his affairs nor hinder nor weaken them, nor act in any other way contrary to his will and his instructions. And that no one should dare to be obstructive about any debt or payment that he owes.

9 That no one in court should make a practice of defending another man in an unlawful manner, by arguing the case weakly through a desire for gain, by hampering a lawful judgment by showing off his skill in pleading, or by presenting a weak case in an attempt to do his client harm. Rather should each man plead for himself, be it a question of tax or debt or some other case, unless he is infirm or unacquainted with pleading; for such men the *missi* or the chief men who are in the court or a judge who knows the case can plead it before the court, or if necessary a man can be provided to plead, who is approved by all parties and has a good knowledge of the case at issue; this, however, should only be done at the convenience of the chief men or *missi* who are present. At all events, it must be done in accordance with justice and the law; and no one should be allowed to impede the course of justice by offering a reward or a fee, by skillful and ill-intentioned flattery, or by the excuse of kinship. And let no one make an unlawful agreement with anyone, but let all men be seriously and willingly prepared to see that justice is done.

10–24 [These sections are all on ecclesiastical matters, dealing with the duties and conduct of clergy, monks, etc.]

25 That the counts and *centenarii* should strive to see that justice is done, and should have as assistants in their duties men in whom they can have full confidence, who will faithfully observe justice and the law, will in no wise oppress the poor, and will not dare, for flattery or a bribe, to conceal in any manner of concealment any thieves, robbers or murderers, adulterers, evil-doers and performers of incantations and auguries, and all other sacrilegious people, but rather will bring them to light, that they may receive correction and punishment according to the law, and that with God's indulgence all these evils may be removed from among our Christian people.

26 That the justices should give right judgment according to the written law, and not according to their private opinions.

27 We ordain that no one in all our kingdom, whether rich or poor, should dare to deny hospitality to pilgrims; that is, no one should refuse a roof, a hearth, and water to any pilgrims who are traveling the country in the service of God, or to anyone who is journeying for love of God or for the salvation of his soul. And if a man should be willing to offer any further benefit to such people, let him know that God will send him the best reward, as he himself said: "Whoso shall receive one such little child in my name receiveth me"; and in another place, "I was a stranger, and ye took me in."[9]

28 Concerning the commissions coming from our lord the emperor. The counts and the *centenarii* should, as they are desirous of the favor of our lord the emperor, provide for the *missi* who are sent upon them with all possible attention, that they may go about their duties without any delay; and he has given instructions to all men that it is their duty to make such provision, that they suffer no delay to occur anywhere, and that they help them to go upon their way with all haste, and make such provision for this as our *missi* may require.

29 Concerning those poor men who owe payment of the royal fine and to whom the lord emperor in his mercy

has given remission; the counts or *missi* are not to have the right for their part to bring constraint upon people so excused.

30 Concerning those whom the lord emperor wishes, with Christ's blessing, to have peace and protection in his kingdom, that is, those who have thrown themselves upon his mercy, those who, whether Christians or pagans, have desired to offer any information, or who from poverty or hunger have sought his intervention; let no one dare to bind them in servitude or take possession of them or dispose of them or sell them, but rather let them stay where they themselves choose, and live there under the lord emperor's protection and in his mercy. If anyone should presume to transgress this instruction, let him know that a man so presumptuous as to despise the lord emperor's orders must pay for it with the loss of his life.

31 For those who administer the justice of our lord the emperor let no one dare to devise harm or injury, nor bring any hostility to bear upon them. Anyone who presumes to do so must pay the royal fine; and if he is guilty of a greater offense, the orders are that he be brought to the king's presence.

32 Murder, by which a great multitude of our Christian people perish, we ordain should be shunned and avoided by every possible means; Our Lord himself forbade hatred and enmity among his faithful, and murder even more. How can a man feel confident that he will be at peace with God, when he has killed the son most close to himself? Or who can believe that Christ Our Lord is on his side, when he has murdered his brother? It is, moreover, a great and unacceptable risk with God the Father and Christ the ruler of heaven and earth to arouse the hostility of men. With men, we can escape for a time by hiding, but even so by some chance of fortune we fall into our enemy's hands; but where can a man escape from God, from whom no secrets are hid? What rashness to think to escape His anger! For this reason we have sought, by every kind of precept, to prevent the people entrusted to us for ruling from perishing as a result of this evil; for he who feels no dread at the anger of God should not receive mild and benevolent treatment from us; rather would we wish a man who had dared to commit the evil act of murder to receive the severest of punishments. Nevertheless, in order that the crime should not increase further, and in order that serious enmity should not arise among Christians when they resort to murders at the persuasion of the Devil,

---

[9] Matthew 18:5; 25:35.

the guilty person should immediately set about making amends, and should with all possible speed pay the appropriate recompense to the relatives of the dead man for the evil he has done to them. And this we firmly forbid, that the parents of the dead man should dare in any way to increase the enmity arising from the crime committed, or refuse to allow peace when the request is made; rather, they should accept the word given to them and the compensation offered, and allow perpetual peace, so long as the guilty man does not delay payment of the compensation. And when a man sinks to such a depth of crime as to kill his brother or a relative, he must betake himself immediately to the penance devised for him, and to do as his bishop instructs him and without any compromising. He should strive with God's help to make full amends, and should pay compensation for the dead man according to the law and make his peace in full with his kinsmen; and once the parties have given their word let no one dare to arouse further enmity on the matter. And anyone who scorns to pay the appropriate compensation is to be deprived of his inheritance pending our judgment.

33 We forbid absolutely the crime of incest. If anyone is stained by wicked fornication he must in no circumstances be let off without severe penalty, but rather should be punished for it in such a way that others will be deterred from committing the same offense, that filthiness may be utterly removed from our Christian people, and that the guilty person himself may be fully freed from it through the penance that is prescribed for him by his bishop. The woman concerned should be kept under her parents' supervision subject to our judgment. And if such people are unwilling to agree to the bishop's judgment concerning their improvement they are to be brought to our presence, mindful of that exemplary punishment for incest imposed by Fricco upon a certain nun.

34 That all should be fully and well prepared for whenever our order or announcement may come. And if anyone then maintains that he is not ready and disregards our instructions he is to be brought to the palace—and not he alone, but all those who presume to go against our edict or our orders.

35 That all bishops and their priests should be accorded all honor and respect in their service of God's will. They should not dare to stain themselves or others with incestuous unions. They should not presume to solemnize marriages until the bishops and priests, together with the elders of the people, have carefully inquired to see if there be any blood relationship between the parties, and should only then give their blessing to the marriage. They should avoid drunkenness, shun greediness, and not commit theft; disputes and quarrels and blasphemies, whether in normal company or in a legal sense, should be entirely avoided; rather, they should live in love and unity.

36 That all men should contribute to the full administration of justice by giving their agreement to our *missi*. They should not in any way give their approval to the practice of perjury, which is a most evil crime and must be removed from among our Christian people. And if anyone after this is convicted of perjury he should know that he will lose his right hand; but he is also to be deprived of his inheritance subject to our judgment.

37 That those who commit patricide or fratricide, or who kill an uncle or a father-in-law or any of their kinsmen, and who refuse to obey and consent to the judgment of our bishops, priests, and other justices, are for the salvation of their souls and for the carrying out of the lawful judgment to be confined by our *missi* and counts in such custody that they will be safe, and will not pollute the rest of the people, until such time as they are brought to our presence. And in the meantime they are not to have any of their property.

38 The same is to be done with those who are arraigned and punished for unlawful and incestuous unions, and who refuse to mend their ways or submit to their bishops and priests, and who presume to disregard our edict.

39 That no one should dare to steal our beasts in our forests; this we have forbidden already on many occasions, and we now firmly ban it again, that no one should do it any more and should take care to keep the faith which everyone has promised to us and desires to keep. And if any count or *centenarius* or vassal of ours or any of our officials should steal our game he must at all costs be brought to our presence to account for it. As for the rest of the people, anyone who steals the game in this way should in every case pay the appropriate penalty, and under no circumstances should anyone be let off in this matter. And if anyone knows that it has been done by someone else, in accordance with the faith he has promised to us to keep and has now to promise again he should not dare to conceal this.

40 Finally, therefore, from all our decrees we desire it to be known in all our kingdom through our *missi* now sent out: among the clergy, the bishops, abbots, priests, deacons, clerks, and all monks and nuns, that each one in his ministry or profession should keep our edict or decree, and when it is right should of his good will offer thanks to the people, give them help, or if need be correct them in some way. Similarly for the laity, in all places everywhere, if a plea is entered concerning the protection of the holy churches, or of widows or orphans or less powerful people, or concerning the host, and is argued on these cases, we wish them to know that they should be obedient to our order and our will, that they maintain observance of our edict, and that in all these matters each man strive to keep himself in God's holy service. This in order that everything should be good and well-ordered for the praise of Almighty God, and that we should give thanks where it is due; that where we believe anything to have gone unpunished we should so strive with all earnestness and willingness to correct it that with God's help we may bring it to correction, to the eternal reward both of ourselves and of all our faithful people. Similarly concerning the counts and *centenarii*, our officers [*ministerialibus*], we wish all the things above mentioned in our deliberations to be known. So be it.

Special capitularies for the *missi*, 802

Capitulary for the missi *for Paris and Rouen*

In Paris, Meaux, Melun, Provins, Estampes, Chartres, and Poissy: Fardulfus and Stephanus. In Le Mans, Exmes, Lisieux, Bayeux, Coutances, Avranches, Evreux and Merey, and for that part of the Seine and Rouen: Bishop Magenardus and Madelgaudus.

Capitulary for the missi *for Orleans*

First, for the city of Orleans on the Seine, by the direct route, then to Troyes, with the whole of its region, then to Langres, from Langres to the town of Besançon in Burgundy, from there to Autun, and afterward to the Loire as far as Orleans: those sent are Archbishop Magnus and Count Godefredus.

1 Concerning the oath of fealty, that all should reaffirm it.

2 Concerning bishops and the clergy, whether they are living according to the canons, and whether they are well acquainted with them and are carrying them out.

3 Concerning abbots, whether they are living according to a rule or according to the canons, and whether they are well acquainted with that rule or those canons.

4 Concerning the monasteries where there are monks, whether they live according to the rule in cases where it is part of their vows.

5 Concerning convents, whether the nuns live according to a rule or to the canons, and concerning their cloisters.

6 Concerning secular laws.

7 Concerning perjury.

8 Concerning murder.

9 Concerning adultery and other unlawful acts, whether committed in bishoprics and monasteries and convents or among laymen.

10 Concerning those men who have plundered our benefices and made up their private holdings. Likewise concerning the property of the churches.

11 Concerning those Saxons who have our benefices in Frankia, in what way they cultivate them, and with what degree of care.

12 Concerning the oppressions of poor free men, who owe military service and are oppressed by the justices.

13 That all men be well prepared for whatever order may come from us.

13a Concerning the preparation of ships around the coast.

13b Concerning the free men who live around the coastal regions; if a message should come to them instructing them to come and give assistance, and they refuse to obey it, each of them must pay 20 shillings, a half to his lord and a half to the people. If one of them is a *lidus* he must pay 15 shillings to the people and give his back to be flogged. If he is a serf he must pay 10 shillings to the people and receive the flogging.

14 Concerning the commissions coming to us and the *missi* sent out by us.

15 Concerning those whom we wish to have peace and protection throughout the kingdoms which by the favor of Christ belong to us.

16 Concerning those men who have been killed in administering our justice.

17 Concerning tithes and ninths and the dues to God's churches, that they should be at pains to pay them and to make good what is wanting.

18 Concerning the ban of our lord the emperor and king, and those things for which it has been our wont to exact a fine, that is, violence offered to churches, to widows or orphans or those unable to defend themselves, and rape, and failure to observe a decree concerning the host, that those who offend against the king in these respects should make full reparation.

18a That they make careful enquiries among the bishops, abbots, counts, abbesses, and all our vassals, to see what degree of mutual harmony and friendship they have in their various districts, or whether there appears to be any discord among them; and that they be careful to report to us the whole truth of these matters, confirmed by their oath. That all of them should have good administrators [*vicedomos*] and advocates.

19 In addition, they ar[...] matter that may be r[...] diction or in that of[...] ows, orphans, min[...] whatever they find[...] take pains to corr[...] what they cannot[...] our presence.

The oath wh[...] forth, being of sound min[...] from my part to his, I am a faithful subject[...] and most pious emperor, Charles, son of King Pippin[...] and Queen Berthana, for the honor of his kingdom, as a man ought lawfully to be toward his lord; so help me God, and these relics of the saints here situated, for all the days of my life with all my will and with what intelligence God has given me, I will so attend and consent.

Again: the oath whereby I affirm. I am a faithful servant of our lord and most pious emperor, Charles, son of King Pippin and Queen Berthana, as a man lawfully ought to be toward his lord, for his kingdom and for his right. And this oath which I have sworn I shall willingly keep to the best of my knowledge and ability, from this day forth, so help me God, who created heaven and earth, and these relics of saints.

20. DHUODA'S HANDBOOK FOR HER SON (*LIBER MANUALIS*)

In 841, not long after the disastrous battle of Fontenoy in which the sons of Louis the Pious (d. 840) fought each other to a bloody stalemate, Dhuoda wrote a treatise of advice for her 15-year-old son William, who was serving King Charles the Bald. This unique text by a Frankish noblewoman shows her education, piety, and deep concern for her family in the tumultuous period of the dissolution of the Carolingian world. Her husband, Bernard of Septimania, had been the closest supporter of Louis the Pious and was firmly in Charles's camp, but Dhuoda feared for her son amid the dangers of the court. Most of the treatise is devoted to William's religious devotion, but Book Three, presented here, focuses on William's reverence to his father, his fealty to his king, and his comportment with other nobles at court. Dhuoda's fears for her son were well-founded—seven years later he revolted against Charles and was eventually killed.

Source: Carol Neel (ed. and trans.), *Handbook for William: A Carolingian Woman's Counsel for Her Son by Dhuoda* (Lincoln: University of Nebraska Press, 1991), 21–42.
Further Reading: See the translator's introduction, pp. ix–xxviii, as well as Marcelle Thiebaux (ed. and trans.), *Dhuoda Handbook for Her Warrior Son:* Liber Manualis,

ambridge Medieval Classics 8 (Cambridge: Cambridge University Press, 1998), 1–39; and Marie Anne Mayeski, *Dhuoda: Ninth Century Mother and Theologian* (Scranton, PA: University of Scranton Press, 1996).

1. On the reverence you should show your father throughout your life.

Now I must do my best to guide you in how you should fear, love, and be faithful to your lord and father, Bernard, in all things, both when you are with him and when you are apart from him. In this Solomon is your teacher and your wisest authority. He chastises you, my son, and says to you in warning, *For God hath made the father* who flourishes in his children *honorable.*[10] And likewise: *He that honoreth his father shall have joy in his own children*[11] and *shall enjoy a long life. He that obeyeth the father shall be a comfort to his mother.*[12] *As one that layeth up* good things,[13] so is he who honors his father. *He that feareth the Lord, honoreth his parents.*[14] So honor thy father, my son, and pray for him devoutly, *that thou mayest be longlived upon the land,*[15] with a full term of earthly existence. *Remember that thou hadst not been born* but through him.[16] In every matter be obedient to your father's interest and heed his judgment.[17] If by God's help you come to this, *support the old age of thy father and grieve him not in his life.*[18] *Despise him not when thou art in thy strength.*[19]

May you never do this last, and may the earth cover my body before such a thing might happen. But I do not believe that it will. I mention it not because I fear it but rather so that you may avoid it so completely that such a crime never comes to your mind, as I have heard that it indeed has done among many who are not like you. Do not forget the dangers that befell Elias's sons, who disobediently scorned the commands of their father and for this met with a bitter death.[20] Nor should I fail to mention

the tree of Absalom, who rebelled against his father and whom a base death brought to a sudden fall. Hung from an oak and pierced by lances, he ended his earthly life in the flower of his youth, with a groan of anguish. Lacking as he did an earthly kingdom, he never reached that highest of kingdoms promised to him.[21]

What of the many more who behave as he did? Their path is perilous. May those who perpetrate such evil suffer accordingly. It is not I who condemn them, but Scripture that promises their condemnation, threatening them terribly and saying, *Cursed is he that honoreth not his father.*[22] And again, *He who curseth his father, dying let him die*[23] basely and uselessly. If such is the punishment for harsh, evil words alone, what do you think will happen to those who inflict real injury upon their parents and insult the dignity of their fathers? We hear of many in our times who, thinking their present circumstances unjust, consider such crimes without taking into account the past. On them and on those like them fall hatred, jealousy, disaster, and calamity, and *nourishment to their envy.*[24] They lose rather than keep those goods of others that they seek, and they are scarcely able even to keep their own property. I say these things not because I have seen them happen, but because I have read about such matters in books. I have heard of them in the past, you hear about them yourself, and I am hearing them even now. Consider what will happen in the future to those who treat others in this fashion. But God has the power to bring even these people—if there are such—to lament their evil ways and, in their conversion, to do penance and be worthy of salvation. May anyone who behaves so stay away from you, and may God give him understanding.

Everyone, whoever he may be, should consider this, my son: if the time comes that God finds him worthy to give him children of his own, he will not wish them to be rebellious or proud or full of greed, but humble and quiet and full of obedience, so that he rejoices to see them. He who was a son before, small and obedient to his father, may then be fortunate in his own fatherhood. May he who thinks on these things in the hope that they will

---

[10] Ecclesiasticus 3:3.

[11] Ecclesiasticus 2:6.

[12] Ecclesiasticus 3:7.

[13] Ecclesiasticus 3:5.

[14] Ecclesiasticus 3:8.

[15] Ecclesiasticus 20:12.

[16] Ecclesiasticus 7:30.

[17] Compare Ecclesiasticus 3:2.

[18] Ecclesiasticus 3:14.

[19] Ecclesiasticus 3:15.

[20] 1 Kings 4:11.

[21] Compare 2 Kings 18:15.

[22] Deuteronomy 27:16.

[23] Leviticus 20:9.

[24] Genesis 37:8.

happen consider too what I have said above. Then "all his limbs" will work "in concert, peacefully."[25]

Hear me as I direct you, my son William, and "listen carefully," follow the "instructions . . . of a father." Heed the words of the holy Fathers, and *bind them in thy heart*[26] by frequent reading so that years *of life may be multiplied to thee*[27] as you grow continually in goodness. For *they that wait upon*[28] God, blessing him, obeying the Fathers and complying freely with their precepts—such men *shall inherit the land.*[29] If you listen to what I say above and if you put it into worthy practice, not only will you have success here on this earth, but also you will be found worthy to possess with the saints what the Psalmist describes: *I believe to see the good things of the Lord in the land of the living.*[30] So that this other land may be your inheritance, my son, I pray that he who lives eternally may deign to prepare you to dwell there.

2. On the same topic, on reverence for your father.

In the human understanding of things, royal and imperial appearance and power seem pre-eminent in the world, and the custom of men is to account those men's actions and their names ahead of all others, as though these things were worthy of veneration and as though worldly power were the highest honor. This attitude is testified in the words of him who said, *whether it be to the king as excelling, or to the governors.*[31] But despite all this, my wish is as follows, my son. In the smallness of my understanding—but also according to God's will—I caution you to render first to him whose son you are special, faithful, steadfast loyalty as long as you shall live. For it is a fixed and unchangeable truth that no one, unless his rank comes to him from his father, can have access to another person at the height of power.

So I urge you again, most beloved son William, that first of all you love God as I have written above. Then love, fear, and cherish your father. Keep in mind that your worldly estate proceeds from his. Recognize that

from the most ancient times, men who have loved their fathers and have been truthfully obedient to them have been found worthy to receive God's benediction from those fathers' hands.

3. On the examples of the early Fathers.

We read that Sem, the son of Noah, reached heaven because he loved his father, and so did his brother Japheth. Their father said over their heads as he blessed them: may God bless Sem and Japheth, and may he dwell in their tents;[32] may they prosper, may they flourish, and may they be enriched in all good things. What shall I say about Cham and others like him?[33]

Is it not necessary for you to know? For it is very useful to discern the meaning of these examples. Let us think upon them always, turning toward those who have been good.

In obeying his father, Isaac was found worthy to share with his wife and descendants many goods in this world, for he received that father's benediction. Isaac is also called *laughter*[34] in holy Scripture, or "rejoicing," and "rejoicing" is a fitting name for one such as he, just as "mourning" is rightly applied to an idle, confused, and profligate man. So too Jacob, because he loved and obeyed his father, was found worthy to be snatched away from many tribulations and pressing difficulties. He received double and triple benediction from God and from his earthly father, and also from his mother and an angel. It was said to him, *I will bless thee, and I will multiply* your name as *the stars of heaven.*[35] *You will be blessed and you will be called Israel,*[36] *for if thou hast been strong against God, how much more shalt thou prevail against* men?[37]

Consider, my son, how strong those are in the secular world who are worthy of God's blessing because of their parents' merits and because of their own filial obedience. If such was the case for Jacob, then you too should fight, seek, struggle, and strive manfully in all situations that you too may be worthy to receive at least that blessing from him who is called God and to receive your

---

25 Benedict, Rule 34.

26 Proverbs 16:20.

27 Proverbs 4:10.

28 Psalm 36:9.

29 Psalm 36:9.

30 Psalm 26:13.

31 1 Peter 2:13–14.

---

32 Compare Genesis 9:26–27.

33 Compare Genesis 9:22.

34 Genesis 21:16.

35 Genesis 22:17.

36 Genesis 35:10.

37 Genesis 32:28.

inheritance along with Jacob. For it is according to Jacob's model that faults are washed away and vices overcome; all his enemies submitted to the weight of his gentleness as if they wore yokes in his service.[38] The creator of the world gave Jacob a wife, children, and much material wealth. We read of him that he was always satisfied and rich in this world and that he pleased God in every way.

And what shall I say of Joseph, Jacob's son, who was so loving and obedient to his father that he would have been willing to die for him if God and that father's merits had not protected him? Joseph was betrayed and accused because of his obedience to his father; he was sent to his brothers, and they sold him. But he feared and avoided fornication with women, maintaining chastity of the mind for God's sake and of the body for his earthly lord's sake. Thus he was worthy to be loved more than all the other servants of his lord. He was imprisoned, he was beaten, and he suffered greatly—all these things for his father's sake, and throughout he gave thanks to God. Finally he was set free of this swarm of troubles and hardships. He became the greatest of counselors and interpreters of dreams; he was raised to great authority and crowned with the highest power. In the royal hall, when he shone forth as the second in command on account of his merits, he was higher in rank than all the rest.

He was called *Joseph . . . a growing son, a growing son*[39] and the Egyptians changed his name to ruler of the world and savior[40] because of the goodness of his great love. Beautiful in demeanor, beautiful in spirit, beautiful in appearance, he was still more beautiful in understanding, chaste in body and humble in heart. And what else shall I say? Eminent and rich in this world, he was pleasing in everything to God and man alike. Ruling his father and his brothers, governing all of Egypt, he ended his earthly life in peace. Walking *from virtue to virtue*,[41] he was found worthy in his humility, chastity, and obedience to be joined to God, shining forth in heaven and ruling with the saints in glory. And all this because of his devotion to his father.

Many others who have been obedient to God and mindful of the commands of a devoted father have been honored and respected in the secular world and have safely reached that heavenly reward for which they struggled. May what happened to them happen also for you if the good Lord grants you children. But what else shall I write for you about that humble respect I have described above? I beseech and I caution you that you act worthily toward deserving individuals. Always do good works. And always grow and increase in him who is called God, the maker of heaven and earth, about whom it is written: and he was subject to his parents.[42] May the redeemer of the human race cause you to grow, to progress, and to be enlarged in age and wisdom before God and men.[43] May Jesus Christ, our Lord in whom all good things are possible and who reigns eternally, deign to grant these things to you. Amen.

4. Direction on your comportment toward your lord.

You have Charles[44] as your lord; you have him as lord because, as I believe, God and your father, Bernard, have chosen him for you to serve at the beginning of your career, in the flower of your youth. Remember that he comes from a great and noble lineage on both sides of his family. Serve him not only so that you please him in obvious ways, but also as one clearheaded in matters of both body and soul. Be steadfastly and completely loyal to him in all things.

Think on that excellent servant of the patriarch Abraham. He traveled a great distance to bring back a wife for his master's son.[45] Because of the confidence of him who gave the command and the wise trustworthiness of him who followed it, the task was fulfilled. The wife found great blessing and great riches in her many descendants. What shall I say of the attitude of Joab, of Abner, and of many others toward the king David?[46] Facing dangers on their king's behalf in many places, they desired with all their might to please their lord more than themselves. And what of those many others in holy Scripture who faithfully obeyed their lords' commands? Because of their watchful strength they were found worthy to flourish in this world. For we know that, as Scripture tells, all honor and authority are given by God. Therefore we should serve our lords faithfully, without ill will, without reluctance, and without sluggishness. As we read, *there is no*

[38] Compare Jeremiah 27:12.
[39] Genesis 49:22.
[40] Compare Genesis 49:22.
[41] Psalm 83:8.
[42] Compare Luke 2:51.
[43] Compare Luke 2:52.
[44] Charles the Bald (823–877).
[45] Genesis 24.
[46] Compare 3 Kings 2.

power but from God: and he . . . that resisteth the power, resisteth the ordinance of God.[47]

That is why, my son, I urge you to keep this loyalty as long as you live, in your body and in your mind. For the advancement that it brings you will be of great value both to you and to those who in turn serve you. May the madness of treachery never, not once, make you offer an angry insult. May it never give rise in your heart to the idea of being disloyal to your lord. There is harsh and shameful talk about men who act in this fashion. I do not think that such will befall you or those who fight along-side you because such an attitude has never shown itself among your ancestors. It has not been seen among them, it is not seen now, and it will not be seen in the future.

Be truthful to your lord, my son William, child of their lineage. Be vigilant, energetic, and offer him ready assistance as I have said here. In every matter of importance to royal power take care to show yourself a man of good judgment—in your own thoughts and in public—to the extent that God gives you strength. Read the sayings and the lives of the holy Fathers who have gone before us. You will there discover how you may serve your lord and be faithful to him in all things. When you understand this, devote yourself to the faithful execution of your lord's commands. Look around as well and observe those who fight for him loyally and constantly. Learn from them how *you may* serve him. Then, informed by their example, with the help and support of God, you will easily reach the celestial goal I have mentioned above. And may your heavenly Lord God be generous and benevolent toward you. May he keep you safe, be your kind leader and your protector. May he deign to assist you in all your actions and be your constant defender. *As it shall be the will* of God *in heaven so be it done.*[48] Amen.

5. On taking counsel.

If God should someday bring you to such a point that you are found worthy to be called to the council of the magnates, consider carefully on what, when, to whom, and how you should offer worthy and appropriate comment. Act with the advice of those who encourage you to behave loyally in body and in soul. It is written: do everything with counsel, *and thou shalt not repent when thou hast done.*[49] Here "everything" refers not to

evil deeds offensive to good judgment, but to lofty and generous actions such as enhance the health of soul and body and are beyond reproach; such deeds are useful and steady, of long-enduring effect. As someone said, *what I have said is determined.*[50]

Those who do metalwork, when they begin to pound out gold to make it into leaf, wait for the best and most suitable day, weather, and temperature. Then the gold that they work for decoration, brilliant and sparkling even among the finest metals, may shine still more brightly. In the same way, the thought of those in council should in all matters follow the well-reasoned pattern known to the wise. For the speech of one who has good understanding is whiter than snow, sweeter than honey, purer than gold or silver. Why? Because, as Scripture says, from the mouth of a wise man comes honey.[51] The eloquence of a great man is therefore a favor greater than silver and gold[52] because his lips draw from the honeycomb[53] and his words are *pure words . . . tried by the fire, purged.*[54]

There are no riches where stupidity reigns, and nothing is wanting, nothing an obstacle, in matters where gentle speech prevails.[55] Whoever tries to be numbered among the wise can be welcome to both God and man and pleasing in every way to his earthly lord. For he will be known as true as gold, seen as whiter than snow. It is written: the mouths of the wise will be bleached whiter than snow,[56] and their lips will be the lips of exaltation.[57] Such are the lips of those who, with thoughtful counsel, offer speech useful to both God and men and enduring in Christ after its good effect is accomplished.

As for you, my son, believe in God, fear him, and love him. Do not hesitate to cling to him in the flower of your youth. Seek his wisdom and he will grant it to you. For the Apostle James says, *But if any of you want wisdom, let him ask of God, who giveth to all men abundantly, and upbraideth not,* but let him ask *nothing wavering,* and *it shall be given him,*[58] for God wishes to be petitioned. For the Lord says, encouraging us, *Ask, and it shall be given you: seek, and you shall find: knock, and it shall be opened*

[47] Romans 13:1–2.
[48] 1 Maccabees 3:60.
[49] Ecclesiasticus 32:34.
[50] 2 Kings 19:29.
[51] Compare Psalm 118:103.
[52] Compare Proverbs 22:1.
[53] Compare Canticles 4:11.
[54] Psalm 117.
[55] Compare Ecclesiasticus 6:5.
[56] Compare Psalm 50:9.
[57] Compare Psalm 62:6.
[58] James 1:5–6.

to you.[59] I believe confidently in that Lord's generous mercy, freely given. For he who beseeches the Lord with the worthy, pure love of the heart may ask to be given wisdom, counsel, and those other things necessary for the body. Such a man may then believe that God will open to him and that the Lord will give to him.[60]

Therefore, my son, pray and seek of the Lord, just as a certain man used to pray to him in song. Say with that poet: to you be praise, honor, and power. You who are rich in all things, *give me wisdom*. And again, *Give me wisdom, that sitteth by thy throne, and cast me not off from among thy children.*[61] Send *wisdom out from the throne of thy majesty, that she may be with me, and may labor with me,*[62] so that I may *discern between good and evil* and be able to judge which is better.[63] Love this wisdom, even from your youth, and seek it often as you invoke God. And if the good Lord should give it to you, cherish it, and it will embrace you in return. If you have wisdom, you will be the more blessed.

I urge you to make every effort to associate not only with older men who love God and seek wisdom but also with youths who do so, for maturity is rooted in the flower of youth. As someone says, *The things that thou hast not gathered in thy youth, how shalt thou find them in old age?*[64] *So* seek this in the Lord and say: God, teach me therefore from my youth, and unto old age and gray hairs[65] my good father will not desert me.[66] You will be blessed, my son, if you are made learned by him and if you are worthy to be instructed in his law. Indeed, Samuel and David were judges even as boys in the flower of youth according to the custom of the Fathers, and they were again as old men.[67] They were great counselors to kings in the secular world, and they faithfully gave advice to the leaders of the Gentiles and foreign people. They deserved the victor's palm because of their worthy merits.

Think on the Fathers who went before us; think about Joseph before Pharaoh,[68] Daniel before Nabuchodonosor,

Baltassar, and Darius and the leaders of the Medes and the Persians.[69] Without abandoning their own ways, these Fathers were always helpful in council. Do not forget Jethro, Moses' kinsman, and how he gave important counsel,[70] or how Achior advised Holofernes, prince of the Gentiles,[71] or how many more of the ancients faithfully gave excellent counsel to their friends and those around them. In freeing themselves, they were found worthy both of spiritual salvation and of the bounty of those they counseled. Indeed, these Fathers shine forth in the sacred Scriptures, praised much more than others. Why? *Because God hath tried them, and found them worthy,*[72] humble and pure in mind and body, informed in their understanding, so that the Lord is known to have joined them, pure as gold, to himself. There is no doubt that they, like the sacrifice of the holocaust,[73] are brought together with him in his kingdom in spirit and in body along with all the saints.

What shall I, the unworthy, unlucky, and insignificant Dhuoda, say then of you, *my son?* I pray that he who strengthened those men and others like them, he who is called God, may also increase the strength of your manhood now and always. *Nevertheless as it shall be the will of God in heaven so be it done*[74] always in respect to you.

6. More on the same topic. On counselors.

There are some who consider themselves counselors and are not, for they think themselves wise even when this is untrue. I *speak as one less wise: I am more.*[75] But this is not the fault of him in whom all good flourishes. For there are those who give good counsel and do not do it in a good way but in a way neither useful to themselves nor uplifting to another. Why? Because the counsel of such men does not lead to the highest, perfect good of heaven. And there are many who give bad counsel, but without effect. This happens in many, various ways. There were in former times many worthy, good, and truthful men, but today most people are unlike those ancients in many

---

[59] Matthew 7:7.

[60] Compare Mark 11:24.

[61] Wisdom 9:4.

[62] Wisdom 9:10.

[63] Compare Psalm 70:17–189.

[64] Ecclesiasticus 25:5.

[65] Compare 3 Kings 3:9.

[66] Compare 3 Kings 3:9.

[67] Compare Benedict, Rule 63.

[68] Genesis 41:13ff.

[69] Daniel 2:27ff, 5:17, 6:3.

[70] Exodus 18:14–23.

[71] Judith 5:5ff.

[72] Wisdom 3:5.

[73] Wisdom 3:6.

[74] 1 Maccabees 3:60.

[75] 2 Corinthians 11:23.

ways. What does this mean for us? Many things are clear in this secular world. For Scripture says, *and because iniquity hath abounded, the charity of many shall grow cold.*[76] As things are now, one does not know whom to choose as a counselor or whom one ought first to believe, and for many the hope of finding help from anyone remains uncertain. Read the *Synonyms.*[77]

But you must not despair in this, my son. There are many descended from these ancients who still, with God's help, are willing and able to give counsel that is good, welcome, and appropriate in respect to both themselves and their lords. And all these things happen through him who is called the Most High. For Scripture says, Is *there no physician* in Egypt *or balm in Galaad,*[78] clear water in Canaan or counselor in Israel? There is indeed, and clear understanding reveals itself in *many* men. God, who gives light to the world and is the angel of good counsel, knows his own. He shows them the words that bring the soul's salvation. May he who was then among the ancients and is now among the living, who is in you, goes out from you, and returns to you, who directs you to fight alongside a worthy, high king to carry out that earthly lord's command—may that God cause you to arrive at that high, right counsel. Amen.

7. Special direction on the same topic.

For you to be such a man depends entirely on the judgment and the power of omnipotent God. If, with the aid of the highest creator, you come to the time that I have mentioned above,[79] fear immoral men and seek out worthy ones. Flee evil men and find good ones.[80] Do not take counsel with a man of ill will or a weak-spirited man or a wrathful man. For he will corrupt you like tin,[81] and under his command you will never rest secure. For the wrath and the envy that come easily to him draw him at once, headlong, to the depths.

Let not your fate be like Achitofel's[82] or like Aman's,[83] bad and arrogant men whose counsels were worthless

and who, when they gave bad advice to their lord, fell headlong in both spirit and body to their deaths. For I wish, my son, that you take pleasure in fighting on your lord's behalf, as did such men as Doeg the Edomite[84] and the humble Mardochai.[85] Achitophel offered Absalom the bad counsel that he should rebel against his father, David—and Achitophel did so in order to win the son's favor. But by the will of God,[86] Achitophel's evil counsels were brought to nothing.[87] But Chusai[88] and Doeg, a strong man who firmly held his ground against another determined man, remained unshakable in their counsel. On the other hand Aman, on account of the pride in his envious spirit, gave evil counsel to Assuerus so that sons of Israel were killed.[89] But Mardochai, praying for God's help to liberate himself and his people, gave the same king good counsel, the evidence of loyalty, in order to free and to vindicate himself.[90] Mardochai began, "Consider, O king."

By God's providence, one man merits salvation with his people. Another, a proud man, goes away empty along with all his house. He is hung on the gallows that in his envy he has prepared for the humble man, so that this evil is turned upon its designer. All by himself he has brought his life, even his body, to a worse end. There is fulfilled in him and in those like him what is said: *He hath conceived sorrow, and brought forth iniquity. He hath opened a pit . . . and fallen into it.*[91] For he who had prepared evil for his innocent brother has now rushed headlong and straightaway into death. God, who is good and who in his goodness spares the wicked, rightly desires to bring all men to himself through penance. *For he knoweth both the deceiver, and him that is deceived by the deceiver.*[92]

Therefore, my son William, fear immoral men and seek out worthy ones. Flee evil men like those mentioned here, but attach yourself to good men seeking after worthy goals. They offer counsel in the most useful of ways, in their true subjection to the wishes of their lords, and they are found worthy to receive fitting reward both from God and in the secular world. I pray that such counsel as

---

[76] Matthew 24:12.

[77] Isidore of Seville, *Synonyma* 2.44.

[78] Jeremiah 8:22.

[79] That is, if William should become one of the king's counselors.

[80] Compare Isidore, *Synonyma* 2.43.

[81] Compare Isidore, *Synonyma* 2.43.

[82] 2 Kings 16:15ff.

[83] Esther 6:4ff.

[84] 1 Kings 21:7, 22:9.

[85] Esther 8:2ff.

[86] Compare 2 Kings 17:14.

[87] Compare 2 Kings 17:14.

[88] 2 Kings 15:32ff.

[89] Esther 6:6ff.

[90] Compare Esther 2:22.

[91] Psalm 7:15–16.

[92] Psalm 7:15–16.

has been in those great men may grow in you now, every day, always, my best of sons.

8. Regarding your lord's family.

As for the great and famous relations and associates of your royal lord—those who are descended from his illustrious father's side as well as those related to him by marriage—fear, love, honor, and cherish them if you and those who fight alongside you are found worthy to serve them in the royal and imperial court or anywhere else you may act on their behalf. In all undertakings in their interest maintain a pure, fitting, and steadfast obedience to them, as well as good faith in the execution of your duties.

Remember how David comported himself toward Jonathan, the son of the king Saul. In every way, throughout his life, he was a pure, faithful, and true supporter of both the father and the son, and also their children, not only during their lives but also after their deaths. Even after their destruction the sweetness of his great love caused him to mourn them with sorrowful tears, greatly lamenting and saying, *How are the valiant fallen in battle*[93] and *the weapons of war perished.*[94] And also, *I grieve for thee, my brother Jonathan: exceedingly beautiful, and amiable to me above the love of women,*[95] *swifter than eagles, stronger than lions.*[96] And again, my best of children, *the arrow of Jonathan never turned back.*[97] In these and other instances David was filled with grief for the king's son, and with his retainers he mourned deeply over Jonathan's ruin. May you and those who fight alongside you avoid such a fate.

I am having this copied out as an example for you. For when David recovered, as if consoled by the great loyalty of his love for them, he praised his dead friends in another voice, with sighing, *Saul and Jonathan, lovely, and comely in their life, even in death they were not divided.*[98] Many who faithfully obeyed the commandments of their lords and their lords' relations are abundantly and honorably praised in sacred Scriptures. Read the book of Kings and the books of the other Fathers, and you will find many.

---

[93] 2 Kings 1:25.
[94] 2 Kings 1:27.
[95] 2 Kings 1:26.
[96] 2 Kings 1:23.
[97] 2 Kings 1:22.
[98] 2 Kings 1:23.

So, my son William, bear patiently the yoke that governs a servant and be faithful to your lord Charles—whatever sort of lord he may be—and to his worthy relations of both sexes and to all those of royal origins. It is fitting for you and for all those who fight under their royal power to do so, and I wish that you serve them to good ends, faithfully, with all your might. For as we believe, God chose them and established them in royal power, granting them glory almost as great in its likeness to the ancients' as that promised to Abraham, Isaac, and Jacob,[99] and to their worthy children and descendants.

May the omnipotent Father—our strong King, the glorious Highest—make them peaceful and harmonious, seeking concord after the manner of their fathers in this earthly realm. Then they may shine in prosperity and rule, protect, and govern the world and its people with strength in the service of God and his saints. And they may hold and defend our people from the blows of enemies pressing all around, uniting the holy church of God the more firmly in Christ and his true religion. May they see the children of their sons pleasing God in worthy fashion, growing and flourishing, and aiming for heaven through many cycles of the years, persevering in this course until they come happily to the end of their lives. As for you, after you have reached the end of this present life, may he who gives all recompense and all bounty bring you to rest in the kingdom of heaven with those Fathers whom I have mentioned. May he bring you to his kingdom and his glory—you who struggle here to render faithful service both to your several earthly lords and to that singular Lord who gives fitting reward for your merits from his own riches. And may he unite you happily to Christ.

9. Regarding the magnates.

As for the magnates and their counselors—and all those like them who serve faithfully—show them your love, affection, and service often. Do so to them together and individually, to whomever is important at court. Learn attentively from the model of their distinction and adhere to it firmly. For in a house as great as the king's there are, there have been, and there will be, if the good Lord so commands, many conversations. There, one who wishes can learn from others humility, charity, chastity, patience, gentleness, modesty, sobriety,

---

[99] Compare Genesis 15:4ff.

discretion, and other virtues, as well as the desire to do good.

So, my son, while you are a young boy still growing,[100] learn from those elders whose understanding is rich whatever good you can with the Father's help so you may be pleasing to God before all else and then be useful to man. I urge you to strive to act among your associates, peers, and faithful friends so that your life may hold to a good course, marked with no shame of disloyalty to your lords but with eagerness for good action, in a laudable fashion, worthy and proper. May that God who makes the tongues of infants speak in his praise—as it is written, *out of the mouths of infants*[101]—himself cause you, filled with the eloquence of worthy, noble men who fear the Lord, to climb to the ranks of heaven.

10. That you accommodate yourself to great and to lesser men.

I need not point out to you that great men as well as lesser should follow the examples of their lords and of the highest magnates. Far from me as you are, you realize that constantly yourself. Still, never doubt that even lesser folk improve themselves after the model of their betters. I urge you not to hesitate to attach yourself to them—and them to you—by large and small favors.

God is the maker of all good things in heaven and earth, but he deigned to show his presence even here below for the sake of the least of his creatures. For as the learned say, even though he is the Most High and the creator of all things, he deigned to take on the form of a servant.[102] He raises up the powerful so that they may be cast down to the depths, and he exalts the humble "in order then to raise them up to a higher state. It is he, as the prophet says, who is the littlest one multiplying to a thousand, the weak one who becomes the strongest nation." He is great among the least of men, the feeble; he is powerful and manly. We believe in one God, creator, shepherd, and governor of our bodies and our souls, namely that one about whom I have written above. We receive all things from him, whatever seems to be within our power. Every higher creature with the faculty of reason should undoubtedly, whether he is greater or lesser than another, serve and praise his maker; such is fitting.

And according to the authority of Scripture, the earth with all that is born of her, *the old with the younger,*[103] should bless God and give him praise.

There is a short saying: *Let every spirit praise the Lord.*[104] For it is he who loves the human race, and he does not fail to enrich through his gifts both the great and the small, according to his measure and on the scale of their merits. For he is *not a respecter of persons*, but in all things, when he is besought, he is present to those who fear him[105] and who do his will.

And if he who is so great acts thus even toward the least of men, what should we who are ourselves of small importance do for those who are even lesser? Those who can give aid should do so and—according to the words and injunctions of the apostle—carry burdens for each other,[106] the strong for the weak, the capable for those who are not. Then the weak may climb along with the strong, participating in their strength, to that heavenly height promised our forefathers. For the same apostle says: Now you *that are stronger* and more powerful *ought to bear the infirmities of the weak,*[107] so that your *abundance may supply their want*[108] and their poverty.

My son, although you may be the least in stature among those who fight alongside you, you are nevertheless steadfast in your mind. Do not hesitate, I therefore urge you, to examine closely and to imitate the exemplary strength and model of those great men of whom you have read above. Consider great men as high above you, your equals as your betters, and those like you as ahead of you, so that in your attachment to them you may advance the dignity of your ancestors. Rejoice in deep humility, I beseech you, that they all have been set before you as your examples.

For instance, consider the image, metaphorically expressed, of the man about whom it is written, *his hand will be against all men, and all men's hands against him.*[109] If we understand this short description in a good sense, then I urge that you be such a man in all respects. Then your hand will be ready for worthy action, and you will do your best now and always to give service and honor—not only in words but in deeds, and with gentle

---

[100] Compare Genesis 49:22.

[101] Psalm 8:3.

[102] Compare Philippians 2:7.

---

[103] Psalm 148:12.

[104] Psalm 150:5.

[105] Acts 10:34–35.

[106] Compare Galatians 6:2.

[107] Romans 15:1.

[108] 2 Corinthians 8:14.

[109] Genesis 16:12.

speech—to great men, to lesser men, to those who are your equals, and likewise to the least of men. For it is written about our obligation to give, *God loveth a cheerful giver.*[110] And it is said about words that a good speech is better than the *best gift.*[111] So you must do both things. If you strive to apply yourself with good will toward all, there will be accomplished in you what is written above. And may your hand, giving free service, be against all in order to give, and may all hands be against you to help you or to reward you according to the merit of your actions.

Love all so that you may be loved by all, and cherish them that you may be cherished. If you love all, all will love you. If you—who are singular—love them, then they—who are plural—will love you. It is written in Donatus' *Art of Poetry*, "I love you and I am loved by you, I kiss you and am kissed by you, I cherish you and am cherished by you, I respect and am respected by you." And again, "I, of me or by me, of me or from me, and O, by me" and more of the same, "them, of them or by them, O, by them," and many other relevant things.[112]

Therefore, my son William, cherish and show respect to whatever one or many persons you wish to respect you. Love, revere, stand by, and honor all, so that you may be found worthy to receive appropriately honorable recompense in all the changeable situations of the world. Toward our edification in this regard a certain learned author offers a brief comparison—an important one, extraordinarily clear in its meaning—with dumb animals. He says in the forty-first Psalm, *As the hart panteth.* For this is what harts do when groups of them begin to cross seas or wide streams with churning waves—they lower their necks one after the other, each putting his head and horns on the back of the previous one, so that as they each rest a little they all may the more easily cross the swift current. The harts have such intelligence and such commensurate discretion that, when they perceive that the one in front is weakening, the leader becomes a follower and eventually the last in line so that the others may assist and support him; then they choose another to go first. Thus, as one individual takes the place of another, each feels the brotherly fellowship of love run through them all. Always careful that the head and antlers

of any one of their kind not be plunged into the flood, the harts manage to hold up his head and to keep his antlers visible.

The point of this is not obscure to the learned, for everything is immediately clear in their sight. In the harts' mutual support—in their changing places in line—they show that human beings too must have the brotherly fellowship of love for greater and lesser men alike, in all ways and in all circumstances. We read that this was fulfilled in the past by many men, especially among the holy apostles and those like them. It is written, *For neither was there any one needy among them,*[113] *but all things were common unto them.*[114] They had *one heart and one soul*[115] in God, always feeling brotherly compassion for each other in Jesus Christ.

Just as the harts support and sustain each other's heads and antlers, so those who have faith in Christ hold up their hearts and keep their minds always on him. He who was born king of David's seed for the salvation of the human race and descended to the depth of this sea of battering waves has raised his horn to liberate his people.[116] Acting of his grace, he has found those who were lying in darkness, and rising from that depth he has visited them[117] and raised them to the heights. He offers his example lest we be lost in the turmoil of the deep sea or in the blinding mud of desire and cupidity, so that we may hold up our hearts in perseverance and say with the apostle, *But our conversation is in heaven.*[118]

What of the lions and boars and other sensate animals? And what of the vine clinging to the earth or the elm reaching toward the sky, that edify us in their turn? There are many useful examples available to men. Read what is said in the appropriate books, and you will find out. *Speak to the earth, and it shall answer thee*, it is written, and *ask . . . the beasts, and they shall teach thee; and the birds of the air, and they shall tell thee . . . and the fishes of the sea shall tell.*[119] The meaning of this passage is indeed useful, and it is clear to some who know it. For there is one Creator and Restorer. He has seen fit to

---

[110] 2 Corinthians 8:14.

[111] James 1:17.

[112] An obscure reference to a versified version of Donatus's grammar.

[113] Acts 4:34.

[114] Acts 4:32.

[115] Acts 4:32.

[116] Compare Luke 1:69.

[117] Compare Luke 1:78.

[118] Philippians 3:20.

[119] Job 12:7–8.

choose man before all the other beings to be in charge of them, according to a certain poet. As he says in his verses:

A virgin, he created the earth; a virgin,
    he created a virgin man,
And he was later made man of another virgin.
Alas, oh grief! The virgin man was corrupted
Oh grief, alas!—the virgin woman was corrupted,
Yielding, both of them, to the serpent.[120]

Likewise the same poet:

On that account he will leave his father
    and mother,
And will cleave to his wife.
The two will be one flesh,
Commanding all that is subject to them,
Raising their estate by the use of reason.

And again:

He who gave to man all the things
That heaven and earth and sea generate
In sky and stream and field
Whatever the eye can see or hand feel
This he set under their sway, and they under his.[121]

The meaning of this, my son William, is that the Highest, the omnipotent one, saw fit that man be fashioned out of the mud of the earth to replenish the number of his angels and to be joined to their high rank. Granting to man the use of all things, God chose him to enjoy the great glory of eternity in his Lord's company. For man God willed that he be born, suffer, rise again, ascend to heaven, so that according to the measure of their goodness he might join great and lesser men to himself and bring them to his heavenly kingdom.

What more could I or might I say to you by way of example of those who are of differing status—subjects or equals or even those of low estate—but joined together by love? With God's help, you know this already, and you will always be able to learn more concerning the standard of him who made all life. Great and greatly to be praised,[122] granting his bounty to the mighty and the

small, may he cause you and all those mentioned above, as well as those who like them adhere to Christ, to be joined to him. And then may you come to that Lord who holds the mighty in his embrace and gathers in the small, praising them in saying, *Suffer the little children to come unto me . . . for of such is the kingdom of* heaven.[123] And may this happen with the help and grace of him who reigns without end in heaven. Amen.

11. On respect for priests.

Priests are to be revered, my son, because they have been chosen for God's ministry and because, in holding sacred orders, they intercede for our sins. So fear God and honor his priests with all your soul. Love them and revere them. It is they who bless the chrism and the oil. It is they who baptize the people in the faith of Holy Trinity, uniting them with the holy Church of God. It is they who consecrate the bread and the wine in the likeness of the body and blood of our Lord Jesus Christ, preparing the table and giving us communion *unto remission of sins*[124] and for the health of the body.

They are called sacerdotes, "priests," in order to sanctify or consecrate them after the example of him who said, Be holy because I am holy.[125] And again, *Follow peace with all men, and holiness: without which . . .*[126] and so forth. They are called priests, for the Prophet says, *You shall be called the priests of the Lord* our God.[127] They will wear down the Gentiles' strength, and *they shall eat the sins of my people.*[128] They are the shepherds who do not fail to feed the flock of the Lord through words and examples and who invite the people to the kingdom of God so that they do not hesitate to enter, but say with the Psalmist: *Come let us adore and fall down: and weep before the Lord that made us. For he is the Lord our God: and we are the people* and the sheep *of his pasture.*[129]

Priests are also called *presbyteri* for the reason that they are ready and prepared for the work of God; for in this word we use *prae* for *ante*, "before," as the Psalmist says: I have seen the Lord before,[130] that is through the

---

[123] Mark 10:14.

[124] Matthew 26:28.

[125] Leviticus 11:44.

[126] Hebrews 12:14.

[127] Isaiah 61:6.

[128] Hosea 4:8.

[129] Psalm 94:6–7.

[130] Compare Psalm 15:8.

---

[120] Presumably an unknown Carolingian poet. Only the final verse quoted here is by Prudentius.

[121] Prudentius, *Cathemerinon* 3:36–40.

[122] Augustine, *Confessions* 1.1; compare Psalm 144:3.

contemplation of the mind I have seen him in advance. We mean something similar when we say "precursor," that is, one who goes before and precedes, or takes his place before. Thus it is the priests among us who—on account of their worthy merits—approach the altar, warning us to have a ready heart and that *our conversation is in heaven*.[131] They are the path through the example of whose preaching we travel confidently toward our heavenly fatherland through the practice of good works.

Bishops are called *episcopi* and "overseers" because they admonish us always to be alert in our direction and goal. For *epi* in Greek is *super*, "over," in Latin. *Scopon* in Greek, in the same fashion, is *intuitio* or *destinatio*, "sight" or "objective," in Latin. And so it is the responsibility of bishops to reveal each man to others, and our responsibility to observe and to obey those bishops. For priests are also called *pontifices* because we cross to our fatherland through them as on a *pons*, a "bridge," across a river. That is, we cross and do not tarry in the malice of the heart as in churning mud. We are corrected through penance and amends, and with God's help we touch upon no foreign shore. It is written, *they went back another way into their country*.[132]

Bishops, after the model of the true and sublime Lord, are the bearers of authority above, below, within, and outside. They have authority above for the reason that they give protection by looking out afar, as they take up a point of observation at a distance. For through their learning and by the example of their chastisement, the Lord gathers us together from far-off lands. And bishops have authority below because they are the feet that bring peace, announce good tidings, preach salvation, and speak to Sion.[133] They have authority within because we are imbued with the example of their worth and wisdom; we are made learned and satisfied by them. And they have authority outside because through their constant prayer, staying as they do close to God, we are found worthy to be surrounded, fortified, protected, and kept safe, so that evil spirits do not seize us. Only thus we are able to direct ourselves toward him who appeared in the world and who was made our salvation and our support, so that he might recall fallen man to the heavenly fatherland.

And what may I say of those who are so worthy of reverence? My spirit shrinks from this task. It is priests who, according to the example of the holy apostles, bind and loose (*compare Matthew 18:18*) and *they eat the sins of the people*.[134] They are closer and nearer to God. They are the fishermen and the hunters, as the Prophet says, *Behold I will send my fishers . . . and they shall fish them: and . . . I will send my hunters, and they shall hunt them*.[135] They seize the prize from the hands of others, that is from unclean spirits, and by penance they join those they have captured to the company of their heavenly fatherland. These priests fashion and assemble the holy altar to stand in its proper place. For Scripture says: and the priests and Levites brought in the altar of the Lord into its place, *into the holy of holies under the wings of the cherubim*.[136] For such are the properties of priests' titles. Although the names applied to them vary according to their rank and activity, still they are properly called priests or keepers of vessels, that is, of the souls that belong to God. For what better can we call the ranks of the priesthood than the company to be joined with the ranks of the angels and of the citizens of heaven? For they are called angels, as the prophet Zacharias says, *the lips of the priest . . . keep knowledge, and* the people *seek the law at his mouth: because he is the angel of the Lord*, and not just an angel but the angel *of hosts*.[137]

What can be more sublime than the angels and archangels? Because of their merits they are so agile as to reach the sacred windows in their flight[138] as do the watchful doves. Glorying in their worthy virtues, deservedly—in a fashion that is clear to understand—they are called the friends of God. Why? Because they are filled with the fervor of charity. Their living example never ceases to inform the many. As Scripture says, they are clothed in justice,[139] joined with the company of the saints. Joyful and holy and flourishing in Christ, they are found worthy, with the acquisition of a double treasure, to reach the sublime kingdom of heaven.

Since priests have so many and such great names and virtues that their dignity in the secular world is so brilliant, I urge you to render them, worthy as they are, as much honor as you can. As for those whose personal merit is not adequate to their sacred office—even if you realize this about them—do not hastily judge them but shrink from condemning their way of life, as many do.

---

[131] Philippians 3:20.

[132] Matthew 2:12.

[133] Compare Isaiah 52:7.

[134] Hosea 4:8.

[135] Jeremiah 16:16.

[136] 3 Kings 8:6.

[137] Malachi 2:7.

[138] Compare Isaiah 60:8.

[139] Compare Psalm 131:9.

Think on David. When he cut the border of Saul's cloak he was sorry.[140] And so we should not condemn priests, my son. God knows their hearts and the hearts of all who struggle in the secular world. Their fruit and their achievement are known to be worthy from their appearance, their speech, their understanding, and their life. As it is written, *by their fruits you shall know them.*[141]

What more shall I say? The Lord knows his own.[142] Still, take as your models those priests whom you find to be the better among them, more clearheaded in word and deed. Such men, even more than others, announce to us the word of God; they are the people chosen for his holy inheritance.[143] Listen to what they say, consider it, accomplish it, and think back upon it often. Wherever you encounter such priests, act humbly toward them and revere them—not only them but also the angels who go before them. For as sacred Scripture says, their angels always see the face of the Father.[144] May you dine often, if you can, with them and with hungry pilgrims. As I have said above, do not hesitate to entrust yourself into the hands of honorable priests. Find in them, among all those loyal to you, counselors when you have need. Listen to those who you see are especially close to God. Let them give food and drink to the poor from your hand and your table, and you will receive your reward in the aftermath.

So, my son William, as I have already said, revere those worthy priests who are God's servants. They are the chosen of God, and they are his helpers and his worshipers. If their behavior is not as it should be, do not—as is written—revile them. The sacred Scripture says in part of them: *touch ye not my anointed,* that is, those touched by my chrism; *do not evil to my prophets,*[145] that is, my priests. For in the house of the Lord *there are many mansions,*[146] and the stars of heaven do not gleam so brightly. For *star differeth from star in glory,*[147] and the just are brighter than the others because of the variety of their merits. In the same way there are differences among priests. Some *instruct many* through the example of their good works, drawing laymen along with them to Christ

as stars for all eternity,[148] as we believe. And this is God's gift. But revere them, my son, as I have said, and if you are remiss in something, correct it. *For there is no man who sinneth not*[149] even if his life is as short as a single day.[150] But there is only one creator, shaper, ruler, and governor. On account of God and as his gift, the Lord's words come forth from the priest, for he grants this to us not according to our sins but according to his ancient mercy. In offering us this release, the Lord is called good, gentle, and merciful; he is, he has been, he will always be. May you know that it is he in whom, always and everywhere, true and learned priests find their understanding.

Offer them your true confession as best you know how—in privacy, with sighing, and with tears. As the learned authors say, true confession liberates the soul from death,[151] and prevents it from going to hell. Do not hesitate, I urge you, to entrust your mind and body to the hands of priests. When you are busy or at rest, or whatever you do or is done to you, always ask and pray that they deign to pray for you, interceding with that God who chose them as his people's intercessors in this world. Then you may deserve to be found worthy, as you devote half your days to penance[152] through true amends and worthy reparation, to be granted what he has promised to his saints.

May that true priest who is pontifex for eternity[153] bring you to true and worthy progress as you study and struggle in earthly service and as you follow the good examples of the ministers of his holy church. Through the help and grace of that God who reigns through all time, amen.

Questions for Study

In Carolingian culture, leaders were responsible for the mistakes (and sins) of their followers. In what ways do the sources reveal how the elite navigated this expectation? How does the image of Charlemagne compare with that of the later life of Alfred?

---

[140] Compare 1 Kings 24:5–6.

[141] Matthew 7:16.

[142] Compare 2 Timothy 2:19.

[143] Compare Psalm 32:12.

[144] Compare Matthew 11:10.

[145] Psalm 104:15.

[146] John 14:2.

[147] 1 Corinthians 15:41.

[148] Compare Daniel 12:3.

[149] 3 Kings 8:46.

[150] Compare Job 14:5.

[151] Compare Isidore, *Synonyma* 1.53.

[152] Compare Psalm 54:24.

[153] Compare Hebrews 5:6.

The Tenth Century

21. LIUDPRAND OF CREMONA

A CHRONICLE OF OTTO'S REIGN

Liudprand (Liudbrand) of Cremona (ca. 920–972) was raised in the court of King Hugo of Italy before becoming chancellor of King Berengar II. After breaking with Berengar, he found favor with his rival, Otto I, who would soon become king of Italy. In the service of Otto, Liudprand became bishop of Cremona and was sent on various diplomatic missions. He was the author of a history of Italy, Germany, and Byzantium between 888 and 949 directed against Berengar, which he called *Antapodosis* (Retaliation), an account of his unsuccessful attempt to arrange a marriage for Otto II with a Byzantine princess, and the following text, a justification of Otto I's Italian policy.

Source: F.A. Wright, *The Works of Liudprand of Cremona* (London: George Routledge and Sons, 1930).
Further Reading: Robert Levine, "Liudprand of Cremona: History and Debasement in the Tenth Century," *Mittellateinisches Jahrbuch* 26 for 1991 (1992): 70–84.

Ch. I. Berengar and Adalbert were reigning, or rather raging, in Italy, where, to speak the truth, they exercised the worst of tyrannies, when John, the supreme pontiff and universal pope, whose church had suffered from the savage cruelty of the aforesaid Berengar and Adalbert, sent envoys from the holy Church of Rome, in the persons of the cardinal deacon John and the secretary Azo, to Otto, at that time the most serene and pious king and now our august emperor, humbly begging him, both by letters and a recital of facts, for the love of God and the holy apostles Peter and Paul, whom he hoped would remit his sins, to rescue him and the holy Roman Church entrusted to him from their jaws, and restore it to its former prosperity and freedom. While the Roman envoys were laying these complaints, Waldpert, the venerable archbishop of the holy church of Milan, having escaped half-dead from the mad rage of the aforesaid Berengar and Adalbert, sought the powerful protection of the above-mentioned Otto, at that time king and now our august emperor, declaring that he could no longer bear or submit to the cruelty of Berengar and Adalbert and Willa, who contrary to all human and divine law had appointed Manasses bishop of Arles to the see of Milan. He said that it was a calamity for his church thus to intercept a right that belonged to him and to his people. After Waldpert came Waldo bishop of Como, crying out that he also had suffered a like insult at the hands of Berengar, Adalbert, and Willa. With the apostolic envoys there also arrived some members of the laity, among them the illustrious marquess Otbert, asking help and advice from his most sacred majesty Otto, then king now emperor.

Ch. II. The most pious king was moved by their tearful complaints, and considered not himself but the cause of Jesus Christ. Therefore, although it was contrary to custom, he appointed his young son Otto as king, and leaving him in Saxony collected his forces and marched in haste to Italy. There he drove Berengar and Adalbert from the realm at once, the more quickly inasmuch as it is certain that the holy apostles Peter and Paul were fighting under his flag. The good king brought together what had been scattered and mended what had been broken, restoring to each man his due possessions. Then he advanced on Rome to do the same again.

Ch. III. There he was welcomed with marvelous ceremony and unexampled pomp, and was anointed as emperor by John the supreme bishop and universal pope. To the church he not only gave back her possessions but bestowed lavish gifts of jewels, gold, and silver. Furthermore Pope John and all the princes of the city swore solemnly on the most precious body of Saint Peter that they would never give help to Berengar and Adalbert. Thereupon Otto returned to Pavia with all speed.

Ch. IV. Meanwhile Pope John, forgetful of his oath and the promise he had made to the sacred emperor, sent to Adalbert asking him to return and swearing that he would assist him against the power of the most sacred emperor. For the sacred emperor had so terrified this Adalbert, persecutor of God's churches and of Pope John, that he had left Italy altogether and had gone to Fraxinetum and put himself under the protection of the Saracens. The righteous emperor for his part could not understand at all why Pope John was now showing such affection to the very man whom previously he had attacked in bitter hatred. Accordingly he called together some of his intimates and sent off to Rome to inquire if this report was true. On his messengers' arrival they got this answer, not from a few chance informants, but from all the citizens of Rome:— "Pope John hates the most sacred emperor, who freed him from Adalbert's clutches, for exactly the same reason that the devil hates his creator. The emperor, as we have learned by experience, knows, works and loves the things of God: he guards the affairs of church and state with his sword, adorns them by his virtues, and purifies them by his laws. Pope John is the enemy of all these things. What we say is a tale well known to all. As witness to its truth take the widow of Rainer his own vassal, a woman with whom John has been so blindly in love that he has made her governor of many cities and given to her the golden crosses and cups

that are the sacred possessions of St. Peter himself. Witness also the case of Stephana, his father's mistress, who recently conceived a child by him and died of an effusion of blood. If all else were silent, the palace of the Lateran, that once sheltered saints and is now a harlot's brothel, will never forget his union with his father's wench, the sister of the other concubine Stephania. Witness again the absence of all women here save Romans: they fear to come and pray at the thresholds of the holy apostles, for they have heard how John a little time ago took women pilgrims by force to his bed, wives, widows, and virgins alike. Witness the churches of the holy apostles, whose roof lets the rain in upon the sacrosanct altar, and that not in drops but in sheets. The woodwork fills us with alarm, when we go there to ask God's help. Death reigns within the building, and, though we have much to pray for, we are prevented from going there and soon shall be forced to abandon God's house altogether. Witness the women he keeps, some of them fine ladies who, as the poet says, are as thin as reeds by dieting, others everyday buxom wenches. It is all the same to him whether they walk the pavement or ride in a carriage and pair. That is the reason why there is the same disagreement between him and the holy emperor as there is of necessity between wolves and lambs. That he may go his way unchecked, he is trying to get Adalbert, as patron, guardian, and protector."

Ch. V. When the envoys on their return gave this report to the emperor, he said:—"He is only a boy, and will soon alter if good men set him an example. I hope that honorable reproof and generous persuasion will quickly cure him of these vices; and then we shall say with the prophet:—'This is a change which the hand of the Highest has brought.'"[1] He added:—"The first thing required by circumstances is that we dislodge Berengar from his position on Montefeltro. Then let us address some words of fatherly admonition to the lord pope. His sense of shame, if not his own wishes, will soon effect a change in him for the better. Perchance if he is forced into good ways, he will be ashamed to get out of them again."

Ch. VI. This done, the emperor went on board ship and sailed down the Po to Ravenna. Thence he advanced to Montefeltro, sometimes called St Leo's Mountain, and besieged the fort in which Berengar and Willa had taken refuge. Thereupon the aforesaid Pope John sent Leo, then the venerable chief notary of the holy Roman Church and now in that same see successor to Saint Peter chief of the apostles, together with Demetrius, one of the most

---

[1] Psalm 77:10.

illustrious of the Roman princes, as envoy to the holy emperor. By their mouths he declared that it was not surprising if in the heat of youth he had hitherto indulged in childish follies; but now the time had come when he would fain live in a different fashion. He also cunningly alleged that the holy emperor had sheltered two of his disloyal subordinates, Bishop Leo and the cardinal deacon John, and that he was now breaking his sworn promise by letting them take an oath of allegiance not to the pope but to the emperor. To the envoys the emperor gave this answer: "I thank the pope for the change and improvement in his ways that he promises. As for the violation of pledges that he charges me with, judge yourselves if the accusation be true. We promised to restore all the territory of Saint Peter that might fall into our hands: and for that reason we are now striving to drive Berengar with all his household from yonder fort. How can we restore this territory to the pope, if we do not first wrest it from the hands of violent men and bring it under our control? As for Bishop Leo and the cardinal deacon John, his disloyal subordinates, whom he accuses us of having welcomed, we have neither seen them in these days nor welcomed them. The lord pope sent them to Constantinople to do us damage, and on their way, we are told, they were taken prisoners at Capua. We are also informed that with them was arrested a certain Saleccus, a Bulgarian by birth and an Hungarian by training, who is an intimate friend of the lord pope, and also a reprobate named Zacheus, a man quite ignorant of all literature sacred or profane, whom the lord pope has recently consecrated as bishop, with the intention that he should preach to the Hungarians a campaign against us. We would not have believed that the lord pope would have acted thus, whoever told us; but his letter, sealed with leaden seals and bearing his signature, compels us to think that it is true."

Ch. VII. This done, the emperor sent Landohard the Saxon bishop of Minden and Liudprand the Italian bishop of Cremona to Rome in company with the pope's envoys, to satisfy the lord pope that no blame attached to him. Furthermore the righteous emperor bade the soldiers of their guard to prove the truth of his words in single combat if the pope refused to believe him. The aforesaid bishops Landohard and Liudprand came before the lord pope at Rome, and although they were received with all due honor they saw clearly with what scorn and indifference he was prepared to treat the holy emperor. They explained everything in order, as they had been told to do, but the pope refused to be satisfied either with an oath or with a single combat and persisted in being obdurate. Still, a week later he craftily sent John, bishop

of Narni, and Benedict, cardinal deacon, back to the lord emperor with his envoys, thinking that by their tricks he could delude a man whom it is exceptionally difficult to deceive. Before they got back, however, Adalbert at the pope's invitation had left Fraxinetum and reached Civita Vecchia; whence he set out for Rome and there, so far from being repudiated by the pope, as he should have been, received from him an honorable welcome.

Ch. VIII. While these things were going on, the fierce heat of the dog days kept the emperor away from the hills of Rome. But when the sun had entered the sign of the Virgin and brought a temperate change, he collected his forces, and at the secret invitation of the Romans drew near to the city. Yet why do I say "secret," when the greater part of the Roman princes forced their way into the castle of St. Paul and giving hostages invited the holy emperor to enter. Why make a long tale? When the emperor pitched his camp in the vicinity, the pope and Adalbert made their escape together from Rome. The citizens welcomed the holy emperor and all his men into their town, promising again to be loyal and adding under a strong oath that they would never elect or ordain a pope except with the consent and approval of the august Caesar Otto the lord emperor and his son King Otto.

Ch. IX. Three days later at the request of the bishops and people of Rome a synod was held in the church of St Peter, attended by the emperor and the Italian archbishops. The deacon Rodalf acted in place of Ingelfred patriarch of Aquileia, who had been seized by a sudden sickness in that city; Waldpert came from Milan, Peter from Ravenna; Archbishop Adeltac and Landohard, bishop of Minden, represented Saxony; Otker, bishop of Spires, France. The Italian bishops were Hubert of Parma, Liudprand of Cremona, Hermenard of Reggio; the Tuscans, Conrad of Lucca, Everard of Arezzo, the bishops of Pisa, Sienna, Florence, Pistoia, Peter of Camerino, the bishop of Spoleto; the Romans, Gregory of Albano, Sico of Ostia, Benedict of Porto, Lucidus of Gavio, Theophylact of Palestrina, Wido of Selva Candida, Leo of Velletri, Sico of Bieda, Stephen of Cervetri, John of Nepi, John of Tivoli, John of San Liberato, Romanus of Ferentino, John of Norma, John of Veroli, Marinus of Sutri, John of Narni, John of Sabina, John of Gallese, the bishops of Civita, Castellana, Alatri, Orte, John of Anagni, the bishop of Trevi, Sabbatinus of Terracina. There were also present: Stephen cardinal archpriest of the parish Balbina, Dominic of the parish Anastasia, Peter of the parish Damascus, Theophylact of the parish Chrysogonus, John of the parish Equitius, Peter of the parish Pamachius, Adrian of the parish Caecilia, Adrian of the parish Lucina, Benedict of the parish Sixtus,

Theophylact of the parish Four Crowned Saints, Stephen of the parish Sabina, Benedict cardinal archdeacon, John deacon, Bonofilius chief cardinal deacon, George second cardinal deacon, Stephen assistant, Andrew treasurer, Sergius chief warden, John sacristan, Stephen, Theophylact, Adrian, Stephen, Benedict, Azo, Adrian, Romanus, Leo, Benedict, Leo, Leo, Leo notaries, Leo chief of the school of singers, Benedict subdeacon in charge of the offertories, Azo, Benedict, Demetrius, John, Amicus, Sergius, Benedict, Urgo, John, Benedict subdeacon and steward, Stephen arch-acolyte with all the acolytes and district deacons. Representing the princes of Rome were Stephen son of John, Demetrius Meliosi, Crescenti de Caballo Marmoreo, John Mizina, Stephen de Imiza, Theodore de Rufina, John de Primicerio, Leo de Cazunuli, Rihkard, Pietro de Capanaria, and Benedict with his son Bulgamin. The commoner Peter, also called Imperiola, together with the whole body of Roman soldiery was in attendance.

Ch. X. When all had taken their seats and complete silence was established, the holy emperor began thus: "How fitting it would have been for the lord Pope John to be present at this glorious holy synod. I ask you, holy fathers, to give your opinion why he has refused to attend this great gathering, for you live as he does and share in all his interests." Thereupon the Roman bishops and the cardinal priests and deacons together with the whole population said:—"We are surprised that your most holy wisdom deigns to ask us this question: even the inhabitants of Iberia and Babylonia and India know the answer to it. John is not now even one of those who come in sheep's clothing and within are ravening wolves: his savageness is manifest, he is openly engaged in the devil's business, and he makes no attempt at disguise." The emperor replied:—"It seems to us right that the charges against the pope should be brought forward seriatim, and that the whole synod should then consider what course we should adopt." Thereupon the cardinal priest Peter got up and testified that he had seen the pope celebrate mass without himself communicating. John bishop of Narni and John cardinal deacon then declared that they had seen the pope ordain a deacon in a stable and at an improper season. Benedict cardinal deacon with his fellow deacons and priests said that they knew the pope had been paid for ordaining bishops and that in the city of Todi he had appointed a bishop for ten years. On the question of his sacrilege, they said, no inquiries were necessary; knowledge of it was a matter of eyesight not of hearsay. As regards his adultery, though they had no visual information, they knew for certain that he had carnal acquaintance with Rainer's widow, Stephana his father's concubine, the widow Anna,

and his own niece, and that he had turned the holy palace into a brothel and resort for harlots. He had gone hunting publicly; he had blinded his spiritual father Benedict who died of his injuries; he had caused the death of cardinal subdeacon John by castrating him; he had set houses on fire and appeared in public equipped with sword, helmet, and cuirass. To all this they testified; while everyone, clergy and laity alike, loudly accused him of drinking wine for love of the devil. At dice, they said, he asked the aid of Jupiter, Venus, and the other demons; he did not celebrate Matins nor observe the canonical hours nor fortify himself with the sign of the cross.

Ch. XI. When he had heard this, as the Romans could not understand his native Saxon tongue, the emperor bade Liudprand bishop of Cremona to deliver the following speech in the Latin language to all the Romans. Accordingly he got up and began thus: "It often happens, and we know it by experience that men set in high positions are besmirched by the foul tongue of envy: the good displease the bad, even as the bad displease the good. For this reason we still regard as doubtful the charge against the pope which the cardinal Benedict read out and communicated to you, and we are uncertain whether it originated from zeal for righteousness or from impious envy. Therefore, unworthy as I am, by the authority of the position that has been granted me I call upon you all by the Lord God, whom no one, even if he wishes, can deceive, and by His Holy Mother the pure Virgin Mary, and by the most precious body of the chief of apostles, in whose church this is now being read, cast no foul words against the lord pope nor accuse him of anything that he has not really done and that has not been witnessed by men on whom we can rely." Thereupon the bishops, the priests, the deacons, the rest of the clergy, and the whole Roman people cried out as one man:—"If Pope John has not committed all the shameful crimes that the deacon Benedict read out to us and done things even worse and more disgusting than those, may the most blessed Peter, whose verdict closes the gates of Heaven against the unworthy and opens them for the righteous, never free us from the chains of our sins: may we be held fast in the bonds of anathema and at the last day be set on the left hand with those who said to the Lord God: 'Depart from us, we would have no knowledge of thy ways.' If you do not give us credence, at least you ought to believe the army of our lord the emperor, against whom the pope advanced five days ago, equipped with sword, shield, helmet, and cuirass. It was only the intervening waters of the Tiber that saved him from being taken prisoner in that garb." Then the holy emperor said:—"There are as many witnesses to that as there are fighting men in our army." So the holy synod pronounced: "If it please the holy emperor, let a letter be sent to the lord pope, that he come here and purge himself from all these charges." Thereupon a letter was sent to him as follows:—

Ch. XII. "To the supreme pontiff and universal pope lord John, Otto, august emperor by the grace of God, together with the archbishops and bishops of Liguria, Tuscany, Saxony, and France, sends greeting in the name of the Lord. When we came to Rome in God's service and inquired of your sons, the Roman bishops, cardinal priests, and deacons, and the whole body of the people besides, concerning your absence, and asked them what was the reason that you were unwilling to see us, the defenders of your church and your person, they brought out such foul and filthy tales about you that we should be ashamed of them, even if they were told about actors. That your highness may not remain in complete ignorance we set down some of them briefly here; for though we would fain give them all seriatim, one day is not enough. Know then that you are charged, not by a few men but by all the clergy and laity alike, of homicide, perjury, sacrilege, and of the sin of unchastity with your own kinswoman and with two sisters. They tell me too something that makes me shudder, that you have drunk wine for love of the devil, and that in dice you have asked the help of Jupiter, Venus, and the other demons. Therefore we earnestly beg your paternal highness not to refuse under any pretense to come to Rome and clear yourself of all these charges. If perchance you fear the violence of a rash multitude, we declare under oath that no action is contemplated contrary to the sanction of the holy canons."

Ch. XIII. After reading this letter, the pope sent the following reply: "Bishop John, servant of God's servants, to all the bishops. We hear say that you wish to make another pope. If you do, I excommunicate you by Almighty God, and you have no power, to ordain no one or celebrate mass."

Ch. XIV. When this answer was read in the holy synod, the following clergy, who had been absent at the previous meeting, were present: from Lorraine, Henry archbishop of Trèves; from Aemilia and Liguria, Wido of Modena, Gezo of Tortona, Sigulf of Piacenza. The synod returned the following reply to the lord pope:—"To the supreme pontiff and universal lord pope John, Otto, august emperor by the grace of God, and the holy synod assembled at Rome in God's service, send greeting in the Lord's name. At our last meeting of the sixth of November we sent you a letter containing the charges made against you by your accusers and their reasons for bringing them. In the same letter we asked your highness to come to Rome,

as is only just, and to clear yourself from these allegations. We have now received your answer, which is not at all of a kind suited to the character of this occasion but is more in accordance with the folly of rank indifference. There could be no reasonable excuse for not coming to the synod. But messengers from your highness ought certainly to have put in an appearance here, and assured us that you could not attend the holy synod owing to illness or some such insuperable difficulty. There is furthermore a sentence in your letter more fitting for a stupid boy than a bishop. You excommunicated us all if we appointed another bishop to the see of Rome, and yet gave us power to celebrate the mass and ordain clerical functionaries. You said:—'You have no power to ordain no one.' We always thought, or rather believed, that two negatives make an affirmative, if your authority did not weaken the verdict of the authors of old. However, let us reply, not to your words, but to your meaning. If you do not refuse to come to the synod and to clear yourself of these charges, we certainly are prepared to bow to your authority. But if—which Heaven forbid!—under any pretense you refrain from coming and defending yourself against a capital charge, especially when there is nothing to stop you, neither a sea voyage, nor bodily sickness, nor a long journey, then we shall disregard your excommunication, and rather turn it upon yourself, as we have justly the power to do. Judas, who betrayed, or rather who sold, Our Lord Jesus Christ, with the other disciples received the power of binding and loosing from their master in these words:—'Verily I say unto you, Whatsoever ye shall bind on earth shall be bound in Heaven: and whatsoever ye shall loose on earth shall be loosed in Heaven.' As long as Judas was a good man with his fellow disciples, he had the power to bind and loose. But when he became a murderer for greed and wished to destroy all men's lives, whom then could he loose that was bound or bind that was loosed save himself, whom he hanged in the accursed noose?" This letter was written on the twenty-second day of November and sent by the hand of the cardinal priest Adrian and the cardinal deacon Benedict.

Ch. XV. When these latter arrived at Tivoli, they could not find the pope: he had gone off into the country with bow and arrows, and no one could tell them where he was. Not being able to find him they returned with the letter to Rome and the holy synod met for the third time. On this occasion the emperor said: "We have waited for the pope's appearance, that we might complain of his conduct toward us in his presence: but since we are now assured that he will not attend, we beg you earnestly to listen to an account of his treacherous behavior. We hereby inform you, archbishops, bishops, priests, deacons, clerics, counts, judges, and people, that Pope John being hard pressed by Berengar and Adalbert, our revolted subjects, sent messengers to us in Saxony, asking us for the love of God to come to Italy and free him and the church of St. Peter from their jaws. We need not tell you how much we did for him with God's assistance: you see it today for yourselves. But when by my help he was rescued from their hands and restored to his proper place, forgetful of the oath of loyalty which he swore to me on the body of St. Peter, he got Adalbert to come to Rome, defended him against me, stirred up tumults, and before my soldiers' eyes appeared as leader in the campaign equipped with helmet and cuirass. Let the holy synod now declare its decision." Thereupon the Roman pontiffs and the other clergy and all the people replied: "A mischief for which there is no precedent must be cauterized by methods equally novel. If the pope's moral corruption only hurt himself and not others, we should have to bear with him as best we could. But how many chaste youths by his example have become unchaste? How many worthy men by association with him have become reprobates? We therefore ask your imperial majesty that this monster, whom no virtue redeems from vice, shall be driven from the holy Roman Church, and another be appointed in his place, who by the example of his goodly conversation may prove himself both ruler and benefactor, living rightly himself and setting us an example of like conduct." Then the emperor said: "I agree with what you say; nothing will please me more than for you to find such a man and to give him control of this holy universal see."

Ch. XVI. At that all cried with one voice:—"We elect as our shepherd Leo, the venerable chief notary of the holy Roman Church, a man of proved worth deserving of the highest sacerdotal rank. He shall be the supreme and universal pope of the holy Roman Church, and we hereby reprobate the apostate John because of his vicious life." The whole assembly repeated these words three times, and then with the emperor's consent escorted the aforesaid Leo to the Lateran Palace amid acclamations, and later at the due season in the church of St. Peter elevated him to the supreme priesthood by holy consecration and took the oath of loyalty toward him.

Ch. XVII. When this had been arranged the most holy emperor, hoping that he could stay at Rome with a few men and not wishing the Roman people to be burdened with a great army, gave many of his soldiers leave to return home. John, the so-called pope, hearing of this and knowing how easily the Romans could be bribed, sent messengers to the city, promising the people all the wealth of St. Peter and the churches, if they would fall upon the pious

emperor and the lord Pope Leo and impiously murder them. Why make a long tale? The Romans encouraged, or rather ensnared by the fewness of the emperor's troops and animated by the promised reward, at once sounded their trumpets and rushed in hot haste upon the emperor to kill him. He met them on the bridge over the Tiber, which the Romans had barricaded with wagons. His gallant warriors, well trained in battle with fearless hearts and fearless swords, leaped forward among the foe, like hawks falling on a flock of birds, and drove them off in panic without resistance. No hiding place, neither basket nor hollow tree trunk nor filthy sewer, could protect them in their flight. Down they fell, and as usually happens with such gallant heroes, most of their wounds were in the back. Who of the Romans then would have escaped from the massacre, had not the holy emperor yielded to the pity, which they did not deserve, and called off his men still thirsting for the enemies' blood.

Ch. XVIII. After they were all vanquished and the survivors had given hostages, the venerable Pope Leo fell at the emperor's feet and begged him to give the hostages back and rely on the people's loyalty. At the request of the venerable Pope Leo the holy emperor gave back the hostages, although he knew that the Romans would soon start the trouble I am about to relate. He also commended the pope to the Romans' loyalty, a lamb entrusted to wolves; and leaving Rome hastened toward Camerino and Spoleto where he had heard that Adalbert was to be found.

Ch. XIX. Meanwhile the women, with whom the so-called pope John was accustomed to carry on his voluptuous sports, being many in numbers and noble in rank, stirred up the Romans to overthrow Leo, whom God and they themselves had chosen as supreme and universal pope, and bring John back again into Rome. This they did; but by the mercy of God the venerable Pope Leo escaped from their clutches and with a few attendants made his way to the protection of the most pious emperor Otto.

Ch. XX. The holy emperor was bitterly grieved at this insult, and to avenge the expulsion of the lord Pope Leo and the foul injuries done by the deposed John to the cardinal deacon John and the notary Azo, one of whom had his right hand cut off, and the other his tongue, two fingers and his nose, he got his army together again and prepared to return to Rome. But before the holy emperor's forces were all assembled, the Lord decreed that every age should know how justly Pope John had been repudiated by his bishops and all the people, and how unjustly afterwards he had been welcomed back. One night when John was disporting himself with some man's wife outside Rome, the devil dealt him such a violent blow on the temples that he died of the injury within a week. Moreover at the prompting of the devil, who had struck the blow, he refused the last sacraments, as I have frequently heard testified by his friends and kinsmen who were at his death bed.

Ch. XXI. At his death the Romans, forgetful of the oath they had taken to the holy emperor, elected Benedict cardinal deacon as pope, swearing moreover that they would never abandon him but would defend him against the emperor's might. Thereupon the emperor invested the city closely and allowed no one to get out with a whole skin. Siege engines and famine completed the work, and finally in spite of the Romans he got possession of the city again, restored the venerable Leo to his proper place, and bade Benedict the usurper to appear before him.

Ch. XXII. Accordingly the supreme and universal pope the lord Leo took his seat in the church of the Lateran and with him the most holy emperor Otto, together with the Roman and Italian bishops, the archbishops of Lorraine and Saxony, the bishops, priests, deacons, and the whole Roman people whose names will be given later. Before them appeared Benedict, the usurper of the apostolic chair, brought in by the men who had elected him and still wearing the pontifical vestments. To him the cardinal archdeacon Benedict addressed the following charge: "By what authority or by what law, O usurper, are you now wearing this pontifical raiment, seeing that our lord the

venerable Pope Leo is alive and here present, whom you and we elected to the supreme apostolic office when John had been accused and disowned? Can you deny that you swore to our lord the emperor here present that you and the other Romans would never elect nor ordain a pope without the consent of the emperor and his son King Otto?" Benedict replied:—"Have mercy upon my sin." Then the emperor, revealing by his tears how inclined he was to mercy, asked the synod not to pass hasty judgment upon Benedict. If he wished and could, let him answer the questions and defend his case: if he had neither the wish nor the power but confessed his guilt, then let him for the fear of God have some mercy shown to him. Thereupon Benedict flung himself in haste at the feet of the lord Pope Leo and the emperor, and cried out: "I have sinned in usurping the holy Roman see." He then handed over the papal cloak and gave the papal staff which he was holding to Pope Leo, who broke it in pieces and showed it to the people. Next the pope bade Benedict to sit down on the ground and took from him his chasuble and stole. Finally he said to all the bishops: "We hereby deprive Benedict, usurper of the holy Roman apostolic chair, of all pontifical and priestly office: but by reason of the clemency of the lord emperor Otto, by whose help we have been restored to our proper place, we allow him to keep the rank of deacon, not at Rome but in exile, which we now adjudge against him."

22. CLUNIAC CHARTERS

The monastery of Cluny received gifts of land, churches, and monasteries throughout the tenth, eleventh, and twelfth centuries. These and other property transactions were preserved in written form, i.e., in charters. The charters from the tenth century that were preserved at Cluny are among the richest primary sources for that period. Although unprecedented in number, the charters of Cluny are not unlike those made for other monasteries. Except for the Foundation Charter of Cluny, the following were all drawn up for members of one family, later known as the Grossi. The family relationships were as follows:

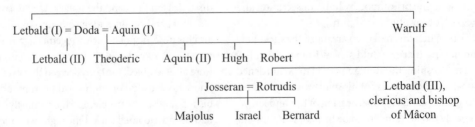

(The Majolus of this family was *not* the same person as the Majolus who was abbot of Cluny 954–994.)

The documents presented here illustrate the ways in which a pious family and a monastery related to one another through the medium of land. These charters raise numerous issues connected with the history of religion; the meaning of property; the uses of written instruments; the uses of land and dependents; the memories that people had of families, land, crimes, and acts of piety; ideas about the Church; and the gift-exchange system of the early Middle Ages.

Sources: E.F. Henderson (ed.), *Select Historical Documents of the Middle Ages* (London: George Bell, 1892), 176–89; A. Bruel, *Recueil des Chartres de l'Abbaye de Cluny* (Paris: Imprimerie Nationale, 1876–84), trans. Barbara Rosenwein.
Further Reading: Barbara H. Rosenwein, *To Be the Neighbor of Saint Peter: The Social Meaning of Cluny's Property, 909–1049* (Philadelphia: University of Pennsylvania Press, 1989).

THE FOUNDATION CHARTER OF CLUNY[2]

To all right thinkers it is clear that the providence of God has so provided for certain rich men that, by means of their transitory possessions, if they use them well, they may be able to merit everlasting rewards. As to which thing, indeed, the divine word, showing it to be possible and altogether advising it, says: "The riches of a man are the redemption of his soul."[3] I, William, count and duke by the grace of God, diligently pondering this, and desiring to provide for my own safety while I am still able, have considered it advisable—nay, most necessary, that from the temporal goods which have been conferred upon me I should give some little portion for the gain of my soul. I do this, indeed, in order that I who have thus increased in wealth may not, perchance, at the last be accused of having spent all in caring for my body, but rather may rejoice, when fate at last shall snatch all things away, in having reserved something for myself. Which end, indeed, seems attainable by no more suitable means than that, following the precept of Christ: "I will make his poor my friends"[4] and making the act not a temporary but a lasting one, I should support at my own expense a congregation of monks. And this is my trust, this my hope, indeed, that although I myself am unable to despise all things, nevertheless, by receiving despisers of the world, whom I believe to be righteous, I may receive the reward of the righteous. Therefore be it known to all who live in the unity of the faith and who await the mercy of Christ, and to those who shall succeed them and who shall continue to exist until the end of the world, that, for the love of God and of our Savior Jesus Christ, I hand over from my own rule to the holy apostles, Peter, namely, and Paul, the possessions over which I hold sway, the town of Cluny, namely, with the court and demesne manor, and the church in honor of St. Mary the mother of God and of St. Peter the prince of the apostles, together with all the things pertaining to it, the vills, indeed, the chapels, the serfs of both sexes, the vines, the fields, the meadows, the woods, the waters and their outlets, the mills, the incomes and revenues, what is cultivated and what is not, all in their entirety. Which things are situated in or about the country of Mâcon, each one surrounded by its own bounds. I give, moreover, all these things to the aforesaid apostles—I, William, and my wife Ingelberga—first for the love of God; then for the soul of my lord king Odo, of my father and my mother; for myself and my wife—for the salvation, namely, of our souls and bodies;—and not least for that of Ava who left me these things in her will; for the souls also of our brothers and sisters and nephews, and of all our relatives of both sexes; for our faithful ones who adhere to our service; for the advancement, also, and integrity of the Catholic religion. Finally, since all of us Christians are held together by one bond of love and faith, let this donation be for all,—for the orthodox, namely, of past, present, or future times.

I give these things, moreover, with this understanding, that in Cluny a regular monastery shall be constructed in honor of the holy apostles Peter and Paul, and that there the monks shall congregate and live according to the rule of St. Benedict, and that they shall possess, hold, have and order these same things unto all time. In such wise, however, that the venerable house of prayer which is there shall be faithfully frequented with vows and supplications, and that celestial converse shall be sought and striven after with all desire and with the deepest ardor; and also that there shall be sedulously directed to God prayers, beseechings and exhortations as well for me

---

as for all, according to the order in which mention has been made of them above. And let the monks themselves, together with all the aforesaid possessions, be under the power and dominion of the abbot Berno, who, as long as he shall live, shall preside over them regularly according to his knowledge and ability. But after his death, those same monks shall have power and permission to elect any one of their order whom they please as abbot and rector, following the will of God and the rule promulgated by St. Benedict,—in such wise that neither by the intervention of our own nor of any other power may they be impeded from making a purely canonical election. Every five years, moreover, the aforesaid monks shall pay to the church of the apostles at Rome ten shillings to supply them with lights; and they shall have the protection of those same apostles and the defense of the Roman pontiff; and those monks may, with their whole heart and soul, according to their ability and knowledge, build up the aforesaid place. We will, further, that in our times and in those of our successors, according as the opportunities and possibilities of that place shall allow, there shall daily, with the greatest zeal to be performed there works of mercy toward the poor, the needy, strangers, and pilgrims. It has pleased us also to insert in this document that, from this day, those same monks there congregated shall be subject neither to our yoke, nor to that of our relatives, nor to the sway of any earthly power. And, through God and all his saints, and by the awful day of judgment, I warn and abjure that no one of the secular princes, no count, no bishop whatever, not the pontiff of the aforesaid Roman see, shall invade the property of these servants of God, or alienate it, or diminish it, or exchange it, or give it as a benefice to any one, or constitute any prelate over them against their will. And that such unhallowed act may be more strictly prohibited to all rash and wicked men, I subjoin the following, giving force to the warning. I adjure ye, o holy apostles and glorious princes of the world, Peter and Paul, and thee, o supreme pontiff of the apostolic see, that, through the canonical and apostolic authority which ye have received from God, ye do remove from participation in the holy church and in eternal life, the robbers and invaders and alienators of these possessions which I do give to ye with joyful heart and ready will; and be ye protectors and defenders of the aforementioned place of Cluny and of the servants of God abiding there, and of all these possessions—on account of the clemency and mercy of the most holy Redeemer. If any one—which Heaven forbid, and which, through the mercy of the God and the protection of the apostles I do not think will happen—whether he be a neighbor or a stranger, no matter what his condition or power, should, through any kind of wild attempt to do any act of violence contrary to this deed of gift which we have ordered to be drawn up for the love of almighty God and for reverence of the chief apostles Peter and Paul; first, indeed, let him incur the wrath of almighty God, and let God remove him from the land of the living and wipe out his name from the book of life, and let his portion be with those who said to the Lord God: Depart from us; and, with Dathan and Abiron whom the earth, opening its jaws, swallowed up, and hell absorbed while still alive, let him incur everlasting damnation. And being made a companion of Judas let him be kept thrust down there with eternal tortures, and, lest it seem to human eyes that he pass through the present world with impunity, let him experience in his own body, indeed, the torments of future damnation, sharing the double disaster with Heliodorus and Antiochus, of whom one being coerced with sharp blows and scarcely escaped alive; and the other, struck down by the divine will, his members putrefying and swarming with vermin, perished most miserably. And let him be a partaker with other sacrilegious persons who presume to plunder the treasure of the house of God; and let him, unless he come to his senses, have as enemy and as the one who will refuse him entrance into the blessed paradise, the key-bearer of the whole hierarchy of the church, and, joined with the latter, St. Paul; both of whom, if he had wished, he might have had as most holy mediators for him. But as far as the worldly law is concerned, he shall be required, the judicial power compelling him, to pay a hundred pounds of gold to those whom he has harmed; and his attempted attack, being frustrated, shall have no effect at all. But the validity of this deed of gift, endowed with all authority, shall always remain inviolate and unshaken, together with the stipulation subjoined. Done publicly in the city of Bourges. I, William, commanded this act to be made and drawn up, and confirmed it with my own hand.

(*Signed by Ingelberga and a number of bishops and nobles.*)

CHARTERS OF THE GROSSI FAMILY

Charter # 802 (March 951)

To all who consider the matter reasonably, it is clear that the dispensation of God is so designed that if riches are used well, these transitory things can be transformed into eternal rewards. The Divine word showed that this was possible, saying "Wealth for a man is the redemption of his soul," and again, "Give alms and all things are yours."[5]

We, that is, I, Doda, a woman, and my son Letbald [II], carefully considering this fact, think it necessary that we share some of the things that were conferred on us, Christ granting, for the benefit of our souls. We do this to make Christ's poor our friends, in accordance with Christ's precept and so that He may receive us, in the end, in the eternal tabernacle.

Therefore, let it be known to all the faithful that we—Doda and my son Letbald—give some of our possessions, with the consent of lord Aquin [I], my husband, for love of God and his holy apostles, Peter and Paul,[6] to the monastery of Cluny, to support the brothers [i.e., monks] there who ceaselessly serve God and His apostles. [We give] an allod that is located in the *pagus*[7] of Mâcon, called Nouville.[8] The serfs [*servi*] that live there are: Sicbradus and his wife, Robert, Eldefred and his wife and children, Roman and his wife and children, Raynard and his wife and children, Teutbert and his wife and children, Dominic and his wife and children, Nadalis with her children, John with his wife and children, Benedict with his wife and children, Maynard with his wife and children, another Benedict with his wife and children, and a woman too . . .[9] with her children.

And we give [land in] another *villa*[10] called Colonge and the serfs living there: Teotgrim and his wife and children, Benedict and his wife and children, Martin and his children, Adalgerius and his wife and children, [and] Sicbradus.

And [we give] a *mansus*[11] in Culey and the serfs there: Andrald and his wife and children, Eurald and his wife and children. And [we give] whatever we have at Chazeux

along with the serf Landrad who lives there. We also give a little harbor on the Aar river[12] and the serfs living there: Agrimbald and Gerald with their wives and children.

In addition, we give an allod in the *pagus* of Autun, in the *villa* called Beaumont and the serfs living there, John, Symphorian, Adalard and their wives and children, in order that [the monks] may, for the love of Christ, receive our nephew, Adalgysus, into their society.[13]

[We give] all the things named above with everything that borders on them: vineyards, fields, buildings, serfs of every sex and age, ingress and egress, with all mobile and immobile property already acquired or to be acquired, wholly and completely. We give all this to God omnipotent and His apostles for the salvation of our souls and for the soul of Letbald [I], the father of my son, and for the salvation of Aquin [I], my husband, and of all our relatives and finally for all the faithful in Christ, living and dead.

Moreover, I, the aforesaid Letbald, unbuckle the belt of war, cut off the hair of my head and beard for divine love, and with the help of God prepare to receive the monastic habit in the monastery [of Cluny]. Therefore, the property that ought to come to me by paternal inheritance I now give [to Cluny] because of the generosity of my mother and brothers. [I do so] in such a way that while [my mother and brothers] live, they hold and possess it. I give a *mansus* in Fragnes, along with the serf Ermenfred and his wife and children, to [my brother] Theoderic, *clericus*,[14] and after his death let it revert to [Cluny]. And I give another *mansus* at Verzé with the serf Girbald and his wife and children to my brother Hugo. In the *pagus* of Autun I give to [my brother] Aquin [II] the allod that is called Dompierre-les-Ormes, and the serf Benedict and his wife and their son and daughter. [I give Aquin also] another allod in Vaux, and the serfs Teutbald and his wife and children and Adalgarius. [I give all this] on condition that, if these brothers of mine [Hugh and Aquin], who are laymen, die without legitimate offspring, all these properties will go to the monastery as general alms.

If anyone (which we do not believe will happen) either we ourselves (let it not happen!) or any other person, should be tempted to bring a claim in bad faith against this charter of donation, let him first incur the wrath of

---

[5] Luke 12:33.

[6] Cluny was dedicated to the apostles Peter and Paul.

[7] A Roman administrative subdivision.

[8] Almost all the places mentioned in these charters are within about ten miles of the monastery of Cluny.

[9] Effaced in the manuscript.

[10] In this region a *villa* was normally not a great estate nor a village, but rather a small district in which many landowners held land.

[11] A *mansus* (plural: *mansi*) was, strictly speaking, a farming unit. In the context of Doda's charter, she is probably thinking of a "demesne mansus," an outsize farming unit that included the *mansi* of dependents.

[12] A tributary of the Rhin (*not* the Rhine) river.

[13] Possibly Adalgysus is to become a monk, but it is more likely that he is to become a special "friend" of the monastery for whom prayers will be said.

[14] I.e., a priest.

God, and let him suffer the fate of Datan and Abiran and of Judas, the traitor of the Lord. And unless he repents, let him have the apostles [Peter and Paul] bar him from the celestial kingdom. Moreover, in accordance with earthly law, let him be forced to pay ten pounds. But let this donation be made firm by us, with the stipulation added. S[ignum][15] of Doda and her son Letbald, who asked that it be done and confirmed. S. of Aquin, who consents. S. of Hugo. S. of Evrard. S. of Walo. S. of Warembert. S. of Maingaud. S. of Giboin. S. of Leotald. S. of Widald. S. of Hemard. S. of Raimbald. Dated in the month of March in the fifteenth year of the reign of King Louis.[16] I, brother Andreas, *levite*,[17] undersign at the place for the secretary.

Charter # 1460 (November 12, 978— November 11, 979)[18]

I, Majolus, humble abbot [of Cluny] by the will of God, and the whole congregation of brothers of the monastery of Cluny. We have decided to grant something from the property of our church to a certain cleric, named Letbald [III] for use during his lifetime, and we have done so, fulfilling his request.

The properties that we grant him are located in the *pagus* of Mâcon, in the *ager*[19] of Grevilly, in a *villa* called Colonge: *mansi*, vineyards, land, meadows, woods, water, and serfs of both sexes, and whatever else we have in that place, which came to us from Raculf.[20] And we grant two *mansi* at Boye and whatever we have there. And in Massy, one *mansus*. And in "Ayrodia,"[21] in a place called Rocca, we give *mansi* with vineyards, land, woods, water, and serfs of every sex and age; and we grant all the property

of Chassigny [a place near Lugny that has disappeared]: vineyards, land, meadows, woods, water, mills, and serfs and slaves. And at "Bussiacus" [near St-Huruge], similarly [we grant] *mansi*, vineyards, lands, meadows, and woods. And at "Ponciacus"[22] [we give] *mansi*, vineyards, land. Just as Raculf gave these things to us in his testament, so we grant them to [Letbald] on the condition that he hold them while he lives and after his death these things pass to Cluny. And let him pay 12 denars every year to mark his taking possession [*in vestitura*].

We also grant to him other property that came from lord Letbald [I], his uncle: a *mansus* at La Verzée and another at Bassy and another at Les Légères, and again another in Fragnes and another in Chazeux. And again a *mansus* in the *pagus* of Autun, at Dompierre-les-Ormes and another in Vaux and the serfs and slaves of both sexes that belong to those *mansi*. Let him hold and possess these properties as listed in this *precaria*[23] for as long as he lives. And when his mortality prevails—something no man can avoid—let this property fall to [Cluny] completely and without delay. [Meanwhile] let him pay 12 denars every year, on the feast day of apostles Peter and Paul.

I have confirmed this decree with my own hand and have ordered the brethren to corroborate it, so that it will have force throughout his lifetime. S. of lord Majolus, abbot. S. of Balduin, monk. S. of Vivian. S. of John. S. of Arnulf. S. of Costantinus. S. of Tedbald. S. of Joslen. S. of Grimald. S. of Hugo. S. of Rothard. S. of Ingelbald. S. of Achedeus. S. of Vuitbert. S. of Ingelman. Dated by the hand of Rothard, in the twenty-fifth year of the reign of King Lothar.

Charter # 1577 (November 12, 981— November 11, 982)

To this holy place, accessible to our prayers [et cetera].[24] I, Rotrudis, and [my husband] Josseran, and my sons,

---

[15] Usually laymen did not sign charters; rather they made marks or signs (their *signum*) which were copied by the scribe in front of their name. The S refers to this sign.

[16] A Carolingian king of the area that would later become France between 936–954.

[17] I.e., a deacon.

[18] This charter is dated in this way because the scribe dated it in the twenty-fifth year of the reign of King Lothar, the son of King Louis, whose rule began on November 12, 954.

[19] The *pagus* of Mâcon was divided into subdivisions called *agri* (singular: *ager*). There were perhaps ten or more *villae* in each *ager*.

[20] Raculf was probably a member of this family whose precise relationship has not been established.

[21] Not identified.

[22] Not identified.

[23] This document is in fact an excellent example of a precarial donation. It was a conditional grant of land *by* the monastery to someone outside of the monastery for his (or her) lifetime.

[24] A formula considered so commonplace that it did not need to be fully written out. Consider the formula today, "Sincerely yours," which is so familiar that the full sentence, "Be assured that I remain sincerely yours" (or something on that order), is usually left out.

all of us give to God and his holy apostles, Peter and Paul, and at the place Cluny, half of a church[25] that is located in the *pagus* of Mâcon, named in honor of St. Peter, with everything that belongs to it, wholly and completely, and [property in] the *villa* that is called Curtil-sous-Buffières. There [we give] a field and a meadow that go together and have the name *ad Salas*. This land borders at the east on a *via publica*[26] and a man-made wall; at the south on a meadow; at the west on a *via publica*, and similarly at the north. [I make this gift] for the salvation of the soul of my husband Josseran, and [for the soul of my son] Bernard. Done at Cluny. Witnesses: Rotrudis, Josseran, Bernard, Israel, Erleus, Hugo, Odo, Raimbert, Umbert. Ingel-bald wrote this in the twenty-eighth year of the reign of King Lothar.

Charter # 1845 (990–991)

By the clemency of the Savior a remedy was conceded to the faithful: that they could realize eternal returns on His gifts if they distributed them justly. Wherefore, I, Majolus,[27] in the name of God, give to God and his holy apostles Peter and Paul and at the place Cluny some of my property which is located in the county of Lyon, in the *villa* "Mons." It consists of a *mansus indominica-tus*[28] with a serf named Durannus and his wife, named Aldegard, and their children, and whatever belongs or appears to belong to this *mansus*, namely fields, vineyards, meadows, woods, pasturelands, water and water courses, that is already acquired or will be acquired, whole and complete. I make this donation first for my soul and for my burial [in Cluny's cemetery] and for the soul of my father Josseran and of my mother Rotrudis and of my brothers, and for the souls of my *parentes*[29] and for the salvation of all the departed faithful, so that all may profit in common. [I give it] on the condition that I may hold and possess it while I live, and that every

year I will pay a tax of 12 denars on the feast day of the Prince of the Apostles [i.e., St. Peter]. After my death, let [the property] go to Cluny without delay.

But if anyone wants to bring any bad-faith claim against this donation, let him first incur the wrath of the Omnipotent and all His saints; and unless he returns to his senses, let him be thrust into hell with the Devil. As in the past, let this donation remain firm and stable, with the stipulation added. Done publicly at Cluny. S. of Majolus, who asks that it be done and confirmed. S. of Bernard, S. of Israel, S. of Arleius, S. of Bernard, S. of Hubert. Aldebard, *levite* wrote this in the fourth year of the reign of Hugh [Capet].

Charter # 2508 (994–1030?)[30]

Notice of a quitclaim that took place at Cluny in the presence of lord Rainald, venerable prior at that place; and of other monks who were there, namely Walter, Aymo, Amizon, Warner, Lanfred, Locerius, Giso; and of noblemen: Witbert, Robert, Ildinus, Gislebert, Bernard, and Hugo. In the first place, let all, present and future, know that a long and very protracted quarrel between the monks of Cluny and Majolus[31] finally, by God's mercy, came to this end result: first that he [Majolus] quit his claim to the land which Oddo and Teza [Oddo's] daughter[32] destined for us and handed over by charter: the woods in *Grandi Monte* with its borders [as follows]: on the east [it borders on] its own inheritance [namely] passing between mountains and through wasteland and across the castle of Teodoric; on the south [it borders on] *terra francorum*;[33] on the west and north [it borders on] land of St. Peter. [Majolus] draws up this notice at this time so that he may reunite himself with the favor of St. Peter and the brothers, and so that he may persevere in future as a faithful servant in the service of St. Peter. S. Hugo, S. Witbert, S. Robert, S. Ildinus, S. Gislebert, S. Bernard.

---

[25] Churches could be given in whole or in part, and with or without their tithes (which often belonged not to the holder of the church but to the local bishop).

[26] A dirt road. There was a very extensive network of roads in the area around Cluny, left from the Roman period.

[27] *Not* the abbot.

[28] This is the "demesne mansus" referred to above.

[29] Meaning much more than a nuclear family, but perhaps not quite as much as a clan.

[30] The scribe did not give a date. But we know that Rainald was prior at Cluny beginning in 994, and that Majolus died ca. 1030; these give us, respectively, the *terminus post quem* and the *terminus ante quem* of the document.

[31] The same man as the donor above.

[32] These were probably relatives of Majolus.

[33] Probably land of free peasants.

Charter # 2946 (?1018–1030)[34]

In the name of the incarnate Word. I, Raimodis, formerly the wife of the lord Wichard, now dead, and now joined in matrimony to lord Ansedeus, my husband; with the consent and good will [of Ansedeus], I give or rather give again some land which is called Chazeux to St. Peter and Cluny. [I give it] for the soul of my husband Wichard. This land once belonged to St. Peter and Cluny. But the abbot and monks gave it as a precarial gift to lord Letbald [III], a certain cleric who afterwards became bishop of Mâcon. Letbald, acting wrongly, alienated [the land] from St. Peter and gave it to Gauzeran to make amends for killing Gauzeran's relative, Berengar.

Therefore I give it again to St. Peter for the soul of my husband Wichard, and for Gauzeran, Wichard's father. I also give a slave named Adalgarda and her children, and [I give] the whole inheritance for the soul of my husband Wichard, and of my daughter Wiceline, and for my own soul.

If anyone wants to bring false claim against this donation, let him not prevail, but let him pay a pound of gold into the public treasury. S. of Raimodis, who asked that this charter be done and confirmed. S. of Ansedeus. S. of another Ansedeus. S. of Achard. S. of Walter. S. of Costabulus. S. of Ugo.

---

[34] This date is suggested, on the basis of other charters elsewhere that tell us at what date Raimodis, the donor in this charter, became a widow.

Glossary

Many specialized and technical terms appearing within only one document are defined in the notes to that document. The following terms appear more frequently.

anathema/to anathematize: a curse consigning one to damnation

augur: Roman religious officials thought to predict future events by observing the flights of birds

bailiff: official charged with public administrative authority; executes writs and processes, distrains, and arrests

catechumens: those receiving instruction in preparation for baptism

cellarers: member of a monastery responsible for supplies and provisions

centenarius (pl. centenarii): an agent of a count responsible for a jurisdiction termed a "hundred"

compline: last of the monastic liturgical hours

demesne: portion of a manor worked by peasants for the direct profit of the lord

ealdorman: a high-ranking Anglo-Saxon royal official, roughly equivalent to a count

fisc: originally the public treasury of Rome, but its meaning is extended to any imperial or royal treasury

hide: a measurement of land sufficient to support one peasant household

lauds: the second of the monastic liturgical hours, said around dawn

letter patent: legal document conferred by a monarch granting title or right

margrave: title, which became hereditary, given to rulers of principalities on the borders of the Holy Roman Empire (the Marches).

matins: the first of the monastic liturgical hours, said around midnight

master of the soldiery (*magister militum*): a top-level military commander in the late Roman empire

missus (pl. missi): Carolingian court officer, normally a count or bishop, charged with delivering imperial judgments and acting as investigator in high-level disputes

none: a monastic liturgical hour, sung in the mid-afternoon

pallium: a narrow cloth band, worn over the shoulders, presented by the pope to metropolitan archbishops

patrimony: any land, estate, or goods inherited after the death of the father

prime: a monastic liturgical hour, sung in the early morning

prebend: a clerical income from church estates

precarial holdings: land offered in exchange for service, but revocable by lender

prefect: civic official responsible for the administration of a city, roughly equivalent to mayor

presbyter: originally an elder in the early Christian community; in time applied to priests, the ordained clergy subordinate to bishops

prior: second-ranking member of monastery, below abbot

reeve: English chief royal magistrate of town or district (shire-reeve); more generally a local overseer (sometimes of large estates)

rescript: written command sent out by imperial authorities in answer to problem or question

sanctuary: in medieval law, a church or holy place designated as a place of refuge where fugitives could find immunity from their secular pursuers

seneschal: in the Frankish period, a household officer; later a high royal official responsible for military and judicial administration; equivalent of bailiff

sext: a monastic liturgical hour, sung at midday

sextaria: a measure of land differing regionally

synod: meeting of clergy to discuss ecclesiastical affairs

terce: a monastic liturgical hour, sung in the mid-morning

usufruct: the legal right to the goods normally produced from the land, without actual ownership of it

vespers: a monastic liturgical hour, sung in the evening

wergeld: price to be paid to the family or the lord of a slain person; set by social standing or proximity to the king

Sources

Dutton, Paul Edward (ed. and trans.), "The Life of Charlemagne" from *Charlemagne's Courtier: The Complete Einhard* (Toronto: University of Toronto Press, 2003). © University of Toronto Press 2003. Reprinted by permission of the University of Toronto Press and Paul Edward Dutton.

Gutenbrunner, Sigfried (trans.), excerpts from *Von Hildebrand und Hadubrand: Lied—Sage—Mythos* (Heidelberg: Winter, 1976). Reprinted by permission of the publisher.

Hillgarth, J.N. (trans.), excerpts from *Christianity and Paganism, 350–750* (Philiadelphia: University of Pennsylvania Press, 1986).

Hutton, Maurice (trans.), Tacitus, *Dialogus, Agricola, Germania* (London: Heineman, 1914). Rev. D. LePan, 1989. Reprinted by permission of Don LePan.

Loyn, H.R., and John Percival, excerpts from *The Reign of Charlemagne: Documents on Carolingian Government and Administration* (New York: St. Martin's Press, 1975).

McNamara, JoAnn, John Halborg, and E. Gordon Whatley, "Balthid, Queen of Neustria (d. ca 680)," in *Sainted Women of the Dark Ages* (Charlotte, NC: Duke University Press, 1992). Copyright 1992, Duke University Press. All rights reserved. Republished by permission of the copyright holder. www.dukepress.edu.

McNeill, John, and Helena M. Gamer, excerpts from *Medieval Handbooks of Penance: A Translation of the* Principal Libri Poenitentiales *and Selections from Related Documents* (New York: Columbia University Press, 1938). Copyright © 1938 Columbia University Press. Reprinted with permission of the publisher.

Musurillo, H.R. (trans.), excerpts from *The Acts of the Christian Martyrs* (Oxford: Claredon Press, 1972). Reprinted by permission of Oxford University Press.

Neel, Carol (ed. and trans.), excerpts from *Handbook for William: A Carolingian Woman's Counsel for Her Son by Dhouda* (Lincoln: University of Nebraska Press, 1991). Reprinted by permission of the University of Nebraska Press. English translation copyright 1991 by the University of Nebraska Press. French edition titled *Manuel por mon fils*, edited by Pierre Riché, copyright 1975 by Les Éditions du Cerf.

Périn, Patrick, and Laure-Charlotte Feffer, "The Tomb of Childeric" and "Father of Clovis" from *Les Francs*, vol. I: *À la conquête de la Gaule*, trans. Joelle Faveau (Paris: Colin, 1987). Reprinted by permission of Patrick Périn and Laure-Charlotte Feffer.

Pharr, Clyde (trans.) with Theresa Sherrer Davidson and Mary Brown Pharr, excerpts from *The Theodosian Code and Novels, and the Sirmondian Constitutions* (Princeton, NJ: Princeton University Press, 1952). Copyright © 1952. Republished with permission of Princeton University Press via Copyright Clearance Center, Inc.

Whitelock, Dorothy (ed.), "Laws of Ethelbert," "Dooms," "Letter to Edward the Elder," and "The Anglo-Saxon Chronicle" from *English Historical Documents 500–1042*, vol. I (London: Eyre & Spottiswoode, 1955). Copyright © 1955 Eyre & Spottiswoode. Reproduced by permission of Taylor & Francis Books UK.

Zimmerman, Odo John (ed. and trans.), excerpts from *Saint Gregory the Great, Dialogues* (New York: Fathers of the Church, Inc., 1959).

IMAGES

Treasure of Pouan. Anonyme, Trésor de Pouan, inv.860.19. 1à14. Cliché: Musée des Beaux-Arts et d'Archéologie de Troyes.

Zoomorphic purse clasps. Bibliotheque Nationale, Paris, France.

Two gold bees cloisonné with garnet. © BnF, Dist. RMN-Grand Palais/Art Resource, NY.

The signet ring of Childeric I. Copy of the ring of the Frankish King Childeric (c. 481–482). © Ashmolean Museum, University of Oxford, UK/Bridgeman Images.

Reconstruction of the scramsax sheath. Objects found in the tomb of Childeric I at Tournay (chromolitho), French School, (19th century). Private Collection. © Look and Learn/Bridgeman Images.

Frankish battle-ax. Bibliotheque Nationale, Paris, France.

Signet ring and gold bracelet. Belt and shoe buckles and applique. Gold bracelet and belt buckles, from princely burial of Germanic warrior. © De Agostini Picture Library/G. Dagli Orti/Bridgeman Images.

Selection of jewellery from the Treasure of Childeric (gold and garnet), Merovingian (5th century). © Bibliotheque Nationale, Paris, France/Bridgeman Images.

Gold bracelet and belt buckle, from princely burial of Germanic warrior. © De Agostini Picture Library/ G. Dagli Orti/Bridgeman Images.

Hilt and mouth of the sheath of Childeric's sword. © Photos 12/Alamy.

Reconstruction of the sheath of the sword. Bibliotheque Nationale, Paris, France.

Anglo-Saxon–type buckle with zoomorphic and anthropomorphic design, sixth century. © KIK-IRPA, Brussels (Belgium), cliché N550. Royal Institute for Cultural Heritage.

PLATES

1. © Foto Marburg/Art Resource, NY.
2. Late sixth–seventh century tombstone depicting knight, from Hornhausen, Germany. Landesmuseum fuer Vorgeschichte, Halle, Germany. © DeA Picture Library/Art Resource, NY.
3. Ann Münchow/Domkapital Aachen. © Domarchiv Aachen.
4. Courtesy of Stiftbibliothek St. Gallen.
6. © Ashmolean Museum, University of Oxford, UK/ Bridgeman Images.
7. © Scala/White Images/Art Resource, NY.
8. Saint Petersburg, National Library of Russia, lat. Q. v. I. 18. © Erich Lessing/Art Resource, NY.